PRENTICE HALL
LITERATURE

Timeless Voices, Timeless Themes

BRONZE LEVEL

Prentice
Hall

Upper Saddle River, New Jersey
Glenview, Illinois
Needham, Massachusetts

ISBN 0-13-054787-5

3 4 5 6 7 8 9 10 11   06 05 04 03 02

Cover: *The Picnic Grove,* Martha Walter, David David Gallery, Philadelphia/SuperStock

ACKNOWLEDGMENTS

Grateful acknowledgment is made to the following for copyrighted material:

Allyn & Bacon, Inc. "Making Fantasy Real" by Zena Sutherland, from *Children and Books.* Copyright © 1997. Reprinted by permission of Allyn & Bacon.

Miriam Altshuler Literary Agency "The Treasure of Lemon Brown" by Walter Dean Myers from *Boy's Life Magazine,* March 1983. Copyright © 1983 by Walter Dean Myers. Reprinted by permission of Miriam Altshuler Literary Agency, on behalf of Walter Dean Myers.

AMG *A Christmas Carol: Scrooge and Marley* by Israel Horovitz, an adaptation of Charles Dickens's *A Christmas Carol.* Copyright © 1994 by Fountain Pen, Inc. All rights reserved.

Bantam Books, a division of Random House, Inc. "The Eternal Frontier" from *Frontier* by Louis L'Amour, photographs by David Meunch. Copyright © 1984 by Louis L'Amour Enterprises, Inc. Used by permission of Bantam Books, a division of Random House, Inc.

Susan Bergholz Literary Services, New York "Four Skinny Trees" from *The House on Mango Street.* Copyright © 1984 by Sandra Cisneros. Published by Vintage Books, a division of Random House, Inc., and in hardcover by Alfred A. Knopf in 1994. Reprinted by permission of Susan Bergholz Literary Services, New York. All rights reserved.

Brandt & Hochman Literary Agents, Inc. "The Third Wish" from *Not What You Expected: A Collection of Short Stories* by Joan Aiken. Copyright © 1974 by Joan Aiken. Reprinted by permission of Brandt & Hochman Literary Agents, Inc.

Curtis Brown, Ltd. "Suzy and Leah" by Jane Yolen. Copyright © 1994 by Jane Yolen. First appeared in *American Girl Magazine,* published by The Pleasant Company. Reprinted by permission of Curtis Brown, Ltd. "Ribbons" by Laurence Yep, copyright © 1992 by Laurence Yep, from *American Girl,* Jan/Feb 1992.

Cahner Business Information "Review: 'A Christmas Carol'" by Michael Speier from *Variety,* November 22, 1999. Copyright © 2001 Cahner Business Information, a division of Reed Elsevier, Inc.

Clarion Books/Houghton Mifflin Company Excerpt from *The Midwife's Apprentice* by Karen Cushman. Copyright © 1995 by Karen Cushman. Reprinted by permission of Clarion Books/Houghton Mifflin Company. All rights reserved.

Don Congdon Associates, Inc. "All Summer in a Day" by Ray Bradbury, published in *The Magazine of Fantasy and Science Fiction,* March 1, 1954. Copyright © 1954, renewed 1982 by Ray Bradbury. Reprinted by permission of Don Congdon Associates, Inc. "The Third Level" by Jack Finney, published in *Collier's,* October 7, 1950. Copyright © 1950 by Crowell Collier, renewed 1977 by Jack Finney.

Michael Courlander for the Emma Courlander Trust "All Stories Are Anansi's" from *The Hat-Shaking Dance and Other Ashanti Tales from Ghana* by Harold Courlander with Albert Kofi Prempeh. Copyright © 1957 by Harcourt, Inc.; 1985 by Harold Courlander. Used by permission.

Dell Publishing, a division of Random House, Inc., and Curtis Brown, Ltd. "The Luckiest Time of All" from *The Lucky Stone* by Lucille Clifton. Copyright © 1979 by Lucille Clifton. Used by permission of Dell Publishing, a division of Random House Children's Publishing, and Curtis Brown, Ltd. All rights reserved.

Farrar, Straus & Giroux, Inc. "Seal" from *Laughing Time: Collected Nonsense* by William Jay Smith. Copyright © 1955, 1957, 1990 by William Jay Smith. Reprinted by permission of Farrar, Straus & Giroux, Inc. "The Cat Who Thought She Was a Dog and the Dog Who Thought He Was a Cat" from *Naftali the Storyteller and His Horse, Sus* by Isaac Bashevis Singer. Copyright © 1973, 1976 by Isaac Bashevis Singer. Excerpt from *A Wrinkle in Time* by Madeleine L'Engle, copyright © 1962 by Madeleine L'Engle Franklin.

(Acknowledgments continue on page R43, which constitutes an extension of this copyright page.)

PRENTICE HALL
LITERATURE

Timeless Voices, Timeless Themes

COPPER

BRONZE

SILVER

GOLD

PLATINUM

THE AMERICAN EXPERIENCE

THE BRITISH TRADITION

CONTRIBUTING AUTHORS

The contributing authors guided the direction and philosophy of *Prentice Hall Literature: Timeless Voices, Timeless Themes*. Working with the development team, they helped to build the pedagogical integrity of the program and to ensure its relevance for today's teachers and students.

Kate Kinsella

Kate Kinsella, Ed.D., is a faculty member in the Department of Secondary Education at San Francisco State University. A specialist in second-language acquisition and adolescent reading and writing, she teaches coursework addressing language and literacy development across the secondary curricula. She has taught high-school ESL and directed SFSU's *Intensive English Program* for first-generation bilingual college students. She maintains secondary classroom involvement by teaching an academic literacy class for second-language learners through the University's *Step to College* partnership program. A former Fulbright lecturer and perennial institute leader for TESOL, the California Reading Association, and the California League of Middle Schools, Dr. Kinsella provides professional development nationally on topics ranging from learning-style enhancement to second-language reading. Her scholarship has been published in journals such as the *TESOL Journal,* the *CATESOL Journal,* and the *Social Studies Review.* Dr. Kinsella earned her M.A. in TESOL from San Francisco State University and her Ed.D. in Second Language Acquisition from the University of San Francisco.

Kevin Feldman

Kevin Feldman, Ed.D., is the Director of Reading and Early Intervention with the Sonoma County Office of Education (SCOE). His career in education spans thirty-one years. As the Director of Reading and Early Intervention for SCOE, he develops, organizes, and monitors programs related to K–12 literacy and prevention of reading difficulties. He also serves as a Leadership Team Consultant to the California Reading and Literature Project and assists in the development and implementation of K–12 programs throughout California. Dr. Feldman earned his undergraduate degree in Psychology from Washington State University and has a Master's Degree in Special Education, Learning Disabilities, and Instructional Design from U.C. Riverside. He earned his Ed.D. in Curriculum and Instruction from the University of San Francisco.

Colleen Shea Stump

Colleen Shea Stump, Ph.D., is a Special Education supervisor in the area of Resources and Inclusion for Seattle Public Schools. She served as a professor and, since 1993, as chairperson for the Department of Special Education at San Francisco State University. She continues as the lead consultant in the area of collaboration for the California State Improvement Grant and travels the state of California providing professional development training in the areas of collaboration, content literacy instruction, and inclusive instruction. Dr. Stump earned her doctorate at the University of Washington, her M.A. in Special Education from the University of New Mexico, and her B.S. in Elementary Education from the University of Wisconsin–Eau Claire.

Joyce Armstrong Carroll

In her forty-year career, Joyce Armstrong Carroll, Ed. D., has taught on every grade level from primary to graduate school. In the past twenty years, she has trained teachers in the teaching of writing. A nationally known consultant, she has served as president of TCTE and on NCTE's Commission on Composition. More than fifty of her articles have appeared in journals such as *Curriculum Review, English Journal, Media & Methods, Southwest Philosophical Studies, English in Texas,* and the *Florida English Journal.* With Edward E. Wilson, Dr. Carroll co-authored *Acts of Teaching: How to Teach Writing* and co-edited *Poetry After Lunch: Poetry to Read Aloud.* She co-directs the New Jersey Writing Project in Texas.

Edward E. Wilson

A former editor of *English in Texas,* Edward E. Wilson has served as a high-school English teacher and a writing consultant in school districts nationwide. Wilson has served on both the Texas Teacher Professional Practices Commission and NCTE's Commission on Composition. Wilson's poetry appears in Paul Janeczko's anthology *The Music of What Happens.* With Dr. Carroll, he co-wrote *Acts of Teaching: How to Teach Writing* and co-edited *Poetry After Lunch: Poetry to Read Aloud.* Wilson co-directs the New Jersey Writing Project in Texas.

PROGRAM ADVISORS

The program advisors provided ongoing input throughout the development of *Prentice Hall Literature: Timeless Voices, Timeless Themes*. Their valuable insights ensure that the perspectives of the teachers throughout the country are represented within this literature series.

Diane Cappillo
English Department Chair
Barbara Goleman Senior High School
Miami, Florida

Anita Clay
Language Arts Instructor
Gateway Institute of Technology
St. Louis, Missouri

Ellen Eberly
Language Arts Instructor
Catholic Memorial High School
West Roxbury, Massachusetts

Nancy Fahner
L.A.M.P. Lansing Area Manufacturing
   Partnership
Ingham Intermediate School District
Mason, Michigan

Terri Fields
Instructor of Language Arts,
   Communication Arts, and Author
Sunnyslope High School
Phoenix, Arizona

Susan Goldberg
Language Arts Instructor
Westlake Middle School
Thornwood, New York

Margo L. Graf
English Department Chair, Speech,
   Yearbook, Journalism
Lane Middle School
Fort Wayne, Indiana

Christopher E. Guarraia
Language Arts Instructor
Lakewood High School
Saint Petersburg, Florida

V. Pauline Hodges
Teacher, Educational Consultant
Forgan High School
Forgan, Oklahoma

Karen Hurley
Language Arts Instructor
Perry Meridian Middle School
Indianapolis, Indiana

Lenore D. Hynes
Language Arts Coordinator
Sunman-Dearborn Community
   Schools
Sunman, Indiana

Linda Kramer
Language Arts Instructor
Norman High School North
Norman, Oklahoma

Thomas S. Lindsay
Assistant Superintendent of Schools
Mannheim District 83
Franklin Park, Illinois

Agathaniki (Niki) Locklear
English Department Chair
Simon Kenton High School
Independence, Kentucky

Ashley MacDonald
Language Arts Instructor
South Forsyth High School
Cumming, Georgia

Mary Ellen Mastej
Language Arts Instructor
Scott Middle School
Hammond, Indiana

Nancy L. Monroe
English, Speed Reading Teacher
Bolton High School
Alexandria, Louisiana

Jim Moody
Language Arts Instructor
Northside High School
Fort Smith, Arkansas

David Morris
Teacher of English, Writing,
   Publications, Yearbook
Washington High School
South Bend, Indiana

Rosemary A. Naab
English Department Chair
Ryan High School
Archdiocese of Philadelphia
Philadelphia, Pennsylvania

Ann Okamura
English Teacher
Laguna Creek High School
Elk Grove, California

Tucky Roger
Coordinator of Languages
Tulsa Public Schools
Tulsa, Oklahoma

Jonathan L. Schatz
English Teacher/Team Leader
Tappan Zee High School
Orangeburg, New York

John Scott
Assistant Principal
Middlesex High School
Saluda, Virginia

Ken Spurlock
Assistant Principal, Retired
Boone County High School
Florence, Kentucky

Dr. Jennifer Watson
Secondary Language Arts
   Coordinator
Putnam City Schools
Oklahoma City, Oklahoma

Joan West
Assistant Principal
Oliver Middle School
Broken Arrow, Oklahoma

Contents in Brief

Learn About Literature

Themes in Literature

Literary Genres

Resources

Indexes

UNIT 1

THEME: *Independence and Identity*

SKILLS WORKSHOPS

UNIT 2

THEME: *Common Threads*

SKILLS WORKSHOPS

UNIT 3

THEME: *What Matters*

SKILLS WORKSHOPS

UNIT 4

THEME: *Meeting Challenges*

SKILLS WORKSHOPS

UNIT 5

THEME: *Just for Fun*

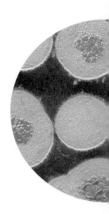

SKILLS WORKSHOPS

GENRE: *Short Story*

SKILLS WORKSHOPS

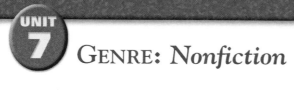

UNIT 7 GENRE: *Nonfiction*

SKILLS WORKSHOPS

UNIT 8

GENRE: *Drama*

SKILLS WORKSHOPS

UNIT 9

GENRE: *Poetry*

(continued)

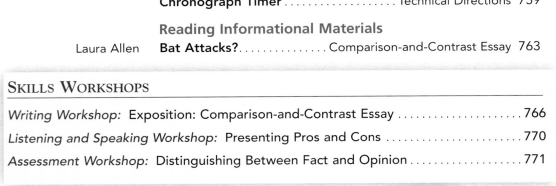

UNIT 10

GENRE: *Legends, Folk Tales, and Myths*

SKILLS WORKSHOPS

Complete Contents by Genre

Complete Contents by Genre

Poetry

MYTHS, LEGENDS, AND FOLK TALES

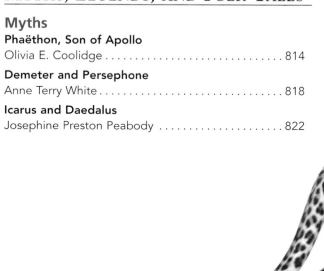

COMPARING LITERARY WORKS

Reading Informational Material

Connections

CONNECTIONS (CONTINUED)

HOW TO READ LITERATURE

WRITING WORKSHOPS

LISTENING AND SPEAKING WORKSHOPS

ASSESSMENT WORKSHOPS

Learn About Literature

Forms of Literature

Novel and Novella • Short Story • Nonfiction •
Poetry • Drama • Folk Literature

Just as there are different types of sports, like basketball or swimming, so there are different forms of literature. Each form, called a genre (zhän′ rə)**, has its own characteristics. In this introduction, you can learn about these genres. Keep these terms in mind:**

- **Prose** is writing that is organized in sentences and paragraphs. Prose can be further categorized as *fiction*—writing based on imagination—and *nonfiction*—writing about real people, places, objects, or events.

- **Poetry** is writing that uses rhythms and is organized in lines and groups of lines called stanzas.

Novel and Novella

Novels and **novellas** are long works of fiction that tell a story about imaginary people called characters who live in a made-up world. A novella is briefer than a novel, and both works are longer than a short story. However, both forms convey a message about life and have the same literary elements that short stories do.

- **How do these lines raise interest in the central character, Tom Sawyer, at the start of this novel?**

"Tom!"
No answer.
"Tom!"
No answer.
FROM *THE ADVENTURES OF TOM SAWYER,*
MARK TWAIN
PRENTICE HALL LITERATURE LIBRARY

Short Story

A **short story** is a brief work of fiction that tells a story about imaginary characters. Like longer forms of fiction, the story usually conveys a message about life.

- **What do you learn about the world of this story from its first sentence?**

Once there was a man who was driving in his car at dusk on a spring evening through part of the forest of Savernake.
FROM "THE THIRD WISH," JOAN AIKEN, PAGE 168

Nonfiction

Nonfiction is literature about real-life events or the world of ideas. Nonfiction can inform, persuade, or entertain.

- **What might be the purpose of this nonfiction passage?**

. . . Frankly, I don't believe that the task of bringing us all together can be accomplished by government. What we need now is soul force—the efforts of people. . . .
FROM "ALL TOGETHER NOW," BARBARA JORDAN, PAGE 532

> *"I read for pleasure, and that is the moment at which I learn most."*
>
> —*Margaret Atwood*

Poetry

Poetry is literature written in verse form. Poetry may have regular rhythms, and it is often presented in lines and groups of lines called stanzas, rather than in paragraphs. Poetry can say a lot in a few words. Whether telling a story or focusing on a single moment, a poem is alive in every line with feeling, thought, and observation.

○ **What word-pictures does James Stephens pack into the poetic lines at right?**

Drama

Drama, which can be written in prose or poetry, tells a story through the words and actions of actors who impersonate the characters on stage. In the text of a drama, the characters' words are indicated through dialogue. In addition to dialogue, a drama includes stage directions that tell actors how to move and speak.

○ **In what ways is the appearance of this dramatic text different from the appearance of a short story?**

STEVE. What was that? A meteor?

DON. [*Nods*] That's what it looked like. I didn't hear any crash though, did you?

STEVE. [*Shakes his head*] Nope. I didn't hear anything except a roar.

MRS. BRAND. [*From her porch*] Steve? What was that?

FROM "THE MONSTERS ARE DUE ON MAPLE STREET," ROD SERLING, PAGE 666

Gleaming in silver are the hills!
Blazing in silver is the sea!
And a silvery radiance spills
Where the moon drives royally!

Clad in silver tissue, I
March magnificently by!
"WASHED IN SILVER," JAMES STEPHENS, PAGE 713

Folk Literature

Most works of prose or poetry travel from the author's imagination to a page. **Folk literature** makes a different and longer journey, from the mouths of many tellers to the ears of many listeners. Folk literature—including myths, folk tales, and legends—is shaped by a group or culture over many years before being written down. Also, this type of literature expresses the hopes and values of the culture that creates it.

○ **What does the beginning of this myth reveal about the value that the ancient Greeks placed on cleverness and ingenuity? Explain your answer.**

Among all those mortals who grew so wise that they learned the secrets of the gods, none was more cunning than Daedalus.

He once built, for King Minos of Crete, a wonderful Labyrinth of winding ways. . . .

FROM "ICARUS AND DAEDALUS," JOSEPHINE PRESTON PEABODY, PAGE 822

Short Stories

*Plot and Conflict • Characters •
Point of View • Setting • Theme*

The short stories in this book will take you to fictional worlds as far away as India and as close as the family next door. By introducing you to new people in a variety of situations, these stories will touch your heart, challenge your mind, and stretch your imagination. No two of these tales are exactly alike. However, they all share common elements. This introduction will help you understand the elements of short stories.

Plot and Conflict

The **plot** of a story is a sequence of events linked by cause and effect, which means that earlier events advance the plot by bringing about later ones. A typical plot, diagrammed below, involves a **conflict** or problem. As the problem worsens, the story builds to the point of greatest tension, the climax. Then, the problem is solved and the story ends.

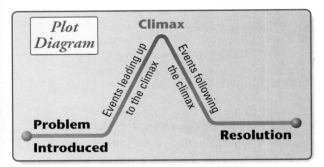

Plot Diagram
Climax
Events leading up to the climax
Events following the climax
Problem Introduced
Resolution

● **What conflict is identified in this passage from a short story?**

> Darzee and his wife only cowered down in the nest without answering . . . Then inch by inch out of the grass rose up the head and spread hood of Nag, the big black cobra . . ."
>
> FROM "RIKKI-TIKKI-TAVI,"
> RUDYARD KIPLING, PAGE **408**

Characters

The **characters** in a short story are the people or animals who take part in the action. To bring them to life, authors use characterization, revealing them through their thoughts, words, speech patterns, and actions or through the narrator's descriptions of them. *Flat characters* have just one or a few traits, while *round characters* have many traits. Similarly, *static characters* do not change, while *dynamic characters* change in the course of a story.

● **Do the details in the passage from this story suggest that Harry is a static or a dynamic character? Why?**

> For years, after school, Harry had always stopped in to see his father at work. Many of Harry's friends stopped there, too, to spend a few cents choosing penny candy from the giant bins or to sample Mr. Tillian's latest batch of roasted peanuts. Mr. Tillian looked forward to seeing his son and his son's friends every day. He liked the company.
>
> When Harry entered junior high school, though, he didn't come by the candy and nut shop as often. Nor did his friends. They were older and they had more spending money. . . .
>
> FROM "PAPA'S PARROT," CYNTHIA RYLANT, PAGE **438**

> *"The key to a short story is tension."*
> —William Trevor

Point of View

The **point of view** is the vantage point from which a story is told. Here are three common points of view:

- *First person,* when the narrator is involved in the action and refers to himself or herself as "I."
- *Third person,* when the narrator is outside the action and refers to characters as "he" or "she."
- *Omniscient* (äm nish´ ənt) *third person,* when the narrator knows every character's thoughts.

○ **What clues to the point of view can you find in this early paragraph from a story?**

I went down that way on my way to school one spring morning. It was out of my way but I wanted to see if Walter was there.
FROM "STOLEN DAY," SHERWOOD ANDERSON, PAGE 494

Setting

Every story has a **setting**, the place and time of the action. A story's setting can be anywhere in any time.

○ **What do you learn about the time and place of the action from the opening of this story?**

The dark sky, filled with angry, swirling clouds, reflected Greg Ridley's mood as he sat on the stoop of his building. His father's voice came to him again . . .
FROM "THE TREASURE OF LEMON BROWN," WALTER DEAN MYERS, PAGE 475

Theme

In stories, literary elements work together to convey a **theme**, an insight into life. Certain recurring themes appear in many stories because they have meaning for numbers of readers. One such theme is the value of courage and loyalty.

Authors communicate themes in different ways, sometimes stating them directly. More often, however, writers imply or suggest the theme through what happens to the characters. To formulate an implied theme, consider clues like the meaning of a story's title, how a character solves a problem, and passages—especially near the end—that convey powerful emotions.

○ **If you were trying to formulate the implied theme of Laurence Yep's "Ribbons," why might you focus on this passage near the end of the story?**

Suddenly I felt as if there were an invisible ribbon binding us, tougher than silk and satin, stronger even than steel; and it joined her [the speaker's grandmother] to Mom and Mom to me.

I wanted to hug her so badly that I just did. Though she was stiff at first, she gradually softened in my arms. . . .
FROM "RIBBONS," LAURENCE YEP, PAGE 466

Nonfiction

Autobiography • Biography • Exposition • Essay • Informational Text

Nonfiction introduces you to a wide variety of real people and places—some that are familiar to you and some that are far from your experience. Through the essays, biographies, and articles in this textbook, you can enjoy new experiences, consider new ideas, and learn new concepts. The terms defined on these pages will help you discover the characteristics and varied purposes of nonfiction.

Autobiography

An **autobiography** is the story of part or all of a person's life, written by that person. As a story, a narrative of events, it shares certain characteristics with fiction, such as characters, point of view, setting, and theme. Unlike fiction, however, it presents a version of what actually happened to the author rather than describing a made-up world. The author's purposes for telling this life story may be to teach lessons in life, to tell how he or she developed, to entertain, or any combination of these.

⦿ **What does this passage from Russell Baker's autobiography reveal about his purposes for writing?**

The flaw in my character which she had already spotted was lack of "gumption." My idea of a perfect afternoon was lying in front of the radio rereading my favorite Big Little Book, *Dick Tracy Meets Stooge Viller.* My mother despised inactivity. Seeing me have a good time in repose, she was powerless to hide her disgust. "You've got no more gumption than a bump on a log," she said.

FROM "NO GUMPTION," RUSSELL BAKER, PAGE **554**

Biography

In a **biography**, an author tells the story of someone else's life. Biographies have been written about many famous historical and contemporary people, but they can also be written about relatively unknown people, too. Like an autobiography, this literary form is a factual prose narrative with elements such as plot, characters, setting, and theme. It can also share many of the purposes of autobiography, such as teaching and entertaining. With biography, however, there is often a special emphasis on explaining the causes and effects of a subject's actions.

⦿ **This passage comes from a biographical essay on baseball player Nolan Ryan. What does the author indicate is a cause of Ryan's long career?**

Ryan's physical conditioning has kept him going long after most players his age have retired. He stays fit during the winter, and during the season, maintains a workout schedule of weightlifting, throwing, and running that almost never changes. The times are very different from his early days in baseball, when all a pitcher did between starts was throw enough each day to stay loose.

FROM "NOLAN RYAN," WILLIAM W. LACE, PAGE **572**

> *". . . essayists tell the truth. They just say what they think, as nicely or as brutally as they can."*
> —Robert Winder

Exposition

An **expository essay** presents and explains information. Exposition helps writers share ideas about a variety of subjects.

⊙ **What specific aspect of poetry do you think this passage from an expository essay addresses?**

What is poetry? . . . Many have suspected that it was invented as a school subject, because you have to take exams on it. But that is not what poetry is or why it is still around. . . .
FROM "HOW TO ENJOY POETRY," JAMES DICKEY, PAGE 544

Essay

Essays, brief prose works that are based on fact, can be defined by their different purposes.

- **Descriptive** essays present people or places using vivid, sensory details.
- **Personal** essays provide an informal account of an important episode from a person's life.
- **Persuasive** essays develop arguments to show why readers should think or act in a certain way.

⊙ **Who is the subject of this personal essay?**

During the next few weeks Miss Ryan overcame my fears of tall, energetic teachers as she bent over my desk to help me with a word in the pre-primer. . . . Frequently she burst into happy announcements to the whole class. "Ito can read a sentence," . . .
FROM *BARRIO BOY,* ERNESTO GALARZA, PAGE 523

Informational Text

Imagine you had a friendly guide who could help you buy the right clothes, discover what is happening in the world, learn a subject, or master a sport. **Informational texts** are such a guide. Ranging from instructional manuals and signs to textbooks and newspapers, the informational writing you encounter in your daily life can help you perform necessary tasks or enjoy your recreation.

⊙ **One type of informational text is a press release, an announcement that an organization makes available to the media. What does this information from a press release tell you about the purpose of a new exhibition?**

From R&B came soul, funk, disco and rap—all important African American music forms that still resonate with energy and excitement today.

The Rock and Roll Hall of Fame and Museum honors the men and women who have made unique contributions to the evolution of rock and roll in our new exhibit, "Let the Good Times Roll: A Tribute to Rhythm & Blues."
FROM "NEW EXHIBIT: LET THE GOOD TIMES ROLL," PAGE 489

Drama

Dialogue and Stage Directions •
Characterization • Plot and Conflict • Theme

The word *drama* comes from the Greek word *dran*, meaning "to do" or "to act." It is this doing or acting quality that makes drama unique in literature. While plays share many elements with prose fiction and poetry—plot, character, setting, and theme—the greatest difference is that drama is designed to be presented by actors on a stage before an audience. The terms defined on these pages will help you discover the characteristics of drama.

Dialogue and Stage Directions

Much more than fiction writers, playwrights tell a story through **dialogue**, the words of the characters placed next to their names. They support the dialogue with **stage directions**, bracketed instructions about sets and actors' movements and emotions. By seeing a stage in your mind as you read, you can use the dialogue and stage directions to create an imaginary performance.

● What effect would the music and lighting have on this scene from *A Christmas Carol*?

SCENE 1 [*Ghostly music in auditorium.*
A single spotlight on JACOB MARLEY,
D.C. *He is ancient: awful, dead-
eyed. He speaks straight out to
auditorium.*]

MARLEY. [*Cackle-voiced*] My name is
Jacob Marley and I am dead. [*He
laughs.*] Oh, no, there's no doubt
that I am dead. . . .

FROM *A CHRISTMAS CAROL: SCROOGE AND
MARLEY,* ISRAEL HOROVITZ, PAGE **600**

Characterization

Characterization is the process of creating fictional characters. In drama, characterization depends on the dialogue and stage directions. Playwrights reveal what characters are like through the characters' own words, what the characters do, how they look and move, and what others say about them. Any or all of these sources will provide clues to a character's traits, emotions, and changes.

● In this scene from *A Christmas Carol*, the miser Scrooge is talking to The Ghost of Christmas Present. Which parts of the dialogue and stage directions hint that Scrooge is becoming a less selfish character?

SCROOGE. I went forth last night on compulsion, and learnt a lesson which is working now. Tonight, if you have aught to teach me, let me profit by it.

PRESENT. Touch my robe.
[SCROOGE *walks cautiously to*
PRESENT *and touches his robe.*]

FROM *A CHRISTMAS CAROL: SCROOGE AND
MARLEY,* ISRAEL HOROVITZ, PAGE **600**

Plot and Conflict

As in a short story, the **plot** in a drama is a linked sequence of events involving a **conflict,** a struggle between opposing forces. The problem or conflict is introduced, tension builds to its greatest point, the climax, and then the problem is solved.

Plays are especially suited to showing conflicts that result in action. You can learn about each character's conflicts through the dialogue and action. In addition, you can see the plot unfold and advance with each passing scene.

● **Which words suggest that the playwright wants the actor to use gestures and a tone of voice that reveal an inner conflict?**

> **S**TEVE. Go ahead, Tommy. We'll be right back. And you'll see. That wasn't any ship or anything like it. That was just a . . . a meteor or something. Likely as not—[*He turns to the group, now trying to weight his words with an optimism he obviously doesn't feel but is desperately trying to instill in himself as well as the others.*] No doubt it did have something to do with all this power failure and the rest of it. Meteors can do some crazy things. Like sunspots.
>
> FROM "THE MONSTERS ARE DUE ON MAPLE STREET," ROD SERLING, PAGE 666

Theme

Changes that a main character experiences can be clues to the play's **theme**, its central idea about life. As an individual reader, you can explore the play's theme by testing it against your own experience and, if possible, by discussing it with classmates. If you attend a performance, you can discuss the meaning, or theme, of the play with others who watched the performance.

● **In what way do the inner changes that Scrooge expresses in this speech point toward the theme of *A Christmas Carol*?**

> **S**CROOGE. . . . Oh, Good Spirit, I see by your wavering hand that your good nature intercedes for me and pities me. Assure me that I yet may change these shadows that you have shown me by an altered life!
>
> [FUTURE'S *hand trembles; pointing has stopped.*]
>
> I will honor Christmas in my heart and try to keep it all the year. I will live in the Past, the Present, and the Future. The Spirits of all Three shall strive within me. I will not shut out the lessons that they teach.
>
> FROM "A CHRISTMAS CAROL: SCROOGE AND MARLEY," ISRAEL HOROVITZ, PAGE 600

Poetry

Narrative and Lyric Poetry • Form •
Rhythm and Rhyme • Sound Devices •
Figurative Language

There are almost as many definitions of poetry as there are poets. Poetry can appear in neat stanzas or it can look almost like prose on a page. It can tell a story, express an idea, convey an emotion, describe a setting, or examine a situation. The terms defined on these pages will help you discover the characteristics of poetry.

Narrative and Lyric Poetry

Like a short story, a **narrative poem** tells a story using plot, characters, setting, and theme. However, a narrative poem tells a story more musically than prose fiction does. It uses sounds and rhythms to make the story memorable.

A **lyric poem** does not tell a story. Instead, it expresses the thoughts and feelings of the poem's speaker, the one who says its words. Once, lyric poems were actually sung or chanted to the accompaniment of a stringed instrument called a lyre. Today, they rely on their own music of rhythm and sound.

● **What details of appearance and sound make the beginning of this narrative poem different from a prose narrative?**

There are strange things done in the
     midnight sun
   By the men who moil for gold;
The Arctic trails have their secret tales
     That would make your
     blood run cold . . .

FROM "THE CREMATION OF SAM MCGEE,"
ROBERT SERVICE, PAGE **708**

Form

Poetic **form** refers to the shape and appearance of the poem in lines and stanzas on the page. The basic unit of poetic form is the **line**, a group of words extending toward the right margin. In their varied lengths, however, lines of poetry differ from lines of prose, which automatically continue until they reach a set right margin.

Poets often group lines into **stanzas**, which may repeat regularly. Stanzas in a poem are something like paragraphs in prose, although paragraphs usually vary more in size.

With the tools of line and stanza, poets build poems of many different shapes. Often, a chosen form helps convey the meaning or feeling a poet wants to express.

● **In what way does the beginning of this concrete poem begin to resemble its subject, a seal?**

See how he dives
  From the rocks with a zoom!
    See how he darts
       Through his watery room
      Past crabs and eels
      And green seaweed,
     Past fluffs of sandy
    Minnow feed!

FROM "SEAL," WILLIAM JAY SMITH, PAGE **720**

> *". . . a poem . . . begins in delight and ends in wisdom."*
>
> —Robert Frost

Rhythm and Rhyme

Two elements that give poetry its musical quality are rhythm and rhyme.

- **Rhythm** is the pattern of stressed (´) and unstressed (˘) syllables, as in this example:

  Ĭt wăs mánў ănd mánў ă yéar ăgó . . .

- **Rhyme** is the linking of sounds at the ends of words. For example, *ago* and *know* are rhyming words.

⬤ **What rhythm and rhyme do you find in this passage from "Annabel Lee"?**

And so, all the nighttide, I lie down
    by the side
Of my darling, my darling, my life
    and my bride . . .
FROM "ANNABEL LEE," EDGAR ALLAN POE, PAGE 728

Sound Devices

In addition to rhythm and rhyme, these **sound devices** also make poetry musical:

- **Alliteration** is the repetition of nearby consonant sounds in stressed syllables, as in *Full fathom five thy father lies.*

- **Onomatopoeia** is the use of words, such as *whirr,* whose sound suggests their meaning.

⬤ **Which words in this passage create alliteration?**

Nothing of him that doth fade
But doth suffer a sea change . . .
FROM "FULL FATHOM FIVE," WILLIAM SHAKESPEARE, PAGE 736

Figurative Language

Poems use **figurative language**, words not meant in their exact dictionary sense, to describe and to take you by surprise. Each type of figurative language is based on a comparison of apparently unlike items:

Type	Description	Example
Simile	Uses *like* or *as* to compare two apparently unlike items	"And the muscles of his brawny arms/Are strong as iron bands."
Metaphor	Describes one thing as if it were another, apparently unlike thing	"The fog comes/ on little cat feet."
Personification	Gives human qualities to something nonhuman	A poem describing a volcano as if it were a woman

⬤ **Which type of figurative language does this passage contain?**

They love to see the flaming forge,
    And hear the bellows roar,
And catch the burning sparks that fly
    Like chaff from a threshing floor.
FROM "THE VILLAGE BLACKSMITH," HENRY WADSWORTH LONGFELLOW, PAGE 748

Folk Literature

Legend • Folk Tale • Myth • Fable

Folk literature develops in every culture, reflecting the history and beliefs of the people who create it. Most often, folk literature is part of an oral tradition in which stories are told, revised, and retold as they are passed from one generation to the next. These stories explain important events in the history of a people or the natural world. In addition, they reflect cultural values and they entertain. The terms defined on these pages will help you discover the characteristics of folk literature.

Legend

A **legend** is a story about the past believed to be based on real events or people. However, if a legend is in some way based on history, it is a version of history seen through a strange magnifying glass. In a legend, everything looks bigger and stranger than usual. Nature does things that seem beyond nature, or supernatural. Human characters are larger than life, as if they were forces of nature.

● **Which details in this first paragraph suggest that this Mexican legend is based on history?**

Before the Spaniards came to Mexico and marched on the Aztec capital of Tenochtitlan there were two volcanoes to the southeast of that city. The Spaniards destroyed much of Tenochtitlan and built another city in its place and called it Mexico City. It is known by that name still, and the pass through which the Spaniards came to the ancient Tenochtitlan is still there, as are the volcanoes on each side of that pass. . . .

FROM "POPOCATEPETL AND IXTLACCIHUATL," RETOLD BY JULIET PIGGOTT, PAGE **778**

Folk Tale

The **folk tale** is a story passed on by word of mouth through a culture for the purpose of teaching ideas and values. The lessons of folk tales reflect the hopes and wisdom of the tellers and listeners. As you read folk tales, use a chart like the one here to identify the story with the culture that created it.

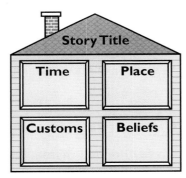

Story Title

| Time | Place |
| Customs | Beliefs |

● **How does this passage from an African American folk tale about slavery reflect the hopes of tellers and listeners alike?**

There was a great outcryin. The bent backs straightened up. Old and young who were called slaves and could fly joined hands. . . . They rose on the air. . . . Way above the plantation, way over the slavery land. Say they flew away to *Free-dom*. . . .

FROM "THE PEOPLE COULD FLY," RETOLD BY VIRGINIA HAMILTON, PAGE **798**

Myth

A **myth** is a fictional tale that explains the actions of gods, the interactions with gods and humans, or the causes of natural phenomena. Unlike legends, myths have little historical truth and involve supernatural elements. Every culture has its collection of myths. Among the most well known are the myths of ancient Greece and Rome.

As a member of a scientifically minded society, you may read these "explanations" with disbelief. However, a story that is not scientifically true can still contain other kinds of truth, including instruction about actions and their consequences or about the ways people can interact with others successfully.

⬤ **The myth of Phaëthon describes a young man who defies the will of the gods. In this final paragraph from the myth, what natural fact do the details explain?**

Unhappy Clymene and her daughters wandered over the whole earth seeking the body of the boy they loved so well. When they found him, they took him and buried him. Over his grave they wept and could not be comforted. At last the gods in pity for their grief changed them into poplar trees, which weep with tears of amber in memory of Phaëthon.

FROM "PHAËTHON, SON OF APOLLO," RETOLD BY OLIVIA E. COOLIDGE, PAGE 814

Fable

Fables, brief stories that teach a lesson called a **moral**, are like the cartoons of folk literature. These tales are cartoonlike in their humor, brevity, simplicity, and frequent use of talking animals to make a point about life.

Whether in a cartoon or a fable, talking animals exhibit human failings. The creators of fables may have realized that people often find it easier to learn about their weaknesses if these faults are disguised in entertaining stories about animals.

⬤ **What types of people do the fox and the crow in this fable portray?**

A Fox once saw a Crow fly off with a piece of cheese in its beak and settle on a branch of a tree. "That's for me, as I am a Fox," said Master Reynard, and he walked up to the foot of the tree.

"Good day, Mistress Crow," he cried. "How well you are looking today . . . let me but hear one song from you that I may greet you as the Queen of Birds."

The Crow lifted up her head and began to caw her best. . . .

FROM "THE FOX AND THE CROW," AESOP, PAGE 803

UNIT 1

Independence and Identity

Untitled, Steve Dininno

Exploring the Theme

One of the most rewarding searches you will ever conduct is the search to discover the qualities that make you an individual. The literature in this unit will introduce you to people of all generations who have explored the challenges and experienced the rewards of striving toward independence and identity.

◄ **Critical Viewing** What makes the bicyclists individuals? What makes them part of a group? **[Distinguish]**

Why Read Literature?

As you read the selections in this unit, you will explore the theme of independence and identity from a variety of angles. In addition to exploring the theme, you will have other purposes for reading as well. Preview three of the purposes you might set before reading the works in this unit.

Read for the love of literature.

When Walt Whitman wrote his first book of poetry, *Leaves of Grass*, publishers thought it was terrible and did not want to publish it! Whitman set his own type and paid the printer with his own money. Today, Whitman is recognized as having had a powerful and positive influence on American poetry. Read part of the first poem in *Leaves of Grass*, **"Song of Myself,"** page 38, to form your own opinion about Whitman's work.

Emily Dickinson is often grouped with Whitman as one of the greatest American poets. Yet, she claimed that she never read Walt Whitman's work because she heard it was "disgraceful." Compare her work to his when you read **"I'm Nobody,"** page 39.

Read for information.

One of the early English child-labor laws stated that children under fourteen could not work more than twelve hours. Today, children have more free time—or do they? Read the *Time* article **"Burning Out at Nine?"** on page 33 to find out more about how young Americans spend their time.

Many people tried to find out about their ancestors after reading Alex Haley's book *Roots* or watching the TV mini-series it inspired. Read **"My Furthest-Back Person,"** page 46, to find out how Haley followed the difficult path back through his family's history.

Read to be entertained.

Jack Finney wrote the science-fiction novel that inspired the horror movie *Invasion of the Body Snatchers*. Most of his work is not as frightening but just as unusual. Give yourself goosebumps by considering an unsettling possibility when you read **"The Third Level,"** page 64.

Most animals do not recognize their own reflections. Birds who have established a territory will often do battle with the "enemy" they see reflected in a window. For a humorous adventure involving reflections and misunderstandings, read **"The Cat Who Thought She Was a Dog and the Dog Who Thought He Was a Cat,"** page 6.

 Take It to the Net

Visit the Web site for online instruction and activities related to each selection in this unit.

www.phschool.com

How to Read Literature

Use Literal Comprehension Strategies

Reading is similar to athletics. Just as you need to be in good physical shape to play basketball or baseball, you need to be in good mental shape to read. As you read the selections in this unit, use the following strategies to help you succeed at the reading game.

1. Clarify word meanings.

When you come across unfamiliar words or words that can have more than one meaning, look for clues to the word's meaning in the surrounding sentences or paragraphs. Clues that clarify word meanings include the following:

- **Definition**—the meaning of the word is explained
- **Example**—one or more words indicate the category the word names
- **Restatement**—a word or phrase says the same thing in a different way
- **Contrast**—another word shows what the unfamiliar word is not

Use new words to make them a natural part of your vocabulary.

2. Use roots and affixes.

Break a word into its parts to find a part you can recognize and pronounce. The root is the most basic part of a word that has meaning after the added parts that change its meaning are removed. Affixes are the added parts. Look at the example at right.

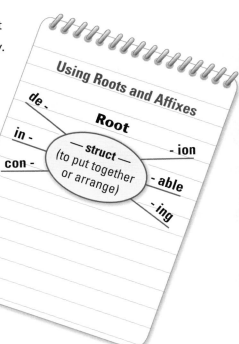

Using Roots and Affixes

de -
in -
con -

Root

— struct —
(to put together or arrange)

- ion
- able
- ing

3. Recognize figures of speech.

Figures of speech are expressions not meant to be taken literally. Look for what the words actually mean.

If a writer writes "It was raining cats and dogs," you know that cats and dogs were not falling from the sky. Instead, this unusual expression indicates that rain is falling heavily. Recognizing figures of speech will help you avoid misunderstandings.

4. Break down long sentences.

Find the main parts of the sentence that tell *who* or *what* the sentence is about and what happens—even if the writer has separated these two main parts with descriptions or additional details.

As you read the selections in this unit, review the reading strategies and look at the notes in the side columns. Use the suggestions to apply the strategies for literal comprehension.

Prepare to Read

The Cat Who Thought She Was a Dog and the Dog Who Thought He Was a Cat

Peasant shows his wife her reflection in the mirror, undated painting

Preview

Connecting to the Literature

The characters in "The Cat Who Thought She Was a Dog and the Dog Who Thought He Was a Cat" are unconcerned with appearances until they see their reflections in a mirror. As you read this story, think about how much appearance influences your opinion of yourself and others.

Background

The characters in this story are peasant farmers who have little money for items that are not necessary for their survival. Because mirrors are not necessary for survival, the Skibas have no experience with them. This unfamiliarity with mirrors leads to confusion and conflict when they first discover one.

Literary Analysis
The Moral of a Story

Some short stories have a **moral,** a lesson or guide for living, that you can apply to your own life. The author or a character may directly state the moral, or the moral may be suggested by what the characters learn. As you read the story, look for the lesson it teaches. Use the following focus questions to help you:

1. What do the characters learn from their experiences?

2. How can the lesson the characters learn be applied to life?

Connecting Literary Elements

The moral of a story is often indicated by the way a conflict or problem is worked out. A **conflict** is a struggle between two opposing forces. It may occur between two characters, within a character with two opposing feelings or needs, or between a character and an outside force, such as nature. The following example shows a conflict between two animal characters from this story:

> So great was the distress of Burek and Kot that for the first time in their lives, they turned on each other. Burek took a bite out of Kot's throat and Kot hissed and spat at him and clawed his muzzle.

Reading Strategy
Clarifying Word Meanings

As you read, you will sometimes come across words or phrases that are unfamiliar or that have more than one meaning. **Clarify**—get a clearer understanding of—word meanings by using additional information in the text around the unfamiliar word. Following are two types of clues to look for in surrounding text:

- **Restatement** words or phrases that say the same thing in a different way
- **Explanation** direct statements that tell what a word means or add information that makes the meaning more clear

Use a chart like the one shown to clarify word meanings as you read.

Clarification Chart

Unfamiliar Word	...he said a half *gulden*
Explanation	...he said a half gulden, <u>which was a lot of money for poor peasants</u>
Clarification	A gulden is an amount of money

Vocabulary Development

enthralled (en thrôld´) v. fascinated; charmed (p. 7)

protruded (prō trōōd´ id) v. stuck out; extended (p. 9)

console (kən sōl´) v. comfort; make less sad (p. 9)

afflicted (ə flik´ tid) v. received pain or suffering (p. 9)

vanity (van´ ə tē) n. too much pride in one's appearance (p. 9)

anguish (aŋ´ gwish) n. great suffering; agony (p. 10)

The Cat Who Thought She Was a Dog and the Dog Who Thought He Was a Cat

~ ISAAC BASHEVIS SINGER

"Then Came a Dog and Bit the Cat" from Had Gadya (Tale of a Goat), 1919, E. Lissitzky, The Jewish Museum, New York, New York

▲ **Critical Viewing** Singer includes humorous touches in his story. What details does this artist use to create humor? Explain. [**Analyze**]

Once there was a poor peasant, Jan Skiba by name. He lived with his wife and three daughters in a one-room hut with a straw roof, far from the village. The house had a bed, a bench bed, and a stove, but no mirror. A mirror was a luxury for a poor peasant. And why would a peasant need a mirror? Peasants aren't curious about their appearance.

But this peasant did have a dog and a cat in his hut. The dog was named Burek and the cat Kot. They had both been born within the same week. As little food as the peasant had for himself and his family, he still wouldn't let his dog and cat go hungry. Since the dog had never seen another dog and the cat had never seen another cat and they saw only each other, the dog thought he was a cat and the cat thought she was a dog. True, they were far from being alike by nature. The dog barked and the cat meowed. The dog chased rabbits and the cat lurked after mice. But must all creatures be exactly like their own kind? The peasant's children weren't exactly alike either. Burek and Kot lived on good terms, often ate from the same dish, and tried to mimic each other. When Burek barked, Kot tried to bark along, and when Kot meowed, Burek tried to meow too. Kot occasionally chased rabbits and Burek made an effort to catch a mouse.

The peddlers who bought groats,[1] chickens, eggs, honey, calves, and whatever was available from the peasants in the village never came to Jan Skiba's poor hut. They knew that Jan was so poor he had nothing to sell. But one day a peddler happened to stray there. When he came inside and began to lay out his wares, Jan Skiba's wife and daughters were bedazzled by all the pretty doodads. From his sack the peddler drew yellow beads, false pearls, tin earrings, rings, brooches, colored kerchiefs, garters, and other such trinkets. But what <u>enthralled</u> the women of the house most was a mirror set in a wooden frame. They asked the peddler its price and he said a half gulden, which was a lot of money for poor peasants. After a while, Jan Skiba's wife, Marianna, made a proposition to the peddler. She would pay him five groshen a month for the mirror. The peddler hesitated a moment. The mirror took up too much space in his sack and there was always the danger it might break. He, therefore, decided to go along, took the first payment of five groshen from Marianna, and left the mirror with the family. He visited the region often and he knew the Skibas to be honest people. He would gradually get his money back and a profit besides.

---

1. **groats** (grōtz) *n.* coarsely cracked grains, especially wheat, buckwheat, oats, or barley.

Reading Strategy
Clarifying Word Meanings
What explanation helps you clarify the meaning of *nature* as it is used here?

enthralled (en thrôld´) *v.* fascinated; charmed

☑**Reading Check**
What does Marianna buy?

La Cour d' une Ferme (The Farmyard), Marc Chagall

▲ **Critical Viewing** What details in this painting illustrate that Singer's story is set in a rural area far from a village? **[Support]**

The mirror created a commotion in the hut. Until then Marianna and the children had seldom seen themselves. Before they had the mirror, they had only seen their reflections in the barrel of water that stood by the door. Now they could see themselves clearly and they began to find defects in their faces, defects they had never noticed before. Marianna was pretty but she had a tooth missing in front and she felt that this made her ugly. One daughter discovered that her nose was too snub and too broad; a second that her chin was too narrow and too long; a third that her face was sprinkled with freckles. Jan Skiba too caught a glimpse of himself in the mirror and grew displeased by his thick lips and his teeth, which <u>protruded</u> like a buck's. That day, the women of the house became so absorbed in the mirror they didn't cook supper, didn't make up the bed, and neglected all the other household tasks. Marianna had heard of a dentist in the big city who could replace a missing tooth, but such things were expensive. The girls tried to <u>console</u> each other that they were pretty enough and that they would find suitors, but they no longer felt as jolly as before. They had been <u>afflicted</u> with the <u>vanity</u> of city girls. The one with the broad nose kept trying to pinch it together with her fingers to make it narrower; the one with the too-long chin pushed it up with her fist to make it shorter; the one with the freckles wondered if there was a salve² in the city that could remove freckles. But where would the money come from for the fare to the city? And what about the money to buy this salve? For the first time the Skiba family deeply felt its poverty and envied the rich.

But the human members of the household were not the only ones affected. The dog and the cat also grew disturbed by the mirror. The hut was low and the mirror had been hung just above a bench. The first time the cat sprang up on the bench and saw her image in the mirror, she became terribly perplexed. She had never before seen such a creature. Kot's whiskers bristled, she began to meow at her reflection and raised a paw to it, but the other creature meowed back and raised her paw too. Soon the dog jumped up on the bench, and when he saw the other dog he became wild with rage and shock. He barked at the other dog and showed him his teeth, but the other barked back and bared his fangs too. So great was the distress of Burek and Kot that for the first time in their lives they turned on each other. Burek took a bite out of Kot's throat and Kot hissed and spat at him and clawed his muzzle. They both started to bleed and the sight of blood aroused them so that they nearly killed or crippled each other. The members of the household barely managed to separate them. Because a dog is stronger than a cat,

protruded (prō trōōd′ id) v. stuck out; extended

console (kən sōl′) v. comfort; make less sad

afflicted (ə flik′ tid) v. received pain or suffering

vanity (van′ ə tē) n. very proud of one's appearance

☑**Reading Check**
What problems does the mirror cause?

---

2. **salve** (sav) n. lotion or ointment used to soothe or heal.

Burek had to be tied outside, and he howled all day and all night. In their <u>anguish</u>, both the dog and the cat stopped eating.

When Jan Skiba saw the disruption the mirror had created in his household, he decided a mirror wasn't what his family needed. "Why look at yourself," he said, "when you can see and admire the sky, the sun, the moon, the stars, and the earth, with all its forests, meadows, rivers, and plants?" He took the mirror down from the wall and put it away in the woodshed. When the peddler came for his monthly installment, Jan Skiba gave him back the mirror and in its stead, bought kerchiefs and slippers for the women. After the mirror disappeared, Burek and Kot returned to normal. Again Burek thought he was a cat and Kot was sure she was a dog. Despite all the defects the girls had found in themselves, they made good marriages. The village priest heard what had happened at Jan Skiba's house and he said, "A glass mirror shows only the skin of the body. The real image of a person is in his willingness to help himself and his family and, as far as possible, all those he comes in contact with. This kind of mirror reveals the very soul of the person."

anguish (aṉʹ gwish) *n.* great suffering; agony

Review and Assess

Thinking About the Selection

1. **Respond:** What are some ways in which your life would be different without mirrors?

2. **(a) Recall:** List some of the goods that the peddler shows Marianna and her daughters. **(b) Compare and Contrast:** What is similar about all these goods? **(c) Deduce:** Why do the Skibas usually avoid buying goods such as these?

3. **(a) Recall:** Before the Skibas buy a mirror, how do the dog and the cat act toward each other? **(b) Compare and Contrast:** How does their behavior change after the Skibas buy a mirror? **(c) Deduce:** Why does their behavior change?

4. **(a) Compare and Contrast:** How are the humans' reactions to the mirror similar to and different from the animals' reactions? **(b) Generalize:** Does the mirror have a positive or negative effect on the humans and the animals? **(c) Apply:** What are some positive and negative effects of mirrors on people in general?

5. **(a) Analyze:** In what ways does the mirror change the Skibas' opinion of themselves? **(b) Infer:** Why does the mirror change their opinion? **(c) Make a Judgment:** Did Jan make the right decision in returning the mirror? Explain.

Isaac Bashevis Singer

(1904–1991)

As a boy in Poland, Isaac Bashevis Singer became fascinated with the events and people he encountered in his home town of Warsaw. As a writer, Singer created characters based on the real people he recalled from his past.

Singer's respect for the past is also shown in the language in which he chose to write. Although he allowed his works to be translated into a number of languages, Singer usually wrote in Yiddish, the language of his childhood.

Singer came to the United States in 1935 and, over the years, became famous for his novels and stories, which were often based on what he saw and heard as a boy. He won the Nobel Prize for Literature in 1978.

Review and Assess

Literary Analysis

The Moral of a Story

1. What do the characters learn from their experiences?
2. How can the lesson the characters learn be applied to life?
3. In a chart like the one shown, give three examples from the story that illustrate the moral, and explain how they illustrate the point.

Examples	Explanation
1.	1.
2.	2.
3.	3.

Connecting Literary Elements

4. What is the main conflict in the story?
5. How does the conflict turn out?
6. Using a chart like the one shown, replace each word or phrase with information from the story.

Reading Strategy

Clarifying Word Meanings

7. What restatements or explanations help you clarify the meaning of *groshen* (page 7) by restating its meaning in other words?
8. *Absorbed* can mean "soaked up" or "totally focused on." Using clues from the first paragraph on page 9, clarify the meaning of *absorbed* as it is used in this story.

Extend Understanding

9. **(a) Science Connection:** Explain what a mirror can and cannot show about a person. **(b) Assess:** Do people today value appearances too much, too little, or just enough? Explain.

Quick Review

The **moral** of a story is the lesson that it teaches. To review moral, see page 5.

Conflict is the struggle between two opposing forces in a story. To review conflict, see page 5.

To **clarify the meaning** of a word is to make its meaning clear.

 Take It to the Net

www.phschool.com
Take the interactive self-test online to check your understanding of these selections.

Integrate Language Skills

Vocabulary Development Lesson

Word Analysis: Latin Prefix *pro-*

In this story you met a character whose teeth *protruded*. The Latin prefix *pro-* can mean "in front of" or "forward or before in place or time." The Latin base *-trude* means "to thrust or jut out." Teeth that *protrude* jut out in front of the lip.

Explain how each italicized *pro-* word in the following paragraph includes the meaning "before, ahead, in front of" or "forth."

Today, factories *produce* mirrors. Advertisers *promote* them by showing models holding mirrors. The ads indirectly *promise* people that they will look like models if they buy mirrors.

Spelling Strategy

The *gw* sound following *n*, as in *anguish*, is spelled *gu*. Write words containing the *gu* spelling of the *gw* sound that fit the following definitions.

1. Human speech: l____?____
2. To lose energy: lan____?____sh

Concept Development: Clarify Word Meaning

On your paper, write the word or phrase that could be used to clarify the meaning of the first word through restatement.

1. enthralled: **(a)** fascinated, **(b)** stalled, **(c)** enjoyed
2. console: **(a)** help, **(b)** comfort, **(c)** go alone
3. afflicted: **(a)** troubled, **(b)** calmed, **(c)** beaten
4. protruded: **(a)** intruded, **(b)** stuck out, **(c)** protected
5. vanity: **(a)** beauty, **(b)** large mirror, **(c)** excessive pride
6. anguish: **(a)** tears, **(b)** suffering, **(c)** anger

Grammar Lesson

Nouns

A **noun** is a word that names a person, animal, place, thing, or idea. Singer uses the following kinds of nouns in his story.

Person:	peasant, daughter	Animal:	cat, rabbit
Thing:	mirror, trinket	Idea:	soul, rage
Place:	village, city		

▶ *For more practice, see page R28, Exercise A.*
Practice Write the nouns in these sentences. Tell what kind of item each names.

1. The peasant had a dog and a cat in his hut.
2. The peddlers never came to the hut.
3. There was a mirror in his sack.
4. All day, the women looked into the mirror.
5. The family felt true distress.

Writing Application Choose a noun from the story that names a person, another that names a place, and one that names a thing or idea. Use each noun in an original sentence.

W/*G Prentice Hall Writing and Grammar Connection: Chapter 14, Section 1*

Writing Lesson

Fable That Teaches a Lesson

Write a **fable** that suggests a lesson that can be applied to life. Use Singer's cat and dog, or develop animal characters of your own.

Prewriting   Choose the lesson you want to teach, such as the importance of teamwork. Plan story events that will demonstrate the lesson. Jot down the order of events.

Drafting   Introduce the characters and the conflict. Then, create a sequence of events—tell the events in time order, leading up to the point at which the conflict is settled. Finally, tell how the conflict turns out. Reveal the lesson of the fable in the words of one of the characters.

Revising   Review your draft, and use a squiggly line to underline each word or phrase that connects one event to the next. Look for places that are lacking squiggly lines. Add transition words like those in the sample below.

Model: Sequence of Events

After a few minutes,

At night Mitzi heard a coyote howl. She ran to warn the hens.

She dashed toward the chicken coop and she barked.

Suddenly, a large shadow appeared. Mitzi stopped running.

> The italicized time words move the action forward in a logical sequence.

Prentice Hall Writing and Grammar Connection: Chapter 4, Section 4

Extension Activities

Listening and Speaking Using the Skiba household as an example, deliver a **lecture** to your class on the dangers of placing too much value on appearances.

1. Organize your lecture around a few main points that will influence an audience of classmates.

2. Show the problems that can occur, using examples to which your classmates can relate their own experiences.

Research and Technology Use the Internet and science textbooks to find out how mirrors work. Share your findings in a **science presentation**. Include pictures and diagrams.

Writing As a reporter for the local village paper, write an **article** about the strange events at the Skiba house. Begin with a lead paragraph that tells readers *who, what, when, where,* and *how.*

 **Take It to the Net**   www.phschool.com

Go online for an additional research activity using the Internet.

Prepare to Read

Two Kinds

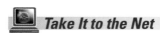

Take It to the Net

Visit www.phschool.com
for interactive activities
and instruction related to
"Two Kinds," including

- background
- graphic organizers
- literary elements
- reading strategies

Preview

Connecting to the Literature

Most people love to star in their own daydreams of greatness.
However, when someone has different dreams for you than you have for
yourself, you may feel divided. This is the problem the main character
faces in Amy Tan's "Two Kinds."

Background

In 1949, the Communist party seized control of China, following years
of civil war. Like the mother in "Two Kinds" a number of Chinese who
feared the communists fled to the United States. Many of them lost
everything except their hopes for a better future. They placed these hopes
on the shoulders of the children born in the new land. Pay attention to
how the daughter in "Two Kinds" deals with her mother's expectations.

Literary Analysis

Characters' Motives

Characters' motives are the emotions or goals that drive characters to act one way or another. Some powerful motives are love, anger, and hope. In this example, the words in italics show the narrator's motives.

> The girl staring back at me was *angry, powerful*. . . . I had new thoughts, willful thoughts, or rather thoughts filled with lots of won'ts. I *won't* let her change me, I promised myself. I *won't be what I'm not.*

As you read, notice how the different motives of the narrator and her mother influence their actions.

Connecting Literary Elements

A character's motives and actions are influenced by **character traits,** the individual qualities that make each character unique. For example, in "Two Kinds," the daughter is young and strong-willed. Use the following focus questions to analyze the character traits of the mother and daughter in "Two Kinds":

1. What traits do the mother and daughter share?

2. What traits make them different from each other?

Reading Strategy

Using Roots and Affixes

When you come across an unfamiliar word, break the word into parts to help you recognize and pronounce it.

- A **root** is the base of a word that has meaning by itself.
- The **affixes** are the word parts that come before or after the root and influence its meaning.

Look at the examples in the chart shown. Create a similar chart. As you come across unfamiliar words in your reading, separate the words into roots and affixes.

Word Identification

Word	Root	Affixes
uneventful	*event*	un, ful
government	*govern*	ment
retirement	*retire*	ment
impatient	*patient*	im

Vocabulary Development

prodigy (präd´ ə jē) *n.* child of unusually high talent (p. 17)

reproach (ri prōch´) *n.* disgrace; blame (p. 18)

mesmerizing (mez´ mər īz´ iŋ) *adj.* hypnotizing (p. 20)

sauciness (sô´ sē nes) *n.* liveliness; boldness; spirit (p. 20)

conspired (kən spīrd´) *v.* planned together secretly (p. 23)

debut (dā byoo´) *n.* first performance in public (p. 23)

devastated (dev´ ə stā tid) *v.* destroyed; completely upset (p. 25)

fiasco (fē as´ cō) *n.* complete failure (p. 25)

Two Kinds
from The Joy Luck Club

Amy Tan

My mother believed you could be anything you wanted to be in America. You could open a restaurant. You could work for the government and get good retirement. You could buy a house with almost no money down. You could become rich. You could become instantly famous.

"Of course you can be <u>prodigy</u>, too," my mother told me when I was nine. "You can be best anything. What does Auntie Lindo know? Her daughter, she is only best tricky."

America was where all my mother's hopes lay. She had come here in 1949 after losing everything in China: her mother and father, her family home, her first husband, and two daughters, twin baby girls. But she never looked back with regret. There were so many ways for things to get better.

We didn't immediately pick the right kind of prodigy. At first my mother thought I could be a Chinese Shirley Temple.[1] We'd watch Shirley's old movies on TV as though they were training films. My mother would poke my arm and say, "Ni kan" [nē kän]— You watch. And I would see Shirley tapping her feet, or singing a sailor song, or pursing her lips into a very round O while saying, "Oh my goodness."

"*Ni kan*," said my mother as Shirley's eyes flooded with tears. "You already know how. Don't need talent for crying!"

---

1. **Shirley Temple** American child star of the 1930s, she starred in her first movie at age three and won an Academy Award at age six.

◀ **Critical Viewing** San Francisco's Chinatown, seen here, uses both the English and Chinese languages. How might such a mix affect the narrator's sense of herself? **[Speculate]**

prodigy (präd´ ə jē) *n.* child of unusually high talent

Literary Analysis
Characters' Motives
In what way might these details contribute to the mother's motives?

Reading Check
Whom did the narrator's mother want her to be like?

Soon after my mother got this idea about Shirley Temple, she took me to a beauty training school in the Mission district[2] and put me in the hands of a student who could barely hold the scissors without shaking. Instead of getting big fat curls, I emerged with an uneven mass of crinkly black fuzz. My mother dragged me off to the bathroom and tried to wet down my hair.

"You look like Negro Chinese," she lamented, as if I had done this on purpose.

The instructor of the beauty training school had to lop off these soggy clumps to make my hair even again. "Peter Pan is very popular these days," the instructor assured my mother. I now had hair the length of a boy's, with straight-across bangs that hung at a slant two inches above my eyebrows. I liked the haircut and it made me actually look forward to my future fame.

In fact, in the beginning, I was just as excited as my mother, maybe even more so. I pictured this prodigy part of me as many different images, trying each one on for size. I was a dainty ballerina girl standing by the curtains, waiting to hear the right music that would send me floating on my tiptoes. I was like the Christ child lifted out of the straw manger, crying with holy indignity. I was Cinderella stepping from her pumpkin carriage with sparkly cartoon music filling the air.

In all of my imaginings, I was filled with a sense that I would soon become *perfect*. My mother and father would adore me. I would be beyond reproach. I would never feel the need to sulk for anything.

But sometimes the prodigy in me became impatient. "If you don't hurry up and get me out of here, I'm disappearing for good," it warned. "And then you'll always be nothing."

Every night after dinner, my mother and I would sit at the Formica kitchen table. She would present new tests, taking her examples from stories of amazing children she had read in *Ripley's Believe It or Not*, or *Good Housekeeping*, *Reader's Digest*, and a dozen other magazines she kept in a pile in our bathroom. My mother got these magazines from people whose houses she cleaned. And since she cleaned many houses each week, we had a great assortment. She would look through them all, searching for stories about remarkable children.

The first night she brought out a story about a three-year-old boy who knew the capitals of all the states and even most of the European countries. A teacher was quoted as saying the little boy could also pronounce the names of the foreign cities correctly.

"What's the capital of Finland?" my mother asked me, looking at the magazine story.

---

2. **Mission district** residential district in San Francisco, California.

reproach (ri prōch´) n. blame

Reading Strategy
Using Roots and Affixes
What is the root of *unbreakable*?

All I knew was the capital of California, because Sacramento was the name of the street we lived on in Chinatown. "Nairobi!"[3] I guessed, saying the most foreign word I could think of. She checked to see if that was possibly one way to pronounce "Helsinki" [hel sin´ kē] before showing me the answer.

The tests got harder—multiplying numbers in my head, finding the queen of hearts in a deck of cards, trying to stand on my head without using my hands, predicting the daily temperatures in Los Angeles, New York, and London.

One night I had to look at a page from the Bible for three minutes and then report everything I could remember. "Now Jehoshaphat had riches and honor in abundance and . . . that's all I remember, Ma," I said.

Mandarin Square: Badge with peacock-insignia-3rd civil rank. China, 17th–20th century, Unknown artist, Yale University Art Gallery

And after seeing my mother's disappointed face once again, something inside of me began to die. I hated the tests, the raised hopes and failed expectations. Before going to bed that night, I looked in the mirror above the bathroom sink and when I saw only my face staring back—and that it would always be this ordinary face—I began to cry. Such a sad, ugly girl! I made high-pitched noises like a crazed animal, trying to scratch out the face in the mirror.

And then I saw what seemed to be the prodigy side of me—because I had never seen that face before. I looked at my reflection, blinking so I could see more clearly. The girl staring back at me was angry, powerful. This girl and I were the same. I had new thoughts, willful thoughts, or rather thoughts filled with lots of won'ts. I won't let her change me, I promised myself. I won't be what I'm not.

So now on nights when my mother presented her tests, I performed listlessly, my head propped on one arm. I pretended to be bored. And I was. I got so bored I started counting the bellows of the foghorns out on the bay while my mother drilled me in other areas. The sound was comforting and reminded me of the cow jumping over the moon. And the next day, I played a game with myself, seeing if my mother would give up on me before eight bellows. After a while I usually counted only one, maybe two bellows at most. At last she was beginning to give up hope.

Two or three months had gone by without any mention of my being a prodigy again. And then one day my mother was watching

▲ Critical Viewing
Which characters in the story are best suggested by this peacock, a symbol of arrogance and pride? **[Connect]**

✔**Reading Check**

How does the daughter feel as the tests go on?

---

3. **Nairobi** (nī rō´ bē) capital of Kenya, a country in east central Africa.

The Ed Sullivan Show[4] on TV. The TV was old and the sound kept shorting out. Every time my mother got halfway up from the sofa to adjust the set, the sound would go back on and Ed would be talking. As soon as she sat down, Ed would go silent again. She got up, the TV broke into loud piano music. She sat down. Silence. Up and down, back and forth, quiet and loud. It was like a stiff embraceless dance between her and the TV set. Finally she stood by the set with her hand on the sound dial.

She seemed entranced by the music, a little frenzied piano piece with this <u>mesmerizing</u> quality, sort of quick passages and then teasing lilting ones before it returned to the quick playful parts.

"*Ni kan*," my mother said, calling me over with hurried hand gestures. "Look here."

I could see why my mother was fascinated by the music. It was being pounded out by a little Chinese girl, about nine years old, with a Peter Pan haircut. The girl had the <u>sauciness</u> of a Shirley Temple. She was proudly modest like a proper Chinese child. And she also did this fancy sweep of a curtsy, so that the fluffy skirt of her white dress cascaded slowly to the floor like the petals of a large carnation.

In spite of these warning signs, I wasn't worried. Our family had no piano and we couldn't afford to buy one, let alone reams of sheet music and piano lessons. So I could be generous in my comments when my mother bad-mouthed the little girl on TV.

"Play note right, but doesn't sound good! No singing sound," complained my mother.

"What are you picking on her for?" I said carelessly. "She's pretty good. Maybe she's not the best, but she's trying hard." I knew almost immediately I would be sorry I said that.

"Just like you," she said. "Not the best. Because you not trying." She gave a little huff as she let go of the sound dial and sat down on the sofa.

The little Chinese girl sat down also to play an encore of "Anitra's Dance" by Grieg.[5] I remember the song, because later on I had to learn how to play it.

Three days after watching *The Ed Sullivan Show*, my mother told me what my schedule would be for piano lessons and piano practice. She had talked to Mr. Chong, who lived on the first floor of our apartment building. Mr. Chong was a retired piano teacher and my mother had traded housecleaning services for weekly lessons and a piano for me to practice on every day, two hours a day, from four until six.

When my mother told me this, I felt as though I had been sent to hell. I whined and then kicked my foot a little when I couldn't stand it anymore.

---

4. *The Ed Sullivan Show* popular variety show, hosted by Ed Sullivan, that ran from 1955 to 1971.
5. *Grieg* (grēg) Edvard Grieg (1843–1907), Norwegian composer.

mesmerizing
(mez´ mər īz´ iŋ) *adj.*
hypnotizing

sauciness (sô´ sē nes) *n.*
liveliness; boldness; spirit

Literary Analysis
Characters' Motives and Character Traits
What does this conversation indicate about the difference between the mother's and daughter's traits and motives?

Chinese Girl Under Lanterns, Winson Trang

▲ **Critical Viewing** How does the contrast between the modern and the traditional in this painting reflect the title of Tan's story? **[Connect]**

"Why don't you like me the way I am? I'm *not* a genius! I can't play the piano. And even if I could, I wouldn't go on TV if you paid me a million dollars!" I cried.

My mother slapped me. "Who ask you be genius?" she shouted. "Only ask you be your best. For you sake. You think I want you be genius? Hnnh! What for! Who ask you!"

"So ungrateful," I heard her mutter in Chinese. "If she had as much talent as she has temper, she would be famous now."

Mr. Chong, whom I secretly nicknamed Old Chong, was very strange, always tapping his fingers to the silent music of an invisible orchestra. He looked ancient in my eyes. He had lost most of the hair on top of his head and he wore thick glasses and had eyes that always looked tired and sleepy. But he must have been younger than I thought, since he lived with his mother and was not yet married.

I met Old Lady Chong once and that was enough. She had this peculiar smell like a baby that had done something in its pants. And her fingers felt like a dead person's, like an old peach I once found in the back of the refrigerator; the skin just slid off the meat when I picked it up.

Reading Check

What happens after the mother and daughter see the pianist on television?

Two Kinds ◆ 21

I soon found out why Old Chong had retired from teaching piano. He was deaf. "Like Beethoven!"[6] he shouted to me. "We're both listening only in our head!" And he would start to conduct his frantic silent sonatas.

Our lessons went like this. He would open the book and point to different things, explaining their purpose: "Key! Treble! Bass! No sharps or flats! So this is C major! Listen now and play after me!"

And then he would play the C scale a few times, a simple chord, and then, as if inspired by an old, unreachable itch, he gradually added more notes and running trills and a pounding bass until the music was really something quite grand.

I would play after him, the simple scale, the simple chord, and then I just played some nonsense that sounded like a cat running up and down on top of garbage cans. Old Chong smiled and applauded and then said, "Very good! But now you must learn to keep time!"

So that's how I discovered that Old Chong's eyes were too slow to keep up with the wrong notes I was playing. He went through the motions in half-time. To help me keep rhythm, he stood behind me, pushing down on my right shoulder for every beat. He balanced pennies on top of my wrists so I would keep them still as I slowly played scales and arpeggios.[7] He had me curve my hand around an apple and keep that shape when playing chords. He marched stiffly to show me how to make each finger dance up and down, staccato[8] like an obedient little soldier.

He taught me all these things, and that was how I also learned I could be lazy and get away with mistakes, lots of mistakes. If I hit the wrong notes because I hadn't practiced enough, I never corrected myself. I just kept playing in rhythm. And Old Chong kept conducting his own private reverie.

So maybe I never really gave myself a fair chance. I did pick up the basics pretty quickly, and I might have become a good pianist at that young age. But I was so determined not to try, not to be anybody different that I learned to play only the most ear-splitting preludes, the most discordant hymns.

Over the next year, I practiced like this, dutifully in my own way. And then one day I heard my mother and her friend Lindo Jong both talking in a loud bragging tone of voice so others could hear. It was after church, and I was leaning against the brick wall wearing a dress with stiff white petticoats. Auntie Lindo's daughter, Waverly, who was about my age, was standing farther down the wall about

Reading Strategy
Using Roots and Affixes
Identify the root and two affixes in *unreachable*. What does each one contribute to the word's meaning?

Literary Analysis
Characters' Motives
What motive does the daughter have for learning to play piano badly?

---

6. **Beethoven** (bā´ tō´ vən) Ludwig van Beethoven (1770–1827), German composer who began to lose his hearing in 1801. By 1819, he was completely deaf. Some of his greatest pieces were written when he was deaf.

7. **arpeggios** (är pej´ ē ōz) *n.* notes in a chord played in quick succession instead of at the same time.

8. **staccato** (stə kät´ ō) *adv.* played crisply, with distinct breaks between notes.

five feet away. We had grown up together and shared all the close-ness of two sisters squabbling over crayons and dolls. In other words, for the most part, we hated each other. I thought she was snotty. Waverly Jong had gained a certain amount of fame as "Chinatown's Littlest Chinese Chess Champion."

"She bring home too many trophy," lamented Auntie Lindo that Sunday. "All day she play chess. All day I have no time do nothing but dust off her winnings." She threw a scolding look at Waverly, who pretended not to see her.

"You lucky you don't have this problem," said Auntie Lindo with a sigh to my mother.

And my mother squared her shoulders and bragged: "Our prob-lem worser than yours. If we ask Jing-mei wash dish, she hear nothing but music. It's like you can't stop this natural talent."

And right then, I was determined to put a stop to her foolish pride.

A few weeks later, Old Chong and my mother <u>conspired</u> to have me play in a talent show which would be held in the church hall. By then, my parents had saved up enough to buy me a secondhand piano, a black Wurlitzer spinet[9] with a scarred bench. It was the showpiece of our living room.

For the talent show, I was to play a piece called "Pleading Child" from Schumann's[10] *Scenes from Childhood*. It was a simple, moody piece that sounded more difficult than it was. I was supposed to memorize the whole thing, playing the repeat parts twice to make the piece sound longer. But I dawdled over it, playing a few bars and then cheating, looking up to see what notes followed. I never really listened to what I was playing. I daydreamed about being some-where else, about being someone else.

The part I liked to practice best was the fancy curtsy: right foot out, touch the rose on the carpet with a pointed foot, sweep to the side, left leg bends, look up and smile.

My parents invited all the couples from the Joy Luck Club[11] to witness my <u>debut</u>. Auntie Lindo and Uncle Tin were there. Waverly and her two older brothers had also come. The first two rows were filled with children both younger and older than I was. The littlest ones got to go first. They recited simple nursery rhymes, squawked out tunes on miniature violins, twirled Hula Hoops, pranced in pink ballet tutus, and when they bowed or curtsied, the audience would sigh in unison, "Awww," and then clap enthusiastically.

---

9. **spinet** (spin' it) *n.* small, upright piano.
10. **Schumann** (shoō' män) Robert Alexander Schumann (1810–1856), German composer.
11. **Joy Luck Club** four Chinese women who have been meeting for years to socialize, play games, and tell stories from the past.

When my turn came, I was very confident. I remember my childish excitement. It was as if I knew, without a doubt, that the prodigy side of me really did exist. I had no fear whatsoever, no nervousness. I remember thinking to myself, This is it! This is it! I looked out over the audience, at my mother's blank face, my father's yawn, Auntie Lindo's stiff-lipped smile, Waverly's sulky expression. I had on a white dress layered with sheets of lace, and a pink bow in my Peter Pan haircut. As I sat down I envisioned people jumping to their feet and Ed Sullivan rushing up to introduce me to everyone on TV.

And I started to play. It was so beautiful. I was so caught up in how lovely I looked that at first I didn't worry how I would sound. So it was a surprise to me when I hit the first wrong note and I realized something didn't sound quite right. And then I hit another and another followed that. A chill started at the top of my head and began to trickle down. Yet I couldn't stop playing, as though my hands were bewitched. I kept thinking my fingers would adjust themselves back, like a train switching to the right track. I played this strange jumble through two repeats, the sour notes staying with me all the way to the end.

When I stood up, I discovered my legs were shaking. Maybe I had just been nervous and the audience, like Old Chong, had seen me go through the right motions and had not heard anything wrong at all. I swept my right foot out, went down on my knee, looked up and smiled. The room was quiet, except for Old Chong, who was beaming and shouting, "Bravo! Bravo! Well done!" But then I saw my mother's face, her stricken face. The audience clapped weakly, and as I walked back to my chair, with my whole face quivering as I tried not to cry, I heard a little boy whisper loudly to his mother, "That was awful," and the mother whispered back, "Well, she certainly tried."

And now I realized how many people were in the audience, the whole world it seemed. I was aware of eyes burning into my back. I felt the shame of my mother and father as they sat stiffly throughout the rest of the show.

We could have escaped during intermission. Pride and some strange sense of honor must have anchored my parents to their chairs. And so we watched it all: the eighteen-year-old boy with a fake

Reading Strategy
Using Roots and Affixes
When you break the word *envisioned* into parts, what familiar word is hidden inside?

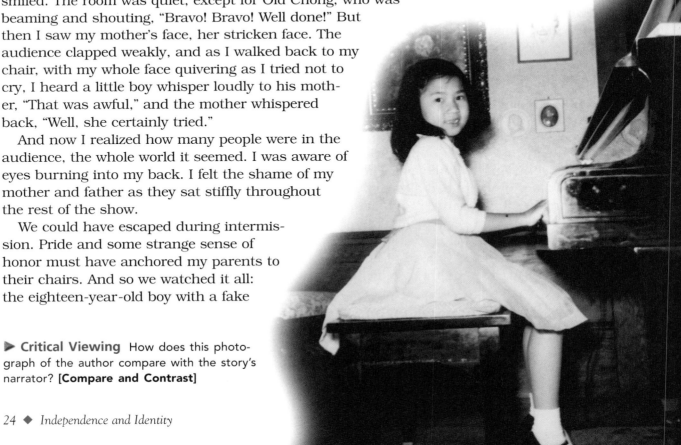

▶ **Critical Viewing** How does this photograph of the author compare with the story's narrator? [**Compare and Contrast**]

mustache who did a magic show and juggled flaming hoops while riding a unicycle. The breasted girl with white makeup who sang from *Madama Butterfly* and got honorable mention. And the eleven-year-old boy who won first prize playing a tricky violin song that sounded like a busy bee.

After the show, the Hsus, the Jongs, and the St. Clairs from the Joy Luck Club came up to my mother and father.

"Lots of talented kids," Auntie Lindo said vaguely, smiling broadly.

"That was somethin' else," said my father, and I wondered if he was referring to me in a humorous way, or whether he even remembered what I had done.

Waverly looked at me and shrugged her shoulders. "You aren't a genius like me," she said matter-of-factly. And if I hadn't felt so bad, I would have pulled her braids and punched her stomach.

But my mother's expression was what <u>devastated</u> me: a quiet, blank look that said she had lost everything. I felt the same way, and it seemed as if everybody were now coming up, like gawkers at the scene of an accident, to see what parts were actually missing. When we got on the bus to go home, my father was humming the busy-bee tune and my mother was silent. I kept thinking she wanted to wait until we got home before shouting at me. But when my father unlocked the door to our apartment, my mother walked in and then went to the back, into the bedroom. No accusations. No blame. And in a way, I felt disappointed. I had been waiting for her to start shouting, so I could shout back and cry and blame her for all my misery.

I assumed my talent-show <u>fiasco</u> meant I never had to play the piano again. But two days later, after school, my mother came out of the kitchen and saw me watching TV.

"Four clock," she reminded me as if it were any other day. I was stunned, as though she were asking me to go through the talent-show torture again. I wedged myself more tightly in front of the TV.

"Turn off TV," she called from the kitchen five minutes later.

I didn't budge. And then I decided. I didn't have to do what my mother said anymore. I wasn't her slave. This wasn't China. I had listened to her before and look what happened. She was the stupid one.

She came out from the kitchen and stood in the arched entryway of the living room. "Four clock," she said once again, louder.

"I'm not going to play anymore," I said nonchalantly. "Why should I? I'm not a genius."

She walked over and stood in front of the TV. I saw her chest was heaving up and down in an angry way.

"No!" I said, and I now felt stronger, as if my true self had finally emerged. So this was what had been inside me all along.

devastated (dev′ ə stā tid) *v.* destroyed; completely upset

fiasco (fē as′ cō) *n.* complete failure

Reading Check

What happens at the talent show?

"No! I won't!" I screamed.

She yanked me by the arm, pulled me off the floor, snapped off the TV. She was frighteningly strong, half pulling, half carrying me toward the piano as I kicked the throw rugs under my feet. She lifted me up and onto the hard bench. I was sobbing by now, looking at her bitterly. Her chest was heaving even more and her mouth was open, smiling crazily as if she were pleased I was crying.

"You want me to be someone that I'm not!" I sobbed. "I'll never be the kind of daughter you want me to be!"

"Only two kinds of daughters," she shouted in Chinese. "Those who are obedient and those who follow their own mind! Only one kind of daughter can live in this house. Obedient daughter!"

"Then I wish I wasn't your daughter. I wish you weren't my mother," I shouted. As I said these things I got scared. It felt like worms and toads and slimy things crawling out of my chest, but it also felt good, as if this awful side of me had surfaced, at last.

"Too late change this," said my mother shrilly.

And I could sense her anger rising to its breaking point. I wanted to see it spill over. And that's when I remembered the babies she had lost in China, the ones we never talked about. "Then I wish I'd never been born!" I shouted. "I wish I were dead! Like them."

It was as if I had said the magic words. Alakazam!—and her face went blank, her mouth closed, her arms went slack, and she backed out of the room, stunned, as if she were blowing away like a small brown leaf, thin, brittle, lifeless.

It was not the only disappointment my mother felt in me. In the years that followed, I failed her so many times, each time asserting my own will, my right to fall short of expectations. I didn't get straight A's. I didn't become class president. I didn't get into Stanford. I dropped out of college.

For unlike my mother, I did not believe I could be anything I wanted to be. I could only be me.

And for all those years, we never talked about the disaster at the recital or my terrible accusations afterward at the piano bench. All that remained unchecked, like a betrayal that was now unspeakable. So I never found a way to ask her why she had hoped for something so large that failure was inevitable.

And even worse, I never asked her what frightened me the most: Why had she given up hope?

For after our struggle at the piano, she never mentioned my playing again. The lessons stopped. The lid to the piano was closed, shutting out the dust, my misery, and her dreams.

So she surprised me. A few years ago, she offered to give me the piano, for my thirtieth birthday. I had not played in all those

Literary Analysis
Characters' Motives
What emotion motivates the mother's actions?

Literary Analysis
Characters' Motives and Characters' Traits What character traits contribute to the daughter's outburst? What are her motives for speaking to her mother in this way?

Reading Strategy
Using Roots and Affixes Into how many parts can you break the word *unspeakable*? What does each part mean? What does the whole word mean?

years. I saw the offer as a sign of forgiveness, a tremendous burden removed.

"Are you sure?" I asked shyly. "I mean, won't you and Dad miss it?"

"No, this your piano," she said firmly. "Always your piano. You only one can play."

"Well, I probably can't play anymore," I said. "It's been years."

"You pick up fast," said my mother, as if she knew this was certain. "You have natural talent. You could been genius if you want to."

"No I couldn't."

"You just not trying," said my mother. And she was neither angry nor sad. She said it as if to announce a fact that could never be disproved. "Take it," she said.

But I didn't at first. It was enough that she had offered it to me. And after that, every time I saw it in my parents' living room, standing in front of the bay windows, it made me feel proud, as if it were a shiny trophy I had won back.

Portrait, Pamela Chin Lee, Courtesy of the artist

❀ ❀ ❀

Last week I sent a tuner over to my parents' apartment and had the piano reconditioned, for purely sentimental reasons. My mother had died a few months before and I had been getting things in order for my father, a little bit at a time. I put the jewelry in special silk pouches. The sweaters she had knitted in yellow, pink, bright orange—all the colors I hated—I put those in moth-proof boxes. I found some old Chinese silk dresses, the kind with little slits up the sides. I rubbed the old silk against my skin, then wrapped them in tissue and decided to take them home with me.

After I had the piano tuned, I opened the lid and touched the keys. It sounded even richer than I remembered. Really, it was a very good piano. Inside the bench were the same exercise notes with handwritten scales, the same secondhand music books with their covers held together with yellow tape.

▲ **Critical Viewing**
Do you think this image accurately portrays the "two kinds" of daughters the mother describes? **[Evaluate]**

✔ **Reading Check**

What does the mother offer the daughter?

I opened up the Schumann book to the dark little piece I had played at the recital. It was on the left-hand side of the page, "Pleading Child." It looked more difficult than I remembered. I played a few bars, surprised at how easily the notes came back to me.

And for the first time, or so it seemed, I noticed the piece on the right-hand side. It was called "Perfectly Contented." I tried to play this one as well. It had a lighter melody but the same flowing rhythm and turned out to be quite easy. "Pleading Child" was shorter but slower; "Perfectly Contented" was longer, but faster. And after I played them both a few times, I realized they were two halves of the same song.

Review and Assess

Thinking About the Selection

1. **Respond:** What advice would you have given the mother and daughter? Why?

2. **(a) Recall:** What child star does the mother hope her daughter can be like? **(b) Infer:** Why does the mother want her daughter to be like this star?

3. **(a) Recall:** In what ways does the mother try to make the daughter a prodigy? **(b) Compare and Contrast:** Compare and contrast the daughter's attitude toward being a prodigy with the mother's attitude. **(c) Draw Conclusions:** How does the difference in their attitudes create problems?

4. **(a) Recall:** Describe the argument that occurs when the mother wants the daughter to return to practicing after the recital. **(b) Analyze:** Why do the daughter's final words in the argument have such a powerful effect on her mother?

5. **(a) Recall:** What gift does the mother give to the daughter on her thirtieth birthday? **(b) Analyze:** What is the meaning of the gift?

6. **(a) Recall:** At the end of the story, what does the daughter discover about the music she had prepared for the recital? **(b) Connect:** In what way does the music reflect the daughter's feelings about herself? **(c) Apply:** What does the daughter's discovery reveal about people in general?

7. **(a) Evaluate:** Do you agree that people can be anything they want to be? Why or why not? **(b) Make a Judgment:** Should the narrator's mother have pushed the daughter as she did? Explain. **(c) Make a Judgment:** Should the narrator have spoken to her mother as she did in the argument after the recital? Explain.

Amy Tan

(b. 1952)
Amy Tan grew up as the second-youngest child in a Chinese American family from California. As a youngster, Tan was pulled between mainstream American culture and the Chinese traditions that her mother kept alive.

Tan showed early signs of being a writer. At age eight, she published an essay entitled "What the Library Means to Me" in a local paper. However, she went to several colleges and held a variety of jobs—from carhop to educational counselor—before achieving great success with her first novel, *The Joy Luck Club*. The novel explores life in a Chinese American community. Nominated for a National Book Award, the novel also inspired a movie of the same title.

Tan's success as a writer has continued with the critically acclaimed novels *The Kitchen God's Wife, The Hundred Secret Senses,* and *The Bonesetter's Daughter.*

Review and Assess

Literary Analysis

Characters' Motives

1. As you read the two story passages in the chart, think about the emotions and goals that drive each **character.** Then, fill in the motive for each character.

	Narrator	Mother
Passage from story	"I was filled with a sense that I would soon become *perfect.* My mother and father would adore me."	"America was where all my mother's hopes lay. She had come here . . . after losing everything in China. . . ."
Motive		

2. Explain how each character is motivated by both self-interest and by concern for the other character.
3. What finally motivates the daughter to rebel against her mother?

Connecting Literary Elements

4. Complete an organizer like this one to show the **character traits** the mother and daughter do and do not share.

5. In what ways do their shared traits contribute to their arguments?

Reading Strategy

Using Roots and Affixes

6. Write each word. Circle the **root** and underline any **affixes.** Explain the meaning of each word as it relates to the roots and affixes.
   (a) assortment   **(b)** remarkable   **(c)** retirement
7. Find three words in the story that have affixes. Explain the meaning of the root and affix in each word.

Extend Understanding

8. **Cultural Connection:** What does this story suggest about struggles that may exist between immigrant parents and their American-born children?

Quick Review

Characters' motives are the emotions or goals that drive characters to act one way or another. To review characters' motives, see page 15.

Character traits are the qualities that make a character unique. To review character traits, see characterization on page 15.

A **root** is the base form of a word that has a meaning of its own. An **affix** is added to the base and changes its meaning. To review roots and affixes, see page 15.

 Take It to the Net

www.phschool.com
Take the interactive self-test online to check your understanding of the selection.

Integrate Language Skills

Vocabulary Development Lesson

Word Analysis: The Suffix -ness

Suffixes, or word endings, are one of the word parts you can use to identify unfamiliar words. *Sauciness* combines the adjective *saucy* ("lively") with the Anglo-Saxon suffix *-ness*, meaning "the quality or condition of."

Use the suffix *-ness* to change the adjectives describing each character into the qualities that each character possesses.

1. Mother: stubborn; hopeful
2. Daughter: rebellious; sad

Spelling Strategy

If the final y in a word is preceded by a consonant, change the y to i when adding the suffix *-ness: sulky* + *-ness* = *sulkiness.*

Write the following words correctly.

1. happy + -ness 2. messy + -ness 3. filthy + -ness

Grammar Lesson

Common and Proper Nouns

This story contains common and proper nouns.

- **Common nouns** name people, places, things, and ideas in general.
- **Proper nouns** name specific people, places, things, and ideas.

A proper noun is capitalized. A common noun is not capitalized unless it is the first word in a sentence.

> PROPER   COMMON
> *Sacramento* was the *name* of
>
> COMMON   PROPER
> the *street* we lived on in *Chinatown.*

Fluency: Word Choice

On your paper, rewrite the following sentences and replace each italicized word or phrase with the word from the vocabulary list on page 15 that has a similar meaning.

1. The *child genius* sat down at the piano for her *first appearance* on stage.
2. Her *hypnotic* performance was beyond *blame,* and her *boldness* won her admirers.
3. The clarinetist sensed that his own efforts were a *failure.*
4. Everything and everyone had *plotted* against him, and he felt *destroyed.*

▶ *For more practice, see page R28, Exercise A.*

Practice On your paper, identify each of the following italicized words as a common noun, a proper noun, or not a noun.

1. She said *Amy* couldn't play the *piano.*
2. The *name* of the *teacher* was Mr. Chong.
3. At the *recital,* the student played a piece by *Schumann.*
4. The girl's mother competed with *Auntie Lindo,* whose daughter played *chess.*
5. Because they weren't living in *China,* she felt more *independent.*

Writing Application Write five sentences about the story, using at least one common noun and one proper noun in each. Identify the nouns you use.

W͜G Prentice Hall Writing and Grammar Connection: Chapter 14, Section 1

Writing Lesson

Story Told by a Different Narrator

"Two Kinds" is a story told by a **first-person narrator**—a narrator who is a character participating in the action. A first-person narrator can include details of what he or she thinks and feels about events. Tan's first-person narrator is the daughter. Retell one of the episodes from the story from the point of view of the mother, focusing on presenting her inner thoughts and feelings.

Prewriting   Choose one of the events in the story. Jot down words that reflect how the mother feels about the events.

Drafting   Write an account of the event. Include only the details that the mother could know.

Model: Different Narrators

Daughter	Mother
So now on nights when my mother presented her test, I performed listlessly, my head propped on one arm. I pretended to be bored.	Every night my daughter seemed more hopeless. She didn't even try! She wouldn't even sit up straight!

Revising   Circle each use of *I* in your narrative. For each use, make sure you have indicated what the mother thinks or feels.

Prentice Hall Writing and Grammar Connection: Chapter 4, Section 4

Extension Activities

Listening and Speaking With a partner, **discuss** why you agree or disagree with the following:

> Doing easily what others find difficult is talent; doing what is impossible for talent is genius.
>
> —Henri Frédéric Amiel

Identify questions you might ask to challenge the statement, as well as reasons from your prior knowledge or experience that can be used to affirm or support the statement. Record the questions and statements that you and your partner identify.

Research and Technology Use encyclopedias, books on China, and the Internet to learn traditional Chinese beliefs and customs about the relationship between parents and children. Write a **summary** of your findings to help students understand why the mother in the story insists on obedience.

 **Take It to the Net**   www.phschool.com

Go online for an additional research activity using the Internet.

READING INFORMATIONAL MATERIALS

About Magazine Articles

Magazines are a form of print media. They may be published weekly, monthly, or even quarterly (four times a year). Some magazines are organized with a very specific audience in mind, such as runners, artists, or movie-lovers. Other magazines provide information on current issues and events that are of interest to a wider and more general audience.

When using magazines as sources of information, ask yourself the following questions:

- Is the writer communicating facts, opinions, or both?
- Is the issue recent enough to provide up-to-date information?
- Does the issue include information from experts?

Reading Strategy

Identify an Author's Argument

In magazines that are written to appeal to a wide and general audience, you will often find articles that comment on an event or issue. When reading these articles, identify the **author's argument**—the point of view or position that the writer presents. To identify the author's argument, notice how the facts and details all seem to lead to a main point. Look also at comments the author includes about the facts. Use a graphic organizer like the one shown here to identify the author's argument in this article and in others you read.

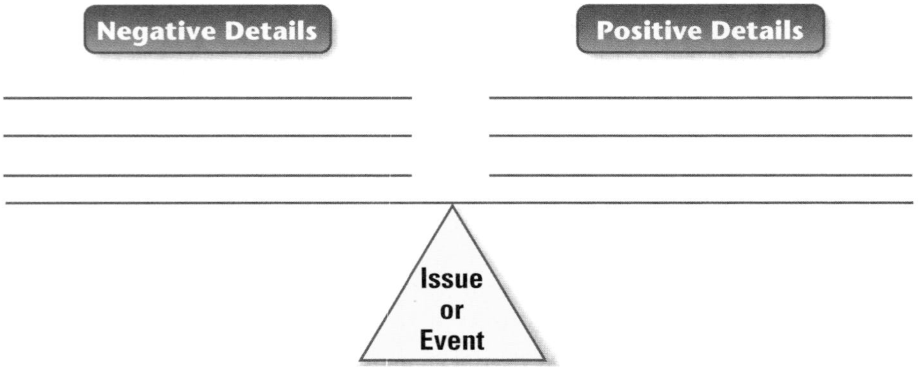

Negative Details	Positive Details
_____	_____
_____	_____
_____	_____

Issue
or
Event

Burning Out at Nine?

Nadya Labi

The writer begins with facts to get the reader's attention and set the stage for her argument.

Steven Guzman is only 12, but he's booked solid. He wakes up at 6 every weekday morning, downs a five-minute breakfast, reports to school at 7:50, returns home at 3:15, hits the books from 5 to 9 (with a break for dinner) and goes to sleep at 10:30. Saturdays are little better: from 9 to 5 he attends a prep program in the hope of getting a scholarship to a private school. Then there are piano lessons and a couple of hours of practice a week. If he's lucky, he'll squeeze in his friends on Sunday. "Sometimes I think, like, since I'm a kid, I need to enjoy my life," he says. "But I don't have time for that."

Remember when enjoying life seemed like the point of childhood? Hah! Researchers at the University of Michigan's Institute for Social Research compiled the 1997 time diaries of 3,586 children nationwide, ages 12 and under. The participants came from virtually every ethnic background and all kinds of households—rich, poor, single parent, dual income.[1] But funnily enough,

Providing the date of the study lets the reader know if the information is up-to-date.

they all sounded a little like Steven.

On average, kids ages 3 to 12 spent 29 hours a week in school, eight hours more than they did in 1981, when a similar study was conducted. They also did more household chores, accompanied their parents on more errands and participated in more of such organized activities as soccer and ballet.

Involvement in sports, in particular, rose almost 50% from 1981 to 1997: boys now spend an average of four hours a week playing sports; girls log half that time. All in all, however, children's leisure time—defined as time left over after sleeping, eating, personal hygiene[2] and attending school or day care—dropped from 40% of the day in 1981 to 25%.

"Children are affected by the same time crunch that affects their parents," says Sandra Hofferth, the

---

1. **dual income** *adj.* having two incomes or salaries.
2. **hygiene** *n.* cleanliness.

November 23, 1998

sociologist[3] who headed the study. A chief reason, she says, is that more mothers are working outside the home. (Nevertheless, children in both dual-income and "male bread-winner" households spent comparable amounts of time interacting with their parents, 19 hours and 22 hours respectively. In contrast, children spent only 9 hours with their single mothers.)

All work and no play could make for some very messed-up kids. Child experts, usually a divided bunch, agree: fun is good. "Play is the most powerful way a child explores the world and learns about himself," says T. Berry Brazelton, a pediatrician[4] at Harvard Medical School who has written a number of books on parenting. Unstructured play encourages independent thinking and allows the young to negotiate[5] their relationships with their peers, but kids ages 3 to 12 spent only 12 hours a week engaged in it.

Brazelton warns, "If we don't pay attention to this, we're going to create obsessive-compulsive[6] people."

The children sampled spent a quarter of their rapidly diminishing[7] "free time" watching television. But that, believe it or not, was one of the findings parents might regard as good news. Kids watched TV for an average of an hour and a half each weekday, the study found, a 25% decline since 1981. The drop parallels the Nielsen ratings, which show that TV viewership by kids ages 2 to 11 has reached its lowest level since the mid-'70s.

But if they're spending less time in front of the TV set, kids aren't replacing it with reading. Despite the campaigning by parents, teachers and Hillary Clinton to get kids more interested in books, the children surveyed spent just over an hour a week reading, little changed from 1981. Let's face it, who's got the time?

> The writer uses information from experts to strengthen her argument.

3. **sociologist** *n.* one who studies human society.
4. **pediatrician** *n.* specialist in children's medicine.
5. **negotiate** *v.* to succeed in moving through.
6. **obsessive-compulsive** *adj.* ruled by persistent ideas, irresistible impulses, or both.
7. **diminishing** decreasing.

November 23, 1998

Checking Comprehension

1. How does this article define "leisure time"?
2. What does the article say are the benefits of unstructured play?
3. How much time does the average child spend in unstructured play?
4. **(a)** Since 1981, what has happened to the amount of time children spend watching television? **(b)** Since 1981, what has happened to the amount of time children spend reading?

Applying the Reading Strategy

Identify an Author's Argument

5. What do you think is the writer's attitude toward children's schedules?
6. What comments in the article reveal her attitude?
7. Do the facts, quotations, and statistics included in the article show mostly positive or negative effects of busy schedules for children?
8. In your own words, make a statement that expresses the author's argument.
9. Which sentence in the article best captures the main point of the author's argument?

Activity

Create a Schedule

Produce a chart that shows your schedule for a week. Include the time you spend eating, getting ready for school, studying, and so on. If possible, use the table function of a word-processing program to design and print your schedule. Calculate how much "leisure time" you have and evaluate how you spend it. Then, decide whether you agree or disagree with the writer of the article.

Contrasting Informational Materials

Newspaper and Magazine Articles

Newspapers and magazines are similar in that both provide current information. However, they are different in some ways. The chart here shows some of their overall differences. Find two news articles on the same topic—one in a newspaper and one in a magazine. Explain to a partner how your articles do or do not illustrate the differences shown here.

Document	Newspaper Article	Magazine Article
Purpose of Document	To provide the latest news	To provide information and analysis
Style	Concise writing style	Varies but is likely to be more wordy than a newspaper
Organization	Generally gives most important facts first and then fills in details	Varies—may be chronological, cause-and-effect, or may build the case for a point in a logical way

Prepare to Read

from Song of Myself ◆ I'm Nobody ◆ Me

Take It to the Net

Visit www.phschool.com
for interactive activities
and instruction related to
these selections, including
- background
- graphic organizers
- literary elements
- reading strategies

Preview

Connecting to the Literature

Decide whether you think the picture on this page suggests independence or loneliness. Then, read the poems. In this group of poems, poets Walt Whitman, Emily Dickinson, and Walter de la Mare use words to explore what it means to be unique, independent, and comfortable with one's self.

Background

It is not surprising that Walt Whitman and Emily Dickinson write about being unique, individual, and separate. Walt Whitman is known for his passion for individual freedom. Emily Dickinson rarely came out of her house, and allowed few visitors to see her in person. Look for details in each poem that capture the poet's individual qualities or beliefs.

Literary Analysis

The Speaker in Poetry

In poetry, the **speaker,** the one who "says" the poem, is not necessarily the poet. Sometimes, the poet creates a character and uses this speaker to express ideas or tell about events that belong to the character, not the poet. Other times, the speaker and the poet may be very similar, or may actually be the same "voice." As you read, listen to the words used, the ideas expressed, and the rhythm of the language to understand who the speakers are and what they are telling you.

Comparing Literary Works

These three poems all focus on the topic of being unique. Each speaker has a different feeling about himself or herself. As you read the poems, use a chart like this one to compare the different feelings expressed by the speakers. Use these focus questions to help you.

1. Does the speaker seem concerned about how others view him or her?

2. Which poem best expresses your idea of individuality?

Speaker's Feelings

"Song of Myself"	"I'm Nobody"	"Me"
Self-contented		

Reading Strategy

Identifying Analogies in Poetry

Poets often express an image or idea through a comparison not meant to be taken literally. One type of comparison is an **analogy**—a comparison that illustrates a point by showing similarities between situations or things that are mostly not alike. In the following example from "Me," the speaker is compared to a tree.

> I shall always be
> My Self—and no other,
> Just me.
> Like a tree.

Look for other analogies in these poems. Think about what each conveys.

Vocabulary Development

assume (ə sōōm′) v. believe to be a fact (p. 38)

loaf (lōf) v. spend time idly (p. 38)

content (kən tent′) adj. happy enough (p. 38)

equal (ē′ kwəl) adj. of the same amount (p. 38)

banish (ban′ ish) v. send away; exile (p. 39)

bog (bäg) n. small marsh or swamp (p. 39)

forlorn (fôr lôrn′) adj. alone and miserable (p. 40)

from *Song of Myself*

Walt Whitman

assume (ə sōōm´) *v.* believe to be a fact

loaf (lōf) *v.* spend time idly

content (kən tent´) *adj.* happy enough

equal (ē´ kwəl) *adj.* of the same amount

Literary Analysis
Speaker in Poetry Do you think these are Whitman's feelings, or the feelings of a character he created?

Walt Whitman

1819–1892

Walt Whitman grew up in Brooklyn, New York, and tried many jobs— from teaching to news reporting. During the Civil War, he nursed his wounded brother and other soldiers.

In his poetry, Whitman abandoned regular rhythm and rhyme in favor of free verse that followed no set pattern.

I celebrate myself,
And what I <u>assume</u> you shall assume,
For every atom belonging to me as good belongs to you.

I <u>loaf</u> and invite my soul,
5   I lean and loaf at my ease . . . .
      observing a spear of summer grass.

     *   *   *

I exist as I am, that is enough,
If no other in the world be aware I sit <u>content</u>,
And if each and all be aware I sit content.

One world is aware, and by far the largest to me,
      and that is myself,
10   And whether I come to my own today
      or in ten thousand or ten million years,
I can cheerfully take it now,
      or with <u>equal</u> cheerfulness I can wait.

I'm Nobody

Emily Dickinson

I'm Nobody! Who are you?
Are you—Nobody—too?
Then there's a pair of us!
Don't tell! they'd banish us—you know!

5   How dreary—to be—Somebody!
How public—like a Frog—
To tell your name—the livelong June—
To an admiring Bog!

banish (ban´ ish) *v.* send away; exile

bog (bäg) *n.* small marsh or swamp

Review and Assess

Thinking About the Selections

1. **Respond:** Would you rather spend an afternoon with the speaker of "Song of Myself" or "I'm Nobody"? Explain.

2. **(a) Recall:** What is the speaker doing in lines four and five of "Song of Myself"? **(b) Interpret:** How is this action a celebration of self?

3. **(a) Recall:** What does Whitman say is the one largest world that is enough? **(b) Infer:** What does this image suggest about Whitman's view of himself? **(c) Apply:** What advice is Whitman passing on to readers?

4. **(a) Recall:** What does Dickinson say will happen if it is revealed that she is a "nobody"? **(b) Infer:** What is her feeling about this action? **(c) Apply:** In what way does Dickinson's poem suggest some of the difficulties celebrities face today?

5. **(a) Draw Conclusions:** For Dickinson, what two key differences make Nobodies better than Somebodies? **(b) Evaluate:** Do you agree that it is better to be Nobody than to be Somebody? Explain.

Emily Dickinson

1830–1886

Unlike Walt Whitman, Emily Dickinson hardly ever ventured outside Amherst, Massachusetts, where she was born. Quietly, however, she was writing the 1,775 poems that would make her famous after her death. In these brief lyrics, she created a poetic self that flashes with humor and intelligence.

Me

Walter de la Mare

As long as I live
I shall always be
My Self—and no other,
Just me.

5 Like a tree.

Like a willow or elder,
An aspen, a thorn,
Or a cypress[1] <u>forlorn</u>.

Like a flower,
10 For its hour
A primrose, a pink,
Or a violet—
Sunned by the sun,
And with dewdrops wet.

15 Always just me.

forlorn (fôr lôrn´) *adj.* alone and miserable

---

1. **cypress** (sī´ prəs) *n.* evergreen, cone-bearing tree whose branches or sprigs are used as a symbol of grief or mourning.

Review and Assess

Thinking About the Selection

1. **Respond:** Would you like to meet the speaker of this poem? Why or why not?

2. **(a) Recall:** In "Me," to what two things does the speaker compare himself or herself? **(b) Connect:** What qualities are shared by the things to which the speaker compares himself or herself?

3. **(a) Recall:** In the first four lines of the poem, what does de la Mare say he shall always be? **(b) Interpret:** What message about people in general does his statement suggest?

4. **(a) Infer:** How does de la Mare feel about being "just me"? **(b) Support:** What specific word choices or details from the poem indicate his feelings? **(c) Apply:** In what ways is a person in society "just me" and more than "just me"?

Walter de la Mare

1873–1956

While still a teenager, Walter de la Mare began working on statistics in a London office. Numbers were part of his daily life. By night, however, he escaped into the world of his imagination, writing poems for adults and children. In the poem "Me," de la Mare writes about the mystery of being one of a kind, not a statistic.

Review and Assess

Literary Analysis

The Speaker in Poetry

1. What specific words and phrases does each **speaker** use to talk about himself or herself? Write them on a chart like the one shown.

Poem	Words and Phrases
"Song of Myself"	
"I'm Nobody"	
"Me"	

2. How would you describe each speaker's feeling about himself or herself?
3. In "Song of Myself," what do the long lines and long sentences indicate about the speaker?
4. In "I'm Nobody," how does the speaker use words humorously to show that Nobodies are special but Somebodies are not?

Comparing Literary Works

5. How much does each speaker concern himself or herself with how other people view him or her? Explain.
6. Which poem do you feel best expresses your idea of individuality? Explain your answer.

Reading Strategy

Identifying Analogies in Poetry

7. **(a)** Complete the chart below by explaining the shared quality expressed by the comparison in the second column. **(b)** Review all of the poems in this section. Find two more **analogies** to add to the chart and explain the shared qualities for each.

Poem	Analogy	Shared Quality
"Song of Myself"	Being me is like being an individual world	

Extend Understanding

8. **History Connection:** Describe a situation in history in which laws or government practices prevented people from expressing their individuality.

Quick Review

The **speaker** of a poem is the poet or a character invented by the poet whom you "hear" as you read the lines. To review the speaker in poetry, see page 37.

An **analogy** is a comparison between two things or situations that are otherwise not alike. To review analogies, see page 37.

 Take It to the Net

www.phschool.com
Take the interactive self-test online to check your understanding of these selections.

Integrate Language Skills

Vocabulary Development Lesson

Word Analysis: Forms of *equal*

Whitman uses *equal* to mean "the same" when he says, "with equal cheerfulness I can wait." Using each word once, choose the form of *equal* that fits best in each blank.

unequal   equals   equality

Poetry is personal, so one poet never exactly ____?____ another. Also, poets are ____?____ in their achievements. However, these three poets, like all fine writers, display an ____?____ of spirit.

Spelling Strategy

The *kw* sound following the *e* in *equal* is spelled *qu*. Fill in the blanks with a suitable word containing the *qu* spelling of the *kw* sound.

1. Often Dickinson's poems ask ____?____ that are hard to answer.
2. Poets living many years ago probably wrote with a ____?____ and ink.

Concept Development: Synonyms

Synonyms are words with similar meanings, such as *exist* and *be*. On your paper, match each word in the first column with the synonym in the second column. To help you, review the vocabulary words on page 37.

1. assume	a. identical
2. loaf	b. sad
3. equal	c. suppose
4. bog	d. swamp
5. forlorn	e. remove
6. banish	f. satisfied
7. content	g. relax

Grammar Lesson

General and Specific Nouns

In using nouns to refer to people, places, or things, imagine that you are operating a movie camera. A **general noun,** like *tree*, is a wide-angle shot that takes in a group of related items. There are many kinds of trees in the group. A **specific noun,** like *oak*, is a close-up shot of a single item. An oak is one type of tree. Notice how De la Mare follows a wide-angle shot (general noun) with a series of quick close-ups (specific nouns):

Example: Like a tree.
          Like a willow or elder,
          An aspen, a thorn,
          Or a cypress forlorn.

▶ *For more practice, see page R28, Exercise A.*
Practice On your paper, indicate whether each italicized noun is general or specific.

1. De la Mare compares human life to that of a *flower*.
2. The poet doesn't mention a *daisy*.
3. He also compares himself to a *tree*.
4. He mentions an *aspen* and a *cypress*.
5. For Dickinson, a Somebody is like a *frog*.

Writing Application Copy the following sentence. Fill in the first blank with a plural general noun. Use three specific nouns in the following blanks.

Three examples of ____?____ are a ____?____, a ____?____, and a ____?____.

W͟G Prentice Hall Writing and Grammar Connection: Chapter 14, Section 1

Writing Lesson

Compare and Contrast Speakers

Write a brief composition in which you compare and contrast two of the speakers from these three poems.

Prewriting Review the poems and select two to compare and contrast. Use a Venn diagram to list the shared and unique qualities of the speakers.

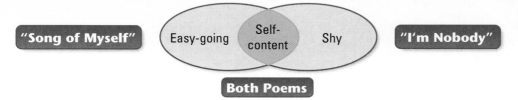

Drafting Begin your composition with a general statement about the way the self is presented in the two poems you have selected. Next, compare the two by pointing out ideas, expressions, or feelings that are similar. Then, contrast by showing ideas, expressions, or feelings that are different in the poems. Finish with a final statement based on your findings.

Revising Review your first sentence, making sure it indicates the general idea you will express in your composition. If necessary, rewrite your first sentence to be consistent with the details you have presented.

Prentice Hall Writing and Grammar Connection: Chapter 8, Section 2

Extension Activities

Listening and Speaking Stage a **poetry contest** among the three poets in which you and your classmates take on the roles of the poets as they read from their work. A panel can rate the performances based on these questions:

- Did the reader pause at commas, dashes, and ellipses?
- Did the reader stop at periods and give proper emphasis to questions and exclamations?
- Did the reader vary the speed at which he or she read?

Research and Technology As these poems suggest, people have individual personalities, but they usually have a unique combination of physical traits as well. Do a **presentation** about how genes contribute to physical characteristics.

- Use library resources to gather facts.
- Include comments by scientists.
- Find visuals to accompany your findings.

 **Take It to the Net** www.phschool.com

Go online for an additional research activity using the Internet.

Prepare to Read

My Furthest-Back Person (*The Inspiration for* Roots)

 Take It to the Net

Visit www.phschool.com for interactive activities and instruction related to "My Furthest-Back Person," including

- background
- graphic organizers
- literary elements
- reading strategies

Preview

Connecting to the Literature

In the essay "My Furthest-Back Person," Alex Haley tells the exciting story of how he traced his African ancestors, some of whom had been brought to the United States as slaves 200 years ago. To understand the difficulty of Haley's search for information, think about the many ways that information is recorded and organized today. Few of these types of records were kept in the 1800s, especially for enslaved Africans.

Background

Alex Haley began research to learn about his African ancestors by searching through government records. In Africa, he found another way people keep records: in the memory of a tribal "historian" who could recite centuries of history!

Literary Analysis

Personal Essay

A **personal essay** is a form of nonfictional prose. The purpose of a personal essay is to allow the writer to share thoughts and reactions to an event or a situation in the writer's own life. The narrator of the essay is the writer, who uses a conversational style and refers to himself or herself with the pronoun *I*. Notice the style and the pronoun in this example.

> *One Saturday in 1965 I happened to be walking* past the National Archives building in Washington. . . .

Look for details throughout the essay that make it seem as though Haley is sitting with you, telling about his experiences.

Connecting Literary Elements

Dialogue is conversation between characters or people. In writing, dialogue is usually set off by quotation marks to indicate a speaker's exact words. In "My Furthest-Back Person," dialogue brings the people in the essay to life and moves Haley's story forward. Use these focus questions to guide you as you read.

1. What important information is conveyed to Haley in the passages that include dialogue?
2. How does the use of people's exact words make the essay personal?

Reading Strategy

Breaking Down Long Sentences

To understand what you read, you must sometimes **break down long sentences** into parts.

- First, find the subject of the sentence—the person or thing that the sentence is about (some sentences will have more than one).
- Then, identify what the sentence is saying about the subject.
- Finally, read the whole sentence, including other groups of words.

Use a chart like this to help you understand the main part and meaning of a sentence.

Word group	What it tells
After about a dozen micro-filmed rolls,	when the action happens
I was beginning to tire,	The subject and the main action

Vocabulary Development

intrigue (in´ trēg) *n.* curiosity and interest (p. 47)

uncanny (un kan´ ē) *adj.* strange; eerie (p. 47)

cherished (cher´ ishd) *adj.* beloved; valued (p. 47)

queried (kwir´ ēd) *v.* asked (p. 48)

eminent (em´ ə nənt) *adj.* distinguished or outstanding (p. 48)

destination (des´ tə nā´ shən) *n.* the place to which something is being sent (p. 54)

My Furthest-Back Person
(The Inspiration for Roots)   Alex Haley

> As a boy, Alex Haley spent his summers on his grand-
> mother's front porch in Henning, Tennessee, listening to her
> and her sisters tell stories of the family's history back
> through the days of slavery. The "furthest-back person" they
> spoke of was an ancestor they called "The African," who was
> kidnapped in his native country, shipped to Annapolis,
> Maryland, and sold into slavery. These stories stayed with
> young Alex throughout his life.

One Saturday in 1965 I happened to be walking past the National Archives building in Washington. Across the interim years I had thought of Grandma's old stories—otherwise I can't think what diverted me up the Archives' steps. And when a main reading room desk attendant asked if he could help me, I wouldn't have dreamed of admitting to him some curiosity hanging on from boyhood about my slave forebears. I kind of bumbled that I was interested in census records of Alamance County, North Carolina, just after the Civil War.

The microfilm rolls were delivered, and I turned them through the machine with a building sense of <u>intrigue</u>, viewing in different census takers' penmanship an endless parade of names. After about a dozen microfilmed rolls, I was beginning to tire, when in utter astonishment I looked upon the names of Grandma's parents: Tom Murray, Irene Murray . . . older sisters of Grandma's as well—every one of them a name that I'd heard countless times on her front porch.

It wasn't that I hadn't believed Grandma. You just *didn't* not believe my Grandma. It was simply so <u>uncanny</u> actually seeing those names in print and in official U.S. Government records.

During the next several months I was back in Washington whenever possible, in the Archives, the Library of Congress, the Daughters of the American Revolution Library. (Whenever black attendants understood the idea of my search, documents I requested reached me with miraculous speed.) In one source or another during 1966 I was able to document at least the highlights of the <u>cherished</u> family story. I would have given anything to have told Grandma, but, sadly, in 1949 she had gone. So I went and told the only survivor of those Henning front-porch storytellers: Cousin Georgia Anderson, now in her 80's in Kansas City, Kan. Wrinkled, bent, not well herself, she was so overjoyed, repeating to me the old stories and sounds; they were like Henning echoes: "Yeah, boy, that African say his name was 'Kin-tay'; he say the banjo was 'ko,' an' the river 'Kamby Bolong,' an' he was off choppin' some wood to make his drum when they grabbed 'im!" Cousin Georgia grew so excited we had to stop her, calm her down, "You go 'head, boy! Your grandma an' all of 'em—they up there watching what you do!"

That week I flew to London on a magazine assignment. Since by now I was steeped in the old, in the past, scarcely a tour guide missed me—I was awed at so many historical places and treasures I'd heard of and read of. I came upon the Rosetta stone in the British Museum, marveling anew at how Jean Champollion, the French archaeologist, had miraculously deciphered its ancient demotic and hieroglyphic texts[1] . . .

---

1. **demotic and hieroglyphic texts** (dē mät´ ik and hī ər ō´ glif´ ik) *adj.* ancient Egyptian writing, using symbols and pictures to represent words.

Literary Analysis
Personal Essay What details in the first two paragraphs show that this is a personal essay?

intrigue (in´ trēg) *n.* curiosity and interest

uncanny (un kan´ ē) *adj.* strange; eerie

cherished (cher´ ishd) *adj.* beloved; valued

Reading Strategy
Breaking Down Long Sentences Identify the subject of the sentence beginning "Since by now..." What does the sentence tell you?

Reading Check

What does Haley find in the microfilm?

The thrill of that just kept hanging around in my head. I was on a jet returning to New York when a thought hit me. Those strange, unknown-tongue sounds, always part of our family's old story . . . they were obviously bits of our original African *"Kin-tay's"* native tongue. What specific tongue? Could I somehow find out?

Back in New York, I began making visits to the United Nations Headquarters lobby; it wasn't hard to spot Africans. I'd stop any I could, asking if my bits of phonetic sounds held any meaning for them. A couple of dozen Africans quickly looked at me, listened, and took off—understandably dubious about some Tennesseean's accent alleging "African" sounds.

My research assistant, George Sims (we grew up together in Henning), brought me some names of ranking scholars of African linguistics. One was particularly intriguing: a Belgian- and English-educated Dr. Jan Vansina; he had spent his early career living in West African villages, studying and tape-recording countless oral histories that were narrated by certain very old African men; he had written a standard textbook, "The Oral Tradition."

So I flew to the University of Wisconsin to see Dr. Vansina. In his living room I told him every bit of the family story in the fullest detail that I could remember it. Then, intensely, he queried me about the story's relay across the generations, about the gibberish of "*k*" sounds Grandma had fiercely muttered to herself while doing her housework, with my brothers and me giggling beyond her hearing at what we had dubbed "Grandma's noises."

Dr. Vansina, his manner very serious, finally said, "These sounds your family has kept sound very probably of the tongue called 'Mandinka.'"

I'd never heard of any "Mandinka." Grandma just told of the African saying *"ko"* for banjo, or *"Kamby Bolong"* for a Virginia river.

Among Mandinka stringed instruments, Dr. Vansina said, one of the oldest was the "*kora.*"

"*Bolong,*" he said, was clearly Mandinka for "river." Preceded by "*Kamby,*" it very likely meant "Gambia River."

Dr. Vansina telephoned an eminent Africanist colleague, Dr. Philip Curtin. He said that the phonetic "*Kin-tay*" was correctly spelled "*Kinte,*" a very old clan that had originated in Old Mali. The Kinte men traditionally were blacksmiths, and the women were potters and weavers.

I knew I must get to the Gambia River.

The first native Gambian I could locate in the U.S. was named Ebou Manga, then a junior attending Hamilton College in upstate Clinton, N.Y. He and I flew to Dakar, Senegal, then took a smaller plane to Yundum Airport, and rode in a van to Gambia's capital, Bathurst.♦ Ebou and his father assembled eight Gambia government officials. I told them Grandma's stories, every detail I could

queried (kwir´ ēd) *v.* asked

Literary Analysis
Personal Essay In what way does this detail about giggling boys make the essay personal?

eminent (em´ ə nənt) *adj.* distinguished or outstanding

remember, as they listened intently, then reacted. "'*Kamby Bolong*' of course is Gambia River!" I heard. "But more clue is your fore-father's saying his name was '*Kinte*.'" Then they told me something I would never ever have fantasized—that in places in the back country lived very old men, commonly called *griots*, who could tell centuries of the histories of certain very old family clans. As for *Kintes*, they pointed out to me on a map some family villages, Kinte-Kundah, and Kinte-Kundah Janneh-Ya, for instance.

The Gambian officials said they would try to help me. I returned to New York dazed. It is embarrassing to me now, but despite Grandma's stories, I'd never been concerned much with Africa, and I had the routine images of African people living mostly in exotic jungles. But a compulsion now laid hold of me to learn all I could, and I began devouring books about Africa, especially about the slave trade. Then one Thursday's mail contained a letter from one of the Gambian officials, inviting me to return there.

Monday I was back in Bathurst. It galvanized me when the officials said that a *griot* had been located who told the *Kinte* clan history—his name was Kebba Kanga Fofana. To reach him, I discovered, required a modified safari: renting a launch to get upriver, two land vehicles to carry supplies by a round-about land route, and employing finally 14 people, including three interpreters and four musicians, since a *griot* would not speak the revered clan histories without background music.

The boat Baddibu vibrated upriver, with me acutely tense: Were these Africans maybe viewing me as but another of the pith-helmets?[2] After about two hours, we put in at James Island, for me to see the ruins of the once British-operated James Fort. Here two centuries of slave ships had loaded thousands of cargoes of Gambian tribespeople. The crumbling stones, the deeply oxidized swivel cannon, even some remnant links of chain seemed all but impossible to believe. Then we continued upriver to the left-bank village of Albreda, and there put ashore to continue on foot to Juffure [jōō′ fōō rā], village of the *griot*. Once more we stopped, for me to see *toubob kolong*, the "white man's well," now almost filled in, in a swampy area with abundant, tall, saw-toothed grass. It was dug two centuries ago to "17 men's height deep" to insure survival drinking water for long-driven, famishing coffles[3] of slaves.

---

2. **pith-helmets** *jargon* tourists or hunters on safari, who typically wore these hard hats.
3. **coffles** (kôf′ əlz) *n.* groups of animals or slaves chained or tied together in a line.

Walking on, I kept wishing that Grandma could hear how her stories had led me to the "*Kamby Bolong*." (Our surviving storyteller Cousin Georgia died in a Kansas City hospital during this same morning, I would learn later.) Finally, Juffure village's playing children, sighting us, flashed an alert. The 70-odd people came rushing from their circular, thatch-roofed, mud-walled huts, with goats bounding up and about, and parrots squawking from up in the palms. I sensed him in advance somehow, the small man amid them, wearing a pillbox cap and an off-white robe—the *griot*. Then the interpreters went to him, as the villagers thronged around me.

And it hit me like a gale wind: every one of them, the whole crowd, was *jet black*. An enormous sense of guilt swept me—a sense of being some kind of hybrid . . . a sense of being impure among the pure. It was an awful sensation.

The old *griot* stepped away from my interpreters and the crowd quickly swarmed around him—all of them buzzing. An interpreter named A.B.C. Salla came to me; he whispered: "Why they stare at you so, they have never seen here a black American." And that hit me: I was symbolizing for them twenty-five millions of us they had never seen. What did they think of me—of us?

Then abruptly the old *griot* was briskly walking toward me. His eyes boring into mine, he spoke in Mandinka, as if instinctively I should understand—and A.B.C. Salla translated:

"Yes . . . we have been told by the forefathers . . . that many of us from this place are in exile . . . in that place called America . . . and in other places."

I suppose I physically wavered, and they thought it was the heat; rustling whispers went through the crowd, and a man brought me a low stool. Now the whispering hushed—the musicians had softly begun playing *kora* and *balafon*, and a canvas sling lawn seat was taken by the *griot*, Kebba Kanga Fofana, aged 73 "rains" (one rainy season each year). He seemed to gather himself into a physical rigidity, and he began speaking the *Kinte* clan's ancestral oral history; it came rolling from his mouth across the next hours . . . 17th- and 18th-century *Kinte* lineage details, predominantly what men took wives; the children they "begot," in the order of their births; those children's mates and children.

Events frequently were dated by some proximate[4] singular physical occurrence. It was as if some ancient scroll were printed indelibly within the *griot's* brain. Each few sentences or so, he would pause for an interpreter's translation to me. I distill here the essence:

---

4. proximate (präks′ ə mət) *adj.* near in time.

◀ **Critical Viewing**
This photograph and the one on page 44 are stills from the television mini-series about Haley's experience. What does the posture of the actors reveal about the relationship between their characters? **[Analyze]**

The *Kinte* clan began in Old Mali, the men generally blacksmiths ". . . who conquered fire," and the women potters and weavers. One large branch of the clan moved to Mauretania from where one son of the clan, Kairaba Kunta Kinte, a Moslem Marabout holy man, entered Gambia. He lived first in the village of Pakali N'Ding; he moved next to Jiffarong village; ". . . and then he came here, into our own village of Juffure."

In Juffure, Kairaba Kunta Kinte took his first wife, ". . . a Mandinka maiden, whose name was Sireng. By her, he begot two sons, whose names were Janneh and Saloum. Then he got a second wife, Yaisa. By her, he begot a son, Omoro."

The three sons became men in Juffure. Janneh and Saloum went off and found a new village, Kinte-Kundah Janneh-Ya. "And then Omoro, the youngest son, when he had 30 rains, took as a wife a maiden, Binta Kebba.

"And by her, he begot four sons—Kunta, Lamin, Suwadu, and Madi . . ."

Sometimes, a "begotten," after his naming, would be accompanied by some later-occurring detail, perhaps as ". . . in time of big water (flood), he slew a water buffalo." Having named those four sons, now the griot stated such a detail.

Reading Check

What does Haley feel when he looks out at the crowd?

"About the time the king's soldiers came, the eldest of these four sons, Kunta, when he had about 16 rains, went away from his village, to chop wood to make a drum . . . and he was never seen again . . ."

Goose-pimples the size of lemons seemed to pop all over me. In my knapsack were my cumulative notebooks, the first of them including how in my boyhood, my Grandma, Cousin Georgia and the others told of the African "*Kin-tay*" who always said he was kidnapped near his village—while chopping wood to make a drum . . .

I showed the interpreter, he showed and told the *griot*, who excitedly told the people; they grew very agitated. Abruptly then they formed a human ring, encircling me, dancing and chanting. Perhaps a dozen of the women carrying their infant babies rushed in toward me, thrusting the infants into my arms conveying, I would later learn, "the laying on of hands . . . through this flesh which is us, we are you, and you are us." The men hurried me into their mosque, their Arabic praying later being translated outside: "Thanks be to Allah for returning the long lost from among us." Direct descendants of Kunta Kinte's blood brothers were hastened, some of them from nearby villages, for a family portrait to be taken with me, surrounded by actual ancestral sixth cousins. More symbolic acts filled the remaining day.

When they would let me leave, for some reason I wanted to go away over the African land. Dazed, silent in the bumping Land Rover, I heard the cutting staccato of talking drums. Then when we sighted the next village, its people came thronging to meet us. They were all—little naked ones to wizened elders—waving, beaming; amid a cacophony of crying out; and then my ears identified their words: "*Meester Kinte! Meester Kinte!*"

Let me tell you something: I am a man. But I remember the sob surging up from my feet, flinging up my hands before my face and bawling as I had not done since I was a baby . . . the jet-black Africans were jostling,[5] staring . . . I didn't care, with the feelings surging. If you really knew the odyssey of us millions of black Americans, if you really knew how we came in the seeds of our

Reading Strategy
Breaking Down Long Sentences Who is "hastened" in the sentence about the family portrait? From where are they hastened?

---

5. **jostling** (jäs´ ling) *v.* bumping and pushing, as in a crowd.

The Purple Quilt (detail), 1986; acrylic on canvas, tie-dyed and printed fabric, 91 x 72, Faith Ringgold, Courtesy of Bernice Steinbaum

▲ **Critical Viewing**
In what way does this quilt give a good representation of Haley's visit to Africa?

forefathers, captured, driven, beaten, inspected, bought, branded, chained in foul ships, if you really knew, you needed weeping . . .

Back home, I knew that what I must write, really, was our black saga, where any individual's past is the essence of the millions'. Now flat broke, I went to some editors I knew, describing the Gambian miracle, and my desire to pursue the research; Doubleday contracted to publish, and Reader's Digest to condense the projected book; then I had advances to travel further.

What ship brought Kinte to Grandma's "'Naplis" (Annapolis, Md., obviously)? The old *griot's* time reference to "king's soldiers" sent me flying to London. Feverish searching at last identified, in British Parliament records, "Colonel O'Hare's Forces," dispatched in mid-1767 to protect the then British-held James Fort whose ruins I'd visited. So Kunta Kinte was down in some ship probably sailing later that summer from the Gambia River to Annapolis.

Now I feel it was fated that I had taught myself to write in the U.S. Coast Guard. For the sea dramas I had concentrated on had given me years of experience searching among yellowing old U.S. maritime records. So now in English 18th Century marine records I finally tracked ships reporting themselves in and out to the

☑ **Reading Check**

What happens after Haley shows his notebook about his ancestor?

Commandant of the Gambia River's James Fort. And then early one afternoon I found that a Lord Ligonier under a Captain Thomas Davies had sailed on the Sabbath of July 5, 1767. Her cargo: 3,265 elephants' teeth, 3,700 pounds of beeswax, 800 pounds of cotton, 32 ounces of Gambian gold and 140 slaves; her destination: "Annapolis."

destination
(des' tə nā' shən) *n.* the place to which something is being sent

That night I recrossed the Atlantic. In the Library of Congress the Lord Ligonier's arrival was one brief line in "Shipping In The Port Of Annapolis—1748–1775." I located the author, Vaughan W. Brown, in his Baltimore brokerage office. He drove to Historic Annapolis, the city's historical society, and found me further documentation of her arrival on Sept. 29, 1767. (Exactly two centuries later, Sept. 29, 1967, standing, staring seaward from an Annapolis pier, again I knew tears.) More help came in the Maryland Hall of Records. Archivist Phebe Jacobsen found the Lord Ligonier's arriving customs declaration listing, "98 Negroes"—so in her 86-day crossing, 42 Gambians had died, one among the survivors being 16-year-old Kunta Kinte. Then the microfilmed Oct. 1, 1767, Maryland Gazette contained, on page two, an announcement to prospective buyers from the ship's agents, Daniel of St. Thos. Jenifer and John Ridout (the Governor's secretary): "from the River GAMBIA, in AFRICA . . . a cargo of choice, healthy SLAVES . . ."

Review and Assess

Thinking About the Selection

1. **Respond:** What questions would you like to ask Haley about his experience?

2. **(a) Recall:** What did Haley find in the National Archives in Washington? **(b) Infer:** Why was his discovery exciting to him? **(c) Interpret:** How was Haley's quest, from the very beginning, both a mental puzzle and an emotional thrill?

3. **(a) Recall:** Describe Haley's reaction to the Rosetta Stone. **(b) Compare and Contrast:** What is similar and different about the African sounds in Haley's family stories and the writing on the Rosetta stone?

4. **(a) Recall:** What does the griot tell Haley about his ancestor Kunta Kinte? **(b) Deduce:** Why does the griot know about Kunta Kinte? **(c) Connect:** In what way are the tales of the griot and the tales of Haley's family like two parts of the same puzzle?

5. **(a) Recall:** What was Haley's reaction when the villagers called out "Meester Kinte"? **(b) Infer:** Why is the moment such an emotional one? **(c) Draw Conclusions:** Why might some people be unable to appreciate the full impact of Haley's experience?

Alex Haley

1921–1992

Alex Haley grew up in Tennessee and Alabama. As a teenager, he joined the Coast Guard to see more of the world. While aboard ships, he began writing sea adventure stories.

After twenty years in the Coast Guard, Haley retired to begin a full-time career as a writer. His best-known work is *Roots: The Saga of an American Family.* "My Furthest-Back Person" explains how he began this book. *Roots,* an immediate bestseller, led to a groundbreaking television mini-series viewed by 140 million people. Together, the book and the mini-series inspired many people to research their own family histories.

Review and Assess

Literary Analysis

Personal Essay

1. Identify one example of each of these characteristics of a **personal essay** in the last six paragraphs of "My Furthest-Back Person." Explain how each makes the essay more personal. **(a)** a sentence using the pronoun *I* **(b)** an event from the life of the person telling the story **(c)** a detail that reveals the person's reaction to events **(d)** a conversational style

2. Use the following chart to compare a personal essay to a short story.

Characteristics of a Personal Essay	Same or Different?	Characteristics of a Short Story
		written in prose
		events in a story do not really happen
		people are invented by the writer
		often includes dialogue or conversations
		may include narrator's reactions

Connecting Literary Elements

3. What important information is conveyed to Haley in the passages that include **dialogue** with Cousin Georgia, Dr. Vansina, Gambian officials, and the *griot*?

4. How does the use of people's exact words make the essay personal?

Reading Strategy

Breaking Down Long Sentences

5. On your paper, underline the main part of the following sentence.
   "When they would let me leave, for some reason I wanted to go away over the African land."

6. What group of words in the following sentence tells how the narrator feels about not having been concerned with Africa?
   "It is embarrassing to me now, but despite Grandma's stories, I'd never been much concerned with Africa, and I had the routine images of African people living mostly in exotic jungles."

Extend Understanding

7. **Extend:** This essay suggests that a person needs to feel part of a larger group. Explain why you agree or disagree.

Quick Review

A **personal essay** is a brief, nonfiction account of an event from the writer's own life, told in a conversational style, and using the pronoun *I*. To review the elements of personal essays, see page 45.

Dialogue is conversation— the exact words of characters or people. To review dialogue, see page 45.

When you **break down long sentences,** you find the subject. Then, you find what the sentence says about the subject.

 Take It to the Net
www.phschool.com
Take the interactive self-test online to check your understanding of the selection.

Integrate Language Skills

Vocabulary Development Lesson

Word Analysis: Anglo-Saxon Prefix *un-*

The Anglo-Saxon prefix *un-* means "not" or "the opposite of." Use these definitions to answer the following questions.

1. Explain why Africa was *unmapped* territory for Haley before he began his research.
2. What *unexpected* information did the Gambian officials give Haley?
3. What incident in Gambia proves that Haley was *unafraid* of showing his emotions?

Spelling Strategy

When you add a prefix to a word, you do not change the spelling of the original word:
un- + canny = uncanny   un- + named = unnamed.
Spell the following words correctly.

1. un- + even   2. re- + place   3. re- + elect

Fluency: Clarify Word Meaning

Answer each question *yes* or *no*. Then, explain your responses. To help you, review the vocabulary words on page 45.

1. If a project is *cherished*, is it valued?
2. Was Alex Haley an *eminent* writer?
3. Was Ghana Haley's *destination* in Africa?
4. Did the *intrigue* of the quest decrease for Haley?
5. Did seeing his great-grandparents' names in census records give Haley an *uncanny* feeling?
6. Is it likely that people *queried* Haley about how to find their own roots?

Grammar Lesson

Collective Nouns

"My Furthest-Back Person" is about individuals and the groups from which they come. Therefore, it is not surprising that Haley uses **collective nouns**—words that have a singular form but name a group of persons, animals, or objects that are considered as a single unit. The italicized words in the following examples are collective nouns.

> **Examples:** The *crowd* surrounded him.
> The Land Rover paused as the *herd* crossed the road.
> The *audience* listened carefully while the storyteller told the old stories.

Other examples of collective nouns are *team*, *jury*, and *class*.

▶ *For more practice, see page R28, Exercise A.*
Practice Write these sentences. Underline the collective noun in each.

1. Haley was interested in the history of his family.
2. In Africa, the crew of the boat took him upriver.
3. He saw the flock of birds circling over the boat.
4. He met many people, and the majority were helpful.
5. A dozen of the African musical instruments he saw were unknown to him.

Writing Application Write sentences with the following collective nouns: *orchestra*, *team*, *army*.

W͜G *Prentice Hall Writing and Grammar Connection: Chapter 14, Section 1*

Writing Lesson

Proposal

Alex Haley probably went to a book publisher and presented a **proposal**—an idea for a project or action that requires assistance or funding. Write a proposal that Haley might have written to the publishers. Include an overall statement of your purpose, what you have done so far, what still needs to be done, and what you need from the publishers.

Prewriting Reread the essay and take notes on Haley's purpose, what he did before making the proposal, what remained to be done, and what he needed most from the publisher.

Drafting Write your proposal. As you draft, balance the different parts of your proposal. Details about what you have done so far should not overshadow details of what remains to be done.

Revising Look for the places where you move from one idea to another. Add transitions to clarify the connections between the ideas.

Model: Add Transitions

My discoveries in Gambia have fired my interest in what else

Although

I might learn about my ancestors.∧I have a lot of

    , I

enthusiasm∧do not have a lot of money.

> The transition *although* shows that the two thoughts contrast with each other.

𝒲𝒢 *Prentice Hall Writing and Grammar Connection: Chapter 7, Section 4*

Extension Activities

Listening and Speaking Interview an older relative or friend to learn about the time period of his or her childhood.

1. Draw up a list of questions beforehand to guide the interview.
2. During the interview, ask follow-up questions. If your subject says school was more difficult in the past, follow up with a question such as, "How many hours a day did you attend?"
3. Present your findings to the class.

Research and Technology Rent one or more of the episodes in the television mini-series *Roots*. Then, in a group of four, write a **review** of the film for classmates. Each group member can discuss a different element of the film, including the acting, set design, costume design, soundtrack, and story.

 **Take It to the Net** www.phschool.com

Go online for an additional research activity using the Internet.

The literature of a culture or time period often reflects trends in public interest. For example, the popularity of science fiction in the 1950s and 1960s reflects the public's interest in science and technology at the beginning of the space age.

Sometimes, literature does not reflect public interest; it creates it. Alex Haley's book *Roots* and the mini-series of the same name caused a surge of interest in genealogy—the study of ancestors and family lines. His work inspired many to take pride and interest in their family history. A public television series was developed to help beginners, especially those who were not of European American descent, to explore family history and genealogy. Alex Haley accepted the position of host and coproducer. Unfortunately, he died before the ten-part series was aired. Nonetheless, the project continued and was highly successful in helping many Americans discover their "roots."

The following selection is the first chapter from the companion book to the PBS series that shares its name: *Ancestors*. It tells the story of the man featured on the first installment of the series.

Victor Edmundo Villaseñor

· · · · · · · · · · · · · ·

from *Ancestors*
Jim and Terry Willard
with Jane Wilson

An inspiring example of the value of family history and genealogy is Victor Edmundo Villaseñor. He has been successful in his search for his roots. Of humble origins, his mother and father came to this country from Mexico and settled on a farm in Southern California. When Victor began his journey into family history, he was faced with common doubts.

The Gomez and Villaseñor Families

E. Escolar
born: 1863
died: 1934
m. 1880
A. Gomez
born: 1861
died: 1911

H. Valdez
born: 1863
died: 1933
m. 1883
S. Villaseñor
born: 1863
died: 1920

O. Ramirez
born: 1880
died: 1958
m. 1838
R. Gomez
born: 1883
died: 1972

L. Gomez
born: 1903
died: 1985
m. 1921
J. S. Villaseñor
born: 1901
died: 1978

A. Villaseñor
born: 1886
died: 1960

M. Villaseñor
born: 1884
died: 1955

L. Villaseñor
born: 1922
died: 1948

C. Villaseñor
born: 1924

V. E. Villaseñor
born: 1928

R. Gomez, Jr.
born: 1899
died: 1962

C. Gomez
born: 1901
died: 1943

G. Gomez
born: 1905
died: 1978

Victor Villaseñor's parents:
Juan Salvador Villaseñor and
Lupe Gomez.

▲ **Critical Viewing** In what ways might a modern-day wedding photograph
be similar to and different from this one? **[Compare and Contrast]**

"When I started my parents' story, I thought that the story of the family down the street was a better story. I didn't think much of my parents' story. But once you really start talking and getting to know people deep inside, an ordinary story can become great and wonderful. *Everyone is special.* I know we've all heard that cliché, but it's really not a cliché. Everyone is born with certain gifts and liabilities. As they live through life, they do heroic things and negative things. As you get to know them, they become heroic for doing the best that they can."

When Victor was a child, his father and grandmother filled Victor's soul with stories of Mexico and the culture from which he came. Victor's father once told him that everyone was Mexican, and if they were not, they wanted to be. In Victor's community, everyone spoke Spanish. When Victor started school, his world was shattered. "I'll never forget it. The teacher put me in the back of the classroom with some other Mexican children. I started talking in Spanish and the teacher screamed, 'No Spanish!' I began to see that everything I had been raised with was wrong."

Victor grew up angry and alienated, ashamed of his Mexican heritage. The stories of his village that he shared with other children were ridiculed. "I felt [my parents] had lied to me. All of the stories were lies."

Victor's father told him of a big snake in his village in Mexico that had eaten children. "Everyone was terrified of it, and my grandfather, a great horseman, fought the serpent on horseback. The serpent was eight feet tall, and he took a tree branch,

▲ **Critical Viewing** Can you imagine a man on horseback like the man in this picture fighting a snake like the one mentioned in the story? **[Assess]**

rammed it down the serpent's throat, and roped and dragged him, like Saint George. My father told me it was true. I thought it was a lie." It wasn't until a trip to the San Diego Zoo, when he was older, that Victor "went to the man that studies snakes and asked him, 'I heard that there is a snake who stands eight feet tall and can attack a man on horseback. Is that possible?' he said, 'Oh yeah. That's the bushmaster.' And I said, 'What?' He said, 'Yeah, they're fourteen feet long and stand up seven feet. Half their length. And if they're sixteen feet, they stand up eight feet. . . . They were fearless. That's why they're basically extinct. They would attack a train, an automobile. So, surely, they'll attack a man on horse-back.' I asked him, "Can they eat a little kid, or a baby pig?' 'Well, a rattlesnake can eat a rabbit, and it's much smaller than the bushmaster, so sure.'" It was then that Victor realized, "My father's stories were true."

Victor went to Mexico at age nineteen to see for himself the land of the stories of his youth. "When I went to Mexico, I could hear them speak Spanish, and then I could see the Indian cultures and the rich colors and the food. All of a sudden, I said 'I am somebody, I come from somewhere. I started to understand that my parents were good people. I had been mad at them all those years, but they hadn't lied to me. The one thing that happened when I started researching my history is that now my parents are my greatest heroes. . . ."

Victor found peace and identity in his family history. He spent sixteen years putting his family history together. He started with stories that he did not believe and an uncertain identity. He came away with a full understanding of himself and a gift for future generations.

Thematic Connection
Is Villaseñor's reaction to family history similar to Haley's reactions? Explain.

Jim and Terry Willard Jane Wilson Victor Edmundo Villaseñor

Jim and Terry Willard hosted the ten-part PBS series *Ancestors*. Before becoming television hosts, they taught high school in Maine. They currently live in Florida.

Jane Wilson was involved in the research, writing, and production of *Ancestors*. She has worked on a number of film and television projects. She lives in Provo, Utah.

In addition to appearing on *Ancestors*, Victor Edmundo Villaseñor has written books about his family history: *Rain of Gold*, *Wild Steps of Heaven*, and *Thirteen Senses*.

Connecting Literature and Culture

1. What details of Alex Haley's experiences might have inspired Villaseñor to begin his own search for his ancestors?
2. In what ways are their searches similar and different?
3. Compare the ways the two men respond to what they find.
4. In what way might seeing Villaseñor's story on television inspire others to begin studying their family history?

Prepare to Read

The Third Level

 Take It to the Net

Visit www.phschool.com for interactive activities and instruction related to "The Third Level," including
- background
- graphic organizers
- literary elements
- reading strategies

Preview

Connecting to the Literature

The narrator of "The Third Level" travels back to 1894 and finds that time period strangely appealing. Based on what you have seen in movies and on television, as well as on what you can assume from the photograph above, what might you like about life in that time?

Background

"The Third Level," a short story by Jack Finney, is set in New York City's Grand Central Station. Completed in 1913 and restored beginning in the late 1990s, Grand Central is one of the world's most famous train stations. The huge main room of the station is connected to railroad platforms, subways, and streets by a series of tunnels. In "The Third Level," one of these tunnels takes an unexpected turn.

Literary Analysis

Time in a Setting

Setting is the time and place in which a story's events occur. In Finney's story, time plays an especially important role, as the main character walks down a corridor in Grand Central Station and discovers that he has been transported back to 1894. In this example, the words in italics help establish that although the narrator is in the same place, the setting has changed.

> . . . I saw the room was *smaller*, there were *fewer ticket windows and train gates*, and the information booth in the center was wood and *old-looking*. . . . The lights were dim and sort of flickering. Then I saw why; *they were open-flame gaslights*.

As you read, look for more details that contrast present and past time.

Connecting Literary Elements

Realistic elements of a story are details that seem as though they could take place or exist in real life. Many of the details that describe Grand Central Station in 1894 are realistic—they are factually correct. **Fantastic elements** of a story are details that could not take place or exist in real life. Use these focus questions to guide you as you read.

1. Which details of setting in "The Third Level" seem real or possible?
2. Which events in the story could not really have happened?

Reading Strategy

Clarifying Word Meanings with Context Clues

In a story like "The Third Level" that has an unusual or unfamiliar setting, you will come across place names, slang, or other words that you do not recognize. Clarify word meanings by using **context clues**—the surrounding words, phrases, and sentences. Often, one of these clues will restate the word or give an example. The diagram on the right shows how to use restatement or examples to clarify word meaning. As you read, use a chart like this one to clarify the meanings of unfamiliar words.

Unfamiliar Word

You have to pay a *premium.*

⬇

Restatement or Example in Text

My $300 bought less than 200 in old-style bills.

⬇

Probable Meaning

The *premium* must be the additional charge for buying old-style money.

Vocabulary Development

psychiatrist (sī kī´ ə trist) *noun used as adj.* medical doctor specializing in illnesses of the mind (p. 64)

arched (ärcht) *adj.* curved (p. 65)

currency (kʉr´ ən sē) *n.* money (p. 67)

premium (prē´ mē əm) *n.* additional charge (p. 67)

▲ **Critical Viewing** List three specific details to prove this photograph was taken in modern New York City. **[Support]**

THE Third Level

Jack Finney

The presidents of the New York Central and the New York, New Haven and Hartford railroads will swear on a stack of time-tables that there are only two. But I say there are three, because I've *been* on the third level at Grand Central Station.[1] Yes, I've taken the obvious step: I talked to a <u>psychiatrist</u> friend of mine, among others. I told him about the third level at Grand Central Station, and he said it was a waking-dream wish fulfillment. He said I was unhappy. That made my wife kind of mad, but he explained that he meant the modern world is full of insecurity, fear, war, worry and all the rest of it, and that I just want to escape. Well, who doesn't? Everybody I know wants to escape, but they don't wander down into any third level at Grand Central Station.

psychiatrist (sī kī˘ ə trist)
noun used as adj. medical doctor specializing in illnesses of the mind

---

1. **Grand Central Station** large train station in New York City.

But that's the reason, he said, and my friends all agreed. Everything points to it, they claimed. My stamp collecting, for example; that's a "temporary refuge from reality." Well, maybe, but my grandfather didn't need any refuge from reality; things were pretty nice and peaceful in his day, from all I hear, and he started my collection. It's a nice collection, too, blocks of four of practically every U.S. issue, first-day covers, and so on. President Roosevelt collected stamps, too, you know.

Anyway, here's what happened at Grand Central. One night last summer I worked late at the office. I was in a hurry to get uptown to my apartment so I decided to take the subway from Grand Central because it's faster than the bus.

Now, I don't know why this should have happened to me. I'm just an ordinary guy named Charley, thirty-one years old, and I was wearing a tan gabardine[2] suit and a straw hat with a fancy band; I passed a dozen men who looked just like me. And I wasn't trying to escape from anything; I just wanted to get home to Louisa, my wife.

I turned into Grand Central from Vanderbilt Avenue, and went down the steps to the first level, where you take trains like the Twentieth Century. Then I walked down another flight to the second level, where the suburban trains leave from, ducked into an <u>arched</u> doorway heading for the subway—and got lost. That's easy to do. I've been in and out of Grand Central hundreds of times, but I'm always bumping into new doorways and stairs and corridors. Once I got into a tunnel about a mile long and came out in the lobby of the Roosevelt Hotel. Another time I came up in an office building on Forty-sixth Street, three blocks away.

Sometimes I think Grand Central is growing like a tree, pushing out new corridors and staircases like roots. There's probably a long tunnel that nobody knows about feeling its way under the city right now, on its way to Times Square, and maybe another to Central Park. And maybe—because for so many people through the years Grand Central *has* been an exit, a way of escape—maybe that's how the tunnel I got into . . . But I never told my psychiatrist friend about that idea.

The corridor I was in began angling left and slanting downward and I thought that was wrong, but I kept on walking. All I could hear was the empty sound of my own footsteps and I didn't pass a soul. Then I heard that sort of hollow roar ahead that means open space and people talking. The tunnel turned sharp left; I went down a short flight of stairs and came out on the third level at Grand Central Station. For just a moment I thought I was back on the second level, but I saw the room was smaller, there were fewer ticket windows and train gates, and the information booth in

Literary Analysis
Time in a Setting
What details of setting does this paragraph provide?

arched (ärcht) *adj.* curved

Reading Strategy
Clarifying Word Meanings How does the second sentence explain the meaning of *corridors*?

Reading Check

Why does Charley decide to take the subway home?

---

2. **gabardine** (gab´ ər dēn´) cloth of wool, cotton, rayon, or other material used for suits and dresses.

the center was wood and old-looking. And the man in the booth wore a green eyeshade and long black sleeve protectors. The lights were dim and sort of flickering. Then I saw why; they were open-flame gaslights.

There were brass spittoons[3] on the floor, and across the station a glint of light caught my eye; a man was pulling a gold watch from his vest pocket. He snapped open the cover, glanced at his watch, and frowned. He wore a derby hat,[4] a black four-button suit with tiny lapels, and he had a big, black, handle-bar mustache. Then I looked around and saw that everyone in the station was dressed like eighteen-ninety-something; I never saw so many beards, sideburns and fancy mustaches in my life. A woman walked in through the train gate; she wore a dress with leg-of-mutton sleeves[5] and skirts to the top of her high-buttoned shoes. Back of her, out on the tracks, I caught a glimpse of a locomotive, a very small Currier & Ives[6] locomotive with a funnel-shaped stack. And then I knew.

To make sure, I walked over to a newsboy and glanced at the stack of papers at his feet. It was the *World*; and the *World* hasn't been published for years. The lead story said something about President Cleveland. I've found that front page since, in the Public Library files, and it was printed June 11, 1894.

I turned toward the ticket windows knowing that here—on the third level at Grand Central— I could buy tickets that would take Louisa and me anywhere in the United States we wanted to go. In the year 1894. And I wanted two tickets to Galesburg, Illinois.

Have you ever been there? It's a wonderful town still, with big old frame houses, huge lawns and tremendous trees whose branches meet overhead and roof the streets. And in 1894, summer evenings

---

3. **spittoons** (spi tōōnz´) jarlike containers into which people spit. Spitting in public was a more accepted habit in the past.
4. **derby hat** stiff felt hat with a round crown and curved brim.
5. **leg-of-mutton sleeves** sleeves that puff out toward the shoulder and resemble a leg of mutton (lamb or sheep).
6. **Currier & Ives** nineteenth-century American printmakers who became famous for their pictures of trains, yachts, horses, and scenes of nature.

were twice as long, and people sat out on their lawns, the men smoking cigars and talking quietly, the women waving palm-leaf fans, with the fireflies all around, in a peaceful world. To be back there with the First World War still twenty years off, and World War II over forty years in the future . . . I wanted two tickets for that.

The clerk figured the fare—he glanced at my fancy hatband, but he figured the fare—and I had enough for two coach tickets, one way. But when I counted out the money and looked up, the clerk was staring at me. He nodded at the bills. "That ain't money, mister," he said, "and if you're trying to skin me you won't get very far," and he glanced at the cash drawer beside him. Of course the money in his drawer was old-style bills, half again as big as the money we use nowadays, and different-looking. I turned away and got out fast.There's nothing nice about jail, even in 1894.

And that was that. I left the same way I came, I suppose. Next day, during lunch hour, I drew three hundred dollars out of the bank, nearly all we had, and bought old-style <u>currency</u> (that *really* worried my psychiatrist friend). You can buy old money at almost any coin dealer's, but you have to pay a <u>premium</u>. My three hundred dollars bought less than two hundred in old-style bills, but I didn't care; eggs were thirteen cents a dozen in 1894.

But I've never again found the corridor that leads to the third level at Grand Central Station, although I've tried often enough.

Louisa was pretty worried when I told her all this, and didn't want me to look for the third level any more, and after a while I stopped; I went back to my stamps. But now we're *both* looking, every weekend, because now we have proof that the third level is still there. My friend Sam Weiner disappeared! Nobody knew where, but I sort of suspected because Sam's a city boy, and I used to tell him about Galesburg—I went to school there—and he always said he liked the sound of the place. And that's where he is all right. In 1894.

Because one night, fussing with my stamp collection, I found—well, do you know what a first-day cover is? When a new stamp is issued, stamp collectors buy some and use them to mail envelopes to themselves on the very first day of sale; and the postmark proves the date. The envelope is called a first-day cover. They're never opened; you just put blank paper in the envelope.

That night, among my oldest first-day covers, I found one that shouldn't have been there. But there it was. It was there because someone had mailed it to my grandfather at his home in Galesburg; that's what the address on the envelope said. And it had been there since July 18, 1894—the postmark showed that— yet I didn't remember it at all. The stamp was a six-cent, dull brown, with a picture of President Garfield. Naturally, when the envelope came to Granddad in the mail, it went right into his

Reading Strategy
Clarifying Word Meanings Using the clerk's reaction as a clue, what do you think was wrong with the narrator's "fancy hatband"?

currency (kŭr′ ən sē) *n.* money

premium (prē′ mē əm) *n.* additional charge

Reading Check
What did Charley confirm by looking at the date on the newspaper?

collection and stayed there—till I took it out and opened it.

The paper inside wasn't blank. It read:

> 941 Willard Street
> Galesburg, Illinois
> July 18, 1894

Charley:

I got to wishing that you were right. Then I got to believing you were right. And, Charley, it's true; I found the third level! I've been here two weeks, and right now, down the street at the Daly's, someone is playing a piano, and they're all out on the front porch singing, "Seeing Nellie home." And I'm invited over for lemonade. Come on back, Charley and Louisa. Keep looking till you find the third level! It's worth it, believe me!

The note was signed *Sam.*

At the stamp and coin store I go to, I found out that Sam bought eight hundred dollars' worth of old-style currency. That ought to set him up in a nice little hay, feed and grain business; he always said that's what he really wished he could do, and he certainly can't go back to his old business. Not in Galesburg, Illinois, in 1894. His old business? Why, Sam was my psychiatrist.

Review and Assess

Thinking About the Selection

1. **Respond:** As it is described, is Galesburg, Illinois, in 1894 a place you would like to go to? Explain.

2. **(a) Recall:** List three details about life in Galesburg.
   (b) Compare and Contrast: Contrast life in the present time of the story and life in Galesburg in 1894. **(c) Support:** What evidence suggests that Charley feels out of place in the present?
   (d) Infer: Why will he feel more at home in the past?

3. **(a) Recall:** Who started the stamp collection? **(b) Infer:** What does the stamp collection represent to the narrator? **(c) Connect:** In what two ways does the stamp collection provide a link to life in Galesburg?

4. **(a) Recall:** How did the narrator's psychiatrist react when the narrator told him about the third level? **(b) Analyze:** How does his psychiatrist's attitude toward the third level change during the story?

5. **(a) Speculate:** Do you think it is helpful or harmful for a person to wish for a different lifestyle from the one he or she is living? Explain.

Jack Finney

(1911–1995)

When you read the writings of Jack Finney, you begin to think he really did learn the secret of time travel. He seemed to map out an escape route from a harsh present to an appealing past. This fantastic idea is at the heart of many of his works, including "The Third Level" and the novel *Time and Again.*

Finney was born in Milwaukee, Wisconsin. After graduating from college, he went to New York City to seek his fortune. While working in advertising, Finney began a second career writing short stories and novels. His science-fiction novel *The Body Snatchers* brought him wider recognition and eventually inspired three film versions.

Review and Assess

Literary Analysis

Time in a Setting

1. Use a diagram like the one shown to compare and contrast the **settings** of Grand Central Station in 1894 and the present.

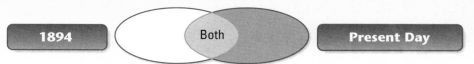

1894   Both   Present Day

2. What details let Charley know that the third level is in the past?
3. What does Sam's letter say that suggests life in Galesburg in 1894 is better than life in modern-day New York City?

Connecting Literary Elements

Decide whether each **story element** in the chart is **realistic** or **fantastic** and then record at least three more story elements.

Story Element	Realistic or Fantastic?
I turned into Grand Central from Vanderbilt Avenue	
Charley, it's true; I found the third level!	

4. Are more elements in the chart realistic or fantastic?
5. What is the most important fantastic element in the chart?
6. Why would a writer create a realistically detailed setting in which to set unrealistic events?

Reading Strategy

Clarifying Word Meanings with Context Clues

Use **context** to define the italicized words. Identify the **clues** you used, and explain your answer.

7. "... where you take trains like the *Twentieth Century*."
8. "The clerk figured the *fare* ... and I had enough for two coach tickets, one way. But when I counted out the money. ..."
9. Find three more difficult or unfamiliar words found in "The Third Level." Identify and explain the context clues that help you discover the meaning.

Extend Understanding

10. **Evaluate:** Some people believe that life in previous times was better than life now. Explain why you agree or disagree.

Quick Review

Setting is the time and place of a story's action. To review setting, see page 63.

Realistic elements of a story are details that seem as though they could take place or exist in real life. **Fantastic elements** are details that could not take place or exist in real life. To review these elements, see page 63.

The **context** of a word is the words, phrases, and sentences that surround the word. To review context clues, see page 63.

 Take It to the Net
www.phschool.com
Take the interactive self-test online to check your understanding of the selection.

Integrate Language Skills

Vocabulary Development Lesson

Word Analysis: Greek Suffix -ist

The Greek suffix *-ist* means "someone who is skilled in or practices." *Psychiatry* deals with illnesses of the mind, so a *psychiatrist* is skilled in curing these illnesses. Write a definition explaining what each of the following people practices.

1. artist
2. chemist
3. novelist
4. violinist
5. florist
6. pianist

Spelling Strategy

Adding the suffix *-ist* to a base word sometimes involves changing the spelling of the base word. Follow these rules when adding *-ist*:

- If the word ends in a silent *e* preceded by a consonant, drop the *e*:
  manicure + *-ist* = manicurist
- If the word ends in *y*, drop the *y* when the *y* sounds like a long *e*:
  psychiatry + *-ist* = psychiatrist

On your paper, add *-ist* to the following words.

1. botany   2. hairstyle   3. zoology   4. type

Fluency: Sentence Completions

On your paper, complete each sentence with one of the following words. To help you, review the words and their meanings on page 63.

psychiatrist	arched
currency	premium

1. Due to its size and curved shape, the ____?____ window lets in more light than the small, narrow window does.
2. When you visit another country, you have to exchange American dollars for foreign ____?____.
3. A ____?____ may help those experiencing extreme sadness or anger.
4. Tickets for the hottest concert of the year were available only at a ____?____ so fewer people bought the tickets than were expected.

Grammar Lesson

Concrete and Abstract Nouns

Concrete nouns refer to physical things that can be seen, heard, tasted, smelled, or touched. **Abstract nouns** refer to ideas, qualities, or feelings that cannot be experienced through the five senses. Look at these nouns from the story:

Concrete: apartment, president, ticket
Abstract: insecurity, fear, worry

An *apartment* can be touched or seen. *Insecurity* can only be described or experienced.

▶ *For more practice, see page R28, Exercise A.*
Practice Identify each of the following as either a concrete or an abstract noun.

1. wish
2. corridor
3. idea
4. mustache
5. envelope

Writing Application Write four sentences about "The Third Level." Include at least one concrete noun in two sentences and at least one abstract noun in the other two.

W͟G Prentice Hall Writing and Grammar Connection: Chapter 14, Section 1

Writing Lesson

Description of a Place

Jack Finney uses vivid descriptive language to re-create the atmosphere, or mood, of a time long gone. Write a description of a place you could use to create an atmosphere for a modern story.

Prewriting If possible, visit the place you have chosen, and take notes on its physical details. Jot down specific words, such as *bustling, tense,* or *dim,* to describe the atmosphere.

Drafting Begin with a vivid detail. Then, build a complete picture of the scene by using words and phrases, such as *above, behind,* and *in front of,* that tell where things are located in space.

Model: Spatial Details

The librarian smiled as she unlocked the *central* doors of the public library on Saturday at 10:00. For a few minutes, she stood *in front of the doors* to take in the stillness. Then she opened a door to let tired-looking mothers come *into the main reading area* with children eager for the story hour.

> Spatial details, such as *central, in front of the doors,* and *into the main reading area,* help bring the library to life.

Revising Reread your draft and replace vague words like *very, really,* or *a lot* with a precise word or phrase. For example, instead of saying "It was a very large building," you could say, "It was a twenty-five story building."

 Prentice Hall Writing and Grammar Connection: Chapter 6, Section 3

Extension Activities

Listening and Speaking When moviemakers, advertisers, and journalists want to create a strong impression, they usually focus on only the positive or negative aspects of their subject. Prepare a chart that shows the positive and negative images of the past as they are used in electronic media, such as movies, advertisements, and television shows. Your chart should include

- the desired effect of each form of media.
- the reality that is not shown.

Use the chart in an **oral presentation** to your class.

Research and Technology Using the Internet or reference books, research train travel in the late 1800s. Using pictures and brief descriptions, prepare a **poster** that compares train travel in the past to air travel today.

Writing Write a letter from Charley asking Sam about Galesburg and the third level. Then, write Sam's response, with details about the 1890s.

 Take It to the Net   www.phschool.com

Go online for an additional research activity using the Internet.

Prepare to Read

A Day's Wait

 Take It to the Net

Visit www.phschool.com
for interactive activities
and instruction related to
"A Day's Wait," including
• background
• graphic organizers
• literary elements
• reading strategies

Preview

Connecting to the Literature

Lying in bed when you are sick can be the worst kind of waiting. In addition to feeling ill and being bored, you also have time to worry. In "A Day's Wait," a young boy experiences this worst kind of waiting.

Background

In "A Day's Wait," by Ernest Hemingway, a doctor measures a boy's temperature in degrees Fahrenheit (°F). On this scale, used in the United States, water freezes at 32°F and boils at 212°F. However, people in many other countries measure temperature in degrees Celsius—a scale at which water freezes at 0°C and boils at 100°C. A confusion about these scales sets off part of the trouble in this story.

Literary Analysis

Internal Conflict

Most fictional stories center on a **conflict**—a struggle between opposing forces. **Internal conflict** takes place within a single character. An inner struggle to overcome fear, control anger, or make a choice produces tension within the character. In this story, the boy struggles between a desire to be brave and the fear and worry he has about his illness.

> "I don't worry," he said, "but I can't keep from thinking."
> "Don't think," I said. "Just take it easy."
> "I'm taking it easy," he said and looked straight ahead. He was evidently holding tight on to himself about something.

As you read "A Day's Wait," look for other signs that the boy is experiencing the tension of an internal conflict.

Connecting Literary Elements

The conflict in a story increases the story's tension until it reaches a **climax,** or turning point. Imagine that two people are pulling on a rubber band. The band stretches tighter until someone lets go or the rubber band snaps. The tension is relieved at that "turning point." At the climax of a story, the outcome of the conflict becomes clear. Identify the conflict and the climax of the story by focusing on these questions.

1. What creates the tension within the boy?
2. At what point is that tension relieved?

Reading Strategy

Identifying Word Roots

Add whole groups of words to your vocabulary by learning **word roots**—the basic forms of words after all the affixes (added parts) have been removed. A word root may come at the beginning, middle, or end of the whole word. Although all roots have a meaning, not all roots are words. Some roots are "bound" or tied to other word parts to make sense. Other word roots are "independent" or free and can stand alone.

Identify and learn about word roots you find in the story by completing a chart like the one shown here.

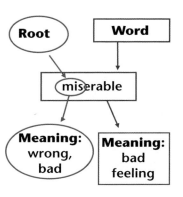

Vocabulary Development

epidemic (ep′ ə dem′ ik) *n.* outbreak of a contagious disease (p. 74)

flushed (flusht) *v.* drove from hiding (p. 75)

covey (kuv′ ē) *n.* small flock of birds (p. 75)

evidently (ev′ ə dent′ lē) *adv.* clearly; obviously (p. 76)

A Day's Wait

ERNEST HEMINGWAY

He came into the room to shut the windows while we were still in bed and I saw he looked ill. He was shivering, his face was white, and he walked slowly as though it ached to move.

"What's the matter, Schatz?"[1]

"I've got a headache."

"You better go back to bed."

"No. I'm all right."

"You go to bed. I'll see you when I'm dressed."

But when I came downstairs he was dressed, sitting by the fire, looking a very sick and miserable boy of nine years. When I put my hand on his forehead I knew he had a fever.

"You go up to bed," I said, "you're sick."

"I'm all right," he said.

When the doctor came he took the boy's temperature.

"What is it?" I asked him.

"One hundred and two."

Downstairs, the doctor left three different medicines in different colored capsules with instructions for giving them. One was to bring down the fever, another a purgative, the third to overcome an acid condition. The germs of influenza can only exist in an acid condition, he explained. He seemed to know all about influenza and said there was nothing to worry about if the fever did not go above one hundred and four degrees. This was a light epidemic of flu and there was no danger if you avoided pneumonia.

Back in the room I wrote the boy's temperature down and made a note of the time to give the various capsules.

"Do you want me to read to you?"

"All right. If you want to," said the boy. His face was very white and there were dark areas under his eyes. He lay still in the bed and seemed very detached from what was going on.

I read aloud from Howard Pyle's *Book of Pirates*; but I could see he was not following what I was reading.

"How do you feel, Schatz?" I asked him.

"Just the same, so far," he said.

▲ Critical Viewing
In this story, a father worries about his son. How might time in a natural setting like this one help the father to stay calm? **[Speculate]**

epidemic (ep´ ə dem´ ik) *n.* outbreak of a contagious disease

---

1. Schatz (shäts) German term of affection, used here as a loving nickname.

I sat at the foot of the bed and read to myself while I waited for it to be time to give another capsule. It would have been natural for him to go to sleep, but when I looked up he was looking at the foot of the bed, looking very strangely.

"Why don't you try to go to sleep? I'll wake you up for the medicine."

"I'd rather stay awake."

After a while he said to me, "You don't have to stay in here with me, Papa, if it bothers you."

"It doesn't bother me."

"No. I mean you don't have to stay if it's going to bother you."

I thought perhaps he was a little lightheaded and after giving him the prescribed capsules at eleven o'clock I went out for a while. It was a bright, cold day, the ground covered with a sleet that had frozen so that it seemed as if all the bare trees, the bushes, the cut brush and all the grass and the bare ground had been varnished with ice. I took the young Irish setter for a little walk up the road and along a frozen creek, but it was difficult to stand or walk on the glassy surface and the red dog slipped and slithered and I fell twice, hard, once dropping my gun and having it slide away over the ice.

We flushed a covey of quail under a high clay bank with overhanging brush and I killed two as they went out of sight over the top of the bank. Some of the covey lit in trees but most of them scattered into brush piles and it was necessary to jump on the ice-coated mounds of brush several times before they would flush. Coming out while you were poised unsteadily on the icy, springy brush they made difficult shooting, and I killed two, missed five, and started back pleased to have found a covey close to the house and happy there were so many left to find on another day.

At the house they said the boy had refused to let anyone come into the room.

"You can't come in," he said. "You mustn't get what I have."

I went up to him and found him in exactly the position I had left him, white-faced, but with the tops of his cheeks flushed by the fever, staring still, as he had stared at the foot of the bed.

I took his temperature.

"What is it?"

"Something like a hundred," I said. It was one hundred and two and four tenths.

"It was a hundred and two," he said.

"Who said so?"

"The doctor."

"Your temperature is all right," I said. "It's nothing to worry about."

"I don't worry," he said, "but I can't keep from thinking."

"Don't think," I said. "Just take it easy."

Literary Analysis
Internal Conflict What details in this dialogue show that the boy is experiencing an intense internal conflict?

Reading Strategy
Identifying Word Roots The root of *prescribed* is *scrib*, meaning "write." What is written when a doctor prescribes capsules?

flushed (flusht) *v.* drove from hiding.
covey (kuv´ē) *n.* small flock of birds

✔**Reading Check**
Why is the boy in bed?

"I'm taking it easy," he said and looked straight ahead. He was evidently holding tight on to himself about something.

"Take this with water."

"Do you think it will do any good?"

"Of course it will."

I sat down and opened the *Pirate* book and commenced to read, but I could see he was not following, so I stopped.

"About what time do you think I'm going to die?" he asked.

"What?"

"About how long will it be before I die?"

"You aren't going to die. What's the matter with you?"

"Oh, yes, I am. I heard him say a hundred and two."

"People don't die with a fever of one hundred and two. That's a silly way to talk."

"I know they do. At school in France the boys told me you can't live with forty-four degrees. I've got a hundred and two."

He had been waiting to die all day, ever since nine o'clock in the morning.

"You poor Schatz," I said. "Poor old Schatz. It's like miles and kilometers. You aren't going to die. That's a different thermometer. On that thermometer thirty-seven is normal. On this kind it's ninety-eight."

"Are you sure?"

"Absolutely," I said. "It's like miles and kilometers. You know, like how many kilometers we make when we do seventy miles in the car?"

"Oh," he said.

But his gaze at the foot of the bed relaxed slowly. The hold over himself relaxed too, finally, and the next day it was very slack and he cried very easily at little things that were of no importance.

evidently (ev′ ə dent′ lē)
adv. clearly; obviously

Literary Analysis
Internal Conflict and Climax Why does the boy's question increase the tension of his conflict?

Ernest Hemingway

(1899–1961)
A true adventurer, Ernest Hemingway based much of his writing on his own experience. He served as an ambulance driver in World War I, worked as a journalist, traveled the world, and enjoyed outdoor sport. His fiction celebrates that spirit of adventure, as well as courage and fortitude. The story "A Day's Wait" captures the quiet bravery of many of Hemingway's characters. His novels include *For Whom the Bell Tolls*, which draws on his war experiences, and *The Sun Also Rises*, which includes his observations of bullfighting in Spain. Hemingway's work is internationally admired, and he won both a Pulitzer Prize and a Nobel Prize for Literature.

Review and Assess

Thinking About the Selection

1. **Respond:** Do you find the boy's actions courageous, touching, or silly? Explain your answer.

2. **(a) Recall:** Why does the boy tell his father to leave the sickroom? **(b) Infer:** What does this reveal about the boy?

3. **(a) Recall:** Why does the boy think he will die? **(b) Interpret:** What is the meaning of the story's title?

4. **(a) Analyze:** Which of the boy's words and actions gave clues that he believed something terrible was wrong? **(b) Evaluate:** Do you think the story is about the boy's bravery or about the boy's fear? **(c) Apply:** In what way did the boy's bravery and/or fear contribute to the problem in the story?

Review and Assess

Literary Analysis

Internal Conflict

1. In your own words, describe the boy's **internal conflict**.
2. Identify two actions and two spoken sentences that show the boy's internal conflict. Explain how the words or actions indicate his inner struggle. Record your answers on a chart like this.

Action	Speech	Explanation

3. How might the story have been different if, right after the doctor's visit, the boy had asked when he would die?

Connecting Literary Elements

4. At what point in the story is the tension of the boy's internal conflict most intense?
5. Use a diagram like the one shown to record three events or conversations that increase the tension and the turning point, or **climax,** of the story.

6. How does the boy's reaction on the following day indicate a release of his tension?

Reading Strategy

Identifying Word Roots

7. The word *position* contains the root *posit*, meaning "place." Identify two other words containing *posit*, and explain what they mean.
8. **(a)** Which **word root** is shared by *kilometer* and *thermometer*?
   (b) What do the whole words have in common?

Extend Understanding

9. **Career Connection:** What are some qualities you think a pediatrician, or young people's doctor, should have? Use examples of the boy's experiences and needs to support your choices.
10. **Take a Position:** Do you think the United States should convert to using the metric system of measurement? Why or why not?

Quick Review

Internal conflict is a struggle within a character between feelings or choices. To review internal conflict, see page 73.

The **climax** is the high point of action in a story, when the tension of the conflict is released and it becomes clear how the situation will turn out. To review climax, see page 73.

A **word root** is a base form of a word after all the affixes, or extra parts, have been removed. To review word root, see page 73.

 Take It to the Net
www.phschool.com
Take the interactive self-test online to check your understanding of the selection.

Integrate Language Skills

Vocabulary Development Lesson

Word Analysis: Latin Root -vid-

The Latin root -vid- means "to see." Complete each sentence below, using one of these words.

video   evident
evidence   evidently

1. Sports analysts review the ___?___ to get a better look at close plays.
2. His white face and tense expression made the boy's fear ___?___.
3. He thought his temperature was ___?___ that he was very sick.
4. ___?___, he misunderstood what the doctor said.

Fluency: Sentence Completion

On your paper, complete these sentences with vocabulary words from the list on page 73.

People in the tiny village were frightened. A terrible ___?___ had caused dozens of people to fall ill. ___?___, a germ had made its way into the water supply. Even a ___?___ of birds, ___?___ from the bushes, appeared to be affected.

Spelling Strategy

The -ent in evident makes the word an adjective—a word used to describe a noun. Many adjectives that end in -ent have a related noun form that ends in -ence, such as evidence. Write the related noun form of each of these words.

1. confident   2. obedient   3. insistent

Grammar Lesson

Pronouns

A **pronoun** is a word that takes the place of a noun or a group of words acting as a noun. Pronouns offer writers another way to identify people, places, and things. For instance, Hemingway uses the nouns "boy" and "Schatz" to refer to his main character, and he uses the pronouns "he" and "him" in place of these nouns.

Here are examples of common pronouns.

Common Pronouns				
I	me	my	hers	herself
she	us	mine	its	themselves
he	you	our	who	whose
it	them	ours	their	myself
we	him	your	which	ourselves
his	they	her	himself	

▶ *For more practice, see page R28, Exercise B.*
Practice On your paper, write the following sentences. Circle the pronouns.

1. As readers, we understand the father's actions.
2. How would you explain it to the boy?
3. The boy finally tells himself that he will survive.
4. It makes him feel much better to know that he will survive.
5. Who will research Hemingway's life?

Writing Application Write four sentences telling the story of "A Day's Wait." Include at least one pronoun in each sentence.

WG Prentice Hall Writing and Grammar Connection: Chapter 14, Section 2

Writing Lesson

Autobiographical Event

"A Day's Wait" tells a story of an experience that at first seems ordinary. Learning what the boy thinks about the event before the happy ending, however, reveals how suspenseful, or tense, the experience was for him. Write an **autobiographical account**— a true story from your own life—about a suspenseful wait that led to a happy ending.

Prewriting   Make a list of successes you have achieved or experiences that have turned out well in the end. Choose one about which you were unsure of the outcome. Use a diagram like the one shown to organize the events to build tension leading up to the high point of your account.

Model: Organize Events Leading Up to the High Point · · ▶ **Turning Point** Rising Action

Drafting   Begin by identifying the situation. Unfold the actions and events during which you felt unsure of the outcome. Include details of your thoughts and reactions. Using your diagram as a guide, lead up to the high point at which you learned how the experience would turn out.

Revising   Review your story to identify places in which you can elaborate by adding details about your thoughts.

W͜G Prentice Hall Writing and Grammar Connection: Chapter 4, Section 2

Extension Activities

Listening and Speaking In a group of four, take turns giving a brief **explanation** to clear up the boy's confusion about his temperature.

As a listener, give constructive feedback to the other speakers. Comment on these things:

- **Content:** Did it make sense? Did the speaker stick to the viewpoint of the boy?
- **Delivery:** Was the speaking clear, well paced, and easy to understand?
- **Overall effect:** What were the strongest points? What could be improved?

Research and Technology Use a computer to make a **chart** showing how Celsius temperatures relate to Fahrenheit temperatures. (If you do not have a computer, develop a chart using poster-board and markers.)

Writing Write two imaginary **journal entries** about the events of the day in "A Day's Wait." Write the first entry as the father and the second as the son.

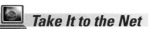 **Take It to the Net**   www.phschool.com

Go online for an additional research activity using the Internet.

Prepare to Read

Was Tarzan a Three-Bandage Man? ◆ Oranges

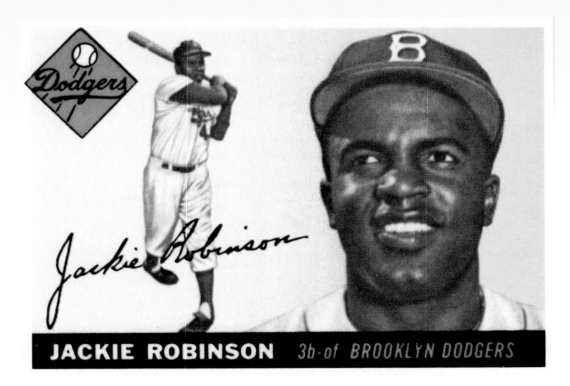

JACKIE ROBINSON 3b·of BROOKLYN DODGERS

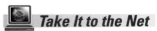
Take It to the Net

Visit www.phschool.com
for interactive activities
and instruction related to
these selections, including
- background
- graphic organizers
- literary elements
- reading strategies

Preview

Connecting to the Literature

Many works of literature tell about the dreams, hopes, and fears of
young people. Connect to the young people in "Was Tarzan a Three-
Bandage Man?" and "Oranges" by identifying feelings you have shared
or similar experiences you have had.

Background

In "Was Tarzan a Three-Bandage Man?" Bill Cosby expresses admiration for two famous African American sports figures—baseball star Jackie
Robinson and boxer Sugar Ray Robinson. In 1947, Jackie Robinson broke
baseball's color barrier. Until then, the major leagues were closed to non-
white players. Sugar Ray Robinson's powerful combination punches won
him six world championships between 1946 and 1958.

Literary Analysis

Anecdote

An **anecdote** is a short, usually personal or autobiographical account. An anecdote can entertain, teach a lesson, or introduce an important person in the writer's life. Although most anecdotes are written in prose, some poems, like Gary Soto's "Oranges," are like anecdotes in poetry.

To appreciate these experiences, focus on the following questions.

1. Why can people relate to the experience?
2. Why does the author share this experience?

Comparing Literary Works

Each of these works shares a memory from the writer's youth. However, one work is written in verse and one work is written in prose (not verse). In addition, the author's purposes, or reasons for writing, are different. Compare and contrast the works in the following areas.

- Form (poetry or prose)   • Author's purpose   • Author's attitude

As you read, notice what is revealed about characters and events through the dialogue.

Reading Strategy

Using Context Clues

Context, the words and phrases surrounding a word, can help you understand a word you might not know. When looking for context clues to help you understand an unfamiliar word, look for a word or words that might mean the same thing or have the opposite meaning of the unfamiliar word. Look at the following example from "Oranges." (The context makes it clear that *released* is the opposite of *took*.)

> I *took* my girl's hand /In mine for two blocks, /Then *released* it . . .
> I turned to the candies /*Tiered* like *bleachers* . . . (the image of
> bleachers at a stadium suggests that *tiered* means "stacked in rows")

Unfamiliar Word	
Context Clues	
Possible Meaning	
Dictionary Meaning	

As you read, list unfamiliar words in a chart like this one. Fill in context clues and a possible meaning. Check the words in a dictionary after reading.

Vocabulary Development

incorporate (in kôr´ pôr āt) *v.* form into a legal business (p. 83)

dejectedly (dē jek´ tid lē) *adv.* sadly; showing discouragement (p. 84)

tourniquets (tʉr´ ni kits) *n.* devices used to stop bleeding in an emergency, as a bandage tightly twisted to stop the flow of blood (p. 84)

rouge (rōōzh) *n.* reddish cosmetic used to color cheeks (p. 85)

tiered (tērd) *adj.* stacked in rows (p. 85)

hissing (his´iŋ) *adj.* making a sound like a prolonged *s* (p. 86)

Was Tarzan a Three-Bandage Man?

Bill Cosby

In the days before athletes had learned how to <u>incorporate</u> themselves, they were shining heroes to American kids. In fact, they were such heroes to me and my friends that we even imitated their walks. When Jackie Robinson, a pigeon-toed[1] walker, became famous, we walked pigeon-toed, a painful form of locomotion unless you were Robinson or a pigeon.

"Why you walkin' like that?" said my mother one day.

"This is Jackie *Robinson's* walk," I proudly replied.

"There's somethin' wrong with his shoes?"

"He's the fastest man in baseball."

"He'd be faster if he didn't walk like that. His mother should make him walk right."

A few months later, when football season began, I stopped imitating Robinson and began to walk bowlegged[2] like a player named Buddy Helm.

"Why you always tryin' to change the shape of your legs?" said my mother. "You keep doin' that an' they'll fall off—an' I'm not gettin' you new ones."

Although baseball and football stars inspired us, our real heroes were the famous prize fighters, and the way to emulate a fighter was to walk around with a Band-Aid over one eye. People with acne walked around that way too, but we hoped it was clear that we were worshipping good fists and not bad skin.

The first time my mother saw me being Sugar Ray, not Jackie Robinson, she said, "What's that bandage for?"

"Oh, nuthin'," I replied.

"Now that's a new kinda stupid answer. That bandage gotta be coverin' somethin'—besides your entire brain."

"Well, it's just for show. I wanna look like Sugar Ray Robinson."

"The fastest man in baseball."

"No, that's a different one."

"You doin' Swiss Family Robinson[3] next?"

"Swiss Family Robinson? They live in the projects?"

"You'd know who they are if you read more books instead of makin' yourself look like an accident. Why can't you try to imitate someone like Booker T. Washington?"[4]

"Who does he play for?"

---

1. **pigeon-toed** (pij´ ən tōd) *adj.* having the feet turned in toward each other.
2. **bowlegged** (bō´ leg ed) *adj.* having legs that are curved outward.
3. **Swiss Family Robinson** fictional family stranded on a desert island.
4. **Booker T. Washington** (1856–1915) African American educator and author.

◄ **Critical Viewing** Why might young boys like Cosby and his friends idolize a man like Sugar Ray Robinson, pictured here? **[Infer]**

incorporate (in kôr´ pôr āt) *v.* form into a legal business

Reading Strategy
Using Context Clues
What clues point to the meaning of the word *emulate*?

Reading Check

Who were the boys' biggest heroes?

"Bill, let's put it this way: you take off that bandage right now or I'll have your father move you up to stitches."

The following morning on the street, I dejectedly told the boys, "My mother says I gotta stop wearin' a bandage. She wants my whole head to show."

"What's wrong with that woman?" said Fat Albert. "She won't let you do *nuthin'*."

"It's okay, Cos," said Junior, "'cause one bandage ain't enough anyway. My brother says the really tough guys wear two."

"One over each eye?" I asked him.

"Or one eye and one nose," he said.

"Man, I wouldn't want to mess with no two-bandage man," said Eddie.

And perhaps the toughest guys of all wore tourniquets around their necks. We were capable of such attire, for we were never more ridiculous than when we were trying to be tough and cool. Most ridiculous, of course, was that our hero worshipping was backwards: we should have been emulating the men who had *caused* the need for bandages.

dejectedly (dē jek´ tid lē) *adv.* sadly; showing discouragement

tourniquets (tur´ ni kits) *n.* devices used to stop bleeding in an emergency, as a bandage tightly twisted to stop the flow of blood

Review and Assess

Thinking About the Literature

1. **Respond:** Would you enjoy having young Cosby as a friend? Why or why not?

2. **(a) Recall:** Who are Cosby's heroes? **(b) Recall:** What does he do to imitate his heroes? **(c) Infer:** Why does the young Cosby admire them?

3. **(a) Recall:** Who does Cosby's mother want Cosby to imitate? **(b) Compare and Contrast:** Compare and contrast the qualities Cosby and his mother admire in a person. **(c) Apply:** Who in today's world would young Cosby and his mother choose as heroes?

4. **(a) Infer:** How does Cosby believe people will view him if he acts like his heroes? **(b) Assess** Does his plan work?

5. **(a) Interpret:** How does Cosby's attitude about "three-bandage men" change in the end? **(b) Infer:** What has Cosby realized? **(c) Interpret:** What does this story suggest about the way famous people influence others?

6. **Speculate:** Do you think it is ever a good idea to try to model someone else's behavior?

Bill Cosby

(b. 1937)
Even as a boy, comedian Bill Cosby showed a talent for comedy. Once described as a student who would rather "clown than study," Cosby later earned a track-and-field college scholarship. Today, his live performances, recordings, and TV shows, such as *Cosby* and *Kids Say the Funniest Things*, have made him an easily recognized, much-loved actor and comic.

Though Cosby idolized boxers in his youth, as shown in this selection, today he promotes achievement in education rather than the boxing ring. He once said, "I think there's a lot to be said for fighting at the blackboard, with a piece of chalk as a weapon."

Three Fruit, Ashton Hinrichs

◀ **Critical Viewing**
This painting of oranges
seems to suit Gary Soto's
poem. What other image
might you suggest?
Defend your choice.
[Extend]

Oranges

GARY SOTO

The first time I walked
With a girl, I was twelve,
Cold, and weighted down
With two oranges in my jacket.
5   December. Frost cracking
Beneath my steps, my breath
Before me, then gone,
As I walked toward
Her house, the one whose
10 Porchlight burned yellow
Night and day, in any weather.
A dog barked at me, until
She came out pulling
At her gloves, face bright
15 With rouge. I smiled,
Touched her shoulder, and led
Her down the street, across
A used car lot and a line
Of newly planted trees,
20 Until we were breathing
Before a drug store. We
Entered, the tiny bell
Bringing a saleslady
Down a narrow aisle of goods.
25 I turned to the candies
Tiered like bleachers,

Literary Analysis
Anecdote In what ways
are these opening lines
similar to the beginning
of a prose (ordinary
language) anecdote?

rouge (rōōzh) *n.* reddish
cosmetic used to color
cheeks

tiered (tērd) *adj.* stacked
in rows

✔**Reading Check**

Where are the speaker
and the girl?

And asked what she wanted—
Light in her eyes, a smile
Starting at the corners
30 Of her mouth. I fingered
A nickel in my pocket,
And when she lifted a chocolate
That cost a dime,
I didn't say anything.
35 I took the nickel from
My pocket, then an orange,
And set them quietly on
The counter. When I looked up,
The lady's eyes met mine,
40 And held them, knowing
Very well what it was all
About.
   Outside,
A few cars <u>hissing</u> past,
45 Fog hanging like old
Coats between the trees.
I took my girl's hand
In mine for two blocks,
Then released it to let
50 Her unwrap the chocolate.
I peeled my orange
That was so bright against
The gray of December
That, from some distance,
55 Someone might have thought
I was making a fire in my hands.

hissing (his´ iŋ) *adj.*
making a sound like
a prolonged *s*

Review and Assess

Thinking About the Selection

1. **Respond:** Which qualities of this poem make it more
or less entertaining than a prose narrative?

2. **(a) Recall:** Where does the speaker take the girl?
(b) Draw Conclusions: Do you think he planned to end up
there? Why or why not?

3. **(a) Recall:** Why is the girl's candy choice a problem for the
speaker? **(b) Interpret:** Soto says the saleslady meets his eyes,
"knowing very well what it was all about." What does the
saleslady know? **(c) Apply:** What does the poem indicate
about relationships between friends and between strangers?

Gary Soto

(b. 1952)
  Gary Soto
grew up in a
working-class
neighborhood
in Fresno,
California.
He began
writing while
in college and uses his
boyhood experiences as
the source of inspiration
for many of his works.
Soto writes short stories,
novels, and poetry—often
for young adults because of
the connection he feels to
his own past.

Review and Assess

Literary Analysis

Anecdotes

1. What detail in the first paragraph of the **anecdote** "Was Tarzan a Three-Bandage Man?" shows that Cosby is sharing a childhood story?

2. Supply at least one detail from "Was Tarzan a Three-Bandage Man?" for each purpose on the chart.

Purpose	Detail
Makes readers laugh.	
Shows that Cosby has changed his attitude toward wearing bandages.	

3. Why can many people relate to Cosby's experiences?

Comparing Literary Works

4. Which form (poetry or prose) allows the writer to include more background information and explanations?

5. How are the authors' purposes similar and different? Explain.

6. How are the authors' attitudes similar and different? Explain.

Reading Strategy

Using Context Clues

Use context clues to clarify the meaning of each italicized word. Then, choose the definition that matches how the italicized word is used in the selection. Explain why the other meaning is not appropriate in this context.

7. "Although baseball and football stars *inspired* us, our real heroes were the famous prize fighters." **(a)** gave us creative ideas **(b)** made us want to be like them

8. "Swiss Family Robinson? They live in the *projects*?" **(a)** activity **(b)** inexpensive housing

9. Find two more difficult or unfamiliar words in the selections and explain how context provides the meaning for each.

Extend Understanding

10. **Apply:** Identify two famous people—in sports or another field—who are good role models. Explain your choices.

Quick Review

An **anecdote** is a short, usually personal or autobiographical account. To review anecdote, see page 81.

To review **form** and **purpose,** see page 81.

Context refers to the words, phrases, and sentences around a word. To review context clues, see page 81.

 Take It to the Net

www.phschool.com

Take the interactive self-test online to check your understanding of these selections.

Integrate Language Skills

Vocabulary Development Lesson

Word Analysis: Anglo-Saxon Suffix -ly

Cosby uses the adverb *dejectedly* to describe how he spoke. The Anglo-Saxon suffix *-ly*, meaning "in this way," usually indicates that a word is an adverb.

Add *-ly* to each word listed here to create an adverb. Then, write a sentence using the new word.

   1. ridiculous   **2.** brave   **3.** complete

Spelling Strategy

In some words that come from French, the *k* sound is spelled *qu*, as in *tourniquet*. On your paper, complete the following words.

   1. Sports equipment used to hit a tennis ball:
       r _ c _ _ _ t

   2. A very old and valuable piece of furniture:
       a _ _ _ _ _ e

Fluency: Word Choice

On your paper, answer these questions and explain each answer.

   1. Which would be a more effective *tourniquet* for a deep cut on the leg—a chair or a belt?

   2. Would you describe someone leaving a funeral as "walking *dejectedly* to the car"?

   3. If you wanted to expand your car-washing business, might you *incorporate* it?

   4. Would you put *rouge* on a cupcake?

   5. Would a five-*tiered* cake be mostly tall or mostly wide?

   6. Identify three things you would describe as *hissing*.

Grammar Lesson

Personal Pronouns

A **personal pronoun** refers to one of three people: the person speaking (first person); the person spoken to (second person); or the person, place, or thing spoken about (third person). This chart shows the most common personal pronouns.

	Singular	Plural
First person	I, me, mine	we, us, our, ours
Second person	you, your, yours	you, your, yours
Third person	he, she, him, her, his, hers, it, its	they, them, their, theirs

Cosby uses a first-person pronoun to identify himself and his friends.

our real heroes were . . . prize fighters.

▶ *For more practice, see page R28, Exercise B.*
Practice Write the personal pronouns in each sentence on your paper. Then, identify each as first, second, or third person.

   1. Cosby and his friends try to act like their heroes.

   2. A boxer is popular with them for a while.

   3. They switch favorites every week.

   4. We also admire actors and celebrities.

   5. The boy was grateful to the saleswoman for her kindness.

Writing Application Write three sentences about Bill and his friends, using one personal pronoun in each sentence. Tell the type of pronoun each is.

 Prentice Hall Writing and Grammar Connection: Chapter 14, Section 2

Writing Lesson

Opinion Essay

Bill Cosby's anecdote raises an important question: Are sports stars good role models? Write an **opinion essay** in which you explain and support your opinion.

Prewriting   Make a chart of the pros and cons of holding athletes up as role models. Jot down the names of athletes whose behavior supports each side. Then, study your list to decide where you stand.

Drafting   Begin your essay by stating your opinion. Support your opinion with reasons. To give depth to your support, use the SEE method. (SEE stands for *Statement, Extension,* and *Elaboration*).

Model: Supporting With SEE

S   Athletes are good role models because they stay fit. Most

E   athletes stay in shape even in the off season. They work out,
and they eat healthy foods so they will be ready when the

E   season comes around again.

The reason is **stated** in the first sentence. The second sentence **extends** by explaining what the writer means in the first sentence. The third sentence **elaborates** on the first two with details of how athletes stay fit.

Revising   Make sure you have supported each reason well, adding examples or explanations. Add an interesting introduction and conclusion.

*W*_{*G*} *Prentice Hall Writing and Grammar Connection: Chapter 7, Section 3*

Extension Activities

Research and Technology   Write a brief **report** about sports images in today's media.

- Jot down descriptions of advertisements that use athletes.

- Decide which of your examples show athletes in a positive way and which show them in a negative way.

- Make a valid generalization—a broad statement that is usually true—about athletes in the media.

Share your statement with a group, and explain how you arrived at this generalization.

Listening and Speaking   With a partner, discuss what makes the mother-son scenes in "Was Tarzan a Three-Bandage Man?" authentic and funny. Then, plan a **role play** of the scenes. Discuss where you should raise your voice, how quickly or slowly you should speak, and what gestures or facial expressions you should use. Role-play the scene for a group of classmates.

 **Take It to the Net**   www.phschool.com

Go online for an additional research activity using the Internet.

Magazine Articles

About Magazine Articles

Magazines are a type of *periodical*, or a publication that is issued at regular intervals, such as weekly or monthly. Magazines usually contain illustrations, advertisements, and a variety of articles by different writers. They often focus on a single topic, such as sports, current events, or travel. For example, the piece here is excerpted from a longer article that Johnette Howard wrote for *Sports Illustrated* magazine in March, 1998. Along with newspapers and Web sites, magazines are a good source of current, up-to-date information.

Reading Strategy

Recognize the Author's Attitude

In a magazine article, the author's attitude is reflected in the way he or she describes and interprets the subject. To recognize the author's attitude, notice the details and events the author chooses to include. Then think about the message the author conveys, either directly or indirectly, through relating this information.

For example, in "Golden Girls," the author admires the members of the 1998 U. S. Women's Hockey Team. She shows this by describing their victory with adjectives such as "spectacular" and "eye-dampening." As you read, use a chart like the one shown to record details that convey the author's admiration and respect for her subject.

Details That Convey Author's Attitude

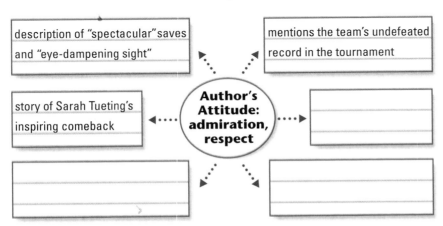

description of "spectacular" saves and "eye-dampening sight"

mentions the team's undefeated record in the tournament

story of Sarah Tueting's inspiring comeback

Author's Attitude: admiration, respect

Golden Girls

Johnette Howard

By the time the clock struck midnight and the pop of champagne corks was heard at the victory party, the game's particulars had begun to fade from conversation. The feelings were what the U.S. women ice hockey players wanted to review: the lumps in their throats, the chills that ran down their spines, the eye-dampening sight of goalie Sarah Tueting high-stepping around the ice like a crazed drum major after the U.S. won the gold medal game 3–1 against archnemesis Canada. Sandra Whyte, Tueting's onetime housemate in Boston, had sealed the victory, nudging in a 40-foot empty-net goal that the sellout crowd in Nagano's Big Hat stadium traced on its excruciatingly slow path to the net with a steadily building roar of *oh-oh-ooOOHH!* "I'm sure all of us will see ourselves celebrating on tape tomorrow and say, 'I did *what?*' said U.S. forward A.J. Mleczko.

"All I could think was, We just won a gold medal—did we not just win a gold medal?" said Tueting, an apple-cheeked Dartmouth junior-to-be who made 21 saves, many of them

> By describing their words and emotions at the victory celebration, Howard lets the reader feel the teams' happiness.

spectacular, in the final, and then floated into both the post-game press conference and the victory party wearing a two-foot-tall foam-rubber Uncle Sam hat that her brother, Jonathon, had tossed onto the ice. Suddenly those despair-filled months in 1996, when Tueting was ready to quit hockey at age 19 because she'd never been invited to a U.S. national team tryout, seemed long, long ago. "I had gone home that summer, taken the Olympic posters off my bedroom wall and told everyone I was through," Tueting said. "Then August came, and I got a letter inviting me to camp. I made the national team. In the space of two weeks I went from quitting hockey to putting my life on hold to chase this dream. And now look."

In winning the six-team inaugural women's Olympic tournament with a 6–0 record, the U.S. team eclipsed Picabo Street[1] as America's feel-good story of the Winter Games. On Sunday, General Mills announced that it had chosen Tueting and her teammates to adorn its post-Olympics Wheaties box. Just hours after the gold medal game on Feb. 17, the *Late Show with David Letterman* rushed 10 of the U.S. players to a Nagano TV studio to read a Top Ten List titled "Cool Things About Winning an Olympic Gold Medal."

Sportswriters walked into the final grousing about having to cover it and walked out gushing that it was the best thing they'd ever seen. A felicitous[2] line by *Washington Post* columnist Michael Wilbon, who called Mleczko "the first leftwinger I've ever had a crush on," was typical.

That stretching sound you hear is attitudes about women athletes continuing to expand. After the 1996 Atlanta Summer Olympics and now the Nagano Games, it's clear that the U.S.'s female athletic heroes don't have to play what Billie Jean King has jokingly called the "good clothes sports"—figure skating, tennis and golf. Women never lacked the strength or will to compete in the grittier sports, just the opportunity. When they get the chance, they can produce stirring results. As the U.S. men's Olympic goalie, Mike Richter of the New York Rangers, said admiringly after watching the U.S. women play Canada, "You felt so good for them, the way they were just bleeding for each other to win every game."

---

1. Picabo (pēk´ ə bōō) **Street** member of the U.S. Women's Ski Team who came back from a serious injury to win a gold medal at the 1998 Olympic Winter Games.
2. felicitous (fə lis´ i təs) *adj.* appropriate or well-chosen.

Here, the writer shows her admiration for one player's perseverance.

The author mentions others who admire and respect the members of the team.

Here, the author shows how even skeptics came to admire the team.

The author shows how the team has had a positive effect on the public's attitudes toward women's sports.

Check Your Comprehension

1. What did the 1998 U. S. Women's Hockey Team accomplish?
2. (a) What was Sarah Tueting's dream in college? (b) Why did she nearly give up on this dream?
3. Why did sportswriters complain about covering the finals?
4. How might this victory affect the dreams of other female athletes?

Applying the Reading Strategy

Recognize the Author's Attitude

5. What details in the article hint at Howard's admiration for the team?
6. Howard calls the hockey team the "feel-good story of the Winter Games." What does this suggest about her attitude toward the team?
7. What is the author's attitude toward the expanding possibilities in women's athletics? How can you tell?

Activity

Examine Media Coverage

In this article, the author explains that "sportswriters walked into the final grousing about having to cover it and walked out gushing that it was the best thing they'd ever seen." In your library or on the Internet, find at least one other article about the team's 1998 Olympic victory. Read the article, and find quotations that reveal the writer's enthusiasm for the game. Record them in a chart like the one shown here.

Source	Writer	Quotation
Washington Post	Michael Wilbon	A. J. Mleczko is "the first leftwinger I've ever had a crush on"

Comparing Informational Materials

Magazine Articles and Internet Sites

The article you just read does not include much information about the hockey games themselves. Find statistics about the 1998 U. S. Women's Hockey Team on the Internet. Do a keyword search to get more information about the games. Then, answer the following questions.

1. What was the final score in each of the U. S. team's six games?
2. Against which teams did the U. S. team play?
3. Overall, how many saves did goalie Sarah Tueting make?

Writing WORKSHOP

Narration: Autobiographical Writing

Narrative writing is writing that tells a story. An **autobiographical narrative** tells the story of an event or person in the writer's life. In this workshop, you will use one of your own experiences to write an autobiographical narrative.

Assignment Criteria Your autobiographical narrative should have the following characteristics:

- clear sequence of events, or plot, involving you the writer
- interesting conflict, problem, or change
- vivid details showing people, setting, and actions
- precise language, including strong nouns and verbs

See the Rubric on page 97 for the criteria on which your autobiographical narrative may be assessed.

Prewriting

Choose a topic. Think about times when you learned something important, overcame a problem, or achieved a goal. One way to begin is to use the **blueprinting** strategy. Make a blueprint or floor plan of a place that is important to you, such as your home or a place where you go with friends. Draw your map, making brief notes on each area about events, people, or activities you associate with the spot. Choose one of these associations you make as the topic for your narrative.

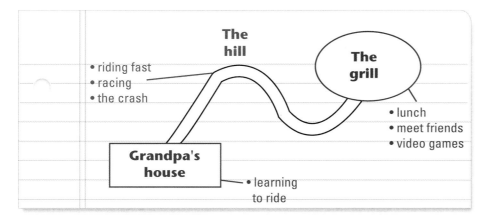

Narrow your topic. Your topic may include many parts. Narrow it down to the most interesting one. A story topic that includes a compelling problem or conflict (a struggle between opposing forces) is usually a good choice.

Student Model

Before you begin drafting your autobiographical narrative, read this student model and review the characteristics of a successful autobiographical narrative.

Alexander Baker
Palos Verdes, California

Bicycle Braking Blues

Crash! Once again, I found myself flying off my bike and toward the grass. At age eight, crashes were an everyday occurrence, and I reminded myself that it was better to practice braking here by the lawn than to risk another episode like "The Club Hill Clobbering."

It all started when I arrived at my grandparents' house in Galesburg to spend the summer. I made many friends in their neighborhood, but they spent most of their time riding bikes, and I didn't have one. Then, my step-grandmother gave me the almost new, metallic green bike that her grandson had outgrown. I was overjoyed to have a bike. . . . I learned to ride it well enough—what I didn't learn was how to use the brakes. On the flat ground near my grandparents' house, I just let the bike slow down until I could put my feet down.

One day, my babysitter took me for lunch at the club grill. She rode my grandfather's golf cart while I rode my bike. When we had to climb the big hill leading up to the club, I walked my bike alongside the cart. After lunch, I mounted my bike while Erika drove Grandpa's golf cart. As we headed toward home, neither of us gave a thought to. . .the HILL.

As we came around the corner of the bike path, I started picking up speed. By the time I realized what was happening, it was too late. "The hill!!" I yelled to Erika. "Your brakes! Use your brakes!" she shouted. With the wind rushing in my ears, I could hardly hear her. Looking down the hill, I saw a golf cart was blocking the path. It seemed to get bigger and closer by the second. "Well," I thought to myself, "it's now or never." I steered my speeding bike toward the grass alongside the path and jumped off sideways. I leapt off and BAM! The world turned upside down and inside out. The next sound I heard was the grumbling of a golf cart engine. It sounded annoyed about the jumble of parts in its path.

The next thing I saw was Erika's face. She was so scared her face was stiff and pale. I stood up to show Erika that I was fine. The only damage I sustained was some dirt on my jeans and the bike survived without too many scratches, too. Also, my pride was hurt. How can you ride a bike if you can never go down a hill? So every day, Erika took me over to the hill and we'd go a little farther up. That way, I learned to brake on a hill, little by little, rather than getting clobbered again!

Alexander hints at the upcoming conflict.

He tells the event in sequence, beginning with where and how he got the bike.

Precise language, such as *grumbling,* creates a specific image in readers' minds.

Details like the expression on Erika's face help readers envision Erika.

Drafting

Create a sequence of events. Begin by identifying the conflict, problem, or change that is at the heart of your narrative. Use a conflict map like the one shown to explore the two sides. In the opening of your narrative, hint at this conflict or change. Then, tell the events leading up to the resolution of the conflict or the moment you recognized the change. At the end of your narrative, tell what the experience meant to you or what you learned.

Use details and dialogue. As you draft your narrative, use precise words—such as *hurled, hesitantly,* and *grin*—to provide details about people's actions, gestures, and expressions. Use dialogue to tell part of the story in the words of the people besides you who participated.

No Dialogue: Derek said he was going to the bakery to buy a cake.

With Dialogue: "I am going to buy the largest, most colorful birthday cake in the world," proclaimed Derek.

Conflict Analysis

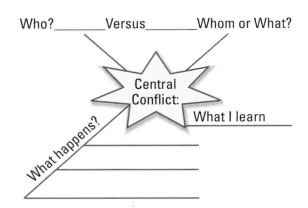

Revising

Revise for connections. Make sure the details in your narrative are connected to the central conflict or change.

Include details about the characters that show the feelings, personality traits, and actions that contribute to or help resolve the conflict.

Model: Making connections

My step-grandmother gave me the bike her grandson had outgrown. I was overjoyed to have a bike like the other kids. ~~All my friends came over to help me learn to ride it.~~ *I learned to ride it well enough—what I didn't learn was how to use the brakes. On the flat ground near my grandparents' house, I just let the bike slow down until I could put my feet down.*

One day, my babysitter took me for lunch at the club grill. After lunch, I mounted my bike while Erika drove Grandpa's golf cart. *As we headed toward home, neither of us gave a thought to...the HILL.*

Revise for word choice. Look for nouns that might leave readers wondering *what kind.* Highlight them, and replace them with **precise nouns**— nouns that name a specific kind of person, place, or thing.

> **Not Precise:** Tom watered the *plant.*
> **Precise:** Tom watered the *rosebush.*

Using a different color, highlight vague verbs and replace them with vivid, **precise verbs**—verbs that tell a very specific action.

> **Not Precise:** Trina *went* to the school.
> **Precise:** Trina *dashed* to the school.

Compare the model and the nonmodel. Why is the model more effective than the nonmodel?

Nonmodel	Model
I got off and BAM! The world turned upside down and inside out. The next thing I heard was the noise of the golf cart engine. It sounded upset about the thing in its path.	I leapt off and BAM! The world turned upside down and inside out. The next sound I heard was the grumbling of the golf cart engine. It sounded annoyed about the jumble of parts in its path.

Publishing and Presenting

Choose one of the following ways to share your writing with classmates or a wider audience.

Present an oral narrative. Use your autobiographical narrative as the basis for an autobiographical narrative presentation.

Make a poster. Design a poster with visuals related to your narrative. You might include photos, artwork, or souvenirs. Arrange these, with a neat copy of your narrative, on posterboard to display in class.

 Prentice Hall Writing and Grammar Connection: Chapter 4, Section 4

Speaking Connection
To learn more about presenting an autobiographical narrative in a speech, see the **Listening and Speaking Workshop: Organizing and Presenting a Narrative Account,** page 98.

Rubric for Self-Assessment

Evaluate your autobiographical narrative using the following criteria and rating scale.

Criteria	Rating Scale Not very				Very
How clearly is the sequence or order of events presented?	1	2	3	4	5
How interesting is the conflict, problem, or change?	1	2	3	4	5
How effectively are details and dialogue used to show people, setting, and action?	1	2	3	4	5
How strong and precise is the language?	1	2	3	4	5

Listening and Speaking WORKSHOP

Organizing and Delivering a Narrative Presentation

The content of an oral, or spoken, **narrative presentation** is prepared and organized in much the same way as a written narrative. This workshop will focus on the specific strategies and techniques for an oral narrative presentation. (To review the characteristics of autobiographical narratives, see the Writing Workshop, pp. 94–97. For fictional narratives such as short stories, see pp. 506–509.) The following strategies will help you give an effective and interesting narrative presentation.

Organize Your Presentation

Like a written narrative, a narrative presentation should tell the events in the story in order, focusing on the central conflict, problem, or experience.

Make notes. For a formal narrative presentation, begin by writing your narrative, including dialogue and descriptive details. If you will be using this written narrative as a script, write it in large print so that you can easily find your place as you glance up and down.

Deliver Your Presentation

Rehearse your delivery. Whether or not you use a script, look up frequently. Use your facial expressions and voice to make the narrative interesting.

- **Vary the volume.** Speak more loudly to express how a coach peps up her team or more softly to tell about a quiet moment, such as how a baby falls asleep.
- **Switch the pitch.** A high voice can show excitement or panic. A low voice might show sternness or tiredness. Also, change the sound of your voice to indicate different speakers in a dialogue.

As you rehearse, think about the pace, tone of voice, and vocabulary that are appropriate for your audience.

Activity:
Storytelling Choose a fictional story you would like to present. (Consider using "The Cat Who Thought She Was a Dog . . ." or "The Third Level" from this unit.) Decide the kind of audience to whom you will make your presentation. Use the strategies in this workshop to organize and deliver your presentation. Ask a partner to give you feedback. Finally, deliver your presentation to the audience you chose.

Presentation Tips for Specific Audiences

Younger audience	Older audience
• Exaggerate emotions and reactions with dramatic facial expressions.	• Use more realistic voices and facial expressions.
• Use short sentences and simple vocabulary.	• Use longer and more varied sentences and a higher level vocabulary.
• Insert questions that invite audience participation.	• Maintain audience attention by changing your position. Stand up, sit down, or move about as you speak. Make frequent eye contact.

Assessment WORKSHOP

Clarifying Word Meanings

In the reading sections of some tests, you may be asked to read a passage and answer questions about word meanings. You may be asked to figure out the meanings of words by using context clues. Use the following strategies to help you.

- Reread the passage to see if the word is explained or defined.
- Look for a description or examples in the passage to help you figure out the meaning.

Test-Taking Strategies

- Try answering the question before looking at the choices. If your answer is one of the choices, select it.
- Eliminate the obviously incorrect answers.

Sample Test Item

Directions: Read the passage, and then choose the letter of the best answer for each item.

We went to a **retrospective** of the work of a local artist and saw examples of her lifetime work. She had expressed herself in several **mediums,** including oils, charcoal, pastels, and watercolor.

1. In this passage, **retrospective** means—
   - **A** biographical movie
   - **B** representative exhibition
   - **C** critical lecture
   - **D** art store
2. The word **mediums** in this passage means—
   - **A** names
   - **B** shows
   - **C** materials
   - **D** decades

Answers and Explanations

For Item 1: The correct answer is *B.* The words "examples of her lifetime work" explain what a retrospective is.

For Item 2: The correct answer is *C.* Oils, charcoal, pastels, and watercolor are examples of materials used in art.

▷ Practice

Directions: Read the passage, and then choose the letter of the best answer for each item.

After her car accident, we visited my aunt in the hospital. She is a bit **prolix,** fond of using twenty words where two would do. Still, her **veracity** is admirable. She admitted that when it came down to a question of responsibility she was **culpable** because she did not notice the stop sign.

1. In this passage, the word **prolix** means—
   - **A** angry
   - **B** wordy
   - **C** distant
   - **D** cheerful
2. The word **culpable** in this passage means—
   - **A** sad
   - **B** angry
   - **C** guilty
   - **D** worried
3. The word **veracity** in this passage means—
   - **A** truthfulness
   - **B** strength
   - **C** dishonesty
   - **D** conversation

Untitled, © David Ridley

Exploring the Theme

No matter how different we may be from people around the world, we share experiences that bring us all together. The literature in this unit will show you just how strong those common threads can be. Through stories, poems, and nonfiction, the authors explore the way people from different backgrounds, age groups, and historical time periods deal with friends and opponents, struggles and successes. Read on—the people you meet in this unit may let you discover new connections to your world!

◀ **Critical Viewing** In what way does the painting illustrate the theme of common threads?

Why Read Literature?

This unit explores the theme of common threads—the threads of experience, ideas, and feelings that may be shared by people from a wide variety of backgrounds. Preview three purposes for reading you might set before reading the works in this unit.

1 Read for the love of literature.

If not for a childhood accident that left her sightless in one eye, Alice Walker might never have turned to writing. Her mother gave Walker a typewriter and she was allowed to write instead of doing chores. Read **"In Search of Our Mothers' Gardens,"** on page 106, to see what came of that early gift.

Rudyard Kipling got an early start at the craft of writing. His first volume of poetry was privately published in 1881 when he was only in his mid-teens! Read his poem **"If—,"** on page 132, to learn what he thinks are the most important qualities of a mature person.

2 Read to be entertained.

Author Gary Soto wrote the words to an unusual opera entitled "Nerd-Landia" for the Los Angeles Opera. In the opera, the main character, Martin, is a nerd who is hopelessly in love with Ceci, a beautiful woman on campus. Enjoy Soto's gentle humor about another young man in love in his short story **"Seventh Grade,"** on page 116.

William Saroyan, who was born and died in Fresno, California, once wrote an entire novel in 38 days. He also wrote a prize-winning play in six days, and during one five-year period in his life he wrote an average of 100 short stories a year! Read his short story **"The Hummingbird That Lived Through Winter,"** on page 146, a heart-warming tale of a boy and an old man who struggle to save the life of a bird.

3 Read for information.

In the past, a false beard or hair dye was enough to disguise a person's identity. With today's new technologies, it is becoming much harder to hide who you are. To learn the latest techniques of verifying a person's identity, read the feature **"Fingerprints and Identity,"** on page 138.

The first baseball game in the world was played in Hoboken, New Jersey—which is also the birthplace of singer Frank Sinatra. Read more about the many faces of this city in Anna Quindlen's article **"Melting Pot,"** on page 122. Originally published as a newspaper column, Quindlen's piece reveals the complexity of relationships in a late-twentieth-century American neighborhood.

Take It to the Net

Visit the Web site for online instruction and activities related to each selection in this unit.
www.phschool.com

How to Read Literature

Use Literal Comprehension Strategies

Before you can play a Mozart concerto or the latest popular song, you must spend time learning to read music—to recognize what those musical marks mean. To accomplish any challenging task, you need to learn the basics and then progress from there.

In reading, you begin with literal comprehension. Once you are sure you understand what the words say, you can begin interpreting and analyzing. Preview the literal comprehension strategies that you will learn in this unit to help you understand what you are reading.

1. Recognize word roots and use word parts.

A word root is the part of a word that reveals its basic meaning. For example, the root of *rebound* (meaning "to jump again") is *bound* (meaning "to jump"). In this unit, you will learn to use word roots and other word parts to help you determine the meaning of unfamiliar words.

2. Interpret idioms.

Decide whether a phrase should be taken literally or not. If your friend tells you she is "in hot water," you know that she is in trouble, not taking a bath. Examples in this unit will teach you to avoid misunderstandings by showing you how to recognize when writers are using figures of speech.

3. Paraphrase.

Restate sentences in your own words. When you paraphrase sentences or paragraphs, you make their meaning clear to yourself. Look at the example of how you might paraphrase a sentence from an Alice Walker essay.

4. Locate information.

Sometimes, your purpose for reading is to locate specific information. Use these techniques to help you accomplish this purpose:

1. Determine what you want to know.

2. List key words related to this topic.

3. As you read, look for these key words to help you gather information related to the topic.

4. Take notes to capture key details.

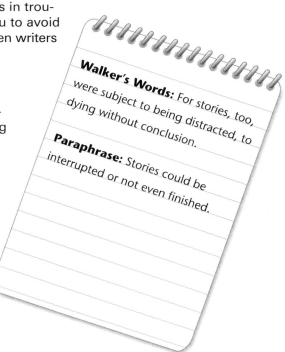

Walker's Words: For stories, too, were subject to being distracted, to dying without conclusion.

Paraphrase: Stories could be interrupted or not even finished.

As you read the selections in this unit, review the reading strategies and look at the notes in the side columns. Use the suggestions to apply the strategies for literal comprehension.

Prepare to Read

from In Search of Our Mothers' Gardens

Preview

Connecting to the Literature

Think about a special someone—your older brother, a grandparent, or maybe your fourth-grade teacher. Somehow, this special person may have changed your life or shaped who you are today. In this essay, Alice Walker shares her memories of the person who had the strongest impact on her life—her mother.

Background

This essay is from *In Search of Our Mothers' Gardens* by Alice Walker. Her parents, like many African Americans in the South, lived the difficult life of sharecroppers. In return for land, seed, and tools, these workers gave landowners a percentage of their crops. Sharecroppers worked long hours and dreamed of buying land of their own. However, many fell into debt and were fortunate if they had enough food for their families.

Literary Analysis

Tribute

Alice Walker's essay is a **tribute,** a literary expression of admiration to honor a special person. A tribute often contains anecdotes, or brief stories, that show the qualities of the honored person and includes an explanation of the subject's importance to the writer. The following lines reveal something about Walker and her mother.

> Guided by my heritage of a love of beauty and a respect for strength—in search of my mother's garden, I found my own.

Connecting Literary Elements

The **theme** of a literary work is the message or truth that the work communicates about life in general. By highlighting a person's admirable qualities, the author of a tribute communicates a general message about what is important or valuable in a person. Think about how Walker's mother's specific qualities suggest a theme about the value of what parents pass on to their children. Focus on these questions as you read:

1. What qualities does Walker admire in her mother?
2. What message does Walker communicate by focusing on the value of these qualities?

Reading Strategy

Recognizing Word Roots

A **word root** is the most basic form of a word. Several words usually "grow" from one root. Because the words share a common root, they also share related meanings. For example, the root *bio* means "life." Words such as *biology* and *biosphere* are related to life, but each has its unique definition. Complete a chart such as the one shown to learn how a single root unlocks the meaning of several words.

As you read the selection, look for examples of words containing the Greek roots shown here.

Root	Meaning of root	Words with root
bio-	"life"	biology biosphere
–nym-	"name"	
–typ-	"model"	

Vocabulary Development

mutilated (myo͞ot´ əl āt´ id) *adj.* damaged or injured (p. 107)

vibrant (vī´ brənt) *adj.* lively (p. 107)

anonymous (ə nän´ ə məs) *adj.* with no name known (p. 107)

profusely (prō fyo͞os´ lē) *adv.* freely or plentifully (p. 108)

radiant (rā´ dē ənt) *adj.* shining brightly (p. 109)

illuminates (i lo͞o´ mə nāts´) *v.* brightens; sheds light on (p. 109)

hindered (hin´ dərd) *adj.* held back (p. 109)

from

In Search of Our Mothers' Gardens

Alice Walker

My mother made all the clothes we wore, even my brothers' overalls. She made all the towels and sheets we used. She spent the summers canning vegetables and fruits. She spent the winter evenings making quilts enough to cover all our beds.

During the "working" day, she labored beside—not behind—my father in the fields. Her day began before sunup, and did not end until late at night. There was never a moment for her to sit down, undisturbed, to unravel her own private thoughts; never a time free from interruption—by work or the noisy inquiries of her many children. And yet, it is to my mother—and all our mothers who were not famous—that I went in search of the secret of what has fed that muzzled and often <u>mutilated</u>, but <u>vibrant</u>, creative spirit that the black woman has inherited, and that pops out in wild and unlikely places to this day.

But when, you will ask, did my overworked mother have time to know or care about feeding the creative spirit?

The answer is so simple that many of us have spent years discovering it. We have constantly looked high, when we should have looked high—and low.

For example: in the Smithsonian Institution[1] in Washington, D.C., there hangs a quilt unlike any other in the world. In fanciful, inspired, and yet simple and identifiable figures, it portrays the story of the Crucifixion. It is considered rare, beyond price. Though it follows no known pattern of quilt-making, and though it is made of bits and pieces of worthless rags, it is obviously the work of a person of powerful imagination and deep spiritual feeling. Below this quilt I saw a note that says it was made by "an <u>anonymous</u> Black woman in Alabama, a hundred years ago."

If we could locate this "anonymous" black woman from Alabama, she would turn out to be one of our grandmothers—an artist who left her mark in the only materials she could afford, and in the only medium her position in society allowed her to use.

And so our mothers and grandmothers have, more often than not anonymously, handed on the creative spark, the seed of the flower they themselves never hoped to see: or like a sealed letter they could not plainly read.

And so it is, certainly, with my own mother.

---

1. Smithsonian Institution group of museums with exhibits in the fields of science, art, and history.

mutilated (myo͞ot′ əl āt′ id) *adj.* damaged or injured

vibrant (vī′ brənt) *adj.* lively and energetic

anonymous (ə nän′ ə məs) *adj.* with no name known

Reading Strategy
Recognizing Word Roots
How is the meaning of *anonymously* related to the meaning of its root, *–nym-* which means *name*.

**Reading Check**

What does Walker believe about the everyday work of women—especially mothers?

Unlike "Ma" Rainey's songs, which retained their creator's name even while blasting forth from Bessie Smith's mouth,[2] no song or poem will bear my mother's name. Yet so many of the stories that I write, that we all write, are my mother's stories. Only recently did I fully realize this: that through years of listening to my mother's stories of her life, I have absorbed not only the stories themselves, but something of the manner in which she spoke, something of the urgency that involves the knowledge that her stories—like her life—must be recorded. It is probably for this reason that so much of what I have written is about characters whose counterparts in real life are so much older than I am.

But the telling of these stories, which came from my mother's lips as naturally as breathing, was not the only way my mother showed herself as an artist. For stories, too, were subject to being distracted, to dying without conclusion. Dinners must be started, and cotton must be gathered before the big rains. The artist that was and is my mother showed itself to me only after many years. This is what I finally noticed:

Like Mem, a character in *The Third Life of Grange Copeland*,[3] my mother adorned with flowers whatever shabby house we were forced to live in. And not just your typical straggly country stand of zinnias, either. She planted ambitious gardens—and still does—with over fifty different varieties of plants that bloom profusely from early March until late November. Before she left home for the fields, she watered her flowers, chopped up the grass, and laid out new beds. When she returned from the fields she might divide clumps of bulbs, dig a cold pit,[4] uproot and replant roses, or prune branches from her taller bushes or trees—until night came and it was too dark to see.

Whatever she planted grew as if by magic, and her fame as a grower of flowers spread over three counties. Because of her creativity with her flowers, even my memories of poverty are seen through a screen of blooms—sunflowers, petunias, roses, dahlias, forsythia, spirea, delphiniums, verbena . . . and on and on.

And I remember people coming to my mother's yard to be given cuttings from her flowers; I hear again the praise showered on her because whatever rocky soil she landed on, she turned into a garden. A garden so brilliant with colors, so original in its design, so magnificent with life and creativity, that to this day people drive by our house in Georgia—perfect strangers and imperfect strangers—and ask to stand or walk among my mother's art.

I notice that it is only when my mother is working in her

2. **"Ma" Rainey's songs . . . Bessie Smith's mouth** Gertrude ("Ma") Rainey, one of America's first blues singers, lived during the early years of the twentieth century. Bessie Smith was a well-known blues singer (1898?–1937), who knew and learned from "Ma" Rainey.
3. **The Third Life of Grange Copeland** the title of a novel by Alice Walker.
4. **cold pit** hole in which seedlings are planted at the beginning of the spring.

Literary Analysis
Tribute What abilities does Walker admire in her mother?

profusely (prō fyo͞os′ lē) *adv.* freely or plentifully

flowers that she is <u>radiant</u>, almost to the point of being invisible—except as Creator: hand and eye. She is involved in work her soul must have. Ordering the universe in the image of her personal conception of Beauty.

Her face, as she prepares the Art that is her gift, is a legacy[5] of respect she leaves to me, for all that <u>illuminates</u> and cherishes life. She has handed down respect for the possibilities—and the will to grasp them.

For her, so <u>hindered</u> and intruded upon in so many ways, being an artist has still been a daily part of her life. This ability to hold on, even in very simple ways, is work black women have done for a very long time.

This poem is not enough, but it is something, for the woman who literally covered the holes in our walls with sunflowers:

They were women then
My mama's generation
Husky of voice—Stout of
Step
With fists as well as
Hands
How they battered down
Doors
And ironed
Starched white
Shirts
How they led
Armies
Headragged[6] Generals
Across mined[7]
Fields
Booby-trapped
Kitchens
To discover books
Desks
A place for us
How they knew what we
Must know
Without knowing a page
Of it
Themselves.

Guided by my heritage of a love of beauty and a respect for

radiant (rā′ dē ənt) *adj.* shining brightly

illuminates (i l o͞o′ mə nāts′) *v.* brightens; sheds light on

hindered (hin′ dərd) *adj.* held back

▼ **Critical Viewing**
How is a garden like a "work of art"? **[Analyze]**

✔ **Reading Check**
When is Walker's mother radiant?

---

5. **legacy** (leg′ ə sē) *n.* something handed down by a parent or an ancestor.
6. **headragged** (hed′ ragd) *adj.* with head wrapped around by a rag or kerchief.
7. **mined** (mīnd) *adj.* filled with buried explosives that are set to go off when stepped on.

strength—in search of my mother's garden, I found my own.

And perhaps in Africa over two hundred years ago, there was just such a mother; perhaps she painted vivid and daring decorations in oranges and yellows and greens on the walls of her hut; perhaps she sang—in a voice like Roberta Flack's[8]—*sweetly* over the compounds of her village; perhaps she wove the most stunning mats or told the most ingenious[9] stories of all the village storytellers. Perhaps she was herself a poet—though only her daughter's name is signed to the poems that we know.

Perhaps Phillis Wheatley's[10] mother was also an artist.

Perhaps in more than Phillis Wheatley's biological life is her mother's signature made clear.

---

8. **Roberta Flack's** Roberta Flack is a contemporary African American singer.
9. **ingenious** (in jēn′ yəs) *adj.* clever and inventive.
10. **Phillis Wheatley's** Phillis Wheatley (1753?–1784) was a poet, considered the first important black writer in America.

Review and Assess

Thinking About the Selection

1. **Respond:** Which of Walker's mother's personal qualities do you most admire? Why?

2. **(a) Recall:** Briefly describe the home and setting in which Walker and her mother lived. **(b) Connect:** How does that setting emphasize the power of her mother's creative spirit? **(c) Apply:** In what way does Walker's mother represent women in general?

3. **(a) Interpret:** What does Walker mean by "We have constantly looked high, when we should have looked high—and low"? **(b) Analyze:** How does the anecdote of the quilt hanging in the Smithsonian Institution clarify Walker's point?

4. **(a) Recall:** What are Walker's mother's skills? **(b) Interpret:** What skills has she passed on? **(c) Synthesize:** In your own words, explain what makes her an artist.

5. **(a) Analyze:** Why does Walker call this essay "In Search of *Our* Mothers' Gardens" instead of "In Search of My Mother's Garden"? **(b) Evaluate:** Explain why one title is more appropriate than the other.

6. **Make a Judgment:** Walker includes useful "creations" such as gardens and quilts in her definition of "art." What is your definition of "art"?

Alice Walker

(b. 1944)

Alice Walker's life has always been shaped by the love and power of women. First, there was Walker's mother, who stood at the center of her large family in rural Georgia and "made a way out of no way." A woman with limited income, she shared her artistic spirit and creations with her family and community. Despite her family's size and limited financial resources, Walker went to college. There, she wrote her first book of poems. Walker's work blossomed after that and became very popular. The novel *The Color Purple*, for example, won the Pulitzer Prize and became a successful movie.

Review and Assess

Literary Analysis

Tribute

1. On a chart like the one shown, identify three qualities that Walker's mother has passed on to Walker.

Walker's Mother		**Alice Walker**
Made Quilts	Creativity →	Writes Poetry
_____	_____ →	_____
_____	_____ →	_____

2. In what ways does Walker's mother contribute to Walker's creativity?
3. What examples does Walker use to show these qualities in her mother?

Connecting Literary Elements

4. What qualities does Walker admire in her mother?
5. What message does Walker communicate by focusing on the value of these qualities?
6. Express Walker's theme based on details from the essay. List details in the categories shown.

Details	1. What does Walker admire in her mother?
	2. What does Walker admire in other women?
	3. How has Walker benefited from their work?
Theme	

Reading Strategy

Recognizing Word Roots

7. (a) What word in the selection has the root -nym-? (b) What other words contain this root?
8. (a) What word in the selection has the root -bio-? (b) What other words contain this root?

Extend Understanding

9. **Art Connection:** What does this essay suggest about the importance of practical arts, such as gardening and quilting, compared with fine arts, such as painting and sculpting?

Quick Review

A **tribute** is a literary expression of admiration or appreciation. To review tributes, see page 105.

Theme is the message about life that a literary work communicates. To review theme, see page 105.

A **word root** is the most basic form of a word. To review word roots, see page 105.

 Take It to the Net
www.phschool.com
Take the interactive self-test online to check your understanding of the selection.

Integrate Language Skills

Vocabulary Development Lesson

Word Analysis: Greek Root -nym-

The word *anonymous* contains the Greek root -nym-, meaning "name." *Anonymous* means "with no name known." On your paper, complete these word equations containing the root -nym-. Then, use the examples to help you define each word.

1. homo (the same) + -nym = ___?___
   Example: there/they're/their
2. anto (the opposite) + -nym = ___?___
   Example: here/there
3. pseudo (fake) + -nym = ___?___
   Example: William Sydney Porter/O. Henry

Spelling Strategy

The -nym- root is always spelled with y, which has a short *i* sound. On your paper, complete each word by adding -nym.

1. acro +   2. topo +   3. syno +

Concept Development: Antonyms

Identify the antonym, or opposite, of the first word in each numbered item.

1. radiant: **a.** dull, **b.** joyful, **c.** shining
2. vibrant: **a.** alive, **b.** weak, **c.** eager
3. illuminates: **a.** lights, **b.** darkens, **c.** explains
4. anonymous: **a.** unknown, **b.** evil, **c.** credited
5. profusely: **a.** scarcely, **b.** frequently, **c.** loudly
6. mutilated: **a.** damaged, **b.** whole, **c.** silly
7. hindered: **a.** aided, **b.** delayed, **c.** frustrated

Grammar Lesson

Pronoun Case

A pronoun takes the place of a noun. It may take the place of the **subject**—the "doer" of the action. It may take the place of the **object**—the receiver of the action or the object of a preposition.

The **case** or form a pronoun takes will change depending on whether it acts as a subject or an object.

Subjective Case	Objective Case
I, we	me, us
you	you
he, she, it, they	him, her, it, them

▶ *For more practice, see page R32, Exercise C.*

Practice On your paper, identify the case of each italicized pronoun.

1. *I* want to visit that beautiful garden.
2. *They* worked from morning 'til night to feed their family.
3. *She* could see *her* weeding the garden.
4. Alice Walker gave *us* new ideas about creativity.
5. *We* read this essay, and it touched *me*.

Writing Application On your paper, write sentences using the personal pronoun forms given.

1. Use two subject pronouns.
2. Use one subject and one object pronoun.
3. Use two object pronouns.

W̶G Prentice Hall Writing and Grammar Connection: Chapter 14, Section 2

Writing Lesson

Write a Tribute

Alice Walker's tribute shows the strong connection between mother and daughter, which can be similar to the connection between artist and teacher. Write a brief tribute to an important person in your life. Include anecdotes, or brief stories, that show your subject demonstrating the qualities you admire.

Prewriting   Choose a person you admire. On a folded piece of paper, list the person's traits, reasons you admire the person, and anecdotes about the person.

Model: Support Statements with Anecdotes

Drafting   Write about each quality the person has, giving the reason you admire the quality and sharing an anecdote to support your point.

Revising   Review your essay. Add a description or example to any quality that you have not supported with an anecdote.

*W*G *Prentice Hall Writing and Grammar Connection: Chapter 6, Section 4*

Extension Activities

Listening and Speaking Walker suggests that a person can find creative outlets in everyday tasks. In a brief **how-to speech,** give step-by-step instructions for performing an activity that is part of your everyday routine.

1. Choose an activity you can explain well.
2. Organize your speech so your classmates will find the order of steps clear and easy to follow.
3. Explain the activity, pointing out steps that require decisions or creative thinking.

Research and Technology Walker's parents and grandparents lived as sharecroppers. With two other students, prepare a **spoken presentation** about the living and working conditions of sharecroppers. Each of you can choose one area to research. Make sure to put information from your sources in your own words. Deliver your presentation to the class. In your presentation, explain the resources you used and the process you followed to find your information. **[Group Activity]**

 **Take It to the Net**   www.phschool.com

Go online for an additional research activity using the Internet.

Prepare to Read

Seventh Grade ◆ Melting Pot

 Take It to the Net

Visit www.phschool.com for interactive activities and instruction related to these selections, including
- background
- graphic organizers
- literary elements
- reading strategies

Preview

Connecting to the Literature

When Victor, the main character in Gary Soto's "Seventh Grade," attempts to impress his classmates by trying to appear smarter than he is, he ends up embarrassing himself instead. What reasons do you think people might have for trying to impress others?

Background

The parents or grandparents of Victor in Gary Soto's story "Seventh Grade" were most likely immigrants from a Latin American country. Since the 1970s, immigrants have been coming to the United States at a faster rate than at any time since the start of the twentieth century. Many of the new arrivals come from Asia, the Pacific Islands, and Latin America. Anna Quindlen's essay, "Melting Pot," describes a city neighborhood—an area strongly affected by constant new arrivals.

Literary Analysis

Tone

The **tone** of a literary work is the writer's attitude toward the subject and characters. The tone can often be described in one word, such as *playful*. This sentence from Anna Quindlen's "Melting Pot" conveys an informal attitude toward the differences between her and her neighbors.

> My children are upstairs in the house next door, having dinner with the Ecuadorian family that lives on the top floor.

Quindlen mentions the nationality of the family in an off-hand way, showing that her attitude toward the subject is casual.

Comparing Literary Works

In both selections, the writers approach the subject of interpersonal differences with a lighthearted tone. Both authors suggest that although people may appear to be very different from one another, they really have a lot in common. Yet, the characters in these selections don't always see things that way. As you read, compare the selections by focusing on the following questions:

1. How do the characters feel about the ways in which they are different from other characters?
2. What do the characters do to try to overcome their differences with other characters?

Reading Strategy

Identifying Idioms

Writers sometimes use expressions that are not meant to be read literally. For example, **idioms** are expressions that have an understood meaning in a particular language or region. If translated word for word, however, the idiom would lose its meaning. The chart here shows an example of an idiom used in the story "Seventh Grade." As you read, create your own chart with other idioms you find.

Idiom

making a face	
Literal	**Actual**
creating or building a face	showing an unusual or different facial expression

Vocabulary Development

elective (ē lek´ tiv) *n.* optional course or subject (p. 116)

conviction (kən vik´ shən) *n.* belief (p. 117)

sheepishly (shēp´ ish lē) *adv.* in a shy or embarrassed way (p. 120)

fluent (floo´ ənt) *adj.* able to write or speak easily and smoothly (p. 122)

bigots (big´ əts) *n.* narrow-minded, prejudiced people (p. 122)

interloper (in´ tər lō´ pər) *n.* one who intrudes on another (p. 124)

Seventh Grade

Gary Soto

On the first day of school, Victor stood in line half an hour before he came to a wobbly card table. He was handed a packet of papers and a computer card on which he listed his one <u>elective</u>, French. He already spoke Spanish and English, but he thought some day he might travel to France, where it was cool; not like Fresno, where summer days reached 110 degrees in the shade. There were rivers in France and huge churches, and fair-skinned people everywhere, the way there were brown people all around Victor.

elective (ē lek´ tiv) *n.*
optional course or subject

Besides, Teresa, a girl he had liked since they were in catechism classes at Saint Theresa's, was taking French, too. With any luck they would be in the same class. Teresa is going to be my girl this year, he promised himself as he left the gym full of students in their new fall clothes. She was cute. And good in math, too, Victor thought as he walked down the hall to his homeroom. He ran into his friend, Michael Torres, by the water fountain that never turned off.

They shook hands, *raza*-style, and jerked their heads at one another in a *saludo de vato*.[1] "How come you're making a face?" asked Victor.

"I ain't making a face, *ese*.[2] This *is* my face." Michael said his face had changed during the summer. He had read a *GQ* magazine that his older brother had borrowed from the Book Mobile and noticed that the male models all had the same look on their faces. They would stand, one arm around a beautiful woman, and *scowl*. They would sit at a pool, their rippled stomachs dark with shadow, and *scowl*. They would sit at dinner tables, cool drinks in their hands, and *scowl*.

"I think it works," Michael said. He scowled and let his upper lip quiver. His teeth showed along with the ferocity of his soul. "Belinda Reyes walked by a while ago and looked at me," he said.

Victor didn't say anything, though he thought his friend looked pretty strange. They talked about recent movies, baseball, their parents, and the horrors of picking grapes in order to buy their fall clothes. Picking grapes was like living in Siberia,[3] except hot and more boring.

"What classes are you taking?" Michael said, scowling.

"French. How 'bout you?"

"Spanish. I ain't so good at it, even if I'm Mexican."

"I'm not either, but I'm better at it than math, that's for sure."

A tinny, three-beat bell propelled students to their homerooms. The two friends socked each other in the arm and went their ways, Victor thinking, man, that's weird. Michael thinks making a face makes him handsome.

On the way to his homeroom, Victor tried a scowl. He felt foolish, until out of the corner of his eye he saw a girl looking at him. Umm, he thought, maybe it does work. He scowled with greater <u>conviction</u>.

In homeroom, roll was taken, emergency cards were passed out, and they were given a bulletin to take home to their parents. The principal, Mr. Belton, spoke over the crackling loudspeaker, welcoming the students to a new year, new experiences, and new friendships. The students squirmed in their chairs and ignored

Reading Strategy
Identifying Idioms
Rephrase Victor's question without using the idiom.

conviction (kən vik´ shən)
n. belief

Reading Check

Why does Victor choose to study French?

---

1. *raza*-style . . . *saludo de vato* (säl o͞o´ do͞ dä bä´ to͞) Spanish gestures of greeting between friends.
2. *ese* (es´ ā) Spanish word for "man."
3. **Siberia** (sī bir´ ē ə) region in northern Asia known for its harsh winters.

▲ **Critical Viewing** Soto describes the students' mood as "sunny" on the first day of school. How does this photograph convey that feeling? **[Connect]**

him. They were anxious to go to first period. Victor sat calmly, thinking of Teresa, who sat two rows away, reading a paperback novel. This would be his lucky year. She was in his homeroom, and would probably be in his English and math classes. And, of course, French.

The bell rang for first period, and the students herded noisily through the door. Only Teresa lingered, talking with the homeroom teacher.

"So you think I should talk to Mrs. Gaines?" she asked the teacher. "She would know about ballet?"

"She would be a good bet," the teacher said. Then added, "Or the gym teacher, Mrs. Garza."

Victor lingered, keeping his head down and staring at his desk. He wanted to leave when she did so he could bump into her and say something clever.

He watched her on the sly. As she turned to leave, he stood up and hurried to the door, where he managed to catch her eye. She smiled and said, "Hi, Victor."

He smiled back and said, "Yeah, that's me." His brown face blushed. Why hadn't he said, "Hi, Teresa," or "How was your summer?" or something nice?

As Teresa walked down the hall, Victor walked the other way, looking back, admiring how gracefully she walked, one foot in front of the other. So much for being in the same class, he thought. As he trudged to English, he practiced scowling.

In English they reviewed the parts of speech. Mr. Lucas, a portly man, waddled down the aisle, asking, "What is a noun?"

"A person, place, or thing," said the class in unison.

"Yes, now somebody give me an example of a person—you, Victor Rodriguez."

Reading Strategy
Identifying Idioms What does Victor actually do when he tries to "catch her eye"?

"Teresa," Victor said automatically. Some of the girls giggled. They knew he had a crush on Teresa. He felt himself blushing again.

"Correct," Mr. Lucas said. "Now provide me with a place."

Mr. Lucas called on a freckled kid who answered, "Teresa's house with a kitchen full of big brothers."

After English, Victor had math, his weakest subject. He sat in the back by the window, hoping that he would not be called on. Victor understood most of the problems, but some of the stuff looked like the teacher made it up as she went along. It was confusing, like the inside of a watch.

After math he had a fifteen-minute break, then social studies, and, finally, lunch. He bought a tuna casserole with buttered rolls, some fruit cocktail, and milk. He sat with Michael, who practiced scowling between bites.

Girls walked by and looked at him.

"See what I mean, Vic?" Michael scowled. "They love it."

"Yeah, I guess so."

They ate slowly, Victor scanning the horizon for a glimpse of Teresa. He didn't see her. She must have brought lunch, he thought, and is eating outside. Victor scraped his plate and left Michael, who was busy scowling at a girl two tables away.

The small, triangle-shaped campus bustled with students talking about their new classes. Everyone was in a sunny mood. Victor hurried to the bag lunch area, where he sat down and opened his math book. He moved his lips as if he were reading, but his mind was somewhere else. He raised his eyes slowly and looked around. No Teresa.

He lowered his eyes, pretending to study, then looked slowly to the left. No Teresa. He turned a page in the book and stared at some math problems that scared him because he knew he would have to do them eventually. He looked to the right. Still no sign of her. He stretched out lazily in an attempt to disguise his snooping.

Then he saw her. She was sitting with a girlfriend under a plum tree. Victor moved to a table near her and daydreamed about taking her to a movie. When the bell sounded, Teresa looked up, and their eyes met. She smiled sweetly and gathered her books. Her next class was French, same as Victor's.

They were among the last students to arrive in class, so all the good desks in the back had already been taken. Victor was forced to sit near the front, a few desks away from Teresa, while Mr. Bueller wrote French words on the chalkboard. The bell rang, and Mr. Bueller wiped his hands, turned to the class, and said, "*Bonjour*."[4]

"*Bonjour*," braved a few students.

"*Bonjour*," Victor whispered. He wondered if Teresa heard him.

Literary Analysis
Tone What details indicate that Soto's attitude toward Victor and Michael is amused but sympathetic?

✔**Reading Check**

Who or what is Victor thinking of during lunch?

---

4. **Bonjour** (bōn zhōōr′) French for "Hello"; "Good day."

Mr. Bueller said that if the students studied hard, at the end of the year they could go to France and be understood by the populace.

One kid raised his hand and asked, "What's 'populace'?"

"The people, the people of France."

Mr. Bueller asked if anyone knew French. Victor raised his hand, wanting to impress Teresa. The teacher beamed and said, "*Très bien. Parlez-vous français?*"[5]

Victor didn't know what to say. The teacher wet his lips and asked something else in French. The room grew silent. Victor felt all eyes staring at him. He tried to bluff his way out by making noises that sounded French.

"La me vave me con le grandma," he said uncertainly.

Mr. Bueller, wrinkling his face in curiosity, asked him to speak up.

Great rosebushes of red bloomed on Victor's cheeks. A river of nervous sweat ran down his palms. He felt awful. Teresa sat a few desks away, no doubt thinking he was a fool. Without looking at Mr. Bueller, Victor mumbled, "Frenchie oh wewe gee in September."

Mr. Bueller asked Victor to repeat what he had said.

"Frenchie oh wewe gee in September," Victor repeated.

Mr. Bueller understood that the boy didn't know French and turned away. He walked to the blackboard and pointed to the words on the board with his steel-edged ruler.

"*Le bateau,*" he sang.

"*Le bateau,*" the students repeated.

"*Le bateau est sur l'eau,*"[6] he sang.

"*Le bateau est sur l'eau.*"

Victor was too weak from failure to join the class. He stared at the board and wished he had taken Spanish, not French. Better yet, he wished he could start his life over. He had never been so embarrassed. He bit his thumb until he tore off a sliver of skin.

The bell sounded for fifth period, and Victor shot out of the room, avoiding the stares of the other kids, but had to return for his math book. He looked <u>sheepishly</u> at the teacher, who was erasing the board, then widened his eyes in terror at Teresa who stood in front of him. "I didn't know you knew French," she said. "That was good."

Mr. Bueller looked at Victor, and Victor looked back. Oh please, don't say anything, Victor pleaded with his eyes. I'll wash your car,

---

Literature
in context Vocabulary Connection

New English Words

At the beginning of the story, Victor and Michael shake hands *raza*-style and give each other a *saludo de vato*. These Spanish terms are not familiar to most English speakers, but the following words originated in Spanish and are now very familiar in English.

tortilla: A thin, flat, round cake made of cornmeal or flour and cooked on a griddle.

fiesta: A celebration or a holiday.

siesta: A brief nap or rest taken after the noon meal.

A fiesta

sheepishly (shēp´ ish lē) *adv.* in a shy or embarrassed way

---

5. *Très bien. Parlez-vous français?* (trā byan pär lā´ voo frän sā´) French for "Very well. Do you speak French?"

6. *Le bateau est sur l'eau* (lə bä tō´ ā soor lō) French for "The boat is on the water."

mow your lawn, walk your dog—anything! I'll be your best student and I'll clean your erasers after school.

Mr. Bueller shuffled through the papers on his desk. He smiled and hummed as he sat down to work. He remembered his college years when he dated a girlfriend in borrowed cars. She thought he was rich because each time he picked her up he had a different car. It was fun until he had spent all his money on her and had to write home to his parents because he was broke.

Victor couldn't stand to look at Teresa. He was sweaty with shame. "Yeah, well, I picked up a few things from movies and books and stuff like that." They left the class together. Teresa asked him if he would help her with her French.

"Sure, anytime," Victor said.

"I won't be bothering you, will I?"

"Oh no, I like being bothered."

"*Bonjour,*" Teresa said, leaving him outside her next class. She smiled and pushed wisps of hair from her face.

"Yeah, right, *bonjour,*" Victor said. He turned and headed to his class. The rose-bushes of shame on his face became bouquets of love. Teresa is a great girl, he thought. And Mr. Bueller is a good guy.

He raced to metal shop. After metal shop there was biology, and after biology a long sprint to the public library, where he checked out three French textbooks.

He was going to like seventh grade.

Review and Assess

Thinking About the Selection

1. **Respond:** What advice would you give Victor about the way he tries to impress Teresa?

2. **(a) Recall:** What does Victor do when Mr. Bueller asks if anyone knows French? **(b) Analyze:** Why does he behave this way?

3. **(a) Recall:** Why does Michael scowl? **(b) Compare:** What is similar about Michael's scowling and Victor's pretending to speak French?

4. **(a) Recall:** How does Victor view Teresa? **(b) Support:** What examples from the story indicate his feelings?

5. **(a) Infer:** What impressions do Victor, Michael, and Mr. Bueller want to make on the other characters? **(b) Draw Conclusions:** How do these impressions prevent the other characters from seeing Victor's, Michael's, and Mr. Bueller's real selves?

6. **(a) Analyze:** What does Victor learn from his experiences? **(b) Apply:** How can you apply that lesson to life in general?

Gary Soto

(b. 1952)
Gary Soto has a lot in common with the character Victor Rodriguez. Soto grew up in Fresno and once harvested crops in the fields of California.

Soto began writing while in college. In the fiction and poetry he's written since, he reaches back to the sense of belonging he felt in Fresno. He often writes for young adults, who he knows are also searching for their own community and their own place.

Melting Pot

Anna Quindlen

"Sunday Afternoon", Ralph Fasanella

My children are upstairs in the house next door, having dinner with the Ecuadorian family that lives on the top floor. The father speaks some English, the mother less than that. The two daughters are <u>fluent</u> in both their native and their adopted languages, but the youngest child, a son, a close friend of my two boys, speaks almost no Spanish. His parents thought it would be better that way. This doesn't surprise me; it was the way my mother was raised, American among Italians. I always suspected, hearing my grandfather talk about the "No Irish Need Apply" signs outside factories, hearing my mother talk about the neighborhood kids, who called her greaseball, that the American fable of the melting pot was a myth. Here in our neighborhood it exists, but like so many other things, it exists only person-to-person.

The letters in the local weekly tabloid[1] suggest that everybody hates everybody else here, and on a macro level they do. The old-timers are angry because they think the new moneyed professionals are taking over their town. The professionals are tired of being blamed for the neighborhood's rising rents, particularly since they are the ones paying them. The old immigrants are suspicious of the new ones. The new ones think the old ones are <u>bigots</u>. Nevertheless, on a micro level most of us get along. We are friendly with the

---

1. **tabloid** (tab′ loid′) *n.* small newspaper.

Ecuadorian family, with the Yugoslavs across the street, and with the Italians next door, mainly by virtue of our children's sidewalk friendships. It took awhile. Eight years ago we were the new people on the block, filling dumpsters with old plaster and lath, . . . (sitting) on the stoop with our demolition masks hanging around our necks like goiters.[2] We thought we could feel people staring at us from behind the sheer curtains on their windows. We were right.

My first apartment in New York was in a gritty warehouse district, the kind of place that makes your parents wince. A lot of old Italians lived around me, which suited me just fine because I was the granddaughter of old Italians. Their own children and grandchildren had moved to Long Island and New Jersey. All they had was me. All I had was them.

I remember sitting on a corner with a group of half a dozen elderly men, men who had known one another since they were boys sitting together on this same corner, watching a glazier install a great spread of tiny glass panes to make one wall of a restaurant in the ground floor of an old building across the street. The men laid bets on how long the panes, and the restaurant, would last. Two years later two of the men were dead, one had moved in with his married daughter in the suburbs, and the three remaining sat and watched dolefully as people waited each night for a table in the restaurant. "Twenty-two dollars for a piece of veal!" one of them would say, apropos of nothing.[3] But when I ate in the restaurant they never blamed me. "You're not one of them," one of the men explained. "You're one of me." It's an argument familiar to members of almost any embattled race or class: I like you, therefore you aren't like the rest of your kind, whom I hate.

Change comes hard in America, but it comes constantly. The butcher whose old shop is now an antiques store sits day after day outside the pizzeria here like a lost child. The old people across the street cluster together and discuss what kind of money they might be offered if the person who bought their building wants to turn it into condominiums. The greengrocer stocks yellow peppers and fresh rosemary for the gourmands, plum tomatoes and broad-leaf parsley for the older Italians, mangoes for the Indians. He doesn't carry plantains, he says, because you can buy them in the bodega.[4]

Sometimes the baby slips out with the bath water. I wanted to throw confetti the day that a family of rough types who propped their speakers on their station wagon and played heavy metal music at 3:00 A.M. moved out. I stood and smiled as the seedy bar at the corner was transformed into a slick Mexican restaurant.

Literary Analysis

Tone What details in the first two paragraphs convey Quindlen's attitude toward the people in her neighborhood?

✓Reading Check

What attitude does Quindlen say most people have toward others who are new or different?

---

2. goiters (goit´ ərz) *n.* swellings in the lower front of the neck caused by an enlarged thyroid gland.

3. apropos (ap´ rə pō´) **of nothing** without connection.

4. bodega (bō dā´ gə) *n.* small Hispanic grocery store.

But I liked some of the people who moved out at the same time the rough types did. And I'm not sure I have that much in common with the singles who have made the restaurant their second home.

Yet somehow now we seem to have reached a nice mix. About a third of the people in the neighborhood think of squid as calamari, about a third think of it as sushi, and about a third think of it as bait. Lots of the single people who have moved in during the last year or two are easygoing and good-tempered about all the kids. The old Italians have become philosophical about the new Hispanics, although they still think more of them should know English. The firebrand community organizer with the storefront on the block, the one who is always talking about people like us as though we stole our houses out of the open purse of a ninety-year-old blind widow, is pleasant to my boys.

Drawn in broad strokes, we live in a pressure cooker: oil and water, us and them. But if you come around at exactly the right time, you'll find members of all these groups gathered around complaining about the condition of the streets, on which everyone can agree. We melt together, then draw apart. I am the grand-daughter of immigrants, a young professional—either an <u>interloper</u> or a longtime resident, depending on your concept of time. I am one of them, and one of us.

interloper (in′ tər lō′ pər) *n.* one who intrudes on another

Review and Assess

Think About the Selection

1. **Respond:** Would you like to live in Anna Quindlen's neighborhood? Why or why not?

2. **(a) Recall:** Identify the different groups in Quindlen's neighborhood. **(b) Connect:** What experiences do most of the residents share? **(c) Interpret:** How do these shared experiences both unite and divide the residents?

3. **(a) Recall:** How does Quindlen feel about her neighbors? **(b) Analyze:** What does Quindlen's choice of a neighborhood reveal about what she finds important?

4. **(a) Recall:** How have Quindlen's children helped her get along with her neighbors? **(b) Draw Conclusions:** What advice would she give on how people of different cultures can get along?

5. **(a) Recall:** How is Quindlen both "one of them" and "one of us"? **(b) Make a Judgment:** Do you think it is possible to belong to both groups? **(c) Apply:** What does this work suggest about the way people live in U.S. city neighborhoods?

Anna Quindlen

(b. 1953)
Anna Quindlen spent five years reporting for *The New York Times,* covering issues relating to her family and her neighborhood. Her regular *Times* columns earned her a Pulitzer Prize in 1992. She left the newspaper to write novels and has published two bestsellers, *One True Thing* and *Black and Blue.*

"Melting Pot" originally appeared in "Life in the 30's," a popular column that Quindlen wrote from 1986 to 1988.

Review and Assess

Literary Analysis

Tone

1. What details in "Seventh Grade" suggest that Soto likes Victor and enjoys his behavior?
2. In your own words, describe the **tone** of "Seventh Grade."
3. On a chart like the one shown, list three details from "Melting Pot" that indicate Quindlen's enjoyment of the diversity in her neighborhood. Explain how each detail reveals her attitude.

Detail	How It Reveals Quindlen's Attitude

Comparing Literary Works

4. How do the characters feel about the ways in which they are different from other characters?
5. What do the characters do to try to overcome their differences with other characters?
6. Create and complete a chart like the one below to compare the ways that characters in these selections deal with the problems they have getting along with other people. On your chart, give two more examples for "Seventh Grade," and two for "Melting Pot."

Selection	Character's Problem	Character's Solution
"Seventh Grade"	Michael wants to be liked by girls at school.	Michael scowls like the men he sees in *GQ* magazine.

Reading Strategy

Identifying Idioms

7. Identify two **idioms** in "Seventh Grade."
8. Explain the difference between the literal and intended meanings of those idioms.
9. Identify and explain one idiom from "Melting Pot."

Extend Understanding

10. **Take a Position:** Do you think young Americans should be required to study more than one language? Why or why not?

Quick Review

A writer's **tone** is his or her attitude toward a subject. To review tone, see page 115.

An **idiom** is an expression that is unique to a region or language and that has a meaning different from its literal meaning. To review idioms, see page 115.

 Take It to the Net
www.phschool.com
Take the interactive self-test online to check your understanding of these selections.

Integrate Language Skills

Vocabulary Development Lesson

Word Analysis: Latin Prefix *inter-*

Quindlen says she fears that some people see her as an *interloper*. Understanding that the Latin prefix *inter-* means "among or between" can help you see that *interloper* means "someone who pushes in between others." On your paper, complete each sentence with one of the words below.

interlock   international   intersect

1. The neighborhood has an ___?___ feel.
2. Many hallways ___?___ in the school.
3. In a jigsaw puzzle, all the pieces ___?___.

Spelling Strategy

English words are often spelled with a *c* for the *k* sound before the vowels *a*, *o*, or *u*, as in *scowl*, and with a *k* before *e* and *i*. On your paper, complete each word correctly.

1. _een   2. s_are   3. _urvy   4. _ind

Fluency: Definitions

A **definition** is the meaning of a word. On your paper, match each numbered word from the literature you just read with its lettered definition.

1. fluent
2. interloper
3. elective
4. bigots
5. conviction
6. sheepishly

a. prejudiced people
b. optional course
c. belief
d. in a shy way
e. intruder
f. able to communicate easily

Grammar Lesson

Action Verbs and Linking Verbs

Verbs are words that express action (*swim*, *throw*) or state of being (*am, is, are, was, were*). An **action verb** tells what action is occurring: Victor *spoke* in French. A **linking verb** joins the subject of a sentence with a word or expression that describes or renames the subject: Victor *sounded* silly. Common linking verbs include *seem, appear, look, sound, stay*, and all forms of *be*. Notice that the following sentence uses both action and linking verbs:

            ACTION VERB   ACTION VERB
Victor didn't *say* anything, though he *thought*

            LINKING VERB
his friend *looked* pretty strange.

▶ *For more practice, see page R28, Exercise C.*
Practice On your paper, identify the action verbs and linking verbs in the following sentences.

1. Quindlen's neighborhood seems busy and vibrant.
2. Many residents are hopeful about the peaceful feelings in the community.
3. Victor already speaks Spanish and English.
4. Mr. Bueller smiled at Victor's behavior.
5. Victor was embarrassed.

Writing Application In a paragraph, describe your first day of seventh grade. Then, circle the action verbs and underline the linking verbs you used.

𝒲𝒢 *Prentice Hall Writing and Grammar Connection: Chapter 15, Sections 1–2*

Writing Lesson

Comparison and Contrast

Victor might have been more prepared for seventh grade if someone had told him what it was like. Include examples from the story and from your experience to write an essay in which you explain what seventh grade is like by comparing and contrasting it with sixth grade.

Prewriting   Review the story and jot down some of Victor's experiences. Use these as the beginning of a list of points you will compare and contrast. Finally, select three or four items that you wish to include in your essay.

Drafting   Develop each point of comparision with an anecdote (brief story), a description, or a specific example.

Model: Develop Each Point

Seventh grade involves more homework than sixth grade.
On a typical school night, I read five pages of science,
a section of social studies, and a short story for English class.
I also do a page of math problems. In sixth grade I usually
had homework in only two subjects each night.

> The writer supports the first sentence with details of homework for each class and a comment about the amount of time spent.

Revising   Ask a peer reviewer to identify comparisons that need more explanation or support. Add details to make your comparisions clearer.

W̶G Prentice Hall Writing and Grammar Connection: Chapter 8, Section 3

Extension Activities

Listening and Speaking Role-play a meeting of a neighborhood improvement board. Two students acting as residents should

- think of a problem, such as disagreement over building a skatepark.
- prepare evidence to support their claims.
- state their problem and support their side.

Others students, acting as board members, should

- prepare and ask probing questions to find out details of the disagreement.
- make suggestions to help the neighbors resolve their differences. **[Group Activity]**

Research and Technology Like Victor's job of picking grapes, employment in an area is often related to a local product or industry. Find the main industry, agricultural products, and businesses of your region. Then, go to your local Chamber of Commerce or job center to see what jobs are available. Present your findings in an **oral report.**

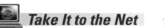 **Take It to the Net**   www.phschool.com

Go online for an additional research activity using the Internet.

Prepare to Read

Fable ◆ If— ◆ Thumbprint

 Take It to the Net

Visit www.phschool.com for interactive activities and instruction related to these selections, including
- background
- graphic organizers
- literary elements
- reading strategies

Preview

Connecting to the Literature

There are moments in our lives when we feel a great sense of accomplishment—passing a tough exam, mastering a rollerblading trick, or getting the lead role in a play. At these times, we celebrate our achievements, determination, and abilities. Connect to the poems in this group by thinking about times you have felt the joy of reaching a goal.

Background

Every person—even an identical twin—is different from everyone else. Although two people may look similar or have similar abilities, the combination of likes and dislikes, strengths and weaknesses, is unique in each person. These poems—"Fable," "If—," and "Thumbprint," by poets Ralph Waldo Emerson, Rudyard Kipling, and Eve Merriam—celebrate that uniqueness.

Literary Analysis

Rhyme

Rhyme—the repetition of sounds at the ends of words—is one of the elements that gives poetry its musical qualities. Rhyme is also used to emphasize or highlight important words and ideas.

There are several types of rhymes:

- **End rhyme** The last word of a line rhymes with the last word of another line. A poem's **rhyme scheme** is the end-rhyme pattern.
- **Exact rhyme** Word endings sound exactly alike, but the beginnings are different, as in *disgrace* and *place*.
- **Half rhymes** Word sounds are similar but not identical, as in *squirrel* and *quarrel*.

Comparing Literary Works

Rhythm—the pattern of stressed (/) and unstressed (∪) syllables—also contributes to the music of poetry. Notice this predictable rhythm:

> ∪ / ∪ / ∪ / ∪ / ∪
> If you can keep your head when all about you
> ∪ / ∪ / ∪ / ∪ / ∪
> Are losing theirs and blaming it on you,

Compare and contrast the ways the poets use rhythm and rhyme. How do rhythm and rhyme affect the impact of each poem?

Reading Strategy

Paraphrasing Figurative Language

Poets often use figurative language—language not meant to be taken literally—to create a striking word picture. Help yourself see the picture by **paraphrasing figurative language**. When you **paraphrase**, you restate lines in your own words.

To fully appreciate each poem, ask yourself the following focus questions:

1. What unusual comparisons or expressions does the poet use?

2. What do the words really mean?

As you read, paraphrase each unusual comparison or expression in a chart like the one shown.

Poet's Words	Paraphrase
I make my own interior weather . . .	I can choose what attitude I will have . . .

Vocabulary Development

spry (sprī) *adj.* full of life; active; nimble (p. 131)

impostors (im päs´ tərz) *n.* people who trick or deceive others by pretending to be what they are not (p. 132)

virtue (vʉr´ choō) *n.* moral goodness (p. 132)

unique (yoō nēk´) *adj.* unlike any other; singular (p. 134)

base (bās) *adj.* lowly; inferior (p. 134)

Fable

Ralph Waldo Emerson

The mountain and the squirrel
Had a quarrel;
And the former called the latter 'Little Prig.'
Bun replied,
5 'You are doubtless very big;
But all sorts of things and weather
Must be taken in together,
To make up a year
And a sphere.
10 And I think it no disgrace
To occupy my place.
If I'm not so large as you,
You are not so small as I,
And not half so <u>spry</u>.
15 I'll not deny you make
A very pretty squirrel track;
Talents differ; all is well and wisely put;
If I cannot carry forests on my back,
Neither can you crack a nut.'

spry (sprī) *adj.* full of life;
active; nimble

Ralph Waldo Emerson

(1803–1882)

Ralph Waldo Emerson had a lifelong motto. This phrase, "Trust yourself," helped direct many of his decisions and actions. Emerson believed in people's inborn judgment—their ability to evaluate the world and make the right choices. From his Boston, Massachusetts, boyhood to his years as a minister, Emerson worked hard at understanding his world. In writing about his ideas, he changed the way many people viewed their place in the world.

Review and Assess

Thinking About the Selection

1. **Respond:** Do you agree or disagree with the squirrel? Why?

2. **(a) Recall:** According to the squirrel, what makes up a year? **(b) Interpret:** Why does the squirrel compare its place in the world to the parts of a year? **(c) Extend:** What are some other comparisons you could make to express the same idea?

3. **(a) Recall:** What are two differences between the squirrel and the mountain? **(b) Draw Conclusions:** What message about the value of the individual does Emerson communicate through these differences? **(c) Evaluate:** Do you think his message is convincing? Why or why not?

4. **Apply:** How might this poem help family members, classmates, or co-workers understand one another better?

If—

Rudyard Kipling

If you can keep your head when all about you
    Are losing theirs and blaming it on you,
If you can trust yourself when all men doubt you,
    But make allowance for their doubting too;
5 If you can wait and not be tired by waiting,
    Or being lied about, don't deal in lies,
Or being hated, don't give way to hating,
    And yet don't look too good, nor talk too wise:

If you can dream—and not make dreams your master;
10   If you can think—and not make thoughts your aim;
If you can meet with Triumph and Disaster
    And treat those two <u>imposters</u> just the same;
If you can bear to hear the truth you've spoken
    Twisted by knaves to make a trap for fools,
15 Or watch the things you gave your life to, broken,
    And stoop and build 'em up with worn-out tools:

If you can make one heap of all your winnings
    And risk it on one turn of pitch-and-toss,
And lose, and start again at your beginnings
20   And never breathe a word about your loss;
If you can force your heart and nerve and sinew
    To serve your turn long after they are gone,
And so hold on when there is nothing in you
    Except the Will which says to them: "Hold on!"

25 If you can talk with crowds and keep your <u>virtue</u>,
    Or walk with Kings—nor lose the common touch,
If neither foes nor loving friends can hurt you,

impostors (im päs´ tərz) *n.* people who trick or deceive others by pretending to be what they are not

virtue (vʉr´ chōō) *n.* moral goodness

If all men count with you, but none too much;
If you can fill the unforgiving minute
30   With sixty seconds' worth of distance run,
Yours is the Earth and everything that's in it,
    And—which is more—you'll be a Man, my son!

Review and Assess

Thinking About the Selection

1. **Respond:** Which of the conditions described in this poem would you find hardest to fulfill? Which might be easiest to fulfill? Explain.

2. **(a) Recall:** Name five conditions that Kipling describes. **(b) Connect:** What is similar about some of the conditions you named?

3. **(a) Recall:** According to Kipling, how should a person regard other people? **(b) Assess:** Do you think this is a reasonable approach to life? Explain.

4. **(a) Recall:** Who are the two "impostors" in the poem? **(b) Interpret:** Why does Kipling advise treating them as impostors?

5. **(a) Draw Conclusions:** What qualities does Kipling value in people? **(b) Interpret:** If one possesses these qualities, what is the result, according to the poem? **(c) Apply:** What general statement about maturity is Kipling making?

6. **Generalize:** Do you think young people today can relate to this poem and benefit from its advice? Why or why not?

Rudyard Kipling

(1865–1936)

"Be brave, and do what needs to be done" would be a suitable motto for Rudyard Kipling. His approach to life may have dated back to growing up in India at a time when it was ruled by the British. In that time and place, a British boy was expected to be brave and to know where he was going. The poem "If—" outlines some of these expectations. "If—" is a tiny part of Kipling's work. His novels, plays, and other writings won him a Nobel Prize for Literature in 1907.

Thumbprint

Eve Merriam

On the pad of my thumb
are whorls, whirls, wheels
in a <u>unique</u> design:
mine alone.
5   What a treasure to own!
My own flesh, my own feelings.
No other, however grand or <u>base</u>,
can ever contain the same.
My signature,
10   thumbing the pages of my time.
My universe key,
my singularity.

Impress, implant,
I am myself,
15   of all my atom parts I am the sum.
And out of my blood and my brain
I make my own interior weather,
my own sun and rain.
Imprint my mark upon the world,
20   whatever I shall become.

unique (yōō nēk´) *adj.*
unlike any other; singular

base (bās) *adj.* lowly;
inferior

Review and Assess

Thinking About the Selection

1. **Respond:** Does this poem come close to stating your life motto? Explain.

2. **(a) Recall:** What is the most important physical feature for the speaker of Merriam's poem? **(b) Analyze:** Why is this feature so precious to her?

3. **(a) Infer:** How does a thumbprint show a person's individuality? **(b) Support:** How does Merriam support the idea that a thumbprint is a key to the universe?

4. **(a) Interpret:** Explain the meaning of the lines "I am myself, of all my atom parts I am the sum." **(b) Assess:** Why do you think people place a high value on individuality?

Review and Assess

Literary Analysis

Rhyme

1. Identify two words of half rhyme in the last four lines of "Fable."
2. Identify two words of exact rhyme in the last four lines of "Fable."
3. What is the rhyme scheme of "Fable"? On a separate sheet of paper, copy and continue the chart below.

Line number	Last word in line	End rhyme
line 1	squirrel	A
line 2	quarrel	A
line 3	Prig	B
line 4	replied	C

4. Complete a similar chart for lines 1–8 of "If—" and of "Thumbprint."

Comparing Literary Works

5. Which poem has the most regular rhyme scheme? Explain.
6. Copy the first eight lines of each poem, and mark the rhythm of stressed (/) and unstressed (∪) beats, as shown.

    ∪   /   /   ∪ ∪ ∪   / ∪
    The mountain and the squirrel
    ∪ ∪ ∪
    Had a quarrel;
    ∪ ∪   / ∪   ∪ ∪ / ∪ ∪ /
    And the former called the latter 'Little Prig.'

7. Which poem has the most regular or predictable rhythm? Explain.

Reading Strategy

Paraphrasing Figurative Language

8. (a) In lines 6–9 of "Fable," what is the "sphere" to which the squirrel refers? (b) Restate these lines in your own words.
9. (a) In line 5 of "Thumbprint," what does the poet mean by "treasure"? (b) Paraphrase lines 1–8.
10. Identify two examples of figurative language in the last eight lines of "If—." Paraphrase the last eight lines.

Extend Understanding

11. **Social Studies Connection:** How might these three poems help people understand one another better?

Quick Review

Rhyme is the repetition of sounds at the ends of words. The rhyme scheme of a poem is its pattern of rhymes. To review rhyme, see page 129.

Rhythm is the pattern of beats, or stresses, in language. To review rhythm, see page 129.

Figurative language is language that is not meant to be taken literally.
Paraphrasing is restating something in your own words.

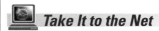 **Take It to the Net**

www.phschool.com
Take the interactive self-test online to check your understanding of these selections.

Integrate Language Skills

Vocabulary Development Lesson

Word Analysis: Latin Prefix *uni-*

The Latin prefix *uni-* means "one." On your paper, explain how the meaning "one" contributes to the meaning of the whole word.

1. union
2. unite
3. universe
4. unit

Spelling Strategy

The word *unique* demonstrates this spelling rule: When using *qu* to make the *k* sound at the end of a word, add an *e*. On your paper, write these words, completing them with the correct spelling of the *k* sound that uses *qu*. Then, use each word in a sentence.

1. mysti___?___
2. techni___?___
3. physi___?___
4. bouti___?___

Fluency: Definitions

On your paper, answer the following questions. Explain each answer.

1. Would a good dancer be a *spry* person?
2. Who is more likely to be *unique* in a group photo—a soccer player in a team picture or a bride posing with her family?
3. Why would an *impostor* use a false name?
4. Is truthfulness a *virtue* or a fault?
5. Would you expect a *base* metal to be valuable?
6. If you have invented a *unique* recipe, is it likely to be found in a cookbook?
7. Would a person who behaves in a *base* way be doing a good deed?
8. Should you strive to expand your *virtues* or get rid of them?

Grammar Lesson

Verb Tenses

Verbs are words that indicate action. Verbs have **tenses,** or different forms, that tell at what time—in the present, in the past, or in the future—something happens.

Present tense: I *make* my own interior weather, . . .
Past tense: The mountain and the squirrel / *Had* a quarrel; / And the former *called* the latter "Little Prig."
Future tense: *I'll [will]* not *deny* you make / A very pretty squirrel track; . . .

▶ *For more practice, see page R32, Exercise B.*
Practice Identify the tense of each verb.

1. She *pressed* her thumb firmly on the inkpad.
2. The advice in "If—" *lingers* in my mind.
3. The mountain and the squirrel *compare* their strengths and weaknesses.
4. The mountain *will respect* the squirrel.
5. Rudyard Kipling *believed* in being brave.

Writing Application Write one sentence for each of the following words in the present tense. Then, rewrite each sentence in the past tense and again in the future tense.

keep   lose   risk   fill   walk

W̶G̶ Prentice Hall Writing and Grammar Connection: Chapter 22, Section 2

Writing Lesson

Persuasive Argument

Make a case for individuality. Write a persuasive composition that explains, for example, whether you should be allowed to decorate your own bedroom.

Prewriting First, write a single sentence in which you state your position. Then, make a list of reasons you feel as you do. Next to each reason on the list, jot down details that illustrate, explain, or support the reason.

Drafting As you draft, use your notes to organize and support your argument. Begin with your second-most important reason. Then, present the rest from least to most important.

Revising Highlight your reasons, and number them in order of importance. If necessary, rearrange them so that they build in importance.

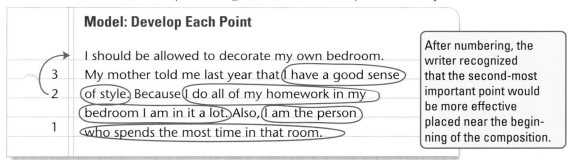

Model: Develop Each Point

I should be allowed to decorate my own bedroom.

3 My mother told me last year that I have a good sense of style. Because I do all of my homework in my bedroom I am in it a lot. Also, I am the person who spends the most time in that room.

2

1

After numbering, the writer recognized that the second-most important point would be more effective placed near the beginning of the composition.

*W*G *Prentice Hall Writing and Grammar Connection: Chapter 7, Section 4*

Extension Activities

Listening and Speaking Choose one of the poems to **read aloud** for the class. Review the poem, paying attention to its punctuation, rhymes, and rhythms. Practice reading the poem aloud in front of a mirror. Focus especially on the following speaking techniques:

- Vary the speed of your voice. Slow down to emphasize key words and lines.
- Speak every word clearly and distinctly.
- Make eye contact with your audience.

After you have read, ask the class to critique your reading in each of the categories you practiced.

Research and Technology In groups of four, research the life and times of Emerson or Kipling. Have some of the group collect and write captions for visuals and others prepare a timeline. Then, put together a presentation, including visual materials. Have each person report part of the group's findings. [**Group Activity**]

Take It to the Net   www.phschool.com

Go online for an additional research activity using the Internet.

CONNECTIONS
Literature and Technology
Fingerprints and Identity

The author of "Thumbprint" speaks of how she treasures her thumbprints because they are like no others. In fact, the unique quality to fingerprints was first observed scientifically as early as the late 1600s. Those observations became the base for the fingerprinting system used today in most English-speaking countries (called the Henry system).

Fingerprint Patterns

In general, there are three basic patterns of fingerprints: arches, loops, and whorls. Experts also check for more specific details, such as ridges that branch or cross. These basic patterns do not change throughout life, and even twins have separate fingerprint patterns.

The Technology of Fingerprinting

The unusual accuracy of fingerprint identification has caused it to become even more widespread in recent years. Computers that read fingerprints now permit users to log on without a password. A photograph of the fingerprint is translated into a digital code, which is then compared to the fingerprint scanned when the user next places a finger on the reader.

Other Forms of Identification

Your body is unique in many other ways as well. Voice verification, for example, is a way of matching your voice with sound patterns kept on file that trace the unique way you speak. One of the advantages of this is that access to computer systems can be gained over the phone. Another new form of identification based on the body's originality is retinal scanning. This is accurate because blood vessels on the back of the retina seldom change in one's lifetime. Expense and the eye's sensitivity, however, keep this form of identification from being more widely used.

Connecting Literature and Technology

1. Does the poet give enough information to identify the type of pattern (arch, loop, or whorl) that her fingerprint has? If so, which is it and where does that information appear in the poem?

2. Eve Merriam calls her thumbprint her signature. How is a signature different from the forms of identification mentioned in this article?

3. What is the difference between "identity" and "identification"? Use details from the poem and this feature in your answer.

Memos

About Memos

A **memorandum**, or memo, is a brief, informal communication between people or groups who share an interest in a common workplace issue. A memo may communicate information about a company policy or regulation, a special meeting, promotions within the company, or other matters that affect all or most of the company's employees, the people in the workplace. Memos sometimes come with attachments—additional documents related to the content of the memo.

Most memos follow a typical format and style.

1. They are written in block format, with each new element beginning at the left margin.
2. The headings clearly state the sender, audience, date, and topic.
3. The sentences are direct and the information is communicated as briefly as possible.
4. They outline any action the receiver of the memo should take.

Reading Strategy

Locate Information in Documents

The headings and text structure of memos can be used to locate information quickly and efficiently. The standard headings indicate the sender, audience, date, topic, copies, and attachments. Use the headings to locate those details.

The body of a memo is broken into short, focused text blocks to make information easy to locate. Each new topic begins a new text block, and some text blocks may have only one sentence. Each text block begins on the left side of the page.

Abbreviations Used in Memos

TO:	identifies the person or people to whom the memo is directed
FR:	**From:** abbreviation for *from*; identifies the person or people sending the memo
RE:	**Regarding:** identifies the subject of the memo
DATE:	identifies the date the memo is sent
cc:	**copies:** identifies others who have received copies
encl:	**enclosure:** In a business letter or with a memo, additional, separate documents called enclosures are sometimes included.

Memorandum

TO: All Employees at Needham Facility
FR: John Charles, Facilities Manager
DATE: 12/1/00
RE: Photo ID's
CC: Captain Schaeffer, Security Chief
         Don Rolds, USR Facilities Manager
         Linda O'Connell, Director of Human Resources

> Although the memo is not addressed to these people, they received copies.

On January 4th and 5th from 3pm to 5pm, I will be taking identification pictures of all the new employees or anyone who is missing their picture on their employee identification badge. Please report to the security office during the specified times if you need a photo taken for your badge. Copies of identification photos will also be sent to Human Resources to be included in the personnel files.

> The most important information is stated in the first paragraph.

Within the next 2 weeks we will be disabling any security badges that do not have photos. After 12/15/00, no one will be admitted to the building without a badge or written authorization. Please make sure that you have a photo on your security badge.

> Additional details and information follow.

My office is located on the second floor, first door on the left after you pass the Human Resources office.

> In a memo a single sentence may be called out as a paragraph to make specific information easy to find.

If you have any questions or need to arrange an alternate time, please e-mail or call me (x1208).

encl. Map to security office.

Check Your Comprehension

1. For how long can employees continue to use badges without photos?
2. Which two groups of employees need to have their photos taken?
3. Why do employees need identification badges?

Applying the Reading Strategy

Locating Information

4. Complete the chart based on the information in the memo.

	Who sent the memo?	On what date was the memo sent?	What is the subject of the memo?	To whom is the memo addressed?	Who else received a copy of the memo?
Answer					
Abbreviation or head used to locate the information					

Activity

Writing a Memo

Write a memo based on the information in the chart below. If possible, use a word-processing program to format the memo.

To:	All members of Community Volunteers Group
From:	Joan Bellows, Secretary
Subject:	New parental or guardian permission form
Date:	January 3, 2001
Subject:	To advise members of the new school policy adopted by the Board of Education that indicates all volunteers must have parents or guardians sign the permission form
Additional Document Enclosed:	A permission form

Contrasting Informational Materials

Memos, Letters, and Notes

Because a memo's purpose is to directly communicate needed information in an efficient and professional style, it is more formal than a note, but it is less formal than a business letter. (See page R16 for an example of a business letter.) Explain why it would be more difficult to locate the details outlined in this memo if they were written in an informal note.

Prepare to Read

Mother to Son ◆ The Courage That My Mother Had
The Hummingbird That Lived Through Winter

Organdy Collar, 1936, Edmund Archer, Whitney Museum of American Art

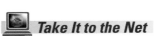

Take It to the Net

Visit www.phschool.com for interactive activities and instruction related to these selections, including
- background
- graphic organizers
- literary elements
- reading strategies

Preview

Connecting to the Literature

In the three selections in this group, writers celebrate the inspiring strength and wisdom of adult family members and friends. Connect to the subjects of the selections by thinking about adults who have guided you or set an example for you.

Background

"The Hummingbird That Lived Through Winter" begins with a hummingbird dying of cold. Hummingbirds are tiny jewel-colored birds. Their quick movements and shiny feathers make them a beautiful sight in summer throughout most of the United States. In winter, hummingbirds travel south, because their tiny bodies are not strong enough to withstand cold winter temperatures.

Literary Analysis

Symbol

A **symbol** is an object that conveys an idea beyond itself. For example, a dove is often used to represent peace. Symbols are used to express ideas in a concrete and memorable way. In the following example, the stairway with tacks in it represents life's struggles.

> Life for me ain't been no crystal stair.
> It's had tacks in it,

Look for symbols in these works by noting items that seem to be of special importance to the speaker. On an organizer like this one, note the details that could also be used to describe something else.

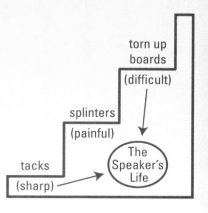

Comparing Literary Works

In "The Courage That My Mother Had" and "Mother to Son," symbols are used to convey messages about courage and determination. Compare and contrast the messages. Use these focus questions to guide you:

1. What qualities do the characters in the two poems share?
2. What are the poets' attitudes toward the characters and the qualities they possess?
3. How do the messages of the poems compare?

Reading Strategy

Using Word Parts

One way to figure out an unfamiliar word is to look for a word part that you recognize. The familiar part can give you a clue to the meaning of the whole word. For example, in the word *transformation*, you can see the familiar word part *form*. **Trans form a tion** Breaking the word into parts reveals a clue that the word might have something to do with the form, or shape, of something.

As you encounter unfamiliar words in these selections, look for word parts that give clues to the meaning of the whole word.

Vocabulary Development

quarried (kwôr´ ēd) *adj.* carved out of the ground (p. 145)

brooch (brōch) *n.* large ornamental pin worn on a blouse or dress (p. 145)

pathetic (pə thet´ ik) *adj.* arousing pity, sorrow, and sympathy (p. 147)

transformation (trans´ fər mā´ shən) *n.* change in condition or outward appearance (p. 147)

MOTHER TO SON

Langston Hughes

Well, son, I'll tell you:
Life for me ain't been no crystal stair.
It's had tacks in it,
And splinters,
5 And boards torn up,
And places with no carpet on the floor—
Bare.
But all the time
I'se been a-climbin' on,
10 And reachin' landin's,
And turnin' corners,
And sometimes goin' in the dark
Where there ain't been no light.
So boy, don't you turn back.
15 Don't you set down on the steps
'Cause you finds it's kinder hard.
Don't you fall now—
For I'se still goin', honey,
I'se still climbin',
20 And life for me ain't been no crystal stair.

Langston Hughes

(1902–1967)

Langston Hughes was one of the main figures in the Harlem Renaissance, a creative movement among African Americans that took place in the 1920s in the New York City community of Harlem.

Hughes was a prolific and varied writer. His more than fifty books include novels, short stories, plays, histories, children's books, and autobiographies. But it is Hughes's poetry for which he is best known. His poems were some of the first to capture the rhythms of jazz, a musical form that was young in his day.

The Courage That My Mother Had

Edna St. Vincent Millay

The courage that my mother had
Went with her, and is with her still:
Rock from New England quarried;
Now granite in a granite hill.

5   The golden brooch my mother wore
She left behind for me to wear;
I have no thing I treasure more:
Yet, it is something I could spare.

Oh, if instead she'd left to me
10   The thing she took into the grave!—
That courage like a rock, which she
Has no more need of, and I have.

quarried (kwôr´ ēd) *adj.* carved out of the ground

brooch (brōch) *n.* large ornamental pin worn on a blouse or dress

Review and Assess

Thinking About the Selections

1. **Respond:** Would you like to know the mothers described in these poems? Why or why not?

2. **(a) Recall:** In "Mother to Son," what does the mother say about her life? **(b) Analyze:** What comparison does she make to develop this point? **(c) Apply:** How does her personal experience influence the advice she gives her son?

3. **(a) Analyze:** What qualities does the mother in "Mother to Son" demonstrate through her words and actions? **(b) Synthesize:** Why does she need these qualities?

4. **(a) Recall:** What has happened to the speaker's mother in "The Courage That My Mother Had"? **(b) Interpret:** Which lines from the poem reveal her fate? **(c) Draw Conclusions:** Why does the speaker need courage more than her mother does?

5. **(a) Recall:** What physical item did the mother leave behind for the speaker? **(b) Interpret:** Why would the speaker rather have her mother's character than the item her mother left her?

Edna St. Vincent Millay

(1892–1950)

Edna St. Vincent Millay was born and raised in Rockland, Maine. The oldest of three girls, she was given books and music lessons by her mother, who encouraged her to lead an artist's life.

Millay began writing poems at five years old, and published her first poem at fourteen. She developed her writing further in college and became a central figure in New York literary circles in the 1920s.

Millay published many volumes of poetry in her lifetime, one of which earned her the first Pulitzer Prize for poetry awarded to a woman.

The *Hummingbird* That Lived Through Winter

William Saroyan

There was a hummingbird once which in the wintertime did not leave our neighborhood in Fresno, California.

I'll tell you about it.

Across the street lived old Dikran [dèk´ rän]. who was almost blind. He was past eighty and his wife was only a few years younger. They had a little house that was as neat inside as it was ordinary outside—except for old Dikran's garden, which was the best thing of its kind in the world. Plants, bushes, trees—all strong, in sweet black moist earth whose guardian was old Dikran. All things from the sky loved this spot in our poor neighborhood, and old Dikran loved *them*.

One freezing Sunday, in the dead of winter, as I came home from Sunday School I saw old Dikran standing in the middle of the street trying to distinguish what was in his hand. Instead of going into our house to the fire, as I had wanted to do,

Literary Analysis
Symbol What symbol that represents life and abundance is found in this paragraph?

I stood on the steps of the front porch and watched the old man. He would turn around and look upward at his trees and then back to the palm of his hand. He stood in the street at least two minutes and then at last he came to me. He held his hand out, and in Armenian he said, "What is this in my hand?"

I looked.

"It is a hummingbird," I said half in English and half in Armenian. Hummingbird I said in English because I didn't know its name in Armenian.

"What is that?" old Dikran asked.

"The little bird," I said. "You know. The one that comes in the summer and stands in the air and then shoots away. The one with the wings that beat so fast you can't see them. It's in your hand. It's dying."

"Come with me," the old man said. "I can't see, and the old lady's at church. I can feel its heart beating. Is it in a bad way? Look again, once."

I looked again. It was a sad thing to behold. This wonderful little creature of summertime in the big rough hand of the old peasant. Here it was in the cold of winter, absolutely helpless and <u>pathetic</u>, not suspended in a shaft of summer light, not the most alive thing in the world, but the most helpless and heartbreaking.

"It's dying," I said.

The old man lifted his hand to his mouth and blew warm breath on the little thing in his hand which he could not even see. "Stay now," he said in Armenian. "It is not long till summer. Stay, swift and lovely."

We went into the kitchen of his little house, and while he blew warm breath on the bird he told me what to do.

"Put a tablespoonful of honey over the gas fire and pour it into my hand, but be sure it is not too hot."

This was done.

After a moment the hummingbird began to show signs of fresh life. The warmth of the room, the vapor of the warm honey—and, well, the will and love of the old man. Soon the old man could feel the change in his hand, and after a moment or two the hummingbird began to take little dabs of the honey.

"It will live," the old man announced. "Stay and watch."

The <u>transformation</u> was incredible. The old man kept his hand generously open, and I expected the helpless bird to shoot upward out of his hand, suspend itself in space, and scare the life out of me—which is exactly what happened. The new life of the little bird was magnificent. It spun about in the little kitchen, going to the window, coming back to the heat, suspending, circling as if it were summertime and it had never felt better in its whole life.

The old man sat on the plain chair, blind but attentive. He listened carefully and tried to see, but of course he couldn't. He kept asking

pathetic (pə thet′ ik) *adj.* arousing pity, sorrow, and sympathy

Reading Strategy
Using Word Parts Into what parts would you break up *tablespoonful*?

transformation (trans′ fər mā′ shən) *n.* change in condition or outward appearance

✓**Reading Check**

Why is the hummingbird dying?

about the bird, how it seemed to be, whether it showed signs of weakening again, what its spirit was, and whether or not it appeared to be restless; and I kept describing the bird to him.

When the bird was restless and wanted to go, the old man said, "Open the window and let it go."

"Will it live?" I asked.

"It is alive now and wants to go," he said. "Open the window."

I opened the window, the hummingbird stirred about here and there, feeling the cold from the outside, suspended itself in the area of the open window, stirring this way and that, and then it was gone.

"Close the window," the old man said.

We talked a minute or two and then I went home.

The old man claimed the hummingbird lived through that winter, but I never knew for sure. I saw hummingbirds again when summer came, but I couldn't tell one from the other.

One day in the summer I asked the old man.

"Did it live?"

"The little bird?" he said.

"Yes," I said. "That we gave the honey to. You remember. The little bird that was dying in the winter. Did it live?"

"Look about you," the old man said. "Do you see the bird?"

"I see humming*birds*," I said.

"Each of them is our bird," the old man said. "Each of them, each of them," he said swiftly and gently.

Reading Strategy
Using Word Parts What word in this sentence is made up of a word root and a prefix?

Review and Assess

Thinking About the Selection

1. **Respond:** Would you have let the hummingbird go again, or would you have tried to keep it inside until spring? Explain.

2. **(a) Recall:** What does Dikran do when he finds the lifeless hummingbird? **(b) Support:** What do his actions reveal about his feelings for nature and living creatures?

3. **(a) Recall:** What does the narrator do to help Dikran? **(b) Interpret:** What does the narrator think about the old man's efforts to save the bird?

4. **(a) Recall:** What does the old man do after the bird gains new life? **(b) Analyze:** Why does he take this action?

5. **(a) Infer:** What do you learn about the two characters in this story from their assumptions about the hummingbird's survival? **(b) Compare and Contrast:** Compare and contrast how the two characters look at the world.

6. **Assess:** How much does it matter if the hummingbird they see in the summer is the same bird as the one they treated? Explain.

William Saroyan

(1908–1981)

William Saroyan was born in Fresno, California, the son of immigrants from Armenia. He spent part of his childhood in an orphanage and left school at fifteen. Although his childhood was difficult, he grew up to write often of his family and other Armenian immigrants he had known as a boy. His play *The Time of Your Life* won a Pulitzer Prize in 1940. Saroyan refused to accept the award, however, because he didn't think it was better than any of his other works.

Review and Assess

Literary Analysis

Symbol

1. What does the mother in "Mother to Son" do despite the tacks and splinters on the staircase?
2. In "The Courage That My Mother Had," what qualities of granite suggest courage?
3. **(a)** What does the hummingbird **symbolize** for Dikran? **(b)** What details help you decide?

Comparing Literary Works

4. What qualities do the mothers in the two poems share?
5. What is different about how these qualities are conveyed to readers?
6. In which poem do we learn more about the mother? Explain.
7. In which poem do we learn more about the speaker?
8. What is similar and different about the messages the two poems convey?

Reading Strategy

Using Word Parts

9. For each word, identify the **word part** or parts you recognize. Explain how these word parts contribute to the overall meanings of the words.

	Word Part	Meaning of Whole Word
(a) guardian		
(b) tablespoonful		
(c) weakening		

10. Besides the word *attentive*, what are two other words that begin with the word part *attend* or *attent*.

Extend Understanding

11. **Science Connection:** From a scientist's view, is it likely that the hummingbird survived the winter? Why or why not?
12. **Evaluate:** **(a)** How do you define courage? **(b)** How important do you think courage is?

Quick Review

A **symbol** is an object that represents an idea beyond itself. To review symbol, see page 143.

Being able to recognize and analyze **word parts** will help you figure out the meanings of unfamiliar words. To review word parts, see page 143.

 Take It to the Net

www.phschool.com
Take the interactive self-test online to check your understanding of these selections.

Integrate Language Skills

Vocabulary Development Lesson

Word Analysis: Latin Prefix *trans-*

A **prefix** is a part of a word added to the beginning of a base word to change or influence its meaning. The Latin prefix *trans-* means "across, through, over, or beyond." Words that contain the prefix usually involve change or movement. Add *trans-* to the following words or word parts. Then, write the letter of the definition of each word.

1. *-late*   2. *-continental*   3. *-lucent*   4. *-form*

   a. change shape
   b. change from one language to another
   c. extending across a continent
   d. allowing light to shine through

Fluency: Sentence Completions

On your paper, complete each sentence with the correct word from the vocabulary list.

1. The little girl's grief over the dead butterfly was ____?____ to behold.
2. The stones were ____?____ nearby.
3. Millay remembers her mother's gold ____?____.
4. The man's efforts caused a ____?____ in the bird.

Spelling Strategy

To form the plural of words ending in *ch*, always add *-es*, as in *brooches*. On your paper, make these words plural.

1. watch   2. church   3. ditch

Grammar Lesson

Parts of Verbs

There are four main forms for every verb, called the **principal parts.** These parts are used to form verb tenses—the forms that show time. The principal parts of a regular verb such as *climb* are *climb* (present tense), *climbing* (present participle), *climbed* (past tense), and *has* or *have climbed* (past participle). The past tense and/or past participles of irregular verbs, such as *be*, are formed in different ways.

Base (present)	Present Participle	Past	Past Participle
reach	reaching	reached	(have, has, had) reached
am, be	being	was, were	(have, has, had) been
go	going	went	(have, had, had) gone

▶ *For more practice, see page R32, Exercise A.*
Practice Copy the following chart on your paper. Then, complete it with the missing principal parts of verbs.

Base (present)	Present Participle	Past	Past Participle
	talking	talked	
	choosing		(have, has, had) chosen
find			(have, has, had) found

Writing Application Write four sentences about one of the selections in this section. In each sentence, use a different principal part of the verb *try*.

W/G *Prentice Hall Writing and Grammar Connection: Chapter 22, Section 1*

Writing Lesson

Prepare a Database

Each of these works communicates a message about courage. Prepare a database—a collection of data or information that can be revised, retrieved, and organized—of works that illustrate or inspire courage.

Prewriting List at least five works in each of the following genres, or types: Movies, Books, Short Stories, True Stories.

Drafting Using one note card for each work, supply information in the categories shown in the model. In a computer database, each category of information is called a "field." Each card, or "record," must have the same fields. If possible, use a computer program to prepare a database from your cards.

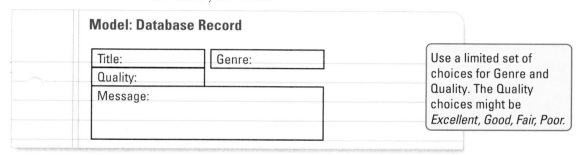

Model: Database Record

Title:
Genre:
Quality:
Message:

Use a limited set of choices for Genre and Quality. The Quality choices might be *Excellent, Good, Fair, Poor.*

Revising Sort your records once by each field. Decide whether you might like to add another field to sort on. If you add a field to one record, add it to all records.

WG Prentice Hall Writing and Grammar Connection: Chapter 7, Section 3

Extension Activities

Listening and Speaking In groups of three, **role-play** a meeting in which Saroyan, Hughes, and Millay give one another advice on life.

1. Choose parts.
2. Reread the works and author biographies.
3. Find examples or explanations from the writer's own experience or work for the statements you plan to make.

Conduct your discussion. Then, point to strengths in each person's interpretation.

Research and Technology Conduct research on the lives of one of the poets. **Summarize** your findings for the class.

Writing Write an **interpretation** of one of the poems that explains how the poem's message applies to contemporary life.

Take It to the Net www.phschool.com

Go online for an additional research activity using the Internet.

READING INFORMATIONAL MATERIALS

Magazine Article

About Magazine Articles

Magazines are a type of periodical, or a publication that is published at regular intervals, such as weekly or monthly. Magazines usually contain illustrations, advertisements, and a variety of articles by different writers. They can focus on events, places, people, or ideas. For example, the article here focuses on the idea of colonizing Mars. It comes from *Newsweek*, a weekly magazine that covers a broad range of news topics. Along with newspapers and Web sites, magazines are a good source of current, up-to-date information.

Reading Strategy

Analyze Analogies

One method writers use to convey ideas is the analogy—a comparison of two unlike things using one or more of their common features. By comparing unfamiliar things with familiar ones, an analogy helps readers understand new ideas.

For example, in "A Colony in the Sky," the writer makes an analogy between transforming Mars and following a simple recipe. In both cases, you mix together "ingredients" and heat them up!

As you read, list at least three analogies you encounter in a graphic organizer like the Analogy Tree shown here.

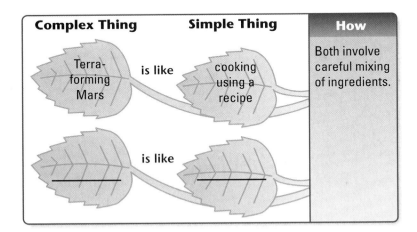

A Colony in the Sky

Kim Stanley Robinson

In the first paragraph, the author introduces his main topic: the colonization of Mars.

One day early in the next century, several people will land on Mars. They will put on spacesuits and leave their vehicle, bounding over red rocks under a pink sky. After this exhilarating day, seen on Earth by billions, they will move into a cluster of habitats already on site. They will spend a year living there making scientific studies, and then they will return to Earth. Another team will cycle in. Back at home we will start to take the base for granted. Nevertheless, something very big will have begun.

Robinson points out some of the benefits of colonizing and studying Mars.

The initial crossing to Mars will be made for a great number of reasons, some of them solid (to see if there really are fossil bacteria there), some of them not (to look for Elvis). Most of the reasons will be scientific and practical; the more we know about the solar system's other planets, the better we will understand Earth, and the safer we will be. It's not heroic but it makes sense, and it is impor-tant. Even if these were the only rea-sons, they would be good enough to send us.

But Mars will never remain just a research site to sharpen Earth man-agement skills. We've been fascinat-ed by the red wanderer ever since our days on the savannah,[1] and even if life at the research station proves to be quite ordinary, the videos they send back will show us a magnificent world of volcanoes and canyons, ice-caps and sand dunes, wind and weather. These wild new landscapes will also look somewhat familiar, especially in comparison to the bone-white moon. This familiar qual-ity is not just superficial, for Mars does resemble Earth in several important ways—general size, pres-ence of water, length of day, range of temperatures—so many similarities,

---

1. **our days on the savannah**: Earliest days of humanity.

Here, Robinson defines the unfamiliar term *terraform:* to alter a planet's surface until Earth's life forms can survive there.

The author makes an analogy between transforming Mars and following a recipe. Both situations require blending and heating "ingredients."

Robinson concludes his essay by explaining how exploring Mars will bring long-term benefits to Earth.

in fact, that some people are beginning to ask if it might be possible to make Mars even more like Earth than it is now. And that's the question that will shift us to the next level of our fascination with the place; the idea that we could live there, that Mars could be "terraformed."

To terraform means to alter a planet's surface until Earth's life forms can survive there. It's a hypothetical discipline[2] at this point, born in science-fiction stories. But in the last 30 years a number of scientists have taken up the concept. Their studies make it clear that the process would be somewhat slower than the cork-popping transformations seen in some recent sci-fi movies; in reality, it would take centuries. But it is an idea that operates within physical reality as we know it. It's possible to do it.

The recipe is simple. Add nitrogen and oxygen to the atmosphere; pump water to the surface; cook for decades, spicing first with cyanobacteria, then with all the rest of Earth's plants and animals, adding them in the order they evolved here. Mars is blessed with all the ingredients called for in the recipe; indeed, Mars turns out to be perfect for terraforming. So, because we have all the life forms here at hand, we can try replaying evolution at extreme fast forward.

Of course it will be more complex than the recipe—it always is. And the process will certainly spiral out of our control. Eventually, however, if all goes well, we will have helped to start a new biosphere.[3] Think of that! It's hard to know how even to characterize such an activity. It would be something like growing a garden, or creating a wilderness, or building a cathedral, or flying seeds over an ocean to drop them on a new island. It would be unlike anything else, a new thing in history.

Some people may believe that such a project is too large or slow or presumptuous[4] for humanity to undertake. But consider our current situation on Earth. There are nearly 6 billion of us now, and the number may double, though we have no good idea how many of us the Earth can support. Many larger species are in danger of extinction unless we protect them from us. We have rearranged much of the land, and we have altered the atmosphere to the point where the global climate in the future will be a matter of legislation and industrial practice. In other words, we are already starting to terraform Earth by necessity to keep it livable. Given this situation, the attempt to terraform Mars does not look so outlandish. Doing it could be regarded as a valuable experiment, with Mars as a giant lab or university, in which we learn how to steward a planet's biosphere for long-term sustainability.[5]

* * *

Humanity's existence on this Earth is a long-term project, . . . and it's important to remember what that means. People will be living here 500 years from now, and they will all be our relatives. These distant children of ours deserve to be given a livable planet to care for in their turn. For their sake we need to work out a sustainable way of life on Earth. Going to Mars will be part of that larger environmental project, and terraforming it will be an education that we will apply at home as we learn it—pausing, from time to time, to look up at our wilderness garden in the sky.

---

2. discipline (dis′ ə plin′) *n.*: Field of science.

3. biosphere (bī′ ō sfir′) *n.*: The zone where life occurs on a planet, including the surface and the atmosphere.

4. presumptuous (prē zump′ cho͞o əs) *adj.*: Too bold.

5. sustainability (sə stān ə bil′ i tē) *n.*: Conditions in which life can survive from one generation to the next.

Check Your Comprehension

1. In what ways does Mars naturally resemble Earth?
2. (a) What does it mean to "terraform" Mars? (b) Explain how this process would take place.
3. How can exploring Mars teach us about life on Earth?

Applying the Reading Strategy

Analyze Analogies

4. Explain how the analogy between terraforming and cooking might put readers at ease.
5. (a) Name the four things to which Robinson compares creating a biosphere. (b) Choose one of these analogies and explain what the two items have in common.
6. Why do you think Robinson uses analogies to communicate the concept of creating a biosphere?
7. (a) Identify one analogy in the next-to-last paragraph. (b) What two items are being compared, and what qualities do they share?
8. Which analogy in the article do you think works best? Why?

Activity

Create an Analogy

Writers use analogies to help readers understand new ideas. In your library, find a magazine article on a scientific topic, such as the greenhouse effect or healthy eating. Read the article and identify a concept that most readers would find unfamiliar. Then, create an analogy that will make the concept easier for readers to understand. Choose something that shares a main characteristic of the concept you are trying to explain.

Contrasting Informational Materials

Magazine Articles and Lab Reports

The magazine article you just read discusses the concept of exploring Mars. However, it does not contain the results of specific studies or experiments done on this issue.

A lab report, on the other hand, explains the procedures and results of a specific science experiment. It includes background on the experiment and the question it attempts to answer; provides a list of materials and an explanation of the procedures; documents the observations made during the experiment; and provides an analysis of the results.

1. Name two characteristics of a lab report that this article shares.
2. Name two ways in which this article is different from a lab report.

Writing WORKSHOP

Description: Descriptive Composition

A **descriptive composition** is an essay that presents a vivid picture of a place, event, object, or person. In this workshop you will write a descriptive composition focused on a topic that interests you.

Assignment Criteria Your descriptive composition should have the following characteristics:

- strong sensory details
- a main impression reinforced by each detail
- clear, consistent organization
- links between sensory details and the feelings or thoughts they inspire
- effective transitions

See the Rubric on page 159 for the criteria on which your descriptive composition may be assessed.

Prewriting

Choose a topic. Make a **timeline** of the important happenings in your life. Then, select as your topic a person, place, or thing related to an event on the timeline.

Gather details. Concentrate on each of the five senses (taste, touch, smell, sight, and hearing) as you generate sensory details on a detail chart. Then, add thoughts and feelings you experience in relation to your topic.

Sight	
Touch	
Taste	
Hearing	
Thoughts and Feelings	

Student Model

Before you begin drafting your descriptive composition, read this student model and review the characteristics of vivid description.

Charity Jackson
Fort Wayne, Indiana

Spring Into Spring

Spring is the perfect time to get outdoors and get active. The spring season brings the freshness of a new beginning. If you've been cooped up all winter, the perfect start to spring is a brisk walk. If you walk during the day, you will feel the sunshine warming up the pavement; a breeze may ruffle your hair; you'll hear the songs of birds that you'd almost forgotten about over the winter. If you walk in the early evening, in the purple-gray dusk, you may even hear the "spring peepers," little frogs that become suddenly vocal around April. You might mistake them for crickets, because they have that same high-pitched monotonous chirping sound, but peepers are more shrill and persistent. Any one of these sensations by itself is enough to raise a little hope that winter is over. If you're lucky enough to experience them all at once on your first spring walk, you'll feel uplifted and energized by the knowledge that soon that stuffy old winter coat can be put in storage for many months.

If you continue to walk, you will experience new additions to the spring line-up. You'll start to smell the earth. As the ground warms up, it gives off a soft, distinct "spring-like" smell. The scent of warm earth says "spring" the way the scent of pine says "winter." Because the ground is warming up, the smell of flowers can't be far behind! The first flowers of spring, though, are more a treat for the eyes than the nose. The brilliant yellow forsythia don't have much of an aroma, but they're so bright, they don't really need one to announce their arrival! The shy hyacinth, which blooms shortly after, is not as easily spotted, but your nose will tell you that the strong perfume in the air means a hyacinth is hiding somewhere nearby. Neighbors working their gardens—some of whom you may not have seen all winter—will call a friendly hello. Everyone seems friendlier at the beginning of spring.

Later in the season, when you begin to hear the growl and grumble of lawnmowers around the neighborhood, you'll know that spring has done its work. When the grass grows tall enough to need mowing, it's time to start thinking about those summer sensations!

Sensory details about sunshine, breezes, birdsongs, and the colors of dusk appeal to the sense of touch, hearing, and sight.

The overall impression of lightness and energy is reinforced to contrast with the stuffy winter coat.

The description is organized in time order—new details are introduced in the order in which they appear as spring progresses.

Here, and at various points in the essay, the writer includes comments on feelings and reactions to what is being described.

Transitions that indicate time help readers follow the chronological organization of the description.

Drafting

Organize your ideas. Present your details in a pattern that will make sense to the reader. Use the chart to select an organizational plan for your composition. Then, draft your composition based on that plan.

Elaborate to create a main impression. Set a mood or use an idea to unify your composition. For example, you might create a feeling of suspense, a calm atmosphere, or a flurry of activity. Focus on details that strengthen this overall impression. Elaborate on these details by depth charging—adding layers of feeling, comparison, or associations to particular details.

Spatial Order:	If you are writing about a place or object, you might use a form of spatial order, such as left to right, front to back, or bottom to top.
Chronological Order:	If you are describing an event, present details in the order they happen.
Order of Importance:	If you are describing to show the significance of your subject, or to allow someone else to evaluate it, begin with your least important details and build up to the most important.

Revising

Revising for organization and transitions. Revise to make the organization of your composition clear. Add transition words and phrases to show the connection between details and ideas. The following are some common transitions used with types of organization.

Chronological Order	Spatial Order	Order of Importance
next, after, later, soon, before, while, during	beside, above, below, near, next to	in addition, primarily, most important, also, significantly

Model:

During the rest of the season,

∧If you continue to walk, you will experience new additions to the spring
Not long after you've heard the peepers,

line-up.∧You'll start to smell the earth. As the ground warms up. it gives off a soft,

distinct "spring-like" smell.

Revise for word choice. Strong descriptive language can add punch to your composition. Highlight vague or empty adjectives like *nice* and *good.* These empty words do not add specific information to your description. Replace them with precise words that tell how or why your subject is *nice* or *good.*

> **Example:** **Vague adjective:** A *bad* wind blew.
> **Precise adjective:** A *ferocious* wind blew.

Compare the nonmodel and the model. Why is the model a more effective description than the nonmodel?

Nonmodel	Model
If you walk in the early evening, in the fading colors of dusk, you may even hear the "spring peepers," little frogs that become suddenly vocal around April. You might mistake them for crickets, because they have that same chirping sound, but peepers are louder.	If you walk in the early evening, in the purple-gray dusk, you may even hear the "spring peepers," little frogs that become suddenly vocal around April. You might mistake them for crickets, because they have that same high-pitched monotonous chirping sound, but peepers are more shrill and persistent.

Publishing and Presenting

Choose one of the following ways to share your writing with class-mates or a wider audience.

Tape-record your composition. Read your description aloud on tape. Add sound effects or background music that reinforces the main impression of your description. Play the tape for a group of classmates or friends.

Post your composition. Put your description on a class bulletin board or post it on a school Web site. Add photos or art if you have any.

WG *Prentice Hall Writing and Grammar Connection: Chapter 6*

Speaking Connection
To learn more about evaluating descriptive language, see the **Listening and Speaking Workshop: Evaluating Advertisements** on page 160.

Rubric for Self-Assessment

Evaluate your descriptive composition using the following criteria and rating scale.

Criteria	Rating Scale Not very				Very
How strong are the sensory details?	1	2	3	4	5
How clear and consistent is the organization?	1	2	3	4	5
How well is elaboration used to strengthen the main impression?	1	2	3	4	5
How effectively are ideas and details connected with transitions?	1	2	3	4	5

Evaluating Advertisements

An **advertisement** is meant to persuade you, a consumer, to do something—perhaps purchase a product or vote for a political candidate. Evaluate the content, logic, and presentation of advertisements to make wise decisions.

Evaluate Content

Like all persuasive writing or speaking, an ad should be based on reliable information and logical reasoning. Use these guidelines to evaluate information and logic.

Challenge the claims and the logic. Some claims may be technically true, but not as powerful as they appear at first. For example, stating that nine out of ten doctors recommend a medication may sound as if all doctors in the country had offered their opinions. However, this claim can be made even if only ten doctors have been interviewed. (For more on faulty claims, see the **Listening and Speaking Workshop**, p. 700.)

Consider the sources. A company's own research may be slanted to favor its products. Facts from well-established research organizations, such as the Food and Drug Administration, are likely to be reliable.

Evaluate Delivery

Advertisements often include speech, sound effects, music, or visual effects. Analyze the effect of these elements.

Analyze the entertainment effect. Dancing dogs, upbeat music, and bottles of ketchup that talk may be entertaining, but they do not give you the information you need about the product to make an informed decision.

Analyze the emotional effect. A car commercial may make it seem as if driving a particular car means you are adventurous or successful. Be aware that advertisers may try to sell a product by associating it with a feeling or quality. Think about whether the product can deliver that feeling or quality.

(Activity:)
Compare Commercials With others, watch several commercials on television. Individually, evaluate the content and delivery using a chart like the one shown. Compare your responses and discuss questions, challenges, and affirmations—points you support or with which you agree.

Be aware that most commercials will contain a mix of facts, effects, and persuasive techniques.

Evaluating an Advertisement

Product	
Facts	
Effects	
Persuasive techniques	
Questions, challenges, or affirmations	
Overall rating	

Assessment WORKSHOP

Analyzing Information

Strategies for Success

Some tests ask you to read a passage and arrange the details in sequential order. These methods will help you answer test questions about sequence.

- Read carefully to determine if the passage is in chronological—time—order.
- If the passage starts with a recent event, read to see if the story goes back to an earlier event.
- If the passage starts in the middle of a story, check to see if it uses flashback to give background information.

Test-Taking Strategies

- Look for clues about time, such as dates or time words like *recently*, *then*, or *first*.
- Skim the question before reviewing the passage.

Sample Test Item

Directions: Read the passage, and then choose the letter of the best answer to the question.

In the 1980s, the Statue of Liberty got new steel supports, a new torch, and a thorough cleaning. She was in good shape for a hundred-year-old woman. Her story began in 1865 when the French decided to give the United States a monument to freedom. Sculptor Frederic-Auguste Bartholdi designed and built the monument. Bartholdi sought help from engineer Alexandre-Gustave Eiffel. When Bartholdi finished the Statue of Liberty, it was taken apart and shipped to New York City. It arrived in 1885 and was dedicated in 1886.

Which event described in the passage happened most recently?

A The Statue of Liberty was dedicated.

B Some Frenchmen decided to build a monument to freedom.

C The Statue of Liberty was taken apart.

D The Statue of Liberty was cleaned.

Answer and Explanation

A happened in 1886, *B* in 1865, *C* in 1885, and *D* in the 1980s. *D* is correct.

▶ Practice

Directions: Read the passage, and then choose the letter of the best answer for each item.

Justin couldn't believe how much work it was just to get his baby brother ready for an outing in the park. After changing Scott's diaper, he'd put sunscreen on him and found a cap to keep the sun out of his eyes. As they were about to leave, Justin realized he should probably take an extra diaper. Then he thought Scott might get hungry, so he packed a snack. Finally, Justin remembered that Dad always took a few toys in case Scott got bored. By the time Justin had squeezed everything into his backpack, Scott needed another diaper change!

1. Before Justin put sunscreen on Scott, he—

   A changed his diaper

   B packed some toys

   C gave Scott a snack

   D found his baseball cap

2. The last thing Justin remembered to pack was—

   A a cap   C diaper

   B toys   D sunscreen

What Matters

A L E R O

Exploring the Theme

To navigate a life filled with options and distractions, each of us has to set priorities and answer a tough question: What matters most? The literature in this unit presents a variety of answers shown through the words of authors and the actions of characters.

◀ **Critical Viewing** What does the painting suggest matters to the artist? Explain. **[Analyze]**

Why Read Literature?

This unit offers works that look at what matters to people—subjects like the struggle between human beings and nature, the idea of war, and how people deal with loss. In addition to reading about the theme, you might have other purposes for reading. Preview three of the purposes you might set before reading the works in this unit.

1

Read for the love of literature.

In 1955, the Vermont state legislature named a mountain in the town of Ripton, Vermont, after Robert Frost. Frost is famous for his poems depicting New England. Discover this poet's New England world by reading his poem **"Stopping by Woods on a Snowy Evening,"** page 226.

Imagine being given 225,000 dollars. That's what happened to poet Sandra Cisneros in 1995, when the MacArthur Foundation awarded her a grant—a sum of money that is "granted," or given, to an individual or group to help them begin or continue a project. Read one of her works, **"Four Skinny Trees,"** on page 230.

2

Read to gain understanding.

Joan Aiken's first published novel was adapted from a work she had written when she was only 17. Enrich your understanding of what matters when you read **"The Third Wish,"** page 168, an unusual love story.

As a young man, Alfred, Lord Tennyson, took part in an unsuccessful revolution against King Ferdinand VII. Read **"The Charge of the Light Brigade,"** page 198, to understand his feelings about courage under fire.

3

Read for information.

Although mountain climbers have been attempting to reach the top of Mount Everest—the world's highest summit—since the beginning of the twentieth century, the first successful ascent did not take place until 1953. Find out the dangers and disasters faced by contemporary climbers when you read an excerpt from Jon Krakauer's **_Into Thin Air_**, page 190.

You probably envision the color of the ocean as green, blue, or maybe gray. Sometimes, however, an event called algal bloom creates what scientists call a "red tide." Read about this worrisome ocean phenomenon in the textbook chapter "Algal Blooms," page 235.

 Take It to the Net

Visit the Web site for online instruction and activities related to each selection in this unit.

www.phschool.com

How to Read Literature

Use Interactive Reading Strategies

When you get truly involved in your reading and read interactively, you will better remember what you read. The strategies in this unit will help you become an interactive reader.

1. Clarify word meanings.

In this unit you will learn strategies for clarifying, or making clear, word meanings and for incorporating new words into your speaking and writing. One way to interact with the text is by jotting down words you do not recognize or words that are used in a way you have not seen before.

2. Make predictions.

A prediction is an educated guess based on details you learn and your experience. The chart here shows how experience and details work together to help a reader make a prediction. As you read, make predictions about story events. Check your predictions against what actually happens.

Detail

Title: "The Third Wish"

My experience

In many stories, characters don't like the way wishes turn out.

Prediction

The character will want to change his wishes.

3. Summarize.

Summarizing is a way of reviewing and restating main events or main points. Strategies in this unit will help you to identify the most important ideas. Then, you can think about the underlying meaning of events and actions.

4. Interpret figurative language.

Interpret the meaning of a work's figures of speech—expressions that are not meant to be interpreted literally. As you read prose and poetry in this unit, notice the effect figurative language has on a work.

Figure of Speech	Interpretation	Effect
They grow down and they grab the earth with their hairy toes and they bite the sky with violent teeth.	The roots hold tight in the earth and the branches create a sharp pointy outline against the sky.	The figures of speech create the impression that the trees are aggressive and tough in the way they grow.

5. Identify cause-and-effect relationships.

Ask yourself whether one event or condition is the reason for, or the result of, another event or condition. Identifying this relationship will deepen your understanding of what happens into an understanding of why it happens.

As you read the selections in this unit, review the reading strategies and look at the notes in the side columns. Use the suggestions to apply the strategies and interact with the text.

Prepare to Read

The Third Wish

Preview

Connecting to the Literature

Imagine that you could have three wishes granted to you. Do you know what your wishes would be? This is the situation of Mr. Peters in "The Third Wish." As you read, think about how his wishes compare with wishes you might make.

Background

"The Third Wish" is, as the title suggests, a story about three wishes. Almost every culture in the world has a traditional tale about a character who is granted three wishes, uses two unwisely, and uses the third wish to undo one or both of the first two.

Literary Analysis

Modern Fairy Tale

Modern fairy tales include elements of traditional fairy tales, including mysterious and fantastic events, magic and wishes, and animals with unusual abilities.

Modern fairy tales differ from traditional fairy tales because they include details related to contemporary life. Look for elements of traditional and modern fairy tales in "The Third Wish."

Connecting Literary Elements

Characterization is the process a writer uses to create and develop a character. There are two types of characterization:

- **Direct characterization:** The writer directly states or describes the character's traits, or characteristics.
- **Indirect characterization:** The writer reveals a character's personality through his or her words and actions, and through the thoughts, words, and actions of other characters.

As you read "The Third Wish," ask yourself these focus questions:

1. What three words directly describe the way Mr. Peters speaks?
2. What two actions of Mr. Peters indirectly show his personality?

Reading Strategy

Clarifying Word Meanings

When you find a word difficult or confusing, **clarify,** or make clear, its meaning by looking for clues in the surrounding text. You might find a restatement—another word or phrase that says almost the same thing. Look also for explanations or examples. In the example, the italicized phrase clarifies the meaning of *preening* by telling what the swan is doing.

> [The swan] put itself to rights with much dabbling and **preening,** *smoothing its feathers with little showers of drops*.

The diagram at right shows how the explanation of what Mr. Peters does clarifies the meaning of *slope*.

Unfamiliar word

Beyond the bank was an open **slope**.

⋮
▼

Possible meanings

field, hill, path

⋮
▼

Clue

Mr. Peters ran down the hill . . .

⋮
▼

Clarification

A *slope* is a *hill.*

Vocabulary Development

extricate (eks′ tri kāt′) *v.* set free (p. 169)

presumptuous (prē zump′ choo əs) *adj.* overconfident; arrogant (p. 169)

composure (kəm pō′ zhər) *n.* calmness of mind (p. 169)

rash (rash) *adj.* thoughtless (p. 170)

remote (ri mōt′) *adj.* far away from everything else (p. 171)

malicious (mə lish′ əs) *adj.* spiteful; hateful (p. 173)

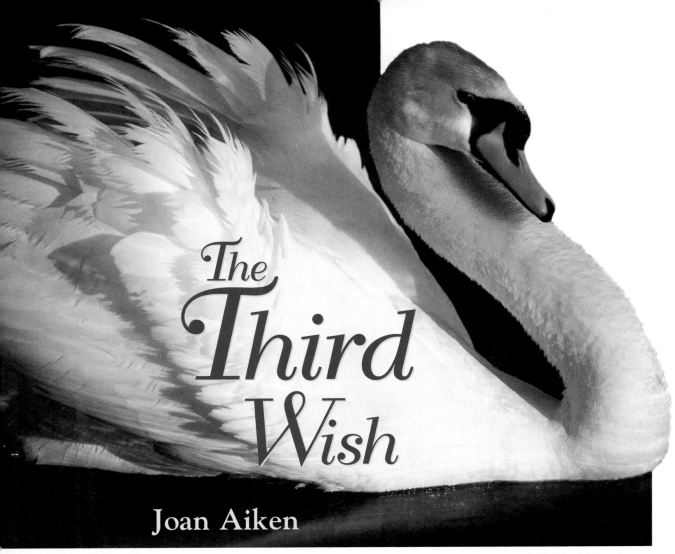

The Third Wish

Joan Aiken

▲ **Critical Viewing**
In this story, a swan has magical powers. What details of the photograph make this swan look powerful? **[Relate]**

Reading Strategy
Clarifying Word Meaning
What words or phrases help you find the meaning of *thrashing*? Clarify its meaning.

Once there was a man who was driving in his car at dusk on a spring evening through part of the forest of Savernake. His name was Mr. Peters. The primroses were just beginning but the trees were still bare, and it was cold; the birds had stopped singing an hour ago.

As Mr. Peters entered a straight, empty stretch of road he seemed to hear a faint crying, and a struggling and thrashing, as if somebody was in trouble far away in the trees. He left his car and climbed the mossy bank beside the road. Beyond the bank was an open slope of beech trees leading down to thorn bushes through which he saw the gleam of water. He stood a moment waiting to try and discover where the noise was coming from, and presently heard a rustling and some strange cries in a voice which was almost human—and yet there was something too hoarse about it at one time and too clear and sweet at another. Mr. Peters ran down the hill and as he neared the bushes he saw something white among them which was trying to extricate itself; coming closer he found that it was a swan that had become entangled in the thorns growing on the bank of the canal.

extricate (eks´ tri kāt´) v. set free

The bird struggled all the more frantically as he approached, looking at him with hate in its yellow eyes, and when he took hold of it to free it, it hissed at him, pecked him, and thrashed dangerously with its wings which were powerful enough to break his arm. Nevertheless he managed to release it from the thorns, and carrying it tightly with one arm, holding the snaky head well away with the other hand (for he did not wish his eyes pecked out), he took it to the verge of the canal and dropped it in.

The swan instantly assumed great dignity and sailed out to the middle of the water, where it put itself to rights with much dabbling and preening, smoothing its feathers with little showers of drops. Mr. Peters waited, to make sure that it was all right and had suffered no damage in its struggles. Presently the swan, when it was satisfied with its appearance, floated in to the bank once more, and in a moment, instead of the great white bird, there was a little man all in green with a golden crown and long beard, standing by the water. He had fierce glittering eyes and looked by no means friendly.

Literary Analysis
Modern Fairy Tale
What mysterious event occurs in this paragraph?

"Well, Sir," he said threateningly, "I see you are presumptuous enough to know some of the laws of magic. You think that because you have rescued—by pure good fortune—the King of the Forest from a difficulty, you should have some fabulous reward."

presumptuous (prē zump´ chōō əs) *adj.* overconfident; arrogant

"I expect three wishes, no more and no less," answered Mr. Peters, looking at him steadily and with composure.

composure (kəm pō´ zhər) *n.* calmness of mind

"Three wishes, he wants, the clever man! Well, I have yet to hear of the human being who made any good use of his three wishes—they mostly end up worse off than they started. Take your three wishes then"—he flung three dead leaves in the air—"don't blame me if you spend the last wish in undoing the work of the other two."

Mr. Peters caught the leaves and put two of them carefully in his briefcase. When he looked up, the swan was sailing about in the middle of the water again, flicking the drops angrily down its long neck.

Mr. Peters stood for some minutes reflecting on how he should use his reward. He knew very well that the gift of three magic wishes was one which brought trouble more often than not, and he had no intention of being like the forester who first wished by mistake for a sausage, and then in a rage wished it on the end of his wife's nose, and then had to use his last wish in getting it off again. Mr. Peters had most of the things which he wanted and was

✔**Reading Check**

What does the King of the Forest give Mr. Peters?

very content with his life. The only thing that troubled him was that he was a little lonely, and had no companion for his old age. He decided to use his first wish and to keep the other two in case of an emergency. Taking a thorn he pricked his tongue with it, to remind himself not to utter <u>rash</u> wishes aloud. Then holding the third leaf and gazing round him at the dusky undergrowth, the primroses, great beeches and the blue-green water of the canal, he said:

"I wish I had a wife as beautiful as the forest."

A tremendous quacking and splashing broke out on the surface of the water. He thought that it was the swan laughing at him. Taking no notice he made his way through the darkening woods to his car, wrapped himself up in the rug and went to sleep.

rash (rash) *adj.* thoughtless

When he awoke it was morning and the birds were beginning to call. Coming along the track towards him was the most beautiful creature he had ever seen, with eyes as blue-green as the canal, hair as dusky as the bushes, and skin as white as the feathers of swans.

"Are you the wife that I wished for?" asked Mr. Peters.

"Yes, I am," she replied. "My name is Leita."

She stepped into the car beside him and they drove off to the church on the outskirts of the forest, where they were married. Then he took her to his house in a <u>remote</u> and lovely valley and showed her all his treasures—the bees in their white hives, the Jersey cows, the hyacinths, the silver candlesticks, the blue cups and the luster bowl for putting primroses in. She admired everything, but what pleased her most was the river which ran by the foot of his garden.

"Do swans come up there?" she asked.

"Yes, I have often seen swans there on the river," he told her, and she smiled.

Leita made him a good wife. But as time went by Mr. Peters began to feel that she was not happy. She seemed restless, wandered much in the garden, and sometimes when he came back from the fields he would find the house empty and she would return after half an hour or so with no explanation of where she had been. On these occasions she was always especially tender and would put out his slippers to warm and cook his favorite dish—Welsh rarebit[1] with wild strawberries—for supper.

One evening he was returning home along the river path when he saw Leita in front of him, down by the water. A swan had sailed up to the verge and she had her arms round its neck and the swan's head rested against her cheek. She was weeping, and as he came nearer he saw that tears were rolling, too, from the swan's eyes.

"Leita, what is it?" he asked, very troubled.

"This is my sister," she answered. "I can't bear being separated from her."

Now he understood that Leita was really a swan from the forest, and this made him very sad because when a human being marries a bird it always leads to sorrow.

---

1. **Welsh rarebit** a dish of melted cheese served on crackers or toast.

Literary Analysis
Modern Fairy Tale
What wish of Mr. Peters has been answered as if by magic?

remote (ri mōt′) *adj.* far away from everything else

✔ **Reading Check**
What happens after Mr. Peters makes his wish?

"I could use my second wish to give your sister human shape, so that she could be a companion to you," he suggested.

"No, no," she cried, "I couldn't ask that of her."

"Is it so very hard to be a human being?" asked Mr. Peters sadly.

"Very, very hard," she answered.

"Don't you love me at all, Leita?"

"Yes, I do, I do love you," she said, and there were tears in her eyes again. "But I missed the old life in the forest, the cool grass and the mist rising off the river at sunrise and the feel of the water sliding over my feathers as my sister and I drifted along the stream."

"Then shall I use my second wish to turn you back into a swan again?" he asked, and his tongue pricked to remind him of the old King's words, and his heart swelled with grief inside him.

"Who will take care of you?"

"I'd do it myself as I did before I married you," he said, trying to sound cheerful.

She shook her head. "No, I could not be as unkind to you as that. I am partly a swan, but I am also partly a human being now. I will stay with you."

Poor Mr. Peters was very distressed on his wife's account and did his best to make her life happier, taking her for drives in the car, finding beautiful music for her to listen to on the radio, buying clothes for her and even suggesting a trip round the world. But she said no to that; she would prefer to stay in their own house near the river.

He noticed that she spent more and more time baking wonderful cakes—jam puffs, petits fours, eclairs and meringues. One day he saw her take a basketful down to the river and he guessed that she was giving them to her sister.

He built a seat for her by the river, and the two sisters spent hours together there, communicating in some wordless manner. For a time he thought that all would be well, but then he saw how thin and pale she was growing.

One night when he had been late doing the account he came up to bed and found her weeping in her sleep and calling:

"Rhea! Rhea! I can't understand what you say! Oh, wait for me, take me with you!"

Then he knew that it was hopeless and she would never be happy as a human. He stooped down and kissed her goodbye, then took another leaf from his notecase, blew it out of the window, and used up his second wish.

Next moment instead of Leita there was a sleeping swan lying across the bed with its head under its wing. He carried it out of the house and down to the brink of the river, and then he said,

Literary Analysis
Modern Fairy Tale and Characterization
What does Mr. Peters's wish reveal about his character?

▲ **Critical Viewing**
What experiences pictured here might Leita miss as a human? [**Analyze**]

"Leita! Leita!" to waken her, and gently put her into the water. She gazed round her in astonishment for a moment, and then came up to him and rested her head lightly against his hand; next instant she was flying away over the trees towards the heart of the forest.

He heard a harsh laugh behind him, and turning round saw the old King looking at him with a <u>malicious</u> expression.

"Well, my friend! You don't seem to have managed so wonderfully with your first two wishes, do you? What will you do with the last? Turn yourself into a swan? Or turn Leita back into a girl?"

"I shall do neither," said Mr. Peters calmly. "Human beings and swans are better in their own shapes."

But for all that he looked sadly over towards the forest where Leita had flown, and walked slowly back to his house.

Next day he saw two swans swimming at the bottom of the garden, and one of them wore the gold chain he had given Leita after their marriage; she came up and rubbed her head against his hand.

malicious (mə lish´ əs) *adj.* spiteful; hateful

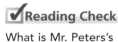 **Reading Check**

What is Mr. Peters's second wish?

Mr. Peters and his two swans came to be well known in that part of the country; people used to say that he talked to swans and they understood him as well as his neighbors. Many people were a little frightened of him. There was a story that once when thieves tried to break into his house they were set upon by two huge white birds which carried them off bodily and dropped them into the river.

As Mr. Peters grew old everyone wondered at his contentment. Even when he was bent with rheumatism[2] he would not think of moving to a drier spot, but went slowly about his work, with the two swans always somewhere close at hand.

Sometimes people who knew his story would say to him:

"Mr. Peters, why don't you wish for another wife?"

"Not likely," he would answer serenely. "Two wishes were enough for me, I reckon. I've learned that even if your wishes are granted they don't always better you. I'll stay faithful to Leita."

One autumn night, passers-by along the road heard the mournful sound of two swans singing. All night the song went on, sweet and harsh, sharp and clear. In the morning Mr. Peters was found peacefully dead in his bed with a smile of great happiness on his face. In his hands, which lay clasped on his breast, were a withered leaf and a white feather.

---

2. **rheumatism** (roo´ me tiz əm) *n.* pain and stiffness of the joints and muscles.

Review and Assess

Thinking About the Selection

1. **Respond:** If you could give advice to Mr. Peters about how to use his third wish, what would you tell him?

2. **(a) Recall:** How does Mr. Peters use his first wish? **(b) Infer:** Why doesn't he wish for riches?

3. **(a) Recall:** Why is Leita sad? **(b) Infer:** How does Mr. Peters feel about his wife's sadness? **(c) Draw Conclusions:** Why does he use his second wish as he does?

4. **(a) Infer:** Who are the two swans singing at the end of the story? **(b) Draw Conclusions:** Why do they sing for Mr. Peters?

5. **(a) Analyze:** Why does Mr. Peters die with a look of happiness on his face? **(b) Draw Conclusions:** How do you think he felt about the wishes he made? **(c) Evaluate:** Do you think he used his wishes wisely?

6. **Apply:** Why do most cultures have traditional tales about wishes that don't work out?

Joan Aiken

(b. 1924)

Born and schooled in England, young Joan Aiken loved to take walks in the fields by her house, creating stories to amuse herself. Aiken was strongly influenced by her father, the American poet Conrad Aiken. Her mother fed her imagination by reading aloud from the works of Charles Dickens, Jane Austen, and other classic English writers.

Joan Aiken's imaginative stories combine pieces of historical fiction, fairy tales, and horror stories and usually deal with fantastic or mysterious events. "The Third Wish" comes from a collection whose title sums up the appeal of Aiken's work—*Not What You Expected.*

Review and Assess

Literary Analysis

Modern Fairy Tale

1. In a chart like the one shown, record three examples from the story of each feature of a **modern fairy tale.**

Mysterious and Fantastic Events	Magic and Wishes	Details About Contemporary Life

2. If you were to rewrite this story as a traditional fairy tale, which details would you have to change?

3. In what way is the ending in "The Three Wishes" similar to and different from the endings of traditional fairy tales?

Connecting Literary Elements

4. What three words directly describe the way Mr. Peters speaks?

5. What two actions of Mr. Peters indirectly show his personality?

6. Use a diagram like the one shown to list three of Leita's character traits. Write whether Aiken reveals each trait through direct or indirect **characterization.**

Leita
very beautiful (direct)

Reading Strategy

Clarifying Word Meaning

7. List two clues in the following sentence that **clarify the meaning** of the italicized word, and then define the word: "Taking a thorn he pricked his tongue with it, to remind himself not to *utter* rash wishes aloud."

8. Explain how restatement helps you clarify the meaning of *content* in the following sentence: "Mr. Peters had most of the things which he wanted and was very *content* with his life."

Extend Understanding

9. **Science Connection:** The swans can live near Mr. Peters because his home is by a river. What are some other characteristics of an ecosystem in which swans can live?

Quick Review

A **modern fairy tale** includes traditional and contemporary details. To review fairy tales, see page 167.

Characterization is the process an author uses to create a character. To review characterization, see page 167.

Clues in the surrounding text can help you **clarify word meanings.**

 Take It to the Net

www.phschool.com
Take the interactive self-test online to check your understanding of the selection.

Integrate Language Skills

Vocabulary Development Lesson

Word Analysis: Latin Suffix -ous

A character in "The Third Wish" describes Mr. Peters as being *presumptuous*. The word *presumptuous* is made by adding the Latin suffix *-ous* to *presume*. The suffix *-ous* means "full of or characterized by." In other words, Mr. Peters is described as being full of presuming, or "arrogant."

Complete each sentence by adding *-ous* to the word in parentheses. Explain how the new word indicates that someone or something is "full of" or "characterized by."

1. The ___?___ firefighter rescued the child. (courage)
2. The clown's ___?___ outfit included huge ears and floppy shoes. (outrage)
3. The actress looked very ___?___. (glamour)

Concept Development: Synonyms

Synonyms are words that are similar in meaning. On your paper, match each word in the first column with its synonym from the second column.

1. extricate	a.	far
2. composure	b.	thoughtless
3. presumptuous	c.	free
4. rash	d.	calmness
5. remote	e.	spiteful
6. malicious	f.	arrogant

Spelling Strategy

When you add *-ous* to words that end with *ce* pronounced like *s*, change the final *e* to *i* before adding the suffix: malice + *-ous* = malicious.

Add *-ous* to the following words.

1. space   2. grace   3. vice

Grammar Lesson

Adjectives

Adjectives are one of the parts of speech. Adjectives modify, or describe, nouns or pronouns. They tell more about the nouns or pronouns they modify by answering the questions *what kind, which one, how many,* and *how much.*

In the following sentence, Aiken uses adjectives to inform the reader about *how many* wishes Mr. Peters expects. She also tells *what kind* of man Mr. Peters is.

Example: "*Three* wishes, he wants, the *clever* man!"

▶ *For more practice, see page R28, Exercise D.*
Practice Copy these sentences. Underline each adjective, and draw an arrow to the word it modifies. Then, tell what question it answers.

1. He climbed the mossy bank beside the road.
2. He had fierce eyes and powerful wings.
3. Leita made him a good wife.
4. Next day he saw two swans.
5. Mr. Peters felt he had enough wishes.

Writing Application Write a paragraph about the story, using the following adjectives.

1. vivid   3. happy
2. careful   4. astonished

𝒲𝒢 *Prentice Hall Writing and Grammar Connection: Chapter 16, Section 1*

Writing Lesson

Modern Fairy Tale

"The Third Wish" contains realistic details of modern life. Choose a traditional fairy tale, and write a retelling of it in a modern setting.

Prewriting   Brainstorm for details that will update the setting and characters.

Drafting   Organize your story with a balanced beginning, middle, and end. Most of the action in the story should occur in the middle. The beginning should briefly introduce the characters and the situation, and the end should briefly bring the story to a close.

Model: Balanced Organization

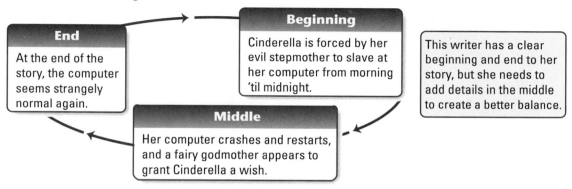

End
At the end of the story, the computer seems strangely normal again.

Beginning
Cinderella is forced by her evil stepmother to slave at her computer from morning 'til midnight.

This writer has a clear beginning and end to her story, but she needs to add details in the middle to create a better balance.

Middle
Her computer crashes and restarts, and a fairy godmother appears to grant Cinderella a wish.

Revising   Rearrange or add details as needed to concentrate the action in the middle of the story. Be sure you have used transitions to link ideas.

WG *Prentice Hall Writing and Grammar Connection: Chapter 5, Section 4*

Extension Activities

Listening and Speaking Present a **news story** that shows Mr. Peters as a local hero. Use details from "The Third Wish" to give examples of Mr. Peters's good deeds and good nature so that your audience will be persuaded to see him as a hero, too.

1. Experiment with the order in which you present the details. You might start with his rescue of the Forest King and lead up to his most selfless act, or you might open with the power of his biggest sacrifice.

2. Practice speaking your news story aloud before presenting it to the class.

Research and Technology Use library resources, such as subject listings in the card catalog or an online catalog, to research fairy tales about wishes from different cultures. Use as key words *fairy tale*, *folk tale*, and *wishes*. Prepare a chart that shows each tale's country of origin, characters, plot summary, and message. Then, use your chart as part of a **presentation** to the class.

 **Take It to the Net**   www.phschool.com

Go online for an additional research activity using the Internet.

Prepare to Read

A Boy and a Man ◆ *from* Into Thin Air

Preview

Connecting to the Literature

Have you felt your heart race as you experienced the thrill of downhill skiing, competitive skateboarding, or white-water rafting? Connect to the danger and excitement of mountain climbing in these selections by relating the physical challenges to one with which you are familiar.

Background

"A Boy and a Man" by James Ramsey Ullman and *Into Thin Air* by Jon Krakauer take place on glaciers. Glaciers are huge "rivers" of ice that have built up over the centuries. Although a glacier is solid, it "flows" a few inches every year. Stress builds as the glacier moves until the surface splits and deep crevasses, or cracks, appear.

Literary Analysis

Conflict with Nature

Conflict is a struggle between opposing sides or forces. It provides the tension, interest, and suspense in prose narratives such as novels, novellas, short stories, and nonfiction accounts.

There are four major types of conflict

- a struggle between characters.
- a struggle between character(s) and nature.
- a struggle between character(s) and society.
- a struggle between two feelings or qualities within a single character.

Both of the narratives in this pair focus on a **conflict with nature**. Look for details that contribute to the conflict in each work.

Comparing Literary Works

These two works share a similar conflict, but they are from different genres, or forms of literature. "A Boy and a Man" is part of the novel *Banner in the Sky.* The excerpt from *Into Thin Air* is part of a full-length nonfiction work. Focus on the following questions to compare and contrast conflicts in the novel excerpt and the nonfiction narrative:

1. Which work contains more factual details about nature?
2. How are descriptions of nature used in each work to make the conflict more intense or dramatic?

Reading Strategy

Making Predictions

Gripping stories such as these keep you wondering what is going to happen next. Based on information the author provides, you can **predict,** or make an informed guess about, the events to follow. The chart shows how details can help you to make a prediction about what a character will do. Use a chart like the one shown here to make predictions at suspenseful points in each narrative.

Possible Outcomes	
Go get help	Stay to help
Details	
1.	
2.	
3.	
Prediction	
Go	Stay

Vocabulary Development

prone (prōn) *adj.* lying face downward (p. 182)

taut (tôt) *adj.* tightly stretched (p. 183)

pummeled (pum´ əld) *v.* pounded; beat (p. 184)

reconnoiter (rē kə noit´ ər) *v.* look around (p. 187)

malevolent (mə lev´ ə lənt) *adj.* wishing evil or harm to others (p. 191)

denigrate (den´ ə grāt´) *n.* discredit; put down; belittle (p. 192)

A Boy and a Man

from Banner in the Sky

James Ramsey Ullman

The crevasse[1] was about six feet wide at the top and narrowed gradually as it went down. But how deep it was Rudi could not tell. After a few feet the blue walls of ice curved away at a sharp slant, and what was below the curve was hidden from sight.

"Hello!" Rudi called.

"Hello—" A voice answered from the depths.

"How far down are you?"

"I'm not sure. About twenty feet, I'd guess."

"On the bottom?"

"No. I can't even see the bottom. I was lucky and hit a ledge."

The voice spoke in German, but with a strange accent. Whoever was down there, Rudi knew, it was not one of the men of the valley.

"Are you hurt?" he called.

---

1. **crevasse** (krə vas´) *n.* deep crack, especially in a glacier.

"Nothing broken—no," said the voice. "Just shaken up some. And cold."

"How long have you been there?"

"About three hours."

Rudi looked up and down the crevasse. He was thinking desperately of what he could do.

"Do you have a rope?" asked the voice.

"No."

"How many of you are there?"

"Only me."

There was a silence. When the voice spoke again, it was still quiet and under strict control. "Then you'll have to get help," it said.

Rudi didn't answer. To get down to Kurtal would take at least two hours, and for a party to climb back up would take three. By that time it would be night, and the man would have been in the crevasse for eight hours. He would be frozen to death.

"No," said Rudi, "it would take too long."

"What else is there to do?"

Rudi's eyes moved over the ice-walls: almost vertical, smooth as glass. "Have you an ax?" he asked.

"No. I lost it when I fell. It dropped to the bottom."

"Have you tried to climb?"

"Yes. But I can't get a hold."

There was another silence. Rudi's lips tightened, and when he spoke again his voice was strained. "I'll think of something." he cried. "I'll think of *something*!"

"Don't lose your head." the voice said. "The only way is to go down for help."

"But you'll—"

"Maybe. And maybe not. That's a chance we'll have to take."

The voice was as quiet as ever. And, hearing it, Rudi was suddenly ashamed. Here was he, safe on the glacier's surface,

Literary Analysis
Conflict with Nature
What are the two sides of the conflict?

Reading Check

What decision does Rudi have to make?

showing fear and despair, while the one below, facing almost certain death, remained calm and controlled. Whoever it was down there it was a real man. A brave man.◆

Rudi drew in a long, slow breath. With his climbing-staff he felt down along the smooth surface of the ice walls.

"Are you still there?" said the voice.

"Yes," he said.

"You had better go."

"Wait—"

Lying flat on the glacier, he leaned over the rim of the crevasse and lowered the staff as far as it would go. Its end came almost to the curve in the walls.

"Can you see it?" he asked.

"See what?" said the man.

Obviously he couldn't. Standing up, Rudi removed his jacket and tied it by one sleeve to the curved end of the staff. Then, holding the other end, he again lay <u>prone</u> and lowered his staff and jacket.

"Can you see it now?" he asked.

"Yes," said the man.

"How far above you is it?"

"About ten feet."

Again the staff came up. Rudi took off his shirt and tied one of its sleeves to the dangling sleeve of the jacket. This time, as he lay down, the ice bit, cold and rough, into his bare chest; but he scarcely noticed it. With his arms extended, all the shirt and half the jacket were out of sight beneath the curve in the crevasse.

"How near are you now?" he called.

"Not far," said the voice.

"Can you reach it?"

"I'm trying."

There was the sound of scraping bootnails; of labored breathing. But no pull on the shirtsleeve down below.

"I can't make it," said the voice. It was fainter than before.

"Wait," said Rudi.

For the third time he raised the staff. He took off his trousers. He tied a trouser-leg to the loose sleeve of the shirt. Then he pulled, one by one, at all the knots he had made: between staff and jacket, jacket and shirt, shirt and trousers. He pulled until the blood pounded in his head and the knots were as tight as his strength could make them. This done, he stepped back from the crevasse to the point where his toes had rested when he lay flat. With feet and hands he kicked and scraped the ice until he had

Literature
in context World Events Connection

♦ **Edward Whymper**

The "brave man" in the novel is based on Edward Whymper who, in 1865, became the first person to reach the summit of the Matterhorn, one of the great peaks of the Alps. On the descent, four of his party were killed when a rope snapped. Ullman himself climbed the Matterhorn. His descriptions of the ice, fear, and danger are based on first-hand experience.

The Matterhorn

prone (prōn) *adj.* lying face downward

made two holes. Then, lying down as before, he dug his toes deep into them. He was naked now, except for his shoes, stockings and underpants. The cold rose from the ice into his blood and bones. He lowered the staff and knotted clothes like a sort of crazy fishing line.

The trousers, the shirt and half of the jacket passed out of sight. He was leaning over as far as he could.

"Can you reach it now?" he called.

"Yes," the voice answered.

"All right. Come on."

"You won't be able to hold me. I'll pull you in."

"No you won't."

He braced himself. The pull came. His toes went <u>taut</u> in their ice-holds and his hands tightened on the staff until the knuckles showed white. Again he could hear a scraping sound below, and he knew that the man was clawing his boots against the ice-wall, trying both to lever himself up and to take as much weight as possible off the improvised lifeline. But the wall obviously offered little help. Almost all his weight was on the lifeline. Suddenly there was a jerk, as one of the knots in the clothing slipped, and the staff was almost wrenched from Rudi's hands. But the knot held. And his hands held. He tried to call down, "All right?" but he had no breath for words. From below, the only sound was the scraping of boots on ice.

How long it went on Rudi could never have said. Perhaps only for a minute or so. But it seemed like hours. And then at last—at last—it happened. A hand came into view around the curve of the crevasse wall; a hand gripping the twisted fabric of his jacket, and then a second hand rising slowly above it. A head appeared. A pair of shoulders. A face was raised for an instant and then lowered. Again one hand moved slowly up past the other.

But Rudi no longer saw it, for now his eyes were shut tight with the strain. His teeth were clamped, the cords of his neck bulged, the muscles of his arm felt as if he were being drawn one by one from the bones that held them. He began to lose his toeholds. He was being dragged forward. Desperately, frantically, he dug in with his feet, pressed his whole body down, as if he could make it part of the glacier. Though all but naked on the ice, he was pouring with sweat. Somehow he stopped the slipping. Somehow he held on. But now suddenly the strain was even worse, for the man had reached the lower end of the staff. The slight "give" of the stretched clothing was gone, and in its place, was rigid deadweight on a length of wood. The climber was close now. But heavy. Indescribably heavy. Rudi's hands ached and burned, as if it were a rod of hot lead that they clung to. It was not a mere man he was holding, but a giant; or a block of granite. The pull was unendurable. The pain

taut (tôt) *adj.* tightly stretched

Reading Strategy
Making Predictions
Predict whether Rudi will or will not be able to hold on to the staff.

 **Reading Check**

What does Rudi do to try to get the climber out of the crevasse?

unendurable. He could hold on no longer. His hands were opening. It was all over.

And then it *was* over. The weight was gone. There was a scraping sound close beneath him; a hand on the rim of ice; a figure pulling itself up onto the lip of the crevasse. The man was beside Rudi, turning to him, staring at him.

"Why—you're just a boy!" he said in astonishment.

Rudi was too numb to move or speak. Taking the staff from him, the man pulled up the line of clothes, untied the knots and shook them out.

"Come on now. Quickly!" he said.

Pulling the boy to his feet, he helped him dress. Then he rubbed and <u>pummeled</u> him until at last Rudi felt the warmth of returning circulation.

"Better?" the man asked, smiling.

Rudi nodded. And finally he was able to speak again. "And you, sir," he said, "you are all right?"

The man nodded. He was warming himself now: flapping his arms and kicking his feet together. "A few minutes of sun and I'll be as good as new."

Nearby, a black boulder lay embedded in the glacial ice, and, going over to it, they sat down. The sunlight poured over them like a warm bath. Rudi slowly flexed his aching fingers and saw that the man was doing the same. And then the man had raised his eyes and was looking at him.

"It's a miracle how you did it," he said. "A boy of your size. All alone."

"It was nothing." Rudi murmured.

"Nothing?"

"I—I only—"

"Only saved my life." said the man.

For the first time, now, Rudi was really seeing him. He was a man of perhaps thirty, very tall and thin, and his face, too, was thin, with a big hawklike nose and a strong jutting chin. His weather-browned cheeks were clean-shaven, his hair black, his eyes deep-set and gray. And when he spoke, his voice was still almost as quiet as when it had been muffled by the ice-walls of the crevasse. He is—what?— Rudi thought. Not Swiss, he knew. Not French or German. English, perhaps? Yes, English. . . . And then suddenly a deep excitement filled him, for he knew who the man was.

"You are Captain Winter?" he murmured.

"That's right."

"And I—I have saved—I mean—"

Rudi stopped in confusion, and the Englishman grinned. "You've saved," he said, smiling, "one of the worst imbeciles that ever

Literary Analysis
Conflict with Nature
What is the moment at which the conflict is most intense?

pummeled (pum´ əld) *v.* pounded; beat

▲ **Critical Viewing** What details of this photograph might inspire Rudi? Explain.
[Speculate]

walked on a glacier. An imbecile who was so busy looking up at a mountain that he couldn't even see what was at his feet."

Rudi was wordless—almost stunned. He looked at the man, and then away in embarrassment, and he could scarcely believe what had happened. The name of Captain John Winter was known through the length and breadth of the Alps. He was the foremost mountaineer of his day, and during the past ten years had made more first ascents of great peaks than any other man alive. Rudi had heard that he had come to Kurtal a few days before. He had hoped that at least he would see him in the hotel or walking by in the street. But actually to meet him—and in this way! To pull him from a crevasse—save him. . . . It was incredible!

Captain Winter was watching him. "And you, son," he asked. "What is your name?"

Somehow the boy got his voice back. "Rudi," he said. "Rudi Matt."

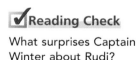

Reading Check

What surprises Captain Winter about Rudi?

"Matt?" Now it was the man's turn to be impressed. "Not of the family of the great Josef Matt?"

"He was my father," Rudi said.

Captain Winter studied him with his gray eyes. Then he smiled again. "I should have known," he said. "A boy who could do what you've done—"

"Did you know my father, sir?"

"No, unfortunately I didn't. He was before my day. But ever since I was a boy I have heard of him. In twenty years no one has come to the Alps and not heard of the great guide, Josef Matt."

Rudi's heart swelled. He looked away. His eyes fixed on the vast mountain that rose before them, and then he saw that Captain Winter was watching it too.

Unconsciously the Englishman spoke his thoughts. "Your father was—" He caught himself and stopped.

"Yes," said Rudi softly, "he was killed on the Citadel."

There was a silence. Captain Winter reached into a pocket and brought out an unbroken bar of chocolate. "Lucky I fell on the other side," he grinned.

He broke the bar in two and handed half to Rudi.

"Oh, no, sir, thank you. I couldn't."

"When I meet a boy your age who can't eat chocolate," said Winter, "I'll be glad to stay in a crevasse for good."

Rudi took it, and they sat munching. The sun was warm on their thawing bodies. Far above, it struck the cliffs and snowfields of the Citadel, so brightly that they had to squint against the glare.

Then there was Winter's quiet voice again. "What do you think, Rudi?"

"Think, sir?"

"Can it be climbed?"

"Climbed? The Citadel?"

"Your father thought so. Alone among all the guides of Switzerland, he thought so." There was another pause. "And I think so too," said Captain Winter.

The boy was peering again at the shining heights. And suddenly his heart was pounding so hard that he was sure the Englishman must be able to hear it. "Is—is that why you have come here, sir?" he asked. "To try to climb the Citadel?"

"Well, now—" Winter smiled. "It's not so simple, you know. For one thing, there's not a guide in the valley who would go with me."

"I have an uncle, sir. He is—"

Literary Analysis
Conflict with Nature
How does the detail about Rudi's father influence the view of nature in the story?

▼ **Critical Viewing**
Based on what you've read, what supplies and equipment do you think these climbers might be carrying? [**Apply**]

"Yes, I know your uncle. Franz Lerner. He is the best in Kurtal, and I've spoken to him. But he would not go. Anything but that, he said. Any other peak, any route, any venture. But not *that*, he said. Not the Citadel."

"He remembers my father—"

"Yes, he remembers your father. They all remember him. And while they love and respect his memory, they all think he was crazy." Winter chuckled softly. "Now they think *I'm* crazy," he added. "And maybe they're right too," he said.

"What will you do, sir?" asked Rudi. "Not try it alone?"

"No, that crazy I'm not." Winter slowly stroked his long jaw. "I'm not certain what I'll do," he went on. "Perhaps I'll go over to the next valley. To Broli. I've been told there is a guide there—a man called Saxo. Do you know him?"

"Yes—Emil Saxo. I have never met him, but I have heard of him. They say he is a very great guide."

"Well, I thought perhaps I'd go and talk with him. After a while. But first I must <u>reconnoiter</u> some more. Make my plans. Pick the route. If there *is* a route."

"Yes, there is! Of course there is!"

Rudi had not thought the words. They simply burst out from him. And now again he was embarrassed as the man looked at him curiously.

"So?" said Captain Winter. "That is interesting, Rudi. Tell me why you think so."

"I have studied the Citadel many times, sir."

"Why?"

"Because—because—" He stopped. He couldn't say it.

"Because you want to climb it yourself?"

"I am not yet a grown man, sir. I know I cannot expect—"

"I wasn't a grown man either," said the Captain, "when I first saw the Citadel. I was younger than you—only twelve—and my parents had brought me here for a summer holiday. But I can still remember how I felt when I looked up at it, and the promise I made myself that some day I was going to climb it." He paused. His eyes moved slowly upward. "Youth is the time for dreams, boy," he murmured. "The trick is, when you get older, not to forget them."

Rudi listened, spellbound. He had never heard anyone speak like that. He had not known a grown man could think and feel like that.

Then Winter asked:

"This east face, Rudi—what do you think of it?"

"Think of it, sir?"

"Could it be climbed?"

Rudi shook his head. "No, it is no good. The long chimney[2] there— you see. It looks all right: it could be done. And to the left, ledges"—

reconnoiter (rē kə noit′ ər) v. look around

Reading Strategy
Making Predictions
What prediction about the captain's search for a guide can you make based on Rudi's remark about the route?

 **Reading Check**

What do Rudi and Captain Winter discuss?

---

2. chimney (chim′ nē) *n.* deep, narrow crack in a cliff face, large enough to climb into.

he pointed—"they could be done too. But higher up, no. They stop. The chimney stops, and there is only smooth rock."

"What about the northeast ridge?"

"That is not good either."

"It's not so steep."

"No, it is not so steep," said Rudi. "But the rocks are bad. They slope out, with few places for holds."

"And the north face?"

Rudi talked on. About the north face, the west ridge, the southwest ridge. He talked quietly and thoughtfully, but with deep inner excitement, for this was the first time in his life that he had been able to speak to anyone of these things which he had thought and studied for so long. . . . And then suddenly he stopped, for he realized what he was doing. He, Rudi Matt, a boy of sixteen who worked in the kitchen of the Beau Site Hotel, was presuming to give his opinions to one of the greatest climbers in the world.

But Captain Winter had been listening intently. Sometimes he nodded. "Go on," he said now, as Rudi paused.

"But I am only—"

"Go on."

And Rudi went on . . .

"That doesn't leave much," said the captain a little later.

"No, sir," said the boy.

"Only the southeast ridge."

"Yes, sir."

"That was the way your father tried, wasn't it?"

"Yes, sir."

"And you believe it's the only way?"

"Yes, sir."

Captain Winter rubbed his jaw for a moment before speaking again. Then—"That also is very interesting to me, Rudi," he said quietly, "because it is what I believe too."

Later, they threaded their way down the Blue Glacier. For a while they moved in silence. Then Captain Winter asked:

"What do you do, Rudi?"

"Do, sir?"

"Are you an apprentice guide? A porter?"

Rudi swallowed. "No sir."

"What then?"

He could hardly say it. "A—dishwasher."

"A dishwasher?"

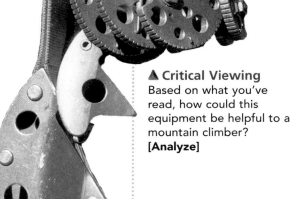

▲ **Critical Viewing**
Based on what you've read, how could this equipment be helpful to a mountain climber? **[Analyze]**

"In the Beau Site Hotel. It is my mother, sir. Since my father died, you see, she is afraid—she does not want—" Rudi swallowed again. "I am to go into the hotel business," he murmured.

"Oh."

Again they moved on without speaking. It was now late afternoon, and behind them the stillness was broken by a great roaring, as sun-loosened rock and ice broke off from the heights of the Citadel.

When they reached the path Rudi spoke again, hesitantly. "Will you please do me a favor, sir," he asked.

"Of course," said Winter.

"Before we come to the town we will separate. And you will please not tell anyone that I have been up here today?"

The Englishman looked at him in astonishment. "Not tell anyone? You save my life, boy, and you want me to keep it a secret?"

"It was nothing, sir. Truly. And if you say that I have been in the mountains, my mother and uncle will hear, and I will be in trouble." Rudi's voice took on a note of urgency. "You will not do it, sir? You will promise—please?"

Winter put a hand on his shoulder. "Don't worry," he said. "I won't get you in trouble." Then he smiled and added: "Master Rudi Matt—dishwasher."

They walked down the path. The sun sank. Behind them, the mountain roared.

Literary Analysis
Conflict with Nature
What does the detail about Rudi's occupation suggest about a conflict in the novel that is not with nature?

James Ramsey Ullman

(1907–1971) Born in the shadow of the mountain-like sky-scrapers of New York City, James Ramsey Ullman developed a love for climbing that made him feel more at home in the Himalayas of Tibet than on New York's crowded streets. Although he personally did not climb Mt. Everest, he was a member of the first American expedition to the mountain.

Ullman was also a talented writer who worked as a reporter and wrote fiction and plays. He combined his love of climbing and his writing skill in *Banner in the Sky*, which won a Newbery Honor award. Five of Ullman's books became films, including *The White Tower*, *River of the Sun*, and *Banner in the Sky*.

Review and Assess

Thinking About the Selection

1. **Respond:** Would you like to know Rudi? Why or why not?

2. **(a) Recall:** Who are the boy and the man referred to in the title of this story? **(b) Analyze:** Explain how the title might also be used to describe two sides of Rudi.

3. **(a) Interpret:** Captain Winter says, "Youth is the time for dreams." What is Rudi's dream? **(b) Infer:** Why has Rudi been unable to fulfill his dream?

4. **(a) Recall:** What advice does Rudi give Captain Winter about climbing the Citadel? **(b) Generalize:** How might giving Captain Winter advice help Rudi solve his own problem?

5. **(a) Infer:** What problems would climbing the Citadel pose for Rudi and Captain Winter? **(b) Contrast:** Explain how their problems are different. **(c) Make a Judgment:** Whose problem is more difficult to solve?

6. **Take a Position:** Should Rudi be allowed to climb in spite of his mother's fears? Explain.

From

Into Thin Air

JON KRAKAUER

In April 1996, writer Jon Krakauer joined an expedition to the top of Mount Everest. Krakauer survived to write a book about his experience, but before the trip was over, eight climbers had lost their lives. Here, Krakauer describes one of the terrifying ordeals of his climb.

If the Icefall required few orthodox climbing techniques, it demanded a whole new repertoire of skills in their stead—for instance, the ability to tiptoe in mountaineering boots and crampons[1] across three wobbly ladders lashed end to end, bridging a heart-stopping chasm. There were many such crossings, and I never got used to them.

At one point I was balanced on an unsteady ladder in the predawn gloaming, stepping tenuously from one bent rung to the next, when the ice supporting the ladder on either end began to quiver as if an earthquake had struck. A moment later came an

---

1. **crampons** (kram′ pənz) *n.* iron spikes on shoes to prevent slipping.

explosive roar as a large serac[2] somewhere close above came crashing
down. I froze, my heart in my throat,
but the avalanching ice passed fifty
yards to the left, out of sight, without
doing any damage. After waiting a few
minutes to regain my composure I
resumed my herky-jerky passage to the
far side of the ladder.

The glacier's continual and often violent state of flux added an element of
uncertainty to every ladder crossing. As
the glacier moved, crevasses would
sometimes compress, buckling ladders
like toothpicks; other times a crevasse
might expand, leaving a ladder dangling
in the air, only tenuously supported,
with neither end mounted on solid ice.
Anchors securing the ladders and lines
routinely melted out when the afternoon
sun warmed the surrounding ice and
snow. Despite daily maintenance, there
was a very real danger that any given
rope might pull loose under body weight.

But if the Icefall was strenuous and
terrifying, it had a surprising allure as
well. As dawn washed the darkness
from the sky, the shattered glacier
was revealed to be a three-dimensional
landscape of phantasmal beauty. The
temperature was six degrees Fahrenheit.
My crampons crunched reassuringly into the glacier's rind. Following
the fixed line, I meandered through a vertical maze of crystalline blue
stalagmites.[3] Sheer rock buttresses seamed with ice pressed in from
both edges of the glacier, rising like the shoulders of a <u>malevolent</u>
god. Absorbed by my surroundings and the gravity of the labor, I lost
myself in the unfettered pleasures of ascent, and for an hour or two
actually forgot to be afraid.

Three-quarters of the way to Camp One, Hall remarked at a
rest stop that the icefall was in better shape than he'd ever seen
it: "The route's a bloody freeway this season." But only slightly
higher, at 19,000 feet, the ropes brought us to the base of a
gargantuan, perilously balanced serac. As massive as a twelve-
story building, it loomed over our heads, leaning 30 degrees past

▲ **Critical Viewing**
What glacial dangers might
exist here? **[Connect]**

malevolent (mə lev´ ə lənt)
adj. wishing evil or harm
to others

**Reading Check**

What are Krakauer's
feelings about the Icefall?

---

2. **serac** (sə rak´) *n.* high, pointed mass of ice.
3. **stalagmites** (stə lag´ mīts´) *n.* cone-shaped mineral deposits.

vertical. The route followed a natural catwalk that angled sharply up the overhanging face: we would have to climb up and over the entire off-kilter tower to escape its threatening tonnage.

Safety, I understood, hinged on speed. I huffed toward the relative security of the serac's crest with all the haste I could muster, but since I wasn't acclimatized my fastest pace was no better than a crawl. Every four or five steps I'd have to stop, lean against the rope, and suck desperately at the thin, bitter air, searing my lungs in the process.

I reached the top of the serac without it collapsing and flopped breathless onto its flat summit, my heart pounding like a jackhammer. A little later, around 8:30 A.M., I arrived at the top of the Icefall itself, just beyond the last of the seracs. The safety of Camp One didn't supply much peace of mind, however: I couldn't stop thinking about the ominously tilted slab a short distance below, and the fact that I would have to pass beneath its faltering bulk at least seven more times if I was going to make it to the summit of Everest. Climbers who snidely denigrate this as the Yak Route, I decided, had obviously never been through the Khumbu Icefall.

denigrate (den´ ə grāt´) n. discredit; put down; belittle

Review and Assess

Thinking About the Selection

1. **Respond:** What thoughts might you have if you were crossing the icefall?

2. **(a) Recall:** What method does the writer use to cross the chasm of the icefall? **(b) Analyze:** Why do you think he never gets used to crossing the chasms?

3. **(a) Infer:** From what you have read, how would you rate Krakauer's skills as a mountaineer? **(b) Support:** How does the text show that being skilled is no guarantee of a climber's safety?

4. **(a) Interpret:** Why does Krakauer continue across the icefall despite his fear? **(b) Draw Conclusions:** What does this tell you about his character? **(c) Evaluate:** Would you want Krakauer with you during an emergency? Why or why not?

5. **(a) Recall:** Why did Krakauer have difficulty climbing the twelve-story serac quickly? **(b) Apply:** Why do climbers stop and camp at various heights on the mountain?

6. **Make a Judgment:** Would you choose the more difficult, but less hazardous route or the easier route with the potential for disaster? Explain.

Jon Krakauer

(b. 1954)
Family outings in Oregon set the stage for Jon Krakauer's interest in mountaineering. By his early twenties, he had attempted several difficult mountain ascents. His first book-length publication, *Eiger Dreams: Ventures Among Men and Mountains,* was a collection of essays about climbing the Eiger, one of the toughest peaks of the Alps. He was well prepared for the challenge of climbing Mt. Everest and writing about it in his best-selling book *Into Thin Air.*

Review and Assess

Literary Analysis

Conflict with Nature

1. Using a chart like the one shown, identify one mental and one physical challenge each character faces.

	Mental Challenge	**Physical Challenge**
Rudi		
Winter		
Krakauer		

2. Identify three details in "A Boy and a Man" that show that a **conflict with nature** can be brutal.

3. Describe the most terrifying environmental threat in the excerpt from *Into Thin Air*.

Comparing Literary Works

4. Which work contains more factual details about nature?

5. How are descriptions, conversations, and factual details used in each narrative? Use an organizer like the one shown to take notes on examples from each work.

Descriptions		**Conversations**		**Factual Details**	
Boy	Thin Air	Boy	Thin Air	Boy	Thin Air

6. What conflicts still remain to be resolved when each excerpt ends?

Reading Strategy

Making Predictions

7. Do you predict that Rudi will climb the Citadel? Explain.

8. What details in the passage from *Into Thin Air* help you predict that Krakauer reaches the summit and returns safely?

Extend Understanding

9. **Career Connection:** Mountain climbing requires mental and physical abilities. Name the mental skills required, and think of three careers that a person with these skills might pursue.

Quick Review

A **conflict** is a struggle between two opposing forces.

A **conflict with nature** is a struggle between a character or characters and a natural element or force. To review conflict, see page 179.

A **prediction** is an informed guess about what will happen and is based on details and experience.

 Take It to the Net
www.phschool.com
Take the interactive self-test online to check your understanding of these selections.

Integrate Language Skills

Vocabulary Development Lesson

Word Analysis: Latin Prefix *mal-*

The Latin prefix *mal-* means "bad" or "badly": *mal* (bad) + *volens* (wish) = *malevolent*, "wishing harm to others."

Write the words formed by adding the prefix *mal-* to the following words. Then, define each new word.

   1. functioned   **2.** nourished   **3.** formed

Spelling Strategy

When you break a word with double consonants at the end of a line, divide it between the two consonants: *pum-meled*. On your paper, divide the following words as if you reached the end of a line.

   1. reconnoiter   **3.** common

   2. allure   **4.** innocent

Fluency: Word Choice

Replace each italicized word or phrase with the vocabulary word that has the same meaning.

prone	reconnoiter
taut	malevolent
pummeled	denigrate

The lieutenant was in the field to **(1)** *investigate* the area that was to be attacked. His body was **(2)** *tense*. He thought that the situation was potentially dangerous, even though he had heard others **(3)** *belittle* the threat. As he lay in a **(4)** *flat* position on the ground, he saw where the **(5)** *evil* enemy had been **(6)** *beaten up* by cannon fire. Knowing the enemy was retreating, the lieutenant felt reassured.

Grammar Lesson

Adjective Placement

Both Ullman and Krakauer make their writing more descriptive by using **adjectives,** words that modify nouns or pronouns. Adjectives can be placed in several different parts of a sentence. Sometimes they come directly before the word they modify. Sometimes they follow linking verbs such as *am, is, are, was,* and *were* to modify the subject of a clause.

Before a Noun: Captain Winter brought out an *unbroken* bar of chocolate.

After a Linking Verb: The journey was *strenuous.*

▶ *For more practice, see page R28, Exercise D.*
Practice Copy these sentences on your paper. Underline each adjective, and draw an arrow to the word it modifies.

   1. He could hear an unfamiliar sound below.
   2. I was lucky and hit a ledge.
   3. You can see that she is afraid.
   4. The climb was terrifying.
   5. I meandered through a vertical maze of crystalline stalagmites.

Writing Application Write a paragraph describing a time when you faced extreme cold, extreme heat, or another serious weather condition. In your paragraph, use three adjectives before nouns and three adjectives following linking verbs.

W͜G *Prentice Hall Writing and Grammar Connection: Chapter 16, Section 1*

Writing Lesson

Persuasive Letter

Write a letter to Rudi's mother persuading her to let Rudi join Captain Winter on a climb up the Citadel.

Prewriting   Review "A Boy and a Man" to gather evidence for these points:

- Rudi is physically capable.
- Rudi has the necessary knowledge.
- Rudi will benefit from the climb.

Drafting   Begin by stating your position: Rudi should accompany the captain to the Citadel. Then, describe the points in support of your argument. Provide evidence for each point.

Model: Supporting an Argument

Rudi should accompany the captain up the Citadel.
He is strong enough for the trip. He has already shown
great physical strength. He supported Captain Winter's weight
while lying flat on his stomach.

> The first supporting point is highlighted in yellow. Evidence is highlighted in blue.

Revising   Find at least one piece of evidence for each point you use in support of your argument. If you cannot find evidence for a point, either add evidence or do not use the point to support your argument.

Prentice Hall Writing and Grammar Connection: Chapter 7, Section 3

Extension Activities

Listening and Speaking The selection "A Boy and a Man" describes a dramatic rescue. Conduct an **interview** with a professional rescue worker, such as a firefighter, police officer, or emergency medical technician.

- List your questions in advance.
- With a partner, practice the interview.

Use the practice interview to learn to ask follow-up questions—questions that draw out additional information, clarification, or evidence about a statement the subject of the interview makes.

Research and Technology Both Rudi and Krakauer face glaciers. Conduct research to find out about the dangers and difficulties associated with climbing or hiking glaciers. Give an oral explanation of what you have learned to the class.

Writing Write a **response** to these two works. In your reponse explain why you preferred the fiction or the nonfiction account.

 Take It to the Net   www.phschool.com

Go online for an additional research activity using the Internet.

Prepare to Read

The Charge of the Light Brigade ◆ The Enemy ◆ *from* Henry V

 Take It to the Net

Visit www.phschool.com
for interactive activities
and instruction related to
these selections, including

- background
- graphic organizers
- literary elements
- reading strategies

Preview

Connecting to the Literature

The works you are about to read give a glimpse into the experience of war. As you read, connect to the literature by focusing on specific details that capture the moments before, during, and after a battle.

Background

Fought between 1853 and 1856, the Crimean War pitted Russia against the armies of Great Britain, France, and what is now Turkey. "The Charge of the Light Brigade," by Alfred, Lord Tennyson, commemorates the Battle of Balaklava, in which about 670 lightly armed British troops charged a heavily armed Russian fortification. Two fifths of the British were killed.

Literary Analysis

Repetition

Repetition is the repeated use of words, phrases, or rhythms. Poets use repetition to add to the music of poetry, to emphasize ideas, and to help establish mood or atmosphere. Read these lines from Tennyson's poem "The Charge of the Light Brigade":

> Theirs not to make reply,
> Theirs not to reason why,
> Theirs but to do and die . . .

The repetition in this example creates rhythm and adds emphasis to the idea that the soldiers had no say in the decision to attack. As you read, look for other repetitions of words, phrases, and rhythms.

Comparing Literary Works

The poems in this group explore the reasons for and the results of war. To compare and contrast the views of war they express, keep the following focus questions in mind as you read.

1. What is similar and different about the images of war in these poems?
2. What feelings about war does each work express or suggest?

Reading Strategy

Using Word Parts

You can use **word parts** to recognize and remember the relationships between words. In "The Enemy," the speaker says, "consent or not/countries choose . . ." *Consent* shares the Latin affix *con-*, which can mean "with or together," with *connect*, meaning "join with or together." This shared affix can help you remember that *consent* means "agreement with."

As you read, look for words that seem to share parts with other words you know. Use a dictionary to confirm that similarities between words indicate shared word parts. Take notes by creating charts like the one shown here.

Word	consent
Origin	Latin *con-*
Other Words With Word Part	connect conflict

Vocabulary Development

dismayed (dis mād´) *adj.* afraid; without confidence (p. 199)

blundered (blun´ dərd) *v.* made a foolish mistake (p. 199)

volleyed (väl´ ēd) *v.* fired together (p. 199)

reeled (rēld) *v.* fell back from a blow (p. 200)

sundered (sun´ dərd) *adj.* broken apart (p. 200)

The Charge

Alfred, Lord Tennyson

Charge of the Light Brigade at the Battle of Balaklava, 1854, Artist Unknown

▲**Critical Viewing** Which words and phrases from the poem can be used to describe this scene? **[Connect]**

of the Light Brigade

1

Half a league,[1] half a league,
Half a league onward,
All in the valley of Death
    Rode the six hundred.
5 "Forward, the Light Brigade!
Charge for the guns!" he said:
Into the valley of Death
Rode the six hundred.

2

"Forward, the Light Brigade!"
10 Was there a man <u>dismayed</u>?
Not though the soldier knew
    Someone had <u>blundered</u>:
Theirs not to make reply,
Theirs not to reason why,
5 Theirs but to do and die,
Into the valley of Death
    Rode the six hundred.

3

Cannon to right of them,
Cannon to left of them,
20 Cannon in front of them
    <u>Volleyed</u> and thundered;
Stormed at with shot and shell,
Boldly they rode and well,
Into the jaws of Death,
25 Into the mouth of Hell
    Rode the six hundred.

---

1. league (lēg) *n.* three miles.

dismayed (dis mād´) *adj.*
afraid; without confidence

blundered (blun´ dərd) *v.*
made a foolish mistake

volleyed (väl´ ēd) *v.*
fired together

✔**Reading Check**

What is the Light
Brigade?

4

Flashed all their sabers bare,
Flashed as they turned in air,
Sab'ring the gunners there,

30 Charging an army, while
    All the world wondered:
Plunged in the battery² smoke
Right through the line they broke:
Cossack and Russian

35 <u>Reeled</u> from the saber stroke
    Shattered and <u>sundered</u>.
Then they rode back, but not,
    Not the six hundred.

5

Cannon to right of them,
40 Cannon to left of them,
Cannon behind them
    Volleyed and thundered;
Stormed at with shot and shell,
While horse and hero fell,

45 They that had fought so well
Came through the jaws of Death,
Back from the mouth of Hell,
All that was left of them,
    Left of six hundred.

6

50 When can their glory fade?
O the wild charge they made!
    All the world wondered.
Honor the charge they made!
Honor the Light Brigade,
55   Noble six hundred!

---

2. **battery** fortification equipped with heavy guns.

reeled (rēld) *v.* fell back from a blow

sundered (sun´ dərd) *adj.* broken apart

Alfred, Lord Tennyson

(1809–1892)

Alfred, Lord Tennyson was the most popular British poet of his day. In 1850, he published *In Memoriam, A.H.H,* a long poem in memory of a friend who had died. This poem impressed Queen Victoria, and she named Tennyson Poet Laureate, or chief poet of England. Many of Tennyson's poems focused on nature. Others dealt with significant historical events. "The Charge of the Light Brigade" was based on a newspaper account of a battle between English and Russian troops.

THE ENEMY

Alice Walker

in gray, battle-scarred Leningrad[1]
a tiny fist unsnapped to show
crumpled heads
of pink and yellow flowers
5 snatched hurriedly on the go
in the cold spring shower—

consent or not
countries choose
cold or hot
10 win or lose
to speak of wars
yellow and red
but there is much
let it be said
15 for children.

---

1. **Leningrad** (len´ in grad´) *n.* important city in the former Soviet Union, renamed St. Petersburg, in 1991.

Review and Assess

Thinking About the Selections

1. **Respond:** Which poem expresses your feelings about war?
2. **(a) Recall:** In the first two stanzas of "The Charge of the Light Brigade," what line sums up the attitude of the men going into battle? **(b) Infer:** What is the spirit of the Light Brigade's cavalrymen as they make their charge? **(c) Interpret:** How is this spirit contradicted by the soldiers' situation?
3. **(a) Recall:** How does the speaker describe the cavalrymen during the battle? **(b) Connect:** What do these descriptions reveal about the speaker's feelings about the soldiers?
4. **(a) Recall:** What is the setting of "The Enemy"? **(b) Interpret:** Why is this setting important in the poem?
5. **(a) Interpret:** Who or what do you think "the enemy" of the title is? **(b) Support:** What details in the poem lead you to this conclusion? **(c) Draw Conclusions:** What do you think Walker thinks about war?
6. **Make a Judgment:** Would Alfred, Lord Tennyson, or Alice Walker make a better war correspondent? Explain.

Alice Walker

(b. 1944)
   Alice Walker was born the eighth and last child in a poor family in Eatonton, Georgia. She developed a love of reading and writing at an early age, and she has gone on to establish herself as one of today's best-known and most-loved writers. In many of her works, she expresses her concerns about social injustice. [For more information on Walker, see page 110.]

from HENRY V
ST CRISPIAN'S DAY SPEECH

William Shakespeare

The following speech is given by King Henry V before he leads his army into battle. His troops are exhausted. The opposing army is much larger and will, it seems, defeat Henry and his troops. Henry attempts to inspire his soldiers by describing how they will be remembered in history for their boldness and bravery in the face of overwhelming odds.

This day is call'd the feast of Crispian:[1]
He that outlives this day, and comes safe home,
Will stand a' tiptoe when this day is named,
And rouse him at the name of Crispian.
5 He that shall live this day, and see old age,
Will yearly on the vigil feast his neighbors,
And say, "To-morrow is Saint Crispian."
Then will he strip his sleeve and show his scars,
And say, "These wounds I had on Crispin's day."

---

1. feast of Crispian St. Crispin's (kris´ pinz) Day, October 25, a religious holiday celebrating two early Christian martyrs.

◀ **Critical Viewing** Laurence Olivier, pictured in armor here, had the title role in the 1944 film version of *Henry V*. What elements of his body language suggest the royalty and leadership the speech conveys? **[Connect]**

☑**Reading Check**

What will the men who live through the battle do every year when they are older?

10 Old men forget; yet all shall be forgot,
    But he'll remember with advantages
    What feats he did that day. Then shall our names,
    Familiar his mouth as household words,
    Harry the King,[2] Bedford and Exeter,
15 Warwick and Talbot, Salisbury and Gloucester,[3]
    Be in their flowing cups freshly rememb'red.
    This story shall the good man teach his son;
    And Crispin Crispian shall ne'er go by,
    From this day to the ending of the world,
20 But we in it shall be remembered—
    We few, we happy few, we band of brothers;
    For he to-day that sheds his blood with me
    Shall be my brother; be he ne'er so vile,
    This day shall gentle his condition;
25 And gentlemen in England, now a-bed,
    Shall think themselves accurs'd they were not here;
    And hold their manhoods cheap whiles any speaks
    That fought with us upon Saint Crispin's day.

---

2. **Harry the King** King Henry V, ruler of England, 1413–1422.
3. **Bedford and Exeter** (eks´ ə tər), **Warwick** (wôr´ ik) **and Talbot**
(tōl´ bət), **Salisbury** (sôlz´ ber´ e) **and Gloucester** (gläs´ tər´) lords in
King Henry V's army.

Review and Assess

Thinking About the Selection

1. **Respond:** Do you agree with the speaker that men who were not at the battle will wish they had been? Why or why not?

2. **(a) Recall:** How does Henry refer to those men who will fight with him in the battle? **(b) Analyze:** What reasons might he have had for referring to them in this way?

3. **(a) Infer:** What does the St. Crispian's Day speech tell you about the character of Henry V? **(b) Speculate:** Do you think his soldiers found him to be an effective motivator? Explain.

4. **Assess:** Henry V's St. Crispian's Day speech is considered by many to be one of the greatest speeches an actor can perform. Based on your reading, why do you think this is so?

5. **Make a Judgment:** **(a)** Do you think the reasons Henry gives for joining the battle are good ones? Explain. **(b) Take a Position:** Under what circumstances, if any, do you feel a leader should ask others to follow him or her into a dangerous situation?

William Shakespeare

(1564–1616)

William Shakespeare was born in Stratford-on-Avon. His father was a successful glove maker and business-man. He studied classical literature and other subjects in school. Shakespeare married Anne Hathaway in 1582. They had three children, two of whom survived to adulthood. Shakespeare started acting professionally when a young man. He began writing plays and eventually became part-owner of the theater company that built the Globe theater in 1599. Most of his many plays were performed there.

[For more information on Shakespeare, see page 736.]

Review and Assess

Literary Analysis

Repetition

1. Give two examples of repeated rhythms and two of repeated words or phrases in the poems. Identify the work in which you found each example.
2. What is the effect of the **repetition** in these lines from "The Charge of the Light Brigade": "Cannon to right of them, / Cannon to left of them, / Cannon in front of them"?
3. What are readers reminded of when "six hundred" is repeated at the end of every stanza?

Comparing Literary Works

Use a chart like the following to take notes before answering questions 4 and 5.

	"The Charge of the Light Brigade"	"The Enemy"	from *Henry V*
Images			
Feelings			

4. What is similar and different about the images of war in these poems?
5. What feelings about war does each work express or suggest?
6. How are the authors' views of war similar, and how are they different?

Reading Strategy

Using Word Parts

On a separate sheet of paper, match each numbered word from science with a word from the poems that shares a **word part**. Then, explain how the meanings of the two words are related. Use a dictionary if necessary.

Words from Science   **Words from Poems**

7. replicate   **a.** dismayed
8. distill   **b.** reply
9. concentrated   **c.** consent

Extend Understanding

10. **Social Studies Connection:** Which of the three poems do you think gives the most realistic vision of war?

Integrate Language Skills

Vocabulary Development Lesson

Word Analysis: Latin Prefix *dis-*

The common Latin prefix *dis-* means "away, apart, not" or the "opposite." Use these words in sentences to demonstrate their meanings.

1. disappear
2. dislike
3. distrust
4. displace
5. displease

Spelling Strategy

When adding *-ed* to a verb with a stressed last syllable, double the final consonant if it is preceded by a vowel:

commit + *-ed* = committed.

Exceptions: words ending in *r, w, x,* and *y*. In those cases, do not double the final letter:

follow + *-ed* = followed

Add *-ed* to the following words.

1. volley + *-ed* =
2. blunder + *-ed* =
3. wonder + *-ed* =
4. regret + *-ed* =

Concept Development: Synonyms and Antonyms

Synonyms are words that are similar in meaning.

Example: battle; conflict

Antonyms are words that are opposite in meaning.

Example: war; peace

Copy each pair of words, and explain whether the words are synonyms or antonyms.

1. dismayed; frightened
2. blundered; repaired
3. volleyed; fired
4. reeled; fell
5. sundered; joined

Grammar Lesson

Possessive Adjectives

Personal pronouns that show ownership—*my, your, his, her, our, their*—are sometimes called **possessive adjectives** because they modify nouns by telling *whose*.

Notice that the pronoun *his* functions as an adjective in this line spoken by Henry V:

Example: "Then will he strip *his* sleeve and show *his* scars, . . ."

▶ *For more practice, see page R32, Exercise C.*

Practice Identify the possessive adjectives in the following lines from the poems. Tell which noun each modifies.

1. Flashed all their sabers bare, . . .
2. When can their glory fade?
3. He that shall live this day, . . . / Will yearly on the vigil feast his neighbors, . . .
4. Then shall our names,/Familiar his mouth as household words, . . .
5. For he to-day that sheds his blood with me / Shall be my brother; . . .

Writing Application In a summary of one of the poems, use *his, their,* and *its*.

𝒲𝒢 *Prentice Hall Writing and Grammar Connection: Chapter 16, Section 1*

Writing Lesson

Factual Account

Choose a battle you have learned about in your Social Studies class. Write a brief factual account of the battle and its outcome.

Prewriting   Use an outline like the one shown to take notes from history texts and online sources. Jot down questions as your outline takes shape.

Model: Outlining

I. Time and place of battle
    A.
    B.
II. Parties involved
    A.
    B.
III. Outcome

> The numbers and letters in an outline vary, according to how many details are noted.

Drafting   Write the details from your outline in complete sentences. Organize your account in paragraphs based on the sections of your outline.

Revising   Double check your draft against your notes to be sure your numbers and names are accurate.

Prentice Hall Writing and Grammar Connection: Chapter 11, Section 2

Extension Activities

Listening and Speaking In a group of three, act out a **debate** among the writers on war. Each writer should address this statement: The most important thing about war is the opportunity it offers for people to show bravery.

1. Find details and quotations from each poem that show the writer's feelings about war.
2. Have each "writer" state his or her position and give supporting reasons and examples.

As a final part of the debate, the writers can support or attack one another's arguments. **[Group Activity]**

Research and Technology View the film *Henry V* (1944), starring Laurence Olivier, and write a **report** on it for the class. In your report, provide classmates with information that will help them better understand the St. Crispian's Day Speech. Explain where in the plot the speech occurs.

Writing Write a **summary** of each poem. In your own words, restate the main ideas and explain what they mean.

 **Take It to the Net**   www.phschool.com

Go online for an additional research activity using the Internet.

CONNECTIONS
Literature and Social Studies

Shakespeare and His World

The St. Crispian's Day speech from *Henry V* focuses on glory, honor, and bravery. Henry inspires his troops by suggesting that simply by participating in the upcoming battle—win or lose—they will become legends. Risking one's life for fame and fortune would not have been a surprising idea for Shakespeare's audiences. Shakespeare lived in a time of intellectual, religious, and political change. Artists, writers, explorers, and scientists were shaking up the world. An ordinary working person could not paint a new style of picture or sail to a new world, but he or she could experience the thrill of bold and daring deeds acted out by characters on stage.

The Renaissance

Shakespeare lived during a time referred to as the Renaissance. The Renaissance (meaning rebirth) is a term used to describe the rich development of Western civilization that occurred after the Middle Ages and reached its height in the fifteenth and sixteenth centuries.

It started in Italy and spread throughout Europe and England. A greater understanding of anatomy allowed Italian artists to begin painting people more realistically. Artists also developed a new awareness of perspective (the appearance of distant objects being smaller than nearby objects) and an appreciation for the effects of color.

The enthusiasm for art and learning during this time period meant that the boy Shakespeare, like other well-to-do boys, attended school. There he learned Latin and Greek and studied classic literature as well as the history of England. Many of Shakespeare's plays are based on events in English history that Shakespeare learned as a boy.

Age of Exploration

Other dramatic changes in Shakespeare's world were the result of the explosion of exploration that followed Christopher Columbus's "discovery" of America. From the middle of the fifteenth century, explorers had traveled from Europe to all corners of the world, sometimes to engage in trade and sometimes to promote religious ideals. They brought back with them goods, maps, and new ideas and information from the places they had visited. Shakespeare would have heard about these voyages, and indeed, used the device of a shipwreck in his play *Twelfth Night.*

Timeline

1503–1506	Leonardo da Vinci paints the *Mona Lisa*
1558	Elizabeth I becomes Queen of England
1563	More than 20,000 Londoners die of the plague
1564	**Shakespeare is born**
1580	Sir Francis Drake returns from circumnavigating the globe
1595	Sir Walter Raleigh explores Orinoco River in South America
1609	Galileo builds the first telescope; Kepler calculates the orbits of the planets
1616	**Shakespeare dies**
1620	Pilgrims land at Plymouth Rock

The discoveries of explorers changed the way Europeans viewed the world in which they lived. The discoveries of scientists forced people to change the way they viewed the universe. Before 1543, most people believed that the sun and the planets revolved around the Earth, the center of the universe. The Polish astronomer Copernicus discovered that the planets, including Earth, revolve around the sun. Although this seems normal to people of today, to people in Elizabethan England, the idea was an almost unimaginable concept.

▲Critical Viewing
In what way does this photo of the new Globe show that people of modern times value the history and tradition of Shakespeare's time? [Analyze]

The Globe Theatre

Although not as sensational as the other changes in Shakespeare's world, a significant change occurred in the way people watched plays. In 1576, the first permanent theatre was built outside the London gates by James Burbage, who called it, simply, The Theatre. Until that time, actors had traveled around the country, performing in the halls of great manor houses and colleges, and on platforms set up in crowded inn-yards.

In 1599, during the last years of Queen Elizabeth's reign, The Theatre was replaced with a new theatre called the Globe. A circular, wooden-framed building, the Globe was built in the classical style of the stone and marble amphitheaters of Rome and Ancient Greece, making it highly distinctive. Audiences could see and hear better in the round theatre than they could in the earlier square or rectangular halls and inn yards used for theatrical performances.

Shakespeare's plays, many of which were first performed at the Globe, are performed at theaters around the world today.

Connecting Literature and Social Studies

1. What ideas in the St. Crispian's Day speech would appeal to an explorer like Sir Walter Raleigh or Sir Francis Drake?

2. What goals might a soldier in Henry's army share with an explorer of Shakespeare's time?

3. Henry speaks of being remembered in history. What people from Shakespeare's time do people remember today? For what are they remembered?

Prepare to Read

The Californian's Tale ◆ Valediction

 Take It to the Net

Visit www.phschool.com
for interactive activities
and instruction related to
these selections, including

- background
- graphic organizers
- literary elements
- reading strategies

Preview

Connecting to the Literature

Open a school yearbook, and you will see rows of smiling young faces. In truth, you know little of the lives that go with the faces. As you read Twain's tale and Heaney's poem, remember that behind every picture lies a story—but it is not necessarily the story you imagine.

Background

The California Gold Rush of 1849 brought thousands to California, eager to strike it rich. Often, men left wives and family behind and lived in terrible conditions as they worked to make their fortunes. With few women around to make life bearable, it is no wonder the prospector in Mark Twain's "The Californian's Tale" saw a woman's presence as a treasure worth more than gold!

Literary Analysis

Local Color

Often the place and time in which a story is set influences the way in which the author develops characters. Writers may use characters' speech or actions to strengthen the impression of a place. **Local color** is the use of details specific to a region, such as

- descriptions of people, places, and things.
- characters' speech, actions, and customs.

In the following example, the italicized words add local color.

> Toward twilight a *big miner from three miles away* came—one of the *grizzled, stranded pioneers*—and gave us warm salutation, clothed in *grave and sober speech*. Then he said:
> "I only *just dropped over to ask about the little madam*, and when is she coming home. Any news from her?"

Use an organizer like the one shown here to note other examples of local color in "The Californian's Tale."

LOCAL COLOR	
Descriptions	1. big miner 2. grizzled pioneers
Speech	1. just dropped over 2. the little madam
Actions/Customs	1. People from 3 miles away just "drop over"!

Comparing Literary Works

Both "The Californian's Tale" and "Valediction" deal with the theme of loss. While both works deal with a similar loss—the loss of a beloved woman—the reactions to the loss are strikingly different. As you read, compare and contrast the ways each man deals with his loss.

Reading Strategy

Summarizing

A **summary** of a story is a brief statement in your own words of the main points and important details. Pause periodically to recall and restate key events. Use these focus questions to help you summarize:

1. What happens before the narrator decides to stay for the party?
2. What happens between Wednesday and the party Saturday?

Vocabulary Development

balmy (bäm´ ē) *adj.* soothing; mild; pleasant (p. 213)

predecessors (pred´ ə ses´ ərz) *n.* those who came before (p. 213)

humiliation (hyo͞o mil´ ē ā´ shən) *n.* embarrassment; feeling of hurt pride (p. 213)

abundant (ə bun´ dənt) *adj.* plentiful (p. 213)

desolation (des´ ə lā´ shən) *n.* loneliness; emptiness; misery (p. 214)

furtive (fʉr´ tiv) *adj.* sneaky (p. 215)

gratify (grat´ i fī´) *v.* to please (p. 215)

apprehensions (ap´ rē hen´ shənz) *n.* fears; anxious feelings (p. 218)

The Californian's Tale

Mark Twain

*T*hirty-five years ago I was out prospecting on the Stanislaus,[1] tramping all day long with pick and pan and horn, and washing a hatful of dirt here and there, always expecting to make a rich strike, and never doing it. It was a lovely region, woodsy, balmy, delicious, and had once been populous, long years before, but now the people had vanished and the charming paradise was a solitude. They went away when the surface diggings gave out. In one place, where a busy little city with banks and newspapers and fire companies and a mayor and aldermen had been, was nothing but a wide expanse of emerald turf, with not even the faintest sign that human life had ever been present there. This was down toward Tuttletown. In the country neighborhood thereabouts, along the dusty roads, one found at intervals the prettiest little cottage homes, snug and cozy, and so cobwebbed with vines snowed thick with roses that the doors and windows were wholly hidden from sight—sign that these were deserted homes, forsaken years ago by defeated and disappointed families who could neither sell them nor give them away. Now and then, half an hour apart, one came across solitary log cabins of the earliest mining days, built by the first gold-miners, the predecessors of the cottage-builders. In some few cases these cabins were still occupied; and when this was so, you could depend upon it that the occupant was the very pioneer who had built the cabin; and you could depend on another thing, too—that he was there because he had once had his opportunity to go home to the States rich, and had not done it; had rather lost his wealth, and had then in his humiliation resolved to sever all communication with his home relatives and friends, and be to them thenceforth as one dead. Round about California in that day were scattered a host of these living dead men—pride-smitten poor fellows, grizzled and old at forty, whose secret thoughts were made all of regrets and longings—regrets for their wasted lives, and longings to be out of the struggle and done with it all.

It was a lonesome land! Not a sound in all those peaceful expanses of grass and woods but the drowsy hum of insects; no glimpse of man or beast; nothing to keep up your spirits and make you glad to be alive. And so, at last, in the early part of the afternoon, when I caught sight of a human creature, I felt a most grateful uplift. This person was a man about forty-five years old, and he was standing at the gate of one of those cozy little rose-clad cottages of the sort already referred to. However, this one hadn't a deserted look; it had the look of being lived in and petted and cared for and looked after; and so had its front yard, which was a garden of flowers, abundant,

---

1. **Stanislaus** (stǎ´ ni slôws) *n.* county, river, and mountain, all located in California.

◄ **Critical Viewing** Based on the clothing in this illustration, what conclusions can you draw about life in the mining camp? **[Draw Conclusions]**

balmy (bäm´ ē) *adj.* soothing; mild; pleasant

Literary Analysis
Local Color What details about the place add local color to the start of the story?

predecessors (pred´ ə ses´ ərz) *n.* those who came before

humiliation (hyōō mil´ ē ā´ shən) *n.* embarrassment; feeling of hurt pride

abundant (ə bun´ dənt) *adj.* plentiful

✔ **Reading Check**
What makes the cottage unusual?

gay, and flourishing. I was invited in, of course, and required to make myself at home—it was the custom of the country.

It was delightful to be in such a place, after long weeks of daily and nightly familiarity with miners' cabins—with all which this implies of dirt floor, never-made beds, tin plates and cups, bacon and beans and black coffee, and nothing of ornament but war pictures from the Eastern illustrated papers tacked to the log walls. That was all hard, cheerless, materialistic <u>desolation</u>, but here was a nest which had aspects to rest the tired eye and refresh that something in one's nature which, after long fasting, recognizes, when confronted by the belongings of art, howsoever cheap and modest they may be, that it has unconsciously been famishing and now has found nourishment. I could not have believed that a rag carpet could feast me so, and so content me; or that there could be such solace to the soul in wall-paper and framed lithographs,[2] and bright-colored tidies[3] and lamp-mats, and Windsor chairs,[4] and varnished what-nots, with sea-shells and books and china vases on them, and the score of little unclassifiable tricks and touches that a woman's hand distributes about a home, which one sees without knowing he sees them, yet would miss in a moment if they were taken away. The delight that was in my heart showed in my face, and the man saw it and was pleased; saw it so plainly that he answered it as if it had been spoken.

"All her work," he said, caressingly; "she did it all herself—every bit," and he took the room in with a glance which was full of affectionate worship. One of those soft Japanese fabrics with which woman drape with careful negligence the upper part of a picture-frame was out of adjustment. He noticed it, and rearranged it with cautious pains, stepping back several times to gauge the effect before he got it to suit him. Then he gave it a light finishing pat or two with his hand, and said: "She always does that. You can't tell just what it lacks, but it does lack something until you've done that—you can see it yourself after it's done, but that is all you know; you can't find out the law of it. It's like the finishing pats a mother gives the child's hair after she's got it combed and brushed, I reckon. I've seen her fix all these things so much that I can do them all just her way, though I don't know the law of any of them. But she knows the law. She knows the why and the how both; but I don't know the why; I only know the how."

He took me into a bedroom so that I might wash my hands; such a bedroom as I had not seen for years: white counterpane, white pillows, carpeted floor, papered walls, pictures, dressing-table, with mirror and pin-cushion and dainty toilet things; and in

desolation (des´ ə lā´ shən) *n.* loneliness; emptiness; misery

Literary Analysis
Local Color What details in this passage develop the local color?

---

2. **lithographs** (li*th*´ ə grafs´) *n.* type of print.
3. **tidies** (tīd´ ēz) *n.* ornamental chair coverings that protect the back, armrests, and headrest.
4. **Windsor chairs** (win´ zər) *n.* wooden chairs popular in the 18th century. They had spreading legs, a back of spindles, and usually a saddle seat.

the corner a wash-stand, with real china-ware bowl and pitcher,[5] and with soap in a china dish, and on a rack more than a dozen towels—towels too clean and white for one out of practice to use without some vague sense of profanation. So my face spoke again, and he answered with gratified words:

"All her work; she did it all herself—every bit. Nothing here that hasn't felt the touch of her hand. Now you would think—But I mustn't talk so much."

By this time I was wiping my hands and glancing from detail to detail of the room's belongings, as one is apt to do when he is in a new place, where everything he sees is a comfort to his eye and his spirit; and I became conscious, in one of those unaccountable ways, you know, that there was something there somewhere that the man wanted me to discover for myself. I knew it perfectly, and I knew he was trying to help me by <u>furtive</u> indications with his eye, so I tried hard to get on the right track, being eager to <u>gratify</u> him. I failed several times, as I could see out of the corner of my eye without being told; but at last I know I must be looking straight at the thing—knew it from the pleasure issuing in invisible waves from him. He broke into a happy laugh, and rubbed his hands together, and cried out:

"That's it! You've found it. I knew you would. It's her picture."

I went to the little black-walnut bracket on the farther wall, and did find there what I had not yet noticed—a daguerreotype-case. It contained the sweetest girlish face, and the most beautiful, as it seemed to me, that I had ever seen. The man drank the admiration from my face, and was fully satisfied.

"Nineteen her last birthday," he said, as he put the picture back; "and that was the day we were married. When you see her—ah, just wait till you see her!"

"Where is she? When will she be in?"

"Oh, she's away now. She's gone to see her people. They live forty or fifty miles from here. She's been gone two weeks to-day."

"When do you expect her back?"

"This is Wednesday. She'll be back Saturday, in the evening—about nine o'clock, likely."

I felt a sharp sense of disappointment.

"I'm sorry, because I'll be gone by then," I said, regretfully.

"Gone? No—why should you go? Don't go. She'll be so disappointed."

She would be disappointed—that beautiful creature! If she had said the words herself they could hardly have blessed me more. I was feeling a deep, strong longing to see her—a longing so supplicating, so insistent, that it made me afraid. I said to myself: "I will go straight away from this place, for my peace of mind's sake."

Reading Strategy
Summarizing What have you learned about the man and his cabin so far?

furtive (fur´ tiv) *adj.* sneaky

gratify (grat´ i fī´) *v.* to please

✔**Reading Check**
Whom does the narrator want to meet?

---

5. **wash-stand, with real china-ware bowl and pitcher** items used for washing before sinks and indoor plumbing were available.

"You see, she likes to have people come and stop with us—people who know things, and can talk—people like you. She delights in it; for she knows—oh, she knows nearly everything herself, and can talk, oh, like a bird—and the books she reads, why, you would be astonished. Don't go; it's only a little while, you know, and she'll be so disappointed."

I heard the words, but hardly noticed them, I was so deep in my thinkings and strugglings. He left me, but I didn't know. Presently he was back, with the picture-case in his hand, and he held it open before me and said:

"There, now, tell her to her face you could have stayed to see her, and you wouldn't."

That second glimpse broke down my good resolution. I would stay and take the risk. That night we smoked the tranquil pipe, and talked till late about various things, but mainly about her; and certainly I had had no such pleasant and restful time for many a day. The Thursday followed and slipped comfortably away. Toward twilight a big miner from three miles away came—one of the grizzled, stranded pioneers—and gave us warm salutation, clothed in grave and sober speech. Then he said:

"I only just dropped over to ask about the little madam, and when is she coming home. Any news from her?"

"Oh yes, a letter. Would you like to hear it, Tom?"

"Well, I should think I would, if you don't mind, Henry!"

Henry got the letter out of his wallet, and said he would skip some of the private phrases, if we were willing; then he went on and read the bulk of it—a loving, sedate, and altogether charming and gracious piece of handiwork, with a postscript full of affectionate regards and messages to Tom, and Joe, and Charley, and other close friends and neighbors.

As the reader finished, he glanced at Tom, and cried out:

Reading Strategy
Summarizing Summarize the reasons why the narrator decides to stay.

"Oho, you're at it again! Take your hands away, and let me see your eyes. You always do that when I read a letter from her. I will write and tell her."

"Oh no, you mustn't, Henry. I am getting old, you know, and any little disappointment makes me want to cry. I thought she'd be here herself, and now you've got only a letter."

"Well, now, what put that in your head? I thought everybody knew she wasn't coming till Saturday."

"Saturday! Why, come to think, I did know it. I wonder what's the matter with me lately? Certainly I knew it. Ain't we all getting ready for her? Well, I must be going now. But I'll be on hand when she comes, old man!"

Late Friday afternoon another gray veteran tramped over from his cabin a mile or so away, and said the boys wanted to have a little gaiety and a good time Saturday night, if Henry thought she wouldn't be too tired after her long journey to be kept up.

"Tired? She tired! Oh, hear the man! Joe, you know she'd sit up six weeks to please any one of you!"

When Joe heard that there was a letter, he asked to have it read, and the loving messages in it for him broke the old fellow all up; but he said he was such an old wreck that that would happen to him if she only just mentioned his name. "Lord, we miss her so!" he said.

Saturday afternoon I found I was taking out my watch pretty often. Henry noticed it, and said, with a startled look:

"You don't think she ought to be here so soon, do you?"

I felt caught, and a little embarrassed; but I laughed, and said it was a habit of mine when I was in a state of expectancy. But he didn't seem quite satisfied; and from that time on he began to show uneasiness. Four times he walked me up the road to a point whence we could see a long distance; and there he would stand, shading his eyes with his hand, and looking. Several times he said:

"I'm getting worried, I'm getting right down worried. I know she's not due till about nine o'clock, and yet something seems to be trying to warn me that something's happened. You don't think anything has happened, do you?"

I began to get pretty thoroughly ashamed of him for his childishness; and at last, when he repeated that imploring question still another time, I lost my patience for the moment, and spoke pretty brutally to him. It seemed to shrivel him up and cow him; and he looked so wounded and so humble after that, that I detested myself for having done the cruel and unnecessary thing. And so I was glad when Charley, another veteran, arrived toward the

Literary Analysis
Local Color How is local color created here?

◀ Critical Viewing
Why would a cabin such as the one pictured here be unusual in the mining camps? **[Connect]**

✔ Reading Check
What is Joe's reaction to the letter?

edge of the evening, and nestled up to Henry to hear the letter read, and talked over the preparations for the welcome. Charley fetched out one hearty speech after another, and did his best to drive away his friend's bodings and <u>apprehensions.</u>

"Anything happened to her? Henry, that's pure nonsense. There isn't anything going to happen to her; just make your mind easy as to that. What did the letter say? Said she was well, didn't it? And said she'd be here by nine o'clock, didn't it? Did you ever know her to fail of her word? Why, you know you never did. Well, then, don't you fret; she'll be here, and that's absolutely certain, and as sure as you are born. Come, now, let's get to decorating—not much time left."

Pretty soon Tom and Joe arrived, and then all hands set about adorning the house with flowers. Toward nine the three miners said that as they had brought their instruments they might as well tune up, for the boys and girls would soon be arriving now, and hungry for a good, old-fashioned break-down. A fiddle, a banjo, and a clarinet—these were the instruments. The trio took their places side by side, and began to play some rattling dance-music, and beat time with their big boots.

It was getting very close to nine. Henry was standing in the door with his eyes directed up the road, his body swaying to the torture of his mental distress. He had been made to drink his wife's health and safety several times, and now Tom shouted:

"All hands stand by! One more drink, and she's here!"

Joe brought the glasses on a waiter, and served the party. I reached for one of the two remaining glasses, but Joe growled, under his breath:

"Drop that! Take the other."

Which I did. Henry was served last. He had hardly swallowed his drink when the clock began to strike. He listened till it finished, his face growing pale and paler; then he said:

"Boys, I am sick with fear. Help me—I want to lie down!"

They helped him to the sofa. He began to nestle and drowse, but presently spoke like one talking in his sleep, and said: "Did I hear horses' feet? Have they come?"

One of the veterans answered, close to his ear: "It was Jimmy Parrish come to say the party got delayed, but they're right up the road a piece, and coming along. Her horse is lame, but she'll be here in half an hour."

"Oh, I'm so thankful nothing has happened!"

He was asleep almost before the words were out of his mouth. In a moment those handy men had his clothes off, and had tucked him into his bed in the chamber where I had washed my hands. They closed the door and came back. Then they seemed preparing to leave; but I said: "Please don't go, gentlemen. She won't know me; I am a stranger."

apprehensions
(ap′ rē hen′ shənz) *n.*
fears; anxious feelings

Literary Analysis
Local Color Which words in the dialogue here help to show local color?

Reading Strategy
Summarizing Identify the three most important facts or events you have learned so far.

They glanced at each other. Then Joe said:

"She? Poor thing, she's been dead nineteen years!"

"Dead?"

"That or worse. She went to see her folks half a year after she was married, and on her way back, on a Saturday evening, the Indians captured her within five miles of this place, and she's never been heard of since."

"And he lost his mind in consequence?"

"Never has been sane an hour since. But he only gets bad when that time of the year comes round. Then we begin to drop in here, three days before she's due, to encourage him up, and ask if he's heard from her, and Saturday we all come and fix up the house with flowers, and get everything ready for a dance. We've done it every year for nineteen years. The first Saturday there was twenty-seven of us, without counting the girls; there's only three of us now, and the girls are all gone. We drug him to sleep, or he would go wild; then he's all right for another year— thinks she's with him till the last three or four days come round; then he begins to look for her, and gets out his poor old letter, and we come and ask him to read it to us. Lord, she was a darling!"

Review and Assess

Thinking About the Selection

1. **(a) Respond:** Were you surprised by the ending of "The Californian's Tale," or did you guess what was coming? Explain your response.

2. **(a) Recall:** In what ways is Henry's house different from the houses of other miners? **(b) Analyze:** Why is Henry's cottage so appealing to the narrator?

3. **(a) Recall:** Where does Henry say his wife is? **(b) Infer:** Why does the narrator wait for her return? **(c) Compare and Contrast:** How are the narrator's feelings about Henry's wife similar to and different from the other characters' feelings?

4. **(a) Infer:** Why do the miners go to such lengths to help Henry? **(b) Infer:** What does their behavior say about their own lives?

5. **(a) Draw Conclusions:** Henry's wife was just nineteen when she disappeared. What do you think she was like? **(b) Support:** Use details from the descriptions in the story and the reactions of the characters to support your conclusion.

6. **Make a Judgment:** Should anyone make an effort to get Henry to recognize the truth? Why or why not?

Mark Twain

(1835–1910)

In his youth, Mark Twain worked as a Mississippi riverboat pilot before heading west to prospect for gold. He never struck it rich through gold, but Twain's experiences in the camps gave him the raw material for writing humorous reports for a local newspaper.

Because Twain loved meeting colorful characters and studying the way that people fool even themselves, life in the prospectors' camps provided him with material to make great stories.

Valediction[1]

Seamus Heaney

Lady with the frilled blouse
And simple tartan[2] skirt,
Since you have left the house
Its emptiness has hurt
5   All thought. In your presence
Time rode easy, anchored
On a smile; but absence
Rocked love's balance, unmoored
The days. They buck and bound
10   Across the calendar
Pitched from the quiet sound
Of your flowertender
Voice. Need breaks on my strand;
You've gone, I am at sea.
15   Until you resume command
Self is in mutiny.

---

1. **valediction** (val´ ə dik´ shən) *n.* the act of saying farewell.
2. **tartan** (tär´ tən) *n.* woolen cloth with plaid pattern, commonly worn in the Scottish Highlands, where each clan has its own plaid.

Review and Assess

Thinking About the Selection

1. **Respond:** Which line in "Valediction" seems saddest to you?
2. **(a) Recall:** Whom is the speaker in the poem addressing?
   (b) Infer: What has happened between the speaker and the person to whom the poem is addressed?
3. **(a) Draw Conclusions:** How does the speaker feel about the situation? **(b) Interpret:** What does the speaker mean by "Until you resume command/Self is in mutiny"?
4. **Make a Judgment:** Do you think the situation identified in the poem is permanent or temporary? Support your answer with details from the poem.
5. **Connect:** Explain how this poem connects to the expression "Absence makes the heart grow fonder."

Seamus Heaney

(b. 1939)
Seamus Heaney is one of Ireland's most beloved contemporary poets. Much of his early work focuses on everyday life in the Irish countryside where he was born. His most recent poetry deals with Irish history, culture, and politics.

Heaney has won numerous awards and honors, including the 1995 Nobel Prize for Literature.

Review and Assess

Literary Analysis

Local Color

1. What details of customs, clothing, and unusual spoken language create **local color** in "The Californian's Tale"?
2. What details in the narrator's descriptions of other characters add to the local color?
3. In "Valediction," what details indicate the clothing styles of the place in which the poem is set?

Comparing Literary Works

4. "The Californian's Tale" and "Valediction" are about men who experience a painful loss. Compare and contrast the works using a Venn Diagram. Use the overlapping portion of the diagram to note similarities in the type of loss and how the men deal with the loss. Use the separate sections to note details that show the differences in the losses and the men's reactions.

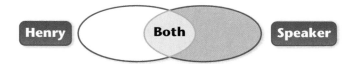

Reading Strategy

Summarizing

5. **Summarize** the events in "The Californian's Tale" that lead Henry to beg the narrator to stay to meet his wife.
6. What happens between Wednesday and Saturday?
7. What happens on Saturday night?
8. Summarize each work by filling in a chart as the directions indicate.

Title	1. Write one significant idea, event, or point from the beginning.	2. Write one significant idea, event, or point from the middle.	3. Write one significant idea, event, or point from the end.
Summary	Write one sentence that contains the ideas and details from sections 1, 2, and 3.		

Extend Understanding

9. **Cultural Connection:** (a) What do "The Californian's Tale" and "Valediction" say about the value of a woman in the home?
   (b) How has this idea of the role of women changed over time?

Quick Review

Local color is the use of detail specific to a region. To review local color, see page 211.

A **summary** of a story is a brief statement in one's own words of the key points and important details of the action.

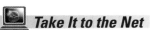 **Take It to the Net**
www.phschool.com
Take the interactive self-test online to check your understanding of these selections.

Integrate Language Skills

Vocabulary Development Lesson

Word Analysis: Latin Suffix *-ify*

The Latin suffix *-ify* indicates that a word is a verb showing action. For example, *gratify* means "to please." Use *-ify* to create a verb from each word below. You may need to drop letters.

1. testimony   **2.** solid   **3.** pure

Spelling Strategy

Use associations to help you remember when to use *t* and when to use *s* when spelling the *shun* sound.

Example: Humiliation and apprehension are different feelings and have different spellings.

Make up sentences that will help you remember the spellings of the following words.

1. association   **2.** desolation   **3.** pretension

Fluency: Word Choice

Answer these questions. Explain each response.

1. How long might a *furtive* glance take?
2. Would a farmer be happy with an *abundant* crop?
3. How could you calm your best friend's *apprehensions*?
4. What was the *predecessor* to digital watches?
5. Would you need mittens on a *balmy* night?
6. What could you do to *gratify* your sister?
7. What is a good way to overcome *humiliation*?
8. Where would you expect to find *desolation*?

Grammar Lesson

Adverbs

An **adverb** is a word that modifies or describes a verb, an adjective, or another adverb. Adverbs provide information by answering the questions *how, when, where, how often,* or *to what extent.* Many adverbs end in the suffix *-ly.* Here are examples from "The Californian's Tale":

They went *away.* (Where did they go?)

"All her work," he said, *caressingly.* (How did he say it?)

"She *always* does that." (When does she do it?)

Certainly I had had no such pleasant time. (To what extent had he not had a pleasant time?)

▶ *For more practice, see page R28, Exercise D.*
Practice Identify each adverb and the word it modifies. Tell what question it answers.

1. Doors were wholly hidden from sight.
2. Thursday followed and slipped comfortably away.
3. "Well, I must be going now."
4. He rose hourly to pace the floor.
5. I began to get pretty thoroughly ashamed of him.

Writing Application Write sentences using the following adverbs. Identify each verb modified.

1. completely   **3.** sadly   **5.** nearly
2. unfortunately   **4.** wisely

W͞G Prentice Hall Writing and Grammar Connection: Chapter 16, Section 2

Writing Lesson

Character Sketch

Write a character sketch of Henry in "The Californian's Tale."

Prewriting   Review the story, taking notes on what you know about Henry. Brainstorm to compile a list of descriptive details that will help you picture him.

Drafting   Now, use your notes and descriptive details to describe how Henry looks, acts, and talks. End with your impression of him, such as "He was certainly a friendly fellow."

Revising   Make five stars out of construction paper. Write one label on each star: Appearance, Actions, Words, Thoughts, Others' reactions. On each star, write appropriate details that are not already included. Look for places in your sketch to add the details.

Appearance

beard   neat   clothes

Model: Descriptive Details

His clothing was neat, and he wore a beard.

Henry was forty-five years old. He thought his wife

was the best woman in the world.

 Prentice Hall Writing and Grammar Connection: Chapter 5, Section 4

Extension Activities

Dramatization With a group, create a **dramatization** of the ending of "The Californian's Tale." Add dialogue to make your scene sound as much like Twain's writing as possible. For an effective presentation,

- vary the intensity of your voice according to Twain's directions in the text.
- express excitement by speeding up your words and raising the pitch of your voice.
- add emphasis by slowing your tempo.

In addition, use gestures and movements indicated by the text. **[Group Activity]**

Research and Technology With a group, create a **multimedia presentation** about the California Gold Rush. Discuss how you will use maps, photographs, newspaper reports, music, and diary entries in your report. When you give your presentation, explain what you learned from your research, and identify the techniques used to achieve the effects your group desired.

Take It to the Net   www.phschool.com

Go online for an additional research activity using the Internet.

Prepare to Read

Stopping by Woods on a Snowy Evening ◆ Miracles ◆ Four Skinny Trees

 Take It to the Net

Preview

Connecting to the Literature

Where you live probably has a big influence on the way you see the world. In the pieces that follow, Robert Frost, Sandra Cisneros, and Walt Whitman describe the settings that surround them and express how these places shape their thoughts and feelings.

Background

Robert Frost, who wrote "Stopping by Woods on a Snowy Evening," is one of America's best-loved poets. Much of his work is set in northern New England. In this region known for its natural beauty, harsh winters, and picture-postcard villages, Frost's speakers confront difficult choices—which road to take, what commitments to honor, how connected each person should be to others.

Literary Analysis
Levels of Meaning

Many works of literature contain different **levels of meaning.** Beyond the literal meaning—what the words actually say—the work may contain deeper meanings. "Four Skinny Trees," for example, is literally about four trees that grow outside a young woman's home. To the author, they represent her personal growth. To readers, they may represent all young people and their struggle to make a place for themselves. As you read, consider the levels of meaning in each work. Take note of your thoughts on an organizer like the one shown.

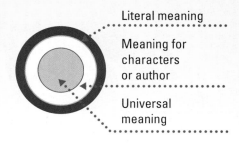

Literal meaning

Meaning for characters or author

Universal meaning

Comparing Literary Works

Compare and contrast the different ideas expressed in the works and the way the ideas are expressed. Think about the following focus questions.

1. What are the similarities and differences in the literal subjects of the works?
2. What deeper levels of meaning does each work communicate?

Reading Strategy
Interpreting Figurative Language

Figurative language is language that is not meant to be read literally. Often, such language is based on a comparison between two apparently unlike items. At first, the comparison may seem surprising, as when Cisneros describes trees as if they are people. However, the more you think about the comparison, the more truth and accuracy you may see in it. To interpret figurative language, identify the items being compared. Then, think about the deeper truth or meaning that the comparison suggests. Some common figures of speech include

- **analogy:** identifying a shared quality between two ideas or situations that are otherwise unlike each other.
- **simile:** comparing one thing to another using *like* or *as*.
- **metaphor:** describing one thing as if it were another.

Vocabulary Development

downy (doun´ ē) *adj.* soft and fluffy (p. 226)

exquisite (eks kwi´ zit) *adj.* very beautiful, especially in a delicate way (p. 229)

distinct (di stiŋkt´) *adj.* separate and different (p. 229)

ferocious (fə rō´ shəs) *adj.* fierce; savage (p. 230)

Stopping by Woods on a Snowy Evening

Robert Frost

Whose woods these are I think I know.
His house is in the village, though;
He will not see me stopping here
To watch his woods fill up with snow.

5   My little horse must think it queer
To stop without a farmhouse near
Between the woods and frozen lake
The darkest evening of the year.

He gives his harness bells a shake
10   To ask if there is some mistake.
The only other sound's the sweep
Of easy wind and <u>downy</u> flake.

downy (doun′ ē) *adj.*
soft and fluffy

The woods are lovely, dark, and deep,
But I have promises to keep,
15   And miles to go before I sleep,
And miles to go before I sleep.

▲ **Critical Viewing** What emotions does a wintry scene like the one pictured here bring out in the speaker of "Stopping by Woods . . ."? **[Infer]**

Review and Assess

Thinking About the Selection

1. **Respond:** In what ways is the setting of this poem like and unlike the place you live?

2. **(a) Recall:** Describe the setting—both the time and the place—of "Stopping by Woods…" **(b) Connect:** How does the description of the time affect the meaning of the poem?

3. **(a) Recall:** Why has the speaker in "Stopping by Woods…" stopped here? **(b) Infer:** What about the place captures his attention?

4. **(a) Recall:** What sights and sounds does the speaker describe? **(b) Synthesize:** What words would you use to describe the feeling of the place? **(c) Apply:** What is the mood, or feeling, of the poem?

Robert Frost

(1874–1963)

Robert Frost was born in San Francisco but moved to New England when he was only eleven. This region would prove to be inspirational for him. Frost's most popular poems describe New England country life and landscapes. Of these, "Stopping by Woods on a Snowy Evening" is considered one of his best. Frost won the Pulitzer Prize four times— more than any other poet.

La Bonne Aventure (*Good Fortune*), 1939, Rene Magritte, Museum Boymans-van Beuningen, Rotterdam

▲ **Critical Viewing**
Identify a line in the poem that relates to this painting. Explain your choice. [**Connect**]

Miracles

WALT WHITMAN

Why, who makes much of a miracle?
As to me I know of nothing else but miracles,
Whether I walk the streets of Manhattan,
Or dart my sight over the roofs of houses toward the sky,
5   Or wade with naked feet along the beach just in the edge
         of the water,
Or stand under trees in the woods,
Or talk by day with any one I love . . .

Or sit at table at dinner with the rest.
Or look at strangers opposite me riding in the car,
10   Or watch honeybees busy around the hive of a summer forenoon[1]
Or animals feeding in the fields,
Or birds, or the wonderfulness of insects in the air,
Or the wonderfulness of the sundown, or of stars shining
          so quiet and bright,
Or the <u>exquisite</u> delicate thin curve of the new moon in spring;
15   These with the rest, one and all, are to me miracles,
The whole referring, yet each <u>distinct</u> and in its place.

To me every hour of the light and dark is a miracle,
Every cubic inch of space is a miracle,
Every square yard of the surface of the earth is spread with
          the same,
20   Every foot of the interior swarms[2] with the same.

To me the sea is a continual miracle,
The fishes that swim—the rocks—the motion of the waves—
the ships with men in them,
What stranger miracles are there?

exquisite (eks kwi′ zit) *adj.*
very beautiful, especially
in a delicate way

distinct (di stiŋkt′) *adj.*
separate and different

---

1. **forenoon** (fôr′ nōōn′) *n.* morning.
2. **swarms** (swôrmz) *v.* is filled or crowded.

Review and Assess

Thinking About the Selection

1. **Respond:** Name something in your environment that is a miracle to you.

2. **(a) Recall:** Which people does the speaker consider to be miracles? **(b) Infer:** Does the speaker enjoy meeting new people? Explain.

3. **(a) Recall:** List five of the physical settings, or places, mentioned in the poem. **(b) Infer:** In what way is the sea a "continual miracle"? **(c) Draw Conclusions:** Do you think the speaker is a contented person? Explain.

4. **(a) Recall:** Name four events that Whitman calls miracles. **(b) Comparison and Contrast:** How does your definition of "miracle" compare with the speaker's definition?

5. **(a) Recall:** What are the questions in the first and last lines of "Miracles"? **(b) Connect:** How would you answer those questions? **(c) Apply:** Based on what you have read in the poem, how do you think the speaker would answer each question?

Walt Whitman

(1819–1892)

Walt Whitman worked at many occupations during his life. He was a printer, carpenter, teacher, and newspaper reporter. Known by many as the father of modern American poetry, Whitman abandoned regular rhyme and rhythm in favor of free verse that followed no set pattern. Because of his unusual style, publishers refused to publish *Leaves of Grass*, his long poem about America. Undiscouraged, Whitman published the first edition himself.

Four Skinny Trees

Sandra Cisneros

They are the only ones who understand me. I am the only one who understands them. Four skinny trees with skinny necks and pointy elbows like mine. Four who do not belong here but are here. Four raggedy excuses planted by the city. From our room we can hear them, but Nenny just sleeps and doesn't appreciate these things.

Their strength is secret. They send <u>ferocious</u> roots beneath the ground. They grow up and they grow down and grab the earth between their hairy toes and bite the sky with violent teeth and never quit their anger. This is how they keep.

Let one forget his reason for being, they'd all droop like tulips in a glass, each with their arms around the other. Keep, keep, keep, trees say when I sleep. They teach.

When I am too sad and too skinny to keep keeping, when I am a tiny thing against so many bricks, then it is I look at trees. When there is nothing left to look at on this street. Four who grew despite concrete. Four who reach and do not forget to reach. Four whose only reason is to be and be.

ferocious (fə rō´ shəs) *adj.* fierce; savage

Sandra Cisneros

(b. 1954)
Sandra Cisneros was born and raised in Chicago. Because her parents were born in Mexico, she grew up speaking English and Spanish. She writes both poetry and fiction about subjects she knows best—memories of her childhood and her Mexican heritage. Her feelings about growing up in the city are reflected in "Four Skinny Trees."

Review and Assess

Thinking About the Selection

1. **Respond:** Do you feel the same way about trees? Explain.

2. **(a) Recall:** Where are the "Four Skinny Trees" in Sandra Cisneros's work located? **(b) Interpret:** In "Four Skinny Trees," the speaker says that she can "hear" the trees from her room. What does this reveal about her relationship with the trees?

3. **(a) Generalize:** According to "Four Skinny Trees," what lessons can the trees teach? **(b) Make a Judgment:** Who can learn those lessons?

Review and Assess

Literary Analysis

Levels of Meaning

1. What is the **literal meaning** of "Stopping by Woods on a Snowy Evening"?
2. Of what do the events of the evening remind the speaker?
3. How can his experience apply to the experiences of people everywhere?
4. What is the purpose of the speaker's list in "Miracles"?
5. How can his feelings and ideas apply to people everywhere?

Comparing Literary Works

6. What are the similarities and differences in the literal subjects of each work?
7. What deeper level of meaning does each work communicate?
8. Use a Venn diagram to compare and contrast the images and ideas in two of the works.

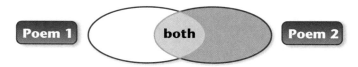

Reading Strategy

Interpreting Figurative Language

9. What does Frost mean when he uses the **metaphor** "and miles to go before I sleep"?
10. Complete a chart like the one shown. Then, explain how Cisneros uses the determination of the trees as an analogy for the determination of people.

Qualities of the four skinny trees that people can have	Challenges the trees face that people face	What the trees do that people can do
Analogy: Trees are like people because . . .		

11. Identify and explain the meaning of a simile in "Four Skinny Trees."

Extend Understanding

12. **Evaluate:** How well do you think most readers can relate to the nature images in these works?

Quick Review

Levels of meaning include the literal meaning, what the words actually say, and deeper meanings. To review levels of meaning, see page 225.

Figurative language is language that is not meant to be taken literally. To review figurative language, including metaphors, similes, and analogies, see page 225.

 Take It to the Net
www.phschool.com
Take the interactive self-test online to check your understanding of these selections.

Integrate Language Skills

Vocabulary Development Lesson

Word Analysis: Forms of *ferocious*

Ferocious is an adjective meaning "fierce" or "savage." Related forms of the word express the same meaning as different parts of speech. Use these forms of *ferocious* to complete each sentence.

ferocious   ferociously   ferocity

1. The roots grew ____?____.
2. The ____?____ roots grew under the concrete.
3. Their ____?____ caused the concrete to crack.

Identify the part of speech for each form of *ferocious*.

Fluency: Word Choice

Write the word that best defines the first word.

1. downy: **(a)** below, **(b)** crusty, **(c)** fluffy
2. ferocious: **(a)** fat, **(b)** fierce, **(c)** famous
3. exquisite: **(a)** small, **(b)** beautiful, **(c)** extra
4. distinct: **(a)** separate, **(b)** loud, **(c)** similar

Spelling Strategy

The *z* sound you hear in *exquisite* is spelled with an *s*. For each clue below, write a word that uses an *s* spelling for a *z* sound.

1. A dry, sandy region: d____?____
2. A loud, disturbing sound: n____?____
3. To create a piece of music: c____?____

Grammar Lesson

Adverbs Modifying Adjectives and Adverbs

Often, **adverbs** modify or describe a verb. They can also modify an adjective or another adverb. The following adverbs are commonly used to modify adjectives and other adverbs: *too, so, very, quite, much, more, rather, usually, almost.* Look at these examples:

Modifying Adjectives: When I am *too* sad and *too* skinny to keep keeping . . . (*How* sad and *how* skinny?)

Modifying Adverbs: The snow falls *more* silently in the forest. (*How* silently?)

▶ *For more practice, see page R28, Exercise D.*
Practice Copy the sentences below. Underline each adverb. Then, identify whether the adverb modifies an adjective, another adverb, or a verb.

1. Frost's poems are extremely popular.
2. Cisneros's piece makes one feel quite lonely.
3. I read Whitman's poem very carefully.
4. Miracles almost never happen to me!
5. The three poets write rather eloquently.

Writing Application For each of the following words, make up a sentence. Include an adverb to modify each listed word.

slowly   happily   tired   warmly   quickly

𝒲𝒢 *Prentice Hall Writing and Grammar Connection: Chapter 16, Section 2*

Writing Lesson

Review

Literary magazines often publish reviews of poetry or prose. Write your own review of one of the works in this section.

Prewriting   Choose one of the three works to review. Make a hexagon as shown. Fill in each segment with your responses.

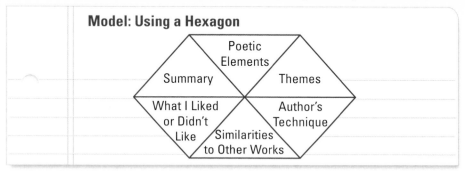

Model: Using a Hexagon

Poetic Elements

Summary

Themes

What I Liked or Didn't Like

Author's Technique

Similarities to Other Works

Drafting   Using the notes in your hexagon, write your insights into the poem. State whether it uses poetic elements effectively, has a meaningful message, and uses language that helps you see or experience the subject of the poem. Support your points with specific examples.

Revising   Eliminate details that do not explain or support your main points.

Prentice Hall Writing and Grammar Connection: Chapter 12, Section 2

Extension Activities

Listening and Speaking   The street scene Cisneros describes would sound much different from Frost's wintry forest. Create a **"sound" environment** to examine how different sounds can influence a listener's reaction to a place.

1. Have each group member choose a distinct place to record sounds.
2. Record the sounds, taking notes on what you saw and felt while recording.

Make one tape to represent your environment and play it for your class. After the presentation, have listeners explain their reactions to the sound effects. **[Group Activity]**

Research and Technology   Conduct a **survey** to determine people's reactions to the theme of "Miracles." Ask your friends and neighbors to identify the everyday events that they consider miracles. Then, classify their responses into categories, such as nature miracles, animal miracles, or people miracles. Finally, develop a spreadsheet or database and chart the miracles to create a statistical response to Whitman's poem.

 **Take It to the Net**   www.phschool.com

Go online for an additional research activity using the Internet.

READING INFORMATIONAL MATERIALS

About Textbooks

A textbook is a nonfiction work that presents instructional information in a particular subject area. Although textbooks can be different from one another in many ways, they have some common features and characteristics.

- **Purpose:** To present information for students—learners. New information is organized and developed around a clearly identified main concept, idea, or topic.
- **Structure:** Most textbooks are organized into sections, chapters, and/or units. The table of contents lists titles of these parts and indicates on what page each one begins.
- **Text format:** Type size, color, and boldfacing are used to highlight key terms or parts of the topic.

Reading Strategy

Analyzing Cause and Effect

The information in a textbook is organized to help students understand and remember facts, concepts, and ideas, as well as the relationships among them. One common relationship is **cause and effect.**

- A **cause** is the reason that an event or condition exists.
- An **effect** is the result of another event or condition.

A social studies text may discuss the causes and effects of a plague in the Middle Ages. A science text may show the causes and effects of an event in nature. As you read, ask yourself the following questions to help you identify cause-and-effect relationships.

- What is the main event or condition in the paragraph or section?
- Does something else have to happen in order for this event to occur or the condition to exist?
- Does something else happen because this event occurred or the condition exists?

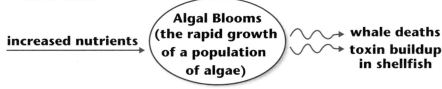

Graphic organizers like the one shown here are a good way to take notes on cause-and-effect relationships.

SECTION 2 Algal Blooms

Figure 1: An algal bloom

Over a five week period one year, the bodies of 14 humpback whales washed up along beaches on Cape Cod, Massachusetts. The whales showed no outward signs of sickness. Their stomachs were full of food. Their bodies contained plenty of blubber to insulate them from changes in water temperature. What caused such healthy-looking animals to die?

When biologists examined the dead whales' tissues, they identified the cause of the puzzling deaths. The whales' cells contained a deadly toxin produced by a dinoflagellate called *Alexandrium tamarense*. For reasons that scientists don't fully understand, the population of these algae grew rapidly in the ocean waters through which the whales were migrating. When the whales fed on the toxin-producing algae or on fishes that had eaten the algae, the toxins reached a deadly level and killed the whales.

Algae are common in both saltwater and freshwater environments on Earth. They float on the surface of the waters and use sunlight to make food. The rapid growth of a population of algae is called an **algal bloom**. The deaths of the humpbacks is one example of the damage that an algal bloom can cause.

Saltwater Blooms

In Figure 1, you see an algal bloom in ocean water. Saltwater algal blooms are commonly called **red tides**. This is because the

The section head identifies that the information in this section relates to algal blooms.

The opening paragraph gives an anecdote, or brief story, that relates to the information in the section.

Boldfaced terms are usually defined in the text. Labeled pictures usually illustrate a concept or definition.

algae that grow rapidly often contain red pigments and turn the color of the water red. But red tides do not always look red. Some red tides are brown, green, or colorless depending on the species of algae that blooms. Dinoflagellates and diatoms are two algae that frequently bloom in red tides.

Scientists are not sure why some saltwater algal populations increase rapidly at times. But red tides occur most often when there is an increase in nutrients in the water. Increases in ocean temperature due to climate changes also affect the occurrence of red tides. Some red tides occur regularly in certain seasons. The cold bottom layers of the ocean contain a lot of nutrients. When the cold water mixes with the surface waters, more nutrients become available to surface organisms. With excess nutrients present in the surface waters, blooms of algae occur.

Red tides are dangerous when the toxins that the algae produce become concentrated in the bodies of organisms that consume the algae. Shellfish feed on large numbers of the algae and store the toxins in their cells. Fishes may also feed on the algae and store the toxins. When people or other large organisms eat these shellfish and fishes, it may lead to serious illness or even death. Public health officials close beaches in areas of red tides and prohibit people from gathering shellfish or fishing.

Integrating Technology

Red tides occur more frequently worldwide today than they did a decade ago. Scientists cannot yet predict when red tides will occur. They use images taken by satellites in space to track how red tides move with ocean currents. Satellite images can also detect increases in ocean temperatures, which may put an area at risk for red tide.

☑ **CHECKPOINT** *Why are red tides often red in color?*

The boldfaced text indicates main ideas and important facts.

Questions within the text help you check your recall of important facts. What is the answer to this question?

Check Your Comprehension

1. What happened to whales along the beaches of Cape Cod, Massachusetts?
2. What did scientists find in the whales' cells?
3. What is an algal bloom?

Applying the Reading Strategy

Analyzing Cause and Effect

4. Identify a chain of at least four events or conditions that led to the deaths of the whales.
5. Identify three conditions that may cause red tides.
6. What is one effect of technology on the study of red tides?

Activity

Take Notes on a Science Text

Use the note-taking suggestions to take notes on algal blooms. When you are finished, discuss your notes with a small group. Evaluate how clear and complete each person's notes are.

Contrasting Informational Materials

Textbooks and Encyclopedias

Find an article about algal blooms in an encyclopedia either in the library or on the Internet. On a separate piece of paper, complete the chart to explain to the class the differences in the way the information on algal blooms is presented in the textbook article and in the encyclopedia article.

Taking Notes

1. **Label the page** with the date and the chapter or section name and number.
2. **Write definitions** of all terms that are boldfaced. Example: **Algal bloom**—rapid growth of a population of algae.
3. **Make an organizer** that shows the causes and effects of the main topic—algal blooms.
4. **Answer any questions** that are in the text or that accompany pictures. Write answers in complete sentences.
5. **Copy facts and explanations** that are formatted with special text.
6. **Summarize** the main ideas presented, labeling each summary with a heading written in colored pen or pencil.

Comparing	Textbook	Encyclopedia
Audience and Purpose	To inform and instruct seventh grade students	To inform general audience of young adults and adults
How is text broken up?		
What do visuals show?		
What examples are given to make topic clearer?		

Cause-and-Effect Essays

About Cause-and-Effect Essays

Exposition is writing that informs or explains. A cause-and-effect essay is expository writing that explains the reasons why something happened or explains the results an event or situation will produce. A cause-and-effect essay might focus on causes, as in an explanation of why days get shorter in the fall, or it might focus on effects, as in an essay on how chemicals affect crops.

Reading Strategy

Analyzing Cause-and-Effect Organization

Although cause-and-effect essays all show causes and effects, the specific organization of an essay may emphasize the type or number of causes and effects. Several ways a cause-and-effect essay may be organized are shown below.

- Several events or circumstances work together to bring about a particular effect.

- A chain of events in which the cause leads to an effect, which becomes a cause for the next event until a final outcome is reached.

- A single event has a wide range of effects.

- Several causes and effects are shown for a significant event or condition.

As you read "How Do Rainmakers Make Rain?" think about which organizer best represents the organization of the article.

How Do Rainmakers Make Rain?

In 1946 Vincent Schaefer and Irving Longmuir started their work at the General Electric Research Laboratories in Schenectady, New York, which proved that rain clouds could be artificially encouraged to produce showers.

Here, the effect that is the focus of the essay is identified.

Clouds are made up of billions of particles of water too small to fall as rain. Only when the droplets grow to a quarter of a millimeter or more will they fall as a fine drizzle. Smaller droplets evaporate before reaching the ground.

One way the droplets grow is by freezing to form particles of ice. In a cloud containing some ice particles and some water droplets, the ice particles grow rapidly as the droplets evaporate and the vapor is transferred to the ice. Since the temperature of clouds is often below freezing it might be expected that the droplets would freeze easily. But the water can be 10 or 20 degrees below freezing (supercooled) without actually freezing.

> Sometimes a condition or effect is listed first and its cause follows.

The reason for this is that the water in clouds is absolutely pure, without any dust or other contaminants which can form the center of an ice crystal. If tiny particles are provided, the droplets freeze, grow quickly until they are large enough to fall, and then melt as the temperature rises, reaching the ground as rain.

> The cause of water not freezing is identified and explained.

Schaefer and Longmuir proved that small particles, usually of silver iodide, added to supercooled clouds could create rapidly growing ice crystals. These particles have been dropped from aircraft, carried by rockets or even released at ground level for air currents to carry them aloft.

> The chain of causes and effects leads to the final outcome: rain is produced.

In the [former] Soviet Union, 70mm artillery guns have been used to fire silver iodide particles into clouds, exploding at the right height to disperse the chemical.

> Here, the practical applications of the causes and effects are addressed.

As long as the clouds are supercooled the technique may work—increasing rainfall by up to a fifth. But since it is impossible to know how much rain would have fallen anyway there are still question marks over the method's economic effectiveness.

Check Your Comprehension

1. What are clouds made of?
2. What happens to small droplets of rain before they reach the ground?
3. Why don't the droplets of water freeze even though the temperature in the clouds is 10 to 20 degrees below freezing?
4. What did Schaefer and Longmuir prove about using silver iodide?
5. What has the (former) Soviet Union used to get silver iodide into clouds?

Applying the Reading Strategy

Analyzing Cause-and-Effect Organization

6. Choose one of the organizers from page 238 and use it to show the cause-and-effect relationships in the essay. Explain why you chose the organizer you did.
7. Why are the cause-and-effect relationships explained in this article important?

Activity

Cause-and-Effect Demonstration

Give a demonstration in which you use a model to show a physical example of cause and effect. For example, you might show the effect of changing the angle at which you throw a tennis ball against a wall. By throwing the ball at different angles and observing the bounce, you can demonstrate that the cause—changing the angle of the throw—has an effect—the angle of the bounce changes as well.

Contrasting Informational Materials

Find a cause-and-effect explanation in your science textbook and another in your social studies textbook. Compare and contrast them using a Venn diagram. Address the categories shown on the diagram.

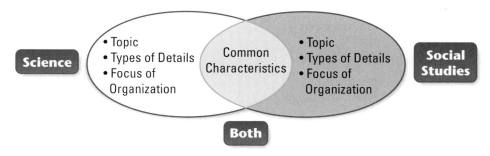

Science

• Topic
• Types of Details
• Focus of Organization

Common Characteristics

• Topic
• Types of Details
• Focus of Organization

Social Studies

Both

Writing WORKSHOP

Expository Writing: Problem-Solution Composition

A **problem-solution composition** identifies and explains a problem and then presents one or more possible solutions to it. In this writing workshop you will propose a solution to a problem that concerns you.

Assignment Criteria. Your problem-solution composition should have the following characteristics:

- a clearly identified and explained problem
- a proposal of a realistic, well-planned solution
- evidence in support of the proposed solution
- logical organization that includes an introduction, a body, and a conclusion
- varied sentence length

See the Rubric on page 245 for the criteria on which your problem-solution composition may be assessed.

Prewriting

Choose a topic. Use **sentence starters** to find a topic. Finish each sentence. Then, choose one of the sentences and its related problem as the subject of your essay.

Narrow your topic by looping. To focus on a problem and solution of manageable size, use the sentence starter to begin looping.

1. Write about the sentence you chose for three or four minutes.
2. "Loop," or circle, the most important or interesting word in what you have written.
3. Write about that word for five minutes.
4. Choose the most interesting or important word in what you have written. Continue looping until you have identified a very specific problem.

Sentence Starters

I would like to help people who . . .
My town or city would be a better place if . . .
What our school really needs is . . .
I would like to be in charge of . . .

Consider your audience as you gather details. Identify the people who can put your proposed solution into action. Focus on this audience, or group of readers. Choose details that will matter to them.

Student Model

Before you begin drafting your problem-solution composition, read this student model and review the characteristics of an effective problem-solution essay.

Chris Lorenz
Oklahoma City, Oklahoma

Manners Mean a Lot

One of the big problems facing today's society is that conflicts break out over the least little thing. The news is full of stories about violence or property damage that occurs because two people who had never before met have a disagreement over a parking space or some equally small matter. In schools, arguments and fights disrupt the school day. The solution to this problem is simple—manners. It may seem humorous or silly to suggest that something we all should have learned as children could solve such a big problem, but it is possible. If everyone used the same manners with strangers as they do with people they like or want to impress, the number of incidents would drop because the number of conflicts would drop.

Manners are a way of showing respect for others. When people use their manners to respect the rights of others, fewer people will feel they have to do anything violent to protect their rights. For example, if you were approaching a door with your grandmother, you probably would not crowd ahead of her. You would slow down to let her pass in front of you so the two of you would not collide in the doorway. You would also do it because it is polite. If drivers applied this politeness when entering or exiting a crowded parking lot, people would get their turn to get in and out. Instead, what most people do is to "crowd ahead"—to be the first one through the door. This lack of manners causes anger and accidents. Applying good manners would eliminate anger and accidents.

In all kinds of situations, using basic manners sets the stage for cooperation instead of conflict. Using the words *please* and *thank you,* addressing people by their names, and speaking in a polite tone of voice will help people avoid many situations in which a confrontation starts simply because someone does not like the way someone else spoke to him or her.

Although manners have changed over the years, they still contain the basic idea that we should show courtesy and respect in our interactions with others. Showing respect through manners is the first step toward reducing conflicts in our society.

In the introduction, the writer clearly identifies the problem.

Here, the writer suggests a solution that everyone can try.

In the body of the essay, the writer offers specific examples and explanations that show why the solution would work.

In the conclusion, the writer restates the problem and her suggested solution. She concludes with a strong statement that shows the importance of trying her solution.

Drafting

Present the problem. In an introductory paragraph, state the problem. Then, briefly outline the solution you propose.

Illustrate the problem and present your plan. In the body of your composition, provide details that illustrate the problem you address. Describe your plan for a solution, step by step. Include support that shows the benefits of each part of your plan. The following types of evidence can be used to illustrate a problem or support a solution.

Write a conclusion. Summarize the solution you propose by reviewing the key steps. Finish with a thought-provoking question or quotation to leave a strong impression in readers' minds.

Types of Evidence

Expert Opinion:
County waste office recommends recycling.

Example:
Landfill in little town has slowed increase since recycling has started.

Reason:
Everyone can do it with just a little effort.

Proposed Solution:
Recycling is one step we can use to reduce landfills.

Facts:
Recycling is done in many counties.

Statistics:
Recycling cans in our county will slow landfill growth by 10%.

Experience:
Our family recycled 100 cans in a week.

Revising

Revise to strengthen support.
Underline each piece of evidence you use to support your proposed solution. Use a different color to underline each type of evidence. Evaluate whether you have supplied sufficient and varied support.

- If you have little underlining, add more evidence.
- If most of your underlining is in one color, add different kinds of evidence.

Model: Strengthening Support

Manners are a way of showing respect for others. When people use their manners to respect the rights of others, fewer people will feel they have to do anything violent to protect their rights. For example, if you were approaching a door with your grandmother, you probably wouldn't crowd ahead of her. If drivers applied politeness when entering or exiting a crowded parking lot, everyone would get their turn to get in and out.

> The writer saw that she had used two reasons, but had given no example. She added an example to strengthen the support of her point.

Revise for sentence variety. Too many short sentences in a row make your writing choppy. Too many long, complicated sentences make it difficult for readers to follow your thoughts. Vary sentence length by combining related ideas in the same sentence. Use short sentences to break the rhythm and emphasize a point.

Choppy: Too few buses are used. Passengers wait too long. We need more public transportation. We need it now.

Varied: Too few buses are used, and passengers wait too long. We need more public transportation. We need it now.

Why is the model more effective than the nonmodel?

Nonmodel	Model
The solution to this problem is simple. Manners are the solution. Maybe that seems humorous or silly. After all, we should have learned manners as children. However, using manners to reduce conflicts is possible.	The solution to this problem is simple—manners. It may seem humorous or silly to suggest that something we all should have learned as children could solve such a big problem, but it is possible.

Publishing and Presenting

Choose one of the following ways to share your writing.

Present a proposal. Present your proposed solution to a group of classmates and ask for feedback.

Write a letter. Rework your composition as a letter to someone who can put your solution into action.

W̶G̶ Prentice Hall Writing and Grammar Connection: Chapter 21, Section 3

 Speaking Connection
To learn more about presenting a proposal, see the **Listening and Speaking Workshop: Presenting a Proposal,** page 246.

Rubric for Self-Assessment

Evaluate your problem-solution composition using the following criteria and rating scale.

Criteria	Rating Scale				
	Not very				Very
How clearly is the problem stated?	1	2	3	4	5
How fully is the problem explained and illustrated?	1	2	3	4	5
How well planned is the solution?	1	2	3	4	5
How effectively is the proposed solution supported?	1	2	3	4	5
How varied are the sentence lengths?	1	2	3	4	5

Listening and Speaking WORKSHOP

Presenting a Proposal

A **proposal** is a plan for a suggested course of action. When you present a proposal, your purpose is to persuade your audience to support your plan—to take the action you suggest. An effective proposal identifies the need for action; states a clear position in suggesting a course of action; and arranges details, descriptions, and examples persuasively in relation to the audience.

Prepare Your Proposal

The following strategies will help you organize and prepare your presentation.

Organize your ideas. Create an outline of the key points in your proposal. Use clear, large print so that you can easily find your place as you glance up and down to speak.

Focus on your audience. Use visuals to illustrate or highlight the information that will be most effective in persuading your audience that your proposal is a good one. Visuals can be displayed as posters or projections or can be handed out at appropriate points in the presentation. The chart shows some ways that visual aids can be used to appeal to the background or interests of a particular audience.

Audience Concern	Effective Visual
Cost	Chart or graph showing cost comparisons
Time	Timeline, schedule, or calendar page showing completion dates of parts of plan
Quality	"Before and after" photographs or drawings

Deliver Your Proposal

Remember these points as you present your proposal.

- **Make eye contact.** Glance down to use the outline as you move from point to point, but look up at the audience and refer to your visuals as you present. Make people in the audience feel as if you are speaking directly to them. Connect with different audience members by making eye contact as you explain your plan.

- **Project your voice.** Speak loudly enough for the people in the back of the room to hear you, but do not shout.

(Activity:)
Field Trip Proposal Prepare a proposal for a class field trip to be presented to a parent-teacher board. This audience will be concerned with costs, safety, and the educational purpose of the trip. Include details, examples, and visual aids that address these concerns.

Assessment WORKSHOP

Analyzing Cause and Effect

The reading sections of some tests require you to analyze a sequence of events in a passage to determine which events caused other events to happen. The following strategies will help you answer such test questions:

- Remember that a cause is an event that brings about another event. An effect is the event that the cause brings about.
- Remember also that one event may be the cause of several effects, and one effect may be the result of several causes.
- Do not confuse sequence or chronological order with cause and effect. One event may happen before a second event and still not be the cause of the second event.

Test-Taking Strategies

- To identify causes and effects, look for signal words such as *because, due to, for this reason,* and *as a result.*
- To test cause and effect, ask yourself whether one event had to happen before a second event could.

Sample Test Item

Directions: Read the passage, and then answer the question that follows.

After a great start this season, the Mudville Tigers slumped during the finals. Ace pitcher Yasmin Jordan was unable to play past the first few games because of an injury. Her replacement, Samantha Jones, was equally gifted, but bad luck hit again, when heavy storms caused the cancellation of many practices. Cancelled practices led to more errors and more losses. As a result, team morale was low. By the time of the finals, the Tigers' spirit was gone and they were playing poorly.

1. Which cause led to low morale?
   A poor playing during the finals
   B losses caused by errors
   C injuries
   D a poor start to the season

Answer and Explanation

1. The correct answer is *B.* A is incorrect because poor playing during the finals was the effect of low morale. C is incorrect, because the pitcher's injury is not a cause of the team's losses. D is incorrect because it contradicts the first sentence.

▷ Practice

Directions: Read the passage, and then answer the question that follows.

Jane looked out the window. The falling snow was beautiful, but it meant that there would be no trip into the city after school today. She sighed. Until she got to the city to buy new art supplies, her special project for art class would have to wait. She had started it early, but it had taken more time and materials than she had anticipated. The project was already late, and now she would have to wait until her mother's next trip into the city. She sighed again but then thought, "At least I'll have more time this weekend for my English report."

1. Which of the following first causes Jane's art project to be late?
   A a late start
   B the snow
   C her trip into the city
   D the size of the project

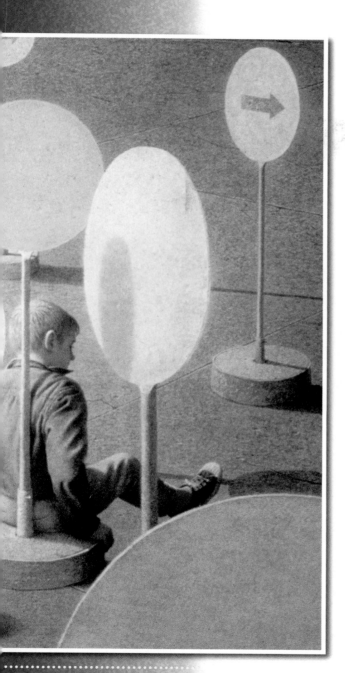

Exploring the Theme

Challenges are a fact of life. The trick to living graciously is to find a way to solve these problems without compromising your beliefs or hurting someone else. The selections in this unit show you a range of problem-solving behaviors. The characters and situations in the literature in this unit may give you some insight into meeting challenges in your own life.

◀ **Critical Viewing** What does this picture suggest about working with others to meet a challenge?

Why Read Literature?

The works in this unit reveal people struggling to deal with challenging situations of many sorts. In addition to finding out how each person solves his or her problem, you might have other purposes for reading. Preview three of the purposes you might set before reading the works in this unit.

1

Read for the love of literature.

Writer Ray Bradbury's work has appeared in over seven hundred anthologies. His writings have also been turned into movies, television shows, sound recordings, and even an opera! Read about his vision of life on the planet Venus in **"All Summer in a Day,"** page 264.

Thomas Hardy published about one thousand poems during his long lifetime! Read one of them, **"The Walk,"** page 299, published shortly after his first wife's death, and experience the beauty of his language.

2

Read to be entertained.

James Thurber's first cartoons were first published only because his friend and coworker E. B. White rescued them out of a waste basket. Enjoy Thurber's humor in cartoons and text in his essay **"The Night the Bed Fell,"** page 254.

3

Read for information.

One ten-year-old boy built twenty bikes in less than six months, using old frames and parts from broken bicycles. Learn why when you read **"Justin Lebo,"** by Phillip Hoose, page 300.

Today's cowboys use the Internet to find work, sell horses, or find out about upcoming cattle drives. For a look at the realities of cowboy life in the past, read **"The Real Story of a Cowboy's Life,"** page 281, by Geoffrey C. Ward.

 Take It to the Net

Visit the Web site for online instruction and activities related to each selection in this unit.

www.phschool.com

How to Read Literature

Use Strategies for Constructing Meaning

To understand a work of literature fully, you must put together details, ideas, events, and relationships. By putting these things together, you build, or construct, meaning. In this unit, you will learn the following strategies for constructing meaning:

1. Identify significant events.

In a narrative, some events are more significant or meaningful than others because they help to move the plot forward or because they reveal something about a character. In this unit you will learn to identify significant events and understand their importance.

2. Compare and contrast characters.

Notice what each character says, thinks, and does, and pay attention to what the author tells you about them. Use these details to analyze the similarities and differences among characters.

In "All Summer in a Day," Margot is described in this way: "Margot stood alone." The rest of the students are "like a feverish wheel, all fumbling spokes." Contrasting these images shows Margot on her own, while her classmates are a group of people acting as one.

3. Identify cause and effect.

Look carefully at the relationship of events. Identify causes—why something happens—and effects—what happens. Look at this example of a cause and an effect from "The Highwayman."

Cause: The highwayman whistles at the window.
Effect: Bess, the landlord's daughter, appears.

4. Draw inferences.

Fill in details the author does not provide by drawing inferences—making logical guesses and assumptions based on the details that are provided, combined with your own knowledge and experience. For example, from the descriptions in "Amigo Brothers," you can infer that Antonio and Felix are very dedicated to their boxing.

> Every chance they had the boys worked out. . . . Early morning sunrises would find them running along the East River Drive.

As you read the selections in this unit, review the reading strategies and look at the notes in the side columns. Use the suggestions to apply the strategies and interact with the text.

Prepare to Read

The Night the Bed Fell

"*Briggs Suffocating*" by James Thurber

Take It to the Net

Visit www.phschool.com for interactive activities and instruction related to "The Night the Bed Fell," including
- background
- graphic organizers
- literary elements
- reading strategies

Preview

Connecting to the Literature

Imagine strolling through a store with a friend, joking about something, and suddenly realizing that the person standing next to you is no longer your friend but rather a complete stranger! In "The Night the Bed Fell," James Thurber shows you what happens when a simple confusion is multiplied by the interpretations of seven different people.

Background

An early accident left writer and cartoonist James Thurber blind in first one eye and then both eyes. This loss of sight led him to develop his own readily identifiable style of simple line drawing. Like the cartoon above, many of his cartoons enhance the humor of the situations he describes.

Literary Analysis

Humorous Essay

Humorous essays are brief works of nonfiction meant to amuse readers. In "The Night the Bed Fell," James Thurber produces a humorous effect by contrasting the reality of a situation with the characters' mistaken views of what is happening. Using an organizer like the one shown, record the different ideas characters have about events in "The Night the Bed Fell."

Connecting Literary Elements

One way that writers create humor is through **characterization.**

- **Characters** are the "actors" in a narrative.
- **Characterization** is the process through which a writer develops a character.

A writer can develop a character through direct description, through the character's actions, words, or thoughts, or through the reactions of other characters. The following example shows characterization through a character's actions and thoughts.

> Old Aunt Melissa Beall (who could whistle like a man with two fingers in her mouth) suffered under the premonition that she was destined to die on South High Street, . . .

Look for other details used to develop characters in "The Night the Bed Fell."

Reading Strategy

Identifying Significant Events

In any narrative, whether humorous or serious, there are **significant events** that move the action forward. Significant events reveal new information, cause other events, change the way a character acts or thinks, or settle a question or problem. Use the following questions as you read:

1. What is the first event that sets the other events in motion?
2. What is one event that increases the misunderstandings?

Vocabulary Development

ominous (äm´ ə nəs) *adj.* threatening (p. 254)

allay (a lā´) *v.* put to rest; calm (p. 255)

fortitude (fôrt´ ə tōōd´) *n.* firm courage (p. 255)

perilous (per´ ə ləs) *adj.* dangerous (p. 256)

deluge (del´ yōōj´) *n.* great flood or rush of anything (p. 257)

pungent (pun´ jənt) *adj.* sharp-smelling (p. 257)

extricate (eks´ tri kāt´) *v.* set free; disentangle (p. 257)

culprit (kul´ prit) *n.* guilty person (p. 257)

What Briggs thinks:
_____

What Mother thinks:
_____

What Father thinks:
_____

What Really Happens: The narrator falls off the cot.

What Roy thinks:
_____

What Herman thinks:
_____

What narrator thinks:
_____

The Night the Bed Fell

JAMES THURBER

I suppose that the high-water mark of my youth in Columbus, Ohio, was the night the bed fell on my father. It makes a better recitation (unless, as some friends of mine have said, one has heard it five or six times) than it does a piece of writing, for it is almost necessary to throw furniture around, shake doors, and bark like a dog, to lend the proper atmosphere and verisimilitude[1] to what is admittedly a somewhat incredible tale. Still, it did take place.

It happened, then, that my father had decided to sleep in the attic one night, to be away where he could think. My mother opposed the notion strongly because, she said, the old wooden bed up there was unsafe: it was wobbly and the heavy headboard would crash down on father's head in case the bed fell, and kill him. There was no dissuading him, however, and at a quarter past ten he closed the attic door behind him and went up the narrow twisting stairs. We later heard <u>ominous</u> creakings as he crawled into bed. Grandfather, who usually slept in the attic bed when he was with us, had disappeared some days before. On these occasions he was usually gone six or eight days and returned growling and out of temper, with the news that the Federal Union[2] was run by a passel of blockheads and that the Army of the Potomac[3] didn't have a chance.

We had visiting us at this time a nervous first cousin of mine named Briggs Beall, who believed that he was likely to cease

Reading Strategy
Identify Significant Events How do you know that the father's decision to sleep in the attic is a significant event?

ominous (äm′ ə nəs) *adj.* threatening

---

1. **verisimilitude** (ver′ ə si mil′ ə tood′) *n.* appearance of being true or real.
2. **Federal Union** northern side during the Civil War. He is under the illusion that the Civil War has not yet ended.
3. **Army of the Potomac** one of the northern armies during the Civil War.

breathing when he was asleep. It was his feeling that if he were not awakened every hour during the night, he might die of suffocation. He had been accustomed to setting an alarm clock to ring at intervals until morning, but I persuaded him to abandon this. He slept in my room and I told him that I was such a light sleeper that if anybody quit breathing in the same room with me, I would wake instantly. He tested me the first night—which I had suspected he would—by holding his breath after my regular breathing had convinced him I was asleep. I was not asleep, however, and called to him. This seemed to <u>allay</u> his fears a little, but he took the precaution of putting a glass of spirits of camphor[4] on a little table at the head of his bed. In case I didn't arouse him until he was almost gone, he said, he would sniff the camphor, a powerful reviver. Briggs was not the only member of his family who had his crotchets.[5] Old Aunt Melissa Beall (who could whistle like a man, with two fingers in her mouth) suffered under the premonition that she was destined to die on South High Street, because she had been born on South High Street and married on South High Street. Then there was Aunt Sarah Shoaf, who never went to bed at night without the fear that a burglar was going to get in and blow chloroform[6] under her door through a tube. To avert this calamity—for she was in greater dread of anesthetics than of losing her household goods—she always piled her money, silverware, and other valuables in a neat stack just outside her bedroom, with a note reading: "This is all I have. Please take it and do not use your chloroform, as this is all I have." Aunt Gracie Shoaf also had a burglar phobia, but she met it with more <u>fortitude</u>. She was confident that burglars had been getting into her house every night for forty years. The fact that she never missed anything was to her no proof to the contrary. She always claimed that she scared them off before they could take anything, by throwing shoes down the hallway. When she went to bed she piled, where she could get at them handily, all the shoes there

allay (a lā´) *v.* put to rest; calm

Literary Analysis
Humorous Essay What is the contrast between the aunts' beliefs and reality?

fortitude (fôrt´ ə tōōd´) *n.* firm courage

Reading Check

What does the narrator say the story will be about?

---

4. **spirits of camphor** liquid with a powerful odor.
5. **crotchets** (kräch´ əts) *n.* peculiar or stubborn ideas.
6. **chloroform** (klôr´ ə fôrm´) *n.* substance used at one time as an anesthetic, or pain-killer, during operations because it can cause a person to pass out.

were about her house. Five minutes after she had turned off the light, she would sit up in bed and say "Hark!" Her husband, who had learned to ignore the whole situation as long ago as 1903, would either be sound asleep or pretend to be sound asleep. In either case he would not respond to her tugging and pulling, so that presently she would arise, tiptoe to the door, open it slightly and heave a shoe down the hall in one direction, and its mate down the hall in the other direction. Some nights she threw them all, some nights only a couple of pair.

But I am straying from the remarkable incidents that took place during the night that the bed fell on father. By midnight we were all in bed. The layout of the rooms and the disposition[7] of their occupants is important to an understanding of what later occurred. In the front room upstairs (just under father's attic bedroom) were my mother and my brother Herman, who sometimes sang in his sleep, usually "Marching Through Georgia" or "Onward, Christian Soldiers." Briggs Beall and myself were in a room adjoining this one. My brother Roy was in a room across the hall from ours. Our bull terrier, Rex, slept in the hall.

My bed was an army cot, one of those affairs which are made wide enough to sleep on comfortably only by putting up, flat with the middle section, the two sides which ordinarily hang down like the sideboards of a drop-leaf table. When these sides are up, it is <u>perilous</u> to roll too far toward the edge, for then the cot is likely to tip completely over, bringing the whole bed down on top of one, with a tremendous banging crash. This, in fact, is precisely what happened about two o'clock in the morning. (It was my mother who, in recalling the scene later, first referred to it as "the night the bed fell on your father.")

Always a deep sleeper, slow to arouse (I had lied to Briggs), I was at first unconscious of what had happened when the iron cot rolled me onto the floor and toppled over me. It left me still warmly bundled up and unhurt, for the bed rested above me like a canopy. Hence I did not wake up, only reached the edge of consciousness and went back. The racket, however, instantly awakened my mother, in the next room, who came to the immediate conclusion that her worst dread was realized: the big wooden bed upstairs had fallen

"Aunt Gracie Shoaf Throwing Shoes" by James Thurber

▲ **Critical Viewing**
How would Gracie Shoaf defend the actions shown in this drawing? **[Analyze]**

perilous (per´ ə ləs) *adj.* dangerous

Reading Strategy
Identify Significant Events How do you know that this crash will be important to the story?

---

7. **disposition** (dis´ pə zish´ ən) *n.* arrangement.

on father. She therefore screamed, "Let's go to your poor father!" It was this shout, rather than the noise of my cot falling, that awakened Herman, in the same room with her. He thought that mother had become, for no apparent reason, hysterical. "You're all right, Mamma!" he shouted, trying to calm her. They exchanged shout for shout for perhaps ten seconds: "Let's go to your poor father!" and "You're all right!" That woke up Briggs. By this time I was conscious of what was going on, in a vague way, but did not yet realize that I was under my bed instead of on it. Briggs, awakening in the midst of loud shouts of fear and apprehension, came to the quick conclusion that he was suffocating and that we were all trying to "bring him out." With a low moan, he grasped the glass of camphor at the head of his bed and instead of sniffing it poured it over himself. The room reeked of camphor. "Ugf, ahfg," choked Briggs, like a drowning man, for he had almost succeeded in stopping his breath under the <u>deluge</u> of <u>pungent</u> spirits. He leaped out of bed and groped toward the open window, but he came up against one that was closed. With his hand, he beat out the glass, and I could hear it crash and tinkle on the alleyway below. It was at this juncture that I, in trying to get up, had the uncanny sensation of feeling my bed above me! Foggy with sleep, I now suspected, in my turn, that the whole uproar was being made in a frantic endeavor to <u>extricate</u> me from what must be an unheard-of and perilous situation. "Get me out of this!" I bawled. "Get me out!" I think I had the nightmarish belief that I was entombed in a mine. "Gugh," gasped Briggs, floundering in his camphor.

By this time my mother, still shouting, pursued by Herman, still shouting, was trying to open the door to the attic, in order to go up and get my father's body out of the wreckage. The door was stuck, however, and wouldn't yield. Her frantic pulls on it only added to the general banging and confusion. Roy and the dog were now up, the one shouting questions, the other barking.

Father, farthest away and soundest sleeper of all, had by this time been awakened by the battering on the attic door. He decided that the house was on fire. "I'm coming, I'm coming!" he wailed in a slow, sleepy voice—it took him many minutes to regain full consciousness. My mother, still believing he was caught under the bed, detected in his "I'm coming!" the mournful, resigned note of one who is preparing to meet his Maker. "He's dying!" she shouted.

"I'm all right!" Briggs yelled to reassure her. "I'm all right!" He still believed that it was his own closeness to death that was worrying mother. I found at last the light switch in my room, unlocked the door, and Briggs and I joined the others at the attic door. The dog, who never did like Briggs, jumped for him—assuming that he was the <u>culprit</u> in whatever was going on—and Roy had to

deluge (del′ yōōj′) *n.* great flood or rush of anything

pungent (pun′ jənt) *adj.* sharp-smelling

extricate (eks′ trə kāt′) *v.* set free; disentangle

culprit (kul′ prit) *n.* guilty person

☑ **Reading Check**

Whose bed falls?

"*Briggs and Rex*" by James Thurber

▲ **Critical Viewing** What part of the story does this picture show? **[Connect]**

throw Rex and hold him. We could hear father crawling out of bed upstairs. Roy pulled the attic door open, with a mighty jerk, and father came down the stairs, sleepy and irritable but safe and sound. My mother began to weep when she saw him. Rex began to howl. "What in the name of heaven is going on here?" asked father.

The situation was finally put together like a gigantic jigsaw puzzle. Father caught a cold from prowling around in his bare feet but there were no other bad results. "I'm glad," said mother, who always looked on the bright side of things, "that your grandfather wasn't here."

Review and Assess

Think About the Selection

1. **Respond:** Do you think you would enjoy visiting a family like James Thurber's? Explain.

2. **(a) Recall:** Who is in the house on the night described?
   (b) Compare: What quality or qualities do these characters share?
   (c) Support: What examples illustrate the shared qualities?

3. **(a) Recall:** Describe the layout of the rooms. **(b) Analyze:** Why is the placement of the rooms in the house important?

4. **(a) Recall:** When did the bed collapse? **(b) Analyze:** In what way does the time of the collapse increase the characters' confusion?

5. **(a) Recall:** What do Briggs, Aunt Sarah Shoaf, and Aunt Gracie Shoaf do before going to bed? **(b) Infer:** What is the narrator's attitude to these actions? **(c) Analyze:** What details show the narrator's attitude?

6. **Evaluate:** Do you think Thurber's essay is funny? Why or why not?

James Thurber
(1894–1961)

According to James Thurber, if you had grown up in his Columbus, Ohio, childhood home, your days would have been filled with absurd and almost unbelievable events. Thurber recounts many of these humorous events in his writings—always with affection for his sometimes silly relatives.

Thurber pursued a long writing career. After working as a newspaper reporter, he found the perfect creative outlet in the literary magazine *The New Yorker*. There, he could write essays that gently poked fun at his family and the rest of the world.

To James Thurber, life's humor came from the contrast between the chaos of the moment and the calm understanding that comes when looking back at it. In writing about his family in "The Night the Bed Fell," Thurber calmly recounts an example of the total confusion he remembers as part of his childhood.

Review and Assess

Literary Analysis

Humorous Essay

1. Contrast what actually happens when the bed falls with what each character thinks happens.
2. Would the essay be as funny if you were as confused about what happened as the characters were? Why or why not? Explain.
3. At the beginning of the **humorous essay,** Thurber writes that he prefers to tell the story orally because he can add physical effects. Do you think such antics would make this funny tale even funnier?

Connecting Literary Elements

4. Which two **characters** are afraid of burglars? Why is this detail important?
5. What details make these characters and their fears humorous?
6. Complete a chart like the one shown to identify different types of **characterization.**

	Direct descriptions	Character's actions	Other characters' reactions
Grandfather			
Briggs Beall			

Reading Strategy

Identifying Significant Events

7. Identify four **significant events** that move the narrative forward in the order in which they happen. Show the significance of the events by completing a chart like the one below for each event.

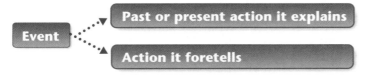

8. What is the first event that sets the other events in motion?
9. What is one event that increases the misunderstandings?

Extending Understanding

10. **Workplace Connection:** What does the story suggest about the importance of being fully alert when making judgments or decisions?

Quick Review

Humorous essays are brief works of nonfiction meant to amuse readers. To review humorous essays, see page 253.

Characters are the "actors" in a narrative. **Characterization** is the process through which a writer develops a character. To review characters and characterization, see page 253.

Significant events reveal new information, cause other events, change the way a character acts or thinks, or settle a question or problem.

 Take It to the Net
www.phschool.com
Take the interactive self-test online to check your understanding of the selection.

Integrate Language Skills

Vocabulary Development Lesson

Word Analysis: Latin Prefix *ex-*

The Latin prefix *ex-* means "out." For example, *exclude* means "to leave out." Match each word to its definition.

1. exalt
2. exceed
3. exhale

a. to go beyond
b. to breathe out
c. to raise high

Spelling Strategy

The *j* sound is often spelled with a *g*, as in *pungent*. When this sound appears at the end of a word, as in *deluge*, always use *ge*. Write words containing the *j* sound spelled with *g*.

1. the trick of pulling a rabbit out of a hat: ma___?____
2. a larger-than-life figure: le___?____
3. a photograph, painting, or moving picture: im___?____

Concept Development: Antonyms

Antonyms are words with opposite meanings. On your paper, write the letter of the word that is most opposite in meaning to the first word.

1. fortitude: **(a)** strength; **(b)** weakness; **(c)** courage
2. ominous: **(a)** favorable; **(b)** dull; **(c)** frightening
3. deluge: **(a)** flood; **(b)** drought; **(c)** shower
4. extricate: **(a)** rescue; **(b)** revolve; **(c)** capture
5. culprit: **(a)** lawyer; **(b)** offender; **(c)** victim
6. perilous: **(a)** risky; **(b)** exciting; **(c)** secure
7. allay: **(a)** partner; **(b)** irritate; **(c)** calm
8. pungent: **(a)** moldy; **(b)** tangy; **(c)** bland

Grammar Lesson

Prepositions

A **preposition** is a part of speech that relates a noun or pronoun that follows it to another word in the sentence. Here are some common prepositions: *above, behind, below, near, into, through, outside, inside, beyond, off, on, over, to, up,* and *with.* Some prepositions—such as *ahead of, because of,* and *in addition to*—consist of more than one word. In the following example, the prepositions are in italics.

On these occasions he returned *out of* temper. Father had been awakened *by* the noise.

I did not realize I was *under* my bed not *on* it.

Practice On your paper, write the prepositions in each sentence.

1. The room was underneath the attic bedroom.
2. Mrs. Thurber slept in that room, too.
3. Two were in the room next to Herman's.
4. Roy slept in a room across the hall from them.
5. The dog, Rex, slept in front of Roy's door.

Writing Application Choose five of the prepositions from this lesson. Write five sentences, each with one or more prepositions, that retell part of Thurber's story from the point of view of one of the other characters.

W̶G̶ Prentice Hall Writing and Grammar Connection: Chapter 17, Section 1

Writing Lesson

Humorous Essay

Write a brief humorous essay based on an experience with confusing or incorrect information. Use some of Thurber's techniques, such as contrast and exaggeration, to produce humor.

Prewriting   Brainstorm with family or friends to recall favorite amusing stories. Once you have chosen your story, list the main events in sequence and circle the climax (the high point) and underline the conclusion.

Drafting   End your essay with a punchy conclusion or a "clincher" that ties all the pieces together. Then, go back to the beginning to narrate the events that lead to the climax and conclusion.

Model: Punchy Conclusion

When I came on stage, I saw my brother glumly shaking his head. Then, I strummed my guitar, I sang, and the audience cheered. Amazed, I saw my bratty big brother stand up, turn around, bow, and with a big grin, mouth the words, "My Kid Brother!"

Revising   Using different colors, highlight the climax, setup (the facts that make the ending believable), and ending of your story.

Prentice Hall Writing and Grammar Connection: Chapter 5, Section 4

Extension Activities

Listening and Speaking With a group of classmates, **dramatize** the confusion in the story at the point when all characters are involved.

1. Choose dialogue, the words of the characters' conversations, that show the misunderstandings.
2. Act out the scene, using movement to add to the confusion.

Follow up with a discussion of how you can modify the words and the movement to increase the confusion.

Research and Technology Some of the confusion in the essay grows out of the fact that the characters are half asleep. **Research** the effect of sleep on the senses. Find out how sensory information can be distorted by the sleeping state. Take notes on the main ideas and the most significant details that you find. Then, share your findings with the class.

 **Take It to the Net**   www.phschool.com

Go online for an additional research activity using the Internet.

Prepare to Read

All Summer in a Day

 Take It to the Net

Visit www.phschool.com for interactive activities and instruction related to "All Summer in a Day," including

- background
- graphic organizers
- literary elements
- reading strategies

Preview

Connecting to the Literature

Watching the sun break through the clouds after a storm, you may feel as if you are welcoming back a good friend. Imagine how you would feel seeing the sun if it had been raining for seven years! This is the situation for schoolchildren in "All Summer in a Day."

Background

"All Summer in a Day" is set on Venus, the second planet from the sun. Today, we know that Venus has a surface temperature of almost 900°F. In 1950, when Ray Bradbury wrote this story, some scientists believed that the clouds of Venus concealed a watery world. That information may have led Bradbury to create a setting of soggy jungles and constant rain.

Literary Analysis

Setting

A story's **setting** is the time and place in which the action of the story occurs. In the example, the details in italics help establish the setting.

> *It had been raining for seven years;* thousands upon thousands of days compounded and filled from one end to the other with rain, *with the drum and gush of water,* . . .

Specific details of time and place may include the year, the season, the weather, and the physical features. As you read "All Summer in a Day," look for details that indicate setting.

Connecting Literary Elements

A **conflict** is a struggle between two opposing forces. In "All Summer in a Day," the rainy setting contributes to the conflict. Children who do not remember the sun are in conflict with one girl who does. (To learn more about conflict, see the Literary Terms Handbook, p. R5.) As you read, think about the following focus questions:

1. What causes conflict between Margo and the other children?
2. What lessons do the children learn as a result of the conflict's outcome?

Reading Strategy

Comparing and Contrasting Characters

Similarities and differences among characters may produce a conflict or may bring characters closer together. **Compare and contrast characters** by identifying similarities and differences in thoughts, feelings, and personalities.

The diagram here compares and contrasts Margot's thoughts about the sun with the other children's thoughts. As you read, use a diagram like this one to note details that show how Margot is similar to or different from the other children.

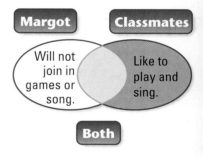

Vocabulary Development

concussion (kən kush′ ən) *n.* violent shaking (p. 264)

slackening (slak′ ən iŋ) *v.* easing; becoming less active (p. 265)

vital (vīt′ 'l) *adj.* necessary to life; critically important (p. 266)

surged (sʉrjd) *v.* moved in a violent swelling motion (p. 266)

tumultuously (too mul′ choo əs lē) *adv.* noisily and violently (p. 269)

resilient (ri zil′ yənt) *adj.* springing back into shape (p. 269)

All Summer in a Day

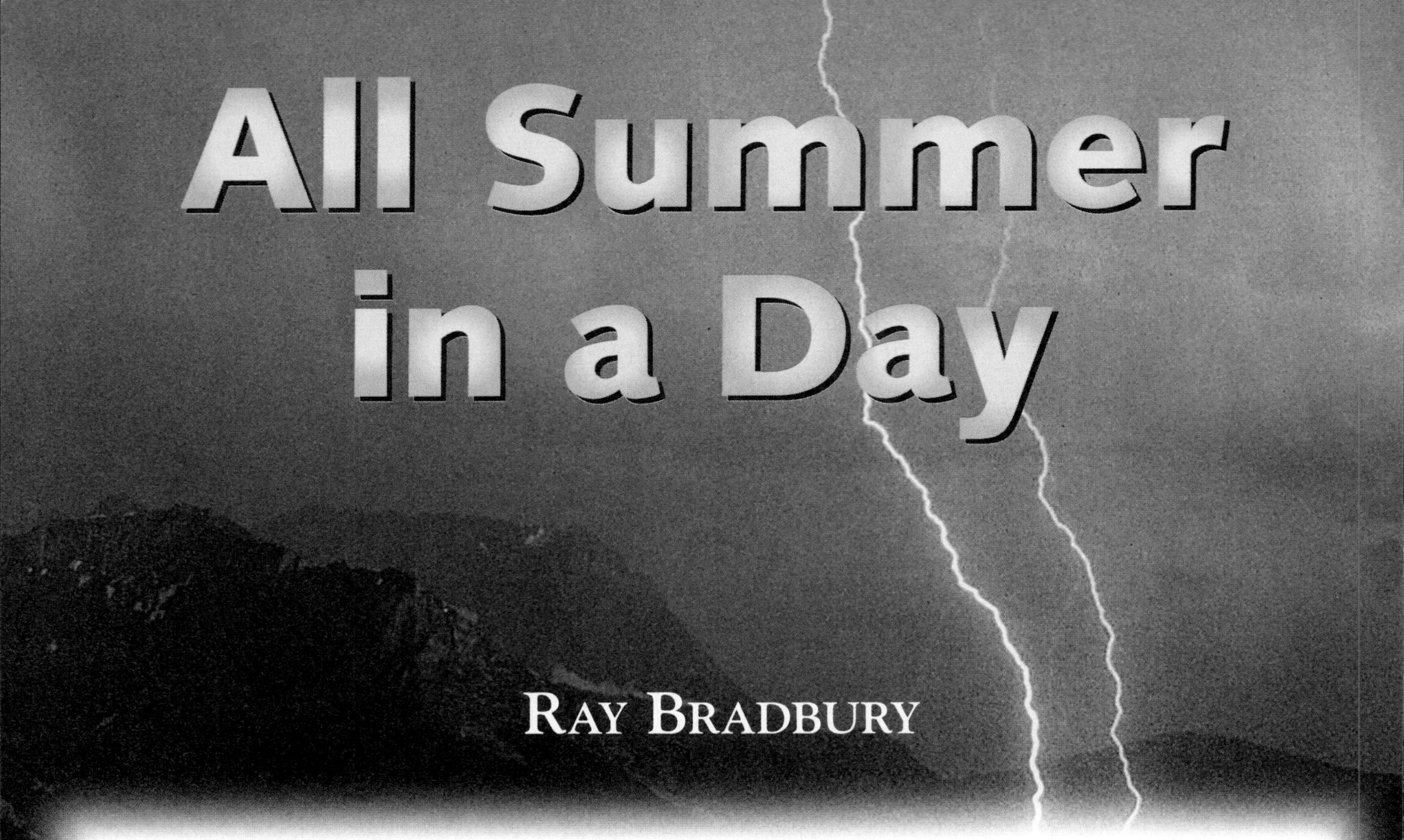

RAY BRADBURY

Ready?"

"Ready."

"Now?"

"Soon."

"Do the scientists really know? Will it happen today, will it?"

"Look, look; see for yourself!"

The children pressed to each other like so many roses, so many weeds, intermixed, peering out for a look at the hidden sun.

It rained.

It had been raining for seven years; thousands upon thousands of days compounded and filled from one end to the other with rain, with the drum and gush of water, with the sweet crystal fall of showers and the <u>concussion</u> of storms so heavy they were tidal waves come over the islands. A thousand forests had been crushed under the rain and grown up a thousand times to be crushed again. And this was the way life was forever on the planet Venus and this was the schoolroom of the children of the rocket men and women who had come to a raining world to set up civilization and live out their lives.

concussion (kən kush´ ən) *n.* violent shaking

"It's stopping, it's stopping!"

"Yes, yes!"

Margot stood apart from them, from these children who could never remember a time when there wasn't rain and rain and rain. They were all nine years old, and if there had been a day, seven years ago, when the sun came out for an hour and showed its face to the stunned world, they could not recall. Sometimes, at night, she heard them stir, in remembrance, and she knew they were dreaming and remembering gold or a yellow crayon or a coin large enough to buy the world with. She knew they thought they remembered a warmness, like a blushing in the face, in the body, in the arms and legs and trembling hands. But then they always awoke to the tatting drum, the endless shaking down of clear bead necklaces upon the roof, the walk, the gardens, the forests, and their dreams were gone.

All day yesterday they had read in class about the sun. About how like a lemon it was, and how hot. And they had written small stories or essays or poems about it:

> I think the sun is a flower,
> That blooms for just one hour.

That was Margot's poem, read in a quiet voice in the still classroom while the rain was falling outside.

"Aw, you didn't write that!" protested one of the boys.

"I did," said Margot. "I did."

"William!" said the teacher.

But that was yesterday. Now the rain was <u>slackening</u>, and the children were crushed in the great thick windows.

"Where's teacher?"

"She'll be back."

"She'd better hurry, we'll miss it!"

They turned on themselves, like a feverish wheel, all fumbling spokes.

Margot stood alone. She was a very frail girl who looked as if she had been lost in the rain for years and the rain had washed out the blue from her eyes and the red from her mouth and the yellow from her hair. She was an old photograph dusted from an album, whitened away, and if she spoke at all her voice would be a ghost. Now she stood, separate, staring at the rain and the loud wet world beyond the huge glass.

"What're you looking at?" said William.

Margot said nothing.

"Speak when you're spoken to." He gave her a shove. But she did not move; rather she let herself be moved only by him and nothing else.

They edged away from her, they would not look at her. She felt them go away. And this was because she would play no games with them in the echoing tunnels of the underground city. If they tagged her and ran, she stood blinking after them and did not follow. When

Literary Analysis
Setting How might the setting described in these opening paragraphs affect the characters?

slackening (slak´ ən iŋ) v. easing; becoming less active

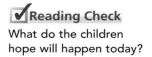
Reading Check
What do the children hope will happen today?

the class sang songs about happiness and life and games her lips barely moved. Only when they sang about the sun and the summer did her lips move as she watched the drenched windows.

And then, of course, the biggest crime of all was that she had come here only five years ago from Earth, and she remembered the sun and the way the sun was and the sky was when she was four in Ohio. And they, they had been on Venus all their lives, and they had been only two years old when last the sun came out and had long since forgotten the color and heat of it and the way it really was. But Margot remembered.

"It's like a penny," she said once, eyes closed.

"No, it's not!" the children cried.

"It's like a fire," she said, "in the stove."

"You're lying, you don't remember!" cried the children.

But she remembered and stood quietly apart from all of them and watched the patterning windows. And once, a month ago, she had refused to shower in the school shower rooms, had clutched her hands to her ears and over her head, screaming the water mustn't touch her head. So after that, dimly, dimly, she sensed it, she was different and they knew her difference and kept away.

There was talk that her father and mother were taking her back to Earth next year; it seemed <u>vital</u> to her that they do so, though it would mean the loss of thousands of dollars to her family. And so, the children hated her for all these reasons of big and little consequence. They hated her pale snow face, her waiting silence, her thinness, and her possible future.

"Get away!" The boy gave her another push. "What're you waiting for?"

Then, for the first time, she turned and looked at him. And what she was waiting for was in her eyes.

"Well, don't wait around here!" cried the boy savagely. "You won't see nothing!"

Her lips moved.

"Nothing!" he cried. "It was all a joke, wasn't it?" He turned to the other children. "Nothing's happening today. Is it?"

They all blinked at him and then, understanding, laughed and shook their heads. "Nothing, nothing!"

"Oh, but," Margot whispered, her eyes helpless. "But this is the day, the scientists predict, they say, they know, the sun . . ."

"All a joke!" said the boy, and seized her roughly. "Hey, everyone, let's put her in a closet before teacher comes!"

"No," said Margot, falling back.

They <u>surged</u> about her, caught her up and bore her, protesting, and then pleading, and then crying, back into a tunnel, a room, a closet, where they slammed and locked the door. They stood looking at the door and saw it tremble from her beating and throwing herself

vital (vīt´ əl) adj. necessary to life; critically important

surged (sʉrjd) v. moved in a violent swelling motion

▲ **Critical Viewing** What aspects of the story's setting do you see in this picture? **[Distinguish]**

against it. They heard her muffled cries. Then, smiling, they turned and went out and back down the tunnel, just as the teacher arrived.

"Ready, children?" She glanced at her watch.

"Yes!" said everyone.

"Are we all here?"

"Yes!"

The rain slackened still more.

They crowded to the huge door.

The rain stopped.

It was as if, in the midst of a film concerning an avalanche, a tornado, a hurricane, a volcanic eruption, something had, first, gone wrong with the sound apparatus, thus muffling and finally cutting off all noise, all of the blasts and repercussions and thunders, and then, second, ripped the film from the projector and inserted in its place a peaceful tropical slide which did not move or tremor. The world ground to a standstill. The silence was so immense and unbelievable that you felt your ears had been stuffed or you had lost your hearing altogether. The children put their hands to their ears. They stood apart. The door slid back and the smell of the silent, waiting world came in to them.

Reading Check
What is the difference between Margot and the other children?

The sun came out.

It was the color of flaming bronze and it was very large. And the sky around it was a blazing blue tile color. And the jungle burned with sunlight as the children, released from their spell, rushed out, yelling, into the springtime.

"Now, don't go too far," called the teacher after them. "You've only two hours, you know. You wouldn't want to get caught out!"

But they were running and turning their faces up to the sky and feeling the sun on their cheeks like a warm iron; they were taking off their jackets and letting the sun burn their arms.

"Oh, it's better than the sun lamps, isn't it?"

Literary Analysis
Setting and Conflict
Explain how the setting is contributing to the conflict.

▼ **Critical Viewing**
How do the emotions of the people in this painting compare with those of the characters in the story? **[Connect]**

"Much, much better!"

They stopped running and stood in the great jungle that covered Venus, that grew and never stopped growing, <u>tumultuously</u>, even as you watched it. It was a nest of octopi, clustering up great arms of fleshlike weed, wavering, flowering in this brief spring. It was the color of rubber and ash, this jungle, from the many years without sun. It was the color of stones and white cheeses and ink, and it was the color of the moon.

The children lay out, laughing, on the jungle mattress, and heard it sigh and squeak under them, <u>resilient</u> and alive. They ran among the trees, they slipped and fell, they pushed each other, they played hide-and-seek and tag, but most of all they squinted at the sun until

tears ran down their faces, they put their hands up to that yellowness and that amazing blueness and they breathed of the fresh, fresh air and listened and listened to the silence which suspended them in a blessed sea of no sound and no motion. They looked at everything and savored everything. Then, wildly, like animals escaped from their caves, they ran and ran in shouting circles. They ran for an hour and did not stop running.

And then—

In the midst of their running one of the girls wailed.

Everyone stopped.

The girl, standing in the open, held out her hand.

"Oh, look, look," she said, trembling.

They came slowly to look at her opened palm.

In the center of it, cupped and huge, was a single raindrop.

She began to cry, looking at it.

They glanced quietly at the sky.

"Oh, Oh."

A few cold drops fell on their noses and their cheeks and their mouths. The sun faded behind a stir of mist. A wind blew cool around them. They turned and started to walk back toward the underground house, their hands at their sides, their smiles vanishing away.

A boom of thunder startled them and like leaves before a new hurricane, they tumbled upon each other and ran. Lightning struck ten miles away, five miles away, a mile, a half mile. The sky darkened into midnight in a flash.

They stood in the doorway of the underground for a moment until it was raining hard. Then they

tumultuously
(tōō mul´ chōō əs lē)
adv. noisily and violently

resilient (ri zil´ yənt) *adj.* springing back into shape

Literary Analysis
Setting and Conflict
How do you think the change in weather will affect the conflict between Margot and her classmates?

✔ **Reading Check**
Why are the children so excited about the sunshine?

closed the door and heard the gigantic sound of the rain falling in tons and avalanches, everywhere and forever.

"Will it be seven more years?"

"Yes. Seven."

Then one of them gave a little cry.

"Margot!"

"What?"

"She's still in the closet where we locked her."

"Margot."

They stood as if someone had driven them, like so many stakes, into the floor. They looked at each other and then looked away. They glanced out at the world that was raining now and raining and raining steadily. They could not meet each other's glances. Their faces were solemn and pale. They looked at their hands and feet, their faces down.

"Margot."

One of the girls said, "Well . . .?"

No one moved.

"Go on," whispered the girl.

They walked slowly down the hall in the sound of cold rain. They turned through the doorway to the room in the sound of the storm and thunder, lightning on their faces, blue and terrible. They walked over to the closet door slowly and stood by it.

Behind the closet door was only silence.

They unlocked the door, even more slowly, and let Margot out.

Ray Bradbury

(b. 1920)

As a boy, Ray Bradbury loved magicians, circuses, and the stories of science-fiction novelist Edgar Rice Burroughs.

In 1950, he published a story about a group of Earth-men struggling on the rainy world of Venus. He wondered how a child would react to the sun's brief appearances on Venus. To answer this question, he wrote "All Summer in a Day."

He has won the World Fantasy Award for Lifetime Achievement and the Grand Master Award from the Science Fiction Writers of America. Bradbury has even had a lunar landmark named in honor of his autobiographical novel, *Dandelion Wine.*

Review and Assess

Thinking About the Selection

1. **(a) Respond:** What is your reaction to the way the other children treat Margot?

2. **(a) Recall:** How does Margot know what the sun is like?
   (b) Infer: Why do the children reject her description of the sun?

3. **(a) Recall:** Why do the children want the teacher to hurry back to the classroom at the beginning of the story? **(b) Infer:** Who is the "leader" of the class when the teacher is out of the room? **(c) Draw Conclusions:** Why do you think all the children go along with the prank that is played against Margot?

4. **(a) Recall:** How do the children react when they realize that Margot missed the sun because of their prank?
   (b) Draw Conclusions: Why do you think they react as they do?
   (c) Generalize: What do the children learn from their experiences?

5. **Make a Judgment:** What, if any, consequences do you think William and the other students should face?

Review and Assess

Literary Analysis

Setting

1. Identify three descriptions or details from the story that indicate or develop setting. Record them on a chart like the one shown here.

Details that indicate time	
Details that indicate place	

2. In your own words, describe the setting of "All Summer in a Day."
3. Explain three ways in which the action of the story might have changed if the setting had been different.

Connecting Literary Elements

4. What poses a **conflict** between Margot and the other children? Fill out the graphic organizer below with details from the story.

5. What do the other children do as a result of the conflict?
6. What lesson do the children learn from the outcome of the conflict?

Reading Strategy

Comparing and Contrasting Characters

7. How does Margot's behavior in playing games and singing songs differ from that of her classmates?
8. How do Margot's words and ways of speaking differ from those of her classmates?
9. What can you tell about Margot's character from her behavior?
10. Compare and contrast the physical effects that the rain has on Margot and her classmates.

Extend Understanding

11. **Science Connection:** Compare details in the story to facts you know about Venus. Does the inaccuracy weaken the story? Why or why not?

Quick Review

Setting is the time and place of a story. To review setting, see page 263.

Conflict is the struggle between two opposing forces. To review conflict, see page 263.

Comparing and contrasting characters involves finding similarities and differences in their personalities and behavior.

 Take It to the Net
www.phschool.com
Take the interactive self-test online to check your understanding of the selection.

Integrate Language Skills

Vocabulary Development Lesson

Word Analysis: Latin Root -vita-

The Latin word root -vita- means "life." Words that contain the root usually have meanings related to life. For example, the word *vital* describes things that have an almost "life or death" importance. Sunshine is *vital* to Margot. It is very important to her health and happiness. Look at these other words that contain the root -vita-.

vitamins   vitality   revitalize

On your paper, match the words with their meanings.

1. A feeling of being alive: ____?____
2. Elements in food that are essential for life: ____?____
3. To give new life to: ____?____

Fluency: Clarify Word Meaning

Read each question aloud. Write and briefly explain an answer to each question.

1. Is water *vital* to life?
2. Is *slackening* rain increasing or decreasing?
3. When a feather lands on the floor, does it produce a *concussion*?
4. Would you describe a baseball as *resilient*?
5. If electricity *surged* through your computer, what effect would it have?
6. If children play *tumultuously*, are they quiet?

Spelling Strategy

In some words, like *tumultuously*, the *choo* sound is spelled *tu*. Pronounce difficult words in syllables as they are spelled: too mul′ choo us lee. Exaggerate the sound in each syllable. Write how you would pronounce each word by syllables.

1. actuality   2. situation   3. fortunate

Grammar Lesson

Prepositional Phrases

A **preposition** relates a noun or pronoun that appears with it to another word in the sentence. A **prepositional phrase** is a group of words that begins with a preposition and ends with a noun or pronoun. The noun or pronoun following a preposition is called the **object of the preposition.**

In the example, the prepositional phrases are in italics. Prepositions are printed in boldface, and objects of prepositions are underlined.

Example: The children pressed **to** *each* <u>other</u>
like *so many* <u>roses</u> . . . peering out **for**
a <u>look</u> **at** *the hidden* <u>sun</u>.

Practice Copy the following sentences, and underline each prepositional phrase.

1. It had been raining for seven years.
2. Margot stood apart from these children.
3. They had read in class about the sun.
4. She would play no games with them in the underground city.
5. The sky filled with clouds in an instant.

Writing Application Add at least two prepositional phrases to each sentence.

1. It rains heavily.
2. One boy spoke.

Prentice Hall Writing and Grammar Connection: Chapter 20, Section 1

Writing Lesson

Setting for a Story

In his story, Bradbury described the setting of Venus as he imagined it might be—wet, rainy, and almost always sunless. Write your own description of a setting.

Prewriting Choose a time and a place—past, present, or future, real or imaginary. Gather sensory details—details about the way the setting looks, sounds, feels, and perhaps even smells!

Drafting Describe the place, incorporating the sensory details you gathered. Organize details to develop a general impression of your setting. Try to *show* rather than *tell* what your setting is like.

Model: Sensory Details in a Setting

Moonlight filtered through the branches of the spruces next to the old mountain trail. A breeze stirred the branches, perfuming the air with the scent of pine. In the distance, a coyote yelped.

> Sensory details, such as *moonlight, the scent of pine, mountain trail,* and *a coyote yelped,* help bring the setting to life.

Revising Review your writing to make sure you have included sensory details. Circle vague words and replace them with more precise words. Proofread for spelling, grammar, and mechanics.

W G Prentice Hall Writing and Grammar Connection: Chapter 5, Section 3

Extension Activities

Listening and Speaking With a group, **role-play the conversation** from the opening of the story among Margot, William, and the other children. Follow these steps to help you organize your task:

1. Choose roles.
2. Review the opening of the story to recall details of the conversation and to sort out who spoke which lines.
3. Role-play the conversation.

Follow up with a discussion in which each participant describes the character he or she played. Other group members should ask questions and respond to the description.

Research and Technology Use an online or printed periodical index (an index of printed materials published on a regular basis) to research information about Venus. Find at least four sources published within the last two years. Using facts that appear in at least two of the sources, make a **comparison chart** comparing Bradbury's imaginary Venus with Venus as scientists understand it today.

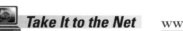 **Take It to the Net**   www.phschool.com

Go online for an additional research activity using the Internet.

Prepare to Read

The Highwayman ◆ The Real Story of a Cowboy's Life

 Take It to the Net

Visit www.phschool.com for interactive activities and instruction related to these selections, including
- background
- graphic organizers
- literary elements
- reading strategies

Preview

Connecting to the Literature

"The Highwayman" makes the life of an outlaw seem daring, romantic, and adventurous. In contrast, in "The Real Story of a Cowboy's Life," Geoffrey Ward tries to replace the romantic adventurous image most people have of a cowboy's life with the reality.

Background

"The Highwayman" takes place when highways were just dirt roads. People would travel by horseback or horse-drawn carriage, stopping at inns to avoid the dangers of isolated highways in the dark of night. Inns provided lodging and care for people and their horses.

Literary Analysis

Suspense

Suspense is the tension or nervous uncertainty about the outcome of events. Suspense can result from not knowing what will happen to a character, or from expecting that something terrible will happen and not knowing when or how the disaster will occur.

In the following passage, the italicized words cause suspense by suggesting that something bad will happen to the highwayman.

> *Yet, if they press me sharply, and harry me through the day,*
> Then look for me by moonlight,

As you read, look for other details that create suspense.

Comparing Literary Works

Literary works that share a common topic may portray that topic in very different ways. In one work, the author's attitude toward the subject may be humorous. In another, it may be respectful and serious. Compare the works in this group by looking for clues to each author's attitude toward the shared subject. As you read, focus on the following questions:

1. In what ways does this work show the romance or reality of its subjects?
2. What common element ties these works together?

Reading Strategy

Identifying Causes and Effects

You will better understand a story if you can identify both

- **causes**—events that bring about other events.
- **effects**—events that result from other events.

The effect of one event can be the cause of another. As you read "The Highwayman," use a diagram like the one shown to record the cause-and-effect chain.

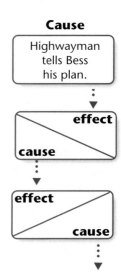

Cause

Highwayman tells Bess his plan.

effect

cause

effect

cause

Vocabulary Development

torrent (tôr´ ənt) *n.* flood (p. 277)

landlord (land´ lôrd) *n.* person who keeps a rooming house, inn, etc. (p. 277)

tawny (tô´ nē) *adj.* tan; yellowish brown (p. 278)

bound (bound) *v.* tied (p. 278)

strive (strīv) *v.* struggle (p. 278)

brandished (bran´ dishd) *adj.* waved in a threatening way (p. 280)

The Highwayman

Alfred Noyes

Part One

The wind was a <u>torrent</u> of darkness among the gusty trees.
The moon was a ghostly galleon[1] tossed upon cloudy seas.
The road was a ribbon of moonlight over the purple moor,[2]
And the highwayman came riding—
5   Riding—riding—
The highwayman came riding, up to the old inn door.

He'd a French cocked-hat on his forehead, a bunch of lace at his chin,
A coat of the claret velvet, and breeches of brown doeskin.
They fitted with never a wrinkle. His boots were up to the thigh.
10 And he rode with a jeweled twinkle,
         His pistol butts a-twinkle,
His rapier hilt[3] a-twinkle, under the jeweled sky.

Over the cobbles he clattered and clashed in the dark innyard.
He tapped with his whip on the shutters, but all was locked and barred.
15 He whistled a tune to the window, and who should be waiting there
But the <u>landlord's</u> black-eyed daughter,
         Bess, the landlord's daughter,
Plaiting a dark red love knot into her long black hair.

And dark in the dark old innyard a stable wicket creaked
20 Where Tim the ostler listened. His face was white and peaked.
His eyes were hollows of madness, his hair like moldy hay,
But he loved the landlord's daughter,
         The landlord's red-lipped daughter.
Dumb as a dog he listened, and he heard the robber say—
25 "One kiss, my bonny[4] sweetheart, I'm after a prize tonight,
But I shall be back with the yellow gold before the morning light;
Yet, if they press me sharply, and harry me through the day,
Then look for me by moonlight,
         Watch for me by moonlight,
30 I'll come to thee by moonlight, though hell should bar the way."

He rose upright in the stirrups. He scarce could reach her hand,
But she loosened her hair in the casement.[5] His face burnt like a
      brand[6]
As the black cascade of perfume came tumbling over his breast;
And he kissed its waves in the moonlight,
35   (O, sweet black waves in the moonlight!)
Then he tugged at his rein in the moonlight, and galloped away to
      the west.

---

1. **galleon** (gal´ ē ən) *n.* large Spanish sailing ship.
2. **moor** (moor) *n.* open, rolling land with swamps.
3. **rapier** (rā´ pē ər) **hilt** large cup-shaped handle of a rapier, which is a type of sword.
4. **bonny** (bän´ ē) *adj.* Scottish for "pretty."
5. **casement** (kās´ mənt) *n.* window frame that opens on hinges.
6. **brand** (brand) *n.* piece of burning wood.

torrent (tôr´ ənt) *n.* flood

landlord (land´ lôrd) *n.* person who keeps a rooming house, inn, etc.

Reading Strategy
Identifying Causes and Effects What is a possible effect of Tim's overhearing the highwayman's plans?

✔**Reading Check**
What did Tim overhear?

Part Two

He did not come in the dawning. He did not come at noon;
And out of the tawny sunset, before the rise of the moon,
When the road was a gypsy's ribbon, looping the purple moor,
40 A redcoat troop came marching—
            Marching—marching—
King George's men[7] came marching, up to the old inn door.

They said no word to the landlord. They drank his ale instead
But they gagged his daughter, and bound her, to the foot of her
            narrow bed.
45 Two of them knelt at her casement, with muskets at their side!
There was death at every window;
            And hell at one dark window;
For Bess could see, through her casement, the road that he would ride.

They had tied her up to attention, with many a sniggering jest.[8]
50 They had bound a musket beside her, with the muzzle
            beneath her breast!
"Now, keep good watch!" and they kissed her. She heard the
            doomed man say—
Look for me by moonlight;
            Watch for me by moonlight;
I'll come to thee by moonlight, though hell should bar the way!

55 She twisted her hands behind her; but all the knots held good!
She writhed her hands till her fingers were wet with sweat or blood!
They stretched and strained in the darkness, and the hours
            crawled by like years,
Till, now, on the stroke of midnight,
            Cold, on the stroke of midnight,
60 The tip of one finger touched it! The trigger at least was hers!

The tip of one finger touched it. She strove no more for the rest.
Up, she stood up to attention, with the muzzle beneath her breast.
She would not risk their hearing; she would not strive again;
For the road lay bare in the moonlight;
65   Blank and bare in the moonlight;
And the blood of her veins, in the moonlight, throbbed to her
            love's refrain.

Tlot-tlot; tlot-tlot! Had they heard it? The horsehoofs ringing clear;
Tlot-tlot, tlot-tlot, in the distance? Were they deaf that they did not
            hear?
Down the ribbon of moonlight, over the brow of the hill,

---

tawny (tô´ nē) *adj.* tan;
yellowish brown

Reading Strategy
**Identifying Causes and
Effects** What causes
troops to set a trap for
the highwayman?

bound (bound) *v.* tied

Literary Analysis
Suspense What is
suspenseful about the
fact that Bess is able to
reach the gun's trigger?

strive (strīv) *v.* struggle

---

7. **King George's men** soldiers serving King George of England.
8. **sniggering** (snig´ ər iŋ) **jest** sly joke.

70 The highwayman came riding—
        Riding—riding—
The redcoats looked to their priming!⁹ She stood up, straight
    and still.

Tlot-tlot, in the frosty silence! Tlot-tlot, in the echoing night!
Nearer he came and nearer. Her face was like a light.
75 Her eyes grew wide for a moment; she drew one last deep breath,
Then her finger moved in the moonlight,
        Her musket shattered the moonlight,
Shattered her breast in the moonlight and warned him—with
    her death.

He turned. He spurred to the west; he did not know who stood
80 Bowed, with her head o'er the musket, drenched with her own blood!
Not till the dawn he heard it, and his face grew gray to hear
How Bess, the landlord's daughter,

---

9. **priming** (prī´ miŋ) *n.* explosive used to set off the charge in a gun.

☑ **Reading Check**
How does Bess warn the highwayman?

▲ **Critical Viewing** What elements of the setting does this illustration capture? **[Connect]**

The landlord's black-eyed daughter,
Had watched for her love in the moonlight, and died in
   the darkness there.

85 Back, he spurred like a madman, shouting a curse to the sky,
With the white road smoking behind him and his rapier
   <u>brandished</u> high.
Blood-red were his spurs in the golden noon; wine-red
   was his velvet coat;
When they shot him down on the highway,
         Down like a dog on the highway,
90 And he lay in his blood on the highway, with a bunch of lace
   at his throat.

· ·

And still of a winter's night, they say, when the wind is in the trees,
When the moon is a ghostly galleon tossed upon cloudy seas,
When the road is a ribbon of moonlight over the purple moor,
A highwayman comes riding—
95   *Riding—riding—*
A highwayman comes riding, up to the old inn door.

Over the cobbles he clatters and clangs in the dark innyard.
He taps with his whip on the shutters, but all is locked and barred.
He whistles a tune to the window, and who should be waiting there
100 *But the landlord's black-eyed daughter,*
         Bess, the landlord's daughter,
Plaiting a dark red love knot into her long black hair.

brandished (bran´ dishd)
adj. waved in a threatening way

Review and Assess

Thinking About the Selection

1. **Respond:** Who do you think was braver—Bess or the highwayman? Why?
2. **(a) Recall:** How does the highwayman communicate his presence to Bess? **(b) Infer:** What does this method of communication indicate about their relationship?
3. **(a) Recall:** Identify three details that make the highwayman appear a romantic or dashing figure. **(b) Compare and Contrast:** How do these details compare with the description of Tim?
4. **(a) Recall:** Besides Bess, who else hears the highwayman's plans? **(b) Infer:** What does this person do after overhearing this information? **(c) Draw Conclusions:** Why?
5. **(a) Recall:** Summarize the events of the poem. **(b) Generalize:** What does the action of the poem suggest about the love between Bess and the highwayman?

Alfred Noyes

(1880–1958)

Alfred Noyes, born in Straffordshire, England, was both a poet and a critic. He wrote frequently about the English countryside and legends. Despite his great love for England's history, Noyes moved to New Jersey to teach at Princeton University. This new location did not stop him from writing poems about English history, especially of legendary figures like Robin Hood.

The Real Story of a Cowboy's Life

Geoffrey C. Ward

A drive's success depended on discipline and planning. According to Teddy Blue[1], most Texas herds numbered about 2,000 head with a trail boss and about a dozen men in charge—though herds as large as 15,000 were also driven north with far larger escorts. The most experienced men rode "point" and "swing," at the head and sides of the long herd; the least experienced brought up the rear, riding "drag" and eating dust. At the end of the day, Teddy Blue remembered, they "would go to the water barrel . . . and rinse their mouths and cough and spit up . . . black stuff. But you couldn't get it up out of your lungs."

---

1. **Teddy Blue** Edward C. Abbot; a cowboy who rode in a successful trail drive in the 1880s.

They had to learn to work as a team, keeping the herd moving during the day, resting peacefully at night. Twelve to fifteen miles a day was a good pace. But such steady progress could be interrupted at any time. A cowboy had to know how to gauge the temperament of his cattle, how to chase down a stray without alarming the rest of the herd, how to lasso a steer using the horn of his saddle as a tying post. His saddle was his most prized possession; it served as his chair, his workbench, his pillow at night. Being dragged to death was the most common death for a cowboy, and so the most feared occurrence on the trail was the night-time stampede. As Teddy Blue recalled, a sound, a smell, or simply the sudden movement of a jittery cow could set off a whole herd.

If . . . the cattle started running—you'd hear that low rumbling noise along the ground and the men on herd wouldn't need to come in and tell you, you'd know—then you'd jump for your horse and get out there in the lead, trying to head them and get them into a mill before they scattered. It was riding at a dead run in the dark, with cut banks and prairie dog holes all around you, not knowing if the next jump would land you in a shallow grave.

Most cowboys had guns, but rarely used them on the trail. Some outfits made them keep their weapons in the chuck wagon to eliminate any chance of gunplay. Charles Goodnight[2] was still more emphatic: "Before starting on a trail drive, I made it a rule to draw up an article of agreement, setting forth what each man was to do. The main clause stipulated[3] that if one shot another he was to be tried by the outfit and hanged on the spot, if found guilty. I never had a man shot on the trail."

Regardless of its ultimate destination, every herd had to ford[4] a series of rivers—the Nueces, the Guadalupe, the Brazos, the Wichita, the Red.

---

2. **Charles Goodnight** cowboy who rode successful trail drives beginning in the 1860s.
3. **stipulated** (stip′ yōō lāt′ id) v. stated as a rule.
4. **ford** (fôrd) v. to cross a river at its low point.

Reading Strategy
Identifying Causes and Effects What might cause a herd to stampede?

▼ **Critical Viewing** How does this photograph suggest the "real story" of a cowboy's life? **[Analyze]**

A big herd of longhorns swimming across a river, Goodnight remembered, "looked like a million floating rocking chairs," and crossing those rivers one after another, a cowboy recalled, was like climbing the rungs of a long ladder reaching north.

"After you crossed the Red River and got out on the open plains," Teddy Blue remembered, "it was sure a pretty sight to see them strung out for almost a mile, the sun shining on their horns." Initially, the land immediately north of the Red River was Indian territory, and some tribes charged tolls for herds crossing their land—payable in money or beef. But Teddy Blue remembered that the homesteaders, now pouring onto the Plains by railroad, were far more nettlesome:

There was no love lost between settlers and cowboys on the trail. Those jay-hawkers would take up a claim right where the herds watered and charge us for water. They would plant a crop alongside the trail and plow a furrow around it for a fence, and then when the cattle got into their wheat or their garden patch, they would come cussing and waving a shotgun and yelling for damages. And the cattle had been coming through there when they were still raising punkins in Illinois.

The settlers' hostility was entirely understandable. The big herds ruined their crops, and they carried with them a disease, spread by ticks and called "Texas fever," that devastated domestic livestock. Kansas and other territories along the route soon established quarantine lines[5], called "deadlines," at the western fringe of settlement, and insisted that trail drives not cross them. Each year, as settlers continued to move in, those deadlines moved farther west.

Reading Strategy
Identifying Causes and Effects What are the causes for the settlers' hostility?

Sometimes, farmers tried to enforce their own, as John Rumans, one of Charles Goodnight's hands, recalled:

Some men met us at the trail near Canyon City, and said we couldn't come in. There were fifteen or twenty of them, and they were not going to let us cross the Arkansas River. We didn't even stop. . . . Old man [Goodnight] had a shotgun loaded with buckshot and led the way, saying: "John, get over on that point with your Winchester and point these cattle in behind me." He slid his shotgun across the saddle in front of him and we did the same with our Winchesters. He rode right across, and as he rode up to them, he said: "I've monkeyed as long as I want to with you," and they fell back to the sides, and went home after we had passed.

There were few diversions on the trail. Most trail bosses banned liquor. Goodnight prohibited gambling, too. Even the songs for which cowboys became famous grew directly out of doing a job, remembered Teddy Blue:

The singing was supposed to soothe [the cattle] and it did; I don't know why, unless it was that a sound they was used to would keep

---

5. quarantine (kwôr´ ən tēn) **lines** *n.* boundaries created to prevent the spread of disease.

them from spooking at other noises. I know that if you wasn't singing, any little sound in the night—it might be just a horse shaking himself—could make them leave the country; but if you were singing, they wouldn't notice it.

The two men on guard would circle around with their horses on a walk, if it was a clear night and the cattle was bedded down and quiet, and one man would sing a verse of song, and his partner on the other side of the herd would sing another verse; and you'd go through a whole song that way. . . . "Bury Me Not on the Lone Prairie" was a great song for awhile, but . . . they sung it to death. It was a saying on the range that even the horses nickered it and the coyotes howled it; it got so they'd throw you in the creek if you sang it.

The number of cattle on the move was sometimes staggering: once, Teddy Blue rode to the top of a rise from which he could see seven herds strung out behind him; eight more up ahead; and the dust from an additional thirteen moving parallel to his. "All the cattle in the world," he remembered, "seemed to be coming up from Texas."

At last, the herds neared their destinations. After months in the saddle—often wearing the same clothes every day, eating nothing but biscuits and beef stew at the chuck wagon, drinking only water and coffee, his sole companions his fellow cowboys, his herd, and his horse—the cowboy was about to be paid for his work, and turned loose in town.

Review and Assess

Thinking About the Selection

1. **Respond:** Which detail in "The Real Story of a Cowboy's Life" surprised you most?

2. **(a) Recall:** What details prove that Teddy Blue likes cattle drives? **(b) Evaluate:** What qualifies him as a reliable source of information?

3. **(a) Recall:** What challenges does the landscape present to cowboys on a drive? **(b) Analyze:** How do conflicts between people add to these challenges?

4. **(a) Recall:** Identify two details that explain how violence is kept to a minimum on the trail. **(b) Interpret:** Based on "The Real Story of a Cowboy's Life," what kind of person do you think succeeds as a cowboy?

5. **(a) Recall:** Why do settlers object to cattle coming through? **(b) Infer:** Why do cowboys object to going around settled areas? **(c) Take a Position:** What solution or compromise would be most fair?

Geoffrey C. Ward

(b. 1940)

Like Alfred Noyes, historian Geoffrey C. Ward writes about his country's past. For Ward, however, the subject is American history, and the means of communication is not a poem but often a television program. Ward has teamed up with filmmaker Ken Burns to create award-winning PBS documentaries like *The Civil War* and a popular series that chronicles the history of baseball.

Review and Assess

Literary Analysis

Suspense

1. Identify three events that increase the **suspense** of "The Highway-man" by suggesting an upcoming problem or disaster. Use a chart like the following.

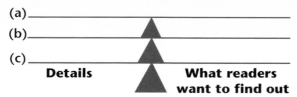

(a) _____

(b) _____

(c) _____

Details   **What readers want to find out**

2. What details in "The Real Story of a Cowboy's Life" might be used in suspenseful writing about a trail drive? Give three examples.

Comparing Literary Works

3. In what ways does each work show the romance or reality of its subjects? Complete a chart like the following to help you answer.

	Romance	Reality
"The Highwayman"		
"The Real Story of a Cowboy's Life"		

4. What common element ties these works together?
5. Do you prefer reading poetry, such as "The Highwayman," or nonfiction, such as "The Real Story of a Cowboy's Life"?

Reading Strategy

Identify Causes and Effects

6. Identify two **causes** and **effects** in "The Highwayman."
7. **(a)** In "The Real Story of a Cowboy's Life," what are some causes of a stampede? **(b)** What are some effects?

Extend Understanding

8. **Career Connection:** What qualities would a successful cowboy need to have? For what other jobs might these qualities be useful?

Quick Review

Suspense is a feeling of nervousness about the outcome of events. To review suspense, see page 275.

A **cause** is what brings about an event or a circumstance.
An **effect** is the result of an event or circumstance.

 Take It to the Net
www.phschool.com
Take the interactive self-test online to check your understanding of these selections.

Integrate Language Skills

Vocabulary Development Lesson

Word Analysis: Compound Nouns

The word *moonlight*, which appears in "The Highwayman," is a **compound noun**—one combining two smaller words, *moon* and *light*. Make five compound nouns from the words below.

lord	way	lamp	land	high
light	ache	heart	quarters	head

Spelling Strategy

In compound adjectives (adjectives combining two words), use a hyphen to separate an adjective and the *-ed* form of a noun. **Example**: *black + eye = black-eyed*. Use the following words to make compound adjectives.

1. red lips
2. black hair
3. brave heart
4. single mind

Concept Development: Antonyms

In your notebook, label each word pair with A for **antonyms** (words with opposite meanings) or S for **synonyms** (words with similar meanings). Choose two of the synonym pairs and find an antonym for the first word of each pair. Check your work in a dictionary or thesaurus.

1. torrent, flood
2. brandished, hid
3. bound, unlocked
4. tawny, tan
5. landlord, tenant
6. strive, try
7. highwayman, outlaw

Grammar Lesson

Hyphens

Punctuation is a set of symbols or marks that are used to indicate the way words work together in sentences. A **hyphen** is a very short line that serves the following purposes.

Purpose	Examples
Joins words in two-word numbers that are less than 100.	twenty-one, eighty-nine
Joins words in two-word fractions used as modifiers.	three-quarter point, two-thirds over
Joins words and word parts.	cocked-hat, red-lipped, all-powerful, ex-student
Shows a break between syllables in a word at the end of a line.	The wind was a torrent of darkness among the gusty trees.

Practice Copy the following sentences onto a piece of paper, and add hyphens where appropriate.

1. She will never have great grandchildren.
2. He is twenty five years old.
3. He loved his beautiful, black eyed Bess.
4. Once across the Wichita River, the cattle had reached the four fifths point of the trip.
5. The fear driven cattle may stampede.

Writing Application Briefly restate what you have learned about cowboys. Every fifth to sixth word, hyphenate the word and start a new line.

WG Prentice Hall Writing and Grammar Connection: Chapter 26, Section 5

286 ◆ *Meeting Challenges*

Writing Lesson

Wanted Poster

Prepare a "wanted poster" that the soldiers might have written to persuade others to help them catch the highwayman.

Prewriting   Review the poem to form a list of words and phrases related to the highwayman. Then, evaluate the **connotations**—the associations of each word or phrase. Place a check mark next to neutral words, a plus sign next to words with positive connotations, and a minus sign next to words with negative connotations. Because you want to portray the highwayman in a negative light, for each neutral or positive word, supply a replacement with negative connotations.

Model: Evaluating Connotations

Words from the poem	Replacements
√ "galloped away"	fled
+ "prize"	loot
– "madman"	(none needed)

> Words in the replacement column have more powerful connotations.

Drafting   Convince readers that the highwayman should be captured by describing him and his actions in a negative way. Use words with negative connotations from your prewriting list.

Revising   Review your poster to see if you can replace other less powerful words with words that have stronger negative connotations.

WG Prentice Hall Writing and Grammar Connection: Chapter 5, Section 3

Extension Activities

Listening and Speaking Give a **persuasive speech** to convince people to help capture the highwayman.

1. On a note card, write a short statement telling why you are in favor of capture.
2. Write your main points in favor of the capture on additional cards. Include solid evidence to back up your position. Use phrases that will remind you of your points—do not write out complete sentences.
3. Give your speech, referring to your cards.

Research and Technology In a group, prepare an **oral presentation** on legendary outlaws. First, research a legendary English highwayman, like Dick Turpin, and a legendary cowboy outlaw, like Jesse James. Share your results with the class, comparing and contrasting the two outlaws to each other and to Noyes's highwayman.

 **Take It to the Net**   www.phschool.com

Go online for an additional research activity using the Internet.

Prepare to Read

Amigo Brothers ◆ The Walk ◆ Justin Lebo ◆ The Rider

Take It to the Net

Visit www.phschool.com
for interactive activities
and instruction related to
these selections, including

• background
• graphic organizers
• literary elements
• reading strategies

Preview

Connecting to the Literature

The characters in "Amigo Brothers" and "Justin Lebo" realize that a small problem or project can sometimes grow into a larger and more complicated challenge. Connect to the selections by remembering a project or problem you have worked on that turned out to be larger and more ambitious than you expected.

Background

"Amigo Brothers" tells the story of two teenage boxers who dream of becoming champions. They both want to represent their boxing club in the annual Golden Gloves tournament. In this competition—probably the most famous amateur boxing event in the United States—local and regional elimination bouts lead to final championship matches.

Literary Analysis

Third-Person Point of View

Point of view is the angle from which a fictional or nonfictional narrative is told. In a narrative told from a **third-person point of view,** the action is conveyed by a narrator who does not participate in the events. There are two types of third-person point of view:

- **Third-person omniscient:** The narrator knows the thoughts of more than one character.
- **Third-person limited:** The narrator knows the thoughts of one character.

"Amigo Brothers" and "Justin Lebo" are both told from the third-person omniscient point of view. However, as you read these narratives, notice which emphasizes a single character's thoughts and which focuses on the thoughts of two characters.

Comparing Literary Works

The characters in these selections confront loneliness, boredom, and competition—problems that face many of us at one time or another. As you compare and contrast the ways in which the characters handle these problems, look for answers to the following focus questions:

1. Which characters come up with a better solution to these problems?
2. Which characters deal with a sense of loneliness arising from a relationship? Compare and contrast their success or failure at solving this problem.

Reading Strategy

Drawing Inferences

An **inference** is a logical guess about information that is not directly stated, based on information that is provided. For example, since Justin Lebo loves to fix bikes, you can infer that he has some mechanical ability. Use an organizer like this one to help you make inferences.

Question	What are some qualities of Justin Lebo's personality?
Detail	He fixes old bikes.
Inference	He is mechanical and intelligent.

Vocabulary Development

devastating (dev′ əs tāt′ iŋ) *adj.* destructive; overwhelming (p. 291)

superimposed (sōō′ pər im pōzd′) *adj.* put or stacked on top of something else (p. 293)

perpetual (pər pech′ ōō əl) *adj.* constant; unending (p. 294)

dispelled (di speld′) *v.* driven away; made to disappear (p. 295)

evading (ē vād′ iŋ) *adj.* keeping away from or avoiding (p. 297)

realign (rē′ ə līn′) *v.* readjust into proper coordination (p. 301)

yield (yēld) *v.* give way to pressure or force (p. 301)

coalition (kō′ ə lish′ ən) *n.* association or organization formed for a specific purpose (p. 305)

Amigo Brothers

Piri Thomas

Antonio Cruz and Felix Vargas were both seventeen years old. They were so together in friendship that they felt themselves to be brothers. They had known each other since childhood, growing up on the lower east side of Manhattan in the same tenement building on Fifth Street between Avenue A and Avenue B.

Antonio was fair, lean, and lanky, while Felix was dark, short, and husky. Antonio's hair was always falling over his eyes, while Felix wore his black hair in a natural Afro style.

Each youngster had a dream of someday becoming lightweight champion of the world. Every chance they had the boys worked out, sometimes at the Boys Club on 10th Street and Avenue A and sometimes at the pro's gym on 14th Street. Early morning sunrises would find them running along the East River Drive, wrapped in sweat shirts, short towels around their necks, and handkerchiefs Apache style around their foreheads.

While some youngsters were into street negatives, Antonio and Felix slept, ate, rapped, and dreamt positive. Between

▶ **Critical Viewing** What does the protective gear in this photograph suggest about boxing? [**Analyze Cause and Effect**]

them, they had a collection of *Fight* magazines second to none, plus a scrapbook filled with torn tickets to every boxing match they had ever attended, and some clippings of their own. If asked a question about any given fighter, they would immediately zip out from their memory banks divisions, weights, records of fights, knock-outs, technical knock-outs,[1] and draws or losses.

Each had fought many bouts representing their community and had won two gold-plated medals plus a silver and bronze medallion. The difference was in their style. Antonio's lean form and long reach made him the better boxer, while Felix's short and muscular frame made him the better slugger. Whenever they had met in the ring for sparring sessions, it had always been hot and heavy.

Now, after a series of elimination bouts,[2] they had been informed that they were to meet each other in the division finals that were scheduled for the seventh of August, two weeks away— the winner to represent the Boys Club in the Golden Gloves Championship Tournament.

The two boys continued to run together along the East River Drive. But even when joking with each other, they both sensed a wall rising between them.

One morning less than a week before their bout, they met as usual for their daily work-out. They fooled around with a few jabs at the air, slapped skin, and then took off, running lightly along the dirty East River's edge.

Antonio glanced at Felix who kept his eyes purposely straight ahead, pausing from time to time to do some fancy leg work while throwing one-twos followed by upper cuts to an imaginary jaw. Antonio then beat the air with a barrage of body blows and short <u>devastating</u> lefts with an overhand jaw-breaking right. After a mile or so, Felix puffed and said, "Let's stop a while, bro. I think we both got something to say to each other."

Antonio nodded. It was not natural to be acting as though nothing unusual was happening when two ace-boon buddies were going to be blasting each other within a few short days.

---

1. technical knock-outs occasions when a fight is stopped because one of the fighters is too hurt to continue, even though he is on his feet.
2. elimination bouts matches in which only the winners go on to fight in other matches.

Literary Analysis
Point of View Of which character(s) does the the narrator know the thoughts?

devastating (dev´ əs tāt´ iŋ) *adj.* destructive; overwhelming

☑**Reading Check**
Why are Antonio and Felix uncomfortable?

They rested their elbows on the railing separating them from the river. Antonio wiped his face with his short towel. The sunrise was now creating day.

Felix leaned heavily on the river's railing and stared across to the shores of Brooklyn. Finally, he broke the silence.

"Man, I don't know how to come out with it."

Antonio helped. "It's about our fight, right?"

"Yeah, right." Felix's eyes squinted at the rising orange sun.

"I've been thinking about it too, *panín*. In fact, since we found out it was going to be me and you, I've been awake at night, pulling punches on you, trying not to hurt you."

"Same here. It ain't natural not to think about the fight. I mean, we both are *cheverote* fighters and we both want to win. But only one of us can win. There ain't no draws in the eliminations."

Felix tapped Antonio gently on the shoulder. "I don't mean to sound like I'm bragging, bro. But I wanna win, fair and square."

Antonio nodded quietly. "Yeah. We both know that in the ring the better man wins. Friend or no friend, brother or no . . ."

Felix finished it for him. "Brother. Tony, let's promise something right here. Okay?"

"If it's fair, *hermano*, I'm for it." Antonio admired the courage of a tugboat pulling a barge five times its welterweight size.

"It's fair, Tony. When we get into the ring, it's gotta be like we never met. We gotta be like two heavy strangers that want the same thing and only one can have it. You understand, don'tcha?"

"*Sí*, I know." Tony smiled. "No pulling punches. We go all the way."

"Yeah, that's right. Listen, Tony. Don't you think it's a good idea if we don't see each other until the day of the fight? I'm going to stay with my Aunt Lucy in the Bronx. I can use Gleason's Gym for working out. My manager says he got some sparring partners with more or less your style."

Tony scratched his nose pensively. "Yeah, it would be better for our heads." He held out his hand, palm upward. "Deal?"

"Deal." Felix lightly slapped open skin.

"Ready for some more running?" Tony asked lamely.

"Naw, bro. Let's cut it here. You go on. I kinda like to get things together in my head."

"You ain't worried, are you?" Tony asked.

"No way, man." Felix laughed out loud. "I got too much smarts for that. I just think it's cooler if we split right here. After the fight, we can get it together again like nothing ever happened."

The amigo brothers were not ashamed to hug each other tightly.

"Guess you're right. Watch yourself, Felix. I hear there's some pretty heavy dudes up in the Bronx. *Suavecito*, okay?"

"Okay. You watch yourself too, *sabe*?"

Reading Strategy
Drawing Inferences
From this conversation, what can you infer about the boys' relationship?

Tony jogged away. Felix watched his friend disappear from view, throwing rights and lefts. Both fighters had a lot of psyching up to do before the big fight.

The days in training passed much too slowly. Although they kept out of each other's way, they were aware of each other's progress via the ghetto grapevine.

The evening before the big fight, Tony made his way to the roof of his tenement. In the quiet early dark, he peered over the ledge. Six stories below the lights of the city blinked and the sounds of cars mingled with the curses and the laughter of children in the street. He tried not to think of Felix, feeling he had succeeded in psyching his mind. But only in the ring would he really know. To spare Felix hurt, he would have to knock him out, early and quick.

Up in the South Bronx, Felix decided to take in a movie in an effort to keep Antonio's face away from his fists. The flick was *The Champion* with Kirk Douglas, the third time Felix was seeing it.

The champion was getting hit hard. He was saved only by the sound of the bell.

Felix became the champ and Tony the challenger.

The movie audience was going out of its head. The challenger, confident that he had the championship in the bag, threw a left. The champ countered with a dynamite right.

Felix's right arm felt the shock. Antonio's face, <u>superimposed</u> on the screen, was hit by the awesome blow. Felix saw himself in the ring, blasting Antonio against the ropes. The champ had to be forcibly restrained. The challenger was allowed to crumble slowly to the canvas.

When Felix finally left the theatre, he had figured out how to psyche himself for tomorrow's fight. It was Felix the Champion vs. Antonio the Challenger.

He walked up some dark streets, deserted except for small pockets of wary-looking kids wearing gang colors. Despite the fact that he was Puerto Rican like them, they eyed him as a stranger to their turf. Felix did a fast shuffle, bobbing and weaving, while letting loose a torrent of blows that would demolish whatever got in its way. It seemed to impress the brothers, who went about their own business.

Finding no takers, Felix decided to split to his aunt's. Walking the streets had not relaxed him, neither had the fight flick. All it had done was to stir him up. He let himself quietly into his Aunt Lucy's apartment and went straight to bed, falling into a fitful sleep with sounds of the gong for Round One.

superimposed
(soō′ pər im pōzd′) *adj.* put or stacked on top of something else

✔ **Reading Check**

What deal do Antonio and Felix reach about their training period before the fight?

Antonio was passing some heavy time on his rooftop. How would the fight tomorrow affect his relationship with Felix? After all, fighting was like any other profession. Friendship had nothing to do with it. A gnawing doubt crept in. He cut negative thinking real quick by doing some speedy fancy dance steps, bobbing and weaving like mercury.[3] The night air was blurred with perpetual motions of left hooks and right crosses. Felix, his *amigo* brother, was not going to be Felix at all in the ring. Just an opponent with another face. Antonio went to sleep, hearing the opening bell for the first round. Like his friend in the South Bronx, he prayed for victory, via a quick clean knock-out in the first round.

Large posters plastered all over the walls of local shops announced the fight between Antonio Cruz and Felix Vargas as the main bout.

The fight had created great interest in the neighborhood. Antonio and Felix were well liked and respected. Each had his own loyal following. Antonio's fans counted on his boxing skills. On the other side, Felix's admirers trusted in his dynamite-packed fists.

Felix had returned to his apartment early in the morning of August 7th and stayed there, hoping to avoid seeing Antonio. He turned the radio on to *salsa* music sounds and then tried to read while waiting for word from his manager.

The fight was scheduled to take place in Tompkins Square Park. It had been decided that the gymnasium of the Boys Club was not large enough to hold all the people who were sure to attend. In Tompkins Square Park, everyone who wanted could view the fight, whether from ringside or window fire escapes or tenement rooftops.

The morning of the fight Tompkins Square was a beehive of activity with numerous workers setting up the ring, the seats, and the guest speakers' stand. The scheduled bouts began shortly after noon and the park had begun filling up even earlier.

The local junior high school across from Tompkins Square Park served as the dressing room for all the fighters. Each was given a separate classroom with desk tops, covered with mats, serving as resting tables. Antonio thought he caught a glimpse of Felix waving to him from a room at the far end of the corridor. He waved back just in case it had been him.

The fighters changed from their street clothes into fighting gear. Antonio wore white trunks, black socks, and black shoes. Felix wore sky blue trunks, red socks, and white boxing shoes. Each had dressing gowns to match their fighting trunks with their names neatly stitched on the back.

The loudspeakers blared into the open windows of the school. There were speeches by dignitaries, community leaders, and great

perpetual (pər pech′ ōō əl) *adj.* constant; unending

Literary Analysis
Point of View In the paragraph beginning, "The fight had created . . .," explain how the details illustrate the third-person omniscient point of view.

---

3. mercury (mur′ kyōō rē) *n.* the element mercury, also known as quicksilver because it is so quick and fluid. This element was named after the Roman god Mercury, who because of his speed and quick thinking served as the messenger of the gods.

boxers of yesteryear. Some were well prepared, some improvised on the spot. They all carried the same message of great pleasure and honor at being part of such a historic event. This great day was in the tradition of champions emerging from the streets of the lower east side.

Interwoven with the speeches were the sounds of the other boxing events. After the sixth bout, Felix was much relieved when his trainer Charlie said, "Time change. Quick knock-out. This is it. We're on."

Waiting time was over. Felix was escorted from the classroom by a dozen fans in white T-shirts with the word FELIX across their fronts.

Antonio was escorted down a different stairwell and guided through a roped-off path.

As the two climbed into the ring, the crowd exploded with a roar. Antonio and Felix both bowed gracefully and then raised their arms in acknowledgment.

Antonio tried to be cool, but even as the roar was in its first birth, he turned slowly to meet Felix's eyes looking directly into his. Felix nodded his head and Antonio responded. And both as one, just as quickly, turned away to face his own corner.

Bong—bong—bong. The roar turned to stillness.

"Ladies and Gentlemen. *Señores y Señoras.*"

The announcer spoke slowly, pleased at his bilingual efforts.

"Now the moment we have all been waiting for—the main event between two fine young Puerto Rican fighters, products of our lower east side. In this corner, weighing 134 pounds, Felix Vargas. And in this corner, weighing 133 pounds, Antonio Cruz. The winner will represent the Boys Club in the tournament of champions, the Golden Gloves. There will be no draw. May the best man win."

The cheering of the crowd shook the window panes of the old buildings surrounding Tompkins Square Park. At the center of the ring, the referee was giving instructions to the youngsters.

"Keep your punches up. No low blows. No punching on the back of the head. Keep your heads up. Understand. Let's have a clean fight. Now shake hands and come out fighting."

Both youngsters touched gloves and nodded. They turned and danced quickly to their corners. Their head towels and dressing gowns were lifted neatly from their shoulders by their trainers' nimble fingers. Antonio crossed himself. Felix did the same.

BONG! BONG! ROUND ONE. Felix and Antonio turned and faced each other squarely in a fighting pose. Felix wasted no time. He came in fast, head low, half hunched toward his right shoulder, and lashed out with a straight left. He missed a right cross as Antonio slipped the punch and countered with one-two-three lefts that snapped Felix's head back, sending a mild shock coursing through him. If Felix had any small doubt about their friendship affecting their fight, it was being neatly <u>dispelled</u>.

Literary Analysis
Point of View If Antonio had told this part of the story, what might be different?

dispelled (dis peld´) v. driven away; made to disappear

 **Reading Check**

Why are so many people in the neighborhood interested in watching the fight?

Antonio danced, a joy to behold. His left hand was like a piston pumping jabs one right after another with seeming ease. Felix bobbed and weaved and never stopped boring in. He knew that at long range he was at a disadvantage. Antonio had too much reach on him. Only by coming in close could Felix hope to achieve the dreamed-of knockout.

Antonio knew the dynamite that was stored in his *amigo* brother's fist. He ducked a short right and missed a left hook. Felix trapped him against the ropes just long enough to pour some punishing rights and lefts to Antonio's hard midsection. Antonio slipped away from Felix, crashing two lefts to his head, which set Felix's right ear to ringing.

Bong! Both *amigos* froze a punch well on its way, sending up a roar of approval for good sportsmanship.

Felix walked briskly back to his corner. His right ear had not stopped ringing. Antonio gracefully danced his way toward his stool none the worse, except for glowing glove burns, showing angry red against the whiteness of his midribs.

"Watch that right, Tony." His trainer talked into his ear. "Remember Felix always goes to the body. He'll want you to drop your hands for his overhand left or right. Got it?"

Antonio nodded, spraying water out between his teeth. He felt better as his sore midsection was being firmly rubbed.

Felix's corner was also busy.

"You gotta get in there, fella." Felix's trainer poured water over his curly Afro locks. "Get in there or he's gonna chop you up from way back."

Bong! Bong! Round two. Felix was off his stool and rushed Antonio like a bull, sending a hard right to his head. Beads of water exploded from Antonio's long hair.

Antonio, hurt, sent back a blurring barrage of lefts and rights that only meant pain to Felix, who returned with a short left to the head followed by a looping right to the body. Antonio countered with his own flurry, forcing Felix to give ground. But not for long.

Felix bobbed and weaved, bobbed and weaved, occasionally punching his two gloves together.

Antonio waited for the rush that was sure to come. Felix closed in and feinted[4] with his left shoulder and threw his right instead. Lights suddenly exploded inside Felix's head as Antonio slipped the blow and hit him with a pistonlike left catching him flush on the point of his chin.

Bedlam[5] broke loose as Felix's legs momentarily buckled. He fought off a series of rights and lefts and came back with a strong right that taught Antonio respect.

▼ **Critical Viewing**
In boxing matches, as in many other sporting events, competitors wear contrasting colors. Why do you think this is true? **[Hypothesize]**

---

4. **feinted** (fānt´ əd) *v.* pretended to make a blow.
5. **Bedlam** (bed´ ləm) *n.* condition of noise and confusion.

Antonio danced in carefully. He knew Felix had the habit of playing possum when hurt, to sucker an opponent within reach of the powerful bombs he carried in each fist.

A right to the head slowed Antonio's pretty dancing. He answered with his own left at Felix's right eye that began puffing up within three seconds.

Antonio, a bit too eager, moved in too close and Felix had him entangled into a rip-roaring, punching toe-to-toe slugfest that brought the whole Tompkins Square Park screaming to its feet.

Rights to the body. Lefts to the head. Neither fighter was giving an inch. Suddenly a short right caught Antonio squarely on the chin. His long legs turned to jelly and his arms flailed out desperately. Felix, grunting like a bull, threw wild punches from every direction. Antonio, groggy, bobbed and weaved, <u>evading</u> most of the blows. Suddenly his head cleared. His left flashed out hard and straight catching Felix on the bridge of his nose.

Felix lashed back with a haymaker,[6] right off the ghetto streets. At the same instant, his eye caught another left hook from Antonio. Felix swung out trying to clear the pain. Only the frenzied screaming of those along ringside let him know that he had dropped Antonio. Fighting off the growing haze, Antonio struggled to his feet, got up, ducked, and threw a smashing right that dropped Felix flat on his back.

Felix got up as fast as he could in his own corner, groggy but still game. He didn't even hear the count. In a fog, he heard the roaring of the crowd, who seemed to have gone insane. His head cleared to hear the bell sound at the end of the round. He was very glad. His trainer sat him down on the stool.

In his corner, Antonio was doing what all fighters do when they are hurt. They sit and smile at everyone.

The referee signaled the ring doctor to check the fighters out. He did so and then gave his okay. The cold water sponges brought clarity to both *amigo* brothers. They were rubbed until their circulation ran free.

Bong! Round three—the final round. Up to now it had been tic-tac-toe, pretty much even. But everyone knew there could be no draw and this round would decide the winner.

This time, to Felix's surprise, it was Antonio who came out fast, charging across the ring. Felix braced himself but couldn't ward off the barrage of punches. Antonio drove Felix hard against the ropes.

The crowd ate it up. Thus far the two had fought with *mucho corazón.* Felix tapped his gloves and commenced

evading (ē vād´ iŋ) *adj.* keeping away from or avoiding

✔**Reading Check**

Why can't the fight be a tie?

---

6. **haymaker** punch thrown with full force.

his attack anew. Antonio, throwing boxer's caution to the winds, jumped in to meet him.

Both pounded away. Neither gave an inch and neither fell to the canvas. Felix's left eye was tightly closed. Claret red blood poured from Antonio's nose. They fought toe-to-toe.

The sounds of their blows were loud in contrast to the silence of a crowd gone completely mute. The referee was stunned by their savagery.

Bong! Bong! Bong! The bell sounded over and over again. Felix and Antonio were past hearing. Their blows continued to pound on each other like hailstones.

Finally the referee and the two trainers pried Felix and Antonio apart. Cold water was poured over them to bring them back to their senses.

They looked around and then rushed toward each other. A cry of alarm surged through Tompkins Square Park. Was this a fight to the death instead of a boxing match?

The fear soon gave way to wave upon wave of cheering as the two *amigos* embraced.

No matter what the decision, they knew they would always be champions to each other.

BONG! BONG! BONG! "Ladies and Gentlemen. *Señores* and *Señoras*. The winner and representative to the Golden Gloves Tournament of Champions is . . ."

The announcer turned to point to the winner and found himself alone. Arm in arm the champions had already left the ring.

Review and Assess

Thinking About the Selection

1. **Respond:** What are the characteristics of an enduring friendship? Give examples from the selection to support your answer.

2. **(a) Recall:** What dream do the boys share? **(b) Analyze:** What do the boys discover is more important to them than their dream?

3. **(a) Recall:** What do the boys agree to do when they face each other in the ring? **(b) Evaluate:** What are the advantages and disadvantages of their agreement?

4. **(a) Analyze:** In what ways does the boys' friendship both help them and hurt them during the fight? **(b) Apply:** Why is it more difficult to compete against a friend than a stranger?

5. **Take a Stand:** What restrictions, if any, do you think there should be on young people participating in contact sports? Explain and support your position.

Piri Thomas

(b. 1928)

In his autobiography, *Down These Mean Streets*, Piri Thomas writes about the challenges of growing up in New York City's Spanish Harlem. Like his characters in "Amigo Brothers," he had struggles to overcome. The road was bumpy until Thomas "dreamt positive."

The Walk

THOMAS HARDY

You did not walk with me
Of late to the hilltop tree
  By the gated ways,
  As in earlier days;
5   You were weak and lame,
  So you never came,
And I went alone, and I did not mind,
Not thinking of you as left behind.

  I walked up there today
10   Just in the former way;
   Surveyed[1] around
   The familiar ground
   By myself again:
   What difference, then?
15 Only that underlying sense
Of the look of a room on returning thence.

1. surveyed (sər vād´) v. looked at in a careful and thorough way.

Review and Assess

Thinking About the Selections

1. **(a) Recall:** What is the change the speaker in "The Walk" must face? **(b) Contrast:** In what way do the speaker's words contrast with the speaker's feelings? **(c) Apply:** For what reasons do people sometimes pretend not to feel sadness or other negative feelings?

2. **(a) Recall:** Why did the speaker used to walk alone?
   (b) Contrast: Why does the speaker walk alone now?
   (c) Interpret: What has the speaker learned?

3. **(a) Infer:** To whom is the speaker addressing the poem?
   (b) Deduce: What has happened to that person?
   (c) Draw Conclusions: What are the speaker's feelings?

Thomas Hardy

(1840–1928)

Thomas Hardy lived during the Victorian era in England. Many considered him the greatest novelist of the period, yet he spent the last three decades of his life writing poetry. Hardy is buried in Westminster Abbey in London.

Justin Lebo

Phillip Hoose

Something about the battered old bicycle at the garage sale caught ten-year-old Justin Lebo's eye. What a wreck! It was like looking at a few big bones in the dust and trying to figure out what kind of dinosaur they had once belonged to.

It was a BMX bike with a twenty-inch frame. Its original color was buried beneath five or six coats of gunky paint. Now it showed up as sort of a rusted red. Everything—the grips, the pedals, the brakes, the seat, the spokes—was bent or broken, twisted and rusted. Justin stood back as if he were inspecting a painting for sale at an auction. Then he made his final judgment: perfect.

Justin talked the owner down to $6.50 and asked his mother, Diane, to help him load the bike into the back of their car.

Reading Strategy
Drawing Inferences
What can you infer about Justin based on his reaction to this bike?

When he got it home, he wheeled the junker into the garage and showed it proudly to his father. "Will you help me fix it up?" he asked. Justin's hobby was bike racing, a passion the two of them shared. Their garage barely had room for the car anymore. It was more like a bike shop. Tires and frames hung from hooks on the ceiling, and bike wrenches dangled from the walls.

At every race, Justin and his father would adjust the brakes and <u>realign</u> the wheels of his two racing bikes. This was a lot of work, since Justin raced flat out, challenging every gear and part to perform to its fullest. He had learned to handle almost every repair his father could and maybe even a few things he couldn't. When Justin got really stuck, he went to see Mel, the owner of the best bike shop in town. Mel let him hang out and watch, and he even grunted a few syllables of advice from between the spokes of a wheel now and then.

Now Justin and his father cleared out a work space in the garage and put the old junker up on a rack. They poured alcohol on the frame and rubbed until the old paint began to <u>yield</u>, layer by layer. They replaced the broken pedal, tightened down a new seat, and restored the grips. In about a week, it looked brand new.

realign (rē´ ə līn´) *v.* readjust into a straight line or into proper coordination

yield (yēld) *v.* give way to pressure or force

✔**Reading Check**

What is Justin's passion?

◀ **Critical Viewing** What does Justin Lebo have in common with the youngsters in this picture? **[Connect]**

Justin wheeled it out of the garage, leapt aboard, and started off around the block. He stood up and mashed down on the pedals, straining for speed. It was a good, steady ride, but not much of a thrill compared to his racers.

Soon he forgot about the bike. But the very next week, he bought another junker at a yard sale and fixed it up, too. After a while it bothered him that he wasn't really using either bike. Then he realized that what he loved about the old bikes wasn't riding them: it was the challenge of making something new and useful out of something old and broken.

Justin wondered what he should do with them. They were just taking up space in the garage. He remembered that when he was younger, he used to live near a large brick building called the Kilbarchan Home for Boys. It was a place for boys whose parents couldn't care for them for one reason or another.

He found "Kilbarchan" in the phone book and called the director, who said the boys would be thrilled to get two bicycles. The next day when Justin and his mother unloaded the bikes at the home, two boys raced out to greet them. They leapt aboard the bikes and started tooling around the semicircular driveway, doing wheelies and pirouettes, laughing and shouting.

The Lebos watched them for a while, then started to climb into their car to go home. The boys cried after them, "Wait a minute! You forgot your bikes!" Justin explained that the bikes were for them to keep. "They were so happy," Justin remembers. "It was like they couldn't believe it. It made me feel good to see them happy."

On the way home, Justin was silent. His mother assumed he was lost in a feeling of satisfaction. But he was thinking about what would happen once those bikes got wheeled inside and everyone saw them. How would all those kids decide who got the bikes? Two bikes could cause more trouble than they would solve. Actually, they hadn't been that hard to build. It was fun. Maybe he could do more. . . .

"Mom," Justin said as they turned onto their street, "I've got an idea. I'm going to make a bike for every boy at Kilbarchan for Christmas." Diane Lebo looked at Justin out of the corner of her eye. She had rarely seen him so determined.

When they got home, Justin called Kilbarchan to find out how many boys lived there. There were twenty-one. It was already June. He had six months to make nineteen bikes. That was almost a bike a week. Justin called the home back to tell them of his plan. "I could tell they didn't think I could do it," Justin remembers. "I knew I could."

Justin knew his best chance was to build bikes almost the way GM or Ford builds cars: in an assembly line. He would start with frames from three-speed, twenty-four-inch BMX bicycles. They were common bikes, and all the parts were interchangeable. If he could

Literary Analysis
Point of View In the paragraph beginning, "On the way home . . .," what details show that the writer is using third-person omniscient point of view?

find enough decent frames, he could take parts off broken bikes and fasten them onto the good frames. He figured it would take three or four junkers to produce enough parts to make one good bike. That meant sixty to eighty bikes. Where would he get them?

Garage sales seemed to be the only hope. It was June, and there would be garage sales all summer long. But even if he could find that many bikes, how could he ever pay for them? That was hundreds of dollars.

He went to his parents with a proposal. "When Justin was younger, say five or six," says his mother, "he used to give some of his allowance away to help others in need. His father and I would donate a dollar for every dollar Justin donated. So he asked us if it could be like the old days, if we'd match every dollar he put into buying old bikes. We said yes."

Justin and his mother spent most of June and July hunting for cheap bikes at garage sales and thrift shops. They would haul the bikes home, and Justin would start stripping them down in the yard.

But by the beginning of August, he had managed to make only ten bikes. Summer vacation was almost over, and school and homework would soon cut into his time. Garage sales would dry up when it got colder, and Justin was out of money. Still, he was determined to find a way.

At the end of August, Justin got a break. A neighbor wrote a letter to the local newspaper describing Justin's project, and an editor thought it would make a good story. One day a reporter entered the Lebo garage. Stepping gingerly through the tires and frames that covered the floor, she found a boy with cut fingers and dirty

Reading Strategy
Drawing Inferences
What do Justin's parents think of his idea? How do you know?

✔Reading Check

What is Justin going to do for the boys who live at Kilbarchan?

▼ Critical Viewing
What skills and abilities are needed to repair a bike? [**Analyze**]

nails, banging a seat onto a frame. His clothes were covered with grease. In her admiring article about a boy who was devoting his summer to help kids he didn't even know, she said Justin needed bikes and money, and she printed his home phone number.

Overnight, everything changed. "There must have been a hundred calls," Justin says. "People would call me up and ask me to come over and pick up their old bike. Or I'd be working in the garage, and a station wagon would pull up. The driver would leave a couple of bikes by the curb. It just snowballed."

By the start of school, the garage was overflowing with BMX frames. Pyramids of pedals and seats rose in the corners. Soon bike parts filled a toolshed in the backyard and then spilled out into the small yard itself, wearing away the lawn.

More and more writers and television and radio reporters called for interviews. Each time he told his story, Justin asked for bikes and money. "The first few interviews were fun," Justin says, "but it reached a point where I really didn't like doing them. The publicity was necessary, though. I had to keep doing interviews to get the donations I needed."

By the time school opened, he was working on ten bikes at a time. There were so many calls now that he was beginning to refuse offers that weren't the exact bikes he needed.

As checks came pouring in, Justin's money problems disappeared. He set up a bank account and began to make bulk orders of common parts from Mel's bike shop. Mel seemed delighted to see him. Sometimes, if Justin brought a bike by the shop, Mel would help him fix it. When Justin tried to talk him into a lower price for big orders, Mel smiled and gave in. He respected another good businessman. They became friends.

The week before Christmas Justin delivered the last of the twenty-one bikes to Kilbarchan. Once again, the boys poured out of the home and leapt aboard the bikes, tearing around the snow.

And once again, their joy inspired Justin. They reminded him how important bikes were to him. Wheels meant freedom. He thought how much more the freedom to ride must mean to boys like these who had so little freedom in their lives. He decided to keep on building.

"First I made eleven bikes for the children in a foster home my mother told me about. Then I made bikes for all the women in a battered women's shelter. Then I made ten little bikes and tricycles for the kids in a home for children with AIDS. Then I made twenty-three bikes for the Paterson Housing <u>Coalition</u>."

In the four years since he started, Justin Lebo has made between 150 and 200 bikes and given them all away. He has been careful to leave time for his homework, his friends, his coin collection, his new interest in marine biology, and of course his own bikes.

Reporters and interviewers have asked Justin Lebo the same question over and over: "Why do you do it?" The question seems to make him uncomfortable. It's as if they want him to say what a great person he is. Their stories always make him seem like a saint, which he knows he isn't. "Sure it's nice of me to make the bikes," he says, "because I don't have to. But I want to. In part, I do it for myself. I don't think you can ever really do anything to help anybody else if it doesn't make you happy."

"Once I overheard a kid who got one of my bikes say, 'A bike is like a book; it opens up a whole new world.' That's how I feel, too. It made me happy to know that kid felt that way. That's why I do it."

coalition (kō′ ə lish′ ən) *n.* association or organization formed for a specific purpose

Review and Assess

Thinking About the Selection

1. **Respond:** What does riding a bicycle mean to you? Explain.

2. **(a) Recall:** How does Justin get started building bikes?
   (b) Infer: Why does he continue? **(c) Draw Conclusions:** What do Justin's actions reveal about his character?

3. **(a) Recall:** How do people find out about Justin's work?
   (b) Analyze: What is it about his project that inspires them?

4. **(a) Recall:** What specific groups of people does Justin help?
   (b) Draw Conclusions: What does he learn from helping them?

5. **(a) Deduce:** Why is Justin uncomfortable talking about his project? **(b) Make a Judgment:** Should Justin be uncomfortable? Explain.

Phillip Hoose

(b. 1947)
Inspired by people who make a difference, Phillip Hoose wrote *It's Our World, Too,* a collection of essays about young people working to help others. Hoose was impressed by the energy, compassion, and creative ideas of these youths. "Justin Lebo" comes from this book.

The RIDER

NAOMI SHIHAB NYE

A boy told me
if he rollerskated fast enough
his loneliness couldn't catch up to him,

the best reason I ever heard
5   for trying to be a champion.

What I wonder tonight
pedaling hard down King William Street
is if it translates to bicycles.

A victory! To leave your loneliness
10 panting behind you on some street corner
while you float free into a cloud of sudden azaleas,
luminous pink petals that have
        never felt loneliness,
no matter how slowly they fell.

▲ **Critical Viewing**
What details of this photograph convey the feelings the poem describes? **[Analyze]**

Review and Assess

Thinking About the Selections

1. **(a) Recall:** What two activities are compared in "The Rider"?
   (b) Compare: What do the two activities have in common?
   (c) Apply: What are two other activities that share these qualities?

2. **(a) Interpret:** In "The Rider," why does the speaker value speed?
   (b) Support: What words show how speed relates to freedom?
   (c) Evaluate: How effective is the image of bike riding to represent freedom?

3. **(a) Synthesize:** In what ways do bicycles help Justin Lebo and the speaker in "The Rider" solve problems? **(b) Apply:** What message do these selections communicate about the importance of recognizing and using your own individual talents?

Naomi Shihab Nye

(b. 1952)
As a teenager, Naomi Shihab Nye probably felt the loneliness described in her poem. Her family moved from Missouri to Israel when Nye was fourteen. Though she now values learning about her Arab heritage, the move was not easy. Nye has published volumes of poetry as well as books for children.

Review and Assess

Literary Analysis

Third-Person Point of View

1. Show how "Amigo Brothers" and "Justin Lebo" are both written from the **third-person omniscient point of view.** Support your answer with details from these narratives.

2. In which narrative, "Amigo Brothers" or "Justin Lebo," does the point of view give you a greater sense of knowing more than one character's thoughts? Explain.

3. In "Amigo Brothers," use a chart like this one to show how the description of the moments before the fight might change if it were told from the first-person point of view by a character participating in the action.

Event	First-Person Narrator
Being escorted to the ring	happening in slow motion, fans chanting my name, feeling excited, nervous
Hearing the applause	
Looking at his opponent/friend	
Hearing the announcer	

Comparing Literary Works

4. Which character would you describe as more selfless, Justin Lebo or the speaker in "The Rider"? Why?

5. Do you think Justin Lebo would agree with the ideas presented in "The Rider"? Why or why not?

6. How do both "Amigo Brothers" and "The Walk" deal with loneliness arising from a relationship?

7. In which selection, "Amigo Brothers" or "The Walk," do the characters solve the problem of loneliness? Explain.

Reading Strategy

Drawing Inferences

8. What personality qualities can you infer Justin has? Give examples of the details on which you base your **inferences.**

9. What event must you infer from details provided in "The Walk"?

Extend Understanding

10. **Sports Safety Connection:** What safety equipment would you recommend for the speaker in "The Rider"? Explain why.

Quick Review

Point of view is the perspective from which events are told. To review point of view, see page 289.

An **inference** is a logical guess about information that is not directly stated, based on information that is provided.

 Take It to the Net
www.phschool.com
Take the interactive self-test online to check your understanding of these selections.

Integrate Language Skills

Vocabulary Development Lesson

Word Analysis: Latin Prefix *re-*

The Latin prefix *re-* means "again." Words that begin with the prefix usually mean that the action or idea of the root word is happening again. For example, when Justin Lebo *realigns* the wheels of a bike, he *aligns them again*.

Use the following words in sentences that show what is happening again.

1. review   3. recall   5. renew
2. recycle   4. reappear   6. reheat

Spelling Strategy

In most cases, you do not need a hyphen to add the prefix *re-* to a word. *Realign* is correct, not *re-align*. On your paper, add *re-* to the following words.

1. paint   3. live   5. build
2. new   4. act   6. enter

Fluency: Definitions

On your paper, match the word on the left with its definition on the right.

1. devastating   a. avoiding
2. superimposed   b. give way to pressure
3. perpetual   c. group formed for common goal
4. dispelled   d. overwhelming; damaging
5. evading   e. never stopping
6. realign   f. put on top of something
7. yield   g. made to disappear
8. coalition   h. adjust so the parts work together

Grammar Lesson

Coordinating Conjunctions

Coordinating conjunctions (*and, but, for, nor, or, so,* and *yet*) connect words, phrases, or sentences of similar kinds. In the following examples, the coordinating conjunctions are circled. The words they connect are italicized.

Nouns: Everyone could view the fight, whether from *ringside* or *fire escapes* or *rooftops*.
Verbs: Mel let him *hang out* and *watch*.
Prepositional Phrases: He stored bicycles *in the garage* and *on the driveway*.
Whole Sentences: *They were common bikes,* and *all the parts were interchangeable.*

▶ *For more practice, see page R29, Exercise F.*
Practice Copy these sentences. Circle the coordinating conjunction in each one. Then, underline the words or groups of words connected by the conjunction.

1. Which do you prefer, biking or skating?
2. Odds were against him, but Justin won.
3. The two friends were athletes, so they worked out together.
4. After school and on weekends, Justin worked.
5. The fight was fierce yet fair.

Writing Application Write a paragraph summarizing one of the selections. In it, use and identify three different coordinating conjunctions.

Prentice Hall Writing and Grammar Connection: Chapter 18, Section 1

Writing Lesson

Volunteering Database

Justin Lebo worked by himself, but your classmates might prefer to join an organization that helps others. Make a database of such organizations. A database is a collection of data, or facts, that can be sorted and organized in different ways, based on what the user asks for. Create an electronic database, or use note cards.

Prewriting   Gather a list of organizations you will include. Identify the categories or "fields" of information that you will provide for each organization to use for sorting.

Drafting   If you have access to a computer, you can either create a database using a special program, or you can use the table feature of a word processing program to produce a document that can be sorted by column. Include a column in which you provide a brief explanation of what each organization does.

Model: Creating a Database

Organization	City	Contact	Address
Healthy Cats	Hawthorne	Burke, M.J.	135 Hill St.
Hidden Valley	Ringwood	Roobey, Vince	15 White St.
Hubert's	Oakland	Goetz, Nikki	27 College Ave.
Indoor Cats	Pine Valley	Butler, Scott	2 Ridge Rd.

The database is sorted alphabetically by the first column. If you were looking for an animal shelter in a particular city, you could sort alphabetically by the second column.

Revising   Print your database out and check the information against your notes, making sure that you have input everything accurately.

 Prentice Hall Writing and Grammar Connection: Chapter 11, Section 2

Extension Activities

Listening and Speaking Give a **persuasive talk** encouraging an audience of local business people to donate money to Justin's project. Give three strong reasons to support your call to action. Provide convincing facts, examples, or anecdotes drawn from the story.

As you speak, make eye contact with the listeners. Let your voice communicate the importance of your cause. Pause now and then to let an important point sink in.

Research and Technology Write a **comparison-and-contrast essay** analyzing similarities and differences between two of the characters in the selections presented here. For example, you might compare Felix to Justin Lebo. Use a computer to create a chart, such as a Venn diagram, to illustrate your essay.

 **Take It to the Net**   www.phschool.com

Go online for an additional research activity using the Internet.

CONNECTIONS
Literature and Culture
Characters and Stereotypes

Fighting Friends

"Amigo Brothers" tells a tale of two boys who manage to maintain their friendship even though they are training to face each other in a boxing match. Think about what your reaction would have been if the story had been about two girls who maintain their friendship even though they are training to face each other in a boxing match. You would probably be surprised. You may even think "Girls don't box!"

Fighting Stereotypes

A stereotype is the categorizing of a whole group of people based on what you may have observed in one or two of the group. Just because the girls you know don't box, doesn't mean all girls don't box. Some girls do. Kate Sekules, the author of *The Boxer's Heart*, trained as a boxer and boxed in competition. In the excerpt that follows, she says that one of the reasons she loves sports is that they help fight stereotypes. Athletes such as soccer star Mia Hamm and basketball player Rebecca Lobo have also helped strengthen the belief that females can be star athletes.

Boys, too, can be stereotyped. The movie *Billy Elliot* tells the story of a boy who wants to learn ballet. In the excerpt from the screenplay, on page 312–313, the father becomes angry after he discovers that Billy has been going to ballet class instead of boxing. Look for evidence of stereotyping in the conversation between the father and Billy.

All Types

Stereotypes can be formed based on gender (whether you are a male or a female), race, age, and religion. If you have ever heard anyone make a sweeping statement about teenagers, then you have heard an example of stereotyping. If you have ever heard a comment that criticizes all older people, then you have heard stereotyping. Any judgment of an entire group based on the characteristics of a few members of the group is a stereotype.

Just because some boys like to box doesn't mean all boys like to box. Just because some girls hate boxing doesn't mean all girls hate boxing. When you read literature, be on the lookout for characters who are shown as stereotypes, for dialogue that reveals beliefs about stereotypes, and for statements that spread stereotypes.

The Boxer's Heart: How I Fell in Love with the Ring

Kate Sekules

Show me a female boxer who wasn't a tomboy and I'll show you a liar. Not that tomboyhood is restricted to embryo pugilists; far from it. Tomboys are everywhere, and they are normal, and they are expected to grow out of it, though many, like me, never quite do. It is not the same for little boys, for whom displaying feminine behavior is taboo. This contradiction implies that qualities customarily associated with masculinity (aggression, drive, forthrightness, ebullience) are useful, whereas those generally tagged feminine (gentleness, kindness, self-deprecation, concern with appearance) are dispensable, verging on undesirable. But that notion is way outdated. A girl child today has role models—rock chicks, Xena, Oprah, Venus and Serena—who synthesize tomboyhood and femininity. Girlpower wasn't available to my generation. For women my age and a decade on either side, being a tomboy was a rebellion against what seemed the weak position; it was a brand of defiance. Personally, I have not finished kicking against a prescribed female role that restricts us. Doors have opened, sure, but what makes me mad is that it's still okay for girls to grow up believing what they weigh and wear is more important than what they know and read, say and do. Sports can cure that. I am fighting stereotypes.

pugilists (pyōō´ ´jil istz) *n.* boxers

taboo (tə bōō) *adj.* forbidden

Kate Sekules

Kate Sekules grew up in London and has sung with a band, been a magazine editor and writer, and has written seven guidebooks about London and New York. In 1992, she moved to New York. In the middle of an aerobics class, the instructor had the students shadow box—throw punches in the air—and Kate was hooked on boxing.

Billy Elliot

Lee Hall

Cut to:
Int. Boxing Hall — Later

Another exercise. MRS WILKINSON *is concentrating her attention on* BILLY. *Billy suddenly sees* DAD *and freezes. His reaction puzzles Mrs. Wilkinson for a second. The music comes to a standstill. Mrs. Wilkinson turns to see* DAD.

DAD. You. Out. Now.

MRS. WILKINSON. I beg your pardon?

The mood has been fractured by DAD'S *aggressive tone. Everybody stares at* DAD. *The girls start to giggle.* BILLY *gives an embarrassed look to* MRS. WILKINSON *and starts to walk out, embarrassed.*

BILLY. Please, Miss. . .

[softly]

. . .don't.

BILLY *exits with* DAD. MRS. WILKINSON *stops in her tracks and watches*

BILLY *follow* DAD *out. She is suddenly lost, running through all the possible courses of action. The class are staring at her, startled by* DAD'S *intrusion. She turns and very calmly says:*

MRS. WILKINSON. All right, which way are we facing?
and carries on with her next exercise as if nothing has happened.

Cut to:
Int. Elliot House — Morning

BILLY *is sitting at one end of the table.* DAD *is sitting at the other staring at* BILLY. GRANDMA *is in the middle eating pork pie, savoring it as if it was the most delicious meal in the world. A long staring match,* DAD *is expecting* BILLY *to apologize.*

DAD. Ballet.

BILLY. What's wrong with ballet?

DAD. What's wrong with ballet?

BILLY. It's perfectly normal.

DAD. Perfectly normal!

GRANDMA. I used to go to ballet.

BILLY. See.

DAD. Aye, for your Nana. For girls. Not for lads, Billy. Lads do football or boxing or. . .wrestling. Not ballet.

BILLY. What lads do wrestling?

DAD. Don't start, Billy.

BILLY. I don't see what's wrong with it.

Connecting Literature and Culture

1. What do Felix and Antonio from "Amigo Brothers" have in common with Kate?
2. Why does Kate believe sports help fight stereotypes?
3. How does Billy's father feel about ballet dancing? Do you agree or disagree? Explain your answer.
4. Explain the shared stereotype with which Kate and Billy struggle.
5. Explain why "Amigo Brothers" is or is not an example of stereotyping.
6. What stereotypes have you encountered in literature or in the media?

Lee Hall

Born in England, Lee Hall explores the connections between art and regular working-class people. *Billy Elliot* was his first movie. He also wrote the screenplay for *Prince of Hearts*, a Masterpiece Theater work that chronicles the fictional adventures of a British prince at university.

READING INFORMATIONAL MATERIALS

Signs

Signs are one of the most basic ways of communicating information. The physical presentation of information is unique—the information is displayed to be accessed at any time by anyone. When you approach a store, you usually see a sign that says "open" or "closed." Without asking a question or opening a book, you have taken in important information. Signs can provide the following types of information:

- Rules
- Warnings
- Hours of operation
- Identifying information

This same information will be available to anyone who approaches the sign at any time. The signs you will read here are from a national park. The first gives information about the Visitor's Center. The sign on page 315 gives detailed information on a historic site along the Oregon Trail. The site is pictured on page 315.

Reading Strategy

Identify Your Purpose

When you read a sign, you usually have a specific purpose—you need particular information about a topic. Clearly identifying your purpose allows you to use the physical presentation to efficiently locate the specific information you need. The physical presentation is how the text looks. The size, color, and arrangement of different parts of the text help you search sections of signs rather than reading word by word.

Practice connecting your purpose to your reading of signs by using a K-W-L chart as you read the signs in this lesson. A K-W-L chart has three columns. Your purpose is reflected in the questions you include in the "What I Want to Know" column.

- **Know** = What I **know**
- **Want** = What I **want** to know
- **Learn** = What I **learned**

K-W-L Chart		
What I know	**What I want to know**	**What I learned**
The store is open.	What time does it close?	It closes at 6:00 P.M.

Although you won't make a chart every time you read a sign, you can consider the same categories without actually writing them down. By identifying in your mind the questions you want answered, you make your reading more efficient.

The National Oregon Trail Center

Open daily 10:00 AM – 5:00 PM

For other times, call (555) 847-3800 for reservations.

All tours by advance reservations only due to on-going winter construction projects in the building

For school outreach classes and tours by reservations only, call (555) 847-3800 or 1-800-448-BEAR.

Admission Prices   Ages 13 & up $6.00 each   Ages 5-12 $4.00 each

Ages under 5 Free   Seniors (65+) $5.00 each

Tour Bus, Education Programs, other Group Rates (15+)

Call 1-800-448-BEAR

The following sign is the text on the marker at the historic site pictured on page 315. The picture on the right shows the marker where the text appears. You will encounter detailed signs like these at historic sites, museums, and nature trails.

pictured on page 315.

Larger letters are used to identify the site.

The Alford-Cameron Gravesite, Bruff's Camp

In a common grave at this site—or in close proximity to it—are buried four emigrants who were killed by a falling tree while on their way to California via the Lassen Trail in 1849. Three of the men were members of the Alford family—the father and two sons; the other was a young friend of one of the sons. Thanks to the detailed account kept by J. Goldsborough Bruff, the man for whom this campsite is named, we know the full story of this tragic event.

A large oak tree, rotted at its base, crashed down upon the four men during a rainstorm as they slept in a tent below. None died instantly; all died agonized deaths within a few hours. The following is a portion of Bruff's account of the burial and the exact words which he inscribed upon the headboards of the common grave:

Italics are used to set off the quotation from the background information.

"…We laid down pine slabs at first, in bottom of the grave; and now cut a hole at the foot, and a gro[o]ve at the head, centrally, and put in a stout ridge pole, about 18 ins: above the breasts of the bodies. The wagon-cover was thrown in over the dead, pine slabs laid along, from the sides to the ridge pole, the ends up, so as to form a roof, and we then filled in and smoothed over the grave.

"I procured the tail-board of a wagon, and scratched and painted together the following inscription, and put it up.

Ormond Alford, aged 54 yrs. and his sons.—
William M., aged 19, and Lorenzo D, aged 15 years
And John W. Cameron, aged 22 yrs.
The 3 first of Kendall Co. Ill.: formerly of
Peru, Clinton Co. N.Y. and the last, of Will Co. Ill.:
Killed by the falling of an oak tree upon them, while asleep in
their tent, near this spot, about 1 A.M. Oct. 31st. 1849.

Epitaph–
Their journey is ended, their toils are all past,
Together they slept, in this false world, their last;
They here sleep together, in one grave entombed,—
Side by side, as they slept, on the night they were doom'd!"

Check Your Comprehension

1. At what time does the Trail Center open?
2. Who is buried at the Alford-Cameron Gravesite at Bruff's Camp?
3. How did they die?
4. How do historians know the story of the site?

Applying the Reading Strategy

Identify Your Purpose

5. **(a)** If you were going to a museum such as the Trail Center, what are three questions you might have? **(b)** What clues in the physical structure of the sign would help you locate that information? **(c)** What are the answers to your questions?
6. **(a)** What information on the marker at the Alford-Cameron Gravesite is called out with special text treatments? **(b)** Why do you think the sign makers treated these sections in special ways?

Activity

Sign Chart

For two days, keep a list of the different kinds of signs you see. Notice the type of information that each sign provides. Make a chart like the one shown here that connects types of signs with the purpose a person might have for reading the sign and the text presentation that helps readers achieve their purpose. Include at least five different kinds of signs.

Type of Sign	Where seen	Possible purposes	Type of information	Presentation	Effect of presentation
Visitor information	Visitor center	To find out hours of operation	Hours, admission, rules, sponsors	Hours called out on separate lines	Makes it easy to see

Comparing Informational Materials

Signs and Instructions

Signs and written instructions can both give directions. These two forms of informational material share this general common purpose, but each has its own unique characteristics. Compare and contrast the two forms by answering these questions.

1. In what ways is the presentation of information on a sign different from the presentation of information in an instruction manual?
2. Identify two purposes for which you would read a sign and two purposes for reading an instruction manual.

READING INFORMATIONAL MATERIALS

Persuasive Essays

About Persuasive Essays

A persuasive essay is a brief work in which a writer presents the case for or against a particular position. Although persuasive essays may differ in content, they share at least two basic similarities. When you read persuasive essays, look for and evaluate the following elements:

- Clear statement of the writer's position on an issue with more than one side.
- Supporting facts, examples, and other details of the writer's position.

When reading persuasive essays critically, you should be aware that the author's purpose is to encourage the reader to accept his or her opinions as true. It is also important to recognize the difference between a **fact**, or a statement that can be proved, and the author's **opinion**, or beliefs that can be supported but not proved.

Reading Strategy

Understanding a Writer's Purpose

A writer's purpose—to entertain, to inform, to argue for a position—affects the facts, arguments, and images he or she uses. Often, a writer has more than one purpose in mind. When you read, try to identify the purpose or purposes of a piece of writing by looking carefully at the writer's choice of language and use of details. If a writer seems to have more than one purpose, identify which is the writer's primary purpose. The chart below outlines several purposes of the essay you are about to read. Considering that the piece is a persuasive essay, you might guess that the primary purpose is to argue for a position. As you read, evaluate how successful L'Amour is in achieving his purpose.

Techniques the Author Uses to Persuade	How I Know
• entertain	• L'Amour uses language and images from the past to entertain as well as inform
• teach	• L'Amour uses this essay to inform the reader of the great advancements people have made and need to continue making
• argue for a position	• L'Amour asks and answers questions in order to show that he is arguing for his position and that his position is right

The Eternal Frontier

Louis L'Amour

The author begins with a question. Then, he answers the question by presenting the position he will support in his essay.

The question I am most often asked is, "Where is the frontier now?"

The answer should be obvious. Our frontier lies in outer space. The moon, the asteroids, the planets, these are mere stepping stones, where we will test ourselves, learn needful lessons, and grow in knowledge before we attempt those frontiers beyond our solar system. Outer space is a frontier without end, the eternal frontier, an everlasting challenge to explorers not [only] of other planets and other solar systems but also of the mind of man.

All that has gone before was preliminary. We have been preparing ourselves mentally for what lies ahead. Many problems remain, but if we can avoid a devastating war we shall move with a rapidity scarcely to be believed. In the past seventy years we have developed the automobile, radio, television, transcontinental and transoceanic flight, and the electrification of the country, among a multitude of other such developments. In 1900 there were 144 miles of surfaced road in the United States. Now there are over 3,000,000. Paved roads and the development of the automobile have gone hand in hand, the automobile being civilized man's antidote to overpopulation.

> L'Amour cites statistics and numerical facts, to support his position.

What is needed now is leaders with perspective; we need leadership on a thousand fronts, but they must be men and women who can take the long view and help to shape the outlines of our future. There will always be the nay-sayers, those who cling to our lovely green planet as a baby clings to its mother, but there will be others like those who have taken us this far along the path to a limitless future.

We are a people born to the frontier. It has been a part of our thinking, waking, and sleeping since men first landed on this continent. The frontier is the line that separates the known from the unknown wherever it may be, and we have a driving need to see what lies beyond…

> Here, L'Amour presents an opinion about human nature that he backs up with facts.

A few years ago we moved into outer space. We landed men on the moon; we sent a vehicle beyond the limits of the solar system, a vehicle still moving farther and farther into that limitless distance. If our world were to die tomorrow, that tiny vehicle would go on and on forever, carrying its mighty message to the stars. Out there, someone, sometime, would know that once we existed, that we had the vision and we made the effort. Mankind is not bound by its atmospheric envelope or by its gravitational field, nor is the mind of man bound by any limits at all.

One might ask—why outer space, when so much remains to be done here? If that had been the spirit of man we would still be hunters and food gatherers, growling over the bones of carrion in a cave somewhere. It is our destiny to move out, to accept the challenge, to dare the unknown. It is our destiny to achieve.

> L'Amour appeals to his readers' sense of pride in the achievements of humankind.

Yet we must not forget that along the way to outer space whole industries are springing into being that did not exist before. The computer age has arisen in part from the space effort, which gave great impetus to the development of computing devices. Transistors, chips, integrated circuits, Teflon, new medicines, new ways of treating diseases, new ways of performing operations, all these and a multitude of other developments that enable man to live and to live better are linked to the space effort. Most of these developments have been so incorporated into our day-to-day life that they are taken for granted, their origin not considered.

If we are content to live in the past, we have no future. And today is the past.

> L'Amour ends his essay with a thought-provoking statement.

Check Your Comprehension

1. What does L'Amour refer to as the "eternal frontier"?
2. What is L'Amour's definition of "frontier"?
3. What kind of leaders does L'Amour say we need now?

Applying the Reading Strategy

Understanding a Writer's Purpose

4. What is L'Amour's specific purpose for writing this essay?
5. What facts and statistics support his purpose?
6. How well do you think L'Amour achieves his purpose?

Activity

Persuasive Essay

L'Amour wrote this essay in the 1980s. Think about how space exploration has changed since then. Using the Internet, newspapers, or magazines, find recent information about the space program. Then, in your own persuasive essay, explain whether or not you think an essay like L'Amour's is still necessary and would still be instrumental in motivating people to continue to support space exploration.

Comparing Informational Materials

Persuasive Essays and Editorials

Look at the chart below, which compares persuasive essays and editorials. Based on this information, could L'Amour's piece have made an effective editorial? Why or why not?

	Persuasive Essays	Editorials
Description	A brief written work	A brief written work generally found in newspapers
Specific Purpose	Presents the case for or against something; used to persuade the reader to believe in the writer's opinion	Gives and supports an opinion on a current issue; sometimes supported by facts; used to persuade the reader to believe in the writer's opinion
Audience	The audience depends on the topic of the essay	People who are interested in current events; people who enjoy reading newspapers

Writing WORKSHOP

Persuasion: Persuasive Composition

A **persuasive composition** is a brief work in which a writer presents the case for or against a particular position. In this workshop, you will choose a position and support it with logical and powerful evidence.

Assignment Criteria. Your persuasive composition should have the following characteristics:

- An issue with more than one "side"
- A clearly stated position on an issue
- Logically organized and well-presented evidence supporting your position
- Statements anticipating and addressing reader concerns and counterarguments

See the Rubric on page 325 for the criteria on which your persuasive composition will be assessed.

Prewriting

Choose a topic. Fold a piece of paper lengthwise in three. In the first column, write a list of issues and ideas that interest you. In the second, write a descriptive word for each. In the third, give an example supporting that description. Review your list, and decide which topic interests you most. Make sure your issue has an opposing side.

Issues and Ideas	Descriptive Word	Examples
Cafeteria food	tasteless	macaroni and cheese
Water pollution	scary	streams polluted by fertilizer runoff
New playground	needed	child hurt falling from slide

Identify your position. Decide where you stand on the issue you have chosen. Remember that you can change your mind as you learn more about your topic. State your opinion in a sentence.

Example: This town needs a new playground.

Gather support for your position. Conduct research either in the library, on the Internet, or by interviewing experts on the topic. Gather the following types of support for your position:

Facts: Statements that can be proven true

Statistics: Facts presented in the form of numbers

Anecdotes: Brief stories that illustrate a point

Quotes from Authorities: Statements of leading experts on the topic

Take notes. Use note cards to record the information you gather. Create a note card for each key piece of information. Indicate your source on each note card. Arrange your note cards in order of importance—from your least to your most important points.

Student Model

Before you begin drafting your persuasive composition, read this student model and review the characteristics of a successful persuasive composition.

Amanda Wintenburg
Daytona Beach, Florida

DECIDE THE FUTURE

To you, voting may seem like just a waste of time, just a mere piece of paper with boxes on it, that you have to go through to mark which person you want for that particular job. But to me, it's something more, much more . . . it's your chance to decide the future. Everyone who is eligible should take advantage of the right to vote.

> In the opening paragraph, the writer points out the two "sides" to the voting issue. Some people think it's not worth the effort; she thinks it is. Then she states her position.

I'm not the only one who thinks voting should be a top priority for people. For years, companies and organizations have supplied numerous reminders and reasons for when and why you vote. You've seen the commercials; they've all told us about it. Although there is no financial profit in convincing people to vote, money is being spent to make sure it happens. That should tell you something.

> Evidence that voting matters is provided here.

Eenie, meenie, miney, mo, . . . maybe you don't want to vote because you feel as if you don't know enough about the candidates to make an informed decision. However, newspapers, television broadcasts, performance records—all these fact-based sources of information are available to the interested voter who wants to make a responsible choice. Find out what the candidates have been doing and what they plan to do. Make your decision based on information.

> Readers' arguments are considered and answered.

In many countries, voting is not an option. The leaders take control rather than being voted into a leadership role. Often leaders who are not elected can be corrupt or tyrannical, because the people can't remove them from power. We are citizens of a free country in which we have the right to vote. Whether or not the system works perfectly, it is better than a system with no voting. Vote because you can. Remind yourself that not everyone is as lucky.

Voting is your chance to make your voice heard. It's your chance to decide the future.

Drafting

State one position; include many facts. State your position clearly and early in one strong sentence. Then present the support you have gathered, starting with your least important points and building toward your most important ones. Bolster the outside support you have gathered by providing the following:

- **Personal anecdotes** Stories from your own experience.
- **Personal knowledge** Things you already know about the topic.
- **Forceful language** Words that will stir readers' emotions.

Appeal to your audience. Use words that your audience will know. If you are writing for teenagers, your language should be informal and fun. If you are writing to a government official, your language should be formal and serious.

Address reader concerns. Anticipate the major arguments against your position. Address them directly; do not avoid them. Look at the example to the right.

Reader concern

"Building a playground will cost way too much!"

Counterargument

"It would cost about $50,000. The state would pay for half. Our goal is to fundraise $25,000. This is a small price to pay for our children's safety."

Revising

Code your evidence. Review the main points in your draft. Use these codes to evaluate your evidence. Can you add more? Do you rely too much on one kind of support?

☆ Anecdote	● Logical argument
✓ Description	■ Expert opinion
▌ Fact or Statistic	▼ Personal observation
▲ Specific example	✳ Powerful language

The codes show that the writer uses a variety of support.

✓ It looks peaceful enough, but the hard metal equipment and concrete benches are dangerous to active kids. ▌ In the summer of 2000, the town Department of Recreation and Safety reports 92 accidents on the Crystal Lake Playground between June 1 and September 1. ■ "It is amazing," says Thomas Bergin, the Town Manager, "There is never an injury-free day." ▌ In the summer of 2000, there were 11 broken arms and legs and 9 cases of stitches. ▼ When I am with my young cousins, I never take them to this park. I am too afraid.

Choose precise words. Use sticky notes to mark places in which you use vague words such as *good, bad, right,* or *wrong.* Replace them with more precise, lively words.

> **Vague:** The playground is in a good place, but it is in bad shape.
>
> **Precise:** The playground has a spectacular view, but it is in dangerous condition.

Compare the model and nonmodel. Why is the model more effective than the nonmodel?

Nonmodel	Model
Eenie, meenie, miney, mo, . . . maybe you don't want to vote because you feel as if you don't know enough about the people to make a good decision. However many good sources of information are available to the interested voter who wants to make the right choice.	*Eenie, meenie, miney, mo, . . . maybe you don't want to vote because you feel as if you don't know enough about the candidates to make an informed decision. However, newspapers, television broadcasts, performance records—all these fact-based sources of information are available to the interested voter who wants to make a responsible choice.*

Publishing and Presenting

Choose one of these ways to share your writing.

Give a speech. Use your persuasive composition as the basis for a speech that you give to your classmates.

Submit a newspaper article. Most newspapers will publish well-written persuasive compositions if they appeal to their audience. Submit your composition and see what happens.

 Prentice Hall Writing and Grammar Connection: Chapter 7.

Speaking Connection

To learn to evaluate persuasive presentations, see the **Listening and Speaking Workshop: Evaluating Persuasive Presentations,** p. 326.

Rubric for Self-Assessment

Evaluate your persuasive composition using the following criteria and rating scale:

Criteria	Rating Scale				
	Not very				Very
Does the issue have more than one "side"?	1	2	3	4	5
How clearly have you stated your position?	1	2	3	4	5
How well have you organized your evidence?	1	2	3	4	5
Is all of your evidence presented clearly?	1	2	3	4	5
How well do you address reader concerns and counterarguments?	1	2	3	4	5

Listening and Speaking WORKSHOP

Evaluating a Persuasive Presentation

A persuasive presentation is organized much as a persuasive composition is. (To review the qualities of successful persuasive compositions, see the writing workshop, pp. 322–325.) This workshop will focus on how to evaluate a persuasive presentation. The following strategies will help you assess the strengths and weaknesses of the presenter's statements.

Evaluate Content

Like its written counterpart, effective persuasive presentations include clear statements of position and plenty of relevant supporting evidence. Listen to every word and be thinking about these ways to evaluate:

Determine the speaker's attitude. How does the speaker feel about his or her subject? Does the speaker rely on emotion, reason, or both?

Listen for a logical organization. Follow the argument from point to point. Listen for the connections between ideas. Listen for a convincing introduction and conclusion.

Listen for strong evidence. Be aware of the anecdotes, descriptions, facts and statistics, and specific examples that support the speaker's position. Is the support convincing? Why or why not?

Respond Constructively

As a listener, it is your job to respond constructively to a persuasive presentation.

- **Ask questions.** Never be afraid to ask questions. You will find out how thoroughly the speaker has researched the topic by probing more deeply.
- **Challenge.** If you disagree with something the presenter has said, do not hesitate to express your opinion. If you suspect a piece of evidence is wrong, challenge it by asking for its source.
- **Offer affirmations.** If you agree with something the presenter has said, it is appropriate to let him or her know. You might share a personal anecdote or observation that affirms the speaker's position and can support future presentations.

Activity:
Presentation and Feedback
With a partner, observe and listen to a persuasive sales pitch, either live or on videotape or television. Use the feedback form to evaluate what you see. Compare and discuss your evaluations.

Feedback Form for Persuasive Composition

Rating System
+ = excellent   ✔ = average   – = weak

Content

Clear position _____

Clear attitude _____

Logical organization _____

Amount of strong evidence _____

Respond honestly to these questions:

What impact did the presentation have on you?

What question does the presentation raise for you?

On what point would you challenge the speaker?

How can you affirm something the speaker has said?

Assessment WORKSHOP

Making Inferences

The reading sections of some tests require you to read a passage and make inferences, or draw logical conclusions, about information not stated directly. Use the following strategies to help you answer such questions:

- Read the text carefully. Look for clues that the author provides, such as time and place, and people's actions, opinions, and reactions.
- Think of similar experiences you have had and draw on your own knowledge.
- Eliminate any possible answers that clearly do not make sense based on the information provided.

Sample Test Item

Read the passage, and then choose the letter of the best answer.

Clara Barton was much younger than her four brothers and sisters. Because she had few playmates, she was very shy as a child. When she was nine, her parents sent her to boarding school, hoping she would overcome her shyness. The opposite happened. After some students laughed at her lisp, she refused to stay at the school. Remarkably, Clara Barton became a teacher herself. When she was refused promotion to the job of principal, she left teaching. She later worked at the U.S. Patent Office, nursed soldiers during the Civil War, and founded the American Red Cross.

The author provides clues to show that—

A Clara Barton saved many lives

B Clara Barton overcame childhood shyness to achieve many things

C Clara Barton could not stick with one job

D everyone admired Clara Barton

Answer and Explanation

There is no evidence to support **A, C,** or **D**. Clues in the text show that Barton was shy and accomplished many things. **B** is correct.

▶ Practice

Read the passage and then choose the letter of the best answer.

Many lonely practice hours in the gym lead up to the moment when the game clock is down to the last few seconds. A player stands alone on the line, pounding the ball a routine three bounces. Was all that practice enough to make the shot with the game on the line? The crowd holds its breath, waiting for his shot.

From this passage you can infer that—

A the article is about basketball.

B the end of the game is being described.

C the player is about to try to shoot a basket.

D all of the above are true.

Snap the Whip, Winslow Homer, Butler Institute of American Art, Youngstown, Ohio.

Exploring the Theme

Words have the power to spark emotion— fear, sadness, surprise, even anger. In this unit, you will find literature to make you laugh. You will meet an unusual cat, a stubborn child, and a newscaster caught in a broadcast gone completely out of control. The behavior of each of these quirky characters produces amusing results. Read on to see how the most common activities can be funny when seen through the eyes of a writer with a sense of humor.

◀ **Critical Viewing** What is the purpose of the activity shown here? **[Deduce]**

Why Read Literature?

The works in this unit will make you laugh, and they might touch you as well. In addition to seeing the humor in each situation, you might have other purposes for reading. Preview three of the purposes you might set before reading the works in this unit.

1 Read for information.

If you think you aren't getting enough exercise, consider how much walking you do every day. You might be getting more exercise than you think. Read the government publication on the health benefits of walking, page 374, to learn about the exercise you can do anytime, any place.

In 1991, hikers in Europe found the body of a 5,300-year-old man. Preserved by the snow, this man has taught archaeologists a great deal about the time in which he lived. Find out more when you read **"The Iceman"** on page 393.

2 Read to be entertained.

Some cultures have thought cats were sacred. Others thought they were evil. Whatever the role, people have always been fascinated by cats. Today, you can even find cats who have Web sites. Read about a brave and social cat in James Herriot's **"Cat on the Go"** on page 342.

Charles Osgood, author of **"Our Finest Hour,"** has written for and appeared on television and radio, has played with well-known orchestras, has received many honorary degrees, and was once named Father of the Year! Read his hilarious account of a newscast that wasn't ready for prime time on page 334.

3 Read for the love of literature.

If you wrote a poem a day from age eight to age twenty-one, you would not have written as many poems as E. E. Cummings did! He wrote more than 5,000 poems in his lifetime. Read his poem about a balloon man who announces the arrival of Spring, **"in Just-,"** page 363.

Lewis Carroll, the eldest son in a family with eleven children, used to entertain his siblings with puppets on strings, called marionettes, that he made himself. Enjoy Carroll's wit and language in his poem **"Father William"** on page 368.

 Take It to the Net

Visit the Web site for online instruction and activities related to each selection in this unit.

www.phschool.com

How to Read Literature

Use Strategies for Reading Critically

Some people think that being critical is the same as being negative. However, being a critical reader does not mean that you necessarily respond negatively to what you read. It means that you take the time to analyze carefully what you read and to consider how effectively an author has put together a piece of writing. In this unit, you will learn strategies for evaluating what you read.

1. Recognize author's purpose.

An author's purpose will influence the type and amount of information provided in a work. Consider the following purposes a writer might be trying to achieve:

- to entertain
- to persuade
- to inform
- to reflect on experiences

Knowing the author's purpose will help you make judgments about his or her reliability and objectivity. In this unit, you will learn strategies for using the author's word choices and the details he or she includes as clues to his or her purpose.

2. Evaluate author's message.

When you evaluate an author's message, you make a judgment about how effectively the writer has proved his or her point. To evaluate the author's message, ask yourself questions like the ones shown on the notepad.

3. Interpret idioms.

Idioms are expressions that have a meaning in a particular language or region. By recognizing and interpreting idioms, you improve your understanding of a work's perspective.

In this unit, you will learn how to get at the meaning of expressions and to appreciate the regional or cultural "seasoning" they give to a work.

Evaluating an Author's Message

- What is the message?
- What supports the message?
- Do I agree or disagree?

4. Identify cause and effect.

Think about how one event causes another. Notice how the cause—an action, feeling, or situation— brings about a result—the effect. Learn to recognize cause-and-effect relationships to

- understand the connections between events.
- judge whether evidence supports a connection between events.

As you read the selections in this unit, review the reading strategies and look at the notes in the side columns. Use the suggestions to apply the strategies and read critically.

Prepare to Read

Our Finest Hour

 Take It to the Net

Visit www.phschool.com for interactive activities and instruction related to "Our Finest Hour," including

- background
- graphic organizers
- literary elements
- reading strategies

Preview

Connecting to the Literature

In his essay "Our Finest Hour," Charles Osgood describes a carefully planned television program that falls apart in front of a nationwide audience. As you read, consider how you might feel if you were in Osgood's position at the time.

Background

Although people who report the news look relaxed, they are actually under a lot of pressure. Because the news is broadcast live, any mistake made by reporters or crew will be seen on TV. Anchors (the main announcers) must handle any mistakes—mispronunciations, technical difficulties, incorrect graphics—as they occur.

Literary Analysis

Humor

Humor is writing that aims to make an audience laugh. Describing real-life bloopers and blunders can make for very effective humor. Often, the humor is a result of the narrator's serious treatment of a ridiculous subject or sequence of events. In this example, Charles Osgood formally presents an absurd combination of details:

> When the commercial was over, I introduced a piece from Washington. What came up was a series of pictures of people who seemed to be dead.

Connecting Literary Elements

Part of the humor in Osgood's essay comes from the bewilderment and confusion he experiences as one thing after another goes wrong. He gives readers a full appreciation of the confusion because he tells events from the **first-person point of view.** He tells events from the perspective of a participant in the action and refers to himself as *I* and *me*.

As you read, consider the effect of point of view by answering the following focus questions:

1. What details would be missing from this essay if it were not told in the first person?
2. How do these details contribute to the humor?

Reading Strategy

Recognizing Author's Purpose

Authors usually write to achieve a **purpose**, or goal, that they have in mind. The purpose might be

- to persuade.
- to entertain.
- to give information.
- to reflect on an experience.

Clues in the text can point to a writer's purpose. For example, an article filled with facts is probably meant to inform. The chart shows types of details and presentations that can indicate an author's purpose. As you read "Our Finest Hour," look for clues of several related purposes that Osgood may have had for writing this essay.

Author's Purpose	Clues
To persuade	strong language; favors one side of an issue
To entertain	silly, humorous, suspenseful, or exciting details
To give information	facts and details
To reflect on an experience	comments by the writer

Vocabulary Development

correspondent (kôr´ ə spän´ dənt) *n.* person hired by a news organization to provide news from a distant place (p. 334)

bewilderment (bē wil´ dər mənt) *n.* state of confusion (p. 336)

Our Finest Hour

Charles Osgood

correspondent
(kôr′ ə spän′ dənt) *n.*
person hired by a news
organization to provide
news from a distant place

Only occasionally do most reporters or <u>correspondents</u> get to "anchor" a news broadcast. Anchoring, you understand, means sitting there in the studio and telling some stories into the camera and introducing the reports and pieces that other reporters do. It looks easy enough. It is easy enough, most of the time . . .

It was back when I was relatively new at CBS News. I'd been in the business a while, but only recently had moved over to CBS News. I was old, but I was new. It was a Saturday night and I was filling in for Roger Mudd[1] on the CBS Evening News. Roger was on vacation. The regular executive producer[2] of the broadcast, Paul Greenberg, was on vacation, too. And so was the regular cameraman and the regular editor and the regular director. Somewhere along the line we had one too many substitutes that night.

I said "Good evening" and introduced the first report and turned to the monitor to watch it. What I saw was myself looking at the monitor. Many seconds passed. Finally there was something on the screen. A reporter was beginning a story. It was not the story I had introduced. Instead, it was a different story by a different reporter. This was supposed to be the second item in the newscast. So I shuffled my script around and made the first piece second and the second piece first. When I came back on camera, I explained what it was we had seen and reintroduced the first piece. Again there was a

Literary Analysis
Humor and Point of View
How does the first-person narration contribute to the humor of the account?

---

1. **Roger Mudd** *CBS News* reporter from 1961 to 1980. He was a backup anchor person for Walter Cronkite during the time of this story.
2. **executive producer** person responsible for the quality of the newscast.

long, awkward pause. I shuffled my papers. I scribbled on the script. I turned to the monitor. Finally, the floor director, who was filling in for the regular floor director, cued me to go on. So I introduced the next report. It didn't come up either, so I said we'd continue in just a moment. Obvious cue for a commercial, I thought, but it took a while to register in the control room. When a commercial did come up, there was a frantic scramble in the studio to reorganize what was left of the broadcast. But by now everything had come undone.

When the commercial was over, I introduced a piece from Washington. What came up was a series of pictures of people who seemed to be dead. One man was slumped over a car wheel. Two or three people were lying in the middle of the street. Another man was propped up against the wall of the building, his eyes staring vacantly into space. Then came the voice of Peter Kalisher. "This was the town where everyone died," he said. I knew nothing whatsoever about this piece. It was not scheduled for the broadcast. Peter Kalisher was in Paris as far as I knew. But there had been nothing on the news wires about everybody in Paris having died. In the "fishbowl," the glassed-in office where the executive producer sits, there were at least three people yelling into telephones. Nobody in there knew anything about this piece either. The story was about some little town in France that was demonstrating the evils of cigarette smoking. Seems the population of the town was the same number as smoking-related deaths in France in a given year. It was a nice story well told, but since nobody in authority at CBS News, New York, had seen it or knew what was coming next, they decided to dump out of it and come back to me.

Reading Strategy
Recognizing Author's Purpose What clues in this paragraph point to the author's purpose?

✔**Reading Check**

Why is this an unusual night for the CBS Evening News?

I, of course, was sitting there looking at the piece with <u>bewilderment</u> written all over my face, when suddenly, in the midst of all these French people pretending to be dead, I saw myself, bewilderment and all.

bewilderment
(bē wil′ dər mənt) *n.* state of confusion

All in all, it was not the finest broadcast CBS News has ever done. But the worst part came when I introduced the "end piece," a feature story that Hughes Rudd had done about raft racing on the Chattahoochee River.[3] Again, when I finished the introduction, I turned to the monitor and, again, nothing happened. Then, through the glass window of the "fishbowl," I heard a loud and plaintive wail. "What is going on?" screamed the fill-in executive producer. I could hear him perfectly clearly, and so could half of America. The microphone on my tie-clip was open. Standing in the control room watching this, with what I'm sure must have been great interest, was a delegation of visiting journalists from the People's Republic of China.[4] They must have had a really great impression of American electronic journalism. The next Monday morning, sitting back at the radio desk where I belonged, I became aware of a presence standing quietly next to my desk. It was Richard Salant, the wise and gentle man who was then president of CBS News. He'd been waiting until I finished typing a sentence before bending over and inquiring softly: "What *was* going on?"

---

3. **Chattahoochee River** (chat ə hoo′ chē) river running south through Georgia and forming part of the borders of Georgia, Alabama, and Florida.
4. **People's Republic of China** official name of China.

Review and Assess

Thinking About the Selection

1. **Respond:** How might you have responded if you had been the anchorperson when this situation occurred?

2. **(a) Recall:** Name three things that go wrong during the newscast. **(b) Interpret:** Why do so many things go wrong?

3. **(a) Recall:** During the newscast, what takes place in the "fishbowl"? **(b) Compare and Contrast:** How is the anchor's experience different from that of the people in the fishbowl?

4. **(a) Hypothesize:** What do you think Osgood learned from this experience? **(b) Speculate:** Why might Osgood have chosen to share this embarrassing story?

5. **Take a Position:** Are there any situations in which newscasters should not report what they know? Explain and defend your position.

Charles Osgood

(b. 1933)
You may be familiar with Charles Osgood from watching the television show *Sunday Morning*, which he began anchoring in 1994. Inspired by listening to the radio as a boy, in the days before TV, Osgood went on to build a distinguished career in news media. He moved from radio work to reporting for TV news, eventually serving as anchor of the CBS Evening News. Though he has reported on serious topics such as politics and the economy, a different side of Osgood comes through on *Sunday Morning* and on his special broadcasts, *Newsbreak* and *The Osgood File*. His wry sense of humor, ability to poke fun at current events, and interest in everyday experiences have endeared him to viewers across the country.

Review and Assess

Literary Analysis

Humor

1. Where does the writer poke fun at people, including himself? Give three examples.
2. On a chart like the one below, record examples of events Osgood uses to create humor by contrasting what was supposed to happen with what did happen.

What should have happened	What did happen

3. **(a)** Which detail do you find funniest? Why? **(b)** How does its placement in the essay affect the humor?
4. How does the title "Our Finest Hour" add to the humor of this essay?

Connecting Literary Elements

5. At what point in the essay do you realize that it is written from the **first-person point of view**? What clue tells you?
6. How does first-person point of view add to the humor?
7. Osgood and the home audience see the broadcast from different perspectives. Use the chart below to compare and contrast these two perspectives.

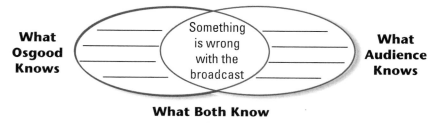

What Osgood Knows — Something is wrong with the broadcast — **What Audience Knows**

What Both Know

Reading Strategy

Recognizing Author's Purpose

8. Find at least three details that show that the **author's purpose** is to entertain the audience.
9. What other purposes might Osgood have?

Extend Understanding

10. **Career Connection:** Why would a news anchor need to have a thorough knowledge of social studies topics?

Quick Review

Humor is writing that is meant to make the audience laugh. To review humor, see page 333.

Point of view is the perspective from which a story is told. In the **first-person point of view**, the writer participates in the action. To review point of view, see page 333.

The **author's purpose** is the goal the writer wants to accomplish. To review author's purpose, see page 333.

 Take It to the Net
www.phschool.com
Take the interactive self-test online to check your understanding of the selection.

Integrate Language Skills

Vocabulary Development Lesson

Word Analysis: Latin Suffix -ment

The Latin suffix -ment means "the condition of." Bewilderment is "the condition of being bewildered." Add -ment to these words, and use each new word in a sentence.

1. excite
2. disappoint
3. content
4. bombard

Spelling Strategy

To avoid mistakes when choosing between one consonant or two, learn the words that use a double consonant r. Copy each clue and write the word it indicates. Underline the related form of words with double consonant r.

1. Interrupting is impolite, so don't ____?____.
2. Someone with whom you correspond is a ____?____.
3. To fix incorrect items is to make them ____?____.

Concept Development: Definitions

On your paper, write the word or phrase whose meaning is closest to that of the first word.

1. correspondent
   (a) one who finds letters
   (b) one who contributes news
   (c) one who speaks out of turn
2. bewilderment
   (a) state of jumbled confusion
   (b) state of inactivity
   (c) state of determination

The following words are defined in the selection. Write the definition of each word as it is used and explained in the essay.

3. anchoring (p. 334)
4. fishbowl (p. 335)

Grammar Lesson

Subjects and Predicates

Every complete sentence has two parts—the subject and the predicate. The **subject** describes whom or what the sentence is about. The **simple subject** is the noun or pronoun that states exactly whom or what the sentence is about. The **predicate** tells something about the subject. The **simple predicate** is the verb or verb phrase that tells what action the subject performs. In this example, the simple subject and simple predicate are circled.

```
┌── SUBJECT ──┐ ┌── PREDICATE ──┐
The floor (director) (cued) me to go on.
```

▶ *For more practice, see page R30, Exercise A.*
Practice Copy the sentences. Underline the subject once and the predicate twice. Circle the simple subject and the simple predicate.

1. We had one too many substitutes.
2. I turned to the monitor.
3. Each problem made the situation worse.
4. The people in the "fishbowl" panicked.
5. The broadcast ended at last.

Writing Application Write five sentences about a humorous experience. In each sentence, underline the subject once and the predicate twice. Circle the simple subject and the simple predicate.

W/G *Prentice Hall Writing and Grammar Connection: Chapter 19, Section 1*

Writing Lesson

Summary of a First-Person Account

A summary is a brief statement of main ideas or events. Summarize Osgood's account of the disastrous broadcast.

Prewriting In your mind, divide the account into beginning, middle, and end. Choose the most important "point" or event from each section.

Drafting Begin your summary by telling the title and author. Then, make a general statement that describes the essay.

Example: "Our Finest Hour" by Charles Osgood is a humorous account of a disastrous newscast.

Continue by writing one sentence about the point or event you have chosen from the beginning, one from the middle and one from the end. Conclude with a sentence in which you tell the meaning or significance of the events.

Revising Revise to make your summary shorter. Look for places where you can use one word instead of two or three.

Model: Revising for Length

Osgood's ~~narrative~~ account ~~of events~~ shows that every ~~type of job or~~
profession has ~~moments of difficulty.~~ *its problems*

W͞G *Prentice Hall Writing and Grammar Connection: Chapter 12, Section 3*

Extension Activities

Listening and Speaking Use Osgood's technique of contrasting ridiculous events with serious delivery to tell the **story** of a real-life humorous experience.

1. Identify the events you want to tell.
2. Experiment with different words and expressions to achieve contrast between serious and ridiculous.
3. Deliver your narrative for a group.

Ask listeners to give feedback on techniques you can use to improve the presentation of your narrative.

Research and Technology With a group, create a school **news show** with at least three stories. Divide tasks of introducing the stories, reporting the stories, and finding visuals for stories. Present your "broadcast" without rehearsal. Discuss how your experience helps you understand the types of mistakes that occur in Osgood's account.

 **Take It to the Net** www.phschool.com

Go online for an additional research activity using the Internet.

Prepare to Read

Cat on the Go

Happy Cat, Christian Pierre

 Take It to the Net

Visit www.phschool.com for interactive activities and instruction related to "Cat on the Go," including
- background
- graphic organizers
- literary elements
- reading strategies

Preview

Connecting to the Literature

In "Cat on the Go," veterinarian James Herriot describes a cat with a remarkable personality. Think about unusual animals you have known—perhaps a dog that performs tricks or a fast-talking parrot—as you read this selection.

Background

Veterinarians must complete a good deal of training before they can be licensed. This includes an in-depth science education and a four-year postgraduate program. Usually veterinarians specialize in small animals, such as house pets, or large animals, such as horses and cows. Like doctors, they sometimes perform surgery. Today's veterinarians have access to far more sophisticated equipment than Herriot did.

Literary Analysis

Character Traits

The qualities that make a person or an animal unique are called
character traits. The girl who finds the injured cat in "Cat on the Go"
has the character trait of sympathy for animals, as shown in this sentence:

> The girl's eyes filled with tears, she stretched out a hand and
> touched the emaciated animal then turned and walked quickly
> to the door.

Keep track of character traits by using a web like this one for each
character, including animals.

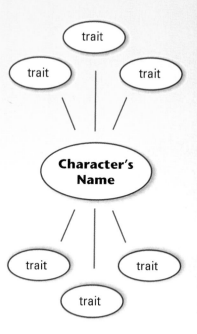

Connecting Literary Elements

One example of a character trait is the way the character speaks. In
"Cat on the Go," many of the characters speak a **dialect**—a form of a language spoken by people in a particular region. In this narrative, the region
is Yorkshire, England. Herriot uses nonstandard spellings to show how the
characters sound. He includes words and expressions that are common in
Yorkshire but seem unusual to other English speakers. The italicized words
in the example give a Yorkshire "flavor" to the character's speech:

> "Aye, but *some folks 'ud say* finders keepers or *summat* like that."

If you have difficulty understanding a nonstandard spelling, try reading
the sentence aloud.

Reading Strategy

Interpreting Idioms

An **idiom** is a word or expression that has meaning in a certain language
or region. Often, it is an expression whose meaning differs from the literal
meaning of its individual words. For example, the idiom "It's raining cats and
dogs," which describes a hard rain, is unrelated to cats or dogs. As you read,
use these focus questions to help you recognize idioms:

1. What unusual expressions does Herriot use?
2. Why does he use these idioms?

Vocabulary Development

grotesquely (grō tesk´ lē) *adv.* in a
strange or distorted way (p. 343)

emaciated (ē mā´ shē āt´ id) *adj.*
extremely thin; starving (p. 343)

inevitable (in ev´ i tə bəl) *adj.* certain
to happen (p. 345)

sauntered (sôn´ tərd) *v.* strolled
(p. 347)

distraught (dis trôt´) *adj.* extremely
upset (p. 348)

despondent (di spän´ dənt) *adj.* lacking hope; depressed (p. 348)

intrigued (in trēg´d´) *v.* fascinated
(p. 349)

surreptitiously (sʉr´ əp tish´ əs lē) *adv.*
secretly (p. 353)

Cat on the Go

James Herriot

▶ Critical Viewing
What human emotions
does the cat in this pho-
tograph seem to convey?
Explain your response.
[Speculate]

One winter evening Tristan shouted up the stairs from the passage far below.

"Jim! Jim!"

I went out and stuck my head over the bannisters. "What is it, Triss?"

"Sorry to bother you, Jim, but could you come down for a minute?" The upturned face had an anxious look.

I went down the long flights of steps two at a time and when I arrived slightly breathless on the ground floor Tristan beckoned me through to the consulting room at the back of the house. A teenage girl was standing by the table, her hand resting on a stained roll of blanket.

"It's a cat," Tristan said. He pulled back a fold of the blanket and I looked down at a large, deeply striped tabby. At least he would have been large if he had had any flesh on his bones, but ribs and pelvis stood out painfully through the fur and as I passed my hand over the motionless body I could feel only a thin covering of skin.

Tristan cleared his throat. "There's something else, Jim."

I looked at him curiously. For once he didn't seem to have a joke in him. I watched as he gently lifted one of the cat's hind legs and rolled the abdomen into view. There was a gash on the ventral surface[1] through which a coiled cluster of intestines spilled <u>grotesquely</u> onto the cloth. I was still shocked and staring when the <u>girl</u> spoke.

"I saw this cat sittin' in the dark, down Brown's yard. I thought 'e looked skinny, like, and a bit quiet and I bent down to give 'im a pat. Then I saw 'e was badly hurt and I went home for a blanket and brought 'im round to you."

"That was kind of you," I said. "Have you any idea who he belongs to?"

The girl shook her head. "No, he looks like a stray to me."

"He does indeed." I dragged my eyes away from the terrible wound. "You're Marjorie Simpson, aren't you?"

"Yes."

"I know your Dad well. He's our postman."

"That's right." She gave a half smile then her lips trembled.

"Well, I reckon I'd better leave 'im with you. You'll be going to put him out of his misery. There's nothing anybody can do about . . . about that?"

I shrugged and shook my head. The girl's eyes filled with tears, she stretched out a hand and touched the <u>emaciated</u> animal then turned and walked quickly to the door.

"Thanks again, Marjorie," I called after the retreating back. "And don't worry—we'll look after him."

---

1. **ventral** (ven´ trəl) **surface** surface near or on the belly.

grotesquely (grō tesk´ le) *adv.* in a strange or distorted way

emaciated (ē mā´ shē āt´ id) *adj.* extremely thin; starving

**Reading Check**

What is wrong with the cat?

In the silence that followed, Tristan and I looked down at the shattered animal. Under the surgery lamp it was all too easy to see. He had almost been disemboweled[2] and the pile of intestines was covered in dirt and mud.

"What d'you think did this?" Tristan said at length. "Has he been run over?"

"Maybe," I replied. "Could be anything. An attack by a big dog or somebody could have kicked him or struck him." All things were possible with cats because some people seemed to regard them as fair game for any cruelty.

Tristan nodded. "Anyway, whatever happened, he must have been on the verge of starvation. He's a skeleton. I bet he's wandered miles from home."

"Ah well," I sighed. "There's only one thing to do. Those guts are perforated in several places. It's hopeless."

Tristan didn't say anything but he whistled under his breath and drew the tip of his forefinger again and again across the furry cheek. And, unbelievably, from somewhere in the scraggy chest a gentle purring arose.

The young man looked at me, round eyed. "My God, do you hear that?"

"Yes . . . amazing in that condition. He's a good-natured cat."

Tristan, head bowed, continued his stroking. I knew how he felt because, although he preserved a cheerfully hard-boiled attitude to our patients he couldn't kid me about one thing: he had a soft spot for cats. Even now, when we are both around the sixty mark, he often talks to me about the cat he has had for many years. It is a typical relationship—they tease each other unmercifully—but it is based on real affection.

"It's no good, Triss," I said gently. "It's got to be done." I reached for the syringe but something in me rebelled against plunging a needle into that mutilated body. Instead I pulled a fold of the blanket over the cat's head.

"Pour a little ether onto the cloth," I said. "He'll just sleep away."

Wordlessly, Tristan unscrewed the cap of the ether bottle and poised it above the head. Then from under the shapeless heap of blanket we heard it again: the deep purring which increased in volume till it boomed in our ears like a distant motorcycle.

Tristan was like a man turned to stone, hand gripping the bottle rigidly, eyes staring down at the mound of cloth from which the purring rose in waves of warm friendly sound.

At last he looked up at me and gulped. "I don't fancy this much, Jim. Can't we do something?"

"You mean, put that lot back?"

"Yes."

Literary Analysis
Character Traits
What character traits does Tristan show in this paragraph?

Reading Strategy
Interpreting Idioms
What is meant by the expression "that lot"? How do you know?

---

2. **disemboweled** (dis´ im bou´ əld) v. lost its intestines.

"But the bowels are damaged—they're like a sieve in parts."

"We could stitch them, couldn't we?"

I lifted the blanket and looked again. "Honestly, Triss, I wouldn't know where to start. And the whole thing is filthy."

He didn't say anything, but continued to look at me steadily. And I didn't need much persuading. I had no more desire to pour ether onto that comradely purring than he had.

"Come on, then," I said. "We'll have a go."

With the oxygen bubbling and the cat's head in the anesthetic mask we washed the whole prolapse[3] with warm saline.[4] We did it again and again but it was impossible to remove every fragment of caked dirt. Then we started the painfully slow business of stitching the many holes in the tiny intestines, and here I was glad of Tristan's nimble fingers which seemed better able to manipulate the small round-bodied needles than mine.

Two hours and yards of catgut[5] later, we dusted the patched up peritoneal[6] surface with sulfanilamide[7] and pushed the entire mass back into the abdomen. When I had sutured muscle layers and skin everything looked tidy but I had a nasty feeling of sweeping undesirable things under the carpet. The extensive damage, all that contamination—peritonitis[8] was <u>inevitable</u>.

"He's alive, anyway, Triss," I said as we began to wash the instruments. "We'll put him onto sulfapyridine and keep our fingers crossed." There were still no antibiotics at that time but the new drug was a big advance.

The door opened and Helen came in. "You've been a long time, Jim." She walked over to the table and looked down at the sleeping cat. "What a poor skinny little thing. He's all bones."

"You should have seen him when he came in." Tristan switched off the sterilizer and screwed shut the valve on the anesthetic machine. "He looks a lot better now."

She stroked the little animal for a moment. "Is he badly injured?"

"I'm afraid so, Helen," I said. "We've done our best for him but I honestly don't think he has much chance."

"What a shame. And he's pretty, too. Four white feet and all those unusual colors." With her finger she traced the faint bands of auburn and copper-gold among the gray and black.

Tristan laughed. "Yes, I think that chap has a ginger Tom somewhere in his ancestry."

Literary Analysis
Character Traits
What traits are shown by the men, who decide to operate on a hopeless case?

inevitable (in ev´ ə tə bəl) *adj.* certain to happen

✔**Reading Check**

What do Tristan and Jim do for the cat?

---

3. **prolapse** (prō´ laps) *n.* internal organ—here, the intestines—that has fallen out of place.
4. **saline** (sā´ līn) *n.* salt solution.
5. **catgut** (kat´ gut´) *n.* tough string or thread used in surgery.
6. **peritoneal** (per´ i tō nē´ əl) *adj.* having to do with the membrane that lines the abdomen.
7. **sulfanilamide** (sul´ fə nil´ ə mīd) *n.* sulfa drugs were used to treat infections before penicillin and other antibiotics were discovered.
8. **peritonitis** (per´ i tō nīt´ is) *n.* inflammation of the abdominal lining.

Helen smiled, too, but absently, and I noticed a broody look about her. She hurried out to the stock room and returned with an empty box.

"Yes . . . yes . . ." she said thoughtfully. "I can make a bed in this box for him and he'll sleep in our room, Jim."

"He will?"

"Yes, he must be warm, mustn't he?"

"Of course."

Later, in the darkness of our bed-sitter,[9] I looked from my pillow at a cozy scene. Sam in his basket on one side of the flickering fire and the cat cushioned and blanketed in his box on the other.

As I floated off into sleep it was good to know that my patient was so comfortable, but I wondered if he would be alive in the morning. . . .

I knew he was alive at 7:30 a.m. because my wife was already up and talking to him. I trailed across the room in my pajamas and the cat and I looked at each other. I rubbed him under the chin and he opened his mouth in a rusty miaow. But he didn't try to move.

"Helen," I said. "This little thing is tied together inside with catgut. He'll have to live on fluids for a week and even then he probably won't make it. If he stays up here you'll be spooning milk into him umpteen times a day."

"Okay, okay." She had that broody look again.

It wasn't only milk she spooned into him over the next few days. Beef essence, strained broth and a succession of sophisticated baby foods found their way down his throat at regular intervals. One lunch time I found Helen kneeling by the box.

"We shall call him Oscar," she said.

"You mean we're keeping him?"

"Yes."

I am fond of cats but we already had a dog in our cramped quarters and I could see difficulties. Still I decided to let it go.

"Why Oscar?"

"I don't know." Helen tipped a few drops of chop gravy onto the little red tongue and watched intently as he swallowed.

One of the things I like about women is their mystery, the unfathomable part of them, and I didn't press the matter further. But I was pleased at the way things were going. I had been giving the sulfapyridine every six hours and taking the temperature night and morning, expecting all the time to encounter the roaring fever, the vomiting and the tense abdomen of peritonitis. But it never happened.

It was as though Oscar's animal instinct told him he had to move as little as possible because he lay absolutely still day after day and looked up at us—and purred.

▼ **Critical Viewing**
What information in the essay suggests Oscar might look like the cat in this photograph?
[Support]

---

9. bed-sitter (bed´ sit´ter) *n.* British term for a one-room apartment.

His purr became part of our lives and when he eventually left his bed, <u>sauntered</u> through to our kitchen and began to sample Sam's dinner of meat and biscuit it was a moment of triumph. And I didn't spoil it by wondering if he was ready for solid food; I felt he knew.

From then on it was sheer joy to watch the furry scarecrow fill out and grow strong, and as he ate and ate and the flesh spread over his bones the true beauty of his coat showed in the glossy medley of auburn, black and gold. We had a handsome cat on our hands.

Once Oscar had fully recovered, Tristan was a regular visitor.

He probably felt, and rightly, that he, more than I, had saved Oscar's life in the first place and he used to play with him for long periods. His favorite ploy was to push his leg round the corner of the table and withdraw it repeatedly just as the cat pawed at it.

Oscar was justifiably irritated by this teasing but showed his character by lying in wait for Tristan one night and biting him smartly[10] in the ankle before he could start his tricks.

From my own point of view Oscar added many things to our menage.[11] Sam was delighted with him and the two soon became firm friends. Helen adored him and each evening I thought afresh that a nice cat washing his face by the hearth gave extra comfort to a room.

Oscar had been established as one of the family for several weeks when I came in from a late call to find Helen waiting for me with a stricken face.

"What's happened?" I asked.

"It's Oscar—he's gone!"

"Gone? What do you mean?"

"Oh, Jim, I think he's run away."

I stared at her. "He wouldn't do that. He often goes down to the garden at night. Are you sure he isn't there?"

"Absolutely. I've searched right into the yard. I've even had a walk round the town. And remember." Her chin quivered. "He . . . he ran away from somewhere before."

I looked at my watch. "Ten o'clock. Yes, that is strange. He shouldn't be out at this time."

As I spoke the front door bell jangled. I galloped down the stairs and as I rounded the corner in the passage I could see Mrs. Heslington, the vicar's[12] wife, through the glass. I threw open the door. She was holding Oscar in her arms.

"I believe this is your cat, Mr. Herriot," she said.

"It is indeed, Mrs. Heslington. Where did you find him?"

---

10. **smartly** (smärt´ lē) *adv.* sharply.
11. **menage** (mā näzh´) *n.* household.
12. **vicar** (vik´ ər) *n.* parish priest.

saundered (sôn´ tərd) *v.* strolled

Literary Analysis
Character Traits What traits are revealed by Tristan and Oscar?

✔**Reading Check**
Where does Oscar live?

She smiled. "Well it was rather odd. We were having a meeting of the Mothers' Union at the church house and we noticed the cat sitting there in the room."

"Just sitting . . .?"

"Yes, as though he were listening to what we were saying and enjoying it all. It was unusual. When the meeting ended I thought I'd better bring him along to you."

"I'm most grateful, Mrs. Heslington." I snatched Oscar and tucked him under my arm. "My wife is <u>distraught</u>—she thought he was lost."

distraught (dis trôt´) *adj.* extremely upset

It was a little mystery. Why should he suddenly take off like that? But since he showed no change in his manner over the ensuing week we put it out of our minds.

Then one evening a man brought in a dog for a distemper[13] inoculation and left the front door open. When I went up to our flat I found that Oscar had disappeared again. This time Helen and I scoured the marketplace and side alleys in vain and when we returned at half past nine we were both <u>despondent</u>. It was nearly eleven and we were thinking of bed when the doorbell rang.

despondent (di spän´ dənt) *adj.* lacking hope; depressed

It was Oscar again, this time resting on the ample stomach of Jack Newbould. Jack was a gardener at one of the big houses. He hiccuped gently and gave me a huge benevolent smile. "Brought your cat, Mr. Herriot."

"Gosh, thanks, Jack!" I said, scooping up Oscar gratefully. "Where the devil did you find him?"

"Well, s'matter o' fact 'e sort of found me."

"What do you mean?"

Jack closed his eyes for a few moments before articulating carefully. "Thish is a big night, tha knows, Mr. Herriot. Darts championship. Lots of t'lads round at t'Dog and Gun—lotsh and lotsh of 'em. Big gatherin'."

"And our cat was there?"

"Aye, he were there, all right. Sitting among t'lads. Shpent t'whole evenin' with us."

"Just sat there, eh?"

"That 'e did." Jack giggled reminiscently. "By gaw 'e enjoyed 'isself. Ah gave 'em a drop out of me own glass and once or twice ah thought 'e was going to have a go at chuckin' a dart. He's some cat." He laughed again.

As I bore Oscar upstairs I was deep in thought. What was going on here? These sudden desertions were upsetting Helen and I felt they could get on my nerves in time.

I didn't have long to wait till the next one. Three nights later he was missing again. This time Helen and I didn't bother to search—we just waited.

---

13. distemper (dis tem´ pər) *adj.* infectious viral disease of young dogs.

He was back earlier than usual. I heard the door bell at nine o'clock. It was the elderly Miss Simpson peering through the glass. And she wasn't holding Oscar—he was prowling on the mat waiting to come in.

Miss Simpson watched with interest as the cat stalked inside and made for the stairs. "Ah, good, I'm so glad he's come home safely. I knew he was your cat and I've been <u>intrigued</u> by his behavior all evening."

"Where . . . may I ask?"

"Oh, at the Women's Institute. He came in shortly after we started and stayed there till the end."

"Really? What exactly was your program, Miss Simpson?"

"Well, there was a bit of committee stuff, then a short talk with lantern slides by Mr. Walters from the water company and we finished with a cake-making competition."

"Yes . . . yes . . . and what did Oscar do?"

She laughed. "Mixed with the company, apparently enjoyed the slides and showed great interest in the cakes."

"I see. And you didn't bring him home?"

"No, he made his own way here. As you know, I have to pass your house and I merely rang your bell to make sure you knew he had arrived."

"I'm obliged to you, Miss Simpson. We were a little worried."

I mounted the stairs in record time. Helen was sitting with the cat on her knee and she looked up as I burst in.

"I know about Oscar now," I said.

"Know what?"

"Why he goes on these nightly outings. He's not running away—he's visiting."

"Visiting?"

"Yes," I said. "Don't you see? He likes getting around, he loves people, especially in groups, and he's interested in what they do. He's a natural mixer."

Helen looked down at the attractive mound of fur curled on her lap. "Of course . . . that's it . . . he's a socialite!"

"Exactly, a high stepper!"

"A cat-about-town!"

It all afforded us some innocent laughter and Oscar sat up and looked at us with evident pleasure, adding his own throbbing purr to the merriment. But for Helen and me there was a lot of relief behind it; ever since our cat had started his excursions there had been the gnawing fear that we would lose him, and now we felt secure.

From that night our delight in him increased. There was endless joy in watching this facet of his character unfolding. He did the social round meticulously, taking in most of the activities of the town. He

intrigued (in trēg d') *v.* fascinated

Literary Analysis
Character Traits What do Oscar's actions tell you about his personality?

Reading Strategy
Interpreting Idioms What expressions would you use in place of "high stepper" and "cat-about-town"?

Reading Check

What does Oscar do every couple of nights?

became a familiar figure at whist drives,[14] jumble sales,[15] school concerts and scout bazaars. Most of the time he was made welcome, but was twice ejected from meetings of the Rural District Council who did not seem to relish the idea of a cat sitting in on their deliberations.

At first I was apprehensive about his making his way through the streets but I watched him once or twice and saw that he looked both ways before tripping daintily across. Clearly he had excellent traffic sense and this made me feel that his original injury had not been caused by a car.

Taking it all in all, Helen and I felt that it was a kind stroke of fortune which had brought Oscar to us. He was a warm and cherished part of our home life. He added to our happiness.

When the blow fell it was totally unexpected.

I was finishing the evening surgery.[16] I looked round the door and saw only a man and two little boys.

"Next, please," I said.

The man stood up. He had no animal with him. He was middle-aged, with the rough weathered face of a farm worker. He twirled a cloth cap nervously in his hands.

"Mr. Herriot?" he said.

"Yes, what can I do for you?"

He swallowed and looked me straight in the eyes. "Ah think you've got ma cat."

"What?"

"Ah lost ma cat a bit since." He cleared his throat. "We used to live at Missdon but ah got a job as plowman to Mr. Horne of Wederly. It was after we moved to Wederly that t'cat went missin'. Ah reckon he was tryin to find 'is way back to his old home."

"Wederly? That's on the other side of Brawton—over thirty miles away."

"Aye, ah knaw, but cats is funny things."

"But what makes you think I've got him?"

He twisted the cap around a bit more. "There's a cousin o' mine lives in Darrowby and ah heard tell from 'im about this cat that goes around to meetin's. I 'ad to come. We've been huntin' everywhere."

"Tell me," I said. "This cat you lost. What did he look like?"

"Gray and black and sort o' gingery. Right bonny[17] 'e was. And 'e was allus goin' out to gatherin's."

14. **whist** (hwist) **drives** attempts to raise money for charities and other purposes by playing the card game whist.
15. **jumble sales** British term for sales of contributed articles to raise money for charity.
16. **surgery** (sur´ jər ē) *n.* British term for "office hours."
17. **bonny** (bän´ ē) *adj.* pretty

▶Critical Viewing Which of Oscar's qualities are shown in this photograph?

Literary Analysis
Character Traits and Dialect Find three phrases that reveal the character's Yorkshire speech patterns.

A cold hand clutched at my heart. "You'd better come upstairs. Bring the boys with you."

Helen was putting some coal on the fire of the bed-sitter.

"Helen," I said. "This is Mr.—er—I'm sorry, I don't know your name."

"Gibbons, Sep Gibbons. They called me Septimus because ah was the seventh in family and it looks like ah'm goin' t'same way 'cause we've got six already. These are our two youngest." The two boys, obvious twins of about eight, looked up at us solemnly.

I wished my heart would stop hammering. "Mr. Gibbons thinks Oscar is his. He lost his cat some time ago."

My wife put down her little shovel. "Oh . . . oh . . . I see." She stood very still for a moment then smiled faintly. "Do sit down. Oscar's in the kitchen, I'll bring him through."

She went out and reappeared with the cat in her arms. She hadn't got through the door before the little boys gave tongue.

"Tiger!" they cried. "Oh, Tiger, Tiger!"

The man's face seemed lit from within. He walked quickly across the floor and ran his big work-roughened hand along the fur.

"Hullo, awd lad," he said, and turned to me with a radiant smile. "It's 'im, Mr. Herriot. It's 'im awright, and don't 'e look well!"

"You call him Tiger, eh?" I said.

"Aye," he replied happily. "It's them gingery stripes. The kids called 'im that. They were brokenhearted when we lost 'im."

As the two little boys rolled on the floor our Oscar rolled with them, pawing playfully, purring with delight.

Sep Gibbons sat down again. "That's the way 'e allus went on wi' the family. They used to play with 'im for hours. By gaw we did miss 'im. He were a right favorite."

I looked at the broken nails on the edge of the cap, at the decent, honest, uncomplicated Yorkshire[18] face so like the many I had grown to like and respect. Farm men like him got thirty shillings a week in those days and it was reflected in the threadbare jacket, the cracked, shiny boots and the obvious hand-me-downs of the boys.

But all three were scrubbed and tidy, the man's face like a red beacon, the children's knees gleaming and their hair carefully slicked across their foreheads. They looked like nice people to me. I didn't know what to say.

Helen said it for me. "Well, Mr. Gibbons." Her tone had an unnatural brightness. "You'd better take him."

The man hesitated. "Now then, are ye sure, Missis Herriot?"

"Yes . . . yes, I'm sure. He was your cat first."

"Aye, but some folks 'ud say finders keepers or summat like that. Ah didn't come 'ere to demand 'im back or owt of t'sort."

"I know you didn't, Mr. Gibbons, but you've had him all those

Literary Analysis
Character Traits What character traits do the narrator and his wife have in common with Sep Gibbons?

Reading Strategy
Interpreting idioms What is a "right favorite"?

Reading Check

Who is Sep Gibbons?

---

18. **Yorkshire** region of northern England

years and you've searched for him so hard. We couldn't possibly keep him from you."

He nodded quickly. "Well, that's right good of ye." He paused for a moment, his face serious, then he stooped and picked Oscar up. "We'll have to be off if we're goin' to catch the eight o'clock bus."

Helen reached forward, cupped the cat's head in her hands and looked at him steadily for a few seconds. Then she patted the boys' heads. "You'll take good care of him, won't you?"

"Aye, missis, thank ye, we will that." The two small faces looked up at her and smiled.

"I'll see you down the stairs, Mr. Gibbons," I said.

On the descent I tickled the furry cheek resting on the man's shoulder and heard for the last time the rich purring. On the front door step we shook hands and they set off down the street. As they rounded the corner of Trengate they stopped and waved, and I waved back at the man, the two children and the cat's head looking back at me over the shoulder.

It was my habit at that time in my life to mount the stairs two or three at a time but on this occasion I trailed upwards like an old man, slightly breathless, throat tight, eyes prickling.

I cursed myself for a sentimental fool but as I reached our door I found a flash of consolation. Helen had taken it remarkably well. She had nursed that cat and grown deeply attached to him, and I'd have thought an unforeseen calamity like this would have upset her terribly. But no, she had behaved calmly and rationally.

It was up to me to do as well. I adjusted my features into the semblance of a cheerful smile and marched into the room.

Helen had pulled a chair close to the table and was slumped face down against the wood. One arm cradled her head while the other was stretched in front of her as her body shook with an utterly abandoned weeping.

I had never seen her like this and I was appalled. I tried to say something comforting but nothing stemmed the flow of racking sobs.

Feeling helpless and inadequate I could only sit close to her and stroke the back of her head. Maybe I could have said something if I hadn't felt just about as bad myself.

You get over these things in time. After all, we told ourselves, it wasn't as though Oscar had died or got lost again—he had gone to a good family who would look after him. In fact he had really gone home.

And of course, we still had our much-loved Sam, although he didn't help in the early stages by sniffing disconsolately where Oscar's bed used to lie then collapsing on the rug with a long lugubrious sigh.

There was one other thing, too. I had a little notion forming in my mind, an idea which I would spring on Helen when the time

Literary Analysis
Character Traits What character traits does Helen show by not making a fuss when Sep and his boys take Oscar?

was right. It was about a month after that shattering night and we were coming out of the cinema at Brawton at the end of our half day. I looked at my watch.

"Only eight o'clock," I said. "How about going to see Oscar?"

Helen looked at me in surprise. "You mean—drive on to Wederly?"

"Yes, it's only about five miles."

A smile crept slowly across her face. "That would be lovely. But do you think they would mind?"

"The Gibbons? No, I'm sure they wouldn't. Let's go."

Wederly was a big village and the plowman's cottage was at the far end a few yards beyond the Methodist chapel. I pushed open the garden gate and we walked down the path.

A busy-looking little woman answered my knock. She was drying her hands on a striped towel.

"Mrs. Gibbons?" I said.

"Aye, that's me."

"I'm James Herriot—and this is my wife."

Her eyes widened uncomprehendingly. Clearly the name meant nothing to her.

"We had your cat for a while," I added.

Suddenly she grinned and waved her towel at us. "Oh aye, ah remember now. Sep told me about you. Come in, come in!"

The big kitchen-living room was a tableau[19] of life with six children and thirty shillings a week. Battered furniture, rows of much-mended washing on a pulley, black cooking range and a general air of chaos.

Sep got up from his place by the fire, put down his newspaper, took off a pair of steel-rimmed spectacles and shook hands.

He waved Helen to a sagging armchair. "Well, it's right nice to see you. Ah've often spoke of ye to t'missis."

His wife hung up her towel. "Yes, and I'm glad to meet ye both. I'll get some tea in a minnit."

She laughed and dragged a bucket of muddy water into a corner. "I've been washin' football jerseys. Them lads just handed them to me tonight—as if I haven't enough to do."

As she ran the water into the kettle I peeped <u>surreptitiously</u> around me and I noticed Helen doing the same. But we searched in vain. There was no sign of a cat. Surely he couldn't have run away again? With a growing feeling of dismay I realized that my little scheme could backfire devastatingly.

It wasn't until the tea had been made and poured that I dared to raise the subject.

"How—" I asked diffidently. "How is—er—Tiger?"

"Oh, he's grand," the little woman replied briskly. She glanced up

---

19. **tableau** (tab´ lō) *n.* dramatic scene or picture.

Literary Analysis
Character Traits
Describe two character traits of Mrs. Gibbons.

surreptitiously
(sur´ əp tish´ əs lē) *adv.*
secretly

Reading Check

Why do Helen and Jim drive to Wederly?

at the clock on the mantelpiece. "He should be back any time now, then you'll be able to see 'im."

As she spoke, Sep raised a finger. "Ah think ah can hear 'im now."

He walked over and opened the door and our Oscar strode in with all his old grace and majesty. He took one look at Helen and leaped onto her lap. With a cry of delight she put down her cup and stroked the beautiful fur as the cat arched himself against her hand and the familiar purr echoed round the room.

"He knows me," she murmured. "He knows me."

Sep nodded and smiled. "He does that. You were good to 'im. He'll never forget ye, and we won't either, will we mother?"

"No, we won't, Mrs. Herriot," his wife said as she applied butter to a slice of gingerbread. "That was a kind thing ye did for us and I 'ope you'll come and see us all whenever you're near."

"Well, thank you," I said. "We'd love to—we're often in Brawton."

I went over and tickled Oscar's chin, then I turned again to Mrs. Gibbons. "By the way, it's after nine o'clock. Where has he been till now?"

She poised her butter knife and looked into space.

"Let's see, now," she said. "It's Thursday, isn't it? Ah yes, it's 'is night for the Yoga class."

Review and Assess

Thinking About the Selection

1. **Respond:** How have you felt when, like the Herriots, you've had to give up something that meant a lot to you?

2. **(a) Recall:** What does the cat do that prevents the men from putting him "out of his misery"? **(b) Connect:** How does this hint at the cat's personality and future actions?

3. **(a) Recall:** Name three things that are done to care for the cat after its operation. **(b) Infer:** What does this say about the personalities of the caretakers? **(c) Criticize:** Were they wise to spend such effort on the cat? Explain your answer.

4. **(a) Recall:** Which three people bring Oscar home to the Herriots after he has gone out to socialize? **(b) Distinguish:** What makes each of these characters distinct?
   (c) Generalize: Based on the characters in the story, describe the community the Herriots live in.

5. **(a) Interpret:** How do the Herriots feel after returning Oscar to the Gibbons family? **(b) Evaluate:** Do you think they made the right choice? Why? **(c) Synthesize:** What does the selection say about the relationship between people and animals?

James Herriot

(1916–1995)
While still in his early twenties, James Herriot became a veterinarian. It wasn't until his fifties that he combined his two loves—animals and writing—into the first of his books, *All Creatures Great and Small*. This work served as the basis for a television series.

Herriot was so dedicated to his work that he never even took a day off at Christmas. At the time he was writing, British veterinarians were not allowed to advertise, so Herriot, who was born James Alfred Wright, adopted a pen name. This allowed him to publish accounts of his experiences.

Herriot continued to work into his seventies. The essay "Cat on the Go" comes from his book *All Things Wise and Wonderful*.

Review and Assess

Literary Analysis

Character Traits

1. What are two of Oscar's **character traits**? Give examples of his behavior that illustrate his traits.

2. Describe two character traits of Septimus. Support your answer with examples from the selection.

3. Helen and Jim share the character trait of respect for people and animals. Give examples of how their words and actions illustrate this trait.

Connecting Literary Elements

4. Complete this chart, giving Standard English "translations" of the **dialect.**

Septimus's Words	Standard English
Aye, ah knaw, but cats is funny things.	
Hello, awd lad.	
It's 'im awright, and don't 'e look well!	
Ah've often spoke of ye to t'missis.	

5. Why does Herriot use nonstandard spelling for some of the character's words?

Reading Strategy

Interpreting Idioms

6. Name three **idioms,** or unusual expressions, that Herriot uses.

7. Use a chart like the one below to decipher the meaning of each expression.

Idiom	Clues	Meaning
hard-boiled attitude	contrasted with a deep affection for cats	realistic, not sentimental
right bonny		
high stepper		
went missing		

Extend Understanding

8. **Career Connection:** Based on what you have read, would you be interested in a career in veterinary medicine? Why or why not?

Quick Review

Character traits are the qualities that make an individual unique. To review character traits, see page 341.

Dialect is the form of a language spoken by a group of people in a particular region. To review dialect, see page 341.

An **idiom** is a use of words particular to a certain language or region. To review idioms, see page 341.

 Take It to the Net
www.phschool.com
Take the interactive self-test online to check your understanding of the selection.

Integrate Language Skills

Vocabulary Development Lesson

Word Analysis: Latin Prefix *in-*

The Latin prefix *in-* often means "not." When Herriot states that infection is *inevitable*, he means it is not avoidable (*evitable* means "avoidable"). Add the prefix *in-* to these words. Then, write sentences using the new words.

1. consistent (following the same pattern)
2. capable (able; skilled)
3. sincere (honest; truthful)

Spelling Strategy

In words such as *distraught*, the letters *gh* are silent. Finish these sentences with words that follow this rule.

1. I th___?___ I asked you to feed the cat.
2. Mrs. Herriot f___?___ back tears.
3. The dr___?___ caused a terrible water shortage.

Fluency: Sentence Completion

Use the vocabulary words from the list on page 341 to complete these sentences.

1. The cat ___?___ into the room gracefully.
2. The movie's complicated plot ___?___ me.
3. The child became so ___?___ that he cried.
4. After a crash diet, he looked ___?___.
5. Intestines spilled ___?___ onto the table.
6. During winter in Alaska, snow is ___?___.
7. Stealing glances, she looked at him ___?___
8. When the cat left, the family became ___?___.

Grammar Lesson

Compound Subjects and Predicates

A **compound subject** is made of two or more subjects that share the same verb.

COMPOUND SUBJECT
[*Tristan* and *I*] looked down at the shattered animal.

A **compound predicate** contains two or more verbs that share the same subject.

COMPOUND PREDICATE
I [*shrugged* and *shook*] my head.

Both compound subjects and compound predicates are joined by conjunctions, such as *and* or *or*, as in the examples above.

▶ *For more practice, see page R30, Exercise A.*
Practice Copy the sentences. Underline compound subjects once and compound predicates twice. Not all sentences have compounds.

1. Tristan unscrewed the cap and held it.
2. Beef essence, strained broth, and baby food found their way down his throat.
3. I ran downstairs and around the corner.
4. Helen and James returned Oscar to Sep and the boys.
5. Oscar runs or walks to the meetings.

Writing Application Write six sentences about the narrative: three with compound subjects and three with compound predicates.

W̶G̶ Prentice Hall Writing and Grammar Connection: Chapter 19, Sections 2 and 3

Writing Lesson

Character Sketch

A character sketch is a written description of a character. It conveys a main impression about a complex character by focusing on his or her major traits. Write a character sketch about a human or animal character in "Cat on the Go."

Prewriting   Choose your character, and then review the story to find his or her three main character traits. Support each trait with details from the text. Use a web like the one below to organize your thoughts.

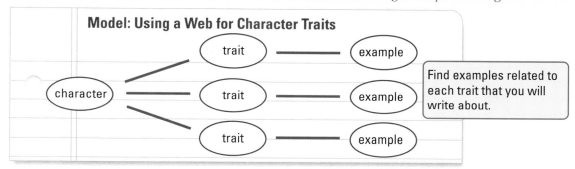

Model: Using a Web for Character Traits

Find examples related to each trait that you will write about.

Drafting   In the introduction, tell who your character is and make a general descriptive statement about the character. In the body of the sketch, discuss the three character traits you listed above. Include brief quotations from the selection to illustrate your points. Conclude by making a statement that pulls together the points you made.

Revising   Make sure you have provided evidence for all three traits. If necessary, provide additional examples of the character's words or actions.

 Prentice Hall Writing and Grammar Connection: Chapter 6, Section 3

Extension Activities

Listening and Speaking **Interview** a veterinarian to find out more about his or her job. As you conduct the interview, look for clues that indicate the speaker's attitude toward the subjects he or she discusses.

1. Listen carefully. Do not interrupt.
2. Ask questions if a word or idea is unfamiliar.
3. Use a tape recorder or take notes.
4. Thank the veterinarian at the end of the interview.

Research and Technology Oscar's trips to meetings and social gatherings would have been easier to plan if he had had a directory of such destinations. In a group, research events and activities in your community. Then, organize the information in a **directory**.

 **Take It to the Net**   www.phschool.com

Go online for an additional research activity using the Internet.

Prepare to Read

The Luckiest Time of All ◆ in Just- ◆ The Microscope
Sarah Cynthia Sylvia Stout Would Not Take the Garbage Out
Father William

 Take It to the Net

Visit www.phschool.com for interactive activities and instruction related to these selections, including
- background
- graphic organizers
- literary elements
- reading strategies

Preview

Connecting to the Literature

The selections in this grouping find humor and happiness in everyday life. As you read, think about whether the quirky characters or comical situations remind you of people you have known or events you have experienced.

Background

Dialect is a form of language spoken by people in a specific region or group. Dialects differ from standard language in pronunciation, grammar, and word choice. In "The Luckiest Time of All," Lucille Clifton uses a dialect from the rural South, including words such as *usta* for "used to" and *nothin* for "nothing." Dialect gives a story the sound of actual speech.

Literary Analysis

Hyperbole

Everyday language is full of **hyperbole**, or exaggeration for effect. When you say, "I haven't seen you for ages" or "I'm hungry enough to eat a horse," you are using hyperbole. Writers use this technique to create humor or emphasize a point. For example, Lucille Clifton uses hyperbole when she describes being chased by a dog:

> He lit out after me and I *flew*!

In the humorous selections that follow, notice how the writers use hyperbole to create humor.

Comparing Literary Works

An **author's style** is the unique and individual way that he or she uses language to express ideas. Hyperbole is just one of many language "tools" a writer can use to develop a unique style. Look at the ways each writer in this group uses language. Compare and contrast the writers' styles by thinking about the following focus questions:

1. How formal or informal is the language in the works?
2. How simple or sophisticated is each writer's vocabulary and sentence structure?

Reading Strategy

Clarifying and Verifying Word Meanings

When you are not sure of a word's meaning, use the context, or surrounding words and sentences, to **clarify**, or clear up, its meaning. Sometimes, you may have an idea about a word's meaning. In these cases, context can help you **verify**, or confirm, the meaning. Use clues like these:

- **Definition:** tells what the word means
- **Example:** shows what the word means
- **Restatement:** uses another word to say the same meaning
- **Contrast:** reveals meaning by showing what the meaning is not

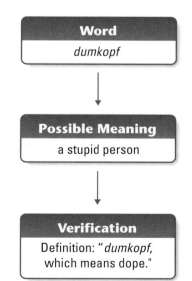

Vocabulary Development

withered (with´ ərd) *adj.* dried up (p. 366)

curdled (kʉr´ dəld) *adj.* thickened; clotted (p. 367)

rancid (ran´ sid) *adj.* spoiled and smelling bad (p. 367)

incessantly (in ses´ ənt lē) *adv.* without stopping (p. 369)

sage (sāj) *n.* very wise person (p. 369)

supple (sup´ əl) *adj.* flexible (p. 369)

The Luckiest Time of All

Lucille Clifton

Mrs. Elzie F. Pickens was rocking slowly on the porch one afternoon when her Great-granddaughter, Tee, brought her a big bunch of dogwood blooms, and that was the beginning of a story.

"Ahhh, now that dogwood reminds me of the day I met your Great-granddaddy, Mr. Pickens, Sweet Tee.

"It was just this time, spring of the year, and me and my best friend Ovella Wilson, who is now gone, was goin to join the Silas Greene. Usta be a kinda show went all through the South, called it the Silas Greene show. Somethin like the circus. Me and Ovella wanted to join that thing and see the world. Nothin wrong at home or nothin, we just wanted to travel and see new things and have high times. Didn't say nothin to nobody but one another. Just up and decided to do it.

"Well, this day we plaited our hair and put a dress and some things in a crokasack[1] and started out to the show. Spring day like this.

"We got there after a good little walk and it was the world, Baby, such music and wonders as we never had seen! They had everything there, or seemed like it.

"Me and Ovella thought we'd walk around for a while and see the show before goin to the office to sign up and join.

"While we was viewin it all we come up on this dancin dog. Cutest one thing in the world next to you, Sweet Tee, dippin and movin and head bowin to that music. Had a little ruffly skirt on itself and up on two back legs twistin and movin to the music. Dancin dancin dancin till people started throwin pennies out of they pockets.

"Me and Ovella was caught up too and laughin so. She took a penny out of her pocket and threw it to the ground where that dog was dancin, and I took two pennies and threw 'em both.

"The music was faster and faster and that dog was turnin and turnin. Ovella reached in her sack and threw out a little pin she had won from never being late at Sunday school. And me, laughin and all excited, reached in my bag and threw out my lucky stone!

"Well, I knew right off what I had done. Soon as it left my hand it seemed like I reached back out for it to take it back. But the stone was gone from my hand and Lord, it hit that dancin dog right on his nose!

"Well, he lit out after me, poor thing. He lit out after me and I flew! Round and round the Silas Greene we run, through every place me and Ovella had walked before, but now that dancin dog was a runnin dog and all the people was laughin at the new show, which was us!

"I felt myself slowin down after a while and I thought I would turn around a little bit to see how much gain that cute little dog was makin on me. When I did I got such a surprise! Right behind me was the dancin dog and right behind him was the finest fast runnin hero in the bottoms of Virginia.

"And that was Mr. Pickens when he was still a boy! He had a length of twine in his hand and he was twirlin it around in the air just like the cowboy at the Silas Greene and grinnin fit to bust.

"While I was watchin how the sun shined on him and made him look like an angel come to help a poor sinner girl, why, he twirled that twine one extra fancy twirl and looped it right around one hind leg of that dancin dog and brought him low.

Literary Analysis
Hyperbole What does Clifton mean by calling the circus show "the world"?

Reading Strategy
Clarifying Word Meaning What restatement does the author use to say "lit out" in other words?

Reading Check

Who saves Mrs. Pickens from the dog?

---

1. crokasack (krō′ kər sak) *usually spelled croker sack, n.* bag made of burlap or similar material.

"I stopped then and walked slow and shy to where he had picked up that poor dog to see if he was hurt, cradlin him and talkin to him soft and sweet. That showed me how kind and gentle he was, and when we walked back to the dancin dog's place in the show he let the dog loose and helped me to find my stone. I told him how shiny black it was and how it had the letter A scratched on one side. We searched and searched and at last he spied it!

"Ovella and me lost heart for shows then and we walked on home. And a good little way, the one who was gonna be your Great-granddaddy was walkin on behind. Seein us safe. Us walkin kind of slow. Him seein us safe. Yes." Mrs. Pickens' voice trailed off softly and Tee noticed she had a little smile on her face.

"Grandmama, that stone almost got you bit by a dog that time. It wasn't so lucky that time, was it?"

Tee's Great-grandmother shook her head and laughed out loud.

"That was the luckiest time of all, Tee Baby. It got me acquainted with Mr. Amos Pickens, and if that ain't luck, what could it be! Yes, it was luckier for me than for anybody, I think. Least mostly I think it."

Tee laughed with her Great-grandmother though she didn't exactly know why.

"I hope I have that kind of good stone luck one day," she said.

"Maybe you will someday," her Great-grandmother said.

And they rocked a little longer and smiled together.

Review and Assess

Thinking About the Selection

1. **Respond:** Have you ever met someone "by chance," the way Elzie met Mr. Pickens? What happened?

2. **(a) Recall:** Why do Ovella and Elzie go to the Silas Greene show? **(b) Infer:** What does this tell you about Elzie as a young woman? **(c) Connect:** In what ways is Elzie similar or different as an older woman?

3. **(a) Recall:** When does Elzie first see Mr. Pickens? **(b) Infer:** What is his real intention in saving Elzie from the dog? **(c) Analyze:** How does Elzie know that Mr. Pickens is a good man?

4. **(a) Recall:** What happens when Elzie throws her lucky stone? **(b) Analyze:** Why does Tee say the stone "wasn't so lucky that time"? **(c) Draw Conclusions:** Why does Elzie call that time "the luckiest time of all"?

5. **(a) Infer:** Would you say that Elzie has been happy with her life? Support your opinion with examples. **(b) Synthesize:** What might Tee learn from her great-grandmother's story?

Lucille Clifton

(b. 1936)
   Lucille Clifton has worked hard to overcome discrimination and become a successful writer. Whether in poetry or prose, she often writes about the value of sharing family traditions. Clifton's best-known work is *Generations*, a poetic memoir based on five generations of her family.

in Just-

E. E. Cummings

in Just-
spring   when the world is mud-
luscious the little
lame balloonman

5   whistles   far   and wee

and eddieandbill come
running from marbles and
piracies and it's
spring

10 when the world is puddle-wonderful

the queer
old balloonman whistles
far   and   wee
and bettyandisbel come dancing

15 from hop-scotch and jump-rope and

it's
spring
and
    the

20   goat-footed

balloonMan   whistles
far
and
wee

Review and Assess

Thinking About the Selections

1. **Respond:** What memories of spring does "in Just-" evoke for you?

2. **(a) Recall:** What event does the poem "in Just-" describe? **(b) Interpret:** What does Cummings mean when he says the world is "mud-luscious" and "puddle-wonderful"? **(c) Analyze:** Why do you think Cummings uses these unusual adjectives?

3. **(a) Recall:** Who are eddieandbill, and what are they doing when they hear the whistle? **(b) Interpret:** What is the effect of Cummings's writing "eddieandbill" instead of "Eddie and Bill?" **(c) Synthesize:** How does Cummings's playful use of language add to his picture of spring?

4. **(a) Interpret:** How does the description of the balloonman change throughout the poem? **(b) Draw Conclusions:** What makes the balloonman appealing to the children?

E. E. Cummings

(1894–1962)

Edward Estlin Cummings's poetry shows his original use of language and uncommon use of punctuation. His style caused much controversy during his lifetime, and this controversy continues today.

The Microscope

Maxine Kumin

Anton Leeuwenhoek was Dutch.
He sold pincushions, cloth, and such.
The waiting townsfolk fumed and fussed
As Anton's dry goods gathered dust.

5   He worked, instead of tending store,
At grinding special lenses for
A microscope. Some of the things
He looked at were:
                    mosquitoes' wings,
the hairs of sheep, the legs of lice,
10 the skin of people, dogs, and mice;
ox eyes, spiders' spinning gear,
fishes' scales, a little smear
of his own blood,
                    and best of all,
the unknown, busy, very small
15 bugs that swim and bump and hop
inside a simple water drop.

Impossible! Most Dutchmen said.
This Anton's crazy in the head.
We ought to ship him off to Spain.
20 He says he's seen a housefly's brain.
He says the water that we drink
Is full of bugs. He's mad, we think!

They called him *dumkopf*, which means dope.
That's how we got the microscope.

▲ **Critical Viewing**
How might Leeuwenhoek's microscope have compared with the one pictured here? Explain. **[Speculate]**

Review and Assess

Thinking About the Selections

1. **Respond:** Do you find microscopes interesting? Why or why not?
2. **(a) Recall:** What is Leeuwenhoek's occupation and what is his hobby? **(b) Compare and Contrast:** Which does Leeuwenhoek seem to enjoy more?
3. **(a) Recall:** What do the townspeople say about Leeuwenhoek? **(b) Infer:** Why do they think he is a "dumkopf"? **(c) Analyze:** What do you know now that they didn't know then?

Maxine Kumin

(b. 1925)
Maxine Kumin writes children's books, fiction, nonfiction, and poetry. She often plays with the lines in her poems to create a look that reflects the subject of her writing.

Sarah Cynthia Sylvia Stout Would Not Take the Garbage Out

Shel Silverstein

Sarah Cynthia Sylvia Stout
Would not take the garbage out!
She'd scour[1] the pots and scrape the pans,
Candy[2] the yams and spice the hams,
5 And though her daddy would scream and shout,
She simply would not take the garbage out.
And so it piled up to the ceilings:
Coffee grounds, potato peelings,
Brown bananas, rotten peas,
10 Chunks of sour cottage cheese.
It filled the can, it covered the floor,
It cracked the window and blocked the door
With bacon rinds[3] and chicken bones,
Drippy ends of ice cream cones,
15 Prune pits, peach pits, orange peel,
Gloppy glumps of cold oatmeal,
Pizza crusts and <u>withered</u> greens,
Soggy beans and tangerines,
Crusts of black burned buttered toast,
20 Gristly bits of beefy roasts . . .
The garbage rolled on down the hall,
It raised the roof, it broke the wall . . .
Greasy napkins, cookie crumbs,
Globs of gooey bubblegum,

withered (with´ ərd) *adj.*
dried up

---

1. scour (skour) *v.* clean by rubbing vigorously.
2. candy (kan´ dē) *v.* coat with sugar.
3. rinds (rīndz) *n.* tough outer layers or skins.

25 Cellophane from green baloney,
  Rubbery blubbery macaroni,
  Peanut butter, caked and dry,
  <u>Curdled</u> milk and crusts of pie,
  Moldy melons, dried up mustard,
30 Eggshells mixed with lemon custard,
  Cold french fries and <u>rancid</u> meat,
  Yellow lumps of Cream of Wheat.
  At last the garbage reached so high
  That finally it touched the sky.
35 And all the neighbors moved away,
  And none of her friends would come to play.
  And finally Sarah Cynthia Stout said,
  "OK, I'll take the garbage out!"
  But then, of course, it was too late
40 The garbage reached across the state,
  From New York to the Golden Gate
  And there, in the garbage she did hate,
  Poor Sarah met an awful fate,
  That I cannot right now relate[4]
45 Because the hour is much too late.
  But children, remember Sarah Stout
  And always take the garbage out!

---

4. relate (ri lāt′) *v.* tell.

curdled (kʉr′ dəld) *adj.*
thickened; clotted

rancid (ran′ sid) *adj.*
spoiled and smelling bad

◀ **Critical Viewing** The
author created the
illustrations accompanying
the poem. How does the
art enhance the humor of
the poem? **[Assess]**

Review and Assess

Thinking About the Selection

1. **Respond:** Do you sympathize more with Sarah or her father?
   Why?
2. **(a) Recall:** What happens to the garbage in Sarah's house?
   (b) Identify Cause and Effect: Why does it happen?
3. **(a) Recall:** What happens at the end of the poem?
   (b) Infer: Why might the poet have left out Sarah's "awful
   fate"? **(c) Speculate:** What do you think happened to
   Sarah?
4. **(a) Recall:** Find two lines in the poem that do not rhyme.
   (b) Interpret: What is the effect of this break in rhyme?
5. **(a) Infer:** What lesson might readers learn from the poem?
   (b) Analyze: Do you think the poet intended to teach a
   lesson? Why or why not? **(c) Generalize:** Can a humorous
   poem teach a lesson? Explain your answer.

Shel Silverstein

(1932–1999)
   Shel Silverstein
was a cartoonist,
a composer, a folk
singer, and a
writer. He is best
known to people
of all ages for two
books of poetry, *Where the
Sidewalk Ends* and *A Light in
the Attic.* Although his
poems are humorous, they
contain a message for all.

Father William

Lewis Carroll

▲ **Critical Viewing** Which stanza or group of lines does this drawing illustrate? **[Connect]**

"You are old, Father William," the young man said,
  "And your hair has become very white;
And yet you <u>incessantly</u> stand on your head—
  Do you think, at your age, it is right?"

incessantly (in ses´ ənt lē) *adv.* without stopping

5   "In my youth," Father William replied to his son,
  "I feared it might injure the brain;
But, now that I'm perfectly sure I have none,
  Why, I do it again and again."
"You are old," said the youth, "as I mentioned before.
10   And have grown most uncommonly[1] fat;
Yet you turned a back-somersault in at the door—
  Pray, what is the reason of that?"

"In my youth," said the <u>sage</u>, as he shook his gray locks,
  "I kept all my limbs very <u>supple</u>
15 By the use of this ointment—one shilling[2] the box—
  Allow me to sell you a couple?"

sage (sāj) *n.* very wise man

supple (sup´ əl) *adj.* flexible

"You are old," said the youth, "and your jaws are too weak
  For anything tougher than suet;[3]
Yet you finished the goose, with the bones and the beak—
20   Pray, how did you manage to do it?"
"In my youth," said his father, "I took to the law,
  And argued each case with my wife;
And the muscular strength, which it gave to my jaw
  Has lasted the rest of my life."

25 "You are old," said the youth, "one would hardly suppose
  That your eye was as steady as ever;
Yet you balanced an eel on the end of your nose—
  What made you so awfully clever?"

✔Reading Check

Why is Father William able
to turn somersaults?

---
1. **uncommonly** (un käm´ ən lē) *adv.* remarkably.
2. **shilling** (shil´ iŋ) *n.* British coin.
3. **suet** (so͞o´ it) *n.* fat used in cooking.

You Are Old Father William II, 1865, Sir John Tenniel

"I have answered three questions, and that is enough,"
30   Said his father. "Don't give yourself airs!
Do you think I can listen all day to such stuff?
      Be off, or I'll kick you downstairs!"

Review and Assess

Thinking About the Selection

1. **Respond:** Which of Father William's replies do you think is the most ridiculous? Why?
2. **(a) Recall:** What four questions does the son ask his father?
   (b) Infer: What do all four questions have in common?
   (c) Draw Conclusions: What does the son believe is appropriate behavior for an older person such as his father?
3. **(a) Recall:** Use details from the poem to describe Father William's appearance. **(b) Support:** How does his appearance make his actions seem especially surprising?
4. **(a) Compare and Contrast:** In what ways is this conversation typical of a conversation between a parent and a child?
   (b) Analyze: In what ways is it unusual for a conversation between a parent and a child?
5. **(a) Infer:** Why does the father refuse to answer more questions at the end? **(b) Make a Judgment:** Do you think he is justified in ending the conversation? Explain.

Lewis Carroll

(1832–1898)

Lewis Carroll is the pen name of Charles Dodgson, a mathematics professor who was born in England. Under his pen name, Dodgson wrote *Alice's Adventures in Wonderland* and *Through the Looking Glass*. His poems are noted for their clever wordplay, nonsensical meanings, and delightfully zany fantasy worlds.

Review and Assess

Literary Analysis

Hyperbole

1. Identify one example of **hyperbole** in each selection.
2. In your opinion, which of Father William's behaviors is exaggerated the most? Explain.
3. Find three examples of hyperbole in "Sarah Cynthia Sylvia Stout." Enter each example in a chart like the one below.

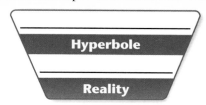

4. Why does hyperbole make people laugh?

Comparing Literary Works

5. How formal or informal is the language in each of these works?
6. To what extent do the writers overstate or understate their points?
7. How simple or sophisticated is each writer's vocabulary and sentence structure?
8. Which **author's style** do you prefer? Why?

Reading Strategy

Clarifying Word Meanings

9. In "The Luckiest Time of All," Elzie says that the dog "lit out after me." Based on the way it is used in the sentence, define the word *lit*.
10. Explain how you clarified the meaning of *lit* in item 9, above.
11. Write a sentence for each of the following words that includes words that define it as it is used in the selection.

    Example: The *youth* spoke to Father William in a way that a *young person* should not speak to an older person.
    - (a) limbs ("Father William")
    - (b) steady ("Father William")
    - (c) fumed ("The Microscope")

Extend Understanding

12. **Community Connection:** What local rules exist in your area to prevent Sarah's situation from actually happening?

Quick Review

Hyperbole is exaggeration for effect. To review hyperbole, see page 359.

An **author's style** is the unique way he or she uses language to express ideas. To review author's style, see page 359.

To **clarify** means to make clear. To **verify** means to confirm.

 Take It to the Net
www.phschool.com
Take the interactive self-test online to check your understanding of these selections.

Integrate Language Skills

Vocabulary Development Lesson

Concept Development: Words With Multiple Meanings

Like *sage*, which can refer to a wise person or an herb, many words in English have multiple meanings. On your paper, explain the different meanings of the italicized words in each set of sentences.

1. Rice is a *staple* in their diet.
   One *staple* can't hold that many pages!
2. Fill the *pitcher* with iced tea.
   Give the *pitcher* the ball.
3. The children are going through a *stage*.
   The children are performing on a *stage*.
4. The world warms up in *Spring*.
   The children *spring* from their hiding places.
   The *spring* was coming through the seat of the chair.

Fluency: Definitions

Explain the answer to each question.

1. Is a faucet that drips *incessantly* wasteful?
2. Is a baseball bat smooth and *supple*?
3. Is *curdled* milk good for drinking?
4. Would you listen to the advice of a *sage*?
5. Might black bananas be *rancid*?
6. Would a *withered* salad be appetizing?

Spelling Strategy

Use word association to help you remember unexpected spellings such as *g* for the *j* sound. Complete each sentence with one of these words: *image, sage, rage.*

1. The ___?___ fades with age.
2. The ___?___ has wisdom and age.
3. Do not ___?___ at increasing age.

Make up your own word association sentence using *age* with *stage*.

Grammar Lesson

Complete and Incomplete Sentences

A **complete sentence** contains two parts: a subject and a verb. It also expresses a complete thought. If a sentence does not meet these requirements, it is an incomplete sentence and may be hard to understand. However, because people often do not speak in complete sentences, dialogue sometimes includes incomplete sentences.

S   V
Complete: Elzie rocked gently on the porch.

S
Incomplete: Spring day like this.

▶ *For more practice, see page R31, Exercise H.*
Practice Copy these examples on your paper. If an item is a complete sentence, underline the subject once and the verb twice. If it is not a sentence, write *incomplete*.

1. Tee brought her great-grandmother a bunch of dogwood blooms.
2. Something like the circus.
3. Between you and me, Father William.
4. When the world is puddle-wonderful.
5. He looked through the lenses.

Writing Application Add a subject or a verb to each incomplete sentence above to make the sentence complete.

W̸G̸ Prentice Hall Writing and Grammar Connection: Chapter 19, Section 1

Writing Lesson

Humorous Poem

Humorous poems can capture the comic side of life, describe absurd situations, or introduce funny characters. Write your own humorous poem about a memorable experience from your life.

Prewriting List words and phrases that describe the details associated with the experience. Use precise verbs that name specific actions. For example, use *tumbled* or *collapsed* instead of *fell*.

Drafting Set the pattern of rhyme you wish to use. If you plan to write without regular rhyme, consider how to shape your poem on the page. Then, refer to your list of key words as you draft your poem.

Revising Fine-tune words and lines to correct rhyme or physical shape. Feel free to create new words if you need them—or create them just for fun.

Model: Imaginative Words in a Poem

Betsy–Esther fussed in a fluster,

She fumed and huffed herself into a bluster.

She stomped until the staircase tumbled,

Until her family's ears were be-numbled.

> Precise verbs (such as *fussed* and *huffed*) and made-up words (such as *be-numbled* instead of *went numb*) can add humor.

W/G *Prentice Hall Writing and Grammar Connection: Chapter 4, Section 2*

Extension Activities

Listening and Speaking With a partner, act out a **dialogue** between two characters from different selections. The words used by each character should reflect the character's unique personality. Use speech, movements, expressions, and gestures to convey his or her characteristics.

Writing Write a **response** in which you tell which of the works you liked best and why.

Research and Technology Using the Internet and other library resources, learn about Leeuwenhoek's invention. Then, write an **explanation** of the significance of the microscope. Include quotations from your research to help you portray a clear and accurate perspective on the subject.

 **Take It to the Net**   www.phschool.com

Go online for an additional research activity using the Internet.

Government Publications

About Government Publications

Government publications are documents published by numerous offices within the federal, state, or local government. They can range from just a few pages to more than 100 pages long, and they are available free of charge or for a small fee. The government issues publications on a wide variety of topics. Some are published to give public access to details of government activity:

- Explanations of new or proposed legislation (laws)
- Details of budgets and spending

Other government publications are published as a public service. These give information that the public may find useful:

- Instructions for evaluating drinking water
- Guidelines for choosing a doctor

The publication on page 375 is published by the President's Council on Physical Fitness and Sports. Different government agencies publish documents on other subjects. Chances are good that, no matter what topic interests you, there is at least one government publication on that subject.

Reading Strategy

Identifying Cause and Effect

As you read the following government publication, look for cause-and-effect relationships among the informational details. Understanding how one behavior or circumstance affects another can help you comprehend and remember what you are reading. The cause-and-effect organization of the pamphlet makes benefits, consequences, and results clear and easy to understand. Use two charts like the one on this page to show the causes and effects you find in relation to walking for exercise and pleasure.

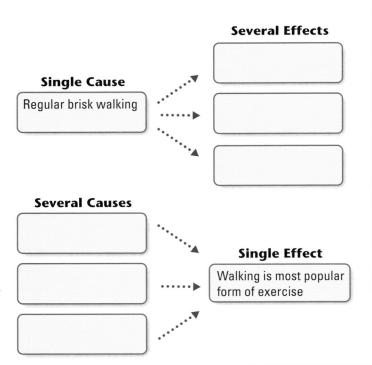

Several Effects

Single Cause

Regular brisk walking

Several Causes

Single Effect

Walking is most popular form of exercise

Walking for Exercise and Pleasure

The President's Council on Physical Fitness and Sports

Walking: An Exercise for All Ages

Walking is easily the most popular form of exercise. Other activities generate more conversation and media coverage, but none of them approaches walking in number of participants. Approximately half of the 165 million American adults (18 years of age and older) claim they exercise regularly, and the number who walk for exercise is increasing every year.

Walking is the only exercise in which the rate of participation does not decline in the middle and later years. In a national survey, the highest percentage of regular walkers (39.4%) for any group was found among men 65 years of age and older.

Unlike tennis, running, skiing, and other activities that have gained great popularity fairly recently, walking has been widely practiced as a recreational and fitness activity throughout recorded history. Classical and early English literature seems to have been written largely by men who were prodigious walkers, and Emerson and Thoreau helped carry on the tradition in America. Among American presidents, the most famous walkers included Jefferson, Lincoln, and Truman.

Walking: The Slower, Surer Way to Fitness

People walk for many reasons: for pleasure . . . to rid themselves of tensions . . . to find solitude . . . or to get from one place to another. Nearly everyone who walks regularly does so at least in part because of a conviction that it is good exercise.

Often dismissed in the past as being "too easy" to be taken seriously, walking recently has gained new respect as a means of improving physical fitness. Studies show that, when done briskly on a regular schedule, it can improve the body's ability to consume oxygen during exertion, lower the resting heart rate, reduce blood pressure, and increase the efficiency of the heart and lungs. It also helps burn excess calories.

Walking burns approximately the same amount of calories per mile as does running, a fact particularly appealing to those who find it difficult to sustain the jarring effects of long distance jogging. Briskly walking one mile in 15 minutes burns just about the same number of calories as jogging an equal distance in 8 1/2 minutes. In weight-bearing activities like walking, heavier individuals will burn more calories than lighter persons. For example, studies show that a 110-pound person burns about half as many calories as a 216-pound person walking at the same pace for the same distance.

In addition to the qualities it has in common with other activities, walking has several unique advantages. Some of these are:

Almost everyone can do it.
You don't have to take lessons to learn how to walk. Probably all you need to do to become a serious walker is step up your pace and distance and walk more often.

You can do it almost anywhere.
All you have to do to find a place to walk is step outside your door. Almost any sidewalk, street, road, trail, park, field, or shopping mall will do. The variety of settings available is one of the things that makes walking such a practical and pleasurable activity.

You can do it almost anytime.
You don't have to find a partner or get a team together to walk, so you can set your own schedule.

> These advantages may be reasons why walking is a popular exercise.

Weather doesn't pose the same problems and uncertainties that it does in many sports. Walking is not a seasonal activity, and you can do it in extreme temperatures that would rule out other activities.

It doesn't cost anything.
You don't have to pay fees or join a private club to become a walker. The only equipment required is a sturdy, comfortable pair of shoes.

Walking for Physical Fitness

Here are some tips to help you develop an efficient walking style:

- Hold head erect and keep back straight and abdomen flat. Toes should point straight ahead and arms should swing loosely at sides.

- Land on the heel of the foot and roll forward to drive off the ball of the foot. Walking only on the ball of the foot, or in a flat-footed style, may cause fatigue and soreness.

- Take long, easy strides, but don't strain for distance. When walking up or down hills, or at a very rapid pace, lean forward slightly.

- Breathe deeply (with mouth open, if that is more comfortable).

> Main points are often set off from the text visually: with italics, heavy dots (called bullets), or as a numbered list.

Listen to Your Body

Listen to your body when you walk. If you develop dizziness, pain, nausea, or any other unusual symptom, slow down or stop. If the problem persists, see your physician before walking again.

The most important thing is simply to set aside part of each day and walk. No matter what your age or condition, it's a practice that can make you healthier and happier.

> When giving instructions, government publications use short paragraphs and clear, direct language.

Check Your Comprehension

1. Approximately what percentage of the American population claims to exercise regularly?
2. Why has walking for exercise not been taken seriously in the past?
3. How does walking compare to running in burning calories?
4. Describe the characteristics of an efficient walking style.

Applying the Reading Strategy

Identifying Cause and Effect

5. What are three reasons that walking is a good exercise choice?
6. What are four effects of walking briskly on a regular schedule?
7. What steps do you need to take in order to become a serious walker?
8. What symptoms are causes for slowing or stopping a walk?

Activity

Directions for Exercise Equipment

A variety of equipment makes it possible to achieve the effects of a brisk walk, even when weather prevents you from going outside. Locate and read written directions about using a treadmill or other piece of exercise equipment you might find in your school gym or at a local gym or health club. Jot down notes about the steps involved in using the equipment safely and effectively, including the correct posture(s) to use, if given. Finally, complete a form like the one shown on this page. Add as many steps as necessary to provide simple but complete directions for using the equipment.

Piece of Equipment _____
Purpose for Using Equipment _____
Directions: _____
1. _____
2. _____
3. _____
Special Recommendations, Cautions, or Warnings: _____
_____

Comparing and Contrasting Informational Materials

Government Publications and Other Public Documents

Public documents such as tax information can usually be obtained on request at post offices and libraries. Find out what public documents can be obtained at your local library and post office. Compare and contrast one of the documents you obtain to the pamphlet on walking. Consider points such as sources, purpose, language level, and probable audience.

Prepare to Read

Zoo ◆ The Hippopotamus ◆ How the Snake Got Poison

Take It to the Net

Visit www.phschool.com
for interactive activities
and instruction related to
these selections, including

- background
- graphic organizers
- literary elements
- reading strategies

Preview

Connecting to the Literature

Which do you find more intriguing—fictional creatures from outer space or creatures such as the hippopotamus that live right here on Earth? In these selections, you will encounter both. As you read, think about what makes each creature unique.

Background

To help organize the study of the animal kingdom, scientists have developed a classification system. Animals are grouped in classes based on shared features. The hippopotamus belongs to the mammal class along with other animals that have backbones, warm blood, and hair. Snakes and other animals that have scales are classified as reptiles.

Literary Analysis

Character's Perspective

A **character's perspective,** the vantage point from which he or she views events, develops from his or her knowledge, abilities, and experiences. For example, in these lines from "Hippopotamus," two very different creatures see things from different perspectives:

> Behold the hippopotamus!
> We laugh at how he looks to us,
> And yet in moments dank and grim
> I wonder how we look to him.

Character	Perspective	Reaction
Humans	Mostly see other humans →	Hippos look funny.
Hippos	Mostly see other hippos →	People probably look funny.

Comparing Literary Works

The **tone** of a literary work is the writer's attitude toward its subject and characters. The tone can often be described in one word, such as *formal, playful,* or *serious.* Compare and contrast the tones of these works based on

- the ways the subjects or characters are presented.
- whether the writer establishes a personal relationship with readers.
- how the writer seems to want the reader to react.

Reading Strategy

Evaluating an Author's Message

The **author's message** is the idea that a writer wants to convey. For example, in "The Hippopotamus," Ogden Nash suggests that animals and humans each find beauty in their own species.

You can **evaluate an author's message** by first identifying the message and then judging whether it is true, clearly reasoned, and well supported. As you read, focus on these questions:

1. What message is each writer conveying?
2. How effectively does the writer support the message with details and examples?

Vocabulary Development

interplanetary (in′ tər plan′ ə ter′ ē) *adj.* between planets (p. 380)

wonderment (wun′ dər ment) *n.* astonishment (p. 380)

awe (ô) *n.* mixed feelings of fear and wonder (p. 380)

immensity (i men′ si tē) *n.* immeasurable largeness or vastness (p. 384)

ZOO

Edward D. Hoch

The children were always good during the month of August, especially when it began to get near the twenty-third. It was on this day that the great silver spaceship carrying Professor Hugo's Interplanetary Zoo settled down for its annual six-hour visit to the Chicago area.

Before daybreak the crowds would form, long lines of children and adults both, each one clutching his or her dollar and waiting with wonderment to see what race of strange creatures the Professor had brought this year.

In the past they had sometimes been treated to three-legged creatures from Venus, or tall, thin men from Mars, or even snake-like horrors from somewhere more distant. This year, as the great round ship settled slowly to earth in the huge tri-city parking area just outside of Chicago, they watched with awe as the sides slowly slid up to reveal the familiar barred cages. In them were some wild breed of nightmare—small, horse-like animals that moved with quick, jerking motions and constantly chattered in a high-pitched tongue. The citizens of Earth clustered around as Professor Hugo's crew quickly collected the waiting dollars, and soon the good Professor himself made an appearance, wearing his many-colored rainbow cape and top hat. "Peoples of Earth," he called into his microphone. The crowd's noise died down and he continued. "Peoples of Earth, this year you see a real treat for your single dollar—the little-known horse-spider

interplanetary
(in′ tər plan′ ə ter′ ē)
adj. between planets

wonderment
(wun′ dər ment)
n. astonishment

awe (ô) *n.* mixed feelings of fear and wonder

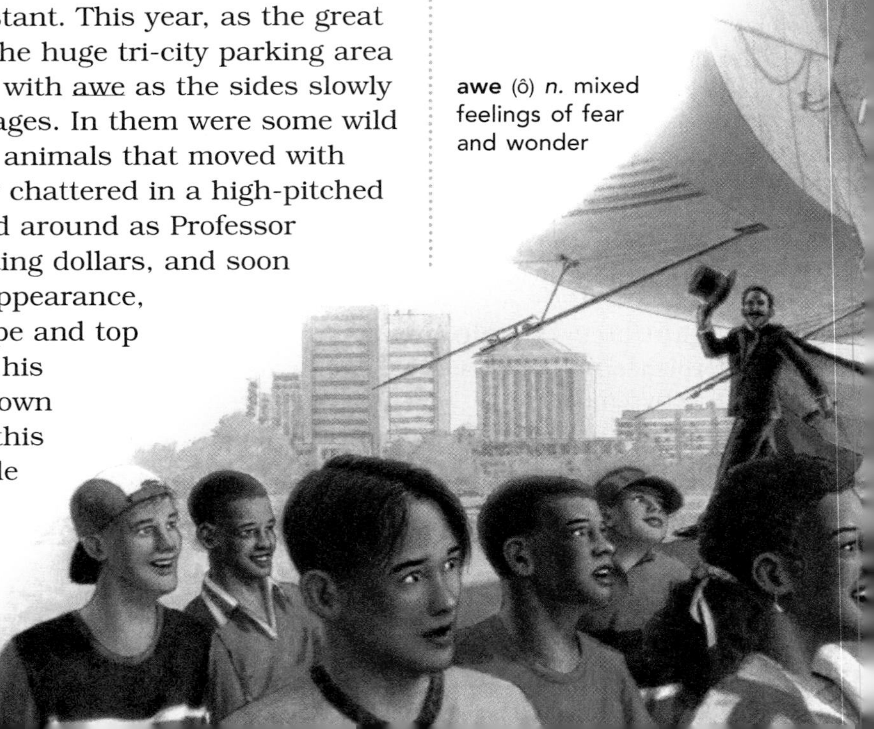

people of Kaan—brought to you across a million miles of space at great expense. Gather around, see them, study them, listen to them, tell your friends about them. But hurry! My ship can remain here only six hours!"

And the crowds slowly filed by, at once horrified and fascinated by these strange creatures that looked like horses but ran up the walls of their cages like spiders. "This is certainly worth a dollar," one man remarked, hurrying away. "I'm going home to get the wife."

All day long it went like that, until ten thousand people had filed by the barred cages set into the side of the spaceship. Then, as the six-hour limit ran out, Professor Hugo once more took the

✔ **Reading Check**

What kind of animals does Professor Hugo keep in his Interplanetary Zoo?

▼ **Critical Viewing** What is each group's reaction to the other? **[Analyze]**

microphone in hand. "We must go now, but we will return next year on this date. And if you enjoyed our zoo this year, telephone your friends in other cities about it. We will land in New York tomorrow, and next week on to London, Paris, Rome, Hong Kong, and Tokyo. Then on to other worlds!"

He waved farewell to them, and as the ship rose from the ground, the Earth peoples agreed that this had been the very best Zoo yet. . . .

Some two months and three planets later, the silver ship of Professor Hugo settled at last onto the familiar jagged rocks of Kaan, and the odd horse-spider creatures filed quickly out of their cages. Professor Hugo was there to say a few parting words, and then they scurried away in a hundred different directions, seeking their homes among the rocks.

In one house, the she-creature was happy to see the return of her mate and offspring. She babbled a greeting in the strange tongue and hurried to embrace them. "It was a long time you were gone. Was it good?"

And the he-creature nodded. "The little one enjoyed it especially. We visited eight worlds and saw many things."

The little one ran up the wall of the cave. "On the place called Earth it was the best. The creatures there wear garments over their skins, and they walk on two legs."

"But isn't it dangerous?" asked the she-creature.

"No," her mate answered. "There are bars to protect us from them. We remain right in the ship. Next time you must come with us. It is well worth the nineteen commocs it costs."

And the little one nodded. "It was the very best Zoo ever. . . ."

Review and Assess

Thinking About the Selection

1. **Respond:** Were you surprised by the ending of Hoch's story? Why or why not?

2. **(a) Recall:** Describe the creatures that Professor Hugo brings to Earth. **(b) Interpret:** Why does the crowd view the creatures as "some wild breed of nightmare"?
   (c) Draw Conclusions: What might this say about the way humans view things that look different from them?

3. **(a) Recall:** Describe how the mother creature greets her family when they return to the planet Kaan.
   (b) Generalize: What kind of family life do they seem to have?
   (c) Compare and Contrast: In what ways are the creatures similar to or different from the humans' view of them?

Edward D. Hoch

(b. 1930)
After graduating from college, Edward Hoch worked as a researcher and copy writer for an advertising agency. The skills he gained in those jobs have served him well as a writer of science-fiction and mystery stories and novels.

The Hippopotamus

Ogden Nash

Behold the hippopotamus!
We laugh at how he looks to us,
And yet in moments dank and grim
I wonder how we look to him.
5 Peace, peace, thou hippopotamus!
We really look all right to us,
As you no doubt delight the eye
Of other hippopotami.

▲ **Critical Viewing**
What features of the hippopotamus might someone find funny? **[Connect]**

Review and Assess

Thinking About the Selection

1. **(a) Analyze:** What is humorous about the poem "The Hippopotamus"? **(b) Support:** What unusual rhymes and words add to the humor in the poem? **(c) Speculate:** Why do you think Nash decided to treat this topic in a humorous way?

2. **(a) Recall:** In "The Hippopotamus," what is the point of view of the hippo? **(b) Analyze:** How does the hippo's point of view differ from that of the speaker? **(c) Synthesize:** What might this selection say about relating to creatures of any kind that are different from us?

Ogden Nash

(1902–1971)
Ogden Nash became famous for his ability to look at life from an unusual angle. Readers of all ages look to his work for fun and insight into life's absurdities. Packed with humor, his wise and witty poems continue to delight.

HOW THE SNAKE GOT POISON

Zora Neale Hurston

Well, when God made de snake he put him in de bushes to ornament de ground. But things didn't suit de snake so one day he got on de ladder and went up to see God.

"Good mawnin', God."

"How do you do, Snake?"

"Ah[1] ain't so many, God, you put me down here on my belly in de dust and everything trods upon me and kills off my generations. Ah ain't got no kind of protection at all."

God looked off towards <u>immensity</u> and thought about de subject for awhile, then he said, "Ah didn't mean for nothin' to be stompin' you snakes

immensity (i men´ si tē) *n.* immeasurable largeness or vastness

---

1. Ah dialect for "I."

lak dat. You got to have some kind of a protection. Here, take dis poison and put it in yo' mouf and when they tromps on you, protect yo'-self."

So de snake took de poison in his mouf and went on back.

So after awhile all de other varmints went up to God.

"Good evenin', God."

"How you makin' it, varmints?"

"God, please do somethin' 'bout dat snake. He' layin' in de bushes there wid poison in his mouf and he's strikin' everything dat shakes de bushes. He's killin' up our generations. Wese skeered to walk de earth."

So God sent for de snake and tole him:

"Snake, when Ah give you dat poison, Ah didn't mean for you to be hittin' and killin' everything dat shake de bush. I give you dat poison and tole you to protect yo'self when they tromples on you. But you killin' everything dat moves. Ah didn't mean for you to do dat."

De snake say, "Lawd, you know Ah'm down here in de dust. Ah ain't got no claws to fight wid, and Ah ain't got no feets to git me out

✔Reading Check

What is the snake's complaint?

◀ Critical Viewing
Does this snake look defenseless?
[Explain]

How the Snake Got Poison ◆ 385

de way. All Ah kin see is feets comin' to tromple me. Ah can't tell who my enemy is and who is my friend. You gimme dis protection in my mouf and Ah uses it."

God thought it over for a while then he says:

"Well, snake, I don't want yo' generations all stomped out and I don't want you killin' every-thing else dat moves. Here take dis bell and tie it to yo' tail. When you hear feets comin' you ring yo' bell and if it's yo' friend, he'll be keerful. If it's yo' enemy, it's you and him."

So dat's how de snake got his poison and dat's how come he got rattles.

Review and Assess

Thinking About the Selection

1. **Respond:** In this folk tale, there are arguments from two conflicting sides. What would you have done? Explain.

2. **(a) Recall:** Find three examples of dialect in the story.
   (b) Assess: Describe the overall effect of dialect.
   (c) Speculate: Why do you think Hurston chose to tell this story in dialect?

3. **(a) Infer:** What is God's first way of giving the snake protection? **(b) Analyze Cause and Effect:** How does this cause a problem for the varmints?

4. **(a) Recall:** What is God's attempt to solve the new problem? **(b) Infer:** How does this affect both the snake and the varmints? **(c) Analyze:** What seems most important to God in deciding how to handle the animals' problems?

5. **(a) Analyze:** Why didn't the varmints and the snake simply work out their problems together? **(b) Speculate:** What might this reveal about people and their ways of interacting? **(c) Apply:** How does this story illustrate the concept of "balance of nature"?

Zora Neale Hurston

(1891–1960)

In addition to writing both fiction and nonfiction, Zora Neale Hurston traveled through the South to collect African American folk tales such as "How the Snake Got Poison." Her writing preserved the exact language of the speaker, allowing Hurston to honor the oral tradition and bring the tales to a wider audience.

Review and Assess

Literary Analysis

Character's Perspective

1. Compare and contrast the **perspective** of the humans and the creatures from Kaan in "Zoo." Note at least two similarities and one difference.
2. How does your understanding of "Zoo" change when you see things from the **perspective** of the creatures from Kaan?
3. Show evidence that God understands the perspective of both the snake and the varmints in "How the Snake Got Poison."

Comparing Literary Works

4. Complete a chart like this one. Write the title of each work in each space that applies. You may have more than one title in a space. You may write a title in more than one space in a category.

Presentation	Silly	Fanciful	Strange
Relationship	Personal		Impersonal
Reaction	Laughter	Thought	Surprise

5. How would you describe the **tone** of each work compared to the others? Give details that support your answer.
6. How can an author's tone, or attitude toward the subject, affect the reader's attitude toward the subject?

Reading Strategy

Evaluating an Author's Message

7. What message is each writer conveying?
8. How effectively does the writer support the message with details and examples?

Extend Understanding

9. **Science Connection:** What facts about the hippopotamus would you include in a scientific description?

Quick Review

A **character's perspective** is the vantage point from which he or she views events. To review character's perspective, see page 379.

The **tone** of a literary work is the author's attitude toward his or her subject and readers. To review tone, see page 379.

The **author's message** is the main idea the author wants to convey. To review author's message, see page 379.

 Take It to the Net
www.phschool.com
Take the interactive self-test online to check your understanding of these selections.

Integrate Language Skills

Vocabulary Development Lesson

Word Analysis: Forms of *wonder*

Wonder has several related words. *Wonder* itself can be a noun or a verb. *Wonderment* is also a noun, and *wondrous* and *wonderful* are adjectives. *Wonderfully* and *wondrously* are adverbs.

On your paper, complete the following sentences with the appropriate form of *wonder*. Choose from *wonderment, wonderful, wondrous,* and *wondrously*.

1. The hippopotamus gazed with ___?___ at me.
2. Snake's poison was ___?___ effective.
3. A human being is a most ___?___ creature.
4. The story was a ___?___ one.

Fluency: Definitions

Explain your answer to each of the following questions.

1. Do the varmints view the snake with *wonderment?*
2. Would you be impressed by the *immensity* of a hippopotamus?
3. Is a flight from New York to Rome *interplanetary?*
4. What inspires a sense of *awe* in you?

Spelling Strategy

Before you add the suffix *-ity* to nouns ending in *e*, drop the *e*: *immense* thus becomes *immensity*. Add *-ity* to each of the following words, and use each new word in a sentence.

1. dense   2. insane   3. scarce

Grammar Lesson

Direct and Indirect Objects

A subject and a verb may require more words to complete their meaning. A **direct object** is the noun or pronoun that receives the action of a verb.

>   VERB   DO
> The creatures wear garments. (*Wear what?*)
>   VERB   DO
> Professor Hugo invited them. (*Invited whom?*)

A sentence with a direct object can also contain an **indirect object**, which names the person or thing that something is given to or done for. Indirect objects appear only before direct objects.

>   VERB   IO   DO
> Snake told *God* his trouble. (*Told to whom?*)

▶ *For more practice, see page R30, Exercise B.*
Practice Identify the direct and indirect objects that appear in the following sentences.

1. We enjoyed our zoo visit this year.
2. Later, God gave the snake a rattle.
3. You told me a joke yesterday.
4. The message reached everyone.
5. They bought the children tickets to the show.

Writing Application Use each of the following verbs in a sentence containing both a direct object and an indirect object. Identify the objects in each sentence.

1. write   3. tell   5. sell
2. send   4. bake

W̶G̶ Prentice Hall Writing and Grammar Connection: Chapter 19, Section 5

Writing Lesson

Summary

A summary of a selection is a brief statement of its overall purpose and most important points. It should be concise and to the point, without including opinions or minor details. Write a summary of one of the selections in this grouping.

Prewriting   After choosing a selection, decide which main ideas you will cover. You might organize them in an outline like the one shown here.

Model: Organize Main Ideas		
Selection:_____		
Beginning	Middle	End

Drafting   Begin by stating the title and author (or reteller) of the selection you choose. Then, tell the most important event from the beginning of the story, one from the middle, and one most important event from the end. Conclude with a single sentence about the message or meaning of the work.

Revising   Ask someone who has not read the selection to read your summary. Have him or her point out anything that is unclear. Revise to make the sequence of events clearer.

W̧G Prentice Hall Writing and Grammar Connection: Chapter 12, Section 2

Extension Activities

Listening and Speaking With a partner, find five unusual facts about an animal. Then, include these facts in a **story** about the animal that does not name the animal. Present the story to your classmates, and have them try to identify your animal. To make your presentation effective and entertaining, use some of the following strategies:

- Include dialogue.
- Use appropriate facial expressions and body movements.
- Include specific facts and details.

Research and Technology Do Internet research to find more works by one of the authors. Read summaries and recommendations online. Then, choose a work to read and **summarize** for the class.

Writing Analyze the **theme** or message of one of the works in an essay. Explain the message and state whether or not you agree with it.

 **Take It to the Net**   www.phschool.com

Go online for an additional research activity using the Internet.

Folk tales like "How the Snake Got Poison" and fables—stories that teach a lesson—often have very specific cultural origins that are revealed in the settings and the way characters talk. The themes, or messages, of fables and folk tales, though, are often universal. In *The Tale of the Unknown Island*, Saramago uses a traditional fable situation—a common person struggling with a king. The fable includes, however, details that suggest modern times.

THE TALE OF THE UNKNOWN ISLAND

JOSÉ SARAMAGO

A man went to knock at the king's door and said, Give me a boat. The king's house had many other doors, but this was the door for petitions. Since the king spent all his time sitting at the door for favors (favors being offered to the king, you understand), whenever he heard someone knocking at the door for petitions, he would pretend not to hear, and only when the continuous pounding of the bronze doorknocker became not just deafening, but positively scandalous, disturbing the peace of the neighborhood (people would start muttering, What kind of king is he if he won't even answer the door), only then would he order the first secretary to go and find out what the supplicant wanted, since there seemed no way of silencing him. Then, the first secretary would call the second secretary, who would call the third secretary, who would give orders to the first assistant who would, in turn, give orders to the second assistant, and so on all the way down the line to the cleaning woman, who, having no one else to give orders to, would half-open the door and ask through the crack, What do you want. The supplicant would state his business, that is, he would wait by the door for his request to trace the path back, person by person, to the king. The king, occupied as usual with the favors being offered him, would take a long time to reply, and it was no small measure of his concern for the happiness and well being of his people that he would, finally, resolve to ask the first secretary for an authoritative opinion in writing, the first secretary, needless to say, would pass on the command to the second secretary, who would pass it to the third secretary, and so on down once again to the cleaning woman, who would give a yes or a no depending on what kind of mood she was in.

However, in the case of the man who wanted a boat, this is not quite what happened. When the cleaning woman asked him through the crack in the door, what do you want the man, unlike all the others, did not ask for a title, a medal, or simply money, he said, I want to talk to the king, You know perfectly well that the king can't come, he's busy at the door for favors, replied the woman, Well, go and tell him that I'm not leaving here until he comes, in person, to find out what I want, said the man, and he lay down across the threshold, covering himself with a blanket against the cold. Anyone wanting to go in or out would have to step over him first. Now this posed an enormous problem, because one must bear in mind that, according to the protocol governing the different doors, only one supplicant could be dealt with at a time, which meant that, as long as there was someone waiting there for a response, no one else could approach and make known their needs or ambitions. At first glance, it would seem that the person to gain most from this article in the regulations was the king, given that the fewer people bothering him with their various tales of woe, the longer he could spend, undisturbed, receiving, relishing and piling up favors. A second glance, however, would reveal that the king was very much the loser, because when people realized the unconscionable amount of time it took to get a reply, the ensuing public protests would seriously increase social unrest, and that, in turn, would have an immediate and negative effect on the flow of favors being offered to the king. In this particular case, as a result of weighing up the pros and cons, after three days, the king went, in person, to the door for favors to find out what he wanted, this troublemaker who had refused to allow his request to go through the proper bureaucratic channels.

The story goes on to tell that the man wants the boat to find an undiscovered island. Although the king at first refuses, again the man's determination and persistence win out. The man is given a boat and, with the help of the cleaning woman and others, sets off on his quest to find the "Unknown Island."

Thematic Connection
What details of this fable are similar to folk tales you have read or heard? What details are different?

José Saramago

(b. 1922)

José Saramago was born to a peasant family in Portugal. His last name should have been De Sousa, but the person who registered his birth gave him the name Saramago, the family nickname. He held various jobs, including car mechanic, civil servant, translator, and critic, but turned to writing full time in 1979. In 1998, Saramago was awarded the Nobel Prize for Literature. In his acceptance speech, he shared his experience with the oral tradition. As a boy, he had been deeply impressed by the folk tales and legends his grandfather told him.

Connecting Literature Across Cultures

1. What do the snake in "How the Snake Got Poison" and the petitioner in "The Tale of the Unknown Island" have in common?
2. In what ways are they different?
3. What lesson could you draw from the story thus far?

About Primary Research Articles

Primary research, unlike research done in a library, is based on first-hand information. Rather than using evidence from books to support their ideas, primary researchers actively collect fresh information about a topic. For example, if you poll your neighborhood to see which television programs are most popular, you are conducting primary research, or gathering new evidence.

Primary research articles are most often found in books, magazines, and newspapers that focus on scientific research and discovery. Reporting discoveries clearly and accurately is very important, so that everyone may benefit from them. Examples of primary research articles are medical reports in journals, such as the *Journal of the American Medical Association*, or accounts of travels and discoveries in faraway places, such as the articles in *National Geographic*.

Don Lessem (b. 1951) has explained prehistoric times in more than a dozen books. In this article, taken from his book *The Iceman*, he explains the discovery and study of the man who came to be called Ötzi. In so doing, he helps the reader understand how scientists reason about their discoveries.

Reading Strategy

Summarize

If you want to describe a piece of writing to someone who has not read it or a movie to someone who has not seen it, you probably do so by **summarizing.** When you summarize, you state briefly in your own words the main points and key details of the action. If you summarize as you read by stopping after each page, paragraph, or episode to note key events, you will improve your understanding of the article.

As you read this selection, pause occasionally to review and restate what has happened so far. This will help you identify the most important ideas. Then, record them in a chart like the one here.

Key Detail	Main Point
Tattoos on Ötzi's body	Religious or status symbol

The Iceman

Don Lessem

The writer's first paragraph describes Ötzi's discovery and outlines his purpose—to describe the objects found with Ötzi and let them show what his life and times were like.

Ötzi and the everyday objects that were found beside him are unique and wonderfully preserved clues to daily life in a time that has long been mysterious. With their help, we can imagine what life might have been like in the Copper Age[1] and how Ötzi lived and died. We can never be certain, but it may have been something like this:

Next, the writer presents additional evidence from other discoveries. Evidence gathered from prehistoric villages suggests that the goods and skills Ötzi brought with him would have been welcome.

Ötzi may have been a shepherd herding sheep, a trader trading stone and metal for tools, or even a medicine man in search of messages from gods. Whatever the reason, Ötzi had hiked high into the mountains. He was strong and well equipped, perhaps a leader among his people. The tattoo lines on his knee, foot, and back may have been religious emblems or a sign of his bravery or status.

Ötzi was a welcome visitor to the villages along his route. If he was a shepherd, he would have brought the villagers meat (since wool was not yet used for clothing). If he was a trader, he would have brought them flint for tools or copper for weapons.

Ötzi may have admired the villagers' talents. They used wheeled wagons and plows to farm. They sewed linen clothes and shoes expertly. They fed him butter and other delicacies.

emblems
(em´ bləmz) *n.* symbols, signs, or badges

delicacies
(del´ i kə sēz) *n.* foods that are rare and tasty

---

1. **Copper Age** (käp´ ər) *n.* period lasting roughly from 6500 B.C. to 3500 B.C., when copper was the most advanced metal in use

The villagers may have been impressed with the hard flints Ötzi had brought—wonderful stones for making daggers and knives—and with his fine ax. But Ötzi would not part with the ax. He had traveled far to the south and traded away many of his belongings to the copper workers for his ax.

Ötzi was handy and so found many uses for his ax. He had been wielding it lately to make a new bow to replace the one he'd traded away or broken. It was a huge bow, taller than he was. It took all his strength to pull the bowstring.

Ötzi had been hunting since he was a child. He had learned to feather his arrows at an angle to make them spin in flight and hold their course. After crossing the mountains, Ötzi planned to finish his new bow and arrows. Then he could hunt in the woods for ibex,[2] deer, and boar, and kill threatening bears and wolves. But for now, his mind was on traveling across the treeless high mountains in the thin, cold air.

In the soft deerskin suit and grass cape made for him by the village tailors, Ötzi was dressed for chill mountain weather. He had stuffed his shoes with mountain grass to protect his feet from the cold. He wore a fur cap on his head.

But the autumn air turned even colder than Ötzi had expected. He huddled in the shelter of a rock hollow. He was too cold and tired to eat the last of the antelope meat and berries he had brought with him.

Ötzi tried to start a fire. He had flint to strike a spark and strips of felt to help the fire along. But far above the tree line,[3] Ötzi could find no branches to keep a fire going. Perhaps falling snow snuffed out the few sparks he had created.

Ötzi's only hope for survival was to move on through the mountain pass and down into the valley. But he was too weak to move. Maybe he was sick or injured.

Ötzi carefully laid his belongings, including his beautiful ax, against the rocks around him. He lay down to sleep on his left side atop a large stone as the snow fell through the frigid air.

Days later, when Ötzi did not appear, other shepherds, or friends from the village, may have come looking for him. If they came upon the spot where he lay down, they would have found only a blanket of snow.

In cold isolation, Ötzi had quietly died. Five thousand years later, his snow blanket was finally removed. At last Ötzi was found, along with his treasures. Their value is beyond measure, for they give us our best view yet of the lost world of our Copper Age ancestors.

---

wielding (wēld´ iŋ) v. using with skill

The writer presents details about Ötzi and items found with him and infers what they may have meant. Note that the writer makes statements such as, "Ötzi had been hunting since he was a child." These are supported by the physical evidence: Ötzi's carefully crafted bow and arrows.

The last paragraphs encourage readers to speculate on the evidence themselves. The evidence presented does not tell the reader whether Ötzi was sick or injured when he lay down in the snow to die. The reader, like the researcher, cannot judge from the evidence.

---

2. ibex (ī´ beks´) n. European wild goats
3. tree line n. elevation above which trees will not grow

Check Your Comprehension

1. What are some possible explanations for Ötzi's traveling so far into the mountains?
2. What evidence is there that Ötzi was probably very strong?
3. Why was Ötzi unable to build a fire to protect himself from the cold?
4. Why would the villagers have had trouble finding Ötzi if they searched for him?

Applying the Reading Strategy

Summarize

5. Where was Ötzi found, and why was he of interest to scientists?
6. What evidence is there that Ötzi was a skilled craftsman?
7. State briefly in your own words the main points and key details that appear in the article relating to Ötzi's death.

Activity

Use Information From Primary Research Articles

Find primary research articles about prehistoric peoples from your state or region. You may find such articles in the library, on a university Web site that focuses on archaeology, or in the *Readers' Guide to Periodical Literature*. Find evidence about where and how people lived in your area 5,000 years ago. Write a summary of your findings.

Comparing and Contrasting Informational Material

Primary Research Articles and Other Types of Articles

Other writings may be based on primary research but use secondary sources rather than firsthand research to present evidence to the reader.

Note the differences between the primary research article you used above to write a summary and the summary itself. As with a research report you might write for a class or for the school newspaper, your summary used a secondary source to provide evidence for readers. Such reports must cite the sources of supporting evidence. Below are some examples of each kind of article.

Primary Research Articles	Articles Using Secondary Sources
Articles in medical journals	Research articles on historical topics
Government or census reports	Biographical articles
Eyewitness newspaper reports	Persuasive writing, such as editorials
Reports of scientific experiments	A comparison of literary works

Writing WORKSHOP

Exposition: Summary

One effective way to take notes or share what you have learned from an essay or article is to write a summary. A **summary** is a brief statement of the main ideas and supporting details presented in a piece of writing. A summary does not include your opinions or judgments; it sticks to the facts. In this workshop, you will learn strategies for writing an effective summary.

Assignment Criteria. A summary should accomplish the following goals:

- Briefly and clearly state the most important points
- Restate ideas in your own words, except for direct quotations
- Indicate the meaning of the material
- Show connections with effective transitions

See the Rubric on page 399 for the criteria on which your summary may be assessed.

Prewriting

Choose a topic. The topics you choose for summaries will depend on your notetaking or reporting needs. To practice writing a summary, choose one of the following.

- an article or essay from this textbook
- a story or essay you have read on your own
- an article from a magazine or newspaper

What's the big idea? From your retelling, identify the "big idea" of the piece you are summarizing. What is the writer writing about? What does he or she say about the subject? Try to write this idea in one or two sentences.

Model: The Big Idea
"Justin Lebo" is about a boy who turns his love of fixing bicycles into a charitable project that benefits hundreds of people.

Review the work to identify names or dates that should be included.

Student Model

Before you begin drafting your summary, read this student model and review the characteristics of a successful summary.

Earvin Santos
Asuza, California

Summary of "Our Finest Hour"

In his essay "Our Finest Hour," newscaster Charles Osgood tells a series of events during one disastrous newscast and explains the causes and effects of those events. First, Osgood sets up the situation. He was new at the station, he was substituting for Roger Mudd, the regular anchor, and several other important members of the news team, such as the camera operator, were also out. Because so many "regulars" were absent, few experienced people were working.

Osgood goes on to tell what happens during the broadcast. His first clue of trouble came after he introduced the first story and the wrong picture came up on the screen. He tries to reorganize his notes and start again, but that just causes more problems. Because the people working with him were also inexperienced, the mess just kept getting bigger each time someone tried to fix the problem. By the time the broadcast went to a commercial, almost everything had been made a mess. Things didn't get any better after the commercial. People in the control room added to the problem by panicking. The final straw came when one of the panicking people cried out in frustration, only to realize too late that a microphone was on and the frustrated cry was broadcast on the news. Throughout the essay, Osgood establishes the cause-and-effect relationships and makes the connections that help readers see how one simple mistake can explode into a complete catastrophe.

Osgood wraps up the essay by telling of a brief conversation he had several days later with the president of the network. A final touch of humor is added to the essay when Osgood tells readers that the president quoted the frustrated cry that had been broadcast. Osgood's essay gives interesting insights into the workings of a newsroom. His experiences illustrate that mistakes and panic are not a good mix. His humor shows that even a famous newscaster knows that mistakes happen, and people shouldn't take themselves too seriously.

The beginning of the summary identifies the title and author of the essay and gives a brief statement of what the essay is about.

After giving the basic information readers need to understand the situation, the writer explains the first important point in his own words: Few experienced people were working.

Rather than retell every single mishap, the writer identifies the next main point: The mess just kept getting bigger.

The writer includes an explanation of how the information is presented.

Finally, the writer concludes by stating in his own words the underlying meaning or significance of the information in the essay.

Drafting

Organize your summary. Begin with a single sentence that includes the name of the work and the name of the writer. Then, write the sentence that tells the "big idea." Follow this up with the main ideas.

Use your own words. Do not be tempted to copy sentences—or even long phrases—from the original work. Write your summary using your own words. This will force you to think about the writer's meaning. One exception to this is direct quotations. For example, if you are summarizing a speech, you may want to include a well-known statement associated with the speech.

Reflect the underlying meaning. Conclude by writing in your own words the meaning or significance of the work.

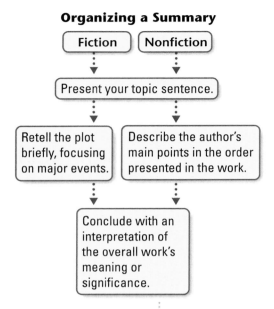

Organizing a Summary

Fiction / Nonfiction

Present your topic sentence.

Retell the plot briefly, focusing on major events. / Describe the author's main points in the order presented in the work.

Conclude with an interpretation of the overall work's meaning or significance.

Model: Telling the Meaning

Geoffrey C. Ward's "The Real Story of a Cowboy's Life" gives an unsentimental view of life on the trail that corrects false impressions people may have from watching cowboy movies.

Revising

Revise to show connections. Make sure your sentences are connected, one to the next, and that your paragraphs flow smoothly as well. Use transitional words to briefly indicate relationships between ideas. The chart below shows common transitional words used to show different relationships between events and ideas.

Common Transitional Words

Time Order	Comparison and Contrast	Order of Importance	Cause and Effect
first	similarly	primarily	therefore
second	on the other hand	significantly	so
then	in contrast	also	as a result
finally	however	in addition	consequently
recently	in the same way		because
simultaneously			

Revise to be brief. Good summaries are brief. Use as few words as possible to cover the main ideas clearly.

- Do not include adjectives that express your opinion.
- Avoid phrases or words that state the obvious.
- Whenever possible, use a word instead of a phrase.

Compare the model and nonmodel. Why is the model more effective than the nonmodel?

Nonmodel	Model
In the *excellent* article, "Origami Tips," the *outstanding writer* Audrey Samuels provides *lots of tips* and many helpful hints *for making origami.*	In the article, "Origami Tips," Audrey Samuels provides many helpful hints.

Publishing and Presenting

Although many of your summaries will be used for your own notes, you may choose to share your summary in one of the following ways. Choose one of these ways to share your writing with classmates or a larger audience.

Organize a class binder. With others, make a binder of summaries organized by topic. Use the binder as a reference for deciding whether reading a complete article would be interesting or useful to you.

Make a recommendation. Include your summary in a personal letter to a friend or relative who you think would enjoy reading the piece you have chosen.

 Prentice Hall Writing and Grammar Connection: Chapter 12, Section 2

 Speaking Connection
To learn more about delivering a summary, see the **Listening and Speaking Workshop: Organizing and Delivering an Oral Summary,** p. 400.

Rubric for Self-Assessment

Evaluate your summary using the following criteria and rating scale:

Criteria	Rating Scale				
	Not very				Very
How clear is the statement of the "big idea" and the main points?	1	2	3	4	5
How accurately does the retelling reflect the original?	1	2	3	4	5
How well does the summary reflect the meaning of the work?	1	2	3	4	5
How effectively are relationships indicated with transitions?	1	2	3	4	5
Is the summary brief?	1	2	3	4	5

Listening and Speaking WORKSHOP

Organizing and Delivering an Oral Summary

Sometimes, you will be asked to present a summary of something you have read. An **oral summary** shares many of the characteristics of a written summary. (To review the qualities of effective written summaries, see the Writing Workshop, pp. 396–399.) The guidelines below will help you plan and organize what you want to say and then help you say it with confidence and skill.

Organize Content

Like its written counterpart, an oral summary should briefly state the main idea of a work, with only as many details as needed to give a complete but concise picture of the work.

Note main idea and significant details. Write the "big idea"—the overall statement of the work's content—on a note card. Similarly, jot brief notes to use in your conclusion about the meaning or significance of the work or ideas in the work. If you want to include a direct quotation, write it word for word, and remember to tell your audience it is a quotation by saying, "I quote."

Show a comprehensive understanding. Do not just string together fact after fact. Ask yourself, "What does all this mean?" Try to convey a genuine understanding of what you have seen or read, not just the surface details.

Plan Delivery

Plan and practice your delivery so that you do not wander from the main points when presenting.

Use your voice well. Be lively and energetic, but enunciate every word. Speak slowly enough for your listeners to catch it all. Use a strong, clear voice that can be heard in the back of the room.

Use visual aids. A flip chart or poster that outlines the main points will help your audience follow your summary. As you indicate relationships between events and ideas, underline key words and phrases.

> **Example:** Because he was <u>buried in snow,</u> the iceman is almost <u>perfectly preserved.</u>

Activity: Summarize the News Choose a news article from a current newspaper or magazine. Be sure your planned summary answers all important questions about the account. Then, deliver your summary in front of your classmates, remembering to use the speaking techniques given above.

Big Idea

"Justin Lebo," by Phillip Hoose, tells the true story of a boy who turns his interest in bikes into a service project.

Conclusion

Justin's experiences show that individuals of any age can help others.

Assessment WORKSHOP

Recognizing Author's Purpose

The reading sections of some tests ask questions that assess your ability to recognize an author's purpose. Use what you have learned about an author's purpose in this unit to answer questions such as these. Read questions carefully to determine which of the following you are being asked to do:

- identify the author's purpose
- evaluate whether the author achieves his or her purpose
- analyze the effect of the purpose on his or her writing

Test-Taking Strategies

- Do not be distracted by choices that are true, but do not identify a purpose.
- Read the entire sentence of each choice to make sure the sentence identifies the correct purpose.

Sample Test Item

Directions: Read the passage, and then choose the letter of the best answer for the item.

Though some may not know it, our class will soon vote on whether formal wear will be required at the annual dance. Many have said that they want to continue the tradition of formal attire. Others say that formal wear is uncomfortable and too expensive for most students. Although the outcome of the vote means a great deal to all of us, the most important thing is for all to cast their votes.

1. In writing this, the author's purpose was to—

A inform readers about the upcoming vote and its importance

B offer an entertaining view of school politics

C encourage a vote for formal clothing

D persuade others to dress up for the dance

Answer and Explanation

Since the letter is neither primarily entertaining nor persuasive, **B**, **C**, and **D** are incorrect. **A** is correct.

▶ Practice

Directions: Read the passages, and then choose the letter of the best answer for the item.

Bill wrote his parents from camp:

I love this place. There is so much to do, and I get to choose my activities. I've tried pottery and working in stained glass. The food is plain but plentiful, and desserts are great. I can't wait to see you on Visitors' Day.

His sister Lillian wrote:

I'm not really enjoying camp. My cabin mates are mean. The activities are OK, but we do the same thing every day. One good thing is the food. Please write back and say I can come home with you after Visitors' Day.

1. The purpose of Lillian's letter is to—

A inform her parents about camp activities

B complain about the food

C persuade her parents to let her come home

D express her feelings about her cabin mates

Negro Boys on Quayside, c. 1880's, David Norslup, © Corcoran Gallery of Art

Exploring the Genre

Short stories carry you to fictional worlds, both strange and familiar. In the pages of a story, you can meet exceptional people or travel to far-off lands. The possibilities are as endless as the bounds of a writer's imagination, so no two stories are ever entirely alike. However, all short stories share these elements:

- **Plot** is the sequence of events that hooks you in and keeps you reading so you will find out what happens.

- **Characters** are the people or animals who take part in the action.

- **Setting** is the time and place of the action.

- **Theme** is the central message expressed in a story.

You will learn about these elements as you read this unit.

◀ **Critical Viewing** What might the older gentleman in this painting be sharing with the young boy?

Why Read Literature?

Fiction is writing that tells about imaginary characters and events. Knowing what fiction is will help you set your purpose for reading short stories. Clearly, people most often read short stories for entertainment, but they may also want to learn about a different culture, explore the theme of a story, or experience the development of the characters in the story. Preview three of the purposes you might set before reading the stories in this unit.

1 Read for the love of literature.

Author William Sydney Porter patterned the hero of one of his stories after a safecracker he met in prison! Porter took the pseudonym O. Henry because he was ashamed of having served a prison stint for a crime that he may or may not have committed. To learn what happens to the safecracker in this story, read **"After Twenty Years,"** page 428.

Because they are known as such fast and fearless hunters, mongooses were imported to islands such as the Virgin Islands to reduce the rat populations in the sugar cane fields. What the plantation owners failed to realize is that mongooses are alert and active all day long, but they sleep at night when the nocturnal rats are on the prowl. Read a fictional story about a heroic mongoose in **"Rikki-tikki-tavi,"** page 408.

2 Read to understand characters.

Jane Yolen, who has been called "the American Hans Christian Andersen," claims that she comes from a long line of story-tellers. She has written more than 200 books for children and young adults. Read her story about two girls from very different backgrounds who find common threads in their lives in **"Suzy and Leah,"** page 448.

3 Read for information.

Over the past fifteen years, more personal computers have been purchased in the United States than automobiles. Read how you can protect yourself from all the other travelers on the information superhighway. Read **"Let the Reader Beware,"** page 503.

The Rock and Roll Hall of Fame is in Cleveland, Ohio. Find out more about this special place that honors musicians when you read **"New Exhibit: Let the Good Times Roll,"** page 489.

 Take It to the Net

Visit the Web site for online instruction and activities related to each selection in this unit.

www.phschool.com

How to Read Literature

Use Strategies for Reading Fiction

Fiction is writing that tells about imaginary characters and events. The genre of fiction includes novels, novellas, and short stories. In this unit, you will learn the following strategies for reading fiction.

1. Predict.

As the events of the story unfold, ask yourself what will happen next. Be on the lookout for clues that hint of events to come. To find out whether your predictions are correct, read on. In this unit, you will learn how to use story patterns to help you predict.

Event: Policeman walks an isolated beat at night.

Predictions: He will meet someone.

He may arrest someone.

He may help someone in need.

2. Identify with a character.

Fiction not only allows you to visit new worlds, but also allows you to experience other lives. Put yourself in the character's place and think about how you would react to the situations that he or she experiences.

3. Draw inferences.

When you read, draw inferences, conclusions based on details the author provides. Jot down notes about characters. Put the details together to draw an inference. As you read the selections in this unit, make inferences about characters based on their actions.

Inference

Bob has lots of diamonds.

✣

Bob brags.

✣

Bob calls Jimmy a plodder.

Bob is conceited!

4. Ask questions.

By **asking questions,** you will focus your attention on the information you need to understand events and characters' actions and motives.

As you read the selections in the unit, review the reading strategies and look at the notes in the side column. Use the suggestions to apply the strategies and interact with the text.

Prepare to Read

Rikki-tikki-tavi

 Take It to the Net

Visit www.phschool.com
for interactive activities
and instruction related to
"Rikki-tikki-tavi," including:

- background
- graphic organizers
- literary elements
- reading strategies

Preview

Connecting to the Literature

You have probably noticed that some animals appear to be natural enemies. "Rikki-tikki-tavi" shows just how fierce the conflict between such enemies can be, and introduces two natural enemies that may be new to you: the mongoose and the cobra.

Background

The Indian cobra can reach six feet in length and six inches around. Cobras feed on small animals. Just before striking, a cobra lifts its body in the air and forms a hood from ribs near its head. The mongoose is a brown, furry animal about fifteen inches long—the perfect size for a cobra's meal. However, the fast, fierce mongoose usually wins any battle with a cobra.

Literary Analysis
Plot

The **plot** is the arrangement of events in a short story. A plot has the following elements:

- **Exposition:** Sets up the situation and introduces the characters.
- **Rising Action:** Events that increase the tension.
- **Climax:** High point of the story at which the eventual outcome becomes clear.
- **Falling Action:** Events that follow the climax.
- **Resolution:** Final outcome is achieved; loose ends are tied up.

Plot is used in other works of fiction, such as a novel, a long work of fiction, and a novella, a work of fiction that is longer than a short story but shorter than a novel. The diagram shows how these elements above work together in a plot.

Connecting Literary Elements

Conflict is a struggle between two opposing forces. Conflict can be external or internal. External conflict is one in which a character struggles against an outside force, such as an another character. Internal conflict is one that takes place within the mind of a character. All of the events in the plot either increase the tension of the conflict or contribute to the resolution. Analyze the conflict by asking yourself the following focus questions:

1. What conflict is revealed at the beginning of the story?
2. What does the snake do to make the conflict worse?

Reading Strategy
Predicting

In a plot, one event leads to another. Analyze the relationships between events by making **predictions**—educated guesses about upcoming actions or events. You can predict by thinking about events that have already happened along with what you have learned about the characters. Also look for details in the story that hint at events to come. As you read ahead, revise your predictions based on new events and information.

Vocabulary Development

revived (ri vīvd´) *v.* came back to consciousness (p. 408)

draggled (drag´ əld) *adj.* wet and dirty (p. 408)

cunningly (kun´ iŋ lē) *adv.* cleverly (p. 418)

mourning (môrn´ iŋ) *adj.* feeling sorrow for the death of a loved one (p. 417)

consolation (kän´ səl ā´ shən) *n.* something that makes you feel better (p. 418)

Rikki-tikki-tavi

RUDYARD KIPLING

This is the story of the great war that Rikki-tikki-tavi fought, single-handed, through the bathrooms of the big bungalow in Segowlee cantonment.[1] Darzee, the tailorbird bird, helped him, and Chuchundra (chōō chun′ drə) the muskrat, who never comes out into the middle of the floor, but always creeps round by the wall, gave him advice; but Rikki-tikki did the real fighting.

He was a mongoose, rather like a little cat in his fur and his tail, but quite like a weasel in his head and his habits. His eyes and the end of his restless nose were pink; he could scratch himself anywhere he pleased, with any leg, front or back, that he chose to use; he could fluff up his tail till it looked like a bottle brush, and his war cry as he scuttled through the long grass, was: *"Rikk-tikk-tikki-tikki-tchk!"*

One day, a high summer flood washed him out of the burrow where he lived with his father and mother, and carried him, kicking and clucking, down a roadside ditch. He found a little wisp of grass floating there, and clung to it till he lost his senses. When he <u>revived</u>, he was lying in the hot sun on the middle of a garden path, very <u>draggled</u> indeed, and a small boy was saying: "Here's a dead mongoose. Let's have a funeral."

"No," said his mother; "let's take him in and dry him. Perhaps he isn't really dead."

They took him into the house, and a big man picked him up between his finger and thumb and said he was not dead but half choked; so they wrapped him in cotton wool, and warmed him, and he opened his eyes and sneezed.

"Now," said the big man (he was an Englishman who had just moved into the bungalow); "don't frighten him, and we'll see what he'll do."

> **Literary Analysis**
> **Plot** What important details about the mongoose are revealed in the exposition?

> **revived** (ri vīvd′) *v.* came back to consciousness
>
> **draggled** (drag′ əld) *adj.* wet and dirty

---

1. **Segowlee cantonment** (sē gou′ lē kan tän′ mənt) *n.* living quarters for British troops in Segowlee, India.

It is the hardest thing in the world to frighten a mongoose, because he is eaten up from nose to tail with curiosity. The motto of all the mongoose family is, "Run and find out"; and Rikki-tikki was a true mongoose. He looked at the cotton wool, decided that it was not good to eat, ran all round the table, sat up and put his fur in order, scratched himself, and jumped on the small boy's shoulder.

"Don't be frightened, Teddy," said his father. "That's his way of making friends."

"Ouch! He's tickling under my chin," said Teddy.

Rikki-tikki looked down between the boy's collar and neck, snuffed at his ear, and climbed down to the floor, where he sat rubbing his nose.

"Good gracious," said Teddy's mother, "and that's a wild creature! I suppose he's so tame because we've been kind to him."

"All mongooses are like that," said her husband. "If Teddy doesn't pick him up by the tail, or try to put him in a cage, he'll run in and out of the house all day long. Let's give him something to eat."

They gave him a little piece of raw meat. Rikki-tikki liked it immensely, and when it was finished he went out into the veranda and sat in the sunshine and fluffed up his fur to make it dry to the roots. Then he felt better.

"There are more things to find out about in this house," he said to himself, "than all my family could find out in all their lives. I shall certainly stay and find out."

Reading Strategy
Predicting Predict what might happen, based on the father's statement.

✔**Reading Check**

Who is Rikki-tikki-tavi and how does he meet Teddy?

◀ **Critical Viewing**
Does the mongoose shown here appear friendly or hostile? Explain. **[Assess]**

He spent all that day roaming over the house. He nearly drowned himself in the bathtubs, put his nose into the ink on a writing table, and burned it on the end of the big man's cigar, for he climbed up in the big man's lap to see how writing was done. At nightfall he ran into Teddy's nursery to watch how kerosene lamps were lighted, and when Teddy went to bed Rikki-tikki climbed up too; but he was a restless companion, because he had to get up and attend to every noise all through the night, and find out what made it. Teddy's mother and father came in, the last thing, to look at their boy, and Rikki-tikki was awake on the pillow. "I don't like that," said Teddy's mother; "he may bite the child." "He'll do no such thing," said the father. "Teddy's safer with that little beast than if he had a bloodhound to watch him. If a snake came into the nursery now—"

But Teddy's mother wouldn't think of anything so awful.

Early in the morning Rikki-tikki came to early breakfast in the veranda riding on Teddy's shoulder, and they gave him banana and some boiled egg; and he sat on all their laps one after the other, because every well-brought-up mongoose always hopes to be a house mongoose some day and have rooms to run about in, and Rikki-tikki's mother (she used to live in the General's house at Segowlee) had carefully told Rikki what to do if ever he came across Englishmen.

Then Rikki-tikki went out into the garden to see what was to be seen. It was a large garden, only half cultivated, with bushes as big as summer houses of Marshal Niel roses, lime and orange trees, clumps of bamboos, and thickets of high grass. Rikki-tikki licked his lips.

◀ **Critical Viewing**
How might a mongoose like Rikki-tikki-tavi know that the cobra pictured here is in a state of attack? **[Interpret]**

"This is a splendid hunting ground," he said, and his tail grew bottlebrushy at the thought of it, and he scuttled up and down the garden, snuffing here and there till he heard very sorrowful voices in a thornbush.

It was Darzee, the tailorbird, and his wife. They had made a beautiful nest by pulling two big leaves together and stitching them up the edges with fibers, and had filled the hollow with cotton and downy fluff. The nest swayed to and fro, as they sat on the rim and cried.

"What is the matter?" asked Rikki-tikki.

"We are very miserable," said Darzee.

"One of our babies fell out of the nest yesterday and Nag ate him."

"H'm!" said Rikki-tikki, "that is very sad—but I am a stranger here. Who is Nag?"

Darzee and his wife only cowered down in the nest without answering, for from the thick grass at the foot of the bush there came a low hiss—a horrid cold sound that made Rikki-tikki jump back two clear feet. Then inch by inch out of the grass rose up the head and spread hood of Nag, the big black cobra, and he was five feet long from tongue to tail. When he had lifted one third of himself clear of the ground, he stayed balancing to and fro exactly as a dandelion tuft balances in the wind, and he looked at Rikki-tikki with the wicked snake's eyes that never change their expression, whatever the snake may be thinking of.

"Who is Nag?" he said. "*I* am Nag. The great god Brahm[2] put his mark upon all our people when the first cobra spread his hood to keep the sun off Brahm...as he slept. Look, and be afraid!"

He spread out his hood more than ever, and Rikki-tikki saw the spectacle mark on the back of it that looks exactly like the eye

2. **Brahm** (bräm) abbreviation of Brahma, the name of the chief god in the Hindu religion.

Literary Analysis
Plot What can you guess about the story's conflict?

✔**Reading Check**

Who is Nag?

part of a hook-and-eye fastening. He was afraid for the minute; but it is impossible for a mongoose to stay frightened for any length of time, and though Rikki-tikki had never met a live cobra before, his mother had fed him on dead ones, and he knew that all a grown mongoose's business in life was to fight and eat snakes. Nag knew that too, and at the bottom of his cold heart he was afraid.

"Well," said Rikki-tikki, and his tail began to fluff up again, "marks or no marks, do you think it is right for you to eat fledglings out of a nest?"

Nag was thinking to himself, and watching the least little movement in the grass behind Rikki-tikki. He knew that mongooses in the garden meant death sooner or later for him and his family; but he wanted to get Rikki-tikki off his guard. So he dropped his head a little, and put it on one side.

"Let us talk," he said. "You eat eggs. Why should not I eat birds?"

"Behind you! Look behind you!" sang Darzee.

Rikki-tikki knew better than to waste time in staring. He jumped up in the air as high as he could go, and just under him whizzed by the head of Nagaina (nə gī´nə), Nag's wicked wife. She had crept up behind him as he was talking, to make an end of him; and he heard her savage hiss as the stroke missed. He came down almost across her back, and if he had been an old mongoose he would have known that then was the time to break her back with one bite; but he was afraid of the terrible lashing return stroke of the cobra. He bit, indeed, but did not bite long enough, and he jumped clear of the whisking tail, leaving Nagaina torn and angry.

Literary Analysis
Plot How does the conflict intensify?

"Wicked, wicked Darzee!" said Nag, lashing up high as he could reach toward the nest in the thornbush; but Darzee had built it out of reach of snakes; and it only swayed to and fro.

Rikki-tikki felt his eyes growing red and hot (when a mongoose's eyes grow red, he is angry), and he sat back on his tail and hind legs like a little kangaroo, and looked all around him, and chattered with rage. But Nag and Nagaina had disappeared into the grass. When a snake misses its stroke, it never says anything or gives any sign of what it means to do next. Rikki-tikki did not care to follow them, for he did not feel sure that he could manage two snakes at once. So he trotted off to the gravel path near the house, and sat down to think. It was a serious matter for him.

Reading Strategy
Predict What do you predict will be the outcome of the conflict? Why?

If you read the old books of natural history, you will find they say that when the mongoose fights the snake and happens to get bitten, he runs off and eats some herb that cures him. That is not true.

The victory is only a matter of quickness of eye and quickness of foot—snake's blow against mongoose's jump—and as no eye can follow the motion of a snake's head when it strikes, that makes things much more wonderful than any magic herb. Rikki-tikki knew he was a young mongoose, and it made him all the more pleased to think that he had managed to escape a blow from behind. It gave him confidence in himself, and when Teddy came running down the path, Rikki-tikki was ready to be petted.

But just as Teddy was stooping, something flinched a little in the dust, and a tiny voice said: "Be careful. I am death!" It was Karait (kə rīt'), the dusty brown snakeling that lies for choice on the dusty earth; and his bite is as dangerous as the cobra's. But he is so small that nobody thinks of him, and so he does the more harm to people.

Rikki-tikki's eyes grew red again, and he danced up to Karait with the peculiar rocking, swaying motion that he had inherited from his family. It looks very funny, but it is so perfectly balanced a gait that you can fly off from it at any angle you please; and in dealing with snakes this is an advantage. If Rikki-tikki had only known, he was doing a much more dangerous thing than fighting Nag, for Karait is so small, and can turn so quickly, that unless Rikki bit him close to the back of the head, he would get the return stroke in his eye or lip. But Rikki did not know: his eyes were all red, and he rocked back and forth, looking for a good place to hold. Karait struck out. Rikki jumped sideways and tried to run in, but the wicked little dusty gray head lashed within a fraction of his shoulder, and he had to jump over the body, and the head followed his heels close.

Teddy shouted to the house: "Oh, look here! Our mongoose is killing a snake"; and Rikki-tikki heard a scream from Teddy's mother. His father ran out with a stick, but by the time he came up, Karait had lunged out once too far, and Rikki-tikki had sprung, jumped on the snake's back, dropped his head far between his fore legs, bitten as high up the back as he could get hold, and rolled away. That bite paralyzed Karait, and Rikki-tikki was just going to eat him up from the tail, after the custom of his family at dinner, when he remembered that a full meal makes a slow mongoose, and if he wanted all his strength and quickness ready, he must keep himself thin.

Literature in context   Science Connection

The Cobra: Fact and Fiction

Although the snakes in this story have fictional abilities and characteristics, many of their qualities are accurately based on the qualities of the real animals. Cobras do have a spectacle-shaped marking on their hood, as shown in the picture below. Cobras are known to enter houses, just as Nag and Nagaina are described doing. (In India and other countries where cobras and mongooses live, mongooses are welcomed around human houses because of their ability to kill cobras.) A female cobra is extremely dangerous and vicious after laying its eggs. Unlike the snakes in this story, however, real cobras do not travel in pairs or work together to hatch their eggs.

✔ Reading Check

What happens when Rikki meets Karait?

He went away for a dust bath under the castor-oil bushes, while Teddy's father beat the dead Karait. "What is the use of that?" thought Rikki-tikki. "I have settled it all"; and then Teddy's mother picked him up from the dust and hugged him, crying that he had saved Teddy from death, and Teddy's father said that he was a providence,[3] and Teddy looked on with big scared eyes. Rikki-tikki was rather amused at all the fuss, which, of course, he did not understand. Teddy's mother might just as well have petted Teddy for playing in the dust. Rikki was thoroughly enjoying himself.

That night, at dinner, walking to and fro among the wineglasses on the table, he could have stuffed himself three times over with nice things; but he remembered Nag and Nagaina, and though it was very pleasant to be patted and petted by Teddy's mother, and to sit on Teddy's shoulder, his eyes would get red from time to time, and he would go off into his long war cry of *"Rikk-tikk-tikki-tikki-tchk!"*

Teddy carried him off to bed, and insisted on Rikki-tikki sleeping under his chin. Rikki-tikki was too well bred to bite or scratch, but as soon as Teddy was asleep he went off for his nightly walk round the house, and in the dark he ran up against Chuchundra the muskrat, creeping round by the wall. Chuchundra is a broken-hearted little beast. He whimpers and cheeps all the night, trying to make up his mind to run into the middle of the room, but he never gets there.

"Don't kill me," said Chuchundra, almost weeping. "Rikki-tikki don't kill me."

"Do you think a snake-killer kills muskrats?" said Rikki-tikki scornfully.

"Those who kill snakes get killed by snakes," said Chuchundra, more sorrowfully than ever. "And how am I to be sure that Nag won't mistake me for you some dark night?"

"There's not the least danger," said Rikki-tikki; "but Nag is in the garden, and I know you don't go there."

"My cousin Chua, the rat, told me—" said Chuchundra, and then he stopped.

"Told you what?"

"H'sh! Nag is everywhere, Rikki-tikki. You should have talked to Chua in the garden."

"I didn't—so you must tell me. Quick, Chuchundra, or I'll bite you!"

Chuchundra sat down and cried till the tears rolled off his whiskers. "I am a very poor man," he sobbed. "I never had spirit enough to run out into the middle of the room. H'sh! I mustn't tell you anything. Can't you *hear,* Rikki-tikki?"

Reading Strategy
Predicting What does Rikki-tikki's war cry make you think might happen?

Reading Strategy
Predicting What can you predict from the conversation between Rikki and Chuchundra?

---

3. a providence (präv´ ə dəns) *n.* a godsend; a valuable gift.

414 ◆ *Short Story*

Rikki-tikki listened. The house was as still as still, but he thought he could just catch the faintest *scratch-scratch* in the world—a noise as faint as that of a wasp walking on a window-pane—the dry scratch of a snake's scales on brickwork.

"That's Nag or Nagaina," he said to himself; "and he is crawling into the bathroom sluice.[4] You're right, Chuchundra; I should have talked to Chua."

He stole off to Teddy's bathroom, but there was nothing there, and then to Teddy's mother's bathroom. At the bottom of the smooth plaster wall there was a brick pulled out to make a sluice for the bath water, and as Rikki-tikki stole in by the masonry curb where the bath is put, he heard Nag and Nagaina whispering together outside in the moonlight.

"When the house is emptied of people," said Nagaina to her husband, "*he* will have to go away, and then the garden will be our own again. Go in quietly, and remember that the big man who killed Karait is the first one to bite. Then come out and tell me, and we will hunt for Rikki-tikki together."

"But are you sure that there is anything to be gained by killing the people?" said Nag.

"Everything. When there were no people in the bungalow, did we have any mongoose in the garden? So long as the bungalow is empty, we are king and queen of the garden; and remember that as soon as our eggs in the melon bed hatch (as they may tomorrow), our children will need room and quiet."

"I had not thought of that," said Nag. "I will go, but there is no need that we should hunt for Rikki-tikki afterward. I will kill the big man and his wife, and the child if I can, and come away quietly. Then the bungalow will be empty, and Rikki-tikki will go."

Rikki-tikki tingled all over with rage and hatred at this, and then Nag's head came through the sluice, and his five feet of cold body followed it. Angry as he was, Rikki-tikki was very frightened as he saw the size of the big cobra. Nag coiled himself up, raised his head, and looked into the bathroom in the dark, and Rikki could see his eyes glitter.

"Now, if I kill him here, Nagaina will know;—and if I fight him on the open floor, the odds are in his favor. What am I to do?" said Rikki-tikki-tavi.

Nag waved to and fro, and then Rikki-tikki-tikki heard him drinking from the biggest water jar that was used to fill the bath. "That is good," said the snake. "Now, when Karait was killed, the big man had a stick. He may have that stick still, but when he comes in to bathe in the morning he will not have

---

4. **sluice** (slo͞os) drain.

Literary Analysis
Plot How does the conflict intensify as Rikki-tikki overhears the conversation?

Reading Check

What are Nag and Nagaina planning to do?

Rikki-tikki-tavi ◆ 415

a stick. I shall wait here till he comes. Nagaina—do you hear me?—I shall wait here in the cool till daytime."

There was no answer from outside, so Rikki-tikki knew Nagaina had gone away. Nag coiled himself down, coil by coil, round the bulge at the bottom of the waterjar, and Rikki-tikki stayed still as death. After an hour he began to move, muscle by muscle, toward the jar. Nag was asleep, and Rikki-tikki looked at his big back, wondering which would be the best place for a good hold. "If I don't break his back at the first jump," said Rikki, "he can still fight; and if he fights—O Rikki!" He looked at the thickness of the neck below the hood, but that was too much for him; and a bite near the tail would only make Nag savage.

"It must be the head," he said at last; "the head above the hood; and, when I am once there, I must not let go."

Then he jumped. The head was lying a little clear of the water jar, under the curve of it; and, as his teeth met, Rikki braced his back against the bulge of the red earthenware to hold down the head. This gave him just one second's purchase,[5] and he made the most of it. Then he was battered to and fro as a rat is shaken by a dog—to and fro on the floor, up and down, and round in great circles: but his eyes were red, and he held on as the body cart-whipped over the floor, upsetting the tin dipper and the soap dish and the fleshbrush, and banged against the tin side of the bath. As he held he closed his jaws tighter and tighter, for he made sure he would be banged to death, and, for the honor of his family, he preferred to be found with his teeth locked. He was dizzy, aching, and felt shaken to pieces when something went off like a thunderclap just behind him; a hot wind knocked him senseless and red fire singed his fur. The big man had been wakened by the noise, and had fired both barrels of a shotgun into Nag just behind the hood.

Rikki-tikki held on with his eyes shut, for now he was quite sure he was dead; but the head did not move, and the big man picked him up and said: "It's the mongoose again, Alice; the little chap has saved our lives now." Then Teddy's mother came in with a very white face, and saw what was left of Nag, and Rikki-tikki dragged himself to Teddy's bedroom and spent half the rest of the night shaking himself tenderly to find out whether he really was broken into forty pieces, as he fancied.

When morning came he was very stiff, but well pleased with his doings. "Now I have Nagaina to settle with, and she will be worse than five Nags, and there's no knowing when the eggs she spoke of will hatch. Goodness! I must go and see Darzee," he said.

---

5. **purchase** (pur´ chəs) *n.* firm hold.

Literary Analysis
Plot How do the father's remarks connect back to the conversation between him and his wife earlier in the story?

Literary Analysis
Plot Why is the death of Nag part of the rising action rather than the resolution?

Without waiting for breakfast, Rikki-tikki ran to the thornbush where Darzee was singing a song of triumph at the top of his voice. The news of Nag's death was all over the garden, for the sweeper had thrown the body on the rubbish heap.

"Oh, you stupid tuft of feathers!" said Rikki-tikki, angrily. "Is this the time to sing?"

"Nag is dead—is dead—is dead!" sang Darzee. "The valiant Rikki-tikki caught him by the head and held fast. The big man brought the bang-stick and Nag fell in two pieces! He will never eat my babies again."

"All that's true enough; but where's Nagaina?" said Rikki-tikki, looking carefully round him.

"Nagaina came to the bathroom sluice and called for Nag," Darzee went on; "and Nag came out on the end of a stick—the sweeper picked him up on the end of a stick and threw him upon the rubbish heap. Let us sing about the great, the red-eyed Rikki-tikki!" and Darzee filled his throat and sang.

"If I could get up to your nest, I'd roll all your babies out!" said Rikki-tikki "You don't know when to do the right thing at the right time. You're safe enough in your nest there, but it's war for me down here. Stop singing a minute, Darzee."

"For the great, the beautiful Rikki-tikki's sake, I will stop," said Darzee. "What is it, O Killer of the terrible Nag!"

"Where is Nagaina, for the third time?"

"On the rubbish heap by the stables, <u>mourning</u> for Nag. Great is Rikki-tikki with the white teeth."

"Bother my white teeth! Have you ever heard where she keeps her eggs?"

"In the melon bed, on the end nearest the wall, where the sun strikes nearly all day. She had them there weeks ago."

"And you never thought it worthwhile to tell me? The end nearest the wall, you said?"

"Rikki-tikki, you are not going to eat her eggs?"

"Not eat exactly; no. Darzee, if you have a grain of sense you will fly off to the stables and pretend that your wing is broken, and let Nagaina chase you away to this bush! I must get to the melon bed, and if I went there now she'd see me."

Darzee was a featherbrained little fellow who could never hold more than one idea at a time in his head; and just because he knew that Nagaina's children were born in eggs like his own, he didn't think at first that it was fair to kill them. But his wife was a sensible bird, and she knew that cobra's eggs meant young cobras later on; so she flew off from the nest, and left Darzee to keep the babies warm, and continue his song about the death of Nag. Darzee was very like a man in some ways.

mourning (môrn′ iŋ) *adj.* feeling sorrow for the death of a loved one

Reading Strategy
Predicting What can you predict from Darzee's words?

✔**Reading Check**

What has Rikki done to Nag?

She fluttered in front of Nagaina by the rubbish heap, and cried out, "Oh, my wing is broken! The boy in the house threw a stone at me and broke it." Then she fluttered more desperately than ever.

Nagaina lifted up her head and hissed, "You warned Rikki-tikki when I would have killed him. Indeed and truly, you've chosen a bad place to be lame in." And she moved toward Darzee's wife, slipping along over the dust.

"The boy broke it with a stone!" shrieked Darzee's wife.

"Well! It may be some consolation to you when you're dead to know that I shall settle accounts with the boy. My husband lies on the rubbish heap this morning, but before night the boy in the house will lie very still. What is the use of running away? I am sure to catch you. Little fool, look at me!"

Darzee's wife knew better than to do *that*, for a bird who looks at a snake's eyes gets so frightened that she cannot move. Darzee's wife fluttered on, piping sorrowfully, and never leaving the ground, and Nagaina quickened her pace.

Rikki-tikki heard them going up the path from the stables, and he raced for the end of the melon patch near the wall. There, in the warm litter about the melons, very cunningly hidden, he found twenty-five eggs, about the size of a bantam's eggs,[6] but with whitish skin instead of shell.

"I was not a day too soon," he said; for he could see the baby cobras curled up inside the skin, and he knew that the minute

---

6. bantam's (ban´ təmz) **eggs** small chicken's eggs.

▶ **Critical Viewing** Basing your answer on the details of this photograph, which animal would you expect to win a match to the death—the cobra or the mongoose? Explain. **[Evaluate]**

Reading Strategy
Predict What do you predict will happen to Darzee's wife? Why?

consolation
(kän´ səl ā´ shən) *n.* something that makes you feel better

cunningly (kun´ iŋ lē) *adv.* cleverly

they were hatched they could each kill a man or a mongoose. He bit off the tops of the eggs as fast as he could, taking care to crush the young cobras, and turned over the litter from time to time to see whether he had missed any. At last there were only three eggs left, and Rikki-tikki began to chuckle to himself, when he heard Darzee's wife screaming:

"Rikki-tikki, I led Nagaina toward the house, and she has gone into the veranda, and—oh, come quickly—she means killing!"

Rikki-tikki smashed two eggs, and tumbled backward down the melon bed with the third egg in his mouth, and scuttled to the veranda as hard as he could put foot to the ground. Teddy and his mother and father were there at early breakfast; but Rikki-tikki saw that they were not eating anything. They sat stone-still, and their faces were white. Nagaina was coiled up on the matting by Teddy's chair, within easy striking distance of Teddy's bare leg, and she was swaying to and fro singing a song of triumph.

"Son of the big man that killed Nag," she hissed, "stay still. I am not ready yet. Wait a little. Keep very still, all you three. If you move I strike, and if you do not move I strike, Oh, foolish people, who killed my Nag!"

Teddy's eyes were fixed on his father, and all his father could do was to whisper, "Sit still, Teddy. You mustn't move. Teddy, keep still."

Then Rikki-tikki came up and cried: "Turn round, Nagaina; turn and fight!"

Literary Analysis
Plot Do you think this scene is the climax or part of the rising action? Why?

✓ **Reading Check**

What does Rikki bring with him to the veranda?

"All in good time," said she, without moving her eyes. "I will settle my account with *you* presently. Look at your friends, Rikki-tikki. They are still and white; they are afraid. They dare not move, and if you come a step nearer I strike."

"Look at your eggs," said Rikki-tikki, "in the melon bed near the wall. Go and look, Nagaina."

The big snake turned half round, and saw the egg on the veranda. "Ah-h! Give it to me," she said.

Rikki-tikki put his paws one on each side of the egg, and his eyes were blood-red. "What price for a snake's egg? For a young cobra? For a young king cobra? For the last—the very last of the brood? The ants are eating all the others down by the melon bed."

Nagaina spun clear round, forgetting everything for the sake of the one egg; and Rikki-tikki saw Teddy's father shoot out a big hand, catch Teddy by the shoulder, and drag him across the little table with the teacups, safe and out of reach of Nagaina.

"Tricked! Tricked! Tricked! *Rikk-tck-tck!*" chuckled Rikki-tikki. "The boy is safe, and it was I—I—I that caught Nag by the hood last night in the bathroom." Then he began to jump up and down, all four feet together, his head close to the floor. "He threw me to and fro, but he could not shake me off. He was dead before the big man blew him in two. I did it. *Rikki-tikki-tck-tck!* Come then, Nagaina. Come and fight with me. You shall not be a widow long."

Nagaina saw that she had lost her chance of killing Teddy, and the egg lay between Rikki-tikki's paws. "Give me the egg, Rikki-tikki. Give me the last of my eggs, and I will go away and never come back," she said, lowering her hood.

"Yes, you will go away, and you will never come back; for you will go to the rubbish heap with Nag. Fight, widow! The big man has gone for his gun! Fight!"

Rikki-tikki was bounding all round Nagaina, keeping just out of reach of her stroke, his little eyes like hot coals. Nagaina gathered herself together, and flung out at him. Rikki-tikki jumped up and backward. Again and again and again she struck, and each time her head came with a whack on the matting of the veranda and she gathered herself together like a watchspring. Then Rikki-tikki danced in a circle to get behind her, and Nagaina spun round to keep her head to his head, so that the rustle of her tail on the matting sounded like dry leaves blown along by the wind.

He had forgotten the egg. It still lay on the veranda, and Nagaina came nearer and nearer to it, till at last, while Rikki-tikki was drawing breath, she caught it in her mouth, turned to the veranda steps, and flew like an arrow down the path, with Rikki-tikki behind her. When the cobra runs for her life, she goes like a whiplash flicked across a horse's neck.

Rikki-tikki knew that he must catch her, or all the trouble would begin again. She headed straight for the long grass by the

Literary Analysis
Plot and Conflict Why is the conflict intensified at this point?

Reading Strategy
Predicting What do you predict will be the outcome of Rikki-tikki's fight with Nagaina? Why?

thornbush, and as he was running Rikki-tikki heard Darzee still singing his foolish little song of triumph. But Darzee's wife was wiser. She flew off her nest as Nagaina came along, and flapped her wings about Nagaina's head. If Darzee had helped they might have turned her; but Nagaina only lowered her hood and went on. Still, the instant's delay brought Rikki-tikki up to her, and as she plunged into the rat hole where she and Nag used to live, his little white teeth were clenched on her tail, and he went down with her—and very few mongooses, however wise and old they may be, care to follow a cobra into its hole. It was dark in the hole; and Rikki-tikki never knew when it might open out and give Nagaina room to turn and strike at him. He held on savagely, and struck out his feet to act as brakes on the dark slope of the hot, moist earth.

Then the grass by the mouth of the hole stopped waving, and Darzee said: "It is all over with Rikki-tikki! We must sing his death song. Valiant Rikki-tikki is dead! For Nagaina will surely kill him underground."

So he sang a very mournful song that he made up all on the spur of the minute, and just as he got to the most touching part the grass quivered again, and Rikki-tikki, covered with dirt, dragged himself out of the hole leg by leg, licking his whiskers. Darzee stopped with a little shout. Rikki-tikki shook some of the dust out of his fur and sneezed. "It is all over," he said. "The widow will never come out again." And the red ants that live between the grass stems heard him, and began to troop down one after another to see if he had spoken the truth.

Rikki-tikki curled himself up in the grass and slept where he was—slept and slept till it was late in the afternoon, for he had done a hard day's work.

"Now," he said, when he awoke, "I will go back to the house. Tell the Coppersmith, Darzee, and he will tell the garden that Nagaina is dead."

The Coppersmith is a bird who makes a noise exactly like the beating of a little hammer on a copper pot; and the reason he is always making it is because he is the town crier to every Indian garden, and tells all the news to everybody who cares to listen. As Rikki-tikki went up the path, he heard his "attention" notes

▲ **Critical Viewing**
What role does Darzee, the tailor-bird, play in the conflict between Rikki-tikki-tavi and Nag? **[Analyze]**

Literary Analysis
Plot How does Darzee's comment add to the tension?

Reading Check

Who wins the battle—Nagaina or Rikki?

like a tiny dinner gong; and then the steady "*Ding-dong-tock! Nag is dead—dong! Nagaina is dead! Ding-dong-tock!*" That set all the birds in the garden singing, and the frogs croaking; for Nag and Nagaina used to eat frogs as well as little birds.

When Rikki got to the house, Teddy and Teddy's mother and Teddy's father came out and almost cried over him; and that night he ate all that was given him till he could eat no more, and went to bed on Teddy's shoulder, where Teddy's mother saw him when she came to look late at night.

"He saved our lives and Teddy's life," she said to her husband. "Just think, he saved all our lives."

Rikki-tikki woke up with a jump, for all the mongooses are light sleepers.

"Oh, it's you," said he. "What are you bothering for? All the cobras are dead; and if they weren't, I'm here."

Rikki-tikki had a right to be proud of himself; but he did not grow too proud, and he kept that garden as a mongoose should keep it, with tooth and jump and spring and bite, till never a cobra dared show its head inside the walls.

Review and Assess

Thinking About the Literature

1. **Respond:** Did you find the story gripping or suspenseful? Why or why not?

2. **(a) Recall:** What is the relationship between Rikki and the two cobras? **(b) Compare:** How do their personalities compare? **(c) Extend:** What makes Rikki a hero?

3. **(a) Recall:** What is the relationship between Nag and Nagaina? **(b) Analyze:** What does Nagaina do to make matters worse for her and Nag? **(c) Draw Conclusions:** Why does this make her a villain?

4. **(a) Recall:** Who is Darzee? **(b) Analyze:** What role does he play? **(c) Compare and Contrast:** Whose approach to life, Darzee's or Rikki's, do you think is more effective? Why?

5. **(a) Support:** How do the animals in the story resemble humans? **(b) Draw Conclusions:** How is "the great war that Rikki-tikki-tavi fought" a battle between good and evil?

6. **(a) Analyze:** "Rikki-tikki-tavi" is among the most widely read short stories ever written. How do you explain the story's enduring popularity? **(b) Evaluate:** Do you think it deserves this standing? Explain.

Rudyard Kipling

(1865–1936)

Rudyard Kipling was born in Bombay, India, to English parents. Though he moved to England when he was six, Kipling remained strongly attached to the land of his birth. In 1882, he returned there as a journalist and began writing the stories that would make him famous.

Published in England, his collections of stories met immediate success, bringing the details of Indian life, especially its landscape and wildlife, to an eager audience. Popularity in America soon followed. Kipling traveled a great deal and wrote several books of stories and poems, many for children. Books such as *The Jungle Book* and *Captains Courageous* were made into successful feature films. Kipling was the first English writer to win the Nobel Prize for Literature. [For more on Kipling, see page 133.]

Review and Assess

Literary Analysis

Plot

1. What relationships are established in the exposition between (a) Rikki and Teddy? (b) Rikki and Nag?
2. What are two **plot** events that increase the tension between Rikki and Nag?
3. Make an organizer like the one shown to identify events that move the plot toward the climax.

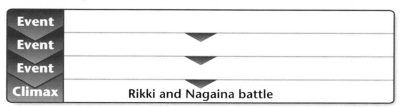

Event	
Event	
Event	
Climax	**Rikki and Nagaina battle**

Connecting Literary Elements

4. Why are Nag and Rikki in **conflict** at the beginning of the story?
5. What does Nag do to make the conflict worse?
6. What is the resolution, or final outcome, of the conflict?

Reading Strategy

Predicting

7. What clues early in the story show that Rikki is capable of facing challenges?
8. Make a chart like the one here to evaluate one prediction you made while reading.

Events and details that support prediction and outcome → What I predicted / What actually happened → Why prediction was or was not accurate

9. (a) List five events that contributed to Nag's death. (b) At which point did you predict that Rikki would kill Nag?

Extend Understanding

10. **Science Connection:** Find three scientific facts about animals that Kipling includes in the story.

Quick Review

Plot is the arrangement of events in a literary work. To review plot, see page 407.

Conflict is the struggle between two opposing forces. To review conflict, see page 407.

A **prediction** is an educated guess based on clues or hints. To review predicting, see page 407.

 Take It to the Net
www.phschool.com
Take the interactive self-test online to check your understanding of the selection.

Integrate Language Skills

Vocabulary Development Lesson

Word Analysis: Latin Root -viv-

The word *revived* contains the Latin root *-viv-*, meaning "life." Explain how "life" fits into the meaning of each of the following words. Then, use each word in a sentence as described below.

    a. vivacious   **b.** vivid

1. Write a sentence about a young man with a lively personality.
2. Write a sentence about a brightly colored bird.

Spelling Strategy

Mourning and *morning* are homophones—they are spelled differently and have different meanings, but they have the same pronunciation. Write the following sentences, correcting the misused homophones.

1. She sat on a peer, fishing.
2. Derek likes to dress in stile.
3. Cara has a flare for designing clothes.

Fluency: Sentence Completions

On your paper, write the vocabulary word that best completes each of the following sentences. To help you, review the vocabulary words on page 407.

1. The contest winner received a trophy, and the other entrants received ___?___ prizes.
2. Her hair was ___?___ from her fall into the pond.
3. He was gloomy because he was ___?___ the death of his turtle.
4. The pirate's treasure chest was ___?___ concealed in a cave behind a waterfall.
5. The wilted plant ___?___ when I watered it and opened the curtains to give it more sunlight.

Grammar Lesson

Simple and Compound Sentences

A **simple sentence** consists of one independent clause (a group of words that has a subject and a verb and can stand by itself as a complete sentence). A **compound sentence** consists of two or more independent clauses. These clauses may be linked by a semicolon or by a word such as *and, but, or, yet,* or *so.*

Simple Sentence

Rikki fights snakes.

Compound Sentence

Independent Clause	Independent Clause
Rikki feared Nag, but	he fought him anyway.

▶ *For more practice, see page R31, Exercise E.*
Practice On your paper, split the following compound sentences into simple sentences.

1. Rikki is curious; he is also brave.
2. Teddy's family might remain in India, or they might return to England.
3. The cobras plotted, and then Nag slipped into the house.
4. Rikki was not afraid, so he did not hesitate.
5. The mongoose hung on, but the snake broke loose.

Writing Application Write a paragraph summarizing one scene in "Rikki-tikki-tavi." Use equal numbers of simple and compound sentences.

W͛G Prentice Hall Writing and Grammar Connection: Chapter 20, Section 2

Writing Lesson

Report on Animals

The mongoose and the cobra are natural enemies. Both are native to India, as the story reveals. Prepare a brief report on the actual relationship of these two animals. Incorporate comparisons and contrasts to the details in the story.

Prewriting Conduct research in the library or on the Internet to gather information about the animals. Find details about their appearance, habitat, diet, and behavior.

Drafting Draft your report using the information you have collected. Describe the animals' natural environment, and show how they fit into it. Give exact details and define any technical terms you use.

Model: Including Details

Although Rikki eats bananas and eggs in the story, bananas are rarely part of a wild mongoose's diet. Mongooses are carnivorous—they eat meat. Rodents, birds, and snakes make up most of their diet.

> The writer defines the term *carnivorous* for readers who are not familiar with the term.

Revising Ask a peer reviewer to read your draft and underline confusing or technical language in red. Incorporate an explanation or definition for each underlined word.

WG *Prentice Hall Writing and Grammar Connection: Chapter 11, Section 3*

Extension Activities

Research and Technology In a group, plan a **presentation** about the author of "Rikki-tikki-tavi," Rudyard Kipling. Include information about major events in his life and his most important literary works. You might also include

- drawings or photos of Kipling and his world.
- a reading from his work.
- a timeline or map showing events in his life.

Use your own words to present the material, unless you are quoting. Present your findings to your class, and when you are finished, take questions from the class.

Listening and Speaking In pairs, role-play a **dialogue** between Rikki-tikki-tavi and either Chuchundra or Darzee. Use the descriptions of the characters from the story to assist you in creating the character's manner of speaking. Think about the tempo and pitch that character might use.

Writing Write an **essay** in which you compare and contrast two of the characters from the story.

 Take It to the Net   www.phschool.com

Go online for an additional research activity using the Internet.

Prepare to Read

After Twenty Years

 Take It to the Net

Visit www.phschool.com for interactive activities and instruction related to the selection, including
- background
- graphic organizers
- literary elements
- reading strategies

Preview

Connecting to the Literature

You have probably had the experience of seeing a friend after a long absence. During your time apart, your looks, interests, or taste in clothing may have changed. Imagine how different someone might look and act if you had not seen him or her for twenty years.

Background

"After Twenty Years," by O. Henry, takes place in New York City in the late 1800s or early 1900s. The city was the largest in the nation, with a population of more than three million. People traveled on foot, on horseback, in horse-drawn carriages, or by trolley, but at night many streets were nearly deserted. Police officers patrolled the streets on foot to deter crime.

Literary Analysis

Surprise Ending

The events in a story usually build to a climax, or high point, and then wind down to a satisfying ending. However, sometimes the writer cleverly plans the ending to be a complete surprise—something the reader did not expect at all. A successful **surprise ending** is startling, but, on second thought, really does make sense. O. Henry is a master of the surprise ending.

As you read this story, think about the following focus questions.

1. What details give hints about the ending?
2. How do you think the story will end?

Connecting Literary Elements

Foreshadowing is the use of clues to hint at later events in a story. These clues create curiosity and anticipation about what will happen as the story unfolds. For example, the sentence "When about midway of a certain block the policeman suddenly slowed his walk" hints that the police officer has seen something suspicious. Use a chart like this one to record clues and suggested outcomes.

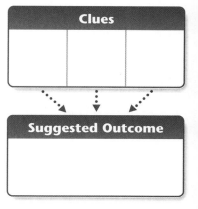

Reading Strategy

Breaking Down Sentences

To grasp the meaning of a long, complex sentence, break it up into groups of words. Use punctuation as a guide when possible. Then, figure out the subject of the sentence (who or what it is about) and the main thing that happens. In the following sentence, the "heart" of the sentence—the subject and the main action—are shown in boldface. The rest of the sentence is broken into logical chunks, which are indicated by commas.

> Trying doors as he went, twirling his club with many intricate and artful movements, turning now and then to cast his watchful eye adown the pacific thoroughfare, **the officer,** with his stalwart form and slight swagger, **made a fine picture of a guardian of the peace.**

Vocabulary Development

spectators (spek´ tāt´ ərz) *n.* onlookers (p. 428)

intricate (in´ tri kit) *adj.* complex; full of complicated detail (p. 428)

destiny (des´ tə nē) *n.* what will necessarily happen; fate (p. 430)

dismally (diz´ məl lē) *adv.* gloomily; miserably (p. 431)

absurdity (ab sur´ də tē) *n.* ridiculousness; foolishness (p. 431)

simultaneously (sī´ məl tā´ nē əs lē) *adv.* at the same time (p. 431)

After Twenty Years

O. Henry

The policeman on the beat moved up the avenue impressively. The impressiveness was habitual and not for show, for <u>spectators</u> were few. The time was barely 10 o'clock at night, but chilly gusts of wind with a taste of rain in them had well nigh[1] depeopled the streets.

Trying doors as he went, twirling his club with many <u>intricate</u> and artful movements, turning now and then to cast his watchful

spectators (spek´ tāt´ ərz) *n.* onlookers

intricate (in´ tri kit) *adj.* complex; full of complicated detail

---

1. well nigh (nī) very nearly.

Nighthawks, 1942, Edward Hopper, The Art Institute of Chicago

eye adown the pacific thoroughfare,[2] the officer, with his stalwart form and slight swagger, made a fine picture of a guardian of the peace. The vicinity was one that kept early hours. Now and then you might see the lights of a cigar store or of an all-night lunch counter; but the majority of the doors belonged to business places that had long since been closed.

When about midway of a certain block the policeman suddenly

2. **pacific thoroughfare** calm street.

▲ **Critical Viewing**
What details in this painting match the setting of the story? **[Connect]**

☑ **Reading Check**
What is the officer doing?

slowed his walk. In the doorway of a darkened hardware store a man leaned, with an unlighted cigar in his mouth. As the policeman walked up to him the man spoke up quickly.

"It's all right, officer," he said, reassuringly. "I'm just waiting for a friend. It's an appointment made twenty years ago. Sounds a little funny to you, doesn't it? Well, I'll explain if you'd like to make certain it's all straight. About that long ago there used to be a restaurant where this store stands—'Big Joe' Brady's restaurant."

"Until five years ago," said the policeman. "It was torn down then."

Reading Strategy
Breaking Down Sentences What is the main action of the sentence beginning "In the doorway"?

The man in the doorway struck a match and lit his cigar. The light showed a pale, square-jawed face with keen eyes, and a little white scar near his right eyebrow. His scarfpin was a large diamond, oddly set.

Literary Analysis
Surprise Ending Foreshadowing What hints does this paragraph give about what might happen next?

"Twenty years ago tonight," said the man, "I dined here at 'Big Joe' Brady's with Jimmy Wells, my best chum, and the finest chap in the world. He and I were raised here in New York, just like two brothers, together. I was eighteen and Jimmy was twenty. The next morning I was to start for the West to make my fortune. You couldn't have dragged Jimmy out of New York; he thought it was the only place on earth. Well, we agreed that night that we would meet here again exactly twenty years from that date and time, no matter what our conditions might be or from what distance we might have to come. We figured that in twenty years each of us ought to have our destiny worked out and our fortunes made, whatever they were going to be."

"It sounds pretty interesting," said the policeman. "Rather a long time between meets, though, it seems to me. Haven't you heard from your friend since you left?"

destiny (des′ tə nē) *n.* what will necessarily happen to any person or thing; fate

"Well, yes, for a time we corresponded," said the other. "But after a year or two we lost track of each other. You see, the West is a pretty big proposition, and I kept hustling around over it pretty lively. But I know Jimmy will meet me here if he's alive, for he always was the truest, stanchest old chap in the world. He'll never forget. I came a thousand miles to stand in this door tonight, and it's worth it if my old partner turns up."

The waiting man pulled out a handsome watch, the lids of it set with small diamonds.

"Three minutes to ten," he announced. "It was exactly ten o'clock when we parted here at the restaurant door."

"Did pretty well out West, didn't you?" asked the policeman.

"You bet! I hope Jimmy has done half as well. He was a kind of plodder, though, good fellow as he was. I've had to compete with some of the sharpest wits going to get my pile. A man gets in a groove in New York. It takes the West to put a razor-edge on him."

The policeman twirled his club and took a step or two.

"I'll be on my way. Hope your friend comes around all right. Going to call time on him sharp?"

"I should say not!" said the other. "I'll give him half an hour at least. If Jimmy is alive on earth he'll be here by that time. So long, officer."

"Good-night, sir," said the policeman, passing on along his beat, trying doors as he went.

There was now a fine, cold drizzle falling, and the wind had risen from its uncertain puffs into a steady blow. The few foot passengers astir in that quarter hurried <u>dismally</u> and silently along with coat collars turned high and pocketed hands. And in the door of the hardware store the man who had come a thousand miles to fill an appointment, uncertain almost to <u>absurdity</u>, with the friend of his youth, smoked his cigar and waited.

About twenty minutes he waited, and then a tall man in a long overcoat, with collar turned up to his ears, hurried across from the opposite side of the street. He went directly to the waiting man.

"Is that you, Bob?" he asked, doubtfully.

"Is that you, Jimmy Wells?" cried the man in the door.

"Bless my heart!" exclaimed the new arrival, grasping both the other's hands with his own. "It's Bob, sure as fate. I was certain I'd find you here if you were still in existence. Well, well, well!— twenty years is a long time. The old restaurant's gone, Bob; I wish it had lasted, so we could have had another dinner there. How has the West treated you, old man?"

"Bully;[3] it has given me everything I asked it for. You've changed lots, Jimmy. I never thought you were so tall by two or three inches."

"Oh, I grew a bit after I was twenty."

"Doing well in New York, Jimmy?"

"Moderately. I have a position in one of the city departments. Come on, Bob; we'll go around to a place I know of, and have a good long talk about old times."

The two men started up the street, arm in arm. The man from the West, his egotism enlarged by success, was beginning to outline the history of his career. The other, submerged in his overcoat, listened with interest.

At the corner stood a drug store, brilliant with electric lights. When they came into this glare each of them turned <u>simultaneously</u> to gaze upon the other's face.

The man from the West stopped suddenly and released his arm.

---

3. Bully *interj.* very well.

dismally (diz´ məl lē) *adv.* gloomily; miserably

absurdity (ab sur´ də tē) *n.* ridiculousness; foolishness

simultaneously (sī´ məl tā´ nē əs lē) *adv.* at the same time

Reading Check

How does Jimmy know that Bob will be waiting for him?

"You're not Jimmy Wells," he snapped. "Twenty years is a long time, but not long enough to change a man's nose from a Roman to a pug."[4]

"It sometimes changes a good man into a bad one," said the tall man. "You've been under arrest for ten minutes, 'Silky' Bob. Chicago thinks you may have dropped over our way and wires us she wants to have a chat with you. Going quietly are you? That's sensible. Now, before we go to the station here's a note I was asked to hand to you. You may read it here at the window. It's from Patrolman Wells."

The man from the West unfolded the little piece of paper handed him. His hand was steady when he began to read, but it trembled a little by the time he had finished. The note was rather short.

Bob: I was at the appointed place on time. When you struck the match to light your cigar I saw it was the face of the man wanted in Chicago. Somehow I couldn't do it myself, so I went around and got a plain clothes man to do the job. Jimmy.

---

4. **change a man's nose from a Roman to a pug** A Roman nose has a high, prominent bridge; a pug nose is short, thick, and turned up at the end.

O. Henry

(1862–1910)

O. Henry is the pen name of William Sydney Porter, a writer famous for his warm, witty short stories about ordinary people. Born in North Carolina, Porter went to Texas to seek his fortune, working at a ranch, a land office, a bank, and a newspaper. For a time he was editor and publisher of a humor magazine. Porter also spent three years in prison for embezzling bank funds (a crime he may not have committed), and in prison he wrote his first short stories.

Porter later moved to New York and continued his writing career, winning great popularity. Many of his stories are based in New York City and are inspired by his time in jail, where he gained an understanding of people on both sides of the law.

Review and Assess

Thinking About the Selection

1. **Respond:** Do you think that Officer Wells did the right thing? Explain your answer.

2. **(a) Recall:** Where is the story set? **(b) Analyze:** Describe the atmosphere, or feeling, of the story, using two details from the story. **(c) Interpret:** How do the setting and the time of day affect the story?

3. **(a) Recall:** How does Bob describe Jimmy—both his strengths and weaknesses? **(b) Infer:** How did Bob spend his time in the West? **(c) Synthesize:** Based on his words and actions, describe Bob's personality.

4. **(a) Support:** What evidence shows that both Bob and Jimmy are proud of their accomplishments?
   (b) Make a Judgment: Who has been more successful, Bob or Jimmy? Explain your answer.

5. **(a) Support:** How much has Jimmy changed over the years? Support your answer with evidence from the story.
   (b) Draw Conclusions: What does this story suggest about the way the passage of time affects people?

6. **Make a Judgment:** Is there such a thing as "lifelong friends"? Explain your answer.

Review and Assess

Literary Analysis

Surprise Ending

1. How do you think things will turn out for Bob? Why?
2. What is surprising about the ending of "After Twenty Years"?
3. On a chart like this one, analyze the last four paragraphs of "After Twenty Years," noting what is surprising in each paragraph.

What Happens	What Is Surprising
1. Man lets go of his friend's arm	It seems that something has gone wrong.

Connecting Literary Elements

4. How does the description of the "man in the doorway" **foreshadow** that he might be a suspicious character?
5. On a chart like this one, list three of Jimmy's actions or characteristics that foreshadow his actions at the story's end.

```
[          ]          [          ]
           Jimmy
[          ]          [ true and staunch ]
```

Reading Strategy

Breaking Down Sentences

6. What are the two subjects of this sentence? How do you know?

   The time was barely 10 o'clock at night, but chilly gusts of wind with a taste of rain in them had well nigh depeopled the streets.

7. Which part of the following sentence tells what the man is doing?

   And in the door of the hardware store the man who had come a thousand miles to fill an appointment, uncertain almost to absurdity, with the friend of his youth, smoked his cigar and waited.

8. Restate the main action of this sentence in your own words.

   The man from the West, his egotism enlarged by success, was beginning to outline the history of his career.

Extend Understanding

9. **Career Connection:** Name three skills that a police officer must have. Note how Officer Wells exemplifies each one.

Quick Review

A **surprise ending** is an unexpected conclusion to a story. To review surprise ending, see page 427.

Foreshadowing is the use of clues to hint at what will happen later in a story. To review foreshadowing, see page 427.

To **break down a sentence,** find the subject and main action of the sentence; then, use punctuation to group words.

 Take It to the Net
www.phschool.com
Take the interactive self-test online to check your understanding of the selection.

Integrate Language Skills

Vocabulary Development Lesson

Word Analysis: Latin Root -spec-

Early in the story, O. Henry uses the word *spectator*, referring to a person who watches. The word comes from the Latin root -spec-, which means "see" or "look." Define each word, incorporating the definition of -spec- into each answer.

1. spectacle
2. prospector
3. respect
4. inspect

Spelling Strategy

Words that describe types of people often end with the sound /ər/, which can be spelled -er (*teacher*) or -or (*professor*). Use the -or spelling when the word is based on a verb that ends in -ate, -ct, or -ess.

Write the word that describes a person who performs each of the following actions.

1. decorate   2. direct   3. process

Fluency: Definitions

Answer the following questions. Explain each answer. To help you, review the vocabulary words on page 427.

1. Can a person avoid his or her *destiny*?
2. Do ordering a book on the Internet and receiving it in the mail happen *simultaneously*?
3. Would you find the *spectators* at a baseball game in the stands or on the field?
4. Is a duck in a three-piece suit an *absurdity*?
5. Would a delighted child regard the perfect birthday gift *dismally*?
6. Which would you describe as *intricate*—a plain sheet of paper or an elaborate piece of lace?

Grammar Lesson

Clauses

A **clause** is a group of words with its own subject and verb. The two major types of clauses are independent clauses and subordinate clauses. An independent (main) clause has a subject and a verb and can stand by itself as a complete sentence. A subordinate clause has a subject and a verb, but it can form only part of a sentence.

Subordinate Clause   Independent Clause
        S   V
| When they came into the glare, |

    S   V
| each of them turned to gaze upon the other. |

▶ *For more practice, see page R30, Exercise D.*
Practice Copy these sentences. Bracket each clause as in the example, and identify each as *independent* or *subordinate*.

1. We agreed that night that we would meet again.
2. If Jimmy is alive on earth, he'll be here.
3. When I see him, I will ask about his life.
4. After he waited twenty minutes, he saw a tall man hurry across the street.
5. When you struck the match, I saw the face of the man wanted in Chicago.

Writing Application Write three sentences about the story, using a subordinate clause and an independent clause in each one.

WG *Prentice Hall Writing and Grammar Connection: Chapter 20, Section 2*

Writing Lesson

Prequel

"After Twenty Years" is centered on the agreement Bob and Jimmy made years ago. Write a prequel—the story before the story, focusing on the conversation in which Bob tells Jimmy he is moving out west and the two men make their agreement.

Prewriting   Make a two-column chart. Use one column for Jimmy's words and expressions. Use the other column for Bob's. Review the story and find examples of their language. Put the examples and any descriptions of their language in your notebook.

Drafting   Draft your story, telling what happens. Add details and actions to show what each character is like. Use plenty of dialogue to show what Jimmy and Bob say.

Model: Dialogue

"Bob," said Jimmy cautiously, "I do not think we should sneak any roses out of Mr. Goldberg's garden."

"Nonsense!" laughed Bob. "Your mother will love them! Let's pick a few for her. Mr. Goldberg will never miss them."

> A character's exact words through dialogue can help show personality, interests, and what the character values.

Revising   Review your draft to make sure you have portrayed each character accurately. Read aloud each passage of dialogue to make sure it sounds like real speech and revise words that do not fit the character.

WG *Prentice Hall Writing and Grammar Connection: Chapter 5, Section 3*

Extension Activities

Listening and Speaking   Write a brief **news bulletin** about the arrest of "Silky" Bob. Then, in the role of a radio announcer, read your bulletin to the class, following these pointers.

1. Speak your words clearly, using good enunciation. Make your consonants sound crisp.
2. Raise and lower your voice for dramatic effect.
3. Speak slowly enough for your audience to follow what you are saying, but not so slowly that they get bored.

Research and Technology   With other classmates, create an **informational display** about New York City in the early twentieth century. Use the Internet and library resources to gather statistics, photos, maps, and interesting information about what the city looked like and how people lived at the time. **[Group Activity]**

 **Take It to the Net**   www.phschool.com

Go online for an additional research activity using the Internet.

Prepare to Read

Papa's Parrot

 Take It to the Net

Visit www.phschool.com
for interactive activities and
instruction related to
"Papa's Parrot," including
- background
- graphic organizers
- literary elements
- reading strategies

Preview

Connecting to the Literature

In "Papa's Parrot," by Cynthia Rylant, a boy discovers the consequences of avoiding something that he should have done. Think about
how the boy must feel as he learns a lesson about taking care of the most
important things in life.

Background

Parrots learn to say words or phrases that are frequently repeated.
While most of a parrot's "vocabulary" is taught on purpose, a parrot sometimes learns sounds or words accidentally. For example, some parrots learn
to make the sound of a ringing telephone because they hear it frequently.

Literary Analysis

Characterization

A writer can reveal characters' personalities in two basic ways:

- **Direct characterization:** The writer tells you the characters' traits through the narrator's direct statements and descriptions. The following example from the story is an example of direct characterization:

  > Rocky was good company.

- **Indirect characterization:** The writer reveals the characters' personalities through their own words, thoughts, and actions, as well as by what other characters say to them or about them. The following example of indirect characterization shows, rather than tells, the reader that Harry likes his father and enjoys spending time with him.

  > For years, after school, Harry had always stopped in to see his father at work.

As you read, notice how characters are revealed directly or indirectly.

Connecting Literary Elements

Character traits are the character's qualities. For example, characters can have qualities such as *dependability*, *intelligence*, or *determination*.

As you read about each character, think about the following questions.

1. What are the traits of the two main characters?
2. What actions or descriptions reveal these traits?

Reading Strategy

Identifying with a Character

Stories give you a chance to live another life for a while. To do this, you **identify with a character.** You put yourself in the character's place and think about how you would react to the situations that he or she experiences.

As you read "Papa's Parrot," identify with either Harry or Papa, the two main characters. Make an organizer like the one shown for each major event. Then, record the character's reaction to it as well as what you would have said or done in the same situation.

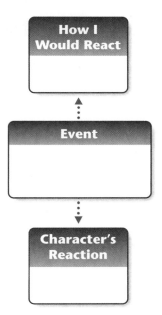

Vocabulary Development

clusters (klus´ tərs) *n.* sets of similar items grouped together; bunches (p. 439)

shipments (ship mənts) *n.* sets of goods or cargo shipped together (p. 440)

resumed (ri zōōmd´) *v.* began again; continued (p. 440)

Papa's Parrot

Cynthia Rylant

*T*hough his father was fat and merely owned a candy and nut shop, Harry Tillian liked his papa. Harry stopped liking candy and nuts when he was around seven, but, in spite of this, he and Mr. Tillian had remained friends and were still friends the year Harry turned twelve.

For years, after school, Harry had always stopped in to see his father at work. Many of Harry's friends stopped there, too, to spend a few cents choosing penny candy from the giant bins or to sample Mr. Tillian's latest batch of roasted peanuts. Mr. Tillian looked forward to seeing his son and his son's friends every day. He liked the company.

When Harry entered junior high school, though, he didn't come by the candy and nut shop as often. Nor did his friends. They were older and they had more spending money. They went to a burger place. They played video games. They shopped for records. None of them were much interested in candy and nuts anymore.

A new group of children came to Mr. Tillian's shop now. But not Harry Tillian and his friends.

The year Harry turned twelve was also the year Mr. Tillian got a parrot. He went to a pet store one day and bought one for more money than he could really afford. He brought the parrot to his shop, set its cage near the sign for maple <u>clusters</u>, and named it Rocky.

Harry thought this was the strangest thing his father had ever done, and he told him so, but Mr. Tillian just ignored him.

Rocky was good company for Mr. Tillian. When business was slow, Mr. Tillian would turn on a small color television he had sitting in a corner, and he and Rocky would watch the soap operas. Rocky liked to scream when the romantic music came on, and Mr. Tillian would yell at him to shut up, but they seemed to enjoy themselves.

The more Mr. Tillian grew to like his parrot, and the more he talked to it instead of to people, the more embarrassed Harry became. Harry would stroll past the shop, on his way somewhere else, and he'd take a quick look inside to see what his dad was doing. Mr. Tillian was always talking to the bird. So Harry kept walking.

◀ **Critical Viewing** What unique ability of parrots is suggested by the combination of the photograph and the title of the story? **[Apply Prior Knowledge]**

Literary Analysis
Characterization
What do you learn about Mr. Tillian through direct characterization in the opening paragraphs?

clusters (klus´ tərs) *n.* sets of similar items grouped together; bunches

✔**Reading Check**
Why is Harry embarrassed by his father?

At home things were different. Harry and his father joked with each other at the dinner table as they always had—Mr. Tillian teasing Harry about his smelly socks; Harry teasing Mr. Tillian about his blubbery stomach. At home things seemed all right.

But one day, Mr. Tillian became ill. He had been at work, unpacking boxes of caramels, when he had grabbed his chest and fallen over on top of the candy. A customer had found him, and he was taken to the hospital in an ambulance.

Mr. Tillian couldn't leave the hospital. He lay in bed, tubes in his arms, and he worried about his shop. New shipments of candy and nuts would be arriving. Rocky would be hungry. Who would take care of things?

Harry said he would. Harry told his father that he would go to the store every day after school and unpack boxes. He would sort out all the candy and nuts. He would even feed Rocky.

So, the next morning, while Mr. Tillian lay in his hospital bed, Harry took the shop key to school with him. After school he left his friends and walked to the empty shop alone. In all the days of his life, Harry had never seen the shop closed after school. Harry didn't even remember what the CLOSED sign looked like. The key stuck in the lock three times, and inside he had to search all the walls for the light switch.

The shop was as his father had left it. Even the caramels were still spilled on the floor. Harry bent down and picked them up one by one, dropping them back in the boxes. The bird in its cage watched him silently.

Harry opened the new boxes his father hadn't gotten to. Peppermints. Jawbreakers. Toffee creams. Strawberry kisses. Harry traveled from bin to bin, putting the candies where they belonged.

"Hello!"

Harry jumped, spilling a box of jawbreakers.

"Hello, Rocky!"

Harry stared at the parrot. He had forgotten it was there. The bird had been so quiet, and Harry had been thinking only of the candy.

"Hello," Harry said.

"Hello, Rocky!" answered the parrot.

Harry walked slowly over to the cage. The parrot's food cup was empty. Its water was dirty. The bottom of the cage was a mess.

Harry carried the cage into the back room.

"Hello, Rocky!"

"Is that all you can say, you dumb bird?" Harry mumbled. The bird said nothing else.

Harry cleaned the bottom of the cage, refilled the food and water cups, and then put the cage back in its place and resumed sorting the candy.

"Where's Harry?"

shipments (ship mənts) *n.* sets of goods or cargo shipped together

Literary Analysis
Characterization What do you learn about Harry through his actions?

Reading Strategy
Identifying with a Character How would you react to doing the job that Harry must do?

resumed (ri zo͞omd′) *v.* began again; continued

Harry looked up.

"Where's Harry?"

Harry stared at the parrot.

"Where's Harry?"

Chills ran down Harry's back. What could the bird mean? It was something from "The Twilight Zone."[1]

"Where's Harry?"

Harry swallowed and said, "I'm here. I'm here, you stupid bird."

"You stupid bird!" said the parrot.

Well, at least he's got one thing straight, thought Harry.

"Miss him! Miss him! Where's Harry? You stupid bird!"

Harry stood with a handful of peppermints.

---

1. **"The Twilight Zone"** science-fiction television series from the 1960s.

Reading Check

What did the parrot ask that made chills run down Harry's back?

"What?" he asked.

"Where's Harry?" said the parrot.

"I'm *here*, you stupid bird! I'm here!" Harry yelled. He threw the peppermints at the cage, and the bird screamed and clung to its perch.

Harry sobbed, "I'm here." The tears were coming.

Harry leaned over the glass counter.

"Papa." Harry buried his face in his arms.

"Where's Harry?" repeated the bird.

Harry sighed and wiped his face on his sleeve. He watched the parrot. He understood now: someone had been saying, for a long time, "Where's Harry? Miss him."

Harry finished his unpacking and then swept the floor of the shop. He checked the furnace so the bird wouldn't get cold. Then he left to go visit his papa.

Review and Assess

Thinking About the Selection

1. **Respond:** Should Harry tell his father what he learned from Rocky? Why or why not?

2. **(a) Recall:** What does Mr. Tillian do for a living?
   (b) Recall: Why do Harry and his friends visit Mr. Tillian after school? **(c) Infer:** Why do Harry and his friends eventually stop visiting Harry's father?

3. **(a) Recall:** Who is Rocky? **(b) Analyze Cause and Effect:** What is Mr. Tillian's motivation, or reason, for buying a parrot? **(c) Analyze:** Why is it significant that Mr. Tillian paid more than he could afford for his parrot?

4. **(a) Analyze:** What can you tell about what motivates Harry from the fact that he walks by his father's shop, looks in, but doesn't stop? **(b) Synthesize:** How has Harry changed since turning twelve?

5. **(a) Recall:** How does Harry react when Rocky says "Where's Harry?" and "Miss him!"? **(b) Analyze:** Why does Harry react as he does?

6. **(a) Synthesize:** Describe Harry's relationship with his father.
   (b) Speculate: How might the father and son relate differently in the future?

7. **(a) Apply:** What does each of the main characters need to understand and accept about the other? **(b) Make a Judgment:** Which character has a greater responsibility to be understanding? Why?

Cynthia Rylant

(b. 1954)

Cynthia Rylant, who grew up in a West Virginia mountain town, originally planned to be a nurse. However, she fell in love with literature in college and switched her major to English.

Later, while working as a librarian, Rylant discovered children's books and was hooked. Her love of books inspired her to write one of her own. Her first book, *When I Was Young in the Mountains*, was published in 1982. It was followed by picture books, novels, short stories, poetry, and biographies. Rylant's 1992 novel, *Missing May*, won a Newbery Award.

Review and Assess

Literary Analysis

Characterization

1. What are two details about Mr. Tillian that are revealed through **direct characterization?**
2. **(a)** Make an organizer like the one shown to record examples of Harry's actions at different ages. **(b)** How does the author use **indirect characterization** to show changes in Harry's personality?

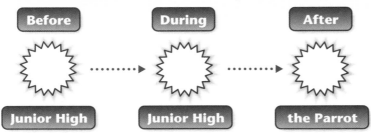

Before ┄┄┄➤ During ┄┄┄➤ After

Junior High   Junior High   the Parrot

Connecting Literary Elements

3. What are two of Harry's **character traits** at age twelve?
4. What are two of Mr. Tillian's character traits?
5. What actions or descriptions reveal each character's traits? Show your answer on a chart like the one below.

	Traits	Actions or descriptions
Harry	1.	
	2.	
Mr. Tillian	1.	
	2.	

Reading Strategy

Identifying With a Character

6. How might you feel if you, like Mr. Tillian, knew that your son was avoiding your shop?
7. If you were in Harry's situation at the end of the story, what changes would you make in your life?
8. What can you learn from Harry's experience to help you?

Extend Understanding

9. **Health Connection:** Why might doctors recommend parrots or other pets for older people who are alone?

Quick Review

In **direct characterization**, the writer tells you the characters' traits. In **indirect characterization**, the writer reveals the characters' traits through their own words, thoughts, and actions, and by what other characters say to or about them. To review **characterization**, see p. 437.

Character traits are a character's qualities. To review character traits, see p. 437.

To **identify with a character,** put yourself in the character's place.

 Take It to the Net
www.phschool.com
Take the interactive self-test online to check your understanding of the selection.

Integrate Language Skills

Vocabulary Development Lesson

Word Analysis: Latin Suffix *-ment*

Mr. Tillian received *shipments* of candy. The word *shipment*, meaning "a group of items shipped together," includes the Latin suffix *-ment*, which can mean "the result of an action or process." Add the Latin suffix *-ment* to each of the following words, and then use each one in a sentence.

1. measure
2. improve
3. govern
4. arrange

Spelling Strategy

Many words contain letters that are not pronounced. These are called silent letters. Write a complete sentence identifying the silent letter in each of these words.

Example: The silent letter in *sign* is *g*.

1. comb
2. knife
3. hymn
4. psychology

Concept Development: Synonyms

On your paper, write the word or phrase whose meaning is closest to that of the first word. To help you, review the vocabulary words and their definitions on p. 437.

1. cluster:
   a. a group,
   b. a strong wind,
   c. a type of small bird
2. shipment:
   a. a harbor for ships,
   b. the lower deck of a ship,
   c. cargo
3. resumed:
   a. assumed,
   b. reached again,
   c. started again

Grammar Lesson

Complex Sentences

A **complex sentence** contains one independent clause, which can stand by itself as a complete sentence, and one or more subordinate clauses. A subordinate clause contains a subject and a verb but cannot stand alone. A subordinate clause starts with a word (or words) that links it to the rest of the sentence. Words that introduce subordinate clauses include *after, although, as, as if, because, before, despite, if, so that, that, until, what, when, where, which, while,* and *who*.

—— SUBORDINATE CLAUSE ——
Although Harry loved his father,

—— INDEPENDENT CLAUSE ——
he was embarrassed by him.

▶ *For more practice, see page R30, Exercise D.*
Practice Copy the sentences. Underline the independent clause. Circle the word that introduces the subordinate clause.

1. While Mr. Tillian lay in his hospital bed, Harry took care of the shop.
2. Harry stopped visiting when he was twelve.
3. It was the parrot that spoke.
4. Harry worked until everything was orderly.
5. Harry fed the parrot before he left.

Writing Application Add a subordinate clause to each sentence.

1. Harry went to the store.
2. The parrot waited for food.
3. Mr. Tillian liked to chat.

W̶G Prentice Hall Writing and Grammar Connection: Chapter 20, Section 2

Writing Lesson

Story Summary

If asked about "Papa's Parrot," you'd probably give a summary, or a brief retelling of events and their meaning. Write a summary of "Papa's Parrot."

Prewriting Create a story outline to organize your thoughts. Briefly describe the setting, major characters, events, and outcome, using an outline like this one. When listing events, include one significant event from the beginning, one from the middle, and one from the end.

> **Model: Story Outline**
>
> Setting: _____   Events: _____
>
> _____
>
> Characters: _____   Outcome: _____
>
> _____

Drafting Write your summary, using information from your outline. Use connecting words such as *because*, *later*, and *however* to show relationships between events. Conclude with a statement about what is learned from story events.

Revising Delete details or events that are not the main event from the beginning, the middle, or the end of the story.

WG Prentice Hall Writing and Grammar Connection: Chapter 12, Section 2

Extension Activities

Listening and Speaking In a small group, prepare a **dramatic reading** of "Papa's Parrot." Divide the text so everyone can present a portion. Rehearse before performing, focusing on these points.

1. Speak clearly and enunciate so that each word is audible.
2. Raise and lower your voice to communicate emotion where appropriate.
3. Slow down and emphasize certain words for effect.
4. Keep your audience involved by making frequent eye contact. **[Group Activity]**

Research and Technology Use the Internet and library resources to find information about the process by which parrots learn to speak. Use the information you find in a brief **report** that explains:

(a) why the parrot knows how to say "Where's Harry" and

(b) why the parrot continues to ask, even though Harry is in the room.

Take It to the Net   www.phschool.com

Go online for an additional research activity using the Internet.

Prepare to Read

Suzy and Leah

 Take It to the Net

Visit www.phschool.com for interactive activities and instruction related to "Suzy and Leah," including
- background
- graphic organizers
- literary elements
- reading strategies

Preview

Connecting to the Literature

When you have a problem, you probably reach out to people close to you for comfort or guidance. In "Suzy and Leah," by Jane Yolen, a young girl is afraid to reach out to others and ask for help.

Background

"Suzy and Leah" is based on true events. The War Refugee Board was established in January 1944 with the goal of rescuing victims of Nazi persecution from death in German-occupied Europe. In one rescue effort, 982 people from eighteen countries were brought to a refugee camp in Oswego, New York.

Literary Analysis

The **setting** of a story is the time and place of the action. In this example from the story, the details in italics help establish the setting of a refugee camp in Oswego, New York.

> Today I walked past *that* place . . . Gosh it is *ugly*! A line of *rickety wooden buildings* just like in the army. And *a fence lots higher than my head. With barbed wire on top.*

The importance of the setting varies. In some stories, the setting is little more than a background. In others, the setting shapes the characters' actions. In "Suzy and Leah," the setting is at first an obstacle to the girls' understanding each other.

Connecting Literary Elements

Sometimes, the **historical context**—the political and social events and trends of the time—plays a key role in a story setting. This story, for example, is set against the backdrop of World War II and Nazi Germany. One of the title characters, Leah, has experienced the violence of war firsthand.

As you read, use the following focus questions to explore the way the war has shaped Leah's thoughts and behavior.

1. How does Leah feel about Suzy and about her new home?
2. How do Leah's experiences of war help explain these feelings?

Reading Strategy

Drawing Inferences

Short-story writers do not tell you everything there is to know about the characters, setting, and events. Instead, they leave it to you to fill in the missing information by **drawing inferences,** or conclusions, based on the material that is provided. To draw inferences, combine information in the text with your own knowledge and understanding and consider what the information might mean. For example, Suzy comments on the prison-like details of the camp. You can infer from her comments and her tone that she is a little frightened by the camp.

As you read, jot down key details and record your inferences in a diagram like the one shown.

Vocabulary Development

refugee (ref′ yoo jē) *n.* person who flees home or country to seek shelter from war or cruelty (p. 448)

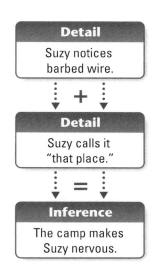

Suzy and Leah

Jane Yolen

August 5, 1944

Dear Diary,

Today I walked past *that* place, the one that was in the newspaper, the one all the kids have been talking about. Gosh, is it ugly! A line of rickety wooden buildings just like in the army. And a fence lots higher than my head. With barbed wire[1] on top. How can anyone—even a <u>refugee</u>—live there?

I took two candy bars along, just like everyone said I should. When I held them up, all those kids just swarmed over to the fence, grabbing. Like in a zoo. Except for this one girl, with two dark braids and bangs nearly covering her eyes. She was just standing to one side, staring at me. It was so creepy. After a minute I looked away. When I looked back, she was gone. I mean gone. Disappeared as if she'd never been.

Suzy

refugee (ref´ yoo jē) *n.* person who flees home or country to seek shelter from war or cruelty

August 5, 1944

My dear Mutti,[2]

I have but a single piece of paper to write on. And a broken pencil. But I will write small so I can tell all. I address it to you, *Mutti,* though you are gone from me forever. I write in English, to learn better, because I want to make myself be understood.

Today another girl came. With more sweets. A girl with yellow hair and a false smile. Yonni and Zipporah and Ruth, my friends, all grabbed for the sweets. Like wild animals. Like . . . like prisoners. But we are not wild animals. And we are no longer prisoners. Even though we are still penned in.

I stared at the yellow-haired girl until she was forced to look down. Then I walked away. When I turned to look back, she was gone. Disappeared. As if she had never been.

Leah

---

1. barbed wire twisted wire with sharp points all along it, used for fences and barriers.
2. Mutti (moo´ tē) German equivalent of Mommy.

September 2, 1944

Dear Diary,

I brought the refugee kids oranges today. Can you believe it—they didn't know you're supposed to peel oranges first. One boy tried to eat one like an apple. He made an awful face, but then he ate it anyway. I showed them how to peel oranges with the second one. After I stopped laughing.

Mom says they are going to be coming to school. Of course they'll have to be cleaned up first. Ugh. My hand still feels itchy from where one little boy grabbed it in his. I wonder if he had bugs.

Suzy

Reading Strategy
Drawing Inferences What can you infer about Suzy's understanding of the refugees from her thoughts and feelings?

September 2, 1944

My dear Mutti,

Today we got cereal in a box. At first I did not know what it was. Before the war we ate such lovely porridge with milk straight from our cows. And eggs fresh from the hen's nest, though you know how I hated that nasty old chicken. How often she pecked me! In the German camp, it was potato soup—with onions when we were lucky, without either onion or potato when we were not. And after, when I was running from the Nazis, it was stale brown bread, if we could find any. But cereal in a box—*that* is something.

I will not take a sweet from that yellow-haired girl, though. She laughed at Yonni. I will not take another orange fruit.

Leah

September 5, 1944

Dear Diary,

So how are those refugee kids going to learn? Our teachers teach in English. This is America, after all.

I wouldn't want to be one of them. Imagine going to school and not being able to speak English or understand anything that's going on. I can't imagine anything worse.

Suzy

▲ **Critical Viewing**
How is the expression on this girl's face different from the way Leah's expression is described? When might Leah have been more like the girl in the photograph?
[Compare and Contrast]

Reading Check

Where do Leah and her friends live?

September 5, 1944

My dear Mutti,

The adults of the Americans say we are safe now. And so we must go to their school. But I say no place is safe for us. Did not the Germans say that we were safe in their camps? And there you and baby Natan were killed.

And how could we learn in this American school anyway? I have a little English. But Ruth and Zipporah and the others, though they speak Yiddish[3] and Russian and German, they have no English at all. None beyond *thank you* and *please* and *more sweets.* And then there is little Avi. How could he go to this school? He will speak nothing at all. He stopped speaking, they say, when he was hidden away in a cupboard by his grandmother who was taken by the Nazis after she swore there was no child in the house. And he was almost three days in that cupboard without food, without water, without words to comfort him. Is English a safer language than German?

There is barbed wire still between us and the world.

Leah

---

3. Yiddish (yid´ ish) *n.* language spoken by eastern European Jews and their descendants. It is written with Hebrew letters and contains words from Hebrew, German, Russian, and Polish.

▲ **Critical Viewing**
This photograph shows the Nazi government overseeing Jews leaving their homes. What do you find most upsetting about the picture?
[Respond]

Literary Analysis
Historical Context How have Leah and Avi been shaped by their experiences with the Nazis?

September 14, 1944

Dear Diary,

At least the refugee kids are wearing better clothes now. And they all have shoes. Some of them still had those stripy pajamas on when they arrived in America.

The girls all wore dresses to their first day at school, though. They even had hair bows, gifts from the teachers. Of course I recognized my old blue pinafore.[4] The girl with the dark braids had it on, and Mom hadn't even told me she was giving it away. I wouldn't have minded so much if she had only asked. It doesn't fit me anymore, anyway.

The girl in my old pinafore was the only one without a name tag, so all day long no one knew her name.

Suzy

Reading Strategy
Drawing Inferences What can you infer about Suzy's character from her remarks about her blue pinafore?

September 14, 1944

My dear Mutti,

I put on the blue dress for our first day. It fit me well. The color reminded me of your eyes and the blue skies over our farm before the smoke from the burning darkened it. Zipporah braided my hair, but I had no mirror until we got to the school and they showed us the toilets. They call it a bathroom, but there is no bath in it at all, which is strange. I have never been in a school with boys before.

They have placed us all in low grades. Because of our English. I do not care. This way I do not have to see the girl with the yellow hair who smiles so falsely at me.

But they made us wear tags with our names printed on them. That made me afraid. What next? Yellow stars?[5] I tore mine off and threw it behind a bush before we went in.

Leah

September 16, 1944

Dear Diary,

Mr. Forest has assigned each of us to a refugee to help them with their English. He gave me the girl with the dark braids, the one without the name tag, the one in my pinafore. Gee, she's as prickly as a porcupine. I asked if I could have a different kid. He said I was the best English student and she already spoke the best English. He wants her to learn as fast as possible so she can help the others. As if she would, Miss Porcupine.

Her name is Leah. I wish she would wear another dress.

Suzy

✔**Reading Check**

What happened to Leah's mother?

---

4. **pinafore** (pin´ ə fôr´) a sleeveless garment worn over a dress, often over a blouse.
5. **yellow stars** Jews were forced to wear fabric stars during the Holocaust to distinguish them from others.

September 16, 1944

My dear Mutti,

Now I have a real notebook and a pen. I am writing to you at
school now. I cannot take the notebook back to the shelter. Someone
there will surely borrow it. I will instead keep it here. In the little cupboard each one of us has been given.

I wish I had another dress. I wish I had a different student helping
me and not the yellow-haired girl.

Leah

Literary Analysis
Setting Why does Leah
assume her notebook is
not safe at the shelter?

September 20, 1944

Dear Diary,

Can't she ever smile, that Leah? I've brought her candy bars and
apples from home. I tried to give her a handkerchief with a yellow
flower on it. She wouldn't take any of them.

Her whole name is Leah Shoshana Hershkowitz. At least, that's the
way she writes it. When she says it, it sounds all different, low and
growly. I laughed when I tried to say it, but she wouldn't laugh with
me. What a grouch.

And yesterday, when I took her English paper to correct it, she
shrank back against her chair as if I was going to hit her or something. Honestly!

Mom says I should invite her home for dinner soon. We'll have
to get her a special pass for that. But I don't know if I want her to
come. It's not like she's any fun at all. I wish Mr. Forest would let
me trade.

Suzy

▼ **Critical Viewing**
What can you infer about
the children in this
photograph? Cite details
that led you to this
inference. **[Infer]**

September 20, 1944

My dear Mutti,

The girl with the yellow hair is called Suzy Ann McCarthy.
It is a silly name. It means nothing. I asked her who she
was named for, and she said, "For a book my mom liked."
A book! I am named after my great-grandmother on my
mother's side, who was an important woman in our village.
I am proud to carry on her name.

This Suzy brings many sweets. But I must call them
candies now. And a handkerchief. She expects me to be
grateful. But how can I be grateful? She treats me like a pet,
a pet she does not really like or trust. She wants to feed me
like an animal behind bars.

If I write all this down, I will not hold so much anger. I have much
anger. And terror besides. *Terror.* It is a new word for me, but an old
feeling. One day soon this Suzy and her people will stop being nice to
us. They will remember we are not just refugees but Jews, and they
will turn on us. Just as the Germans did. Of this I am sure.

Leah

September 30, 1944

Dear Diary,

Leah's English is very good now. But she still never smiles. Especially she never smiles at me. It's like she has a permanent frown and permanent frown lines between her eyes. It makes her look much older than anyone in our class. Like a little old lady.

I wonder if she eats enough. She won't take the candy bars. And she saves the school lunch in her napkin, hiding it away in her pocket. She thinks no one sees her do it, but I do. Does she eat it later? I'm sure they get dinner at the shelter. Mom says they do. Mom also says we have to eat everything on our plates. Sometimes when we're having dinner I think of Leah Shoshana Hershkowitz.

Suzy

▲ **Critical Viewing**
Part of this story is set in a refugee camp, like the one shown here. What details in the photograph are confirmed in Suzy's letters? **[Support]**

September 30, 1944

My dear Mutti,

Avi loves the food I bring home from school. What does he know? It is not even kosher.[6] Sometimes they serve ham. But I do not tell Avi. He needs all the food he can get. He is a growing boy.

I, too, am growing fast. Soon I will not fit into the blue dress. I have no other.

Leah

October 9, 1944

Dear Diary,

They skipped Leah up to our grade, her English has gotten so good. Except for some words, like victory, which she pronounces "wick-toe-ree." I try not to laugh, but sometimes I just can't help it!

Leah knows a lot about the world and nothing about America. She thinks New York is right next to Chicago, for goodness sakes! She can't dance at all. She doesn't know the words to any of the top songs. And she's so stuck up, she only talks in class to answer questions. The other refugees aren't like that at all. Why is it only my refugee who's so mean?

Suzy

✔ **Reading Check**

What does Leah do with her food at lunchtime?

---

6. **kosher** (kō´ shər) *adj.* fit to eat according to the Jewish laws of diet.

October 9, 1944

My dear Mutti,

I think of you all the time. I went to Suzy's house because Mr. Forest said they had gone to a great deal of trouble to get a pass for me. I did not want to go so much, my stomach hurt the whole time I was there.

Suzy's *Mutti* was nice, all pink and gold. She wore a dress with pink roses all over it and it reminded me of your dress, the blue one with the asters. You were wearing it when we were put on the train. And the last time I saw you at the camp with Natan. Oh, *Mutti*, I had to steel my heart against Suzy's mother. If I love her, I will forget you. And that I must never do.

I brought back food from her house, though, for Avi. I could not eat it myself. You would like the way Avi grows bigger and stronger. And he talks now, but only to me. He says, "More, Leah, please." And he says "light" for the sun. Sometimes when I am really lonely I call him Natan, but only at night after he has fallen asleep.

Leah

Literary Analysis
Setting How does being in Suzy's home affect Leah?

October 10, 1944

Dear Diary,

Leah was not in school today. When I asked her friend Zipporah, she shrugged. "She is ill in her stomach," she said. "What did she eat at your house?"

I didn't answer "Nothing," though that would have been true. She hid it all in a handkerchief Mom gave her. Mom said, "She eats like a bird. How does she stay alive?"

Suzy

October 11, 1944

Dear Diary,

They've asked me to gather Leah's things from school and bring them to the hospital. She had to have her appendix out and nearly died. She almost didn't tell them she was sick until too late. Why did she do that? I would have been screaming my head off with the pain.

Mom says we have to visit, that I'm Leah's American best friend. Hah! We're going to bring several of my old dresses, but not my green one with the white trim. I don't want her to have it. Even if it doesn't fit me anymore.

Suzy

October 12, 1944

Dear Diary,

I did a terrible thing. I read Leah's diary. I'd kill anyone who did that to me!

At first it made no sense. Who were *Mutti* and Natan, and why were they killed? What were the yellow stars? What does kosher mean? And the way she talked about me made me furious. Who did she think she was, little Miss Porcupine? All I did was bring candy and fruit and try to make those poor refugee kids feel at home.

Then, when I asked Mom some questions, carefully, so she wouldn't guess I had read Leah's diary, she explained. She said the Nazis killed people, mothers and children as well as men. In places called concentration camps. And that all the Jews—people who weren't Christians like us—had to wear yellow stars on their clothes so they could be spotted blocks and blocks away. It was so awful I could hardly believe it, but Mom said it was true.

How was I supposed to know all that? How can Leah stand any of us? How could she live with all that pain?

Suzy

▲ **Critical Viewing**
The girls pictured here are looking out of a ship's porthole as they prepare to go to America. Which girl has an expression you'd expect to see on Leah's face? Explain.
[Connect]

October 12, 1944

My dear Mutti,

Suzy and her mother came to see me in the hospital. They brought me my notebook so now I can write again.

I was so frightened about being sick. I did not tell anyone for a long time, even though it hurt so much. In the German camp, if you were sick and could not do your work, they did not let you live.

But in the middle of the night, I had so much fever, a doctor was sent for. Little Avi found me. He ran to one of the guards. He spoke out loud for the first time. He said, "Please, for Leah. Do not let her go into the dark."

The doctor tells me I nearly died, but they saved me. They have given me much medicines and soon I will eat the food and they

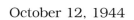

☑ **Reading Check**
What does Suzy learn about Leah's past?

will be sure it is kosher, too. And I am alive. This I can hardly believe. *Alive!*

Then Suzy came with her *Mutti,* saying, "I am sorry. I am so sorry. I did not know. I did not understand." Suzy did a bad thing. She read my notebook. But it helped her understand. And then, instead of making an apology, she did a strange thing. She took a red book with a lock out of her pocket and gave it to me. "Read this," she said. "And when you are out of the hospital, I have a green dress with white trim I want you to have. It will be just perfect with your eyes."

I do not know what this trim may be. But I like the idea of a green dress. And I have a new word now, as well. It is this: *diary.*

A new word. A new land. And—it is just possible—a new friend.
Leah

Review and Assess

Thinking About the Selection

1. **Respond:** How do you think you would have reacted if you had tried to help Leah and she had rejected you?

2. **(a) Recall:** What happened to Leah's mother and brother?
   (b) Interpret: How does Leah come to live in Suzy's town?
   (c) Analyze: What does Leah mean when she says, "There is barbed wire still between us and the world"?

3. **(a) Recall:** How are Suzy and Leah forced to get to know each other? **(b) Analyze:** What do Suzy's reactions to Leah tell you about Suzy? **(c) Analyze:** What do Leah's reactions to Suzy tell you about Leah?

4. **(a) Recall:** Why doesn't Leah eat the food she is given?
   (b) Apply: In what other ways does Leah's experience of the war affect her thoughts and behavior in the story?

5. **(a) Distinguish:** How do Suzy's motivations for offering candy to Leah at the story's beginning differ from her motivations for offering her diary to Leah at the end of the story? **(b) Draw Conclusions:** What has each girl learned from her experience with the other?

6. **(a) Connect:** This story is set decades ago in a difficult time in history. Do you think it teaches lessons that still apply today? Explain. **(b) Make a Judgment:** Why do you think it is or is not important to study events from history? **(c) Extend:** Why do you think it is or is not important to be aware of political events occurring in other countries?

Jane Yolen

(b. 1939)
Jane Yolen's storytelling career began in first grade, when she wrote a class musical about vegetables. Since then, Yolen has written more than two hundred books. She has produced novels, short stories, poems, plays, and essays. She gets her ideas from an "idea file" that she keeps. Whenever a letter, magazine article, or experience gives her the seed of an idea, she saves it in a file. When she is looking for ideas, she reviews the file.

Although Yolen is known mainly for her fantasy stories, she found inspiration in her Jewish heritage to write "Suzy and Leah," the story of a Holocaust survivor. Yolen wrote about the Holocaust so that her own children could understand and remember.

Review and Assess

Literary Analysis

Setting

1. Describe the setting of "Suzy and Leah."
2. Why is the setting of "Suzy and Leah" essential to the story?
3. The girls' different backgrounds and experiences affect the way they think about the time and place in which they live. Use a chart like this one to explain how each element of setting affects each girl.

Suzy	Elements of Setting	Leah
	The war	
	The refugee camp	
	School	

Connecting Literary Elements

4. How does Leah feel about Suzy and her new home?
5. How do Leah's experiences of war help to explain these feelings?
6. In a chart like the one below, record three details from Leah's diary entries, and explain what they reveal about how the war has affected her.

Diary Entry	What It Reveals
But I say no place is safe for us. Did not the Germans say we were safe in their camps?	Helps to explain why Leah is distrustful of Suzy and others who want to help her.

····▸

Reading Strategy

Drawing Inferences

7. Suzy and Leah's first observations of each other end with nearly identical words: "When I looked back, she was gone. . . . Disappeared as if she'd never been." What can you infer from this?
8. Based on her experience with wearing a yellow star, infer why Leah is frightened when she is asked to wear a name tag.
9. What can you infer about Leah based on her attitude toward Suzy's name?

Extend Understanding

10. **Social Studies Connection:** How has this story affected your understanding of the Holocaust?

Quick Review

The **setting** of a story is the time and place of the action. To review setting, see page 447.

The **historical context** of this story is World War II and Nazi Germany. To review the historical context, see the background on page 446.

When you read, you can fill in the missing information by **drawing inferences** based on the material that is provided.

 Take It to the Net
www.phschool.com
Take the interactive self-test online to check your understanding of the selection.

Integrate Language Skills

Vocabulary Development Lesson

Word Analysis: Latin Suffix -ee

The Latin suffix -ee indicates a person who is or receives something. For example, Leah is a refugee. The word *refugee* is formed by adding the suffix -ee to the word *refuge*. Thus, a refugee is a person who seeks or has taken refuge.

Copy the following sentences on your paper. Replace -ed in a word from the first sentence with -ee to create the word that completes the second sentence.

1. Is he employed there? Yes, he's an ___?___.
2. Is she retired? Yes she's a ___?___.
3. Was he inducted in the army? Yes, he's an ___?___.

Concept Development: Definition

1. Choose the best definition of the vocabulary word.

   refugee (a) person needing food, (b) person giving help, (c) person seeking safety

2. Use *refugee* in a sentence about Leah. Include in the sentence an indication of why she seeks safety.

Spelling Strategy

When you add -ee to a word that ends in the letter *e*, drop the final *e* before adding the suffix: *escape* + -ee = *escapee*. If the word ends in a consonant, simply add -ee: *appoint* + -ee = *appointee*.

On your paper, add -ee to the following words.

1. devote	3. trust
2. award	4. absent

Grammar Lesson

Adverb Clauses

An **adverb clause** is a subordinate clause (a group of words that has a subject and a verb but cannot stand alone as a sentence) that functions as an adverb. The entire clause modifies a verb, adjective, or other adverb. Like one-word adverbs, adverb clauses answer the questions *when, where, how, why,* and *to what extent*. Adverb clauses begin with subordinating conjunctions. Common subordinating conjunctions are *after, as, although, because, if, since, when, unless,* and *until*.

When I held them up, all those kids just swarmed over to the fence, grabbing. (Tells when)

▶ *For more practice, see page R30, Exercise D.*
Practice Copy each sentence. Underline each adverb clause, and draw an arrow to the word it modifies. Then, tell what question the adverb clause answers.

1. I write in English because I want to be understood.
2. I stared at the yellow-haired girl until she was forced to look down.
3. He stopped speaking when he was hidden away in a cupboard.
4. If I write all this down, I will not hold so much anger.
5. I had no mirror until we got to the school.

Writing Application Write two sentences about "Suzy and Leah," and include an adverb clause in each.

 Prentice Hall Writing and Grammar Connection: Chapter 20, Section 2

Writing Lesson

Introduction to an Exhibition

Imagine you are helping your local museum prepare an exhibit, or display, about the setting of "Suzy and Leah." Write an introductory brochure to help visitors understand what they will see in the exhibit.

Prewriting   Make a list of questions that the exhibit should answer. Then do library or Internet research, and summarize key information on note cards like the one below. Arrange your cards in a logical order, and use them to write an outline for your brochure.

> **Where?**
>
> The exhibit about Safe Haven, a refugee camp in Oswego, New York.

> Your brochure should answer the questions *who, what, why, where,* and *when* about the topic. Gather answers on note cards like this one.

Drafting   Begin your brochure with the most important facts. End by explaining how the exhibit relates to the historical background.

Revising   Compare your brochure with the information from your sources to make sure that you have conveyed a clear and accurate perspective on your subject.

W̶G Prentice Hall Writing and Grammar Connection: Chapter 11, Section 2

Extension Activities

Listening and Speaking Write an **expository speech** that explains the conditions in the Oswego refugee camp to an audience who is unfamiliar with the topic. After collecting Internet and library research, write your speech so that it appeals to the background and interest of your audience. Use the following techniques:

- define terms that might be unfamiliar
- offer historical context where necessary
- make clear cause-and-effect relationships
- speak slowly and clearly

Research and Technology With a group of class-mates, write a **research report** about the Holocaust. Use Internet, library, and community resources to collect information. Use information from a variety of sources, and make sure your report conveys a clear and accurate perspective on the topic. **[Group Activity]**

 **Take It to the Net**   www.phschool.com

Go online for an additional research activity using the Internet.

CONNECTIONS

Historical Fiction, Past and Present

Young People in Literature

Young people through the ages have often had to face severe difficulties. In "Suzy and Leah," Leah's mother and younger brother were killed while imprisoned in a concentration camp for Jews in Nazi Germany. Like Leah, the heroine of "The Midwife's Apprentice," Alyce, is a homeless child who has to make her own way in the world. However, Alyce lived about a thousand years before Leah. Each of these girls rises above the adversity she is faced with and becomes stronger because of the way she lives her life. As you read the selection, look for similarities and differences between Alyce and Leah.

The Midwife's Apprentice

Karen Cushman

Garden in the interior of a palace: a young lady and her servant, from Recueil de miniatures

Alyce, a homeless child, is taken in by a sharp-tongued midwife (a woman who helps others with childbirth). She makes the girl her apprentice. One day, Alyce finds Edward, another homeless child. Although she is not able to care for him herself, Alyce persuades the cook at the local baron's manor to give the boy a job and a place to stay. Alyce promises Edward that she will return for him when she can. Months pass. Alyce has an argument with the midwife and takes a job working at an inn. Now that she has an income of her own and a place to live, Alyce returns to the manor to reclaim Edward.

▲ **Critical Viewing** Judging from their clothing, which of the women in this painting do you think is of higher social rank? Explain. **[Compare and Contrast; Support]**

While they ate their bread-and-bacon supper, while Alyce helped Edward mound up straw in a corner of the kitchen, while she sat by watching for him to go to sleep, all the while Edward talked of life on the manor. He told her of the silken-robed lords and ladies who came for feasts and rode out to hunt and danced like autumn leaves in the candle-lit great hall, of the visiting knights who clanked their swords against each other as they practiced in the school yard, of the masons who slapped mortar and bricks together to build a great new tower at the corner of the hall that looked to stretch near all the way to heaven. He described the excitement of buying and selling at the great autumn horse fair, the nervous preparations accompanying the arrival of some velvet-shod bishop or priest, and the thrill of watching the baron's men ride out to confront a huge maddened boar who had <u>roamed</u> too close to the village. And he complained at his lot, doing all the smallest tasks, not being allowed to help with the threshing and ploughing, being teased for being so little and <u>frail</u> and tied to Cook's skirts and fit for nothing but gathering eggs. Finally as his eyes looked near to closing, he said, "Tell me a story, Alyce."

"I don't know any stories."

"For sure you do. Everyone does."

"Well, Jennet told me that one night a visiting mayor fell out of bed, hit his head, and thought he was a cat, so he slept all night on the floor watching the mouseholes."

"That is no story, Alyce. Cook tells me stories. A story should have a hero and brave deeds."

"Well then, once there was a boy who for all he was so small and puny was brave enough to do what he must although he didn't like it and was sometimes teased. Is that a story?"

"Close enough, Alyce." And he closed his eyes.

When the moon shone through the misty clouds and two owls hooted in the manor yard, Edward and Alyce slept, each comforted by knowing the other was safe and warm and sheltered and not too very far away.

The next day being the day the woolly black-faced sheep were washed before shearing, Alyce and Edward ate their breakfast down by the river to watch the great event.

Edward finished his breakfast first. "I'm still hungry, Alyce, and there is nothing about here to eat but grass. Do you know if grass is good for people to eat?"

"Try it."

He did. "It be good for exercising my teeth and making my mouth taste better, but it tastes like . . . grass, I would say."

"Then do not eat it."

"What is the best thing you ever ate, Alyce?"

"Hot soup on a cold day, I think."

"Once long ago a monk gave me a fig. It was a wonderful thing, Alyce,

roamed (rōmd) *v.* wandered

frail (frāl) *adj.* delicate or weak

Thematic Connection
Describe Alyce and Edward's relationship.

soft and sweet. After that I had nothing to eat for three days but the smell of the fig on my fingers. Are you ever going to finish that bread, Alyce?"

And Alyce gave him her bread, which is what Edward wanted and Alyce intended all along.

Part of the river had been dammed to form a washing pool. Men stood in the waist-deep water while the hairy shepherds, looking much like sheep themselves, drove the woolly beasts into the water to have their loose fleeces pulled off and then be scrubbed with the strong yellow soap. The river was noisy with the barking of dogs, the bleating of sheep, the calling and cursing of men, and the furious bawling[1] of those lambs separated from their mothers. Edward soon took on the job of matching mothers and babies. He snatched up the bawling lambs and ran from mother to mother until he made up the right pair, whereupon they would knock him out of the way in their hurry to nuzzle each other.

As the day grew hotter the river looked cooler, and finally Alyce tucked her skirt up into her belt and waded in. The weary men were glad of another pair of hands and soon had Alyce helping. First she held the woolly black faces while they were scrubbed, but one old ewe took offense at Alyce's handling and, standing up with her front feet on Alyce's chest, pushed the girl into the water. Alyce, coughing and sputtering, traded jobs with the man who was lathering their backs. Fleeces clean, the sheep swam to the bank and scrambled out of the water, <u>nimble</u> as goats and hungry as pigs.

By midafternoon they were finished. While Edward and the shepherds drove the sheep to their pens across the field, Alyce stretched and wiped her wet hands on her wet skirt. What a wonder, she thought, looking at her hands. How white they were and how soft. The hours of strong soap and sudsy fleece had accomplished what years of cold water never had— her hands were really clean. There was no dirt between her fingers, around her nails, or ground into the lines on her palms. She sat back against a tree, held her hands up before her, and admired them. How clean they were. How white.

Farmyard with woman milking cow, from the Da Costa Book of Hours, Bruges, c. 1515

▲ **Critical Viewing**
What can you infer about medieval life from this painting? **[Infer]**

nimble (nim´ bəl) *adj.* moving quickly and lightly

---

1. bawling (bôl´ iŋ) *n.* loud or angry cries.

Suddenly she sat forward. Was the rest of her then that white and clean under all the dirt? Was her face white and clean? Was Will Russet right—was she even pretty under the dirt? There never had been one pretty thing about her, just skinny arms and big feet and dirt, but lately she had been told her hair was black and curly and her eyes big and sad and she was mayhap even pretty.

Alyce looked about. The washing was done and the sheep driven to the barn to dry off for tomorrow's shearing. The river was empty but for great chunks of the greasy yellow soap floating here and there. Alyce found a spot a bit upriver from the befouled[2] washing pool, pulled off her clothes, and waded in. She rubbed her body with the yellow soap and a handful of sandy gravel until she tingled. Squatting down until the water reached her chin, she washed her hair and watched it float about her until she grew chilled.

Alyce stood up in the shallow water and looked at herself. Much cleaner, although a bit pink and wrinkled from her long soak. And pretty? Mayhap even that, for she had all her teeth and all her limbs, a face unmarked by pox, and perhaps, now, more of happiness and hope than of sadness in those big eyes that even the midwife had remarked on.

She washed her clothes, pulled them on still wet and drippy, and ran for the kitchen to dry a bit before the fire.

Too soon it was time to bid Edward good-bye. "Be assured I will not be far from here, and I promise to come back for Christmas and Easter and your saint's day. And to see when that front tooth grows in again." Edward grinned. He had enjoyed the day, done a man's job, and been carried home on the shoulders of a giant of a shepherd called Hal. He was satisfied with his place at the manor, the <u>devotion</u> of the cook, and the friendship of Alyce. He suddenly felt not so small.

Alyce gave him a hug and a smack and felt that tickling in her throat and stinging in her eyes that meant she might cry again, now she knew how to do it. She went down the path from the manor, stopping every few steps to turn and wave until finally the path curved and Edward was lost from sight and all she could see was the way ahead.

---

2. **befouled** (bē fould´) *adj.* dirty.

Connecting Literature Past and Present

1. What are some of the things both Leah and Alyce have had to do without?

2. Why do you think that both Leah and Alyce feel responsible to the two young boys, Avi and Edward?

3. How believable do you find the characters of Leah and Alyce? What factors influence your reaction?

4. How believable do you find the events? Explain.

Thematic Connection
What discovery does Alyce make in this paragraph?

devotion (di vō´ shən) *n.* loyalty or deep affection

Karen Cushman

(b. 1941)

In stories and poems, Cushman has been taking imaginary journeys to distant lands and earlier ages since she was a girl. She didn't realize people could make a living writing until much later—after she spent time working in museums. At the age of fifty, she finally began writing a novel, which took her more than three years to complete.

Prepare to Read

Ribbons ◆ The Treasure of Lemon Brown

Four Piece Orchestra, 1944, Ben Shahn, 17 1/2 by 23 1/2 inches © Estate of Ben Shahn/Licensed by VAGA, New York, NY

Take It to the Net

Visit www.phschool.com for interactive activities and instruction related to these selections, including

- background
- graphic organizers
- literary elements
- reading strategies

Preview

Connecting to the Literature

In "Ribbons" by Laurence Yep and "The Treasure of Lemon Brown" by Walter Dean Myers, characters discover that by drawing upon an older person's experiences, they gain ideas, information, and skills that can shape their future. Think about a time when you learned something from an older member of your family or community.

Background

In "The Treasure of Lemon Brown," a teenager meets a man who was once a famous blues musician. Blues music, which has strongly influenced other forms of music, such as jazz and rock, is part of the African American musical heritage. Blues lyrics often deal with loneliness, sorrow, and life's other troubles.

Literary Analysis

Theme

A story's **theme** is its central message or insight into life. Occasionally, the theme is stated directly. More often, however, the theme is implied. The writer provides clues to the theme through the words and experiences of the characters, through the events and setting of the story, and through significant objects that represent ideas or people. The following example from "The Treasure of Lemon Brown" shows how an heirloom can strengthen a bond of love between generations.

> ". . . That was my treasure, and when I give it to him he treated it just like that, a treasure. Ain't that something?"

Comparing Literary Works

Although the people in these stories are dealing with very different situations, the themes of both stories address the way older and younger people can strengthen their relationships through love and understanding. Use these focus questions to help you compare and contrast the themes.

1. How are the relationships between Greg and Brown and Stacy and her grandmother similar? How are they different?

2. What is similar and different about how the younger and older characters in these stories enrich each other's lives?

Reading Strategy

Asking Questions

By **asking questions** as you read, you will better understand a story and figure out its theme. For example, you might ask the following questions:

- Why is the author telling me this?
- Why does the character do, say, or think that?
- How does this event fit into what has happened so far?

As you read, jot down questions and answers in a chart like this one.

Question	Answer
Why is grandmother sensitive about her feet?	

Vocabulary Development

sensitive (sen´ sə tiv) *adj.* easily hurt or irritated (p. 467)

meek (mēk) *adj.* timid; not showing anger (p. 467)

coax (kōks) *v.* use gentle persuasion (p. 467)

laborious (lə bôr´ ē əs) *adj.* taking much work or effort (p. 467)

exertion (eg zur´ shən) *n.* physical work (p. 468)

impromptu (im prämp´ tōō´) *adj.* unscheduled; unplanned (p. 476)

ajar (ə jär´) *adj.* open (p. 476)

tentatively (ten´ tə tiv lē) *adv.* hesitantly; with uncertainty (p. 476)

Ribbons

LAURENCE YEP

The sunlight swept over the broad grassy square, across the street, and onto our living-room rug. In that bright, warm rectangle of light, I practiced my ballet. Ian, my little brother, giggled and dodged around me while I did my exercises.

A car stopped outside, and Ian rushed to the window. "She's here! She's here!" he shouted excitedly. "Paw-paw's here!" *Paw-paw* is Chinese for grandmother—for "mother's mother."

I squeezed in beside Ian so I could look out the window, too. Dad's head was just disappearing as he leaned into the trunk of the car. A pile of luggage and cardboard boxes wrapped in rope sat by the curb. "Is that all Grandmother's?" I said. I didn't see how it would fit into my old bedroom.

Mom laughed behind me. "We're lucky she had to leave her furniture behind in Hong Kong." Mom had been trying to get her mother to come to San Francisco for years. Grandmother had finally agreed, but only because the British were going to return the city to the Chinese Communists in 1997. Because Grandmother's airfare and legal expenses had been so high, there wasn't room in the family budget for Madame Oblomov's ballet school. I'd had to stop my daily lessons.

The rear car door opened, and a pair of carved black canes poked out like six-shooters. "Wait, Paw-paw," Dad said, and slammed the trunk shut. He looked sweaty and harassed.

Grandmother, however, was already using her canes to get to her feet. "I'm not helpless," she insisted to Dad.

Ian was relieved. "She speaks English," he said.

"She worked for a British family for years," Mom explained.

Turning, Ian ran toward the stairs. "I've got the door," he cried.

Mom and I caught up with him at the front door and made him wait on the porch. "You don't want to knock her over," I said. For weeks, Mom had been rehearsing us for just this moment. Ian was supposed to wait, but in his excitement he began bowing to Grandmother as she struggled up the outside staircase.

Grandmother was a small woman in a padded silk jacket and black slacks. Her hair was pulled back into a bun behind her head. On her small feet she wore a pair of quilted cotton slippers shaped like boots, with furred tops that hid her ankles.

"What's wrong with her feet?" I whispered to Mom.

"They've always been that way. And don't mention it," she said. "She's <u>sensitive</u> about them."

I was instantly curious. "But what happened to them?"

"Wise grandchildren wouldn't ask," Mom warned.

Mom bowed formally as Grandmother reached the porch. "I'm so glad you're here," she said.

Grandmother gazed past us to the stairway leading up to our second-floor apartment. "Why do you have to have so many steps?" she said.

Mom sounded as <u>meek</u> as a child. "I'm sorry, Mother," she said.

Dad tried to change the subject. "That's Stacy, and this little monster is Ian."

"*Joe sun, Paw-paw,*" I said. "Good morning, Grandmother." It was afternoon, but that was the only Chinese I knew, and I had been practicing it.

Mother had coached us on a proper Chinese greeting for the last two months, but I thought Grandmother also deserved an American-style bear hug. However, when I tried to put my arms around her and kiss her, she stiffened in surprise. "Nice children don't drool on people," she snapped at me.

To Ian, anything worth doing was worth repeating, so he bowed again. "*Joe sun, Paw-paw.*"

Grandmother brightened in an instant. "He has your eyes," she said to Mom.

Mom bent and hefted Ian into her arms. "Let me show you our apartment. You'll be in Stacy's room."

Grandmother didn't even thank me. Instead, she stumped up the stairs after Mom, trying to <u>coax</u> a smile from Ian, who was staring at her over Mom's shoulder.

Grandmother's climb was long, slow, <u>laborious</u>. *Thump, thump, thump.* Her canes struck the boards as she slowly mounted the steps. It sounded like the slow, steady beat of a mechanical heart.

◀ **Critical Viewing** Why are ballet shoes an appropriate visual accompaniment to this story? **[Defend]**

sensitive (sen´ sə tiv) *adj.* easily hurt or irritated

meek (mēk) *adj.* timid; not showing anger

Literary Analysis
Theme How might the grandmother's reaction relate to the story's theme?

coax (kōks) *v.* use gentle persuasion

laborious (lə bôr´ ē əs) *adj.* taking much work or effort

 **Reading Check**
Why does the speaker have to stop her daily ballet lessons?

Mom had told us her mother's story often enough. When Mom's father died, Grandmother had strapped my mother to her back and walked across China to Hong Kong to escape the Communists who had taken over her country. I had always thought her trek was heroic, but it seemed even braver when I realized how wobbly she was on her feet.

I was going to follow Grandmother, but Dad waved me down to the sidewalk. "I need you to watch your grandmother's things until I finish bringing them up," he said. He took a suitcase in either hand and set off, catching up with Grandmother at the foot of the first staircase.

While I waited for him to come back, I inspected Grandmother's pile of belongings. The boxes, webbed with tight cords, were covered with words in Chinese and English. I could almost smell their exotic scent, and in my imagination I pictured sunlit waters lapping at picturesque docks. Hong Kong was probably as exotic to me as America was to Grandmother. Almost without thinking, I began to dance.

Dad came back out, his face red from <u>exertion</u>. "I wish I had half your energy," he said. Crouching, he used the cords to lift a box in each hand.

exertion
(eg zʉr´ shən) *n.*
physical work

I pirouetted,[1] and the world spun round and round. "Madame Oblomov said I should still practice every day." I had waited for this day not only for Grandmother's sake but for my own. "Now that Grandmother's here, can I begin my ballet lessons again?" I asked.

Dad turned toward the house. "We'll see, hon."

Disappointment made me protest. "But you said I had to give up the lessons so we could bring her from Hong Kong," I said. "Well, she's here."

Dad hesitated and then set the boxes down. "Try to understand, hon. We've got to set your grandmother up in her own apartment. That's going to take even more money. Don't you want your room back?"

Poor Dad. He looked tired and worried. I should have shut up, but I loved ballet almost as much as I loved him. "Madame put me in the fifth division even though I'm only eleven. If I'm absent much longer, she might make me start over again with the beginners."

"It'll be soon. I promise." He looked guilty as he picked up the boxes and struggled toward the stairs.

Dad had taken away the one hope that had kept me going during my exile[2] from Madame. Suddenly I felt lost, and the following weeks only made me more confused. Mom started laying down all sorts of new rules. First, we couldn't run around or make noise

---

1. pirouetted (pir´ ōō et´ əd) *v.* whirled around on the point of the toe.
2. exile (eg´ zīl´) *n.* forced absence.

Three Studies of a Dancer in Fourth Position, ©1879/80, Edgar Degas, Art Institute of Chicago

◀ **Critical Viewing**
Which character would be most interested in this drawing? Find a sentence on this page or the previous one to support your answer. **[Connect]**

because Grandmother had to rest. Then we couldn't watch our favorite TV shows because Grandmother couldn't understand them. Instead, we had to watch Westerns on one of the cable stations because it was easier for her to figure out who was the good guy and who was the bad one.

Worst of all, Ian got all of her attention—and her candy and anything else she could bribe him with. It finally got to me on a warm Sunday afternoon a month after she had arrived. I'd just returned home from a long walk in the park with some friends. I was looking forward to something cool and sweet, when I found her giving Ian an ice cream bar I'd bought for myself. "But that was *my* ice cream bar," I complained as he gulped it down.

"Big sisters need to share with little brothers," Grandmother said, and she patted him on the head to encourage him to go on eating.

When I complained to Mom about how Grandmother was spoiling

Reading Strategy
Asking Questions What question could you ask about the narrator at this point?

**Reading Check**

How do things change when Grandmother moves into the house?

Ian, she only sighed. "He's a boy, Stacy. Back in China, boys are everything."

It wasn't until I saw Grandmother and Ian together the next day that I thought I really understood why she treated him so much better. She was sitting on a kitchen chair with her head bent over next to his. She had taught Ian enough Chinese so that they could hold short, simple conversations. With their faces so close, I could see how much alike they were.

Ian and I both have the same brown eyes, but his hair is black, while mine is brown, like Dad's. In fact, everything about Ian looks more Chinese. Except for the shape of my eyes, I look as Caucasian as Dad. And yet people sometimes stare at me as if I were a freak. I've always told myself that it's because they're ignorant and never learned manners, but it was really hard to have my own grandmother make me feel that way.

Even so, I kept telling myself: Grandmother is a hero. She saved my mother. She'll like me just as much as she likes Ian once she gets to know me. And, I thought in a flash, the best way to know a person is to know what she loves. For me, that was the ballet.

Ever since Grandmother had arrived, I'd been practicing my ballet privately in the room I now shared with Ian. Now I got out the special box that held my satin toe shoes. I had been so proud when Madame said I was ready to use them. I was the youngest girl on pointe[3] at Madame's school. As I lifted them out, the satin ribbons fluttered down around my wrists as if in a welcoming caress. I slipped one of the shoes onto my foot, but when I tried to tie the ribbons around my ankles, the ribbons came off in my hands.

I could have asked Mom to help me reattach them, but then I remembered that at one time Grandmother had supported her family by being a seamstress.

Grandmother was sitting in the big recliner in the living room. She stared uneasily out the window as if she were gazing not upon the broad, green lawn of the square but upon a Martian desert.

"Paw-paw," I said, "can you help me?"

Grandmother gave a start when she turned around and saw the ribbons dangling from my hand. Then she looked down at my bare feet, which were callused from three years of daily lessons. When she looked back at the satin ribbons, it was with a

▲ **Critical Viewing**
Review Grandmother's actions as described on this page and the next one. What conclusion can you draw about Grandmother's experiences with ribbons based on this painting? **[Draw Conclusions]**

---

3. **on pointe** (pwant) *n.* dancing on the tip of the toe.

hate and disgust that I had never seen before. "Give those to me." She held out her hand.

I clutched the ribbons tightly against my stomach. "Why?"

"They'll ruin your feet." She lunged toward me and tried to snatch them away.

Angry and bewildered, I retreated a few steps and showed her the shoe. "No, they're for dancing!"

All Grandmother could see, though, was the ribbons. She managed to totter to her feet without the canes and almost fell forward on her face. Somehow, she regained her balance. Arms reaching out, she stumbled clumsily after me. "Lies!" she said.

"It's the truth!" I backed up so fast that I bumped into Mom as she came running from the kitchen.

Mom immediately assumed it was my fault. "Stop yelling at your grandmother!" she said.

By this point, I was in tears. "She's taken everything else. Now she wants my toe-shoe ribbons."

Grandmother panted as she leaned on Mom. "How could you do that to your own daughter?"

"It's not like you think," Mom tried to explain.

However, Grandmother was too upset to listen. "Take them away!"

Mom helped Grandmother back to her easy chair. "You don't understand," Mom said.

All Grandmother did was stare at the ribbons as she sat back down in the chair. "Take them away. Burn them. Bury them."

Mom sighed. "Yes, Mother."

As Mom came over to me, I stared at her in amazement. "Aren't you going to stand up for me?"

But she acted as if she wanted to break any ties between us. "Can't you see how worked up Paw-paw is?" she whispered. "She won't listen to reason. Give her some time. Let her cool off." She worked the ribbons away from my stunned fingers. Then she also took the shoe.

For the rest of the day, Grandmother just turned away every time Mom and I tried to raise the subject. It was as if she didn't want to even think about satin ribbons.

That evening, after the dozenth attempt, I finally said to Mom, "She's so weird. What's so bad about satin ribbons?"

"She associates them with something awful that happened to her," Mom said.

That puzzled me even more. "What was that?"

She shook her head. "I'm sorry. She made me promise never to talk about it to anyone."

The next morning, I decided that if Grandmother was going to be mean to me, then I would be mean to her. I began to ignore her. When she entered a room I was in, I would deliberately turn around and leave.

Reading Strategy
Asking Questions What question could you ask about the grandmother's reaction?

✔**Reading Check**

How does Grandmother react when she sees the ribbons from the ballet shoes?

For the rest of the day, things got more and more tense. Then I happened to go into the bathroom early that evening. The door wasn't locked, so I thought it was unoccupied, but Grandmother was sitting fully clothed on the edge of the bathtub. Her slacks were rolled up to her knees and she had her feet soaking in a pan of water.

"Don't you know how to knock?" she snapped, and dropped a towel over her feet.

However, she wasn't quick enough, because I saw her bare feet for the first time. Her feet were like taffy that someone had stretched out and twisted. Each foot bent downward in a way that feet were not meant to, and her toes stuck out at odd angles, more like lumps than toes. I didn't think she had all ten of them, either.

"What happened to your feet?" I whispered in shock.

Looking ashamed, Grandmother flapped a hand in the air for me to go. "None of your business. Now get out."

She must have said something to Mom, though, because that night Mom came in and sat on my bed. Ian was outside playing with Grandmother. "Your grandmother's very upset, Stacy," Mom said.

"I didn't mean to look," I said. "It was horrible." Even when I closed my eyes, I could see her mangled feet.

I opened my eyes when I felt Mom's hand on my shoulder. "She was so ashamed of them that she didn't like even me to see them," she said.

"What happened to them?" I wondered.

Mom's forehead furrowed as if she wasn't sure how to explain things. "There was a time back in China when people thought women's feet had to be shaped a certain way to look beautiful. When a girl was about five, her mother would gradually bend her toes under the sole of her foot."

"Ugh." Just thinking about it made my own feet ache. "Her own mother did that to her?"

Mom smiled apologetically. "Her mother and father thought it would make their little girl attractive so she could marry a rich man. They were still doing it in some of the back areas of China long after it was outlawed in the rest of the country."

I shook my head. "There's nothing lovely about those feet."

"I know. But they were usually bound up in silk ribbons." Mom brushed some of the hair from my eyes. "Because they were a symbol of the old days, Paw-paw undid the ribbons as soon as we were free in Hong Kong—even though they kept back the pain."

I was even more puzzled now. "How did the ribbons do that?"

Mom began to brush my hair with quick, light strokes. "The ribbons kept the blood from circulating freely and bringing more feeling to her feet. Once the ribbons were gone, her feet ached. They probably still do."

I rubbed my own foot in sympathy. "But she doesn't complain."

"That's how tough she is," Mom said.

Finally the truth dawned on me. "And she mistook my toe-shoe ribbons for her old ones."

Mom lowered the brush and nodded solemnly. "And she didn't want you to go through the same pain she had."

I guess Grandmother loved me in her own way. When she came into the bedroom with Ian later that evening, I didn't leave. However, she tried to ignore me—as if I had become tainted by her secret.

When Ian demanded a story, I sighed. "All right. But only one."

Naturally, Ian chose the fattest story he could, which was my old collection of fairy tales by Hans Christian Andersen. Years of reading had cracked the spine so that the book fell open automatically in his hands to the story that had been my favorite when I was small. It was the original story of "The Little Mermaid"—not the cartoon. The picture illustrating the tale showed the mermaid posed like a ballerina in the middle of the throne room.

"This one," Ian said, and pointed to the picture of the Little Mermaid.

When Grandmother and Ian sat down on my bed, I began to read. However, when I got to the part where the Little Mermaid could walk on land, I stopped.

Ian was impatient. "Come on, read," he ordered, patting the page.

"After that," I went on, "each step hurt her as if she were walking on a knife." I couldn't help looking up at Grandmother.

This time she was the one to pat the page. "Go on. Tell me more about the mermaid."

So I went on reading to the very end, where the Little Mermaid changes into sea foam. "That's a dumb ending," Ian said. "Who wants to be pollution?"

"Sea foam isn't pollution. It's just bubbles," I explained. "The important thing was that she wanted to walk even though it hurt."

"I would rather have gone on swimming," Ian insisted.

"But maybe she wanted to see new places and people by going on the land," Grandmother said softly. "If she had kept her tail, the land people would have thought she was odd. They might even have made fun of her."

When she glanced at her own feet, I thought she might be talking about herself—so I seized my chance. "My satin ribbons aren't like your old silk ones. I use them to tie my toe shoes on when I dance." Setting the book down, I got out my other shoe. "Look."

Grandmother fingered the dangling ribbons and then pointed at my bare feet. "But you already have calluses there."

I began to dance before Grandmother could stop me. After a minute, I struck a pose on half-toe. "See? I can move fine."

She took my hand and patted it clumsily. I think it was the first

Literary Analysis
Theme How might Stacy's insight relate to the theme of the story?

Reading Check

What happened to Grandmother's feet when she was a child?

time she had showed me any sign of affection. "When I saw those ribbons, I didn't want you feeling pain like I do."

I covered her hands with mine. "I just wanted to show you what I love best—dancing."

"And I love my children," she said. I could hear the ache in her voice. "And my grandchildren. I don't want anything bad to happen to you."

Suddenly I felt as if there were an invisible ribbon binding us, tougher than silk and satin, stronger even than steel; and it joined her to Mom and Mom to me.

I wanted to hug her so badly that I just did. Though she was stiff at first, she gradually softened in my arms.

"Let me have my ribbons and my shoes," I said in a low voice. "Let me dance."

"Yes, yes," she whispered fiercely.

I felt something on my cheek and realized she was crying, and then I began crying, too.

"So much to learn," she said, and began hugging me back. "So much to learn."

Review and Assess

Thinking About the Selection

1. **Respond:** What do you think is the hardest part of Stacy's experiences with her grandmother? Explain.

2. **(a) Recall:** What sacrifices does Stacy make as a result of Grandmother's visit? **(b) Speculate:** Why doesn't Grandmother do anything to thank Stacy or make her feel better? **(c) Compare and Contrast:** How does Grandmother's treatment of Ian make Stacy feel even worse?

3. **(a) Recall:** What changes occur in Stacy's house as a result of Grandmother's visit? **(b) Analyze Cause and Effect:** What are Stacy's reasons for feeling a little resentful of her grandmother? **(c) Evaluate:** Does Stacy have good reason to feel resentful? Explain.

4. **(a) Recall:** How does Stacy learn the secret of Grandmother's feet? **(b) Connect:** How do her mother's explanations of Chinese culture affect Stacy's attitude toward her grandmother?

5. **(a) Recall:** Why does Grandmother react so violently to Stacy's ribbons? **(b) Deduce:** How do Stacy and her grandmother eventually come to appreciate each other? **(c) Generalize:** What can you learn from this story about getting along with people from different generations?

Laurence Yep

(b. 1948)

Laurence Yep was born in San Francisco and grew up in an apartment above his family's grocery store. When a high-school teacher encouraged Yep to send out his stories for publication, he decided to become a professional writer. He is the author of more than forty books, including the Newbery Honor Book *Dragonwings*.

Yep learned about his Chinese heritage from his maternal grandmother. Her influence is seen in "Ribbons" and in other works featuring a wise, beloved, and strong-willed grandmother.

The **Treasure** of **Lemon Brown**

WALTER DEAN MYERS

▲ **Critical Viewing**
How do the colors of this painting compare with the mood and description in the story? **[Compare and Contrast]**

The dark sky, filled with angry, swirling clouds, reflected Greg Ridley's mood as he sat on the stoop of his building. His father's voice came to him again, first reading the letter the principal had sent to the house, then lecturing endlessly about his poor efforts in math.

"I had to leave school when I was thirteen," his father had said, "that's a year younger than you are now. If I'd had half the chances that you have, I'd . . ."

Greg had sat in the small, pale green kitchen listening, knowing the lecture would end with his father saying he couldn't play ball with the Scorpions. He had asked his father the week before, and

✔ **Reading Check**

What scene is Greg remembering?

The Treasure of Lemon Brown ◆ 475

his father had said it depended on his next report card. It wasn't often the Scorpions took on new players, especially fourteen-year-olds, and this was a chance of a lifetime for Greg. He hadn't been allowed to play high school ball, which he had really wanted to do, but playing for the Community Center team was the next best thing. Report cards were due in a week, and Greg had been hoping for the best. But the principal had ended the suspense early when she sent that letter saying Greg would probably fail math if he didn't spend more time studying.

"And you want to play *basketball*?" His father's brows knitted over deep brown eyes. "That must be some kind of a joke. Now you just get into your room and hit those books."

That had been two nights before. His father's words, like the distant thunder that now echoed through the streets of Harlem, still rumbled softly in his ears.

It was beginning to cool. Gusts of wind made bits of paper dance between the parked cars. There was a flash of nearby lightning, and soon large drops of rain splashed onto his jeans. He stood to go upstairs, thought of the lecture that probably awaited him if he did anything except shut himself in his room with his math book, and started walking down the street instead. Down the block there was an old tenement[1] that had been abandoned for some months. Some of the guys had held an impromptu checker tournament there the week before, and Greg had noticed that the door, once boarded over, had been slightly ajar.

Pulling his collar up as high as he could, he checked for traffic and made a dash across the street. He reached the house just as another flash of lightning changed the night to day for an instant, then returned the graffiti-scarred building to the grim shadows. He vaulted over the outer stairs and pushed tentatively on the door. It was open, and he let himself in.

The inside of the building was dark except for the dim light that filtered through the dirty windows from the streetlamps. There was a room a few feet from the door, and from where he stood at the entrance, Greg could see a squarish patch of light on the floor. He entered the room, frowning at the musty smell. It was a large room that might have been someone's parlor at one time. Squinting, Greg could see an old table on its side against one wall, what looked like a pile of rags or a torn mattress in the corner, and a couch, with one side broken, in front of the window.

He went to the couch. The side that wasn't broken was comfortable enough, though a little creaky. From the spot he could see the blinking neon sign over the bodega[2] on the corner. He sat awhile, watching the sign blink first green then red, allowing his

Literary Analysis
Theme Do you think Greg's father has communicated his concern effectively?

impromptu (im prämp´ too´) *adj.* unscheduled; unplanned

ajar (ə jär´) *adj.* open

tentatively (ten´ tə tiv lē) *adv.* hesitantly; with uncertainty

---

1. **tenement** (ten´ ə mənt) *n.* old, run-down apartment house.
2. **bodega** (bō dä´ gə) *n.* small grocery store serving a Latino neighborhood.

mind to drift to the Scorpions, then to his father. His father had been a postal worker for all Greg's life, and was proud of it, often telling Greg how hard he had worked to pass the test. Greg had heard the story too many times to be interested now.

For a moment Greg thought he heard something that sounded like a scraping against the wall. He listened carefully, but it was gone.

Outside the wind had picked up, sending the rain against the window with a force that shook the glass in its frame. A car passed, its tires hissing over the wet street and its red taillights glowing in the darkness.

Greg thought he heard the noise again. His stomach tightened as he held himself still and listened intently. There weren't any more scraping noises, but he was sure he had heard something in the darkness—something breathing!

He tried to figure out just where the breathing was coming from; he knew it was in the room with him. Slowly he stood, tensing. As he turned, a flash of lightning lit up the room, frightening him with its sudden brilliance. He saw nothing, just the overturned table, the pile of rags and an old newspaper on the floor. Could he have been imagining the sounds? He continued listening, but heard nothing and thought that it might have just been rats. Still, he thought, as soon as the rain let up he would leave. He went to the window and was about to look when he heard a voice behind him.

"Don't try nothin' 'cause I got a razor here sharp enough to cut a week into nine days!"

Greg, except for an involuntary tremor[3] in his knees, stood stock still. The voice was high and brittle, like dry twigs being broken, surely not one he had ever heard before. There was a shuffling sound as the person who had been speaking moved a step closer. Greg turned, holding his breath, his eyes straining to see in the dark room.

The upper part of the figure before him was still in darkness. The lower half was in the dim rectangle of light that fell unevenly from the window. There were two feet, in cracked, dirty shoes from which rose legs that were wrapped in rags.

"Who are you?" Greg hardly recognized his own voice.

"I'm Lemon Brown," came the answer. "Who're you?"

"Greg Ridley."

"What you doing here?" The figure shuffled forward again, and Greg took a small step backward.

"It's raining," Greg said.

"I can see that," the figure said.

Reading Strategy
Asking Questions What question might you ask based on Greg's reaction to his father's work stories?

✔**Reading Check**
Why does Greg go to the old tenement?

---

3. **involuntary** (in väl′ ən ter′ ē) **tremor** (trem′ ər) n. automatic trembling or shaking.

The person who called himself Lemon Brown peered forward, and Greg could see him clearly. He was an old man. His black, heavily wrinkled face was surrounded by a halo of crinkly white hair and whiskers that seemed to separate his head from the layers of dirty coats piled on his smallish frame. His pants were bagged to the knee, where they were met with rags that went down to the old shoes. The rags were held on with strings, and there was a rope around his middle. Greg relaxed. He had seen the man before, picking through the trash on the corner and pulling clothes out of a Salvation Army box. There was no sign of the razor that could "cut a week into nine days."

"What are you doing here?" Greg asked.

"This is where I'm staying," Lemon Brown said. "What you here for?"

"Told you it was raining out," Greg said, leaning against the back of the couch until he felt it give slightly.

"Ain't you got no home?"

"I got a home," Greg answered.

"You ain't one of them bad boys looking for my treasure, is you?"

▼ Critical Viewing
What role does music play in this story? [Connect]

Four Piece Orchestra, 1944, Ben Shahn, 17 1/2 by 23 1/2 inches © Estate of Ben Shahn/Licensed by VAGA, New York, NY

Lemon Brown cocked his head to one side and squinted one eye. "Because I told you I got me a razor."

"I'm not looking for your treasure," Greg answered, smiling. "*If* you have one."

"What you mean, *if* I have one," Lemon Brown said. "Every man got a treasure. You don't know that, you must be a fool!"

"Sure," Greg said as he sat on the sofa and put one leg over the back. "What do you have, gold coins?"

"Don't worry none about what I got," Lemon Brown said. "You know who I am?"

"You told me your name was orange or lemon or something like that."

"Lemon Brown," the old man said, pulling back his shoulders as he did so, "they used to call me Sweet Lemon Brown."

"Sweet Lemon?" Greg asked.

"Yessir. Sweet Lemon Brown. They used to say I sung the blues so sweet that if I sang at a funeral, the dead would commence to rocking with the beat. Used to travel all over Mississippi and as far as Monroe, Louisiana, and east on over to Macon, Georgia. You mean you ain't never heard of Sweet Lemon Brown?"

"Afraid not," Greg said. "What . . . what happened to you?"

"Hard times, boy. Hard times always after a poor man. One day I got tired, sat down to rest a spell and felt a tap on my shoulder. Hard times caught up with me."

"Sorry about that."

"What you doing here? How come you didn't go on home when the rain come? Rain don't bother you young folks none."

"Just didn't." Greg looked away.

"I used to have a knotty-headed boy just like you." Lemon Brown had half walked, half shuffled back to the corner and sat down against the wall. "Had them big eyes like you got, I used to call them moon eyes. Look into them moon eyes and see anything you want."

"How come you gave up singing the blues?" Greg asked.

"Didn't give it up," Lemon Brown said. "You don't give up the blues; they give you up. After a while you do good for yourself, and it ain't nothing but foolishness singing about how hard you got it. Ain't that right?"

"I guess so."

"What's that noise?" Lemon Brown asked, suddenly sitting upright.

Greg listened, and he heard a noise outside. He looked at Lemon Brown and saw the old man pointing toward the window.

Greg went to the window and saw three men, neighborhood thugs, on the stoop. One was carrying a length of pipe. Greg looked back toward Lemon Brown, who moved quietly across the room to

Reading Strategy

Asking Questions What question comes to mind based on Lemon Brown's words?

Literary Analysis

Theme How might Lemon Brown's attitude about his poor fortunes help Greg put his situation into perspective?

Reading Check

Who is Lemon Brown?

The Treasure of Lemon Brown ◆ 479

the window. The old man looked out, then beckoned frantically for Greg to follow him. For a moment Greg couldn't move. Then he found himself following Lemon Brown into the hallway and up darkened stairs. Greg followed as closely as he could. They reached the top of the stairs, and Greg felt Lemon Brown's hand first lying on his shoulder, then probing down his arm until he finally took Greg's hand into his own as they crouched in the darkness.

"They's bad men," Lemon Brown whispered. His breath was warm against Greg's skin.

"Hey! Rag man!" A voice called. "We know you in here. What you got up under them rags? You got any money?"

Silence.

"We don't want to have to come in and hurt you, old man, but we don't mind if we have to."

Lemon Brown squeezed Greg's hand in his own hard, gnarled fist.

There was a banging downstairs and a light as the men entered. They banged around noisily, calling for the rag man.

"We heard you talking about your treasure." The voice was slurred. "We just want to see it, that's all."

"You sure he's here?" One voice seemed to come from the room with the sofa.

"Yeah, he stays here every night."

"There's another room over there; I'm going to take a look. You got that flashlight?"

"Yeah, here, take the pipe too."

Greg opened his mouth to quiet the sound of his breath as he sucked it in uneasily. A beam of light hit the wall a few feet opposite him, then went out.

"Ain't nobody in that room," a voice said. "You think he gone or something?"

"I don't know," came the answer. "All I know is that I heard him talking about some kind of treasure. You know they found that shopping bag lady with that money in her bags."

"Yeah. You think he's upstairs?"

"HEY, OLD MAN, ARE YOU UP THERE?"

Silence.

"Watch my back, I'm going up."

There was a footstep on the stairs, and the beam from the flashlight danced crazily along the peeling wallpaper. Greg held his breath. There was another step and a loud crashing noise as the man banged the pipe against the wooden banister.[4] Greg could feel his temples throb as the man slowly neared them. Greg thought about the pipe, wondering what he would do when the man reached them—what he *could* do.

Reading Strategy
Asking Questions What questions come to mind for you at this point in the story?

---

4. **banister** (ban´ is tər) *n.* railing along a staircase.

▲ **Critical Viewing** How does a dismal setting like the one in the story and the one in this painting add to the tension of "The Treasure of Lemon Brown"? **[Analyze]**

Then Lemon Brown released his hand and moved toward the top of the stairs. Greg looked around and saw stairs going up to the next floor. He tried waving to Lemon Brown, hoping the old man would see him in the dim light and follow him to the next floor. Maybe, Greg thought, the man wouldn't follow them up there. Suddenly, though, Lemon Brown stood at the top of the stairs, both arms raised high above his head.

"There he is!" A voice cried from below.

"Throw down your money, old man, so I won't have to bash your head in!"

Lemon Brown didn't move. Greg felt himself near panic. The steps came closer, and still Lemon Brown didn't move. He was an eerie sight, a bundle of rags standing at the top of the stairs, his shadow on the wall looming over him. Maybe, the thought came to Greg, the scene could be even eerier.

Greg wet his lips, put his hands to his mouth and tried to make a sound. Nothing came out. He swallowed hard, wet his lips once more and howled as evenly as he could.

"What's that?"

Reading Strategy
Asking Questions What question could you ask about Lemon Brown based on his actions?

✔ **Reading Check**
What do the thugs want from Lemon Brown?

The Treasure of Lemon Brown ◆ 481

As Greg howled, the light moved away from Lemon Brown, but not before Greg saw him hurl his body down the stairs at the men who had come to take his treasure. There was a crashing noise, and then footsteps. A rush of warm air came in as the downstairs door opened, then there was only an ominous silence.

Greg stood on the landing. He listened, and after a while there was another sound on the staircase.

"Mr. Brown?" he called.

"Yeah, it's me," came the answer. "I got their flashlight."

Greg exhaled in relief as Lemon Brown made his way slowly back up the stairs.

"You OK?"

"Few bumps and bruises," Lemon Brown said.

"I think I'd better be going," Greg said, his breath returning to normal. "You'd better leave, too, before they come back."

"They may hang around outside for a while," Lemon Brown said, "but they ain't getting their nerve up to come in here again. Not with crazy old rag men and howling spooks. Best you stay a while till the coast is clear. I'm heading out west tomorrow, out to east St. Louis."

"They were talking about treasures," Greg said. "You *really* have a treasure?"

"What I tell you? Didn't I tell you every man got a treasure?" Lemon Brown said. "You want to see mine?"

"If you want to show it to me," Greg shrugged.

"Let's look out the window first, see what them scoundrels be doing," Lemon Brown said.

They followed the oval beam of the flashlight into one of the rooms and looked out the window. They saw the men who had tried to take the treasure sitting on the curb near the corner. One of them had his pants leg up, looking at his knee.

"You sure you're not hurt?" Greg asked Lemon Brown.

"Nothing that ain't been hurt before," Lemon Brown said. "When you get as old as me all you say when something hurts is, 'Howdy, Mr. Pain, sees you back again.' Then when Mr. Pain see he can't worry you none, he go on mess with somebody else."

Greg smiled.

"Here, you hold this." Lemon Brown gave Greg the flashlight.

He sat on the floor near Greg and carefully untied the strings that held the rags on his right leg. When he took the rags away, Greg saw a piece of plastic. The old man carefully took off the plastic and unfolded it. He revealed some yellowed newspaper clippings and a battered harmonica.

Literary Analysis
Theme What can Greg learn from Lemon Brown's actions?

"There it be," he said, nodding his head. "There it be."

Greg looked at the old man, saw the distant look in his eye, then turned to the clippings. They told of Sweet Lemon Brown, a blues singer and harmonica player who was appearing at different theaters in the South. One of the clippings said he had been the hit of the show, although not the headliner. All of the clippings were reviews of shows Lemon Brown had been in more than 50 years ago. Greg looked at the harmonica. It was dented badly on one side, with the reed holes on one end nearly closed.

"I used to travel around and make money for to feed my wife and Jesse—that's my boy's name. Used to feed them good, too. Then his mama died, and he stayed with his mama's sister. He growed up to be a man, and when the war come he saw fit to go off and fight in it. I didn't have nothing to give him except these things that told him who I was, and what he come from. If you know your pappy did something, you know you can do something too.

"Anyway, he went off to war, and I went off still playing and singing. 'Course by then I wasn't as much as I used to be, not without somebody to make it worth the while. You know what I mean?"

"Yeah," Greg nodded, not quite really knowing.

"I traveled around, and one time I come home, and there was this letter saying Jesse got killed in the war. Broke my heart, it truly did.

"They sent back what he had with him over there, and what it was is this old mouth fiddle and these clippings. Him carrying it around with him like that told me it meant something to him. That was my treasure, and when I give it to him he treated it just like that, a treasure. Ain't that something?"

"Yeah, I guess so," Greg said.

"You *guess* so?" Lemon Brown's voice rose an octave as he started to put his treasure back into the plastic. "Well, you got to guess 'cause you sure don't know nothing. Don't know enough to get home when it's raining."

"I guess . . . I mean, you're right."

"You OK for a youngster," the old man said as he tied the strings around his leg, "better than those scalawags[5] what come here looking for my treasure. That's for sure."

"You really think that treasure of yours was worth fighting for?" Greg asked. "Against a pipe?"

"What else a man got 'cepting what he can pass on to his son, or his daughter, if she be his oldest?" Lemon Brown said. "For a big-headed boy you sure do ask the foolishest questions."

Lemon Brown got up after patting his rags in place and looked out the window again.

---

5. **scalawags** (skal′ ə wagz′) *n.* people who cause trouble; scoundrels.

Reading Check

What is Lemon Brown's treasure?

"Looks like they're gone. You get on out of here and get yourself home. I'll be watching from the window so you'll be all right."

Lemon Brown went down the stairs behind Greg. When they reached the front door the old man looked out first, saw the street was clear and told Greg to scoot on home.

"You sure you'll be OK?" Greg asked.

"Now didn't I tell you I was going to east St. Louis in the morning?" Lemon Brown asked. "Don't that sound OK to you?"

"Sure it does," Greg said. "Sure it does. And you take care of that treasure of yours."

"That I'll do," Lemon said, the wrinkles about his eyes suggesting a smile. "That I'll do."

The night had warmed and the rain had stopped, leaving puddles at the curbs. Greg didn't even want to think how late it was. He thought ahead of what his father would say and wondered if he should tell him about Lemon Brown. He thought about it until he reached his stoop, and decided against it. Lemon Brown would be OK, Greg thought, with his memories and his treasure.

Greg pushed the button over the bell marked Ridley, thought of the lecture he knew his father would give him, and smiled.

Review and Assess

Thinking About the Selection

1. **Respond:** Do you agree with Greg's decision not to tell his father about Lemon Brown? Explain.

2. **(a) Recall:** List five facts you learn about Greg early in the story. **(b) Infer:** Why is Greg angry and upset? **(c) Analyze:** Why doesn't Greg go home when it starts to rain?

3. **(a) Recall:** Why does Greg go into the old tenement building? **(b) Describe:** How does Greg meet Lemon Brown? **(c) Infer:** Why is Lemon Brown in the tenement building?

4. **(a) Recall:** What is the treasure of Lemon Brown? **(b) Infer:** How does Brown react when the thugs break into the building to steal his treasure? **(c) Analyze:** How does Greg's opinion of Lemon Brown change over the course of the story?

5. **(a) Interpret:** Why does Lemon Brown consider the harmonica a treasure? **(b) Generalize:** What does Lemon Brown teach Greg? **(c) Speculate:** Why does Greg smile at the end of the story?

6. **Make a Judgment:** What qualities define a "treasure"?

Walter Dean Myers

(b. 1937)

Born in West Virginia, Walter Dean Myers grew up in the New York City community of Harlem. Although he dreamed of being a professional writer, this seemed impossible because of his poverty and lack of formal education. In the late 1960s, however, his first book won a writing contest and was published. Since then, Myers has published dozens of books and won numerous awards.

Myers has gained wide acclaim for his storytelling as well as his ability to depict believable, well-defined characters—many of whom are young African Americans growing up in urban communities.

Review and Assess

Literary Analysis

Theme

1. What message does "Ribbons" teach about understanding other people's experiences and feelings?
2. Considering what Lemon Brown tells Greg about his "treasure," what would you say is the **theme** of "The Treasure of Lemon Brown"? Explain your answer.
3. How does Myers convey the theme of "The Treasure of Lemon Brown" through the story's title, characters, events, and significant objects? Organize your ideas in a chart like the one below.

Title	Lemon Brown is a treasure, like his harmonica.
Characters	
Events	
Objects	

Theme _____

Comparing Literary Works

4. Compare and contrast the relationships between younger and older people in the two stories.

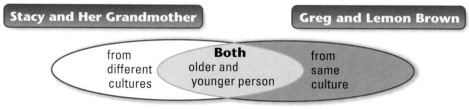

Stacy and Her Grandmother — from different cultures

Both older and younger person

Greg and Lemon Brown — from same culture

5. What is similar and different about how the younger and older characters in these stories enrich each other's lives?

Reading Strategy

Asking Questions

6. (a) At what point while reading "Ribbons" did you have the most questions about the grandmother? (b) What were those questions?
7. (a) What questions about Greg and Lemon Brown were answered for you in the story? (b) What questions about each character did you still have at the end of the story?

Extend Understanding

8. **Career Connection:** How might an understanding of cultural differences—such as those between Stacy and her grandmother—be helpful in the workplace?

Quick Review

A story's **theme** is its central message or insight into life. To review theme, see page 465.

By **asking questions** as you read, you will be better able to understand a story and figure out its theme.

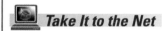 **Take It to the Net**

www.phschool.com

Take the interactive self-test online to check your understanding of these selections.

Integrate Language Skills

Vocabulary Development Lesson

Word Analysis: Latin Root -sens-

The word root -sens- means "feel" or "perceive." On your paper, define each of the following words, using the meaning of -sens- in each definition.

1. sensory
2. insensitive
3. sentiment
4. sentry

Spelling Strategy

Adding the suffix -ious changes a noun into an adjective. If the noun ends in the letter y or e, drop the y or e before adding -ious. For each of the following nouns, write the correct -ious adjective.

1. glory
2. labor
3. victory
4. space

Concept Development: Definitions

On your paper, match each of the following words with its definition. To help you, review the vocabulary words on page 465.

1. tentatively
2. coax
3. ajar
4. laborious
5. impromptu
6. sensitive
7. meek
8. exertion

a. timid
b. slightly open
c. touchy
d. with uncertainty
e. physical work
f. persuade gently
g. unplanned
h. difficult

Grammar Lesson

Adjective Clauses

An **adjective clause** is a subordinate clause (a group of words that has a subject and a verb but cannot stand on its own as a sentence) that functions as an adjective. Just like single-word adjectives, an adjective clause modifies a noun or a pronoun. Adjective clauses usually begin with a relative pronoun (*who, whom, whose, which,* and *that*), which relates that clause to the word it modifies. Adjective clauses may also begin with the subordinating conjunctions *where, when,* and *why.* Look at this example:

There was an old tenement *that had been abandoned for some months.*

(The adjective clause in italics modifies the noun *tenement.*)

▶ *For more practice, see page R31, Exercise I.*
Practice Identify each adjective clause and the word it modifies.

1. He thought of the lecture that awaited him.
2. The inside of the building was dark except for the dim light that filtered through the dirty windows.
3. The person who had been speaking moved a step closer.
4. The person who called himself Lemon Brown peered forward.
5. "I didn't have nothing to give him except these things that told him who I was."

Writing Application Use and identify three adjective clauses in a paragraph summarizing one of the stories.

Prentice Hall Writing and Grammar Connection: Chapter 20, Section 2

Writing Lesson

Brief Interpretation of Theme

The theme of a story is its central message or insight into life. Write an interpretation, or explanation, of the theme of either "Ribbons" or "The Treasure of Lemon Brown."

Prewriting To interpret the theme of a story, think about its important objects, images, ideas, characters, and events. Record such details for the story you chose in a chart like the one below. Then, write a single sentence that expresses the message or lesson of the work.

Theme: _____			
Objects or Images	Ideas	Characters	Events

Drafting Using your notes, begin to draft your essay. Start with your statement of the theme. Then, discuss the story elements and details that led to your interpretation.

Revising Reread your essay, making sure you have supported each point with details from the story. If you have trouble supporting a point, consider revising or deleting it.

 Prentice Hall Writing and Grammar Connection: Chapter 12, Section 2

Extension Activities

Listening and Speaking In "The Treasure of Lemon Brown," Greg meets a man who was once a famous blues musician. Blues music is known for its melancholy sounds and lyrics. Choose a blues song and analyze how the following elements contribute to its overall effect:

- the sounds of the instruments
- the meaning of the lyrics
- other musical devices, such as rhythm, tempo, and repetition

When you finish, share your song and your findings with your class in a presentation.

Research and Technology Stacy's grandmother's feet were bound because of the ideas of beauty of the culture in which she lived. With a group, write a **report** about beauty customs in different cultures. [**Group Activity**]

Writing As Stacy or Greg, write a **diary entry** that describes what you have discovered about yourself and others as a result of the experience described in the story.

 **Take It to the Net**   www.phschool.com

Go online for an additional research activity using the Internet.

Press Release

About Press Releases

A press release is an announcement or statement written specifically to be released to members of the news media. Press releases are issued by government and law enforcement offices, by organizations and institutions, and by prominent individuals when they want a message to receive wide publicity. Press releases are typically brief, from one to three pages long. Examples might include the following:

- a police report relaying the results of a crime investigation to the public;
- a politician announcing her decision to run for high office;
- two corporations announcing that they will merge into one company;
- an orchestra announcing guest conductors and performers for its coming season.

You must read a press release very carefully. Although it may contain facts, a press release is written from the point of view of the person or organization that issued it. This means that it may be less objective than other kinds of public information.

Reading Strategy

Identify the Author's Point of View

An author's point of view is the way he or she thinks about the subject of the writing. Authors may state their point of view directly, or they may imply—suggest—it through the language they use. Sometimes their use of language reveals bias—that is, personal opinions that aren't supported with facts or reliable examples. Consider each pair of phrases in the chart on this page. The phrases convey the same basic information, but the differences in wording reflect the author's feeling about that information.

Author's Point of View	
Athletes who don't practice every day have other interests that are also important to them.	Athletes who don't practice every day are not committed to their sport.
Some people prefer the company of their pets to that of other people.	Some people never socialize but stay cooped up inside with their pets.
The airline matches its competitors in on-time flights.	The airline can do no better than its competitors in on-time flights.

**Rock and Roll
Hall of Fame and Museum
Cleveland, Ohio**

FOR IMMEDIATE RELEASE

New Exhibit: Let the Good Times Roll: A Tribute to Rhythm and Blues

Rock and Roll Hall of Fame

The roots of rhythm and blues are complex and deeply woven into the fabric of American history and culture. Like blues, jazz, and country, R&B was, in part, shaped by events far removed from the music. A look at America in the 1940s and '50s reveals how R&B not only was impacted by the many things going on in this country during these two important post-war decades, but also how R&B reflected them in song and sound.

Rhythm & blues evolved into a generic term describing all forms of black popular music: down home blues, big city jump bands, vocal groups, jazz, urban shouters and torchy night club singers. It was rhythm & blues that provided one of the foundations for rock and roll in the early 1950s and, while rock and roll became the mainstream of popular music, rhythm & blues continued its development into an easily recognizable music form.

From R&B came soul, funk, disco and rap—all important African American music forms that still resonate with energy and exitement today.

The Rock and Roll Hall of Fame and Museum honors the men and women who have made unique contributions to the evolution of rock and roll in our new exhibit, "Let the Good Times Roll: A Tribute to Rhythm & Blues."

Facts About the Rock and Roll Hall of Fame and Museum

The Museum:

The Rock and Roll Hall of Fame and Museum is a 150,000-square-foot facility that serves as the permanent home of the Rock and Roll Hall of Fame. It provides dynamic interactive

This photograph of Chuck Berry is on the cover of an exhibit brochure. What does it suggest about Berry's importance in rhythm-and-blues music? **[Infer]**

exhibits, intimate performance spaces, displays from the museum's permanent collection. Exhibits change periodically and showcase specific rock and roll eras, styles, milestones and the many facets of the music's evolution. It also houses research facilities and features public programming dedicated to the exploration of the music's enduring impact on global culture. It is the world's first museum dedicated to the living heritage of rock and roll music.

Exhibits:

The Museum's exhibits are designed to give the visitor a unique, interactive experience. The Museum's collection is brought to life through a combination of high-tech wizardry and innovative film and video. The Museum offers a comprehensive retrospective on the music's origins, its development, its legends, and its immense impact on global culture.

Another section might describe the structure and activities of the organization.

The exhibitions will take the visitor on a fast-paced journey through the history of rock and roll. They will bring the visitor into the experience, showcasing rock and roll and its impact on society. Major music scenes, specific artists and the music's impact on the way we live will be examined.

Special Features:

Bullets may be used to highlight particular points that the organization wants to emphasize.

- Exhibits on the roots of rock and roll include Gospel, Country, Folk, Blues, and Rhythm and Blues, featuring the Museum's collections.
- Working studio from which visiting radio stations can conduct live broadcasts
- 200-seat indoor theater
- Outdoor area for concerts
- Dramatic new multimedia gallery for the Rock and Roll Hall of Fame

Check Your Comprehension

1. What is the purpose of this press release?
2. What types of music have their origin in rhythm and blues?
3. What single quality makes the Rock and Roll Hall of Fame and Museum unlike any other museum?
4. What do the exhibits in the museum show?
5. What does this press release suggest about what young people can learn from older generations?

Applying the Reading Strategy

Identify the Author's Point of View

6. How do you know the author thinks rhythm-and-blues music is significant?
7. What does the author suggest about the way rock-and-roll music would have developed without rhythm and blues?
8. Why does the author think the new exhibit is important?

Activity

Identify at least two or three musicians who are in the Rock and Roll Hall of Fame. Make a poster showing the contributions to music that earned them a place in the hall of fame.

Contrasting Informational Materials

Press Releases and Reviews

In what way do you think a museum press release is similar to and different from a review? Find a music review and compare it to this press release. Use an organizer like the one shown to evaluate the types of assertions, or claims that are made, and the type and amount of support. If an assertion is supported by related examples, then evaluate the assertion as valid. If the assertion has little support, or if unrelated details are offered as support, then the assertion may be evaluated as weak or invalid.

	Press Release	Review
Assertions		
Support		
Evaluation		

Prepare to Read

Stolen Day

 Take It to the Net

Visit www.phschool.com for interactive activities and instruction related to "Stolen Day," including
- background
- graphic organizers
- literary elements
- reading strategies

Preview

Connecting to the Literature

This story focuses on a character who makes a mistake and then learns an important lesson as a consequence of his action. Connect to the story by thinking of a time when you have made a mistake. What were the consequences of your action, and what lessons did you learn?

Background

In "Stolen Day," a character says he has "inflammatory rheumatism." The term *rheumatism* is used to describe a number of different diseases, including rheumatoid arthritis. In this disease, the joints swell painfully and gradually break down.

Literary Analysis

Point of View

The vantage point from which a story is told is called its **point of view.**

- **First-person point of view:** The narrator is a character who partici-pates in the action of the story. Events are described through that character's eyes. The character uses the words *I* and *me* to refer to himself or herself.
- **Third-person point of view:** The narrator is not a character who participates in the action of the story. The narrator tells events as an outside observer and uses the third-person pronouns *he, she, him, her, they,* and *them* to refer to all characters.

The third-person point of view can be either limited or omniscient.

- **Third-person limited point of view:** The narrator's knowledge is limited to what one of the characters knows.
- **Third-person omniscient point of view:** The narrator knows more than any one single character can know.

"Stolen Day" is told from the first-person point of view. As you read, think about why the author chose to tell the story from this vantage point.

Connecting Literary Elements

Often, the **theme,** or message, of a work can be determined by what a character learns from his or her experiences. When a story is told in the first-person, you are directly involved in the experiences of the character telling the story. As you read, ask yourself the following focus questions:

1. What are the narrator's thoughts and feelings about his experiences?
2. What lesson does he learn about a "stolen day"?

Reading Strategy

Understanding the Author's Purpose

Fiction writers may write for a variety of **purposes.** They may wish to entertain, to teach, to call to action, or to reflect on experiences. Understanding an author's purpose can give you a richer understanding of a selection. As you read, use a chart like the one shown here to note details from the story that fit the different possible purposes of the author.

Vocabulary Development

inflammatory (in flam′ ə tôr′ ē) *adj.* characterized by pain and swelling (p. 494)

solemn (säl′ əm) *adj.* serious; somber (p. 495)

rheumatism (roo′ mə tiz′ əm) *n.* painful condition of the joints and muscles (p. 494)

Stolen Day

SHERWOOD ANDERSON

The Pond, 1985, Adele Alsop, Courtesy of Schmidt Bingham Gallery, NYC

It must be that all children are actors. The whole thing started with a boy on our street named Walter, who had <u>inflammatory rheumatism</u>. That's what they called it. He didn't have to go to school.

Still he could walk about. He could go fishing in the creek or the waterworks pond. There was a place up at the pond where in the spring the water came tumbling over the dam and formed a deep pool. It was a good place. Sometimes you could get some big ones there.

I went down that way on my way to school one spring morning. It was out of my way but I wanted to see if Walter was there.

He was, inflammatory rheumatism and all. There he was, sitting with a fish pole in his hand. He had been able to walk down there all right.

It was then that my own legs began to hurt. My back too. I went on to school but, at the recess time, I began to cry. I did it when the

inflammatory
(in flam′ ə tôr′ ē) *adj.*
characterized by pain
and swelling

rheumatism
(rōō′ mə tiz′ əm) *n.*
painful condition of the
joints and muscles

teacher, Sarah Suggett, had come out into the schoolhouse yard.

She came right over to me.

"I ache all over," I said. I did, too.

I kept on crying and it worked all right.

"You'd better go on home," she said.

So I went. I limped painfully away. I kept on limping until I got out of the schoolhouse street.

Then I felt better. I still had inflammatory rheumatism pretty bad but I could get along better.

I must have done some thinking on the way home.

"I'd better not say I have inflammatory rheumatism," I decided. "Maybe if you've got that you swell up."

I thought I'd better go around to where Walter was and ask him about that, so I did—but he wasn't there.

"They must not be biting today," I thought.

I had a feeling that, if I said I had inflammatory rheumatism, Mother or my brothers and my sister Stella might laugh. They did laugh at me pretty often and I didn't like it at all.

"Just the same," I said to myself, "I have got it." I began to hurt and ache again.

I went home and sat on the front steps of our house. I sat there a long time. There wasn't anyone at home but Mother and the two little ones. Ray would have been four or five then and Earl might have been three.

It was Earl who saw me there. I had got tired sitting and was lying on the porch. Earl was always a quiet, <u>solemn</u> little fellow.

He must have said something to Mother for presently she came.

"What's the matter with you? Why aren't you in school?" she asked.

I came pretty near telling her right out that I had inflammatory rheumatism but I thought I'd better not. Mother and Father had been speaking of Walter's case at the table just the day before. "It affects the heart," Father had said. That frightened me when I thought of it. "I might die," I thought. "I might just suddenly die right here; my heart might stop beating."

On the day before I had been running a race with my brother Irve. We were up at the fairgrounds after school and there was a half-mile track.

"I'll bet you can't run a half-mile," he said. "I bet you I could beat you running clear around the track."

And so we did it and I beat him, but afterwards my heart did seem to beat pretty hard. I remembered that lying there on the porch. "It's a wonder, with my inflammatory rheumatism and all, I didn't just drop down dead," I thought. The thought frightened me a lot. I ached worse than ever.

"I ache, Ma," I said. "I just ache."

Literary Analysis
Point of View How can you tell that the story is being told from a first-person point of view?

solemn (säl´ əm) adj. serious; somber

Reading Check

What do Mother and Father say about Walter's inflammatory rheumatism?

She made me go in the house and upstairs and get into bed.

It wasn't so good. It was spring. I was up there for perhaps an hour, maybe two, and then I felt better.

I got up and went downstairs. "I feel better, Ma," I said.

Mother said she was glad. She was pretty busy that day and hadn't paid much attention to me. She had made me get into bed upstairs and then hadn't even come up to see how I was.

I didn't think much of that when I was up there but when I got downstairs where she was, and when, after I had said I felt better and she only said she was glad and went right on with her work, I began to ache again.

I thought, "I'll bet I die of it. I bet I do."

I went out to the front porch and sat down. I was pretty sore at Mother.

"If she really knew the truth, that I have the inflammatory rheumatism and I may just drop down dead any time, I'll bet she wouldn't care about that either," I thought.

I was getting more and more angry the more thinking I did.

"I know what I'm going to do," I thought; "I'm going to go fishing."

I thought that, feeling the way I did, I might be sitting on the high bank just above the deep pool where the water went over the dam, and suddenly my heart would stop beating.

And then, of course, I'd pitch forward, over the bank into the pool and, if I wasn't dead when I hit the water, I'd drown sure.

They would all come home to supper and they'd miss me.

"But where is he?"

Then Mother would remember that I'd come home from school aching.

She'd go upstairs and I wouldn't be there. One day during the year before, there was a child got drowned in a spring. It was one of the Wyatt children.

Right down at the end of the street there was a spring under a birch tree and there had been a barrel sunk in the ground.

Everyone had always been saying the spring ought to be kept covered, but it wasn't.

So the Wyatt child went down there, played around alone, and fell in and got drowned.

Mother was the one who had found the drowned child. She had gone to get a pail of water and there the child was, drowned and dead.

Literary Analysis
Point of View How does the use of the first-person point of view help you understand the narrator's thoughts and feelings?

▼ **Critical Viewing**
From viewing this picture, what do you think attracts people like the narrator to fishing?

This had been in the evening when we were all at home, and Mother had come running up the street with the dead, dripping child in her arms. She was making for the Wyatt house as hard as she could run, and she was pale.

She had a terrible look on her face, I remembered then.

"So," I thought, "they'll miss me and there'll be a search made. Very likely there'll be someone who has seen me sitting by the pond fishing, and there'll be a big alarm and all the town will turn out and they'll drag the pond."

I was having a grand time, having died. Maybe, after they found me and had got me out of the deep pool, Mother would grab me up in her arms and run home with me as she had run with the Wyatt child.

I got up from the porch and went around the house. I got my fishing pole and lit out for the pool below the dam. Mother was busy— she always was—and didn't see me go. When I got there I thought I'd better not sit too near the edge of the high bank.

By this time I didn't ache hardly at all, but I thought.

"With inflammatory rheumatism you can't tell," I thought.

"It probably comes and goes," I thought.

"Walter has it and he goes fishing," I thought.

I had got my line into the pool and suddenly I got a bite. It was a regular whopper. I knew that. I'd never had a bite like that.

I knew what it was. It was one of Mr. Fenn's big carp.

Mr. Fenn was a man who had a big pond of his own. He sold ice in the summer and the pond was to make the ice. He had bought some big carp and put them into his pond and then, earlier in the spring when there was a freshet, his dam had gone out.

So the carp had got into our creek and one or two big ones had been caught—but none of them by a boy like me.

The carp was pulling and I was pulling and I was afraid he'd break my line, so I just tumbled down the high bank holding onto the line and got right into the pool. We had it out, there in the pool. We struggled. We wrestled. Then I got a hand under his gills and got him out.

He was a big one all right. He was nearly half as big as I was myself. I had him on the bank and I kept one hand under his gills and I ran.

I never ran so hard in my life. He was slippery, and now and then he wriggled out of my arms; once I stumbled and fell on him, but I got him home.

Reading Strategy
Understand Author's Purpose What evidence shows that the author might want to make the reader chuckle?

Reading Check

What happened to the Wyatt child?

So there it was. I was a big hero that day. Mother got a washtub and filled it with water. She put the fish in it and all the neighbors came to look. I got into dry clothes and went down to supper—and then I made a break that spoiled my day.

There we were, all of us, at the table, and suddenly Father asked what had been the matter with me at school. He had met the teacher, Sarah Suggett, on the street and she had told him how I had become ill.

"What was the matter with you?" Father asked, and before I thought what I was saying I let it out.

"I had the inflammatory rheumatism," I said—and a shout went up. It made me sick to hear them, the way they all laughed.

It brought back all the aching again, and like a fool I began to cry.

"Well, I *have* got it—I *have*, I *have*," I cried, and I got up from the table and ran upstairs.

I stayed there until Mother came up. I knew it would be a long time before I heard the last of the inflammatory rheumatism. I was sick all right, but the aching I now had wasn't in my legs or in my back.

Review and Assess

Thinking About the Selection

1. **Respond:** Should the narrator be punished? Why or why not?

2. **(a) Recall:** What inspires the narrator to think he has "inflammatory rheumatism"? **(b) Infer:** Why does the narrator think this would be an appealing disease to have?

3. **(a) Recall:** What happens to the narrator at school? **(b) Interpret:** Why does he stop limping once he leaves school? **(c) Analyze:** Why is it significant that he decides not to tell his family that he has inflammatory rheumatism?

4. **(a) Recall:** What does the narrator do after he gets home? **(b) Infer:** Why does his mother pay him little attention? **(c) Analyze:** What does the narrator mean when he says, "I was having a grand time, having died"?

5. **(a) Recall:** How does his family respond when the boy tells them he has inflammatory rheumatism? **(b) Interpret:** What does the narrator mean at the end of the story when he says, "…but the aching I now had wasn't in my legs or my back"?

6. **(a) Infer:** What are the main character's motivations for pretending to have inflammatory rheumatism? **(b) Evaluate:** Do you think he is fully conscious of his motives? Why or why not? **(c) Generalize:** What does this story suggest about the motivations for peoples' behavior?

Sherwood Anderson

(1876–1941)

As a teenager, Sherwood Anderson was able to attend school only part-time because he had to work to help support his family. Despite his lack of formal education, Anderson became a successful businessman as the manager of a paint factory. He began writing fiction in his spare time.

In 1912, Anderson shocked those who knew him by moving from Elyria, Ohio, to Chicago, where he devoted himself to writing. His most famous book, *Winesburg, Ohio*, was published in 1919. Anderson and his work had a powerful influence on such writers as Ernest Hemingway and William Faulkner.

Review and Assess

Literary Analysis

Point of View

1. What two clues (other than the word *I*) in the first three paragraphs show that "Stolen Day" is a first-person narrative?
2. Using a chart like this, give two examples from the story in which the narrator shares with the reader his true thoughts or feelings about a situation.

Situation		Thoughts or Feelings
"I kept on crying and it worked all right."	···▶	The narrator shows that he is trying to mislead his teacher.

3. Find two places where the narrator pokes fun at his childhood self.
4. How would the story be different if it were told in the third-person?

Connecting Literary Elements

5. What are the narrator's thoughts and feelings about stealing a day? Support your answer with evidence from the story.

Thought   Feeling

Narrator

Thought   Feeling

6. What lesson does he learn about a "stolen day"?

Reading Strategy

Understanding Author's Purpose

7. What are two things the author might have wished to teach his audience?
8. Did the author mean to entertain his audience? Explain your answer.
9. In your own words, what was the author's main purpose in writing this story?

Extend Understanding

10. **Science Connection:** Using the Internet or other library resources, learn more about the causes and symptoms of inflammatory rheumatism. Why might it have been possible for Walter to sometimes go fishing even though he was sick?

Quick Review

A narrative told from **first-person point of view** is told from the perspective of one character who participates in the action of the story. In **third-person limited point of view**, the narrator relates the inner thoughts and feelings of only one character. In **third-person omniscient point of view**, the narrator knows and tells about what each character thinks and feels. To review point of view, see page 493.

The **author's purpose** is the goal he or she wants to achieve through a piece of writing. To review author's purpose, see page 493.

 Take It to the Net
www.phschool.com
Take the interactive self-test online to check your understanding of the selection.

Integrate Language Skills

Vocabulary Development Lesson

Word Analysis: Latin Root -flam-

Inflammatory rheumatism can include a burning sensation in the joints. Once you know that the Latin root -flam- means "flame" or "burn," the name of the disease makes sense. Define each of the following words, incorporating the meaning of -flam-. Use a dictionary if necessary.

    1. inflame   **2.** flammable   **3.** flamboyant

Spelling Strategy

Most words that end with the m sound end with -m or -me. However, a few end with -mn. In these words, the letter n is silent. On your paper, complete each of the following words to form a list of the most common -mn words.

    1. autu__   **2.** conde__   **3.** sole__

Fluency: Word Choice

On your paper, write the following paragraph, filling in each blank with the appropriate vocabulary word from page 493.

    The doctor was ___?___ as she examined the sick boy. She prescribed anti- ___?___ medicine because ___?___ had made his joints swollen, feverish, and painful. The medicine helped.

Read the paragraph aloud. Answer the following questions about the vocabulary words.

    1. Which word begins as if it were spelled *room*?

    2. Which word is probably related in meaning to *inflamed*?

    3. Which word has a silent letter at the end?

Grammar Lesson

Verb Agreement with Collective Nouns

A **collective noun** names a group of people or things. Collective nouns may be either singular or plural.

Use a plural verb form with a collective noun when you refer to the individual parts or members of a group acting separately. In the following examples, the collective noun is italicized and the verb is underlined.

    Plural verb: The *group* <u>wear</u> colorful hats.

Use a singular verb form when you refer to the group acting together as one unit.

    Singular Verb: The *group* <u>appears</u> on the street.

▶ *For more practice, see page R32, Exercise D.*
Practice On your paper, write *correct* if the subject and the verb agree. Write the correct form of the verb if the subject and verb do not agree.

    1. The army march in the parade.

    2. The club argues about the date of the next meeting.

    3. At the thunderclap, the herd scatter in all directions.

    4. The band plays a stirring march.

    5. The group wants different things.

Writing Application For each collective noun below, write a sentence that uses it in the form given in parentheses. Make sure that the verb in each sentence agrees with the subject.

    1. team (plural)   **3.** jury (plural)

    2. crowd (plural)   **4.** class (singular)

*W*G *Prentice Hall Writing and Grammar Connection: Chapter 24, Section 1*

Writing Lesson

Rewriting a Scene in a Different Point of View

Imagine how "Stolen Day" would be different if it were written in the third-person omniscient point of view. Rewrite one scene, changing it to that point of view.

Prewriting Choose one scene, such as the schoolyard or dinner table scene, to rewrite. Give the boy (the main character) a name. Think about how the change in perspective will affect pronouns and content. Begin by using a chart like this one.

Model: Rewrite in Omniscient Third-Person

First-Person Wording	Third-Person Wording	Other Changes
I began to cry.	He began to cry.	Tell what the teachers and classmates thought.

Drafting Rewrite the scene in the third-person omniscient point of view. Quoted dialogue is the only place where you may use *I*. Tell about the experiences of any character in your scene.

Revising Make sure you have included all the important action in the scene. Check for correct third-person pronouns and consistent verb tenses.

W̶G Prentice Hall Writing and Grammar Connection: Chapter 5, Section 2

Extension Activities

Listening and Speaking Think about why the narrator of "Stolen Day" acted as he did. Then, plan a **monologue** that presents these thoughts, speaking as if you were the character.

- Stick to the first-person point of view. Use the word *I*.
- Give three clear reasons for your (the narrator's) actions.
- Project your voice so that everyone can hear you.
- Pause when you need to collect your thoughts.
- Pace yourself to avoid rushing.

Present your monologue to your class.

Research and Technology Through library and Internet research, find statistics about rheumatoid arthritis. Create a **graphic organizer,** by hand or on computer, to chart your findings. Present it to the class.

Writing As the narrator of "Stolen Day," compose a **diary entry** in which you explain your behavior and feelings on this "stolen day."

 **Take It to the Net** www.phschool.com

Go online for an additional research activity using the Internet.

Guidelines

About Guidelines

Guidelines are a written list of recommendations associated with a task. They are addressed to the general reader, and are often informally expressed in a user-friendly tone. Guidelines provide the following information:

- the most efficient or effective method for completing the task
- helpful hints and tips for avoiding problems
- strategies for solving problems

Although guidelines are like instructions in some ways, they have a different organization. Instructions are generally organized in sequential order. Guidelines organize information by category. You do not usually have to perform one step before another.

Reading Strategy

Use Text Features

Like other forms of informative writing, guidelines are formatted with special fonts and text treatments to call out sections and categories of information.

Because guidelines describe processes that are generally unfamiliar to most people, they may contain specialized technical language, or jargon, that is unique to a particular field. Preview the list below before you read the guidelines on the next page. As you read the guidelines, note the words and phrases that are unfamiliar. Make sure that you understand what the language means. Use a dictionary to find the meaning of any terms that do not appear on this page.

Specialized Terms	
Internet	An extensive computer network of individuals, businesses, and instututions
links	An icon or word on a Web page that, when clicked, transfers the user to another Web page or to a different document within the same page
Web site	A set of linked pages on the Internet, reached by typing in an address
Usenet	A worldwide system of discussion groups or newsgroups
newsgroup	An online discussion group where users can post and respond to messages about a specific topic.

LET THE

READER BEWARE

Reid Goldsborough

The title above the introduction summarizes the content of the guidelines as a whole.

Tips for Verifying Information on the Internet

The fact is, the Internet is chock full of rumors, gossip, hoaxes, exaggerations, falsehoods, ruses, and scams. Although the Net can reveal useful, factual information that you'd be hard pressed to find elsewhere, it can also appear to be a gigantic electronic tabloid.[1]

Can you ever trust the Internet? Sure you can. You just need to apply critical thinking in evaluating the information and advice you come across. Here's a six-step approach to doing this.

1. Don't judge a Web site by its appearance.

Note that headings are numbered, and that subtitles provide a summary of the text beneath.

Sure, if a Web site looks professional rather than slopped together, chances are greater that the information within it will be accurate and reliable.

But looks can and do deceive. A flashy site can merely be a marketing front for quack health remedies or an illegal pyramid scheme.

2. Try to find out who's behind the information.

If you're looking at a Web site, check if the author or creator is identified. See if there are links to a page listing professional credentials[2] or affiliations.[3] Be very skeptical if no authorship information is provided.

If you're looking at a message in a Usenet newsgroup or Internet mailing list, see if the author has included a signature—a short, often biographical, description that's automatically appended to the end of messages. Many people include their credentials in their signature or point to their home page, where they provide biographical information.

3. Try to determine the reason the information was posted.

Among those who create Web sites are publishing companies, professional and trade organizations, government agencies, nonprofit

---

1. **tabloid** (tab′ loid′) *n.* newspaper with many pictures and often sensationalized stories
2. **credentials** (kri den′ shəlz) *n.* information that indicates position or authority
3. **affiliations** (ə fil′ ē ā′ shənz) *n.* organizational membership

organizations, for-profit companies, educational institutions, individual researchers, political and advocacy groups, and hobbyists.

Each has its own agenda—sometimes explicit, sometimes hidden. Unearth the agenda and keep it in mind when evaluating the information presented.

Similarly, look behind and between the words posted in Usenet and mailing list discussions. Is the author trying to promote his or her own ends, or be helpful? You can often do both, but not always.

4. Look for the date the information was created or modified.
Unless you're doing historical research, current information is usually more valid and useful than older material.

If the Web site doesn't provide a "last updated" message or otherwise date its content, check out some of its links. If more than a couple are no longer working, the information at the site may no longer be up to date either.

5. Try to verify the same information elsewhere.
This is particularly important if the information is at odds with your previous understanding or if you intend to use it for critical purposes such as an important health, family, or business decision.

Ideally, you should confirm the information with at least two other sources. Librarians and information scientists call this the "principle of triangulation of data." Spending a bit of time validating the material, through the Internet or at a local library, can be well worth the investment.

6. Try to find out how others feel about the reliability and professionalism of the Web site you're looking at.
There are a number of sites that list only sites that have been evaluated by editors or that offer evaluations of other sites. Here are five such sites.

With any information you come across on the Net, the watchword is "Caveat lector"—Let the reader beware.

If you'd like to delve further into the issue of information credibility on the Internet, there are Web sites out there that let you do just that. Here are four good ones.

Selective Listings

About
http://www.about.com

Consumer World
http://www.consumerworld.com/
        pages/internet.html

dmoz
http://dmoz.org

LookSmart
http://www.looksmart.com

Web-Today
http://www.web-today.net

> Important information is presented in boxes for quick reference.

Evaluating Internet Information
http://www.library.mcgill.ca/isearch/isearch6.htm

Evaluating Quality on the Net
http://www.sosig.ac.uk/desire/internet-detective.html

Thinking Critically About World Wide Web Resources
http://www.library.ucla.edu/libraries/college/instruct/web/critical.htm

Internet Source Validation Project
http://www.stemnet.nf.ca/Curriculum/Validate/validate.html

> The author closes with a list of Web locations where an Internet user can find further information.

Check Your Comprehension

1. What is one danger of gathering information on the Internet?
2. How can you check Internet information?
3. Why does the author urge you to look for the date that the information was created or modified?

Applying the Reading Strategy

Analyze Text Features

4. What text features call attention to additional Web sites?
5. Why do the guidelines begin with an introduction?
6. Why does the author present his information in numbered points?

Activity

Use Guidelines

Using the guidelines in the article, evaluate several Web sites. Rate them on their appearance, evidence of authorship, reasons for posting, whether the material is clearly dated, and whether the information can be verified elsewhere. Use a chart like the one below.

Web Site Evaluation Chart					
Site name	Appearance	Authorship	Motive	Clear dates	Verifiable
www.centralhigh.org	OK	Yes	To inform	No	No

Comparing and Contrasting Informational Materials

Guidelines and Instructions

Other documents that help consumers include instruction manuals. Instructions are slightly different from guidelines in purpose and structure. The following list shows some ways that guidelines and instructions differ.

Guidelines

- Intended to be used repeatedly
- Focus on several tasks or goals
- Need not be written in chronological order

Instructions

- Need only be used once
- Focus on a single goal or task
- Always written in strict chronological order

Writing WORKSHOP

Narration: Short Story

A **short story** is a brief, creative, fictional narrative—a retelling of a sequence of events. In this workshop, you will write a short story.

Assignment Criteria Your short story should have the following characteristics:

- One or more complex major characters with any minor characters necessary
- A definite, well-described setting
- A standard plot line that has a beginning, conflict, rising action, climax, and denouement
- A consistent point of view
- Narrative that develops dialogue, suspense, specific actions, movement, gestures, and expressions
- Precise vocabulary and effective word choice

See the Rubric on page 509 for the criteria on which your short story will be assessed.

Prewriting

Choose a topic. Story writer Stephen King says that he always begins with a specific character facing a challenging situation. Try using a "What If?" strategy to get you started. Fill in the blanks of a sentence such as the one shown here. Try a number of situations and choose the one that interests you the most.

What if _____ (describe a person)
suddenly _____ (describe a problem)?

Example: What if I got a kitten for my birthday but suddenly found out that my mom is allergic to cats?

Develop your characters. Decide on your main character—the one who is most complex. Then, develop other major and minor characters.

Identify conflict. To get your story moving, look for a conflict—a struggle between two opposing forces. To identify conflict, ask yourself these questions: What does the main character want? What is preventing him or her from getting it? Use a conflict diagram like the one shown.

Obstacle

Main character

What main character wants

Obstacle

Choose a consistent point of view. Decide who will tell your story. If the narrator is outside the story, tell the story in the third person, using the pronoun *he* or *she.* If the narrator is inside the story, tell it in the first person, using the pronoun *I.* Whichever you choose, be consistent throughout the story.

Student Model

Before you begin drafting your short story, read this portion of a student model and review the characteristics of a successful short story. To read the complete story, go to www.phschool.com.

Megan Gaylor
Broken Arrow, Oklahoma

Late Night Sister

Mr. and Mrs. Boyle were the owners of NIARB, the biggest computer company in the world. At this moment, they were at a company banquet. They knew that their seventeen-year-old son Brad could keep everything under control.

Brad and Chad came in the kitchen sniffing the air. "We're starving, Amber," they bellowed at their sixteen-year-old sister.

"So, what do you want me to do about it?" she asked. "I'm not a bit hungry. Why should I be the one to fix food when I'm not hungry?"

"Because I'm the oldest and I'm in charge, I say you do the cooking tonight. Chad and I will wash the pots and take out the trash, and Fianna can load the dishwasher. C'mon, Amber. You know we can't cook anything that tastes as good as your chicken parmigiana," said Brad.

After dinner, Fianna was in the kitchen loading the dishwasher by herself. Even though she had the easiest job, she always ended up finishing last. Chad, Brad, and Amber were already in the living room watching a movie and laughing their heads off. "Amber, go help Fianna," Brad said suddenly.

*   *   *

Suddenly the TV flickered on and off. In the kitchen, the light dimmed and then brightened. Brad wondered what was going on. He got up and went to the window to look outside. It looked horrible out there. The rain was coming down in waves. Suddenly a sizzling bright light flashed through the living room. Then, the house was dark. The lights wouldn't go on, the television wouldn't go on—nothing that needed electricity would go on.

*   *   *

Amber sighed as she grumbled off toward the basement. "I know, I know, you're in charge cause you're the oldest." Before she reached the basement door, there was a soft knock at the back door. Everyone froze. "Get it," Amber said to Brad. "You're the oldest, and you're in charge."

"Great," said Brad. "Me and my big mouth," Chad whispered, half-scared and half-kidding. So, side by side, Brad and Chad crept to the door, trembling.

The characters are brothers and sisters. Their dialogue should sound like people who know each other very well.

Details about the dinner chores help establish that the setting of the story is a comfortable home.

At first, it seemed as if the conflict might be between Brad and Amber. Now, we realize that the kids will have to pull together to face the real conflict.

Telling that everyone "froze" shows that the family is frightened. It also builds suspense by delaying the climax—the moment when the door is opened.

Drafting

Develop a standard plot line. A plot diagram will help you plan your story, step by step, so that each event connects logically to the next. Most stories follow this standard plot pattern:

The **beginning** introduces the main characters, their basic situation, and the central conflict.

A **conflict** develops during the rising action.

A **climax** is the high point of interest and suspense.

The **resolution** is the outcome of the conflict.

The **denouement** is the wrapping up of the "loose ends" in the plot and an explanation of the final outcome.

Climax

Rising Action

Falling Action

Beginning

Conflict Introduced

Resolution/ Denouement

Define character and setting. Early in your story, make sure that your reader knows exactly when and where the action is taking place. These details of setting are important in creating the mood or feeling you want.

Show rather than tell. Although it is sometimes useful to tell readers something directly, usually you should show them rather than tell them.

> **Example:** Amanda was afraid.
> Amanda crouched in the corner, biting her nails.

As you draft, choose words that accurately describe the mood you want to create.

Revising

Improve your characterization. Cut a five-pointed star out of construction paper and label the points *dialogue, movement, gestures, feelings,* and *expressions.* Slide the star down your draft as you look for places where you can add details that reveal more about characters— their looks, actions, feelings, reactions, and conversation. When you find a place, tape down your star and start over.

feelings

expressions   movement

dialogue   gestures

Brad and Chad came in the kitchen ~~wondering what was for dinner~~. sniffing the air. ~~They hoped Amber would make her famous chicken parmigiana.~~ "We're starving, Amber," they told their sixteen-year-old sister.

"So, what do you want me to do about it?" she asked. "I'm not a bit hungry. Why should I be the one to fix food when I'm not hungry?"

"Because I'm the oldest and I'm in charge, I say you do the cooking tonight. Chad and I will wash the pots and take out the trash, and Fianna can load the dishwasher. C'mon, Amber. You know we can't cook anything that tastes as good as your chicken parmigiana."

> The writer inserts dialogue instead of describing what the characters want.

Revise to improve word choice. Review your draft to find places where you can add details that will bring your ideas to life. Look for vague verbs that you can replace with precise, vivid action verbs.

> **Example:** The sun was hot.
> The sun beat down on us.

Compare the model and nonmodel. Why is the model more effective than the nonmodel?

Nonmodel	Model
Brad and Chad came in the kitche smelling the air. "We're starving, Amber," they told their younger sister.	Brad and Chad came in the kitchen sniffing the air. "We're starving, Amber," they bellowed at their sixteen-year-old sister.

Publishing and Presenting

Choose one of these ways to share your writing with classmates or a larger audience.

Give a reading. Read your story aloud to your classmates, family, or friends. Prepare a poster announcing your reading.

Mail your story to a friend. Mail a copy of your story to someone who would enjoy it. Ask the person to write back, telling you what they liked most about your story.

𝒲𝒢 *Prentice Hall Writing and Grammar Connection: Chapter 5*

Rubric for Self-Assessment

Evaluate your short story using the following criteria and rating scale:

Criteria	Rating Scale Not very				Very
How well are the major and minor characters developed?	1	2	3	4	5
How well is the setting described?	1	2	3	4	5
How well developed is the plot line?	1	2	3	4	5
How consistent is the point of view?	1	2	3	4	5
How well does the narrative develop suspense, dialogue, and action?	1	2	3	4	5
How effective is the choice of words?	1	2	3	4	5

Listening and Speaking WORKSHOP

Giving and Receiving Oral Directions

Every day you **give and receive oral directions,** instructions that are spoken rather than written. The process is a skill that requires close attention to detail and thoughtful listening. The following tips will help you explain and follow directions.

Understand Oral Directions

Following oral directions correctly requires that you understand the speaker's message and carry out the steps in order.

Listen for key words. If your teacher instructs, "Bring two pencils and a blue notebook to class tomorrow," the words *two, pencils,* and *blue notebook* should jump out at you. These key words will help you remember the direction.

Take notes or repeat aloud. If necessary, jot down key words in the order in which they are presented. This is especially effective if the directions are long or complicated and involve many steps. It may also help to repeat the directions aloud to make sure you understand them.

Ask questions at the end. If you have a question, do not interrupt the speaker to ask it. Keep listening. Your question may be answered later in the directions. At the end, however, be sure to ask any questions you may have. It is important that you understand every step.

> ### Understanding Oral Directions
>
> - **Listen for key words.**
>   *Right, left, up, down,*
>   *one, two, red, blue.*
> - **Take notes and repeat steps.**
>   *First, second, third, last.*
> - **Ask questions at the end.**
>   *Which button do I push first?*
> - **Note visual clues.**
>   *He pointed left and then right.*

Give Oral Directions

Explaining oral directions requires patience and a step-by-step approach. Avoid adding any unnecessary details.

Proceed step-by-step. Do not overwhelm your listener with a complex or lengthy explanation or with irrelevant details. Walk the person through the steps one at a time, proceeding slowly and carefully. Give your listener clues to the step-by-step process: *first, second, then, finally.*

Provide visual clues. Visual clues may be helpful. Use gestures, point, and even draw a diagram if it is appropriate.

Restate the directions. A good explanation should include a restatement of the directions. The alternative is to ask the listener to repeat the directions in his or her own words, using key words such as *first* and *last.*

Activity:
Following Technical Directions   With a partner, practice following oral directions by locating two sets of written technical directions for simple mechanical devices such as a CD player or a bicycle pump. While one person reads the directions aloud, the partner should listen and then try using the device by following the directions. Then partners should switch roles.

Assessment WORKSHOP

Predict Probable Actions and Outcomes

The reading sections of some tests require you to read a passage and answer questions about probable outcomes and actions. Use your predicting skills to help you answer such questions.

Sample Test Item

Directions: Read the passage, and then answer the item that follows.

Todd slid into a seat just as the newspaper's representative began to talk. "I have just a few suggestions for you new deliverers. First, look at the map that we have attached to your route list, which is alphabetical by customer's last name. Then plan the most efficient route. Finally, rewrite the list using the order in which you will deliver the papers."

Todd had just begun to follow these directions when Kristina passed his seat. "Are you actually doing that? That's a waste of time. I can figure out my route in my head." Kristina's list, like Todd's, had at least thirty customers on ten different streets. He doubted that anyone could figure out the best route at a glance. But he also knew better than to argue with Kristina. "Come on, my mom will give you a lift," she said. Gratefully, Todd accepted.

1. After he gets home, Todd will most likely—

   A deliver his papers

   B throw away the map he received

   C finish rewriting his route list

   D call Kristina to thank her for the ride

Answer and Explanation

The correct answer is *C.* Todd has already begun following the directions. He clearly wants to prepare for the job, so you can eliminate answers *A* and *B.* Answer *D* is a possibility, but the passage does not suggest that it is a probability.

▶ Practice

Directions: Read the passage, and then answer the items that follow.

Marcie slammed her locker shut and hurried down the hall. She wanted to walk home with Chaney to discuss their weekend plans. Then she remembered that Ms. Weaver was offering extra help in German that afternoon. Marcie hadn't done well on the quiz that day. Ahead, she spied Chaney. "Wait up!" she yelled. Chaney turned. "Oh, hi," she smiled. "I wish we could walk home together, Marcie, but I have to go to Ms. Weaver for some extra help. Today's quiz was murder."

1. Marcie will probably—

   A walk home alone

   B never understand German verbs

   C not see Chaney on the weekend

   D suggest they both go for extra help

2. If she gets extra help from Ms. Weaver, Marcie will probably—

   A miss walking home with Chaney

   B do poorly on her next quiz

   C understand German verbs better

   D neglect her other subjects

Exploring the Genre

The subjects of nonfiction writing are real people, and the events are actual happenings. Nonfiction can tell a true story, explain an idea, and give facts and information. In this unit, you will read the following types of nonfiction:

- A **biography** is the life story of someone written by another person.

- An **autobiography** is a writer's own life story.

- An **expository essay** explains and informs.

- A **personal essay** is an informal account of a person's experiences.

- A **reflective essay** reveals a writer's thoughts about an idea or experience.

- A **narrative essay** is a true story that may focus on a character other than the writer.

- A **persuasive essay** presents an argument and attempts to convince readers of this position.

◀ **Critical Viewing** What symbols and shapes do you find in this painting? How might they relate to nonfiction?

Why Read Literature?

Nonfiction tells about real characters and events or contains the personal views of a real person. People most often read nonfiction to be informed about a subject. However, people may also read nonfiction to learn about other people's lives or to reflect on someone else's thoughts, concerns, or position on a particular subject. Preview three of the purposes you might set before reading the nonfiction pieces in this unit.

1 Read for the love of literature.

Newspapers are an important part of American life. It has been estimated that the typical American will spend an average of two years of his or her life reading newspapers! To read how newspapers played an important role in the life of a paper boy, read **"No Gumption"** by Russell Baker, page 554.

2 Read for information.

Laws are sometimes created to cover very specific situations in a time and place. Sometimes, when circumstances change, the law that covered the situation is left "on the books," even though it is outdated.

For example, in Florida, did you know that if an elephant is left tied to a parking meter, you must pay the parking meter just as you would for a car? Or that in Hartford, Connecticut, it is illegal to cross the street on your hands?

The Bill of Rights is the first ten amendments, or adjustments, to the Constitution. Over the course of history, lawmakers have made additional amendments to ensure that our most important American legal document, the Constitution, stays up-to-date. Read the Bill of Rights, page 539.

3 Read to understand people's concerns.

Chief Dan George began an acting career at age sixty-two and was nominated for an Academy Award for his role in *Little Big Man*. Before this second career began, however, he was a spokesperson for Native American rights and environmental protection, as you can read in **"I Am a Native of North America,"** page 528.

Did you know that rattlesnakes gather in groups to sleep through the winter? Sometimes, up to 1,000 of them will coil up together to keep warm! To read an essay in which one writer's feelings about snakes change from fear and horror to cautious respect, read **"Rattlesnake Hunt"** on page 518.

 Take It to the Net

Visit the Web site for online instruction and activities related to each selection in this unit.
www.phschool.com

How to Read Literature

Use Strategies for Reading Nonfiction

Each day, you are bombarded with facts and ideas from all directions. When you scan a cereal box, read a textbook, or cruise the Internet, you make decisions about what, who, and how much to believe. The strategies you learn in this unit will help you read the nonfiction you encounter every day.

Use organization.

If you recognize how a work of literature is organized, you will be able to read it more easily. In this unit, you will learn some general ways, like the ones shown below, in which authors organize nonfiction:

Chronological Order:	Events are told in the order in which they occur.
Order of Importance:	Details are arranged to lead up to the most significant point.
Spatial Order:	Details are presented to show the physical arrangement.

Understand the author's purpose.

Details in nonfiction work can help you understand why it was written. To identify the author's purpose, look for facts, quotations, and persuasive or humorous language as clues to the author's reason for writing. There may be more than one purpose, but usually one purpose is most important.

Distinguish between fact and opinion.

Readers sometimes assume that an idea in a nonfiction work is a fact when it is just the writer's opinion. To differentiate fact from opinion, ask yourself these questions:

- Can this statement be proven to be true?
- Is this statement someone's personal belief?
- Can this statement be supported by factual evidence?

In this unit, you will practice using the answers to these questions and distinguishing between fact and opinion.

Clues to Author's Purpose
- Silly or exaggerated situations *to amuse*
- Advice to believe or to do something *to persuade*
- Facts or explanations *to inform*

Evaluate support.

An author's message in an essay is supported by the details and examples he or she includes. Learn to evaluate support and to recognize whether writing includes problems such as bias—preconceived attitudes—or stereotypes—the qualities of an individual being used to represent an entire group.

As you read the selections in the unit, review the reading strategies and look at the notes in the side column. Use the suggestions to apply the strategies and interact with the text.

Prepare to Read

Rattlesnake Hunt ◆ *from* Barrio Boy ◆
I Am a Native of North America ◆ All Together Now

Buffalo, 1992. Jaune Smith, Courtesy Steinbaum Krauss Gallery, NYC

 Take It to the Net

Visit www.phschool.com
for interactive activities
and instruction related to
these selections, including
• background
• graphic organizers
• literary elements
• reading strategies

Preview

Connecting to the Literature

The clothes you would wear to a formal event are a different style and fabric from the clothes you would wear to go hiking. Different fabric and styles suit different purposes. Essays, too, are "made" in different ways for different purposes. The essays in this group give you a sampling of the variety of possible essays.

Background

In 1580, the Frenchman Montaigne (män tän´) first used the word *essai* to describe a brief prose work. This French word means "try," and Montaigne's essays were "tries" at understanding. The form caught on, finding its way into the earliest magazines. Today, you can read essays in most magazines, newspapers, textbooks, and literature collections.

Literary Analysis

Essays

An **essay** is a brief prose work written on a particular topic. A **narrative essay** is a true story that may focus on a character other than the writer. An **expository essay** gives information or explanations. A **personal essay** is an informal account of an episode from a person's own life. A **reflective essay** presents a writer's thoughts about ideas or experiences. A **persuasive essay** is a series of arguments presented to convince readers to believe or act in a certain way. Some essays will have qualities of more than one type.

Comparing Literary Works

The type of essay an author writes depends on his or her **purpose,** or reason for writing. If the writer's purpose is to show how a particular event or experience changed his or her viewpoint, the writer might write a narrative essay. Writers may have secondary purposes, in addition to their main purposes. For example, an essay written to inform may also entertain. Compare and contrast these essays by considering the following focus questions.

1. Which of the writers in this group have similar purposes?
2. How do difficulties in the writers' purposes affect the details they include?

Reading Strategy

Evaluating Support

An author's message or conclusion should be backed up by **support**—details and examples that show the truth or validity of the author's main points. Evaluate the support for the messsages in these essays. Judge whether there is enough support and whether it is accurate. Some support may be inaccurate because of the following.

> **Bias:** A preconceived attitude toward an idea, thing, person, group, or situation
> **Stereotyping:** Using one individual or a small group as the representation of the whole group

Main Point	
Support	
Evaluation	
Evidence of Bias or Stereotype	

Use a chart like this to identify the message and the main points in each essay and to note any instances of stereotyping or bias.

Vocabulary Development

desolate (des´ ə lit) *adj.* lonely; solitary (p. 519)

mortality (môr tal´ ə tē) *n.* having to die eventually (p. 520)

formidable (fôr´ mi də bəl) *adj.* impressive (p. 524)

communal (kə myo͞o´ nəl) *adj.* shared by all (p. 528)

tolerant (täl´ ər ənt) *adj.* free from bigotry or prejudice (p. 532)

Rattlesnake Hunt

Marjorie Kinnan Rawlings

Ross Allen, a young Florida herpetologist,[1] invited me to join him on a hunt in the upper Everglades[2]—for rattlesnakes. Ross and I drove to Arcadia in his coupé[3] on a warm January day.

I said, "How will you bring back the rattlesnakes?"

"In the back of my car."

My courage was not adequate to inquire whether they were thrown in loose and might be expected to appear between our feet. Actually, a large portable box of heavy close-meshed wire made a safe cage. Ross wanted me to write an article about his work and on our way to the unhappy hunting grounds I took notes on a mass of data that he had accumulated in years of herpetological research. The scientific and dispassionate detachment of the material and the man made a desirable approach to rattlesnake territory. As I had discovered with the insects and varmints,[4] it is difficult to be afraid of anything about which enough is known, and Ross' facts were fresh from the laboratory.

---

1. **herpetologist** (hʉr′ pə täl′ ə jist) *n.* someone who studies reptiles and amphibians.
2. **Everglades** large region of swampland in southern Florida, about 100 miles long and averaging 50 miles in width.
3. **coupé** (ko͞o pā′) *n.* small two-door automobile.
4. **varmints** (vär′ mənts) *n.* animals regarded as troublesome.

Reading Strategy
Evaluating Support
What kinds of details could be used to support this main point?

◀ **Critical Viewing**
Why is the author afraid of rattlesnakes, like the one pictured here? **[Analyze]**

The hunting ground was Big Prairie, south of Arcadia and west of the northern tip of Lake Okeechobee. Big Prairie is a <u>desolate</u> cattle country, half marsh, half pasture, with islands of palm trees and cypress and oaks. At that time of year the cattlemen and Indians were burning the country, on the theory that the young fresh wire grass that springs up from the roots after a fire is the best cattle forage. Ross planned to hunt his rattlers in the forefront of the fires. They lived in winter, he said, in gopher holes, coming out in the midday warmth to forage, and would move ahead of the flames and be easily taken. We joined forces with a big man named Will, his snake-hunting companion of the territory, and set out in early morning, after a long rough drive over deep-rutted roads into the open wilds.

I hope never in my life to be so frightened as I was in those first few hours. I kept on Ross' footsteps, I moved when he moved, sometimes jolting into him when I thought he might leave me behind. He does not use the forked stick of conventional snake hunting, but a steel prong, shaped like an L, at the end of a long stout stick. He hunted casually, calling my attention to the varying vegetation, to hawks overhead, to a pair of the rare whooping cranes that flapped over us. In mid-morning he stopped short, dropped his stick, and brought up a five-foot rattlesnake draped limply over the steel L. It seemed to me that I should drop in my tracks.

"They're not active at this season," he said quietly. "A snake takes on the temperature of its surroundings. They can't stand too much heat for that reason, and when the weather is cool, as now, they're sluggish."

The sun was bright overhead, the sky a translucent blue, and it seemed to me that it was warm enough for any snake to do as it willed. The sweat poured down my back. Ross dropped the rattler in a crocus sack and Will carried it. By noon, he had caught four. I felt faint and ill. We stopped by a pond and went swimming. The region was flat, the horizon limitless, and as I came out of the cool blue water I expected to find myself surrounded by a ring of rattlers. There were only Ross and Will, opening the lunch basket. I could not eat. Will went back and drove his truck closer, for Ross expected the hunting to be better in the afternoon. The hunting was much better. When we went back to the truck to deposit two more rattlers in the wire cage, there was a rattlesnake lying under the truck.

Ross said, "Whenever I leave my car or truck with snakes already in it, other rattlers always appear. I don't know whether this is because they scent or sense the presence of other snakes, or whether in this arid[5] area they come to the car for shade in the heat of the day."

The problem was scientific, but I had no interest.

That night Ross and Will and I camped out in the vast spaces of the Everglades prairies. We got water from an abandoned well and

---

5. **arid** (ar´ id) *adj.* dry and barren.

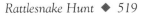

desolate (des´ ə lit) *adj.* lonely; solitary

Reading Strategy
Evaluating Support What evidence do you find that the author has a bias against snakes?

Literary Analysis
Essays What descriptive details does the author give that communicate her discomfort and fear?

Reading Check

How does the narrator feel about snakes?

cooked supper under buttonwood bushes by a flowing stream. The camp fire blazed cheerfully under the stars and a new moon lifted in the sky. Will told tall tales of the cattlemen and the Indians and we were at peace.

Ross said, "We couldn't have a better night for catching water snakes."

After the rattlers, water snakes seemed innocuous[6] enough. We worked along the edge of the stream and here Ross did not use his L-shaped steel. He reached under rocks and along the edge of the water and brought out harmless reptiles with his hands. I had said nothing to him of my fears, but he understood them. He brought a small dark snake from under a willow root.

"Wouldn't you like to hold it?" he asked. "People think snakes are cold and clammy, but they aren't. Take it in your hands. You'll see that it is warm."

Again, because I was ashamed, I took the snake in my hands. It was not cold, it was not clammy, and it lay trustingly in my hands, a thing that lived and breathed and had <u>mortality</u> like the rest of us. I felt an upsurgence of spirit.

The next day was magnificent. The air was crystal, the sky was aquamarine, and the far horizon of palms and oaks lay against the sky. I felt a new boldness and followed Ross bravely. He was making the rounds of the gopher holes. The rattlers came out in the mid-morning warmth and were never far away. He could tell by their trails whether one had come out or was still in the hole. Sometimes the two men dug the snake out. At times it was down so long and winding a tunnel that the digging was hopeless. Then they blocked the entrance and went on to other holes. In an hour or so they made the original rounds, unblocking the holes. The rattler in every case came out hurriedly, as though anything were preferable to being shut in. All the time Ross talked to me, telling me the scientific facts he had discovered about the habits of the rattlers.

"They pay no attention to a man standing perfectly still," he said, and proved it by letting Will unblock a hole while he stood at the entrance as the snake came out. It was exciting to watch the snake crawl slowly beside and past the man's legs. When it was at a safe distance he walked within its range of vision, which he had proved to be no higher than a man's knee, and the snake whirled and drew back in an attitude[7] of fighting defense. The rattler strikes only for paralyzing and killing its food, and for defense.

"It is a slow and heavy snake," Ross said. "It lies in wait on a small game trail and strikes the rat or rabbit passing by. It waits a few minutes, then follows along the trail, coming to the small animal, now dead or dying. It noses it from all sides, making sure that it is its own kill, and that it is dead and ready for swallowing."

---

6. **innocuous** (in näk′ yōō əs) *adj.* harmless.
7. **attitude** (at′ ə tōōd′) *n.* a position or posture of the body.

mortality (môr tal′ ə tē) *n.* having to die eventually

Literary Analysis
Essays What elements of expository writing, or writing that explains, are included here?

A rattler will lie quietly without revealing itself if a man passes by and it thinks it is not seen. It slips away without fighting if given the chance. Only Ross' sharp eyes sometimes picked out the gray and yellow diamond pattern, camouflaged among the grasses. In the cool of the morning, chilled by the January air, the snakes showed no fight. They could be looped up limply over the steel L and dropped in a sack or up into the wire cage on the back of Will's truck. As the sun mounted in the sky and warmed the moist Everglades earth, the snakes were warmed too, and Ross warned that it was time to go more cautiously. Yet having learned that it was we who were the aggressors; that immobility meant complete safety; that the snakes, for all their lightning flash in striking, were inaccurate in their aim, with limited vision; having watched again and again the liquid grace of movement, the beauty of pattern, suddenly I understood that I was drinking in freely the magnificent sweep of the horizon, with no fear of what might be at the moment under my feet. I went off hunting by myself, and though I found no snakes, I should have known what to do.

The sun was dropping low in the west. Masses of white cloud hung above the flat marshy plain and seemed to be tangled in the tops of distant palms and cypresses. The sky turned orange, then saffron. I walked leisurely back toward the truck. In the distance I could see Ross and Will making their way in too. The season was more advanced than at the Creek, two hundred miles to the north, and I noticed that spring flowers were blooming among the lumpy hummocks. I leaned over to pick a white violet. There was a rattlesnake under the violet.

If this had happened the week before, if it had happened the day before, I think I should have lain down and died on top of the rattlesnake, with no need of being struck and poisoned. The snake did not coil, but lifted its head and whirred its rattles lightly. I stepped back slowly and put the violet in a buttonhole. I reached forward and laid the steel L across the snake's neck, just back of the blunt head. I called to Ross:

"I've got one."

He strolled toward me.

"Well, pick it up," he said.

I released it and slipped the L under the middle of the thick body.

"Go put it in the box."

He went ahead of me and lifted the top of the wire cage. I made the truck with the rattler, but when I reached up the six feet to drop it in

Literature in context — Language Connection

Scientific Words From Greek Origins

As we learn in this essay, Ross Allen studies herpetology. The word *herpetology* comes from the Greek words *herpein*, meaning "to creep," and *logos*, meaning "word." Other scientific words derived from Greek and ending with the suffix *-ology* (meaning "science or theory of") include *biology*, the study of animals and plants; *anthropology*, the study of humans; *ichthyology*, the study of fish; and *paleontology*, the study of life forms from the past, especially fossils.

A herpetologist studies snakes and other reptiles.

✔ Reading Check

How are the narrator's feelings changing?

the cage, it slipped off the stick and dropped on Ross' feet. It made no effort to strike.

"Pick it up again," he said. "If you'll pin it down lightly and reach just back of its head with your hand, as you've seen me do, you can drop it in more easily."

I pinned it and leaned over.

"I'm awfully sorry," I said, "but you're pushing me a little too fast."

He grinned. I lifted it on the stick and again as I had it at head height, it slipped off, down Ross' boots and on top of his feet. He stood as still as a stump. I dropped the snake on his feet for the third time. It seemed to me that the most patient of rattlers might in time resent being hauled up and down, and for all the man's quiet certainty that in standing motionless there was no danger, would strike at whatever was nearest, and that would be Ross.

I said, "I'm just not man enough to keep this up any longer," and he laughed and reached down with his smooth quickness and lifted the snake back of the head and dropped it in the cage. It slid in among its mates and settled in a corner. The hunt was over and we drove back over the uneven trail to Will's village and left him and went on to Arcadia and home. Our catch for the two days was thirty-two rattlers.

I said to Ross, "I believe that tomorrow I could have picked up that snake."

Back at the Creek, I felt a new lightness. I had done battle with a great fear, and the victory was mine.

Review and Assess

Thinking About the Selection

1. **Respond:** Would you like to go on a rattlesnake hunt? Why or why not?

2. **(a) Recall:** Why does Rawlings go on the hunt? **(b) Infer:** Why do Rawlings's feelings about snakes change when she holds one?

3. **(a) Recall:** Identify three facts Rawlings learns about rattlers. **(b) Speculate:** What might contribute to Rawlings's feeling of "boldness" on the second day?

4. **(a) Recall:** Note two ways in which Rawlings shows that she has partly overcome her fears. **(b) Draw Conclusions:** Why does the author announce at the end of the hunt that she has won a "victory"?

5. **(a) Analyze:** In what ways does the rattlesnake hunt change how Rawlings thinks about nature and about herself? **(b) Defend:** In what ways does this essay support the idea that knowledge drives away fear?

Marjorie Kinnan Rawlings

(1896–1953)

After starting out as a journalist, Rawlings moved to a rural area in northern Florida where she had bought a tract of orange groves near Cross Creek. Later, she would use this region as the setting of her novel *The Yearling*, which won a Pulitzer Prize and was made into a motion picture. Her writing expresses a deep intimacy with nature. Rawlings also developed an ear for the regional dialect and humor, which she used extensively in her work. Her essay "Rattlesnake Hunt" introduces you to a scary inhabitant of this area.

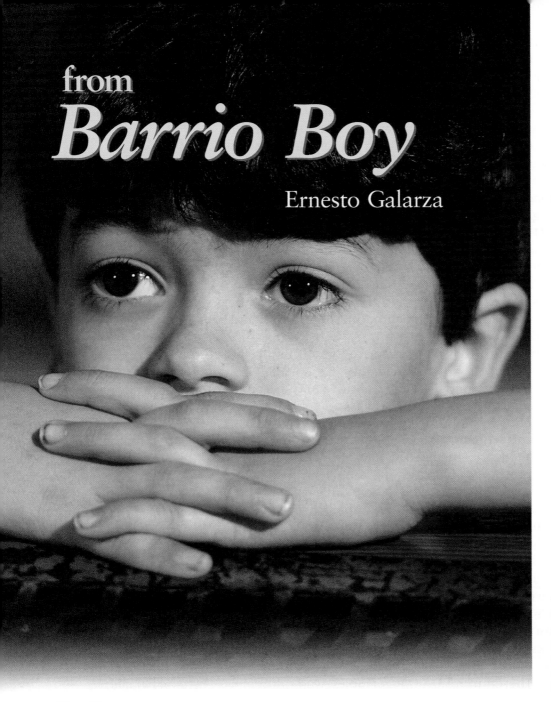

from
Barrio Boy
Ernesto Galarza

◀ **Critical Viewing**
Does this photograph effectively convey the emotions that Ernesto might have felt as he enrolled in a new school? Explain. **[Evaluate]**

My mother and I walked south on Fifth Street one morning to the corner of Q Street and turned right. Half of the block was occupied by the Lincoln School. It was a three-story wooden building, with two wings that gave it the shape of a double-T connected by a central hall. It was a new building, painted yellow, with a shingled roof that was not like the red tile of the school in Mazatlán. I noticed other differences, none of them very reassuring.

✔**Reading Check**

Where do the narrator and his mother go?

We walked up the wide staircase hand in hand and through the door, which closed by itself. A mechanical contraption screwed to the top shut it behind us quietly.

Up to this point the adventure of enrolling me in the school had been carefully rehearsed. Mrs. Dodson had told us how to find it and we had circled it several times on our walks. Friends in the *barrio*[1] explained that the director was called a principal, and that it was a lady and not a man. They assured us that there was always a person at the school who could speak Spanish.

Exactly as we had been told, there was a sign on the door in both Spanish and English: "Principal." We crossed the hall and entered the office of Miss Nettie Hopley.

Miss Hopley was at a roll-top desk to one side, sitting in a swivel chair that moved on wheels. There was a sofa against the opposite wall, flanked by two windows and a door that opened on a small balcony. Chairs were set around a table and framed pictures hung on the walls of a man with long white hair and another with a sad face and a black beard.

The principal half turned in the swivel chair to look at us over the pinch glasses crossed on the ridge of her nose. To do this she had to duck her head slightly as if she were about to step through a low doorway.

What Miss Hopley said to us we did not know but we saw in her eyes a warm welcome and when she took off her glasses and straightened up she smiled wholeheartedly, like Mrs. Dodson. We were, of course, saying nothing, only catching the friendliness of her voice and the sparkle in her eyes while she said words we did not understand. She signaled us to the table. Almost tiptoeing across the office, I maneuvered myself to keep my mother between me and the gringo lady. In a matter of seconds I had to decide whether she was a possible friend or a menace.[2] We sat down.

Then Miss Hopley did a <u>formidable</u> thing. She stood up. Had she been standing when we entered she would have seemed tall. But rising from her chair she soared. And what she carried up and up with her was a buxom superstructure,[3] firm shoulders, a straight sharp nose, full cheeks slightly molded by a curved line along the nostrils, thin lips that moved like steel springs, and a high forehead topped by hair gathered in a bun. Miss Hopley was not a giant in body but when she mobilized[4] it to a standing position she seemed a match for giants. I decided I liked her.

She strode to a door in the far corner of the office, opened it and called a name. A boy of about ten years appeared in the doorway.

---

1. *barrio* (bär´ ē ō) *n.* part of a town or city where most of the people are Hispanic.
2. **menace** (men´ is) *n.* danger; threat.
3. **buxom superstructure** full figure.
4. **mobilized** (mō´ bə līzd´) *v.* put into motion.

formidable (fôr´ mi də bəl) *adj.* impressive

Literary Analysis
Essays In what way does Galarza's honesty about his feelings make the essay seem more personal?

▲ **Critical Viewing** How does the classroom in this photograph compare with the narrator's impressions of school? **[Compare and Contrast]**

He sat down at one end of the table. He was brown like us, a plump kid with shiny black hair combed straight back, neat, cool, and faintly obnoxious.

Miss Hopley joined us with a large book and some papers in her hand. She, too, sat down and the questions and answers began by way of our interpreter. My name was Ernesto. My mother's name was Henriqueta. My birth certificate was in San Blas. Here was my last report card from the Escuela Municipal Numero 3 para Varones of Mazatlán,[5] and so forth. Miss Hopley put things down in the book and my mother signed a card.

As long as the questions continued, Doña[6] Henriqueta could stay and I was secure. Now that they were over, Miss Hopley saw her to the door, dismissed our interpreter and without further ado took me by the hand and strode down the hall to Miss Ryan's first grade.

☑ **Reading Check**

What are the narrator and his mother doing at the school?

---

5. Escuela Municipal Numero 3 para Varones of Mazatlán
(es kwä´ lä mo͞o nē sē päl´ no͞o´ me rō träs pä´ rä bä rō´ nes mä sät län´)
Municipal School Number 3 for Boys of Mazatlán.
6. Doña (dô´ nyä) Spanish title of respect meaning "lady" or "madam."

from *Barrio Boy* ◆ 525

Miss Ryan took me to a seat at the front of the room, into which I shrank—the better to survey her. She was, to skinny, somewhat runty me, of a withering height when she patrolled the class. And when I least expected it, there she was, crouching by my desk, her blond radiant face level with mine, her voice patiently maneuvering me over the awful idiocies of the English language.

During the next few weeks Miss Ryan overcame my fears of tall, energetic teachers as she bent over my desk to help me with a word in the pre-primer. Step by step, she loosened me and my classmates from the safe anchorage of the desks for recitations at the blackboard and consultations at her desk. Frequently she burst into happy announcements to the whole class. "Ito can read a sentence," and small Japanese Ito, squint-eyed and shy, slowly read aloud while the class listened in wonder: "Come, Skipper, come. Come and run." The Korean, Portuguese, Italian, and Polish first graders had similar moments of glory, no less shining than mine the day I conquered "butterfly," which I had been persistently pronouncing in standard Spanish as boo-ter-flee. "Children," Miss Ryan called for attention. "Ernesto has learned how to pronounce *butterfly*!" And I proved it with a perfect imitation of Miss Ryan. From that celebrated success, I was soon able to match Ito's progress as a sentence reader with "Come, butterfly, come fly with me."

Like Ito and several other first graders who did not know English, I received private lessons from Miss Ryan in the closet, a narrow hall off the classroom with a door at each end. Next to one of these doors Miss Ryan placed a large chair for herself and a small one for me. Keeping an eye on the class through the open door she read with me about sheep in the meadow and a frightened chicken going to see the king, coaching me out of my phonetic ruts in words like *pasture*, *bow-wow-wow*, *hay*, and *pretty*, which to my Mexican ear and eye had so many unnecessary sounds and letters. She made me watch her lips and then close my eyes as she repeated words I found hard to read. When we came to know each other better, I tried interrupting to tell Miss Ryan how we said it in Spanish. It didn't work. She only said "oh" and went on with *pasture*, *bow-wow-wow*, and *pretty*. It was as if in that closet we were both discovering together the secrets of the English language and grieving together over the tragedies of Bo-Peep. The main reason I was graduated with honors from the first grade was that I had fallen in love with Miss Ryan. Her radiant, no-nonsense character made us either afraid not to love her or love her so we would not be afraid, I am not sure which. It was not only that we sensed she was with it, but also that she was with us.

Literary Analysis
Essay What details in this selection of Galarza's personal essay help you appreciate the significance of the author's experiences?

Reading Strategy
Evaluating Support What support has the writer provided for the point that he graduated from first grade because of Miss Ryan?

Like the first grade, the rest of the Lincoln School was a sampling of the lower part of town where many races made their home. My pals in the second grade were Kazushi, whose parents spoke only Japanese; Matti, a skinny Italian boy; and Manuel, a fat Portuguese who would never get into a fight but wrestled you to the ground and just sat on you. Our assortment of nationalities included Koreans, Yugoslavs, Poles, Irish, and home-grown Americans.

At Lincoln, making us into Americans did not mean scrubbing away what made us originally foreign. The teachers called us as our parents did, or as close as they could pronounce our names in Spanish or Japanese. No one was ever scolded or punished for speaking in his native tongue on the playground. Matti told the class about his mother's down quilt, which she had made in Italy with the fine feathers of a thousand geese. Encarnación acted out how boys learned to fish in the Philippines. I astounded the third grade with the story of my travels on a stagecoach, which nobody else in the class had seen except in the museum at Sutter's Fort. After a visit to the Crocker Art Gallery and its collection of heroic paintings of the golden age of California, someone showed a silk scroll with a Chinese painting. Miss Hopley herself had a way of expressing wonder over these matters before a class, her eyes wide open until they popped slightly. It was easy for me to feel that becoming a proud American, as she said we should, did not mean feeling ashamed of being a Mexican.

Ernesto Galarza

(1905–1984)
As a child, Ernesto Galarza moved from Mexico to California. His family struggled to make ends meet, but Galarza learned English quickly and won a scholarship for college.

For eleven years, Galarza served as chief of the Division of Labor and Special Information for the Pan American Union. When he returned to California, he fought tirelessly for the rights of American and Mexican farm workers.

After writing several books and articles about the difficult lives of farm workers, Galarza published his autobiography *Barrio Boy*, for which he earned wide acclaim. He also published many books for children.

Review and Assess

Thinking About the Selection

1. **Respond:** What would you do to help a newcomer feel welcome and secure in his or her new school?

2. **(a) Recall:** What is the purpose of Galarza's first visit to the Lincoln School? **(b) Infer:** Why did Galarza feel he had to decide immediately whether Miss Hopley "was a possible friend or a menace"?

3. **(a) Recall:** Why is Galarza afraid of Miss Ryan at first? **(b) Interpret:** What does Galarza mean when he says Miss Ryan "was with it" and "with us"?

4. **(a) Recall:** In what ways does Miss Ryan help him overcome his fears of her and his new class? **(b) Speculate:** In what ways were the seeds of Galarza's success planted in the first grade?

5. **(a) Analyze:** In what ways did the Lincoln School help Galarza realize his dream of "becoming a proud American"? **(b) Generalize:** Using this essay, explain the qualities a person needs to help someone feel at home in a new situation.

I Am a Native of
Chief Dan George

In the course of my lifetime I have lived in two distinct[1] cultures. I was born into a culture that lived in <u>communal</u> houses. My grandfather's house was eighty feet long. It was called a smoke house, and it stood down by the beach along the inlet.[2] All my grandfather's sons and their families lived in this large dwelling. Their sleeping apartments were separated by blankets made of bull rush reeds, but one open fire in the middle served the cooking needs of all. In houses like these, throughout the tribe, people learned to live with one another; learned to serve one another; learned to respect the rights of one another. And children shared the thoughts of the adult world and found themselves surrounded by aunts and uncles and cousins who loved them and did not threaten them. My father was born in such a house and learned from infancy how to love people and be at home with them.

And beyond this acceptance of one another there was a deep respect for everything in nature that surrounded them. My father loved the earth and all its creatures. The earth was his second mother. The earth and everything it contained was a gift from See-see-am[3] . . . and the way to thank this great spirit was to use his gifts with respect.

I remember, as a little boy, fishing with him up Indian River and I can still see him as the sun rose above the mountain top in the early morning . . . I can see him standing by the water's edge with his arms raised above his head while he softly moaned . . . "Thank you, thank you." It left a deep impression on my young mind.

And I shall never forget his disappointment when once he caught me gaffing for fish[4] "just for the fun of it." "My Son," he

> **communal** (kə myoo′ nəl) *adj.* shared by all

> **Literary Analysis**
> **Essays** What thoughts and reflections are included here?

---

1. **distinct** (di stinkt′) *adj.* separate and different.
2. **inlet** (in′ let) *n.* narrow strip of water jutting into a body of land from a river, a lake, or an ocean.
3. **See-see-am** the name of the Great Spirit, or "The Chief Above," in the Salishan language of Chief George's people.
4. **gaffing for fish** using a barbed spear to catch river fish.

said, "the Great Spirit gave you those fish to be your brothers, to feed you when you are hungry. You must respect them. You must not kill them just for the fun of it."

This then was the culture I was born into and for some years the only one I really knew or tasted. This is why I find it hard to accept many of the things I see around me.

I see people living in smoke houses hundreds of times bigger than the one I knew. But the people in one apartment do not even know the people in the next and care less about them.

It is also difficult for me to understand the deep hate that exists among people. It is hard to understand a culture that justifies the killing of millions in past wars, and is at this very moment preparing bombs to kill even greater numbers. It is hard for me to understand a culture that spends more on wars and weapons to kill, than it does on education and welfare to help and develop.

It is hard for me to understand a culture that not only hates and fights its brothers but even attacks nature and abuses her. I see my white brother going about blotting out nature from his cities. I see him strip the hills bare, leaving ugly wounds on the face of mountains. I see him tearing things from the bosom of mother earth as though she were a monster, who refused to share her treasures with him. I see him throw poison in the waters, indifferent to the life he kills there; and he chokes the air with deadly fumes.

My white brother does many things well for he is more clever than my people but I wonder if he knows how to love well. I wonder if he has ever really learned to love at all. Perhaps he only loves the things that are his own but never learned to love the things that are outside and beyond him. And this is, of course, not love at all, for man must love all creation or he will love none of it. Man must love fully or he will become the lowest of the animals. It is the power to love that makes him the greatest of them all . . . for he alone of all animals is capable of love.

Reading Strategy
Evaluating Support Do Chief Dan George's statements contain any bias or stereotyping? Explain.

Reading Check

In what two cultures has Chief Dan George lived?

Buffalo, 1992, Jaune Smith, Courtesy Steinbaum Krauss Gallery, NYC

▲ **Critical Viewing** Based on the ideas he expresses, do you think Chief Dan George would applaud or criticize this collage? Explain. **[Synthesize]**

Love is something you and I must have. We must have it because our spirit feeds upon it. We must have it because without it we become weak and faint. Without love our self-esteem weakens. Without it our courage fails. Without love we can no longer look out confidently at the world. Instead we turn inwardly and begin to feed upon our own personalities and little by little we destroy ourselves.

You and I need the strength and joy that comes from knowing that we are loved. With it we are creative. With it we march tirelessly. With it, and with it alone, we are able to sacrifice for others.

There have been times when we all wanted so desperately to feel a reassuring hand upon us . . . there have been lonely times when we so wanted a strong arm around us . . . I cannot tell you how deeply I miss my wife's presence when I return from a trip. Her love was my greatest joy, my strength, my greatest blessing.

I am afraid my culture has little to offer yours. But my culture did prize friendship and companionship. It did not look on privacy as a thing to be clung to, for privacy builds up walls and walls promote distrust. My culture lived in big family communities, and from infancy people learned to live with others.

My culture did not prize the hoarding of private possessions; in fact, to hoard was a shameful thing to do among my people. The Indian looked on all things in nature as belonging to him and he expected to share them with others and to take only what he needed.

Reading Strategy
Evaluating Support How does Chief Dan George provide support in this passage for his message that we all need love?

Everyone likes to give as well as receive. No one wishes only to receive all the time. We have taken much from your culture . . . I wish you had taken something from our culture . . . for there were some beautiful and good things in it.

Soon it will be too late to know my culture, for integration is upon us and soon we will have no values but yours. Already many of our young people have forgotten the old ways. And many have been shamed of their Indian ways by scorn and ridicule. My culture is like a wounded deer that has crawled away into the forest to bleed and die alone.

The only thing that can truly help us is genuine love. You must truly love us, be patient with us and share with us. And we must love you—with a genuine love that forgives and forgets . . . a love that forgives the terrible sufferings your culture brought ours when it swept over us like a wave crashing along a beach . . . with a love that forgets and lifts up its head and sees in your eyes an answering love of trust and acceptance.

This is brotherhood . . . anything less is not worthy of the name.

I have spoken.

Review and Assess

Thinking About the Selection

1. **Respond:** Do you agree that "the power to love" is the most important human quality? Why or why not?

2. **(a) Recall:** Name three things that people learned from growing up in communal houses. **(b) Compare and Contrast:** Sum up the differences between the "two distinct cultures" in which Chief Dan George lived.

3. **(a) Recall:** What three things puzzle Chief Dan George about his "white brother"? **(b) Interpret:** When Chief Dan George says, "My white brother . . . is more clever than my people," what does he mean by *clever*?

4. **(a) Recall:** Describe the "brotherhood" that Chief Dan George talks about at the end of the essay. **(b) Analyze:** What values does he think are lacking in modern society?

5. **(a) Recall:** According to the author, what makes humans the "greatest of all" creatures? **(b) Assess:** Why do you think Chief Dan George wrote about his culture only in the past tense?

6. **Make a Judgment:** Can people maintain a sense of cultural identity while interacting with another group that does not have the same culture? Explain.

Chief Dan George

(1899–1981)

Chief Dan George was the son of a tribal chief born on a reservation on Vancouver's north shore in 1899 and named "Tes-wah-no," known in English as Dan Slaholt. At age five, he was sent to a mission boarding school where he was not permitted to speak his native language. Dan left school at seventeen and then went on to become a longshoreman, a construction worker, and a school bus driver. The Canadian Broadcasting Company hired Dan to play the role of an aging Indian in one of their series. With that, Dan's long acting career began, and when he was 71, he received an Academy Award nomination for his role in the film *Little Big Man* (1971). Through his celebrity, Chief Dan became a spokesman for native people throughout North America.

All Together Now

Barbara Jordan

When I look at race relations today I can see that some positive changes have come about. But much remains to be done, and the answer does not lie in more legislation. We *have* the legislation we need; we have the laws. Frankly, I don't believe that the task of bringing us all together can be accomplished by government. What we need now is soul force—the efforts of people working on a small scale to build a truly <u>tolerant</u>, harmonious society. And parents can do a great deal to create that tolerant society.

tolerant (täl´ ər ənt) *adj.* free from bigotry or prejudice

Critical Viewing ▶
Does this image reflect the attitude Jordan conveys in her essay?
[Assess]

We all know that race relations in America have had a very rocky history. Think about the 1960s when Dr. Martin Luther King, Jr., was in his heyday and there were marches and protests against segregation[1] and discrimination. The movement culminated in 1963 with the March on Washington.

Following that event, race relations reached an all-time peak. President Lyndon B. Johnson pushed through the Civil Rights Act of 1964, which remains the fundamental piece of civil rights legislation in this century. The Voting Rights Act of 1965 ensured that everyone in our country could vote. At last, black people and white people seemed ready to live together in peace.

But that is not what happened. By the 1990's the good feelings had diminished. Today the nation seems to be suffering from compassion fatigue, and issues such as race relations and civil rights have never regained momentum.

Those issues, however, remain crucial. As our society becomes more diverse, people of all races and backgrounds will have to learn to live together. If we don't think this is important, all we have to do is look at the situation in Bosnia[2] today.

How do we create a harmonious society out of so many kinds of people? The key is tolerance—the one value that is indispensable in creating community.

If we are concerned about community, if it is important to us that people not feel excluded, then we have to do something. Each of us can decide to have one friend of a different race or background in our mix of friends. If we do this, we'll be working together to push things forward.

One thing is clear to me: We, as human beings, must be willing to accept people who are different from ourselves. I must be willing to accept people who don't look as I do and don't talk as I do. It is crucial that I am open to their feelings, their inner reality.

Reading Strategy
Evaluating Support What support does Jordan offer for her assertion that the issue of civil rights is still crucial?

Literary Analysis
Essays How does this paragraph suggest that this is a persuasive essay?

**Reading Check**

What is the topic of Jordan's essay?

---

1. segregation (seg′ rə gā′ shən) *n.* the practice of forcing racial groups to live apart from each other.
2. Bosnia (bäz′ nē ə) *n.* country, located on the Balkan Peninsula in Europe, that was the site of a bloody civil war between different ethnic and religious groups during the 1990s.

What can parents do? We can put our faith in young people as a positive force. I have yet to find a racist baby. Babies come into the world as blank as slates and, with their beautiful innocence, see others not as different but as enjoyable companions. Children learn ideas and attitudes from the adults who nurture them. I absolutely believe that children do not adopt prejudices unless they absorb them from their parents or teachers.

The best way to get this country faithful to the American dream of tolerance and equality is to start small. Parents can actively encourage their children to be in the company of people who are of other racial and ethnic backgrounds. If a child thinks, "Well, that person's color is not the same as mine, but she must be okay because she likes to play with the same things I like to play with," that child will grow up with a broader view of humanity.

I'm an incurable optimist. For the rest of the time that I have left on this planet I want to bring people together. You might think of this as a labor of love. Now, I know that love means different things to different people. But what *I* mean is this: I care about you because you are a fellow human being and I find it okay in my mind, in my heart, to simply say to you, I love you. And maybe that would encourage you to love me in return.

It is possible for all of us to work on this—at home, in our schools, at our jobs. It is possible to work on human relationships in every area of our lives.

Review and Assess

Thinking About the Selection

1. **Respond:** Does this essay inspire you to change your thinking? Explain.

2. **(a) Recall:** How does Jordan summarize the history of race relations from the 1960s to the 1990s? **(b) Interpret:** In your own words, describe what Jordan means by "compassion fatigue."

3. **(a) Recall:** What "one value" is necessary to create "a harmonious society"? **(b) Analyze:** How does the phrase "start small" express two ideas for promoting tolerance?

4. **(a) Recall:** According to Jordan, how do children learn ideas and attitudes? **(b) Interpret:** What does Jordan mean when she says "I have yet to find a racist baby"?

5. **(a) Recall:** What does Jordan suggest that parents do to foster a sense of community? **(b) Evaluate:** Do you think that Jordan's ideas could work to promote tolerance? Explain.

Barbara Jordan

(1936–1996)

Barbara Jordan was the first African American female to serve in the Texas Senate. Elected to Congress in 1972, Jordan was also the first African American congresswoman elected from a southern state. She served three terms and in 1976, became the first African American and the first woman to give the keynote speech at the Democratic National Convention. She returned to Texas as a full professor at the Lyndon B. Johnson School of Public Affairs at the University of Texas.

Review and Assess

Literary Analysis

Essays

1. Develop and complete a chart like the one shown here. You may list the title of an **essay** in more than one category if you can identify characteristics that justify your choices.

Narrative	Expository	Personal	Reflective	Persuasive
"Rattlesnake Hunt"				

Comparing Literary Works

2. Compare and contrast two of the essays by completing an organizer like the one below.

Essay 1				
Compare and contrast	Purpose	Type of essay	Topic	Details included
Essay 2				

3. Which of the writers in this group have similar **purposes?**

4. How do differences in the writers' purposes affect the details they include?

Reading Strategy

Evaluating Support

5. What is the author's bias at the beginning of "Rattlesnake Hunt"?

6. What **support** does Rawlings offer to show readers that her bias was foolish?

7. In what way does the author of *Barrio Boy* support his message about the value of diversity?

8. What is Chief Dan George's message? What examples or illustrations does he use to support it?

9. Does Barbara Jordan offer enough support to persuade you to accept her viewpoint in "All Together Now"? Explain.

Extend Understanding

10. **Apply:** Choose an essay. In what ways can you apply the author's message in the essay to your own life?

Quick Review

An **essay** is a brief prose work in which an author expresses his or her view on a subject. To review essays, see page 517.

An **author's purpose** is his or her reason for writing. To review purpose, see page 517.

To **evaluate support** for an author's message, decide if the details and examples prove the validity of the author's main point. To review support for an author's message, see page 517.

 Take It to the Net
www.phschool.com
Take the interactive self-test online to check your understanding of these selections.

Integrate Language Skills

Vocabulary Development Lesson

Word Analysis: Latin Root -mort-

Explain how the Latin word root -mort-, meaning "death," helps you understand the meaning of each of these words.

1. mortician *n.* funeral director
2. mortal *n.* a being that will eventually die
3. immortal *adj.* deathless; living forever

Spelling Strategy

When spelling the *it* sound at the end of multi-syllable adjectives, you often use the letters *ate*: *desolate, temperate*. Write the words containing the *ate* spelling that fit the following definitions:

1. average, comfortable: mod____?____
2. complex, involved: intri____?____
3. popular flavor: choc____?____

Fluency: Definitions

On your paper, explain your answer to each question. To help you, review the vocabulary words on page 517.

1. Will rattlers be disturbed in a *desolate* place?
2. Do a snake, a rabbit, and a rock all have *mortality*?
3. Does Galarza seem *formidable* to Miss Ryan?
4. Do *communal* houses have things to be shared?
5. Can a *tolerant* attitude help resolve conflicts?

Grammar Lesson

Infinitives and Infinitive Phrases

An **infinitive** is a verb form that can be used as a noun, an adjective, or an adverb. An infinitive usually begins with the word *to*.

Example: Galarza wants *to learn.*

An **infinitive phrase** is an infinitive with modifiers or a complement, all acting together as a single part of speech.

Example: In Chief Dan George's culture, people in communal houses learned from infancy *to live with others.*
Barbara Jordan wants the people of our nation *to build communities of tolerance and equality.*

Practice Copy the infinitive phrase in each of the following sentences. Underline the infinitive.

1. To pick up a rattlesnake was too frightening for Rawlings.
2. His mother waited to see the principal.
3. Miss Ryan wanted to help her students.
4. Chief Dan George's advice, to live in love and brotherhood, is very meaningful.
5. Each of us can decide to have one friend of a different race or background.

Writing Application Write sentences using each of these infinitive phrases.

1. to lose one's fear
2. to become a proud American

W̶G̶ Prentice Hall Writing and Grammar Connection: Chapter 20, Section 1

Writing Lesson

Summary of an Essay

Choose one of the essays in this group and write a summary of it, stating the main points covered in the essay.

Prewriting   Develop a modified outline listing the main points of the essay. First, write the author's message. Then, list each main point and underline it. Write numbered items to recall significant support. Use a modified outline form like the one shown.

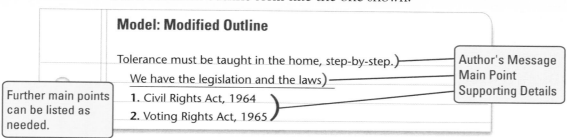

Model: Modified Outline

Tolerance must be taught in the home, step-by-step. — Author's Message

We have the legislation and the laws — Main Point

  1. Civil Rights Act, 1964 — Supporting Details

  2. Voting Rights Act, 1965

Further main points can be listed as needed.

Drafting   Begin your summary with a statement of the author's message in your own words. Then, use your modified outline to help you retell the main points and supporting details. Conclude with a statement of the underlying message or point of the work.

Revising   Add transitional words where necessary to make clear the connection between main points and support.

$\mathcal{W_G}$ *Prentice Hall Writing and Grammar Connection: Chapter 12, Section 2*

Extension Activities

Listening and Speaking Present **a response** to one of the essays.

1. Start with some background information about the writer. Then, speaking slowly and clearly, state the author's message and whether or not you agree or disagree with the message.

2. Next, evaluate whether you feel the author has used enough valid and logical support.

3. Finally, connect the background information and your evaluation of the support to the reasons you agree or disagree with the message.

Research and Technology Prepare and deliver a **group research presentation**, researching some part of history mentioned in these essays, such as the March on Washington. **[Group Activity]**

Writing Write a **persuasive essay** based on the message of one of these works. Among your supporting details, include a quotation from the selection.

 **Take It to the Net**   www.phschool.com

Go online for an additional research activity using the Internet.

READING INFORMATIONAL MATERIALS

Public Documents

About Public Documents

Public documents are any documents that relate to the federal, state, or local government. They are called "public" because they belong to the people as a whole, and every citizen has a right to know what they contain. Public documents include the text of laws, policies, Supreme Court decisions, papers of presidents and governors, and documents related to the various branches of the federal government. The wealth of public documents in our nation's history serve as a kind of historical road map of the United States. Perhaps the best-known public documents are the Declaration of Independence and the Bill of Rights.

Reading Strategy

Previewing

Because many public documents were written long ago or use difficult terms, it is sometimes helpful to preview the document. If an "abstract," or summary, is provided, read that first. Skim the document for words and terms that look unfamiliar. Find out what they mean before reading the document closely.

The Bill of Rights	
1st Amendment	Guarantees freedom of religion, speech, press, assembly, and petition
2nd Amendment	Guarantees the right to bear arms
3rd Amendment	Restricts the manner in which the federal government may house troops in the homes of citizens
4th Amendment	Protects individuals against unreasonable searches and seizures
5th Amendment	Provides that a person must be accused by a grand jury before being tried for a serious federal crime; protects individuals against self-incrimination and against being tried twice for the same crime; prohibits unfair actions by the federal government; prohibits the government from taking private property for public use without paying a fair price for it
6th Amendment	Guarantees persons accused of a crime the right to a swift and fair trial
7th Amendment	Guarantees the right to a jury trial in civil cases tried in federal courts
8th Amendment	Protects against cruel and unusual punishment and excessive bail
9th Amendment	Establishes that the people have rights beyond those stated in the Constitution
10th Amendment	Establishes that all powers not guaranteed to the federal government and not withheld from the states are held by each of the states or their citizens

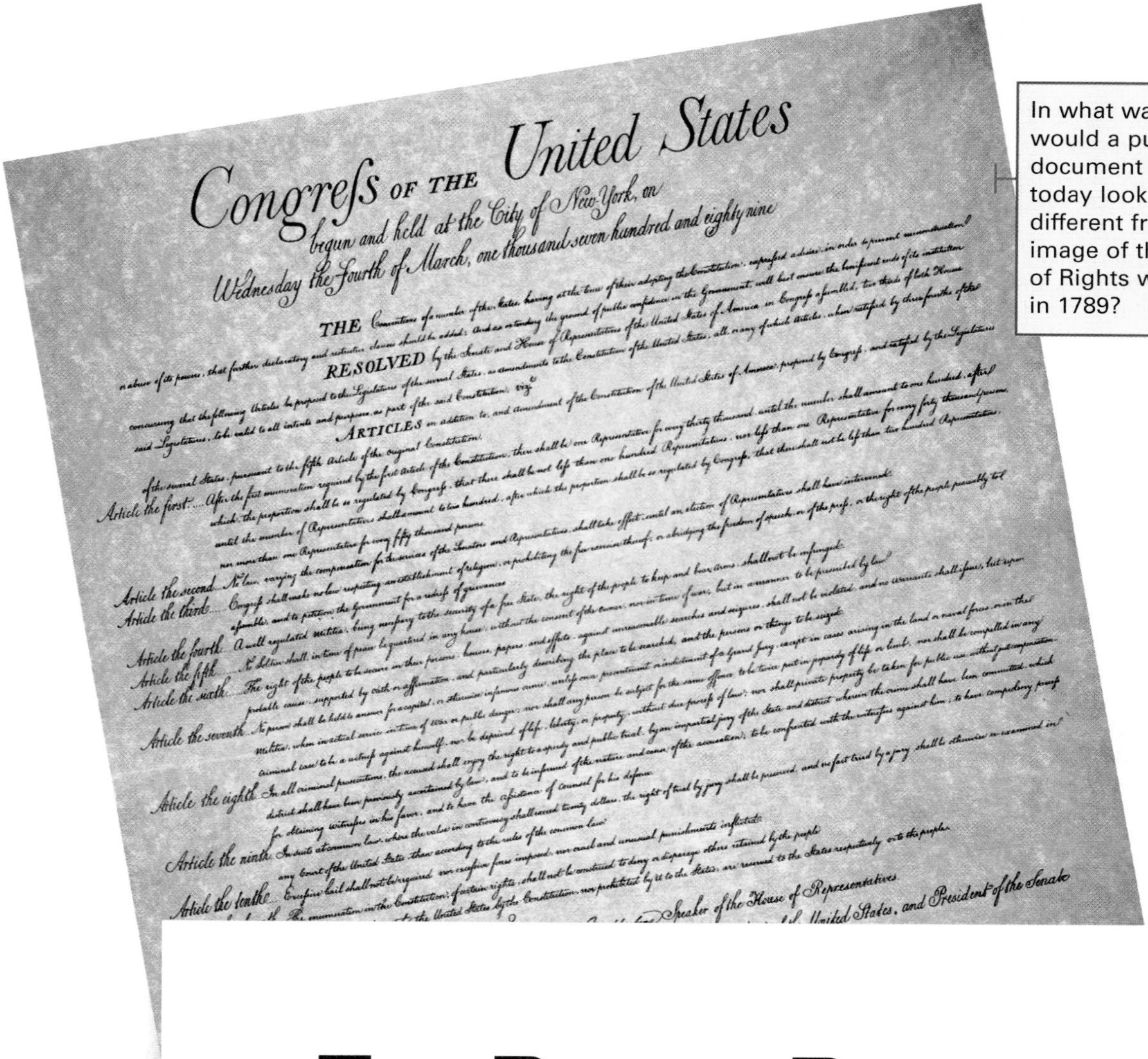

Congress of the United States

begun and held at the City of New York, on Wednesday the fourth of March, one thousand seven hundred and eighty nine

In what ways would a public document written today look different from this image of the Bill of Rights written in 1789?

THE BILL OF RIGHTS

THE FIRST 10 AMENDMENTS TO THE CONSTITUTION AS RATIFIED BY THE STATES

The title of every public document states clearly what information is contained in the document.

Each section of a public document is set off with a heading or section number. Use headings to help you locate information in a long public document.

Amendment I Congress shall make no law respecting an establishment of religion, or prohibiting the free exercise thereof; or abridging[1] the freedom of speech, or of the press; or the right of the people peaceably to assemble, and to petition the Government for a redress[2] of grievances.

Amendment II A well regulated Militia, being necessary to the security of a free State, the right of the people to keep and bear Arms, shall not be infringed[3].

---

1. **abridging** *adj*. reducing in scope or extent; shortening
2. **redress** *n*. a compensation or satisfaction, as for a wrong done
3. **infringed** *v*. broken (as a law or agreement); violated

---

Amendment III No Soldier shall, in time of peace be quartered[4] in any house, without the consent of the Owner, nor in time of war, but in a manner to be prescribed by law.

Amendment IV The right of the people to be secure in their persons, houses, papers, and effects, against unreasonable searches and seizures, shall not be violated, and no Warrants[5] shall issue, but upon probable cause, supported by Oath or affirmation, and particularly describing the place to be searched, and the persons or things to be seized.

Amendment V No person shall be held to answer for a capital,[6] or otherwise infamous crime, unless on a presentment or indictment[7] of a Grand Jury, except in cases arising in the land or naval forces, or in the Militia, when in actual service in time of War or public danger; nor shall any person be subject for the same offense to be twice put in jeopardy of life or limb; nor shall be compelled in any criminal case to be a witness against himself, nor be deprived of life, liberty, or property, without due process of law; nor shall private property be taken for public use, without just compensation.

Amendment VI In all criminal prosecutions, the accused shall enjoy the right to a speedy and public trial, by an impartial jury of the State and district wherein the crime shall have been committed, which district shall have been previously ascertained by law, and to be informed of the nature and cause of the accusation; to be confronted with the witness against him; to have compulsory process for obtaining witnesses in his favor, and to have the Assistance of Counsel[8] for his defense.

Amendment VII In suits at common law, where the value in controversy shall exceed twenty dollars, the right of trial by jury shall be preserved, and no fact tried by a jury, shall be otherwise reexamined in any Court of the United States, than according to the rules of the common law.

Amendment VIII Excessive bail shall not be required, nor excessive fines imposed, nor cruel and unusual punishments inflicted.

Amendment IX The enumeration in the Constitution, of certain rights, shall not be construed[9] to deny or disparage others retained by the people.

Amendment X The powers not delegated[10] to the United States by the Constitution, nor prohibited by it to the States, are reserved to the States respectively, or to the people.

Amendments to the Constitution, as well as most laws, are worded as briefly and directly as possible.

The language of public documents is often difficult. Some words are legal or technical; others contain words no longer in common use.

In most public documents, footnotes are not provided. Sometimes, an appendix, or attachment, gives information. If not, use a dictionary to look up unfamiliar terms.

---

4. **quartered** *v.* assigned to lodgings
5. **warrants** *n.* written authorizations or certifications for something, usually an arrest, seizure, or search
6. **capital** *adj.* involving or punishable by death
7. **indictment** *n.* a written accusation charging one or more persons with a crime, presented by a grand jury to the court when the jury has examined the evidence and found that there is a valid case
8. **counsel** *n.* one or more lawyers representing a client in court
9. **construed** *v.* explained, interpreted
10. **delegated** *adj.* entrusted

Check Your Comprehension

1. Which amendment protects freedom of religion, speech, and the press?
2. Why is the right to keep and bear arms important, according to Amendment II?
3. What must a search warrant describe, according to Amendment IV?
4. Can a United States citizen be tried twice for the same crime? How do you know?
5. Who holds powers that the Constitution does not specifically give to the federal government of the United States? How do you know?

Applying the Reading Strategy

Reviewing

Obviously, you cannot "preview" a document after you have read it. You can, however, review it. When reviewing, use headings to help you recall the main ideas. Write words and terms to be checked and studied. Scan, that is, quickly run your eyes over, the material to locate specific details, terms, dates, names, and so on. Practice reviewing by answering the following questions about the Bill of Rights.

6. How many amendments are in the Bill of Rights?
7. What is the main idea of each one?
8. For which words will you check the meaning?

Activity

Choose one of the ten amendments in the Bill of Rights. In a short essay, paraphrase the amendment, discuss what it means, and then explain your opinion of it.

Comparing Informational Materials

Shared Principles

The Magna Carta is a public document of medieval England that served as a model for the English Constitution, the U.S. Constitution, and other public documents. Locate a copy of the Magna Carta, and, with the help of your teacher, read it. After you have read the document, identify similarities between it and the Bill of Rights. In the right-hand column of a chart like the one shown, write the documents' similarities in regard to each principle listed in the left-hand column.

Shared Principles

Shared Principles	
Personal Freedoms	
Religious Freedom	
Seizure of Property	
Punishment of Individuals	
Due Process of Law	

Prepare to Read

How to Enjoy Poetry

The Starry Night, 1889, Vincent van Gogh, Oil on canvas, 29 x 36 1/4", Collection, The Museum of Modern Art, New York

 Take It to the Net

Visit www.phschool.com for interactive activities and instruction related to "How to Enjoy Poetry," including
- background
- graphic organizers
- literary elements
- reading strategies

Preview

Connecting to the Literature

Shining a bright light on something helps you see all the details of the object. In "How to Enjoy Poetry," James Dickey shows readers how poetry can be the bright light that brings out the detail in ideas and feelings as well as in objects. As you read his advice for enjoying poetry, think about how it will help you "turn on the light."

Background

Thousands of years ago, poets composed and recited long narrative poems. Rhythms, rhymes, and other devices helped them compose and remember these works. Here, Dickey offers advice to modern readers approaching one of the oldest literary forms.

Literary Analysis

Expository Essay

An essay is a brief nonfiction work on a particular topic. **Expository essays** explain, define, or interpret ideas, events, or processes.

In this essay, Dickey explores what poetry is, what it can do, and his own feelings about poetry. To get the most out of the information in his essay, consider these focus questions:

1. What three suggestions does Dickey offer for increasing your enjoyment of poetry?
2. What makes Dickey a reliable source of information about poetry?

Connecting Literary Elements

An **author's argument** is his or her specific position, supported by details and reasons. In an effective argument, you can trace the movement of all main ideas toward a common goal.

Dickey's argument deals with the value of poetry. The main parts of his argument are shown on the organizer. Trace his argument by filling in details from the selection that support each main point of his argument.

Reading Strategy

Recognizing the Organization

The main points of an author's argument are like the framework of a building. Although details and examples are needed to complete the argument, they cannot be put into place in an expository essay until the basic structure is established. The shape of the basic structure is the organization—the arrangement of the main points. Writers choose an organization that allows the pieces to fit together most logically, without gaps or breaks, so that the framework will be strong.

To help you **recognize an author's organization,** consider whether the information is arranged:

- **chronologically**—in the order in which events occur.
- through **order of importance**—in a way that leads up to the most significant point.
- **spatially**—in a specific physical order, left to right, for example.

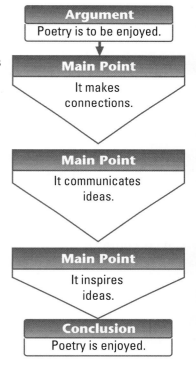

Argument
Poetry is to be enjoyed.

Main Point
It makes connections.

Main Point
It communicates ideas.

Main Point
It inspires ideas.

Conclusion
Poetry is enjoyed.

Vocabulary Development

prose (prōz) *n.* the ordinary form of written language; nonpoetic language (p. 546)

inevitability (in ev′ ə tə bil′ i tē) *n.* certainty (p. 547)

interacts (in′ tər akts′) *v.* affects and is affected by; acts upon and is acted upon by (p. 548)

vital (vīt′ əl) *adj.* essential to life; living (p. 548)

How to Enjoy Poetry

JAMES DICKEY

What is poetry? And why has it been around so long? Many have suspected that it was invented as a school subject, because you have to take exams on it. But that is not what poetry is or why it is still around. That's not what it feels like, either. When you really feel it, a new part of you happens, or an old part is renewed, with surprise and delight at being what it is.

Where Poetry Is Coming From

From the beginning, people have known that words and things, words and actions, words and feelings, go together, and that they can go together in thousands of different ways, according to who is using them. Some ways go shallow, and some go deep.

Your Connection With Other Imaginations

The first thing to understand about poetry is that it comes to you from outside you, in books or in words, but that for it to live, something from within you must come to it and meet it and complete it. Your response with your own mind and body and memory and emotions gives the poem its ability to work its magic; if you give to it, it will give to you, and give plenty.

When you read, don't let the poet write down to you; read up to him. Reach for him from your gut out, and the heart and muscles will come into it, too.

Which Sun? Whose Stars?

The sun is new every day, the ancient philosopher Heraclitus[1] said. The sun of poetry is new every day, too, because it is seen in different ways by different people who have lived under it, lived with it, responded to it. Their lives are different from yours, but by means of the special spell that poetry brings to the *fact* of the sun—everybody's sun; yours, too—you can come into possession of many suns: as many as men and women have ever been able to imagine. Poetry makes possible the deepest kind of personal possession of the world.

Literary Analysis
Expository Essay How do the questions prepare you for what you might learn in the essay?

---

1. Heraclitus (her´ ə klī´ təs) Greek philosopher who lived about 500 B.C.

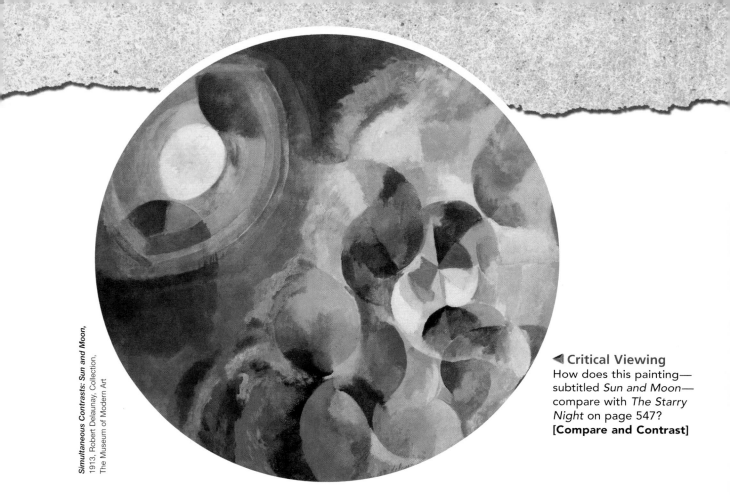

Simultaneous Contrasts: Sun and Moon,
1913, Robert Delaunay, Collection,
The Museum of Modern Art

◀ **Critical Viewing**
How does this painting—
subtitled *Sun and Moon*—
compare with *The Starry
Night* on page 547?
[Compare and Contrast]

The most beautiful constellation in the winter sky is Orion [ō rī´ ən], which ancient poets thought looked like a hunter, up there, moving across heaven with his dog Sirius [sir´ ē əs]. What is this hunter made out of stars hunting for? What does he mean? Who owns him, if any-body? The poet Aldous Huxley[2] felt that he did, and so, in Aldous Huxley's universe of personal emotion, he did.

Up from among the emblems of the wind into its heart of power,
The Huntsman climbs, and all his living stars
Are bright, and all are mine.

Where to Start

The beginning of your true encounter with poetry should be simple. It should bypass all classrooms, all textbooks, courses, examinations, and libraries and go straight to the things that make your own existence exist: to your body and nerves and blood and muscles. Find your own way—a secret way that just

Reading Strategy
Recognizing the Organization How does the heading of this section help you recognize that the organization of the essay may be chronological?

✔**Reading Check**

What is the reader's job when reading poetry?

---

2. **Aldous Huxley** English poet, essayist, and novelist (1894–1963).

maybe you don't know yet—to open yourself as wide as you can and as deep as you can to the moment, the *now* of your own existence and the endless mystery of it, and perhaps at the same time to one other thing that is not you, but is out there: a handful of gravel is a good place to start. So is an ice cube—what more mysterious and beautiful *interior* of something has there ever been?

As for me, I like the sun, the source of all living things, and on certain days very good-feeling, too. "Start with the sun," D. H. Lawrence[3] said, "and everything will slowly, slowly happen." Good advice. And a lot *will* happen.

What is more fascinating than a rock, if you really feel it and *look* at it, or more interesting than a leaf?

Horses, I mean; butterflies, whales;
Mosses, and stars; and gravelly
Rivers, and fruit.

Oceans, I mean; black valleys; corn;
Brambles, and cliffs; rock, dirt, dust,
ice . . .

Go back and read this list—it is quite a list, Mark Van Doren's[4] list!—item by item. Slowly. Let each of these things call up an image out of your own life.

Think and feel. What moss do you see? Which horse? What field of corn? What brambles are *your* brambles? Which river is most yours?

The Poem's Way of Going

Part of the spell of poetry is in the rhythm of language, used by poets who understand how powerful a factor rhythm can be, how compelling and unforgettable. Almost anything put into rhythm and rhyme is more memorable than the same thing said in <u>prose</u>. Why this is, no one knows completely, though the answer is surely rooted far down in the biology by means of which we exist; in the circulation of the blood that goes forth from the heart and comes back, and in the repetition of breathing. Croesus [krē′ səs] was a rich Greek king, back in the sixth century before Christ, but this tombstone was not his:

No Croesus lies in the grave you see;
I was a poor laborer, and this suits me.

That is plain-spoken and definitive. You believe it, and the rhyme helps you believe it and keep it.

---

3. **D. H. Lawrence** English poet and novelist (1885–1930).
4. **Mark Van Doren** American poet, teacher, and critic (1894–1972).

Literary Analysis
Expository Essay What specific suggestions does Dickey provide for beginning the process of enjoying poetry?

prose (prōz) *n.* the ordinary form of written language; nonpoetic language

Literary Analysis
Expository Essay What factual information is included here?

The Starry Night, 1889, Vincent van Gogh, Oil on canvas, 29 x 36 1/4", Collection, The Museum of Modern Art, New York

▲ **Critical Viewing** Dickey says that a poet in some ways "owns" what he or she describes. In Dickey's sense of the word, does Vincent van Gogh "own" the night sky he painted here? **[Assess]**

Some Things You'll Find Out

Writing poetry is a lot like a contest with yourself, and if you like sports and games and competitions of all kinds, you might like to try writing some. Why not?

The possibilities of rhyme are great. Some of the best fun is in making up your own limericks. There's no reason you can't invent limericks about anything that comes to your mind. No reason. Try it.

The problem is to find three words that rhyme and fit into a meaning. "There was a young man from . . ." *Where* was he from? What situation was he in? How can these things fit into the limerick form—a form everybody knows—so that the rhymes "pay off," and give that sense of completion and <u>inevitability</u> that is so deliciously memorable that nothing else is like it?

inevitability
(in ev′ ə tə bil′ i tē) *n.*
certainty

☑ **Reading Check**

What two elements of poetry are appealing for reasons that cannot be fully explained?

How It Goes With You

The more your encounter with poetry deepens, the more your experience of your own life will deepen, and you will begin to see things by means of words, and words by means of things.

You will come to understand the world as it <u>interacts</u> with words, as it can be re-created by words, by rhythms and by images.

You'll understand that this condition is one charged with <u>vital</u> possibilities. You will pick up meaning more quickly—and you will *create* meaning, too, for yourself and for others.

Connections between things will exist for you in ways that they never did before. They will shine with unexpectedness, wide-openness, and you will go toward them, on your own path. "Then . . . ," as Dante[5] says, ". . . Then will your feet be filled with good desire." You will know this is happening the first time you say, of something you never would have noticed before, "Well, would you look at *that*! Who'd 'a thunk it?" (Pause, full of new light)

"*I* thunk it!"

---

5. **Dante** (dän´ tā) Italian poet (1265–1321).

interacts (in´ tər akts´) *v.* affects and is affected by; acts upon and is acted upon by

vital (vīt´ əl) *adj.* essential to life; living

Review and Assess

Thinking About the Literature

1. **Respond:** How do you know when you like a poem? What reasons do you generally give?

2. **(a) Recall:** A poem comes to you from outside, Dickey says, but what does he say is required for the poem to live?
   (b) Interpret: What does Dickey mean when he says that a poem "lives"?

3. **(a) Recall:** According to Dickey, how is the sun of poetry new every day? **(b) Interpret:** How does this newness help the reader of poetry take "personal possession of the world"?

4. **(a) Recall:** What processes of the human body does Dickey discuss in relation to the rhythm and rhyme of poetry?
   (b) Infer: In what way could the rhythm of poetry be related to human biology?

5. **(a) Recall:** What does Dickey say will happen "the more your encounter with poetry deepens"? **(b) Apply:** Dickey says you can enjoy poetry more by focusing on yourself and also on "one other thing that is not you." Which other thing would you choose? Why?

6. **Make a Judgment:** Is the study of poetry more, less, or equally important as the study of other subjects, such as math, science, or social studies?

James Dickey

(1923–1997)

James Dickey lived a life packed with adventure. Born in Atlanta, Georgia, he was a football player and motorcycle enthusiast as a young man. During World War II, he served as a radar operator. Then, for a period in the 1950s, he worked for advertising agencies in Atlanta and New York.

Dickey's literary life was active, too. In prize-winning volumes of poetry, like *Buckdancer's Choice*, he spoke of animals, hunting, and his wartime experiences. He also wrote many prose works, such as the novel *Deliverance*, which was made into a movie.

Review and Assess

Literary Analysis

Expository Essay

1. Identify three suggestions that Dickey offers for increasing your enjoyment of poetry.
2. What details does Dickey include about his own feelings for poetry?
3. What makes Dickey a reliable source of information about poetry?
4. Break down the parts of Dickey's **expository essay** by completing a graphic organizer like the one shown below.

What is poetry?	What can it do?	Author's conclusion

Connecting Literary Elements

5. What is Dickey's **argument?**
6. Trace the development of his argument by identifying his main points.

Reading Strategy

Recognizing the Organization

7. What are the first three headings in Dickey's essay?
8. What do the headings suggest about his **organization?**
9. Arrange the points in the essay in chronological order by adding the missing steps to an organizer like the one shown. Add sections if necessary.

Background	→		→	Reading the poem	→	

Extend Understanding

10. **Science Connection: (a)** Do you think a poem could include images and ideas from the sciences? Why or why not? **(b)** Have you ever read a poem that focused on one aspect of nature or science? Describe the poem.

Quick Review

An **expository essay** is a short piece of nonfiction writing that explains a subject. To review expository essays, see pages 517 and 543.

An **author's argument** is his or her specific position. To review author's argument, see page 543.

The **organization** of a work is the arrangement of main points. To review organization, see page 543.

Take It to the Net

www.phschool.com

Take the interactive self-test online to check your understanding of the selection.

Integrate Language Skills

Vocabulary Development Lesson

Word Analysis: Latin Prefix *inter-*

The Latin prefix *inter-* means "between" or "among." In his essay, Dickey uses the word *interacts*, meaning "affects and is affected by another."

Match each *inter-* word in the first column with its definition in the second column.

1. interview
2. interlock
3. international
4. Internet
5. interchange

   a. concerning relations among nations
   b. a meeting between people
   c. to make a firm joining between things
   d. to change places with each other
   e. a system of connections among computers

Concept Development: Analogies

On your paper, write the vocabulary word that best completes each analogy.

1. *Invigorates* is to *exhausts* as ___?___ is to *avoids*.
2. *Tree* is to *plant* as ___?___ is to *writing*.
3. ___?___ is to *unnecessary* as *early* is to *late*.
4. *Simplicity* is to *complexity* as ___?___ is to *impossibility*.

Spelling Strategy

When you change certain adjectives ending in *-able* to their noun forms ending in *-ility*, you drop the *-le* ending. For example, inevitable + *-ility* = inevitability.

On your paper, add *-ility* to correctly spell the noun forms of these adjectives:

1. probable
2. irritable
3. durable
4. reliable

Grammar Lesson

The Four Functions of Sentences

Sentences are classified into four categories based on their function. Note these examples from the selection.

- **Declarative** (making statements): The possibilities of rhyme are great.
- **Interrogative** (asking questions): What is poetry?
- **Imperative** (giving commands): Don't let the poet write down to you; read up to him.
- **Exclamatory** (calling out or exclaiming): "I thunk it!"

▶ *For more practice, see page R30, Exercise A.*
Practice On your paper, identify which function each of these sentences performs.

1. What does he mean?
2. Some ways go shallow, and some go deep.
3. Try it.
4. I really enjoyed that poem!
5. New connections between things will exist for you.

Writing Application Write sentences that serve each of the four functions. Include the words *enjoy poetry* in each sentence.

Prentice Hall Writing and Grammar Connection: Chapter 22, Section 1

Writing Lesson

Essay of Inspiration

Choose an activity that you care about as much as James Dickey cares about poetry. Then, write three paragraphs of an essay in praise of this pursuit. Tell readers why this activity is so rewarding and what they can do to appreciate it.

Prewriting   Jot down three main points to convey. Brainstorm for a list of experiences you have had that support your main points. Then, choose an organization, such as chronological order or order of importance.

Model: Order of Importance

③ Running a long-distance race, like a 10K, is the best way I know to prove to yourself that you can do anything.

① Long-distance running keeps your body in good shape.

② You meet people from all over the country in long-distance races.

> After choosing order of importance, the writer numbered the main ideas from least important to most important.

Drafting   Begin by writing an introduction that presents your topic. In the body of your essay, write your main points in the order that fits your organization. Follow each main point with supporting details.

Revising   Underline each main point. Evaluate whether the main points are presented in the order suited to your organization. Make sure supporting details are grouped with their main points. If necessary, revise to strengthen organization by moving sections related to a main point.

W̶G Prentice Hall Writing and Grammar Connection: Chapter 7, Section 3

Extension Activities

Research and Technology Design an **Internet Home Page** for poetry with a small group of classmates. Include ideas from Dickey's essay to encourage people to read more poetry.

- Assign sections of the page for each member of the group to write.
- Create links to other Web pages.
- Create graphics to go on the page.

Ask an experienced adult to help your group launch your Home Page. **[Group Activity]**

Listening and Speaking In small groups, deliver an **oral summary** of Dickey's essay.

1. Choose a poem to illustrate his ideas.
2. In your own words, outline his main points and most important supporting details.
3. Conclude with a statement of the underlying message of Dickey's essay.

 **Take It to the Net**   www.phschool.com

Go online for an additional research activity using the Internet.

Prepare to Read

No Gumption ◆ *from* An American Childhood

Take It to the Net

Visit www.phschool.com
for interactive activities
and instruction related to
these selections, including

- background
- graphic organizers
- literary elements
- reading strategies

Preview

Connecting to the Literature

These selections are self-portraits that use words instead of paint. The authors paint a picture of a significant event in their lives that reveals some of their values and beliefs. As you read, think about an important event you might explore in an essay about your own life.

Background

"No Gumption" is set during the Depression, a period of economic troubles that began in 1929 when the value of stocks fell rapidly. By 1933, one out of every four workers in the United States was unemployed. This was why Russell Baker's mother considered a good job so important. It was not until the early 1940s that the economy recovered completely.

Literary Analysis
Autobiography

In an **autobiography**—a narrative of a person's life written by that person—a writer tells some or all significant events from his or her life. An autobiography reveals the writer's

- struggles, values, and ideas.
- thoughts and reactions that an observer could not reveal.

In this passage, Baker describes how he decides to become a writer.

> I had never met a writer, had shown no previous urge to write, and hadn't a notion how to become a writer, but I loved stories and thought that making up stories must surely be almost as much fun as reading them.

As you read, enjoy the stories that the authors tell you, but look deeper. Ask yourself about the author's struggles and beliefs.

Comparing Literary Works

The subject of an autobiography, or the main character, is as different from selection to selection as one person is from the next. Baker and Dillard reveal their unique personalities by describing experiences that helped to shape their values and ideas. Compare and contrast these autobiographical accounts by thinking about these focus questions:

1. What kind of experience does each writer relate?
2. Which writer's account of a childhood memory seems more connected to his or her life as an adult?

Reading Strategy
Understanding the Author's Purpose

An **author's purpose** is his or her reason for writing. Writers of autobiographies have many different reasons for telling their life stories. Their purposes might include explaining themselves and their values, teaching lessons about life, entertaining, or a combination of these. As you read, use a chart like the one here to determine the authors' purpose.

Passage	Possible Purpose
The flaw in my character . . . was lack of "gumption."	To explain himself To entertain by making fun of himself

Vocabulary Development

gumption (gump´ shən) *n.* courage; enterprise (p. 554)

paupers (pô´ pərz) *n.* people who are very poor (p. 555)

crucial (kroo´ shəl) *adj.* of great importance (p. 556)

aptitude (ap´ tə tood´) *n.* talent; ability (p. 558)

translucent (trans loo´ sənt) *adj.* able to transmit light but no details of things on the other side (p. 563)

compelled (kəm peld´) *v.* forced (p. 564)

perfunctorily (pər funk´ tə rə lē) *adv.* without enthusiasm; routinely (p. 565)

NO GUMPTION

Russell Baker

I began working in journalism when I was eight years old. It was my mother's idea. She wanted me to "make something" of myself and, after a level-headed appraisal[1] of my strengths, decided I had better start young if I was to have any chance of keeping up with the competition.

The flaw in my character which she had already spotted was lack of "gumption." My idea of a perfect afternoon was lying in front of the radio rereading my favorite Big Little Book,[2] *Dick Tracy Meets Stooge Viller.* My mother despised inactivity. Seeing me having a good time in repose, she was powerless to hide her disgust. "You've got no more gumption than a bump on a log," she said. "Get out in the kitchen and help Doris do those dirty dishes."

My sister Doris, though two years younger than I, had enough gumption for a dozen people. She positively enjoyed washing dishes, making beds, and cleaning the house. When she was only seven she could carry a piece of short-weighted cheese back to the A&P, threaten the manager with legal action, and come back triumphantly with the full quarter-pound we'd paid for and a few ounces extra thrown in for forgiveness. Doris could have made something of herself if she hadn't been a girl. Because of this defect,

gumption (gump´ shən) *n.* courage; enterprise

THE SATURDAY EVENING POST

November 27, 1937

5c. the Copy

WATER BUKIT

THIS PEACE IS A CHEAT—By JOHN GUNTHER

---

1. appraisal (ə prāz´ əl) *n.* judgment of something's or someone's quality.
2. Big Little Book a small, inexpensive illustrated book that often portrayed the adventures of comic-strip heroes like Dick Tracy.

however, the best she could hope for was a career as a nurse or schoolteacher, the only work that capable females were considered up to in those days.

This must have saddened my mother, this twist of fate that had allocated all the gumption to the daughter and left her with a son who was content with Dick Tracy and Stooge Viller. If disappointed, though, she wasted no energy on self-pity. She would make me make something of myself whether I wanted to or not. "The Lord helps those who help themselves," she said. That was the way her mind worked.

She was realistic about the difficulty. Having sized up the material the Lord had given her to mold, she didn't overestimate what she could do with it. She didn't insist that I grow up to be President of the United States.

Fifty years ago parents still asked boys if they wanted to grow up to be President, and asked it not jokingly but seriously. Many parents who were hardly more than paupers still believed their sons could do it. Abraham Lincoln had done it. We were only sixty-five years from Lincoln. Many a grandfather who walked among us could remember Lincoln's time. Men of grandfatherly age were the worst for asking if you wanted to grow up to be President. A surprising number of little boys said yes and meant it.

I was asked many times myself. No, I would say, I didn't want to grow up to be President. My mother was present during one of these interrogations.[3] An elderly uncle, having posed the usual question and exposed my lack of interest in the Presidency, asked, "Well, what *do* you want to be when you grow up?"

I loved to pick through trash piles and collect empty bottles, tin cans with pretty labels, and discarded magazines. The most desirable job on earth sprang instantly to mind. "I want to be a garbage man," I said.

My uncle smiled, but my mother had seen the first distressing evidence of a bump budding on a log. "Have a little gumption, Russell," she said. Her calling me Russell was a signal of unhappiness. When she approved of me I was always "Buddy."

When I turned eight years old she decided that the job of starting me on the road toward making something of myself could no longer be safely delayed. "Buddy," she said one day, "I want you to come home right after school this afternoon. Somebody's coming and I want you to meet him."

When I burst in that afternoon she was in conference in the parlor with an executive of the Curtis Publishing Company. She

3. **interrogations** (in ter´ ə gā´ shənz) *n.* situations where a person is formally questioned.

◀ **Critical Viewing** How do the boys in this illustration from the 1930s differ from Baker? How are they the same? **[Compare and Contrast]**

Reading Strategy
Understanding Author's Purpose Which portions of this paragraph indicate that Baker is showing himself as less than perfect in order to entertain the reader?

paupers (pô´ pərz) *n.* people who are very poor

Literary Analysis
Autobiography What do these details reveal about Russell's character?

✔ **Reading Check**
What is Russell's mother worried about?

introduced me. He bent low from the waist and shook my hand. Was it true as my mother had told him, he asked, that I longed for the opportunity to conquer the world of business?

My mother replied that I was blessed with a rare determination to make something of myself.

"That's right," I whispered.

"But have you got the grit, the character, the never-say-quit spirit it takes to succeed in business?"

My mother said I certainly did.

"That's right," I said.

He eyed me silently for a long pause, as though weighing whether I could be trusted to keep his confidence, then spoke man-to-man. Before taking a <u>crucial</u> step, he said, he wanted to advise me that working for the Curtis Publishing Company placed enormous responsibility on a young man. It was one of the great companies of America. Perhaps the greatest publishing house in the world. I had heard, no doubt, of the *Saturday Evening Post*?

Heard of it? My mother said that everyone in our house had heard of the *Saturday Post* and that I, in fact, read it with religious devotion.

Then doubtless, he said, we were also familiar with those two monthly pillars of the magazine world, the *Ladies Home Journal* and the *Country Gentleman*.

Indeed we were familiar with them, said my mother.

Representing the *Saturday Evening Post* was one of the weightiest honors that could be bestowed in the world of business, he said. He was personally proud of being a part of that great corporation.

My mother said he had every right to be.

Again he studied me as though debating whether I was worthy of a knighthood. Finally: "Are you trustworthy?"

My mother said I was the soul of honesty.

"That's right," I said.

The caller smiled for the first time. He told me I was a lucky young man. He admired my spunk. Too many young men thought life was all play. Those young men would not go far in this world. Only a young man willing to work and save and keep his face washed and his hair neatly combed could hope to come out on top in a world such as ours. Did I truly and sincerely believe that I was such a young man?

"He certainly does," said my mother.

"That's right," I said.

He said he had been so impressed by what he had seen of me that he was going to make me a representa-tive of the Curtis Publishing Company. On the following Tuesday, he said, thirty freshly printed copies of the *Saturday Evening Post* would be delivered at our door.

crucial (krōō′ shəl) *adj.* of great importance

▼ **Critical Viewing**
How does your image of Russell Baker compare with this photograph of him with his sister?
[Compare and Contrast]

I would place these magazines, still damp with the ink of the presses, in a handsome canvas bag, sling it over my shoulder, and set forth through the streets to bring the best in journalism, fiction, and cartoons to the American public.

He had brought the canvas bag with him. He presented it with reverence fit for a chasuble.[4] He showed me how to drape the sling over my left shoulder and across the chest so that the pouch lay easily accessible[5] to my right hand, allowing the best in journalism, fiction, and cartoons to be swiftly extracted and sold to a citizenry whose happiness and security depended upon us soldiers of the free press.

The following Tuesday I raced home from school, put the canvas bag over my shoulder, dumped the magazines in, and, tilting to the left to balance their weight on my right hip, embarked on the highway of journalism.

We lived in Belleville, New Jersey, a commuter town at the northern fringe of Newark. It was 1932, the bleakest year of the Depression. My father had died two years before, leaving us with a few pieces of Sears, Roebuck furniture and not much else, and my mother had taken Doris and me to live with one of her younger brothers. This was my Uncle Allen. Uncle Allen had made something of himself by 1932. As salesman for a soft-drink bottler in Newark, he had an income of $30 a week; wore pearl-gray spats,[6] detachable collars, and a three-piece suit; was happily married; and took in threadbare relatives.

With my load of magazines I headed toward Belleville Avenue. That's where the people were. There were two filling stations at the intersection with Union Avenue, as well as an A&P, a fruit stand, a bakery, a barber shop, Zuccarelli's drugstore, and a diner shaped like a railroad car. For several hours I made myself highly visible, shifting position now and then from corner to corner, from shop window to shop window, to make sure everyone could see the heavy black lettering on the canvas bag that said *The Saturday Evening Post*. When the angle of the light indicated it was suppertime, I walked back to the house.

"How many did you sell, Buddy?" my mother asked.

"None."

"Where did you go?"

"The corner of Belleville and Union Avenues."

"What did you do?"

"Stood on the corner waiting for somebody to buy a *Saturday Evening Post*."

▲ **Critical Viewing**
Does this picture fit your idea of Baker's mother? Explain. **[Connect]**

Literary Analysis
Autobiography What struggle is revealed in the details about the family situation?

Reading Check

What job does Russell have?

---

4. **chasuble** (chaz′ ə bəl) *n.* sleeveless outer garment worn by priests.
5. **accessible** (ak ses′ ə bəl) *adj.* easy to get.
6. **spats** (spats) *n.* pieces of cloth or leather that cover the upper part of the shoe or ankle.

"You just stood there?"

"Didn't sell a single one."

"For God's sake, Russell!"

Uncle Allen intervened. "I've been thinking about it for some time," he said, "and I've about decided to take the *Post* regularly. Put me down as a regular customer." I handed him a magazine and he paid me a nickel. It was the first nickel I earned.

Afterwards my mother instructed me in salesmanship. I would have to ring doorbells, address adults with charming self-confidence, and break down resistance with a sales talk pointing out that no one, no matter how poor, could afford to be without the *Saturday Evening Post* in the home.

I told my mother I'd changed my mind about wanting to succeed in the magazine business.

"If you think I'm going to raise a good-for-nothing," she replied, "you've got another think coming." She told me to hit the streets with the canvas bag and start ringing doorbells the instant school was out next day. When I objected that I didn't feel any aptitude for salesmanship, she asked how I'd like to lend her my leather belt so she could whack some sense into me. I bowed to superior will and entered journalism with a heavy heart.

My mother and I had fought this battle almost as long as I could remember. It probably started even before memory began, when I was a country child in northern Virginia and my mother, dissatisfied with my father's plain workman's life, determined that I would not grow up like him and his people, with calluses on their hands, overalls on their backs, and fourth-grade educations in their heads. She had fancier ideas of life's possibilities. Introducing me to the *Saturday Evening Post*, she was trying to wean me as early as possible from my father's world where men left with lunch pails at sunup, worked with their hands until the grime ate into the pores, and died with a few sticks of mail-order furniture as their legacy. In my mother's vision of the better life there were desks and white collars, well-pressed suits, evenings of reading and lively talk, and perhaps—if a man were very, very lucky and hit the jackpot, really made something important of himself—perhaps there might be a fantastic salary of $5,000 a year to support a big house and a Buick with a rumble seat[7] and a vacation in Atlantic City.

And so I set forth with my sack of magazines. I was afraid of the dogs that snarled behind the doors of potential buyers. I was timid about ringing the doorbells of strangers, relieved when no one came to the door, and scared when someone did. Despite my mother's instructions, I could not deliver an engaging sales pitch. When a door opened I simply asked, "Want to buy a *Saturday Evening Post*?" In

---

7. **rumble seat** in early automobiles, an open seat in the rear of the car that could be folded shut.

aptitude (ap′ tə tōōd′) *n.* talent; ability

Reading Strategy
Understanding Author's Purpose What do you think is Baker's purpose in telling this story about his first job?

Literary Analysis
Autobiography What details are revealed in this passage that only Baker and no one else would know?

Belleville few persons did. It was a town of 30,000 people, and most weeks I rang a fair majority of its doorbells. But I rarely sold my thirty copies. Some weeks I canvassed the entire town for six days and still had four or five unsold magazines on Monday evening; then I dreaded the coming of Tuesday morning, when a batch of thirty fresh *Saturday Evening Posts* was due at the front door.

"Better get out there and sell the rest of those magazines tonight," my mother would say.

I usually posted myself then at a busy intersection where a traffic light controlled commuter flow from Newark. When the light turned red I stood on the curb and shouted my sales pitch at the motorists.

"Want to buy a *Saturday Evening Post?*"

One rainy night when car windows were sealed against me I came back soaked and with not a single sale to report. My mother beckoned to Doris.

"Go back down there with Buddy and show him how to sell these magazines," she said.

Brimming with zest, Doris, who was then seven years old, returned with me to the corner. She took a magazine from the bag, and when the light turned red she strode to the nearest car and banged her small fist against the closed window. The driver, probably startled at what he took to be a midget assaulting his car, lowered the window to stare, and Doris thrust a *Saturday Evening Post* at him.

"You need this magazine," she piped, "and it only costs a nickel."

Her salesmanship was irresistible. Before the light changed half a dozen times she disposed of the entire batch. I didn't feel humiliated. To the contrary. I was so happy I decided to give her a treat. Leading her to the vegetable store on Belleville Avenue, I bought three apples, which cost a nickel, and gave her one.

"You shouldn't waste money," she said.

"Eat your apple." I bit into mine.

"You shouldn't eat before supper," she said. "It'll spoil your appetite."

Back at the house that evening, she dutifully reported me for wasting a nickel. Instead of a scolding, I was rewarded with a pat on the back for having the good sense to buy fruit instead of candy. My mother reached into her bottomless supply of maxims[8] and told Doris, "An apple a day keeps the doctor away."

By the time I was ten I had learned all my mother's maxims by

---

8. **maxims** (mak´ simz) *n.* wise sayings.

▼ **Critical Viewing** Do you think this magazine would be easy or difficult to sell? Why? **[Connect]**

©The Curtis Publishing Company, Illustrator: Norman Rockwell

✔ **Reading Check**

What skill does Doris have that Russell doesn't?

heart. Asking to stay up past normal bedtime, I knew that a refusal would be explained with, "Early to bed and early to rise, makes a man healthy, wealthy, and wise." If I whimpered about having to get up early in the morning, I could depend on her to say, "The early bird gets the worm."

The one I most despised was, "If at first you don't succeed, try, try again." This was the battle cry with which she constantly sent me back into the hopeless struggle whenever I moaned that I had rung every doorbell in town and knew there wasn't a single potential buyer left in Belleville that week. After listening to my explanation, she handed me the canvas bag and said, "If at first you don't succeed . . ."

Three years in that job, which I would gladly have quit after the first day except for her insistence, produced at least one valuable result. My mother finally concluded that I would never make something of myself by pursuing a life in business and started considering careers that demanded less competitive zeal.

One evening when I was eleven I brought home a short "composition" on my summer vacation which the teacher had graded with an A. Reading it with her own schoolteacher's eye, my mother agreed that it was top-drawer seventh grade prose and complimented me. Nothing more was said about it immediately, but a new idea

▼ **Critical Viewing**
Which character in these illustrations seems the most like Doris? Explain.
[Connect]

560

had taken life in her mind. Halfway through supper she suddenly interrupted the conversation.

"Buddy," she said, "maybe you could be a writer."

I clasped the idea to my heart. I had never met a writer, had shown no previous urge to write, and hadn't a notion how to become a writer, but I loved stories and thought that making up stories must surely be almost as much fun as reading them. Best of all, though, and what really gladdened my heart, was the ease of the writer's life. Writers did not have to trudge through the town peddling from canvas bags, defending themselves against angry dogs, being rejected by surly strangers. Writers did not have to ring doorbells. So far as I could make out, what writers did couldn't even be classified as work.

I was enchanted. Writers didn't have to have any gumption at all. I did not dare tell anybody for fear of being laughed at in the schoolyard, but secretly I decided that what I'd like to be when I grew up was a writer.

Review and Assess

Thinking About the Selection

1. **Respond:** Do you agree with Baker's mother that Baker has no "gumption"? Why or why not?

2. **(a) Recall:** What are two main qualities of young Baker's personality? **(b) Interpret:** Give two examples of his actions that reveal these qualities. **(c) Analyze:** How do these qualities prevent Baker from being a good salesperson?

3. **(a) Recall:** Why does Baker's mother get him a job as a newsboy? **(b) Infer:** What goals does Baker's mother set for him as a child? **(c) Compare and Contrast:** Compare Baker's own aims in life as a child with the goals his mother sets for him.

4. **(a) Analyze:** Give two examples that show Baker's sense of humor about his poor salesmanship. **(b) Connect:** What does Baker's sense of humor about his failures reveal about his personality?

5. **(a) Recall:** What inspires Baker's mother's new plan for his career? **(b) Infer:** How does Baker react to this idea? **(c) Analyze:** How much of the idea for Baker's new career comes from him, and how much comes from his mother?

6. **(a) Evaluate:** What are the benefits and drawbacks for a young person having a paying job? **(b) Take a Position:** Do you think young people should or should not have after-school jobs? Explain.

Russell Baker

(b. 1925)

As a newspaper columnist and author, Russell Baker has found humor in the news and in his own life story. You'll see how Baker's humor emerges even as he writes about problems he faced early in life. As a result of the country's failing economy, his family moved often in search of better opportunities.

Eventually, Baker went on to a successful career in journalism. He won a Pulitzer Prize for his "Observer" column in *The New York Times* and another for his autobiography *Growing Up,* from which this essay comes.

from An American Childhood

Annie Dillard

Some boys taught me to play football. This was fine sport. You thought up a new strategy for every play and whispered it to the others. You went out for a pass, fooling everyone. Best, you got to throw yourself mightily at someone's running legs. Either you brought him down or you hit the ground flat out on your chin, with your arms empty before you. It was all or nothing. If you hesitated in fear, you would miss and get hurt: you would take a hard fall while the kid got away, or you would get kicked in the face while the kid got away. But if you flung yourself wholeheartedly at the back of his knees—if you gathered and joined body and soul and pointed them diving fearlessly—then you likely wouldn't get hurt, and you'd stop the ball. Your fate, and your team's score, depended on your concentration and courage. Nothing girls did could compare with it.

Boys welcomed me at baseball, too, for I had, through enthusiastic practice, what was weirdly known as a boy's arm. In winter, in the snow, there was neither baseball nor football, so the boys and I threw snowballs at passing cars. I got in trouble throwing snowballs, and have seldom been happier since.

On one weekday morning after Christmas, six inches of new snow had just fallen. We were standing up to our boot tops in snow on a front yard on trafficked Reynolds Street, waiting for cars. The cars traveled Reynolds Street slowly and evenly; they were targets all but wrapped in red ribbons, cream puffs. We couldn't miss.

I was seven; the boys were eight, nine, and ten. The oldest two Fahey boys were there—Mikey and Peter—polite blond boys who lived near me on Lloyd Street, and who already had four brothers and sisters. My parents approved Mikey and Peter Fahey. Chickie McBride was there, a tough kid, and Billy Paul and Mackie Kean too, from across Reynolds, where the boys grew up dark and furious, grew up skinny, knowing, and skilled. We had all drifted from our houses that morning looking for action, and had found it here on Reynolds Street.

It was cloudy but cold. The cars' tires laid behind them on the snowy street a complex trail of beige chunks like crenellated castle walls.[1] I had stepped on some earlier; they squeaked. We could have wished for more traffic. When a car came, we all popped it one. In the intervals between cars we reverted to the natural solitude of children.

I started making an iceball—a perfect iceball, from perfectly white snow, perfectly spherical, and squeezed perfectly <u>translucent</u> so no snow remained all the way through. (The Fahey boys and I considered it unfair actually to throw an iceball at somebody, but it had been known to happen.)

I had just embarked on the iceball project when we heard tire chains come clanking from afar. A black Buick was moving toward us down the street. We all spread out, banged together some regular snowballs, took aim, and, when the Buick drew nigh, fired.

---

1. **chunks like crenellated** (kren´ əl āt´ əd) **castle walls** The snow was in rows of square clumps like the notches along the top of castle walls.

Reading Strategy
Understanding Author's Purpose How do these details suggest that Dillard's purpose might be to share an observation or insight?

translucent (trans loo´ sənt) *adj.* able to transmit light but no detail of things on the other side

Reading Check

What are Annie and her friends doing?

A soft snowball hit the driver's windshield right before the driver's face. It made a smashed star with a hump in the middle.

Often, of course, we hit our target, but this time, the only time in all of life, the car pulled over and stopped. Its wide black door opened; a man got out of it, running. He didn't even close the car door.

He ran after us, and we ran away from him, up the snowy Reynolds sidewalk. At the corner, I looked back; incredibly, he was still after us. He was in city clothes: a suit and tie, street shoes. Any normal adult would have quit, having sprung us into flight and made his point. This man was gaining on us. He was a thin man, all action. All of a sudden, we were running for our lives.

Wordless, we split up. We were on our turf; we could lose ourselves in the neighborhood backyards, everyone for himself. I paused and considered. Everyone had vanished except Mikey Fahey, who was just rounding the corner of a yellow brick house. Poor Mikey, I trailed him. The driver of the Buick sensibly picked the two of us to follow. The man apparently had all day.

He chased Mikey and me around the yellow house and up a back-yard path we knew by heart: under a low tree, up a bank, through a hedge, down some snowy steps, and across the grocery store's delivery driveway. We smashed through a gap in another hedge, entered a scruffy backyard and ran around its back porch and tight between houses to Edgerton Avenue; we ran across Edgerton to an alley and up our own sliding woodpile to the Halls' front yard; he kept coming. We ran up Lloyd Street and wound through mazy back-yards toward the steep hilltop at Willard and Lang.

He chased us silently, block after block. He chased us silently over picket fences, through thorny hedges, between houses, around garbage cans, and across streets. Every time I glanced back, choking for breath, I expected he would have quit. He must have been as breathless as we were. His jacket strained over his body. It was an immense discovery, pounding into my hot head with every sliding, joyous step, that this ordinary adult evidently knew what I thought only children who trained at football knew: that you have to fling yourself at what you're doing, you have to point yourself, forget yourself, aim, dive.

Mikey and I had nowhere to go, in our own neighborhood or out of it, but away from this man who was chasing us. He impelled us for-ward; we <u>compelled</u> him to follow our route. The air was cold; every breath tore my throat. We kept running, block after block; we kept improvising, backyard after backyard, running a frantic course and choosing it simultaneously, failing always to find small places or hard places to slow him down, and discovering always, exhilarated, dismayed, that only bare speed could save us—for he would never give up, this man—and we were losing speed.

He chased us through the backyard labyrinths of ten blocks before he caught us by our jackets. He caught us and we all stopped.

compelled
(kəm peld') v. forced

Critical Viewing ▶
In what two ways is this photograph of a snow-covered bicycle a good choice for this selection?
[Support]

We three stood staggering, half blinded, coughing, in an obscure hilltop backyard: a man in his twenties, a boy, a girl. He had released our jackets, our pursuer, our captor, our hero: he knew we weren't going anywhere. We all played by the rules. Mikey and I unzipped our jackets. I pulled off my sopping mittens. Our tracks multiplied in the backyard's new snow. We had been breaking new snow all morning. We didn't look at each other. I was cherishing my excitement. The man's lower pants legs were wet; his cuffs were full of snow, and there was a prow of snow beneath them on his shoes and socks. Some trees bordered the little flat backyard, some messy winter trees. There was no one around: a clearing in a grove, and we the only players.

It was a long time before he could speak. I had some difficulty at first recalling why we were there. My lips felt swollen; I couldn't see out of the sides of my eyes; I kept coughing.

"You stupid kids," he began <u>perfunctorily</u>.

We listened perfunctorily indeed, if we listened at all, for the chewing out was redundant, a mere formality, and beside the

perfunctorily
(per fuŋk´ tə rə lē) *adv.*
without enthusiasm;
routinely

✓**Reading Check**

Why are Annie and her
friend chased?

point. The point was that he had chased us passionately without giving up, and so he had caught us. Now he came down to earth. I wanted the glory to last forever.

But how could the glory have lasted forever? We could have run through every backyard in North America until we got to Panama. But when he trapped us at the lip of the Panama Canal, what precisely could he have done to prolong the drama of the chase and cap its glory? I brooded about this for the next few years. He could only have fried Mikey Fahey and me in boiling oil, say, or dismembered us piecemeal, or staked us to anthills. None of which I really wanted, and none of which any adult was likely to do, even in the spirit of fun. He could only chew us out there in the Panamanian jungle, after months or years of exalting pursuit. He could only begin, "You stupid kids," and continue in his ordinary Pittsburgh accent with his normal righteous anger and the usual common sense.

If in that snowy backyard the driver of the black Buick had cut off our heads, Mikey's and mine, I would have died happy, for nothing has required so much of me since as being chased all over Pittsburgh in the middle of winter—running terrified, exhausted—by this sainted, skinny, furious red-headed man who wished to have a word with us. I don't know how he found his way back to his car.

Review and Assess

Thinking About the Selection

1. **Respond:** Would you want the young Annie Dillard as a friend? Why or why not?

2. **(a) Recall:** How does Dillard describe playing football with the boys? **(b) Interpret:** What connection does Dillard make between playing football and being chased for throwing a snowball? **(c) Analyze:** What qualities does Dillard enjoy and value in everyday activities?

3. **(a) Recall:** What are Dillard and her friends doing "On one weekday morning after Christmas"? **(b) Describe:** Describe the way the man chases Dillard and her friend. **(c) Interpret:** Why does Dillard call the man who chased her "our hero"?

4. **(a) Recall:** What does the man do when he catches Dillard and her friend? **(b) Infer:** How do his actions cause this "hero" to come "down to earth"? **(c) Analyze:** In general, what does the young Dillard value and not value in adults?

5. **(a) Analyze:** Which of Dillard's values or beliefs does this event in her life reveal? **(b) Evaluate:** Does this episode from Dillard's early life have a larger meaning, or is it just an entertaining story? Explain.

Annie Dillard

(b. 1945)
As a child, Annie Dillard loved reading, drawing, and observing the natural world. While attending college in Virginia, she lived near a creek in a valley of the Blue Ridge Mountains. In 1974, she published *Pilgrim at Tinker Creek*, which describes her explorations of that environment. The book won the Pulitzer Prize for Nonfiction.

This essay comes from *An American Childhood*, Dillard's autobiographical account of growing up in Pittsburgh, Pennsylvania.

Review and Assess

Literary Analysis

Autobiography

1. Explain how Baker's humorous confession of his faults makes him more appealing to his readers.
2. Explain how the chase scene from Dillard's **autobiography** reveals her passionate approach to life.
3. What do the two selections show about the values of their authors? Record your answers in a chart like the one below.

Comparing Literary Works

4. What kind of experience does each writer relate?
5. Which writer's account of a childhood memory seems more connected to his or her life as an adult?
6. In what ways are the key events in "No Gumption" and the excerpt from *An American Childhood* similar? In what ways are they different? Write your answers in a Venn diagram like this one.

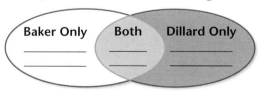

Reading Strategy

Understanding the Author's Purpose

7. What might Baker be trying to teach by showing his failures as well as his successes?
8. What does Dillard herself seem to learn about "concentration and courage" from the chase?
9. Why do you think Dillard wants to share this lesson?

Extend Understanding

10. **Career Connection:** Russell Baker's interest in writing eventually led to his career as a writer. What interest of yours could lead to a career? Explain.

Quick Review

An **autobiography** is a form of nonfiction in which a person tells his or her own life story, or part of it. To review autobiography, see page 553.

The **author's purpose** is his or her reason for writing. To review author's purpose, see page 553.

 Take It to the Net
www.phschool.com
Take the interactive self-test online to check your understanding of these selections.

Integrate Language Skills

Vocabulary Development Lesson

Word Analysis: Latin Root -pel-

The word *compelled* contains the Latin root *-pel-*. This root means "to push" or "to drive." Explain the meaning of each of the following words. Use a dictionary to check your definitions.

1. repel   2. propel   3. expel

Spelling Strategy

When studying or spelling multisyllable words, pronounce each syllable to avoid skipping letters. Practice pronouncing and spelling these words from the selections:

ap•ti•tude   trans•lu•cent   per•func•to•ri•ly

Unscramble the letters of the mixed-up syllables of each word. Circle the syllable that is missing a letter. Then, write the whole word correctly.

1. deut•pa•t   2. rep•ot•nuf•yl•ir

Concept Development: Antonyms

Choose the word or phrase that is an **antonym,** or opposite, of each numbered word:

1. gumption: **(a)** spunk **(b)** laziness **(c)** loveliness
2. paupers: **(a)** clerks **(b)** puppets **(c)** billionaires
3. crucial: **(a)** unimportant **(b)** essential **(c)** facial
4. aptitude: **(a)** test **(b)** inability **(c)** capacity
5. translucent: **(a)** admitting light **(b)** filled with light **(c)** not admitting light
6. compelled: **(a)** jailed **(b)** left alone **(c)** dreamed
7. perfunctorily: **(a)** excitedly **(b)** deliberately **(c)** jokingly

Grammar Lesson

Participles and Participial Phrases

A **participle** is a verb form that acts as an adjective, modifying a noun or a pronoun. Present participles end in *-ing*. Past participles usually end in *-ed* but may have an irregular ending, such as *-en* in *spoken*. Notice how the present participle modifies the noun in the following example.

Present participle

I could not deliver an *engaging* sales pitch.

A **participial phrase** consists of a participle and its modifiers. The entire phrase acts as an adjective. Notice how the participial phrase modifies the pronoun in the following example.

Participial phrase

Brimming with zest, she returned with me.

▶ *For more practice, see page R30, Exercise C.*
Practice Identify the participles and participial phrases. Then, indicate the words they modify.

1. Doris banged her fist against the closed window.
2. She threw herself at his running legs.
3. Dazed by exhaustion, we froze in our tracks.
4. They ran up the sliding woodpile.

Writing Application Combine each pair of sentences by using a participle or participial phrase.

1. He dreaded the magazines. They were wrapped.
2. She escaped. She was running fast.

W̶G̶ Prentice Hall Writing and Grammar Connection: Chapter 20, Section 1

Writing Lesson

Comparison-and-Contrast Essay

Write a comparison-and-contrast essay about the young Russell Baker and the young Annie Dillard. Choose three or four points that show how Baker and Dillard are similar or different.

Prewriting Jot down examples to support each of your three or four points. Points of comparison or contrast might include gumption, favorite activities, and interaction with adults.

Drafting Begin by introducing the two writers you are comparing. Referring to your notes, write a paragraph for each point of comparison or contrast.

Model: Paragraph Outline

Paragraph Comparing Characters' "Gumption"

- Baker lacks it—give examples
- Dillard has it—give examples

Paragraph Comparing Interaction

- Baker in awe of adults—give examples
- Dillard not as concerned with adults—give examples

Revising Be sure that your essay has an introduction that explains your purpose and a conclusion that summarizes your findings. Use transitions between paragraphs.

*W*G *Prentice Hall Writing and Grammar Connection: Chapter 8, Sections 1–7*

Extension Activities

Research and Technology With classmates, give a **presentation** on the Depression, the time in which Baker spent his childhood. Use some or all of the following resources:

- film clips
- photographs
- speeches
- recordings
- news stories
- books

Before your presentation, rehearse with your team to be sure that your information paints a clear and accurate picture of the era. Write a summary of your presentation to hand out to classmates.

Listening and Speaking With a partner, act out a **scene** in which the young Russell Baker meets the young Annie Dillard. Review their autobiographical accounts for clues about how they would relate to each other. Then, reveal these attitudes in your dialogue.

 **Take It to the Net**   www.phschool.com

Go online for an additional research activity using the Internet.

Prepare to Read

Nolan Ryan

Take It to the Net

Visit www.phschool.com
for interactive activities
and instruction related to
"Nolan Ryan," including

- background
- graphic organizers
- literary elements
- reading strategies

Preview

Connecting to the Literature

The media provide so much information about athletes that their private lives are often public knowledge—often revealing less-than-inspiring details. In "Nolan Ryan," author William W. Lace focuses on the strengths and achievements of his celebrity athlete subject—one of the greatest pitchers in the history of major league baseball.

Background

Numbers do not tell the whole story of a life. However, you can suggest people's achievements with statistics, a numerical measure of what they have accomplished. Nolan Ryan's statistics include major league records for number of strikeouts (5,714) and total years of service (27).

Literary Analysis

Biography

A **biography** is the story of all or part of someone's life, told by someone else. Usually, authors write about a famous subject—someone known and interesting to many people. Biographies

- tell you facts about a person's life.
- give a picture of the significance of these facts in the person's life.

Connecting Literary Elements

When personal opinions come through in a piece of nonfiction writing such as a biography, the **author's bias** is revealed. Recognizing bias while you read will help you sort out fact from opinion. These elements are signs of author's bias:

- **Loaded words**, such as "*sloppy* losing pitcher"
- **Stereotypes**, such as "*absent-minded professor*"
- **One-sided arguments**, those that present only one point of view on the subject
- **Generalizations**, such as "All sports are violent," or other broad statements based on only a few instances or examples.

Use these focus questions to guide you as you read:

1. What elements of the author's bias are found in the biography?
2. Overall, is the author biased for or against Ryan? Explain.

Reading Strategy

Distinguishing Fact and Opinion

- A **fact** is something that has actually happened and can be proved true.
- An **opinion** is a person's belief or judgment. It may be supported by factual evidence, but it cannot be proven.

As you read the selection, use the questions on the chart to distinguish between facts and opinions.

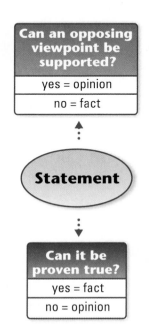

Vocabulary Development

wholesome (hōl′ səm) *adj*. promoting health; healthful (p. 574)

hostility (häs til′ ə tē) *n*. anger; unfriendliness (p. 575)

endorsements (en dôrs′ mənts) *n*. statements supporting a particular product, as in an advertisement (p. 576)

obscure (əb skyoor′) *adj*. not well known (p. 576)

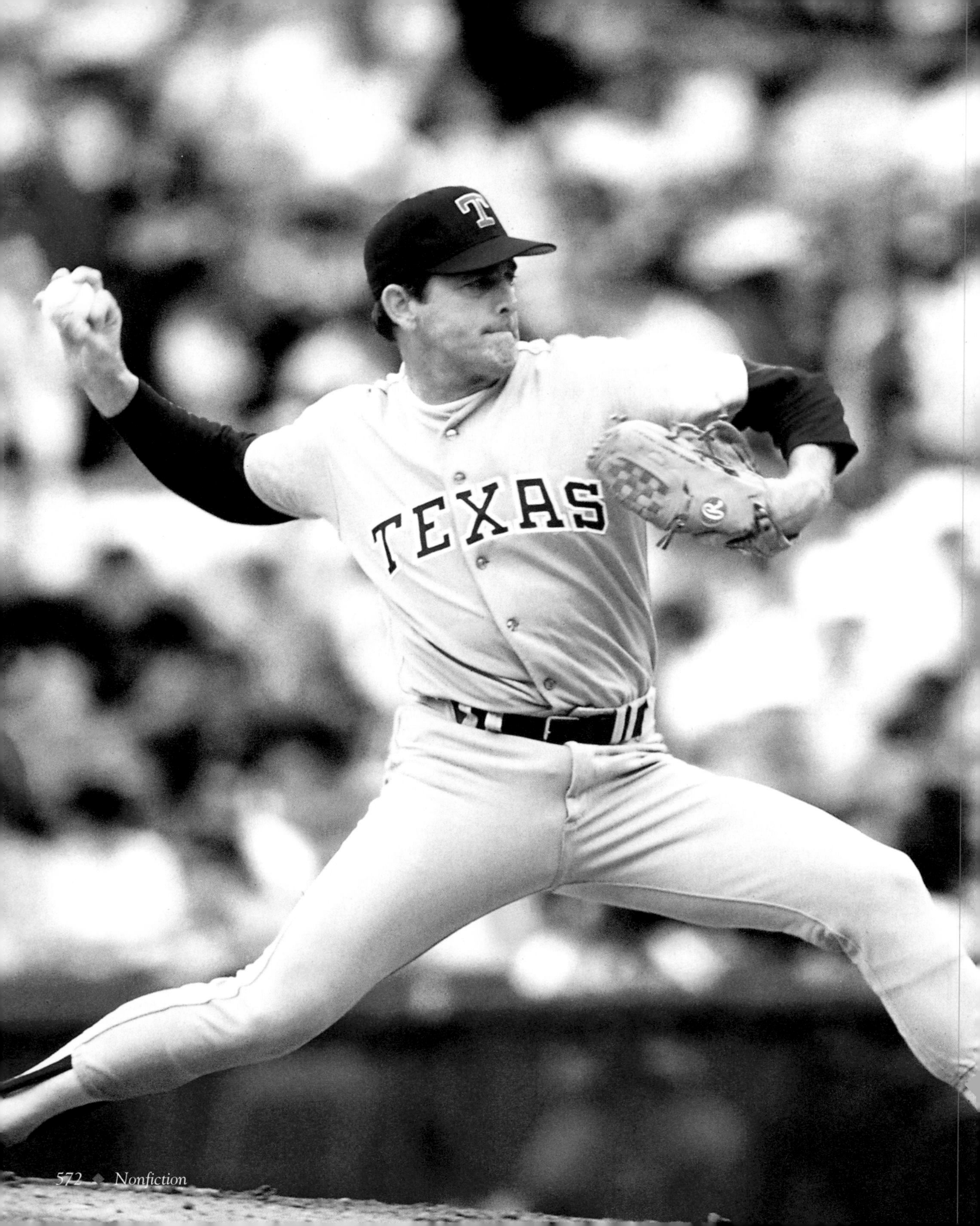
TEXAS

NOLAN RYAN

William W. Lace

A generation has passed since Nolan Ryan threw his first major league pitch. His fellow players are sometimes just as eager as fans to get his autograph. Texas third baseman Steve Buchele, a southern California native, said, "There wasn't anything more exciting than coming to the games and watching Nolan pitch."

How has Ryan lasted so long? He claims that it's a combination of physical condition and mental attitude.

Ryan has always taken good care of his body. Even after the biggest of games, like his seventh no-hitter, he was up early, working out. "We're working against the clock," he told a reporter. "I can't do this forever. I haven't got much time."

Reading Strategy
Distinguishing Fact and Opinion How do you know the first sentence of this paragraph is a fact?

✔**Reading Check**

How do other ballplayers feel about Ryan?

◀ **Critical Viewing** What does Ryan's facial expression tell you about the act of pitching? **[Draw Conclusions]**

He learned a balanced, healthy diet from his mother, who took pride in putting <u>wholesome</u> meals on the Ryan family table. Even as a young player he was careful about what he ate. He's even more careful now, avoiding meats like bacon or sausage, cream soups, and any other food high in fat. He doesn't eat fried foods and doesn't often eat large meals. When he snacks, he usually chooses fruit.

Ryan's physical conditioning has kept him going long after most players his age have retired. He stays fit during the winter, and

wholesome (hōl′ səm) *adj.* promoting health; healthful

▼ **Critical Viewing** Ryan is carried off the field after throwing his record-breaking seventh no-hitter. What details in this photograph tell you this is a historic moment? **[Analyze]**

during the season, maintains a workout schedule of weightlifting, throwing, and running that almost never changes. The times are very different from his early days in baseball, when all a pitcher did between starts was throw enough each day to stay loose.

Mental fitness probably has been just as important. Even after 26 major-league seasons, baseball is still fun and challenging to Ryan. Yet, even though it's his living, baseball isn't his whole life. He spends as much time at home with his family as he can. He is keenly interested in cattle raising and operates three ranches in addition to his property near Alvin. He has many other business interests and spends much time on charity work.

The talented pitcher has not allowed fame and fortune to change his personality, as many star athletes have. Ryan remains what he always was—a modest, uncomplicated, man from a middle-class, family-centered background.

"I still represent small-town Texas, and that's fine with me," he once said. "I'm still like the people who lived where I grew up. I've kept my roots. I'm proud of that."

If you didn't know differently, you'd think Ryan was the man next door, working hard to put food on the table and tires on the car. "If you saw him in a shopping mall or talked to him in the grocery store, you'd think he was just another middle-aged guy," said a member of the Rangers' organization.

He's a nice guy off the field, but not necessarily on it. Baseball is still much more than just a game to Ryan. His drive to excel, to win, to help his team is still strong. But Nolan is able to confine this drive to the playing field.

"When I'm out on the mound I don't consider myself a very nice person," he wrote. "I almost hate the players I'm pitching against. I get to feeling a lot of <u>hostility</u>. Normally, I'm a very quiet and reserved person with a peaceful outlook on things. But when I'm pitching I'm anything but that."

Ryan wants to be known and remembered as a "gamer," a player who goes all out in every game. He's not afraid to pitch inside to a batter who tries to gain an advantage by standing closer to home plate. He'll make a batter have to duck or leap backward to teach him not to "crowd" the plate.

With so many accomplishments so late in his career, Ryan is more famous as a Texas Ranger than he ever was as a Met, Angel, or Astro. There are crowds of fans and autograph seekers wherever the Rangers go. And Ryan's importance to the Rangers goes far beyond his pitching record. He's the player people come to see.

In its first 17 seasons, the Texas franchise[1] had 17 sellout crowds. In three seasons with Nolan Ryan, the team had 15, mostly on nights

---

1. **franchise** (fran´ chīz´) *n.* team.

Literary Analysis
Biography and Bias What details or words reveal the author's bias?

hostility (häs til´ ə tē) *n.* anger; unfriendliness

**Reading Check**

Describe Ryan's personality.

Ryan pitched. Souvenir program sellers know they can make three times their usual amount when he's on the mound. People hope the programs will turn out to be mementos from another no-hitter.

Ryan is possibly the best-known person in the state of Texas. Watch television, listen to radio, read a newspaper, drive down a freeway, and you'll see or hear Ryan in ads for everything from air-lines to blue jeans. He earns an estimated $1 million to $2 million a year from such <u>endorsements</u>.

Ryan holds almost 50 major league records from the important (strikeouts, no-hitters) to the <u>obscure</u> (most assists by a pitcher in a five-game National League Championship Series). Some, like the ones for most walks and wild pitches in a career, he'd rather not have.

Numbers, however, can't begin to explain the excitement Ryan brings to every game. You know you'll see history made with every strikeout. You may be in on something truly spectacular, like a no-hitter. And Ryan's accomplishments are even more enjoyable because of the kind of person he is as well as the kind of pitcher.

In a country full of sports stars, he somehow stands out. Jim Murray of the *Los Angeles Times* wrote that even though we may have seen Mantle, Mays, Aaron, Rose, and all the rest, "I have a feel-ing when they talk of the second half of the 20th century in baseball, the most frequently heard question by our generation will be, 'Did you ever see Nolan Ryan pitch?'"

endorsements (en dôrs′ mənts) *n.* statements sup-porting a particular prod-uct, as in an advertisement

obscure (əb skyo͝or′) *adj.* not well known

Review and Assess

Thinking About the Selection

1. **Respond:** Do you admire Nolan Ryan? Why or why not?

2. **(a) Recall:** What activities does Ryan do off the ball field? **(b) Connect:** Why are these activities just as important to his career as what he does on the field?

3. **(a) Recall:** What is Ryan's state of mind when on the ball field? **(b) Infer:** What do you think enables Ryan to let go of this feeling when he steps off the field?

4. **(a) Recall:** What is the meaning of "gamer"? **(b) Speculate:** Do you think all players in professional sports should be "gamers"? Explain.

5. **(a) Recall:** What changed for the Rangers after Ryan came to the team? **(b) Infer:** What does this indicate about Ryan's importance to the team? **(c) Draw Conclusions:** What are the special qualities that make Ryan different from other sports stars?

6. **Take a Stand:** **(a)** Do you think athletes have a responsibility to act as role models? Why or why not? **(b)** Do other celebrities have this responsibility? Why or why not?

William W. Lace

(b. 1942)

A native of Fort Worth, Texas, William W. Lace worked for newspapers before joining the University of Texas at Arlington as sports informa-tion director. Later, he became the director of col-lege relations for a junior college in Fort Worth.

Lace and his wife, Laura, a public school librarian, live in Arlington, Texas, with their two children. His wife and her book-hungry students inspired Lace to write about Nolan Ryan for young people.

Review and Assess

Literary Analysis

Biography

1. Make a chart like the one shown to take notes on what you have learned about Nolan Ryan's life.

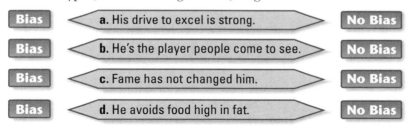

Statement	Source
Ryan holds almost 50 major league records.	Author

2. What have you learned about Nolan Ryan, the baseball player?
3. What have you learned about Nolan Ryan, the person?

Connecting Literary Elements

4. What elements of the author's bias are found in the biography?
5. Evaluate each of the statements below as biased or unbiased. If biased, tell whether the bias is shown through loaded words, stereotypes, one-sided arguments, or generalizations.

Bias		No Bias
Bias	**a.** His drive to excel is strong.	**No Bias**
Bias	**b.** He's the player people come to see.	**No Bias**
Bias	**c.** Fame has not changed him.	**No Bias**
Bias	**d.** He avoids food high in fat.	**No Bias**

6. Overall, is the author biased for or against Ryan's qualities? Explain.

Reading Strategy

Distinguishing Fact and Opinion

7. Identify three facts about Ryan's career from the selection.
8. Identify two opinions about Ryan's personality from the selection.
9. Would you say the selection relies more on facts or on opinions? Explain.

Extend Understanding

10. **Physical Education Connection:** What activities could you do that might help you train to become a good baseball player?

Quick Review

A **biography** is the story of all or part of someone's life told by someone else. To review biography, see page 571.

The **author's bias** is the author's personal opinion about the subject. To review author's bias, see page 571.

A **fact** is something that can be proved.

An **opinion** is a person's judgment or belief. To review fact and opinion, see page 571.

 Take It to the Net
www.phschool.com
Take the interactive self-test online to check your understanding of the selection.

Integrate Language Skills

Vocabulary Development Lesson

Word Analysis: Latin Prefix *ob-*

Lace writes that some of Ryan's major league records are "obscure." *Obscure* combines the Latin prefix *ob-*, meaning "against," "over," or "completely," with a word part meaning "to cover or conceal." An obscure record is one that is completely concealed or not well known.

Use the meaning of *ob* to define the italicized words:

1. The stadium was *oblong* rather than rectangular.
2. She *observed* that she should find a seat close to the field.
3. Nothing *obstructed* her view.
4. It was *obvious* that the game would be sold out.

Grammar Lesson

Appositives and Appositive Phrases

An **appositive** is a noun or pronoun placed after another noun or pronoun to identify, rename, or explain it.

An **appositive phrase** is an appositive and the words that modify it. Appositives and appositive phrases are set off by commas or dashes, as in these examples:

Appositive: Ryan, *the pitcher,* reached the mound.

Appositive Phrase: Ryan watched what he ate even in his youth, *the most carefree time of life*.

Appositive Phrase: Ryan—*a modest man*—is respected by his teammates.

Fluency: Definitions

On your paper, match each word in the first column with its definition in the second column.

1. endorsements
2. hostility
3. obscure
4. wholesome

a. feeling of unfriendliness
b. healthful
c. not famous
d. grants of approval

Spelling Strategy

Some words have unexpected silent letters. For example, *wholesome* gives no sound clue that it begins with *w*. Practice spelling these words from the selection that have silent letters.

1. weight   2. know   3. height   4. wrote

Match each numbered word above with the lettered word below that has the same silent letter. Write each pair.

a. wring   b. light   c. knelt   d. neighbor

▶ *For more practice, see page R30, Exercise C.*
Practice Identify the appositive or appositive phrase in each of these sentences.

1. Ryan's mother, a great influence in his life, taught him about eating well.
2. The Rangers, a Texas team, hired Ryan after he had played on several other teams.
3. Ryan's other interests—cattle raising and charity work—take up some of his spare time.
4. Ryan's seventh no-hitter—one for the records—brought the team a victory.
5. Steve Buchele, a southern California native, was Ryan's teammate.

Writing Application Write five sentences about someone you admire, using an appositive or appositive phrase in each sentence.

𝒲𝒢 *Prentice Hall Writing and Grammar Connection: Chapter 20, Section 1*

Writing Lesson

Biography

Write a short biography of a friend, family member, or neighbor. Because the person is someone you know well, you can provide both facts and insights about him or her.

Prewriting Prepare a list of people you know well. Choose your subject. Draw up a list of questions about the subject's life. Interview your subject and others who know the person well.

Drafting Review your interview notes and decide on your perspective—the point of view you will take regarding your subject. In your introduction, make a general statement that communicates your perspective. In the body of your biography, include examples and quotations to support your statements about the person.

Revising Highlight the sentences in your introduction that indicate your focused perspective throughout your essay, and delete details that do not contribute to this perspective.

Model: Focus Your Perspective

My great-aunt Estelle has always been a survivor. In her childhood, she and her family worked hard as sharecroppers. ~~She liked taking walks by the creek.~~ As a young mother, she kept a cheerful, loving attitude in spite of financial difficulties. Yet even as her energy level slows down in her older years, she still has a hearty laugh and a warm smile.

> The circled sentence is deleted because it does not help focus the writer's perspective on Estelle—that she is to be admired for keeping a positive attitude in the face of hardship.

WG *Prentice Hall Writing and Grammar Connection: Chapter 6, Section 4*

Extension Activities

Listening and Speaking As the emcee at a formal dinner, present Nolan Ryan with a lifetime achievement award.

1. In your **presentation,** state clearly why you think Ryan deserves the prize.
2. Describe his areas of achievement and back up your statements with facts.

Writing Write a **response** to Ryan's biography in which you explain whether you share the author's admiration for Ryan.

Research and Technology In a small group, research the game of baseball. Begin by making an **outline.** Divide research tasks based on the outline. After the research is completed, evaluate and revise the outline to incorporate new information or to reorder categories based on what you have discovered. **[Group Activity]**

 Take It to the Net www.phschool.com

Go online for an additional research activity using the Internet.

CONNECTIONS
Literature and Sports

Themes of Competition and Commitment

Nolan Ryan is known not only for his major league records and twenty-seven years of service to baseball, he's also known for being a modest and respectable person. In the 1998 baseball season, two other well-respected players, Sammy Sosa of the Chicago Cubs and Mark McGwire of the St. Louis Cardinals, made international headlines as they competed for the most major-league home runs in a season. As you read the following article by Sammy Sosa, look for similarities and differences in the way he and Nolan Ryan approach their game.

Mi Amigo, Mark

Sammy Sosa

In my home country, the Dominican Republic, we have always taken great pride in our ability to survive tough times while staying true to our core values of family, faith and hard work. Sometimes it is an outside event, such as the devastation[1] caused by Hurricane Georges last September, that inspires us to reach further inside ourselves and do our best. In the process, I think we learn something about ourselves that prepares us to be even stronger for our next challenge.

Early in this year's baseball season, I would hardly have imagined that it would be a historic home-run race with Mark McGwire that would show me the example you can be to others when you push your individual limits.

Before the season started, I made a commitment to take my game to a higher level. I have always been a power hitter, but I felt I could become a more selective batter. Sometimes I tried too hard to do too much. I would go to home plate and swing hard at almost everything instead of having the

---

1. **devastation** (dev´ əs tā´ shən) *n.* destruction.

calm to wait for the right pitch. My new goal was to be a greater offensive threat. With patience, an improved swing and a sharper eye, I felt I could bring more to the batter's box and be an even steadier performer for my team, the Chicago Cubs.

Early in the season, people were looking at McGwire and Ken Griffey, Jr., to hit a lot of homers, but after I slugged 20 in June, I found myself not far behind. While I was happy to be on a roll, I was more pleased that my team was winning. By late July, as I passed Ken, the media started to hype a rivalry between Mark and me. If there was one, it was the best kind—friendly and professional. I motivated Mark and he motivated me. That's what good competition is all about—two people trying to go out there and be their best. I think Mark is a great human being, and I think people could see the respect and admiration that developed between us and that while we were rivals, we were having fun.

Some tried to suggest that our popularity was divided along racial lines. I never felt that at all. I was treated well by everyone from the commissioner of baseball and the people in his office, to the Cubs organization and especially the fans. Everywhere I played, people of all races greeted me warmly and cheered me on, just as people of all races cheered for Mark.

What I hope people will remember most about 1998 is that it was a great season for baseball and for home runs. The fans supported Mark and me all year long and we gave them an exciting and memorable season.

It's unlikely that next year will be so extraordinary—but who knows? I'm not thinking about it. There are a lot of people in my homeland who are now suffering in the wake of the hurricane, and I am trying to help in ways that I can. I'm just glad that 1998 was so terrific and that Mark and I were able to bring so much joy to a sport that we love. The two of us were in Los Angeles recently to have our picture taken, and we got to spend some time together. And that's another thing I'm happy about this year. I've made a real friend in Mark.

Thematic Connection
How did Sosa think he could become a better player?

Sammy Sosa

(b. 1968)
Sammy Sosa, the fifth of seven children, grew up in a poor family in the Dominican Republic. As a kid, he sold oranges and shined shoes to help earn income for his family. In his spare time, he and his friends played baseball using milk cartons as gloves, tree branches as bats, and rolled-up socks as balls. When Sosa was sixteen, his talent was noticed at a baseball camp, and he joined the major leagues. Sosa played for the Texas Rangers and the Chicago White Sox before joining the Chicago Cubs in 1992. He wears the number 21 in honor of Roberto Clemente, the first Latino baseball player to enter the Hall of Fame.

Connecting Literature and Sports

1. How does Sosa feel about McGwire?
2. What is Sosa's attitude toward the home-run record?
3. What attitude would you expect Nolan Ryan to have about a home-run record?
4. Are Sosa's and Ryan's views of competition and commitment similar or different? Explain.

Research Reports

About Research Reports

A research report presents information that is gathered from reference books, observations, interviews, or other sources. A good research report does not simply repeat information. It guides readers through the topic, showing them why each fact matters and creating an overall picture of the subject. When reading research reports critically, it is necessary to pay close attention to the following:

- An overall focus or main idea
- Information gathered from a variety of sources
- Clear organization and smooth transitions
- Facts and details to support each main point
- Accurate, complete citations identifying sources

Reading Strategy

Asking Questions

As you read a research report, you will probably understand it better if you ask yourself questions about the people, events, and other details. Then, keep reading to see if you can figure out the answers.

Look at the following chart that contains details from the selection "Pandas." Read the information that is given. Then, think of a question that you might ask yourself in response. Copy this chart into your notebook. While you are reading "Pandas," write down any questions you have regarding the text. As you read, look for answers to your questions.

Detail	Question	Answer
"[The giant panda] is also one of the rarest [animals]."	Why have pandas become so rare?	Pandas have become rare because hunters kill them.
"There are few people living in this part of China." "This leaves no food for the pandas until new plants grow from the seeds." "However, the hunters still manage to smuggle a few panda skins out of China."	Why don't people live in this part of China?	

Pandas

Gillian Standring

Introducing Pandas The giant panda is one of the best-known animals in the world. It is also one of the rarest. In 1990 there were only about one thousand giant pandas living wild in China, and only fifteen in zoos outside China. So if you have seen pandas in a zoo, you are very lucky.

. . . The first living pandas outside China were brought to the United States in 1936 and to Britain in 1938 (Angel 16–24). Ever since, the giant panda has been of great interest to scientists, zookeepers, and all animal lovers. Because it is so popular and so unusual, it was chosen as the symbol of the World Wildlife Fund (WWF), the world's best-known conservation organization.

Life in the Wild Pandas, unlike people, prefer to be cool and damp. Hot, dry weather is bad for them (Dudley 29). High up in the mountains of Sichuan in southwest China, there are thick, misty forests where it is always cool and damp. Pandas spend most of the year in these forests. In winter they come down to the lower slopes to get away from the deep snow and freezing cold. There are few people living in this part of China.

Pandas are famous for eating bamboo. Their food grows all around them in the bamboo forests, so they never have to hunt for it. However, they like to eat only a few kinds of bamboo, and their digestion is not very good, so they spend almost all the day just eating (Angel 37–39). Pandas also eat grasses, roots, bulbs, and tree bark. Sometimes they catch little cane rats and fish. They often take long drinks from mountain streams and rivers.

Why Are Pandas So Rare? Giant pandas have probably never been common anywhere. There are several reasons for this. They do not produce many babies. As we have seen, they can live only in cool bamboo forests. Each panda needs a big area of forest to itself, and even large areas of suitable mountain forest have room for only a few pandas (Laidler 109–113).

Pandas also need plenty of their favorite bamboo. This plant has a very unusual way of growing. For perhaps a hundred years, bamboo plants spread by underground branches. Then suddenly, all the bamboo plants over a wide area flower, make seeds, and die. This leaves no food for the pandas until new plants grow from the seeds. Many pandas die of starvation when this happens, as it did in 1975–6 (Schaller 137).

For thousands of years, the giant panda's homeland in southwest China was very hard for people to reach, so it was left undisturbed for pandas and other wildlife. Now the millions of Chinese people need more land for their farms and villages. Modern roads help them to reach even the farthest mountains of Sichuan. As the people cut down the mountain forest, the pandas have fewer unspoiled bamboo groves to live in.

> The first paragraph establishes the main idea—that the giant panda is a rare and special animal.

> Standring sets up a clear organization by presenting information on the life of the panda and then moving to the reasons they are rare and endangered.

Another reason why pandas are rare is that people have captured them from the wild. . . . The People's Republic of China banned the hunting of pandas in 1962. Now zoos can obtain pandas only as a gift from the Chinese people or from other zoos (Catton 110–111).

However, panda-hunting still goes on in spite of the ban. The pandas are not captured to be taken to zoos but are killed for their skins. Panda fur is too coarse to use for fur coats, but some people like to have a panda skin to decorate their home. In Japan people will pay a great deal (over $200,000) to have a black-and-white panda skin rug on the floor (Catton 110–115).

Of course, this hunting is against the law, and if the hunters are caught they are imprisoned for life or even sentenced to death. However, the hunters still manage to smuggle a few panda skins out of China. They take the risk because they are well paid by the people who want the panda skins.

Saving the Panda Although pandas are in danger from hunting, the main threat to them is the loss of their bamboo forests (Dudley 31–33). There is some good news for pandas, however. The Chinese people and international conservation organizations are working hard to protect them. Now there are thirteen special panda reserves in China, where some 800 pandas are living in safety. The reserves were created to protect the pandas and the bamboo forests they need. The cutting down of bamboo and felling of trees by people is strictly controlled. Armed guards patrol the reserves to protect the pandas from hunters and to ensure that local people do not destroy the trees (Schaller 231–233).

> Facts and details support the point that organizations are working to protect pandas.

> Standring uses the standard format for internal citations for all facts that are not common knowledge.

Besides protecting the pandas, it is important to tell the local people why these animals are so special. So the people from 5,000 villages in Sichuan are taught about the need to protect pandas and how to care for starving pandas. They are told why they should not cut down trees and bamboo. If a panda causes damage to the local people's farm crops, the people are paid to cover the damage (Laidler 188–189).

The largest reserve, at Wolong, was created in 1975. In 1980, the Chinese government and WWF built a special panda-breeding and research center there (Laidler 177).

The Future for Pandas . . . [T]he giant panda's urgent need for help has brought together conservation workers, vets, scientists, zookeepers, and animal lovers from all over the world. The Chinese people and conservation organizations have managed to protect large areas of bamboo forest and guard the pandas that live in them. We have already found some ways of helping pandas to survive by studying them in the wild and in captivity.

If we can give enough support to the efforts to save pandas, perhaps in the next century there will be more pandas in the world than now. Then the panda on the WWF badge will be the symbol of a success story in wildlife conservation.

Works Cited
Angel, Heather. *Pandas.* Stillwater, MN: Voyageur Press, 1998.
Catton, Chris. *Pandas.* New York: Facts on File, 1990.
Dudley, Karen. *Giant Pandas.* Austin, TX: Raintree Steck-Vaughn, 1997.
Laidler, Keith and Liz. *Pandas: Giants of the Bamboo Forest.* London: BBC Books, 1992.
Schaller, George B. *The Last Panda.* Chicago: University of Chicago Press, 1993.

Check Your Comprehension

1. What conservation organization chose the giant panda as its symbol?
2. What kind of place do pandas need to live in?
3. What kinds of food do pandas eat?
4. What are three reasons why pandas have become so rare?
5. How are the Chinese people protecting the giant pandas?

Applying the Reading Strategy

Asking Questions

6. What question would you ask yourself after reading the first paragraph? Why?
7. What questions might you ask about the panda reserves in China? Why?

Activity

Develop Questions for Research

Reading a research report will give you information about a specific topic. The text will also give you the answers to some questions, but it may raise other questions in your mind.

Create a chart like the one shown here. Identify three details from "Pandas," record the questions you might ask based on those details, and make a note of possible sources to investigate. This information can be used for your own research report in the future.

Detail	Pandas are one of the rarest animals in the world.
Question	What other animals are extremely rare?
Where I can find out	Internet

Comparing Informational Material

Research Reports and News Articles

When writing a research report, it is necessary to look at a number of sources to find enough information to write a well-researched paper. Another type of informational material that requires some research is a news article. Although a news article's research may come from a variety of sources, it differs from a research report in a number of ways. The topics of news articles are almost always about current events; however, unlike a research report, a news article does not require citations of sources.

Find a recent news article about either pandas or another animal. Read the article and summarize it for the class. Explain the differences in format between the news article and the research report, "Pandas."

Writing WORKSHOP

Research: Research Report

A **research report** combines information gathered from a variety of reliable sources to present a clear and accurate picture of a topic or to answer a question. In this workshop, you will learn how to prepare and present research in a formal report.

Assignment Criteria Your research report should have the following characteristics:

- An overall topic or question to be investigated
- A thesis statement giving the writer's viewpoint or perspective
- Evidence gathered from a variety of reliable sources to support each point
- A logical organization
- Accurate citations and a bibliography

See the Rubric on page 591 for the criteria on which your Research Report may be assessed.

Prewriting

Choose and narrow a topic. List people, places, events, and current issues. Jot down historical events, inventions, technology, and discoveries that interest you. Review your list, and circle possible topics. Then, narrow your topic.

For example, "whales" is too broad a topic for a research paper. You can focus your topic by asking yourself questions such as "What problems do whales face?" or "What makes whales unique?" The answers to your questions should lead to a **thesis statement**—a statement in which you express the main point or focus of your research.

> **Education**
> Papp, p.5
>
> Only the upper classes could read.
>
> Most of the common people in Shakespeare's time could not read.

> Papp, Joseph and Kirkland, Elizabeth
>
> **Shakespeare Alive!**
>
> New York: Bantam Books, 1988.

Example
Thesis Statement: Whales are among the most intelligent mammals on Earth.

Gather evidence and take notes. Find information that supports your thesis statement by conducting research in a variety of print and electronic sources. Use note cards and source cards so that you can easily organize and reference information.

- Write only one note per card. Label the card with a category for organization. Note the source and page number for every note you take.

Use technology. In addition to using technology for finding information, you can use technology for taking notes. You can photocopy articles and copyright pages, you can print articles from the Internet, or you can enter notes and source information directly onto a "notes" disk.

Student Model

Before you begin drafting, read this portion of a student model and review the characteristics of a successful research report. To read a full report, see www.phschool.com.

Laura Agajanian
Santa Clarita, California

Hatching Chirpers

A hen's egg is an amazing thing. Sitting in the nest, it seems as if it is an inanimate, or lifeless, object, but it contains everything that is needed to make a chick. In order for the chick to grow inside the egg, however, the right external conditions are needed. Under normal circumstances, these conditions are provided by the hen. They can also be reproduced and regulated in an incubator. My investigation was to discover whether the hen or the incubator would more efficiently and effectively provide the right external conditions. My hypothesis is that an incubator can provide the right external conditions more effectively and efficiently. Let's find out.

A chicken egg should take about twenty-one days to incubate, or take form. During that time, the eggs must be kept warm. The ideal temperature is between 99 and 100 degrees Fahrenheit. In addition, the eggs must be rotated, or turned, every eight to twelve hours. If they remain in one position for longer than that, the chick can become stuck to one side of the egg and may not form properly (Johnson 14–16).

Usually, the temperature and the turning are handled by the hen that sits on the nest. She regulates the temperature of the eggs by getting off the nest or standing above the eggs if the eggs begin to get too warm. When they have had some time to cool, she gets back on the nest. The hen turns the eggs by poking at them with her beak until each egg rolls a little to one side, eventually turning from its original position (Scott).

An incubator performs these same functions. The temperature inside the incubator is measured and regulated by a thermostat that tells the heater when to turn on and when to turn off. In this way, the temperature of the eggs is kept at a constant 99 degrees. The eggs sit on a device that rolls them every eight hours. This device is controlled by an electronic timer. It is dependable because it is automatic and does not require a person to push a button for the eggs to turn. It is more efficient than a hen, because all the eggs get turned equally and consistently (*Little Giant* 2–6).

In the first paragraph, the writer identifies her main topic, the question she is investigating. In this science report, she gives a hypothesis—a proposition that the research will prove or disprove. This statement gives her perspective or viewpoint on the topic.

Accurate facts and details gathered through the formal research process are presented. Since these are specific statistics that a reader might want to check, the writer gives the source.

The report is organized to give balanced information about both methods being investigated.

Based on the fact that conditions in the incubator are more consistent and controlled, I concluded that an incubator sets the ideal conditions more efficiently, and I hypothesized that it would hatch eggs more effectively. To test my hypothesis, I observed four hens sitting on a total of twenty-four eggs and placed twenty-four eggs in an incubator. Each egg was marked with a small *x* so that I could observe how frequently and completely each egg was turned. Chart A shows specific observations over a twenty-five day period.

> Detailed information that would interrupt the flow of the report is presented in a separate chart for readers to reference as needed.

Chart A

Day	Incubator Observations	Nest Observations
Day 1	**6:45 AM:** After placing the turner in the incubator, I put the 24 eggs on the turner. The temperature leveled off at 100 degrees. The eggs have warmed up quickly. **5:33 PM:** The turner is working efficiently—eggs are tilted appropriately.	**7:10 AM:** After placing the 24 eggs on the nests in the cage, I put food and water in the cage. Then, I placed the hens in the cage. **6:01 PM:** All hens are on the eggs.
Day 5	X marks on the eggs show that eggs have made a complete turn.	X marks on the eggs show that the eggs were not turned completely since I last checked.
Day 10	The turner seems to be tilting the eggs efficiently—X marks show a complete turn.	X marks show that 18 eggs were turned, but 6 were not.
Day 15	The temperature of the eggs is at a steady 100 degrees.	Two hens have moved off the nest for a brief time. Temperature of the eggs right now is 97 degrees.
Day 25	The incubator has hatched thirteen out of the twenty-four eggs.	The hens have hatched ten out of the twenty-four eggs.

In general, the incubator eggs received much more consistent attention to their condition. The machine did not need to stop to eat or exercise, as the hens did. The marks on the eggs showed that the eggs under the hens did not always get completely turned. Sometimes, some of the eggs were turned and some were not. In addition, the hens sometimes left the nest for as long as an hour. When the temperature of the eggs was measured after a hen had been gone a long time, the egg temperature was sometimes as low as 97 degrees.

After twenty-five days, the hens had hatched ten out of the twenty-four eggs, and the incubator had hatched thirteen. The difference between the two numbers is not great enough to say that one way of incubating is more effective than the other. The incubator is definitely more efficient at delivering ideal conditions than the hens were. However, since the increased efficiency does not result in a higher number of hatches, maybe "ideal" conditions are not required for a successful hatch.

> The writer concludes by explaining whether the research did or did not support her original hypothesis.

Bibliography

Johnson, Sylvia A. *Inside an Egg*. Minneapolis: Lerner Publications Company, 1982.

Kruse Poultry Feed. *Care and Feeding of Baby Chicks.*

Little Giant Instruction Manual for Still Air Incubator and Automatic Egg Turner. Miller Mfg. Co., So. St. Paul, MN, 1998.

Scott, Wyatt. Personal Interview. 1 Dec. 2000.

Selsam, Millicent E. *Animals as Parents*. Canada: George J. McLeod Limited, 1965.

> In the bibliography, the writer lists all the works from which she gathered information used in her report. Some teachers prefer a "Works Cited" list, in which you list only the sources that you actually cite, or note, in your research report.

Drafting

Evaluate your thesis statement. Compare your thesis statement to your researched information. If your researched information does not support the thesis statement, you may adjust your thesis statement based on what you have learned.

Develop a formal outline. Group your notes by category. Use Roman numerals (I, II, III) to number your most important points. Under each Roman numeral, use capital letters (A, B, C) for the supporting details.

Prepare to credit sources. When you include a direct quotation, present an original idea that is not your own, or report a fact that is available in only one source or is not common knowledge, you must include documentation. As you draft,

- circle ideas or words that are not your own.
- use parentheses to note the author's last name and the page numbers of the material used.

Later, you can use this record to create formal citations.

Title of Your Report
I. First main point
A. First supporting detail
B. Second supporting detail
II. Second main point
A. First supporting detail
B. Second supporting detail

Revising

Revise to improve organization. Look over your draft and analyze your organization to see if it matches your outline.

1. Mark each paragraph with the Roman numeral and capital letter from your outline and designate the subject of the paragraph.

2. If all the paragraphs with the same Roman numeral are not next to each other, figure out if the change is an improvement in organization or not. If not, correct it.

Revise to vary sentence lengths. Underline your sentences in alternating colors so you can easily see differences in length. Combine short, choppy sentences or break up longer sentences if there are too many of either.

Example

Having teeth allows these whales to eat chewy food. These foods include squid and octopus. These creatures are abundant in the cold southern waters.

Having teeth allows these whales to eat chewy foods such as squid and octopus, which are abundant in the cold southern waters.

Publishing and Presenting

Choose one of these ways to share your writing with classmates or a larger audience.

Teach a lesson. Use your research report as the basis for an oral presentation on your topic. Keep your audience in mind as you prepare your presentation.

- If you are presenting to younger students, evaluate which terms and concepts will need to be explained in simpler language or illustrated with visuals.

- If you are presenting to people your own age, think about what your friends and classmates would need to have explained.

Create a resource center. Combine your research report with those of your classmates to create an information resource center in your classroom.

Create a reference list. Your research writing should document your sources of information. A works cited page provides readers with full bibliographic information on each source that you cite in your paper.

Since standards for documentation are set by several organizations, identify the format that your teacher prefers. Following that format, check that each entry is complete and properly punctuated. (For more information, see Citing Sources, page R14.)

 Prentice Hall Writing and Grammar Connection: Chapter 11, Section 4

Speaking Connection

To learn strategies for delivering a research report as a speech, see the Listening and Speaking Workshop: Delivering a Research Presentation, page 592.

Rubric for Self-Assessment

Evaluate your research report using the following criteria and rating scale:

Criteria	Rating Scale				
	Not very				Very
How clearly is the viewpoint or perspective stated in the thesis statement?	1	2	3	4	5
How reliable are the sources?	1	2	3	4	5
How varied are the sources?	1	2	3	4	5
How well is each point supported by facts, details, and evidence?	1	2	3	4	5
How clearly is the writing organized?	1	2	3	4	5
How consistently is quoted and paraphrased information credited?	1	2	3	4	5
How consistently does the bibliography follow an approved format?	1	2	3	4	5

Listening and Speaking WORKSHOP

Delivering a Research Presentation

Delivering a **research presentation** has many of the same characteristics as preparing a research report. (To review the characteristics of a research report, see the Writing Workshop, pp. 586–591.) To turn your report into a successful presentation, use some of the strategies suggested here.

Plan Your Content

Because they contain many facts and details, research presentations require detailed notes and careful preparation.

Expand your outline. Use an outline as your script. Refer to the points on the outline to keep your presentation organized. Add to your "outline script" any specific quotations or statistics that you want to mention. Underline or highlight any details that need to be read especially carefully.

Deliver Effectively

To deliver an effective research presentation, take time to rehearse using speaking techniques that will keep the audience interested and engaged.

Speak clearly and slowly. Without shouting, use a strong, clear voice that can be heard in the back of the room. Speak slowly so your listeners can hear *every word* you say.

Use visual aids. Visual aids, such as photographs, charts, graphs, diagrams, or maps, can give your presentation variety. If you are comparing data, you might display a spreadsheet— a multi-column table that exhibits numerical information in columns and rows. Show slides, videotapes, or objects when appropriate.

Answer questions. At the end of your presentation, invite your audience to ask questions. If you cannot answer a question, suggest a resource that may help, or write down the question and answer it later.

Activity:
Research Presentation Choose a topic that you wrote about in a research report. Review your presentation for places to add visual aids, such as photographs, charts, graphs, diagrams, or maps. Plan a presentation using the tips listed here.

Using Visual Aids

To Show . . .

• **Organization**, use an outline to help your audience follow your points

• **Statistical information**, use a bar graph to show increases and decreases in amounts

• **Physical characteristics**, present slides, videos, or photographs

Assessment WORKSHOP

Distinguishing Between Fact and Opinion

The reading sections of some tests require you to read a passage and answer multiple-choice questions about facts and opinions. You have learned in this unit that a fact can be proven true. An opinion can be supported but not proven.

Sample Test Item

There are many things to see and do in Washington, D.C. You can visit the Washington Monument, the Capitol, and the White House. You could spend weeks exploring the many museums that are part of the Smithsonian Institution. The best is the National Museum of American History, where you can see George Washington's false teeth. Some of the city's spots, such as the Vietnam Veterans Memorial, are thought-provoking. For a blend of fun and education, everyone should see Washington, D.C., at least once.

1. Which of these is a FACT in the passage?
   A Washington, D.C., is a fascinating city.
   B At the National Museum of American History, you can see George Washington's false teeth.
   C The Vietnam Veterans Memorial is thought-provoking and fun.
   D Everyone should see Washington, D.C., once.

Answer and Explanation

A, C, and *D* cannot be shown to be true. They are the speaker's opinions. *B* is correct.

Practice

Read the following passage and answer the questions.

No student at my school should ever have a boring afternoon. There are after-school activities for every interest. Athletes can run track or play basketball. The Math Team challenges mathematicians to put their skills to work. There are clubs for readers, history buffs, and cooks. The Chess Club is best. I've improved my game tremendously since joining. With all of these activities, maybe we need a Free-Time Club for those who just want to relax!

1. Which of these statements is an OPINION?
   A There is a club for readers.
   B Athletes can run track.
   C No student at my school should ever have a boring afternoon.
   D I have improved my chess game since joining the Chess Club.

2. Which is a FACT expressed in the passage?
   A The best activity is the Chess Club.
   B Athletes can run track or play basketball.
   C Maybe we need a Free-Time Club.
   D After-school activities cover every interest.

UNIT 8 Drama

Performers, Freshman Brown

Exploring the Genre

Reading drama can give your imagination a workout. You become part of the action as you read what the characters say and follow their actions on the stage or screen. Noticing the stage directions will also give your imagination a boost, helping you get a mental picture of the setting and of how the characters speak and look as they deliver their lines.

◀ **Critical Viewing** What elements in the painting show that the people are performers on stage? **[Analyze]**

Why Read Literature?

As you read a drama, you can visualize how the words and actions on the page come to life on a stage or screen. To help you understand and remember dramatic works, set different purposes for your reading. Review the three purposes you might set before reading the dramas and reviews in this unit.

1 Read for the love of literature.

Readers have been associating Christmas with *A Christmas Carol* by Charles Dickens since the story was published in 1843. It is said that one street vendor in London was heard to cry out when she learned that Dickens had died in 1870, "Dickens dead! Then will Father Christmas die, too?" Read the dramatized version—*A Christmas Carol: Scrooge and Marley,* p. 600—to see why Scrooge, Marley, and the other classic characters of the story have become so familiar to readers for more than 150 years.

3 Read for information.

A literary critic predicted in 1858 that "Fifty years hence, . . . our children will wonder why their ancestors thought Charles Dickens was a great writer." Yet, Dickens is still popular today, and the critics have changed their opinion! Read what several reviewers had to say about performances of *A Christmas Carol: Scrooge and Marley,* p. 659, to see how times have changed.

2 Read to be entertained.

Do scary stories, movies, or television shows make your heart beat a little faster? Rod Serling's eerie television dramas in the series *The Twilight Zone* provided viewers with an unusual and frightening view of the world each week. You can find out how it feels to be inside the Twilight Zone yourself when you read **"The Monsters Are Due on Maple Street,"** p. 666.

Take It to the Net
Visit the Web site for online instruction and activities related to each selection in this unit.
www.phschool.com

How to Read Literature

Use Strategies for Reading Drama

Reading drama is different from reading other writing since drama is written to be performed. The story is told mostly through what actors say (dialogue) and what they do (action). Use the stage directions to understand what is happening while the characters are talking or while they are silent.

1. Picture the action.

Stage directions will help you picture the action of a play. Use the stage directions to picture Scrooge's expression and hear his voice.

> **SCROOGE.** [*Panicked*] Fly, but I am a mortal and cannot fly!
> —from *A Christmas Carol: Scrooge and Marley*, Act I

Reading stage directions can also help you picture when and where the events in a drama take place and how the characters' surroundings look on stage.

2. Ask questions.

The best way to read drama is to get actively involved in the action. Ask yourself questions and look for the answers as you read. For example, you might ask yourself: *Why did the character say or do that?* or *What caused this to happen?* What questions might come to mind as you read the lines below?

> [PROLOGUE: MARLEY *stands spotlit,* L. *He speaks directly to the audience.*]
> **MARLEY.** My ghostly friend now leads my living partner through the city's streets.
> —from *A Christmas Carol: Scrooge and Marley*, Act II

Thinking of answers to your questions will put you right into the action of the drama.

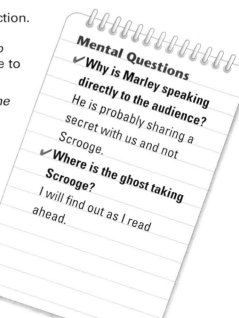

Mental Questions

✔ **Why is Marley speaking directly to the audience?**
He is probably sharing a secret with us and not Scrooge.

✔ **Where is the ghost taking Scrooge?**
I will find out as I read ahead.

3. Predict what is going to happen.

When reading drama, novels, novellas, short stories and narrative nonfiction, make predictions—educated guesses. As you read further, see if your predictions were correct.

> **STEVE.** What was that? A meteor?
> **DON.** [*Nods*] That's what it looked like. I didn't hear any crash though, did you?
> **STEVE.** [*Shakes his head*] Nope. I didn't hear anything except a roar.
> —from "The Monsters Are Due on Maple Street," Act I

As you read the selections in this unit, review the strategies for reading drama and look at the notes in the side column. Use the suggestions to help you interact with the text.

Prepare to Read

A Christmas Carol: Scrooge and Marley, Act I
adapted from A Christmas Carol

 Take It to the Net

Visit www.phschool.com
for interactive activities
and instruction related to
the selection, including

- background
- graphic organizers
- literary elements
- reading strategies

Preview

Connecting to the Literature

In Charles Dickens's novel *A Christmas Carol*, a greedy, mean-spirited man named Scrooge has a life-changing experience. This adaptation for the stage, by Israel Horovitz, dramatizes that experience. Put yourself in Scrooge's place as you read. Would you react as he does?

Background

A Christmas Carol is set in nineteenth-century England, a time of rapid industrial growth. In this booming economy, the wealthy lived in luxury, but the poor and the working class suffered. Dickens's novel, from which this drama was adapted, shows sympathy for the situation of these people and suggests a way in which it might be changed.

Literary Analysis

Elements of Drama

A **drama** is a story written to be performed. Like other stories, a drama has characters, a setting, and a plot. However, a drama has two specific characteristics that set it apart from **prose**—the ordinary form of writing that is neither poetry nor drama.

- **Presentation of Dialogue:** Conversations between characters. Characters' names are written before the words they speak.
- **Stage Directions:** Words not spoken by characters. Stage directions describe the set, the special effects, and the way characters look and move.

Connecting Literary Elements

A **novel** is a full-length fictional narrative with characters, a setting, a conflict, and a plot. This play is an adaptation of Charles Dickens's novel *A Christmas Carol.* **Dramatic adaptations**—such as movies, musicals, and plays like this one—make use of the plot, characters, and setting of the novels on which they are based. The writing must be changed or adapted, however, so that the story can be delivered through dialogue and movement. As you read, think about the following focus questions.

1. In what ways is a drama similar to a novel?
2. What parts of this drama probably reflect changes made for a staged version of the story?

Reading Strategy

Picturing the Action

Reading a drama is different from seeing one on stage. To **picture** in your mind what a performance of *A Christmas Carol* might be like, use the details the playwright provides in the stage directions. Keep track of descriptions telling what the characters and the set look like in each scene. Use a chart like this one, adding characters as they make their entrances.

Stage Directions

Scene 1	
Character	Setting

Vocabulary Development

implored (im plôrd´) *v.* asked or begged earnestly (p. 602)

morose (mə rōs´) *adj.* gloomy; ill-tempered (p. 603)

destitute (des´ tə tōōt´) *adj., used as n.* people living in complete poverty (p. 606)

misanthrope (mis´ ən thrōp´) *n.* person who hates everyone (p. 609)

void (void) *n.* total emptiness (p. 609)

ponderous (pän´ dər əs) *adj.* very heavy; bulky (p. 611)

benevolence (bə nev´ ə ləns) *n.* kindliness (p. 611)

A Christmas Carol: Scrooge and Marley

Israel Horovitz

from A Christmas Carol by Charles Dickens

Act I

THE PEOPLE OF THE PLAY

JACOB MARLEY, a specter

EBENEZER SCROOGE, not yet dead, which is to say still alive

BOB CRATCHIT, Scrooge's clerk

FRED, Scrooge's nephew

THIN DO-GOODER

PORTLY DO-GOODER

SPECTERS (VARIOUS), carrying money-boxes

THE GHOST OF CHRISTMAS PAST

FOUR JOCUND TRAVELERS

A BAND OF SINGERS

A BAND OF DANCERS

LITTLE BOY SCROOGE

YOUNG MAN SCROOGE

FAN, Scrooge's little sister

THE SCHOOLMASTER

SCHOOLMATES

FEZZIWIG, a fine and fair employer

DICK, young Scrooge's co-worker

YOUNG SCROOGE

A FIDDLER

MORE DANCERS

SCROOGE'S LOST LOVE

SCROOGE'S LOST LOVE'S DAUGHTER

SCROOGE'S LOST LOVE'S HUSBAND

THE GHOST OF CHRISTMAS PRESENT

SOME BAKERS

MRS. CRATCHIT, Bob Cratchit's wife

BELINDA CRATCHIT, a daughter

MARTHA CRATCHIT, another daughter

PETER CRATCHIT, a son

TINY TIM CRATCHIT, another son

SCROOGE'S NIECE, Fred's wife

THE GHOST OF CHRISTMAS FUTURE, a mute Phantom

THREE MEN OF BUSINESS

DRUNKS, SCOUNDRELS, WOMEN OF THE STREETS

A CHARWOMAN

MRS. DILBER

JOE, an old second-hand goods dealer

A CORPSE, very like Scrooge

AN INDEBTED FAMILY

ADAM, a young boy

A POULTERER

A GENTLEWOMAN

SOME MORE MEN OF BUSINESS

THE PLACE OF THE PLAY   Various locations in and around the City of London, including Scrooge's Chambers and Offices; the Cratchit Home; Fred's Home; Scrooge's School; Fezziwig's Offices; Old Joe's Hide-a-Way.

THE TIME OF THE PLAY   The entire action of the play takes place on Christmas Eve, Christmas Day, and the morning after Christmas, 1843.

Scene 1

[*Ghostly music in auditorium. A single spotlight on* JACOB MARLEY, D.C. *He is ancient; awful, dead-eyed. He speaks straight out to auditorium.*]

MARLEY. [*Cackle-voiced*] My name is Jacob Marley and I am dead. [*He laughs.*] Oh, no, there's no doubt that I am dead. The register of my burial was signed by the clergyman, the clerk, the undertaker . . . and by my chief mourner . . . Ebenezer Scrooge . . . [*Pause; remembers*] I am dead as a doornail.

[*A spotlight fades up, Stage Right, on* SCROOGE, *in his counting-house,[1] counting. Lettering on the window behind* SCROOGE *reads:* "SCROOGE AND MARLEY, LTD." *The spotlight is tight on* SCROOGE'*s head and shoulders. We shall not yet see into the offices and setting. Ghostly music continues, under.* MARLEY *looks across at* SCROOGE; *pitifully. After a moment's pause*]

I present him to you: Ebenezer Scrooge . . . England's most tight-fisted hand at the grindstone, Scrooge! a squeezing, wrenching, grasping, scraping, clutching, covetous, old sinner! secret, and self-contained, and solitary as an oyster. The cold within him freezes his old features, nips his pointed nose, shrivels his cheek, stiffens his gait; makes his eyes red, his thin lips blue; and speaks out shrewdly in his grating voice. Look at him. Look at him . . .

[SCROOGE *counts and mumbles.*]

SCROOGE. They owe me money and I will collect. I will have them jailed, if I have to. They owe me money and I will collect what is due me.

[MARLEY *moves towards* SCROOGE; *two steps. The spotlight stays with him.*]

MARLEY. [*Disgusted*] He and I were partners for I don't know how many years. Scrooge was my sole executor, my sole administrator, my sole assign, my sole residuary legatee,[2] my sole friend and my sole mourner. But Scrooge was not so cut up by the sad event of my death, but that he was an excellent man of business on the very day of my funeral, and solemnized[3] it with an undoubted bargain. [*Pauses again in disgust*] He never painted out my name from the window. There it stands, on the window and above the warehouse door: Scrooge and Marley. Sometimes people new to our business call him Scrooge and sometimes they call him Marley. He answers to both names. It's all the same to him. And it's cheaper than painting in a new sign, isn't it? [*Pauses; moves closer to*

Literary Analysis
Elements of Drama and Adaptations
What part of a novel's plot would reveal this background information about the situation and characters?

---

1. **countinghouse** office for keeping financial records and writing business letters.
2. **my sole executor** (ig zek′ yə tər), **my sole administrator, my sole assign** (ə sīn′), **my sole residuary legatee** (ri zij′ ōō wer′ ē leg′ ə tē′) legal terms giving one person responsibility to carry out the wishes of another who has died.
3. **solemnized** (säl′ əm nīzd′) *v.* honored or remembered. Marley is being ironic.

SCROOGE] Nobody has ever stopped him in the street to say, with gladsome looks, "My dear Scrooge, how are you? When will you come to see me?" No beggars <u>implored</u> him to bestow a trifle, no children ever ask him what it is o'clock, no man or woman now, or ever in his life, not once, inquire the way to such and such a place. [MARLEY *stands next to* SCROOGE *now. They share, so it seems, a spotlight.*] But what does Scrooge care of any of this? It is the very thing he likes! To edge his way along the crowded paths of life, warning all human sympathy to keep its distance.

[*A ghostly bell rings in the distance.* MARLEY *moves away from* SCROOGE, *now, heading* D. *again. As he does, he "takes" the light:* SCROOGE *has disappeared into the black void beyond.* MARLEY *walks* D.C., *talking directly to the audience. Pauses*]

The bell tolls and I must take my leave. You must stay a while with Scrooge and watch him play out his scroogey life. It is now the story: the once-upon-a-time. Scrooge is busy in his counting-house. Where else? Christmas eve and Scrooge is busy in his counting-house. It is cold, bleak, biting weather outside: foggy withal: and, if you listen closely, you can hear the people in the court go wheezing up and down, beating their hands upon their breasts, and stamping their feet upon the pavement stones to warm them . . .

[*The clocks outside strike three.*]

Only three! and quite dark outside already: it has not been light all day this day.

[*This ghostly bell rings in the distance again.* MARLEY *looks about him. Music in.* MARLEY *flies away.*]

[N.B. *Marley's comings and goings should, from time to time, induce the explosion of the odd flash-pot.* I.H.]

Scene 2

[*Christmas music in, sung by a live chorus, full. At conclusion of song, sound fades under and into the distance. Lights up in set: offices of Scrooge and Marley, Ltd.* SCROOGE *sits at his desk, at work. Near him is a tiny fire. His door is open and in his line of vision, we see* SCROOGE's *clerk,* BOB CRATCHIT, *who sits in a dismal tank of a cubicle, copying letters. Near* CRATCHIT *is a fire so tiny as to barely cast a light: perhaps it is one pitifully glowing coal?* CRATCHIT *rubs his hands together, puts on a white comforter[4] and tries to heat his hands around his candle.* SCROOGE's *NEPHEW enters, unseen.*]

SCROOGE. What are you doing, Cratchit? Acting cold, are you? Next, you'll be asking to replenish your coal from my coal-box, won't you?

---

4. **comforter** (kum′ fər tər) *n.* long, woolen scarf.

implored (im plôrd′) *v.* asked or begged earnestly

Literary Analysis
Elements of Drama and Novels What information here would be found in the novel? What details are specific to the drama?

Well, save your breath, Cratchit! Unless you're prepared to find employ elsewhere!

NEPHEW. [*Cheerfully; surprising* SCROOGE] A merry Christmas to you, Uncle! God save you!

SCROOGE. Bah! Humbug![5]

NEPHEW. Christmas a "humbug," Uncle? I'm sure you don't mean that.

SCROOGE. I do! Merry Christmas? What right do you have to be merry? What reason have you to be merry? You're poor enough!

NEPHEW. Come, then. What right have you to be dismal? What reason have you to be <u>morose</u>? You're rich enough.

SCROOGE. Bah! Humbug!

NEPHEW. Don't be cross, Uncle.

SCROOGE. What else can I be? Eh? When I live in a world of fools such as this? Merry Christmas? What's Christmastime to you but a time of paying bills without any money; a time for finding yourself a year older, but not an hour richer. If I could work my will, every idiot who goes about with "Merry Christmas" on his lips, should be boiled with his own pudding, and buried with a stake of holly through his heart. He should!

NEPHEW. Uncle!

SCROOGE. Nephew! You keep Christmas in your own way and let me keep it in mine.

NEPHEW. Keep it! But you don't keep it, Uncle.

SCROOGE. Let me leave it alone, then. Much good it has ever done you!

NEPHEW. There are many things from which I have derived good, by which I have not profited, I daresay. Christmas among the rest. But I am sure that I always thought of Christmas time, when it has come round—as a good time: the only time I know of, when men and women seem to open their shut-up hearts freely, and to think of people below them as if they really were fellow-passengers to the grave, and not another race of creatures bound on other journeys. And therefore, Uncle, though it has never put a scrap of gold or silver in my pocket, I believe that it *has* done me good, and that it *will* do me good; and I say, God bless it!

[*The* CLERK *in the tank applauds, looks at the furious* SCROOGE *and pokes out his tiny fire, as if in exchange for the moment of impropriety.* SCROOGE *yells at him.*]

SCROOGE. [*To the clerk*] Let me hear another sound from you and

morose (mə rōs´) *adj.* gloomy; ill-tempered

**Reading Check**
How does Scrooge feel about Christmas?

---

5. **Humbug** (hum´ bug´) *interj.* nonsense!

you'll keep your Christmas by losing your situation. [*To the nephew*] You're quite a powerful speaker, sir. I wonder you don't go into Parliament.[6]

NEPHEW. Don't be angry, Uncle. Come! Dine with us tomorrow.

SCROOGE. I'd rather see myself dead than see myself with your family!

NEPHEW. But, why? Why?

SCROOGE. Why did you get married?

NEPHEW. Because I fell in love.

SCROOGE. That, sir, is the only thing that you have said to me in your entire lifetime which is even more ridiculous than "Merry Christmas"! [*Turns from* NEPHEW] Good afternoon.

NEPHEW. Nay, Uncle, you never came to see me before I married either. Why give it as a reason for not coming now?

SCROOGE. Good afternoon, Nephew!

NEPHEW. I want nothing from you; I ask nothing of you; why cannot we be friends?

SCROOGE. Good afternoon!

NEPHEW. I am sorry with all my heart, to find you so resolute. But I have made the trial in homage to Christmas, and I'll keep my Christmas humor to the last. So A Merry Christmas, Uncle!

SCROOGE. Good afternoon!

NEPHEW. And A Happy New Year!

SCROOGE. Good afternoon!

NEPHEW. [*He stands facing* SCROOGE.] Uncle, you are the most . . . [*Pauses*] No, I shan't. My Christmas humor is intact . . . [*Pause*] God bless you, Uncle . . . [NEPHEW *turns and starts for the door; he stops at* CRATCHIT's *cage.*] Merry Christmas, Bob Cratchit . . .

CRATCHIT. Merry Christmas to you sir, and a very, very happy New Year . . .

SCROOGE. [*Calling across to them*] Oh, fine, a perfection, just fine . . . to see the perfect pair of you: husbands, with wives and children to support . . . my clerk there earning fifteen shillings a week . . . and the perfect pair of you, talking about a Merry Christmas! [*Pauses*] I'll retire to Bedlam![7]

NEPHEW. [*To* CRATCHIT] He's impossible!

CRATCHIT. Oh, mind him not, sir. He's getting on in years, and he's alone. He's noticed your visit. I'll wager your visit has warmed him.

Literary Analysis
Elements of Drama
What does the dialogue reveal about Scrooge and his relationship with his nephew?

---

6. **Parliament** (pär′ lə mənt) national legislative body of Great Britain, in some ways like the American Congress.
7. **Bedlam** (bed′ ləm) hospital in London for the mentally ill.

NEPHEW. Him? Uncle Ebenezer Scrooge? *Warmed?* You are a better Christian than I am, sir.

CRATCHIT. [*Opening the door for* NEPHEW; *two* DO-GOODERS *will enter, as* NEPHEW *exits*] Good day to you, sir, and God bless.

NEPHEW. God bless . . . [*One man who enters is portly, the other is thin. Both are pleasant.*]

CRATCHIT. Can I help you, gentlemen?

THIN MAN. [*Carrying papers and books; looks around* CRATCHIT *to* SCROOGE] Scrooge and Marley's, I believe. Have I the pleasure of addressing Mr. Scrooge, or Mr. Marley?

SCROOGE. Mr. Marley has been dead these seven years. He died seven years ago this very night.

PORTLY MAN. We have no doubt his liberality[8] is well represented by his surviving partner . . . [*Offers his calling card*]

---

8. **liberality** (lib´ ər al´ i tē) generosity.

▲ **Critical Viewing**
The character above heats his hands over a small flame in his office. What does this action communicate to the audience about the setting? **[Infer]**

 **Reading Check**

What invitation does Scrooge's nephew offer?

A Christmas Carol: Scrooge and Marley, Act I ◆ 605

SCROOGE. [*Handing back the card; unlooked at*] . . . Good afternoon.

THIN MAN. This will take but a moment, sir . . .

PORTLY MAN. At this festive season of the year, Mr. Scrooge, it is more than usually desirable that we should make some slight provision for the poor and <u>destitute</u>, who suffer greatly at the present time. Many thousands are in want of common necessities; hundreds of thousands are in want of common comforts, sir.

SCROOGE. Are there no prisons?

PORTLY MAN. Plenty of prisons.

SCROOGE. And aren't the Union workhouses still in operation?

THIN MAN. They are. Still. I wish that I could say that they are not.

SCROOGE. The Treadmill[9] and the Poor Law[10] are in full vigor, then?

THIN MAN. Both very busy, sir.

SCROOGE. Ohhh, I see. I was afraid, from what you said at first, that something had occurred to stop them from their useful course. [*Pauses*] I'm glad to hear it.

PORTLY MAN. Under the impression that they scarcely furnish Christian cheer of mind or body to the multitude, a few of us are endeavoring to raise a fund to buy the Poor some meat and drink, and means of warmth. We choose this time, because it is a time, of all others, when Want is keenly felt, and Abundance rejoices. [*Pen in hand; as well as notepad*] What shall I put you down for, sir?

SCROOGE. Nothing!

PORTLY MAN. You wish to be left anonymous?

SCROOGE. I wish to be left alone! [*Pauses; turns away; turns back to them*] Since you ask me what I wish, gentlemen, that is my answer. I help to support the establishments that I have mentioned: they cost enough: and those who are badly off must go there.

THIN MAN. Many can't go there; and many would rather die.

SCROOGE. If they would rather die, they had better do it, and decrease the surplus population. Besides—excuse me—I don't know that.

THIN MAN. But you might know it!

SCROOGE. It's not my business. It's enough for a man to understand his own business, and not to interfere with other people's. Mine occupies me constantly. Good afternoon, gentlemen!

destitute (des´ tə toōt´) *adj. used as n.* people living in complete poverty

Literary Analysis
Elements of Drama
What do you learn about Scrooge from this dialogue?

---

9. the Treadmill (tred´ mil´) kind of mill wheel turned by the weight of persons treading steps arranged around it; this device was used to punish prisoners in jails.
10. the Poor Law the original 17th-century Poor Laws called for overseers of the poor in each parish to provide relief for the needy. The New Poor Law of 1834 made the workhouses in which the poor sometimes lived and worked extremely harsh and unattractive. They became a symbol of the misery of the poor.

[SCROOGE *turns his back on the gentlemen and returns to his desk.*]

PORTLY MAN. But, sir, Mr. Scrooge . . . think of the poor.

SCROOGE. [*Turns suddenly to them. Pauses*] Take your leave of my offices, sirs, while I am still smiling.

[*The* THIN MAN *looks at the* PORTLY MAN. *They are undone. They shrug. They move to the door.* CRATCHIT *hops up to open it for them.*]

THIN MAN. Good day, sir . . . [*To* CRATCHIT] A merry Christmas to you, sir . . .

CRATCHIT. Yes. A Merry Christmas to both of you . . .

PORTLY MAN. Merry Christmas . . .

[CRATCHIT *silently squeezes something into the hand of the* THIN MAN.]

THIN MAN. What's this?

CRATCHIT. Shhhh . . .

[CRATCHIT *opens the door; wind and snow whistle into the room.*]

THIN MAN. Thank you, sir, thank you.

[CRATCHIT *closes the door and returns to his workplace.* SCROOGE *is at his own counting table. He talks to* CRATCHIT *without looking up.*]

SCROOGE. It's less of a time of year for being merry, and more a time of year for being loony . . . if you ask me.

CRATCHIT. Well, I don't know, sir . . .

[*The clock's bell strikes six o'clock.*]

Well, there it is, eh, six?

SCROOGE. Saved by six bells, are you?

CRATCHIT. I must be going home . . . [*He snuffs out his candle and puts on his hat.*] I hope you have a . . . very very lovely day tomorrow, sir . . .

SCROOGE. Hmmm. Oh, you'll be wanting the whole day tomorrow, I suppose?

CRATCHIT. If quite convenient, sir.

SCROOGE. It's not convenient, and it's not fair. If I was to stop half-a-crown for it, you'd think yourself ill-used, I'll be bound?

[CRATCHIT *smiles faintly.*]

CRATCHIT. I don't know, sir . . .

SCROOGE. And yet, you don't think me ill-used when I pay a day's wages for no work . . .

CRATCHIT. It's only but once a year . . .

SCROOGE. A poor excuse for picking a man's pocket every 25th of December! But I suppose you must have the whole day. Be here all the earlier the next morning!

Reading Strategy
Picture the Action
What action is indicated by the stage directions? What do you think Bob Cratchit has done?

✔**Reading Check**

Why is Cratchit taking a day off?

CRATCHIT. Oh, I will, sir. I will. I promise you. And, sir . . .

SCROOGE. Don't say it, Cratchit.

CRATCHIT. But let me wish you a . . .

SCROOGE. Don't say it, Cratchit. I warn you . . .

CRATCHIT. Sir!

SCROOGE. Cratchit!

[CRATCHIT *opens the door.*]

CRATCHIT. All right, then, sir . . . well . . . [*Suddenly*] Merry Christmas, Mr. Scrooge!

[*And he runs out the door, shutting same behind him.* SCROOGE *moves to his desk; gathering his coat, hat, etc. A* BOY *appears at his window. . . .*]

BOY. [*Singing*] "Away in a manger . . ."

[SCROOGE *seizes his ruler and whacks at the image of the* BOY *outside. The* BOY *leaves.*]

SCROOGE. Bah! Humbug! Christmas! Bah! Humbug! [*He shuts out the light.*]

A note on the crossover, following Scene 2:

[SCROOGE *will walk alone to his rooms from his offices. As he makes a long slow cross of the stage, the scenery should change. Christmas music will be heard, various people will cross by* SCROOGE, *often smiling happily.*

There will be occasional pleasant greetings tossed at him.]

SCROOGE, *in contrast to all, will grump and mumble. He will snap at passing boys, as might a horrid old hound.*

Reading Strategy
Picturing the Action
What details in the stage directions help you picture the actions that emphasize the difference between Scrooge and other people?

◀ **Critical Viewing** What emotion does each actor express in these photographs? Describe the tone of voice that the actors might use to convey this emotion. **[Speculate]**

In short, SCROOGE*'s sounds and movements will define him in contrast from all other people who cross the stage: he is the* <u>misanthrope</u>, *the malcontent, the miser. He is* SCROOGE.

This statement of SCROOGE*'s character, by contrast to all other characters, should seem comical to the audience.*

During SCROOGE*'s crossover to his rooms, snow should begin to fall. All passers-by will hold their faces to the sky, smiling, allowing snow to shower them lightly.* SCROOGE, *by contrast, will bat at the flakes with his walking-stick, as might an insomniac swat at a sleep-stopping, middle-of-the-night swarm of mosquitoes. He will comment on the blackness of the night, and, finally, reach his rooms and his encounter with the magical specter:*[11] MARLEY, *his eternal mate.*]

misanthrope
(mis´ ən thrōp´) *n.* person who hates or distrusts everyone

void (void) *n.* total emptiness

✓ **Reading Check**

What does Scrooge see in the door knocker?

Scene 3

SCROOGE. No light at all . . . no moon . . . that is what is at the center of a Christmas Eve: dead black: <u>void</u> . . .

[SCROOGE *puts his key in the door's keyhole. He has reached his rooms now. The door knocker changes and is now* MARLEY*'s face. A musical sound; quickly: ghostly.* MARLEY*'s image is not at all angry, but looks at* SCROOGE *as did the old* MARLEY *look at* SCROOGE. *The hair is curiously stirred; eyes wide open, dead: absent of focus.* SCROOGE *stares wordlessly here. The face, before his very eyes, does* deliquesce.[12] *It is a knocker again.* SCROOGE *opens the door and checks the back of same, probably for* MARLEY*'s pigtail. Seeing nothing but screws and nuts,* SCROOGE *refuses the memory.*]

Pooh, pooh!

[*The sound of the door closing resounds throughout the house as thunder. Every room echoes the sound.* SCROOGE *fastens the door and walks across the hall to the stairs, trimming his candle as he goes; and then he goes slowly up the staircase. He checks each room: sitting room, bedrooms, slumber-room. He looks under the sofa, under the table: nobody there. He fixes his evening gruel on the hob,*[13] *changes his jacket.* SCROOGE *sits near the tiny low-flamed fire, sipping his gruel. There are various pictures on the walls:*

---

11. specter (spek´ tər) *n.* ghost.
12. deliquesce (del´ i kwes´) *v.* melt away.
13. gruel (grōō´ əl) **on the hob** (häb) thin broth warming on a ledge at the back or side of the fireplace.

all of them now show likenesses of MARLEY. SCROOGE *blinks his eyes.*]

Bah! Humbug!

[SCROOGE *walks in a circle about the room. The pictures change back into their natural images. He sits down at the table in front of the fire. A bell hangs overhead. It begins to ring, of its own accord. Slowly, surely, begins the ringing of every bell in the house. They continue ringing for nearly half a minute.* SCROOGE *is stunned by the phenomenon. The bells cease their ringing all at once. Deep below* SCROOGE, *in the basement of the house, there is the sound of clanking, of some enormous chain being dragged across the floors; and now up the stairs. We hear doors flying open.*]

Bah still! Humbug still! This is not happening! I won't believe it!

[MARLEY'S GHOST *enters the room. He is horrible to look at: pigtail, vest, suit as usual, but he drags an enormous chain now, to which is fastened cash-boxes, keys, padlocks, ledgers, deeds, and heavy purses fashioned of steel. He is transparent.* MARLEY *stands opposite the stricken* SCROOGE.]

How now! What do you want of me?

MARLEY. Much!

SCROOGE. Who are you?

MARLEY. Ask me who I *was.*

SCROOGE. Who *were* you then?

MARLEY. In life, I was your business partner: Jacob Marley.

SCROOGE. I see . . . can you sit down?

MARLEY. I can.

SCROOGE. Do it then.

MARLEY. I shall. [MARLEY *sits opposite* SCROOGE, *in the chair across the table, at the front of the fireplace.*] You don't believe in me.

SCROOGE. I don't.

MARLEY. Why do you doubt your senses?

SCROOGE. Because every little thing affects them. A slight disorder of the stomach makes them cheat. You may be an undigested bit of beef, a blot of mustard, a crumb of cheese, a fragment of an underdone potato. There's more of gravy than of grave about you, whatever you are!

[*There is a silence between them.* SCROOGE *is made nervous by it. He picks up a toothpick.*]

Humbug! I tell you: humbug!

[MARLEY *opens his mouth and screams a ghosty, fearful scream. The scream echoes about each room of the house. Bats fly, cats screech,*

Reading Strategy
Picturing the Action
Why are the items attached to Marley's chains significant enough to mention in the stage directions?

Reading Strategy
Picturing the Action
How do Scrooge's actions indicate his feelings?

lightning flashes. SCROOGE *stands and walks backwards against the wall.* MARLEY *stands and screams again. This time, he takes his head and lifts it from his shoulders. His head continues to scream.* MARLEY'*s face again appears on every picture in the room: all screaming.* SCROOGE, *on his knees before* MARLEY.]

Mercy! Dreadful apparition,[14] mercy! Why, O! why do you trouble me so?

MARLEY. Man of the worldly mind, do you believe in me, or not?

SCROOGE. I do. I must. But why do spirits such as you walk the earth? And why do they come to me?

MARLEY. It is required of every man that the spirit within him should walk abroad among his fellow-men, and travel far and wide; and if that spirit goes not forth in life, it is condemned to do so after death. [MARLEY *screams again; a tragic scream; from his ghosty bones.*] I wear the chain I forged in life. I made it link by link, and yard by yard. Is its pattern strange to you? Or would you know, you, Scrooge, the weight and length of the strong coil you bear yourself? It was full as heavy and long as this, seven Christmas Eves ago. You have labored on it, since. It is a <u>ponderous</u> chain.

[*Terrified that a chain will appear about his body,* SCROOGE *spins and waves the unwanted chain away. None, of course, appears. Sees* MARLEY *watching him dance about the room.* MARLEY *watches* SCROOGE; *silently.*]

SCROOGE. Jacob. Old Jacob Marley, tell me more. Speak comfort to me, Jacob . . .

MARLEY. I have none to give. Comfort comes from other regions, Ebenezer Scrooge, and is conveyed by other ministers, to other kinds of men. A very little more, is all that is permitted to me. I cannot rest, I cannot stay, I cannot linger anywhere . . . [*He moans again.*] my spirit never walked beyond our countinghouse—mark me!—in life my spirit never roved beyond the narrow limits of our money-changing hole; and weary journeys lie before me!

SCROOGE. But you were always a good man of business, Jacob.

MARLEY. [*Screams word "business"; a flash-pot explodes with him.*] BUSINESS!!! Mankind was my business. The common welfare was my business; charity, mercy, forbearance, <u>benevolence</u>, were, all, my business. [SCROOGE *is quaking.*] Hear me, Ebenezer Scrooge! My time is nearly gone.

SCROOGE. I will, but don't be hard upon me. And don't be flowery, Jacob! Pray!

ponderous (pän´ dər əs) *adj.* very heavy; bulky

benevolence (bə nev´ ə ləns) *n.* kindliness

 **Reading Check**

Why does Marley visit Scrooge?

---

14. apparition (ap´ ə rish´ ən) *n.* ghost.

▲ **Critical Viewing** How does this actor's appearance compare to the description of Marley in the stage directions? **[Connect]**

MARLEY. How is it that I appear before you in a shape that you can see, I may not tell. I have sat invisible beside you many and many a day. That is no light part of my penance. I am here tonight to warn you that you have yet a chance and hope of escaping my fate. A chance and hope of my procuring, Ebenezer.

SCROOGE. You were always a good friend to me. Thank'ee!

MARLEY. You will be haunted by Three Spirits.

SCROOGE. Would that be the chance and hope you mentioned, Jacob?

MARLEY. It is.

SCROOGE. I think I'd rather not.

MARLEY. Without their visits, you cannot hope to shun the path I tread. Expect the first one tomorrow, when the bell tolls one.

SCROOGE. Couldn't I take 'em all at once, and get it over, Jacob?

MARLEY. Expect the second on the next night at the same hour. The third upon the next night when the last stroke of twelve has ceased to vibrate. Look to see me no more. Others may, but you may not. And look that, for your own sake, you remember what has passed between us!

[MARLEY *places his head back upon his shoulders. He approaches the window and beckons to* SCROOGE *to watch. Outside the window, specters fly by, carrying money-boxes and chains. They make a confused sound of lamentation.* MARLEY, *after listening a moment, joins into their mournful dirge. He leans to the window and floats out into the bleak, dark night. He is gone.*]

SCROOGE. [*Rushing to the window*] Jacob! No, Jacob! Don't leave me! I'm frightened!

[*He sees that* MARLEY *has gone. He looks outside. He pulls the shutter closed, so that the scene is blocked from his view. All sound stops. After a pause, he re-opens the shutter and all is quiet, as it should be on Christmas Eve. Carolers carol out of doors, in the distance.* SCROOGE *closes the shutter and walks down the stairs. He examines the door by which* MARLEY *first entered.*]

No one here at all! Did I imagine all that? Humbug! [*He looks about the room.*] I did imagine it. It only happened in my foulest dream-mind, didn't it? An undigested bit of . . .

[*Thunder and lightning in the room; suddenly*]

Sorry! Sorry!

[*There is silence again. The lights fade out.*]

Reading Strategy
Picturing the Action
What details in the stage directions help you envision the action? [**Connect**]

**Reading Check**
Who does Marley say is going to visit Scrooge?

Scene 4

[*Christmas music, choral, "Hark the Herald Angels Sing," sung by an onstage choir of children, spotlighted,* D.C. *Above,* SCROOGE *in his bed, dead to the world, asleep, in his darkened room. It should appear that the choir is singing somewhere outside of the house, of course, and a use of scrim[15] is thus suggested. When the singing is ended, the choir should fade out of view and* MARLEY *should fade into view, in their place.*]

MARLEY. [*Directly to audience*] From this point forth . . . I shall be quite visible to you, but invisible to him. [*Smiles*] He will feel my presence, nevertheless, for, unless my senses fail me completely, we are—you and I—witness to the changing of a miser: that one, my partner in life, in business, and in eternity: that one: Scrooge. [*Moves to staircase, below* SCROOGE] See him now. He endeavors to pierce the darkness with his ferret eyes.[16] [*To audience*] See him, now. He listens for the hour.

[*The bells toll.* SCROOGE *is awakened and quakes as the hour approaches one o'clock, but the bells stop their sound at the hour of twelve.*]

SCROOGE. [*Astonished*] Midnight! Why this isn't possible. It was past two when I went to bed. An icicle must have gotten into the clock's works! I couldn't have slept through the whole day and far into another night. It isn't possible that anything has happened to the sun, and this is twelve at noon! [*He runs to window; unshutters same; it is night.*] Night, still. Quiet, normal for the season, cold. It is certainly not noon. I cannot in any way afford to lose my days. Securities come due, promissory notes,[17] interest on investments: these are things that happen in the daylight! [*He returns to his bed.*] Was this a dream?

[MARLEY *appears in his room. He speaks to the audience.*]

MARLEY. You see? He does not, with faith, believe in me fully, even still! Whatever will it take to turn the faith of a miser from money to men?

SCROOGE. Another quarter and it'll be one and Marley's ghosty friends will come. [*Pauses; listens*] Where's the chime for one? [*Ding, dong*] A quarter past [*Repeats*] Half-past! [*Repeats*] A quarter to it! But where's the heavy bell of the hour one? This is a game in which I lose my senses! Perhaps, if I allowed myself another short doze . . .

---

15. **scrim** (skrim) *n.* light, semitransparent curtain.
16. **ferret eyes** a ferret is a small, weasellike animal used for hunting rabbits; this expression means to look persistently, the way a ferret hunts.
17. **promissory** (präm´ i sôr´ ē) **notes** written promises to pay someone a certain sum of money.

Reading Strategy
Picture the Action
Why is it helpful to have stage directions at the beginning of each scene?

Reading Strategy
Picturing the Action
Why are stage directions about Marley's appearances and disappearances especially important?

MARLEY . . . Doze, Ebenezer, doze.

[*A heavy bell thuds its one ring; dull and definitely one o'clock. There is a flash of light.* SCROOGE *sits up, in a sudden. A hand draws back the curtains by his bed. He sees it.*]

SCROOGE. A hand! Who owns it! Hello!

[*Ghosty music again, but of a new nature to the play. A strange figure stands before* SCROOGE—*like a child, yet at the same time like an old man: white hair, but unwrinkled skin, long, muscular arms, but delicate legs and feet. Wears white tunic; lustrous belt cinches waist. Branch of fresh green holly in its hand, but has its dress trimmed with fresh summer flowers. Clear jets of light spring from the crown of its head. Holds cap in hand. The Spirit is called* PAST.]

Are you the Spirit, sir, whose coming was foretold to me?

PAST. I am.

MARLEY. Does he take this to be a vision of his green grocer?

SCROOGE. Who, and what are you?

PAST. I am the Ghost of Christmas Past.

SCROOGE. Long past?

PAST. Your past.

SCROOGE. May I ask, please, sir, what business you have here with me?

PAST. Your welfare.

SCROOGE. Not to sound ungrateful, sir, and really, please do understand that I am plenty obliged for your concern, but, really, kind spirit, it would have done all the better for my welfare to have been left alone altogether, to have slept peacefully through this night.

PAST. Your reclamation, then. Take heed!

SCROOGE. My what?

PAST. [*Motioning to* SCROOGE *and taking his arm*] Rise! Fly with me! [*He leads* SCROOGE *to the window.*]

SCROOGE. [*Panicked*] Fly, but I am a mortal and cannot fly!

PAST. [*Pointing to his heart*] Bear but a touch of my hand here and you shall be upheld in more than this!

[SCROOGE *touches the spirit's heart and the lights dissolve into sparkly flickers. Lovely crystals of music are heard. The scene dissolves into another. Christmas music again*]

Scene 5

[SCROOGE *and the* GHOST OF CHRISTMAS PAST *walk together across an open stage. In the background, we see a field that is open; covered by*

Literary Analysis
Elements of Drama and Novel What details of this description probably come from the novel?

✔**Reading Check**

Who has appeared to Scrooge during Scene 4?

a soft, downy snow: a country road.]

SCROOGE. Good Heaven! I was bred in this place. I was a boy here!

[SCROOGE *freezes, staring at the field beyond.* MARLEY'S *ghost appears beside him; takes* SCROOGE'S *face in his hands, and turns his face to the audience.*]

MARLEY. You see this Scrooge: stricken by feeling. Conscious of a thousand odors floating in the air, each one connected with a thousand thoughts, and hopes, and joys, and care long, long forgotten. [*Pause*] This one—this Scrooge—before your very eyes, returns to life, among the living. [*To audience, sternly*] You'd best pay your most careful attention. I would suggest rapt.[18]

[*There is a small flash and puff of smoke and* MARLEY *is gone again.*]

PAST. Your lip is trembling, Mr. Scrooge. And what is that upon your cheek?

SCROOGE. Upon my cheek? Nothing . . . a blemish on the skin from the eating of overmuch grease . . . nothing . . . [*Suddenly*] Kind Spirit of Christmas Past, lead me where you will, but quickly! To be stagnant in this place is, for me, unbearable!

PAST. You recollect the way?

SCROOGE. Remember it! I would know it blindfolded! My bridge, my church, my winding river! [*Staggers about, trying to see it all at once. He weeps again.*]

PAST. These are but shadows of things that have been. They have no consciousness of us.

[*Four jocund travelers enter, singing a Christmas song in four-part harmony—"God Rest Ye Merry Gentlemen."*]

SCROOGE. Listen! I know these men! I know them! I remember the beauty of their song!

PAST. But, why do you remember it so happily? It is Merry Christmas that they say to one another! What is Merry Christmas to you, Mr. Scrooge? Out upon Merry Christmas, right? What good has Merry Christmas ever done you, Mr. Scrooge? . . .

SCROOGE. [*After a long pause*] None. No good. None . . . [*He bows his head.*]

PAST. Look, you, sir, a school ahead. The schoolroom is not quite deserted. A solitary child, neglected by his friends, is left there still.

[SCROOGE *falls to the ground; sobbing as he sees, and we see, a small boy, the young* SCROOGE, *sitting and weeping, bravely, alone at his desk: alone in a vast space, a void.*]

Literary Analysis
Elements of Drama Are Scrooge's emotions revealed more clearly through dialogue or stage directions at this point?

---

18. rapt (rapt) *adj.* giving complete attention; totally carried away by something.

SCROOGE. I cannot look on him!

PAST. You must, Mr. Scrooge, you must.

SCROOGE. It's me. [*Pauses; weeps*] Poor boy. He lived inside his head . . . alone . . . [*Pauses; weeps*] poor boy. [*Pauses; stops his weeping*] I wish . . . [*Dries his eyes on his cuff*] ah! it's too late!

PAST. What is the matter?

SCROOGE. There was a boy singing a Christmas Carol outside my door last night. I should like to have given him something: that's all.

PAST. [*Smiles; waves his hand to* SCROOGE] Come. Let us see another Christmas.

[*Lights out on little boy. A flash of light. A puff of smoke. Lights up on older boy*]

SCROOGE. Look! Me, again! Older now! [*Realizes*] Oh, yes . . . still alone.

[*The boy—a slightly older* SCROOGE—*sits alone in a chair, reading. The door to the room opens and a young girl enters. She is much, much younger than this slightly older* SCROOGE. *She is, say, six, and he is, say, twelve. Elder* SCROOGE *and the* GHOST OF CHRISTMAS PAST *stand watching the scene, unseen.*]

FAN. Dear, dear brother, I have come to bring you home.

BOY. Home, little Fan?

FAN. Yes! Home, for good and all! Father is so much kinder than he ever used to be, and home's like heaven! He spoke so gently to me one dear night when I was going to bed that I was not afraid to ask him once more if you might come home; and he said "yes" . . . you should; and sent me in a coach to bring you. And you're to be a man and are never to come back here, but first, we're to be together all the Christmas long, and have the merriest time in the world.

BOY. You are quite a woman, little Fan!

[*Laughing; she drags at boy, causing him to stumble to the door with her. Suddenly we hear a mean and terrible voice in the hallway, Off. It is the* SCHOOLMASTER.]

SCHOOLMASTER. Bring down Master Scrooge's travel box at once! He is to travel!

FAN. Who is that, Ebenezer?

BOY. O! Quiet, Fan. It is the Schoolmaster, himself!

[*The door bursts open and into the room bursts with it the* SCHOOLMASTER.]

SCHOOLMASTER. Master Scrooge?

BOY. Oh, Schoolmaster. I'd like you to meet my little sister, Fan, sir . . .

Reading Strategy
Picturing the Action
What abrupt change in Scrooge is shown through his action here?

Literary Analysis
Elements of Drama and Novel What additional information about Scrooge's family might be included in the novel? Why do you think it is not included here?

Reading Check

Where is Scrooge when his sister arrives to take him home?

[*Two boys struggle on with* SCROOGE'S *trunk.*]

FAN. Pleased, sir . . . [*She curtsies.*]

SCHOOLMASTER. You are to travel, Master Scrooge.

SCROOGE. Yes, sir. I know sir . . .

[*All start to exit, but* FAN *grabs the coattail of the mean old* SCHOOL-MASTER.]

BOY. Fan!

SCHOOLMASTER. What's this?

FAN. Pardon, sir, but I believe that you've forgotten to say your goodbye to my brother, Ebenezer, who stands still now awaiting it . . . [*She smiles, curtsies, lowers her eyes.*] pardon, sir.

SCHOOLMASTER. [*Amazed*] I . . . uh . . . harumph . . . uhh . . . well, then . . . [*Outstretches hand*] Goodbye, Scrooge.

BOY. Uh, well, goodbye, Schoolmaster . . .

[*Lights fade out on all but* BOY *looking at* FAN; *and* SCROOGE *and* PAST *looking at them.*]

SCROOGE. Oh, my dear, dear little sister, Fan . . . how I loved her.

PAST. Always a delicate creature, whom a breath might have withered, but she had a large heart . . .

SCROOGE. So she had.

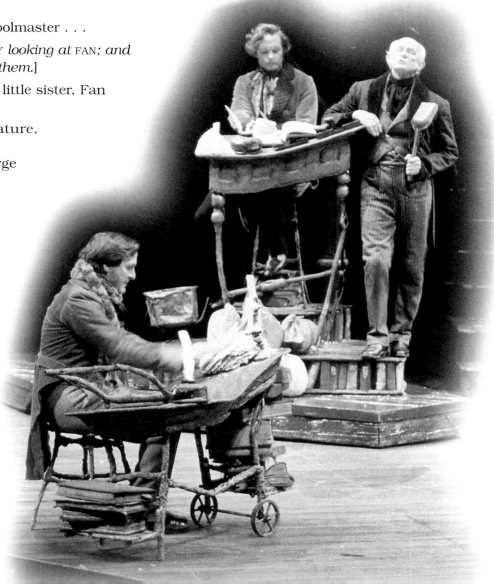

▶ **Critical Viewing**
Without knowing about the action of the scene, what can you infer about the relationship of the characters? **[Infer]**

PAST. She died a woman, and had, as I think, children.

SCROOGE. One child.

PAST. True. Your nephew.

SCROOGE. Yes.

PAST. Fine, then. We move on, Mr. Scrooge. That warehouse, there? Do you know it?

SCROOGE. Know it? Wasn't I apprenticed[19] there?

PAST. We'll have a look.

[*They enter the warehouse. The lights crossfade with them, coming up on an old man in Welsh wig:* FEZZIWIG.]

SCROOGE. Why, it's old Fezziwig! Bless his heart; it's Fezziwig, alive again!

[FEZZIWIG *sits behind a large, high desk, counting. He lays down his pen; looks at the clock: seven bells sound.*]

Quittin' time . . .

FEZZIWIG. Quittin' time . . . [*He takes off his waistcoat and laughs; calls off*] Yo ho, Ebenezer! Dick!

[DICK WILKINS *and* EBENEZER SCROOGE—*a young man version—enter the room.* DICK *and* EBENEZER *are* FEZZIWIG'S *apprentices.*]

SCROOGE. Dick Wilkins, to be sure! My fellow-'prentice! Bless my soul, yes. There he is. He was very much attached to me, was Dick. Poor Dick! Dear, dear!

FEZZIWIG. Yo ho, my boys. No more work tonight. Christmas Eve, Dick. Christmas, Ebenezer!

[*They stand at attention in front of* FEZZIWIG; *laughing*]

Hilli-ho! Clear away, and let's have lots of room here! Hilli-ho, Dick! Chirrup, Ebenezer!

[*The young men clear the room, sweep the floor, straighten the pictures, trim the lamps, etc. The space is clear now. A fiddler enters, fiddling.*]

Hi-ho, Matthew! Fiddle away . . . where are my daughters?

[*The fiddler plays. Three young daughters of* FEZZIWIG *enter followed by six young male suitors. They are dancing to the music. All employees come in: workers, clerks, housemaids, cousins, the baker, etc. All dance. Full number wanted here. Throughout the dance, food is brought into the feast. It is "eaten" in dance, by the dancers.* EBENEZER *dances with all three of the daughters, as does* DICK. *They compete for the daughters, happily, in the dance.* FEZZIWIG *dances with*

Reading Strategy
Picturing the Action How do you picture Scrooge as a young man?

Literary Analysis
Elements of Drama
Why are lengthy stage directions needed here?

Reading Check

Who is Fezziwig?

---

19. apprenticed (ə pren′ tist) *v.* receiving instruction in a trade as well as food and housing or wages in return for work.

his daughters. FEZZIWIG *dances with* DICK *and* EBENEZER. *The music changes:* MRS. FEZZIWIG *enters. She lovingly scolds her husband. They dance. She dances with* EBENEZER, *lifting him and throwing him about. She is enormously fat. When the dance is ended, they all dance off, floating away, as does the music.* SCROOGE *and the* GHOST OF CHRISTMAS PAST *stand alone now. The music is gone.*]

PAST. It was a small matter, that Fezziwig made those silly folks so full of gratitude.

SCROOGE. Small!

PAST. Shhh!

[*Lights up on* DICK *and* EBENEZER]

DICK. We are blessed, Ebenezer, truly, to have such a master as Mr. Fezziwig!

YOUNG SCROOGE. He is the best, best, the very and absolute best! If ever I own a firm of my own, I shall treat my apprentices with the same dignity and the same grace. We have learned a wonderful lesson from the master, Dick!

DICK. Ah, that's a fact, Ebenezer. That's a fact!

PAST. Was it not a small matter, really? He spent but a few pounds[20] of his mortal money on your small party. Three or four pounds, perhaps. Is that so much that he deserves such praise as you and Dick so lavish now?

SCROOGE. It isn't that! It isn't that, Spirit. Fezziwig had the power to make us happy or unhappy; to make our service light or burdensome; a pleasure or a toil. The happiness he gave is quite as great as if it cost him a fortune.

PAST. What is the matter?

SCROOGE. Nothing particular.

PAST. Something, I think.

SCROOGE. No, no. I should like to be able to say a word or two to my clerk just now! That's all!

[EBENEZER *enters the room and shuts down all the lamps. He stretches and yawns. The* GHOST OF CHRISTMAS PAST *turns to* SCROOGE; *all of a sudden.*]

PAST. My time grows short! Quick!

[*In a flash of light,* EBENEZER *is gone, and in his place stands an* OLDER SCROOGE, *this one a man in the prime of his life. Beside him stands a young woman in a mourning dress. She is crying. She speaks to the man, with hostility.*]

Literary Analysis
Elements of Drama What is revealed through dialogue about Scrooge's feelings for Fezziwig?

---

20. **pounds** (poundz) *n.* common type of money used in Great Britain.

WOMAN. It matters little . . . to you, very little. Another idol has displaced me.

MAN. What idol has displaced you?

WOMAN. A golden one.

MAN. This is an even-handed dealing of the world. There is nothing on which it is so hard as poverty; and there is nothing it professes to condemn with such severity as the pursuit of wealth!

WOMAN. You fear the world too much. Have I not seen your nobler aspirations fall off one by one, until the master-passion, Gain, engrosses you? Have I not?

SCROOGE. No!

MAN. What then? Even if I have grown so much wiser, what then? Have I changed towards you?

WOMAN. No . . .

MAN. Am I?

WOMAN. Our contract is an old one. It was made when we were both poor and content to be so. You *are* changed. When it was made, you were another man.

MAN. I was not another man: I was a boy.

WOMAN. Your own feeling tells you that you were not what you are. I am. That which promised happiness when we were one in heart is fraught with misery now that we are two . . .

SCROOGE. No!

WOMAN. How often and how keenly I have thought of this, I will not say. It is enough that I have thought of it, and can release you . . .

SCROOGE. [*Quietly*] Don't release me, madame . . .

MAN. Have I ever sought release?

WOMAN. In words. No. Never.

MAN. In what then?

WOMAN. In a changed nature; in an altered spirit. In everything that made my love of any worth or value in your sight. If this has never been between us, tell me, would you seek me out and try to win me now? Ah, no!

SCROOGE. Ah, yes!

MAN. You think not?

WOMAN. I would gladly think otherwise if I could, heaven knows! But if you were free today, tomorrow, yesterday, can even I believe that you would choose a dowerless girl[21]—you who in

Literary Analysis
Elements of Drama
What personality change in Scrooge is revealed in the dialogue?

Reading Check
What does the woman tell Scrooge about himself?

---

21. a dowerless (dou´ ər les) **girl** a girl without a dowry, the property or wealth a woman brought to her husband at marriage.

your very confidence with her weigh everything by Gain; or, choosing her, do I not know that your repentance and regret would surely follow? I do; and I release you. With a full heart, for the love of him you once were.

SCROOGE. Please, I . . . I . . .

MAN. Please, I . . . I . . .

WOMAN. Please. You may—the memory of what is past half makes me hope you will—have pain in this. A very, very brief time, and you will dismiss the memory of it, as an unprofitable dream, from which it happened well that you awoke. May you be happy in the life that you have chosen for yourself . . .

SCROOGE. No!

WOMAN. Yourself . . . alone . . .

SCROOGE. No!

WOMAN. Goodbye, Ebenezer . . .

SCROOGE. Don't let her go!

MAN. Goodbye.

SCROOGE. No!

[*She exits.* SCROOGE *goes to younger man: himself.*]

You fool! Mindless loon! You fool!

MAN. [*To exited woman*] Fool. Mindless loon. Fool . . .

SCROOGE. Don't say that! Spirit, remove me from this place.

PAST. I have told you these were shadows of the things that have been. They are what they are. Do not blame me, Mr. Scrooge.

SCROOGE. Remove me! I cannot bear it!

[*The faces of all who appeared in this scene are now projected for a moment around the stage: enormous, flimsy, silent.*]

Leave me! Take me back! Haunt me no longer!

[*There is a sudden flash of light: a flare. The* GHOST OF CHRISTMAS PAST *is gone.* SCROOGE *is, for the moment, alone onstage. His bed is turned down, across the stage. A small candle burns now in* SCROOGE'S *hand. There is a child's cap in his other hand. He slowly crosses the stage to his bed, to sleep.* MARLEY *appears behind* SCROOGE, *who continues his long, elderly cross to bed.* MARLEY *speaks directly to the audience.*]

MARLEY. Scrooge must sleep now. He must surrender to the irresistible drowsiness caused by the recognition of what was. [*Pauses*] The cap he carries is from ten lives past: his boyhood cap . . . donned atop a hopeful hairy head . . . askew, perhaps, or at

Literary Analysis
Elements of Drama
What do you learn about Scrooge's past from the dialogue here?

a rakish angle. Doffed now in honor of regret.[22] Perhaps even too heavy to carry in his present state of weak remorse . . .

[SCROOGE *drops the cap. He lies atop his bed. He sleeps. To audience*]

He sleeps. For him, there's even more trouble ahead. [*Smiles*] For you? The play house tells me there's hot cider, as should be your anticipation for the specter Christmas Present and Future, for I promise you both. [*Smiles again*] So, I pray you hurry back to your seats refreshed and ready for a miser—to turn his coat of gray into a blazen Christmas holly-red.

[*A flash of lightning. A clap of thunder. Bats fly. Ghosty music.* MARLEY *is gone.*]

---

22. donned . . . regret To *don* and *doff* a hat means to put it on and take it off, *askew* means "crooked," and *at a rakish angle* means "having a dashing or jaunty look."

Charles Dickens

(1812–1870)

Charles Dickens spent most of his life in London, England. When Dickens was twelve years old, his father was sent to jail for not paying his debts. For several months, young Charles did not attend school and worked in a factory for twelve hours a day, six days a week.

At age fifteen, Dickens went to work as a law clerk. Later, he became a reporter, and in 1833 he began writing humorous sketches for newspapers and magazines. His first serialized novel, *The Pickwick Papers*, met with huge success, bringing fame to Dickens at the age of twenty-four. His later novels, including *Oliver Twist* and *David Copperfield*, established Dickens as one of England's great novelists.

Review and Assess

Thinking About the Literature

1. **Respond:** In your opinion, what is the meanest thing Scrooge does in Act I? Explain your answer.

2. **(a) Recall:** Who is Jacob Marley? **(b) Analyze:** What clues does Marley give about his personality as a living person? **(c) Compare:** When Marley was living, in what ways were he and Scrooge alike?

3. **(a) Recall:** What scenes from his past does Scrooge visit? **(b) Compare and Contrast:** Which memories are happy ones and which are not? **(c) Draw Conclusions:** What does each event contribute to his current attitude and personality?

4. **(a) Recall:** What human visitors does Scrooge receive at the beginning of the act? **(b) Connect:** What similarities do you see in the purposes of all of the visitors? **(c) Generalize:** What is Scrooge's attitude toward other people?

5. **(a) Deduce:** What does Scrooge value? **(b) Evaluate:** Why isn't Scrooge a happy man?

6. **(a) Analyze:** What hints are given that Scrooge may change for the better? **(b) Assess:** Do you think people's personalities can change dramatically?

7. **(a) Deduce:** What effect have Scrooge's past experiences had on the person he has become? **(b) Take a Position:** Based on his past experiences, should Scrooge be excused for his current behavior? Explain.

Review and Assess

Literary Analysis

Elements of Drama

1. Give examples of **dialogue** that show the three character traits of the old Scrooge listed on the chart.

Character Trait	Dialogue
miserliness	
rudeness	
narrow-mindedness	

2. Find three examples of special effects in the **stage directions**. What does each contribute to the drama?

Connecting Literary Elements

3. List two details from the play that clearly have been added as part of the process of adapting the novel as a play. How do these details affect the drama?

4. Prepare a Venn diagram like the one shown. On your diagram, place the following characteristics in the appropriate spaces to show if they are unique to drama, unique to novels, or shared by both. **(a)** characters **(b)** stage directions **(c)** descriptions of setting **(d)** narrative point of view **(e)** plot developed through action and dialogue **(f)** plot developed through action, dialogue, and narration **(g)** theme

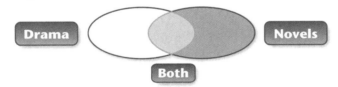

Drama — Both — Novels

Reading Strategy

Picturing the Action

5. Why are the stage directions necessary for you to envision Scrooge's reaction to his younger self alone in the schoolroom?

6. How do the stage directions help you picture the action at Fezziwig's party?

Extend Understanding

7. **Career Connection:** Name three ways in which the office where Scrooge and Cratchit work differs from a modern office.

Quick Review

Elements of **drama** include dialogue and stage directions. To review the elements of drama, see page 599.

A **dramatic adaptation of a novel** reworks the same story, setting, and characters for performance. To review adaptations, see page 599.

To **picture the action** of a drama, pay attention to details in the stage directions that set the scene and describe characters.

 Take It to the Net
www.phschool.com
Take the interactive self-test online to check your understanding of the selection.

Integrate Language Skills

Vocabulary Development Lesson

Word Analysis: Latin Root -bene-

The Latin word root *-bene-* (as in *benevolence*) means "good." Define each italicized word.

1. Exercise is *beneficial* to health.
2. We *benefited* from her wise advice.

Fluency: Word Choice

Write the following paragraph, filling in each blank with a vocabulary word.

The ___?___ beggar ___?___ the unhappy rich man to show some ___?___. "Don't be a ___?___ ! Helping others will make your troubles feel less ___?___. You won't feel so ___?___ if you let compassion fill the ___?___."

Spelling Strategy

Remembering the spelling of a root can help you spell words correctly. For example, if you know that *bene* is part of *beneficial*, you can easily recognize that *benificial* is incorrectly spelled. Unscramble the letters to spell other words that contain the root *bene*. (Unscramble *bene* first so you have fewer "mystery" letters to worry about.) Use each word in a sentence.

1. bleevenonce
2. beteinf
3. labeenfici

Grammar Lesson

The Active Voice

In sentences with verbs in the active voice, the subject is the "doer" of the action:

$$s$$
Active Voice: Marley <u>haunts</u> Scrooge.

In sentences with verbs in the passive voice, the receiver of the action is the subject of the sentence, and a form of the verb *to be* is added:

$$s$$
Passive Voice: Scrooge <u>is haunted</u> by Marley.

To produce clear, direct writing, use the active voice most of the time. Write sentences in which the subject *acts* rather than *is acted upon*.

▶ *For more practice, see page R28, Exercise C.*
Practice Revise the sentences with verbs in the passive voice, changing them to active voice.

1. A donation is given to the poor by Cratchit.
2. The poor are offered nothing by Scrooge.
3. Holiday spirit is enjoyed by the Cratchits.
4. The two men are left wondering.
5. Scrooge is visited by the Ghost of Christmas Past.

Writing Application Write a paragraph describing the action in one scene of *A Christmas Carol*. Use verbs in the active voice.

𝒲𝒢 *Prentice Hall Writing and Grammar Connection: Chapter 22, Section 2*

Extension Activities

Speaking and Listening In small groups, assign parts and then prepare and perform **readings of scenes** from *A Christmas Carol*. Take turns as performers and audience. Listeners should analyze the readings and provide feedback. **[Group Activity]**

Writing Write a **prose narrative** of one of the scenes in this act. Include dialogue and descriptions of characters as well as an account of events.

Prepare to Read

A Christmas Carol: Scrooge and Marley, Act II

Literary Analysis

Characterization

Characterization is the act of creating and developing a character. In drama, character traits—the qualities of characters—are revealed through what they say, what is said about them, and their own actions. As you read Act II, think about the following focus questions.

1. Where does dialogue show insights into character?
2. Where does an action or gesture show character?

Connecting Literary Elements

A character's **motives** are the reasons for his or her actions. Motives are usually related to what a character wants, needs, or feels. Common general motives are shown below.

- fear
- love
- greed
- honor

As you read, look for specific motives for characters' actions.

Reading Strategy

Asking Questions

To understand the traits, actions, and motives of characters, ask yourself questions.

- Why did the character do that?
- What did the character mean by that comment?
- How is the character feeling?

Use a chart like this one to jot down questions as you read Act II. Fill in the answers as you read further.

Q	
A	
Q	
A	
Q	
A	

Vocabulary Development

astonish (ə stän′ ish) v. amaze (p. 627)

compulsion (kəm pul′ shən) n. a driving, irresistible force (p. 629)

severe (sə vir′) adj. harsh (p. 629)

meager (mē′ gər) adj. of poor quality; small in amount (p. 631)

threadbare (thred′ ber′) adj. worn; shabby (p. 631)

audible (ô′ də bəl) adj. loud enough to be heard (p. 637)

gnarled (närld) adj. knotty and twisted (p. 638)

dispelled (dis peld′) v. scattered and driven away; made to vanish (p. 649)

A Christmas Carol: Scrooge and Marley

◆❖◆

Act II

Scene 1

[*Lights. Choral music is sung. Curtain.* SCROOGE, *in bed, sleeping, in spotlight. We cannot yet see the interior of his room.* MARLEY, *opposite, in spotlight equal to* SCROOGE'S. MARLEY *laughs. He tosses his hand in the air and a flame shoots from it, magically, into the air. There is a thunder clap, and then another; a lightning flash, and then another. Ghostly music plays under. Colors change.* MARLEY'S *spotlight has gone out and now reappears, with* MARLEY *in it, standing next to the bed and the sleeping* SCROOGE. MARLEY *addresses the audience directly.*]

MARLEY. Hear this snoring Scrooge! Sleeping to escape the nightmare that is his waking day. What shall I bring to him now? I'm afraid nothing would <u>astonish</u> old Scrooge now. Not after what he's seen. Not a baby boy, not a rhinoceros, nor anything in between would astonish Ebenezer Scrooge just now. I can think of nothing . . . [*Suddenly*] that's it! Nothing! [*He speaks confidentially.*] I'll have the clock strike one and, when he awakes expecting my second messenger, there will be no one . . . nothing. Then I'll have the bell strike twelve. And then one again . . . and then nothing. Nothing . . . [*Laughs*] nothing will . . . astonish him. I think it will work.

[*The bell tolls one.* SCROOGE *leaps awake.*]

SCROOGE. One! One! This is it: time! [*Looks about the room*] Nothing!

[*The bell tolls midnight.*]

Midnight! How can this be? I'm sleeping backwards.

[*One again*]

Good heavens! One again! I'm sleeping back and forth! [*A pause.* SCROOGE *looks about.*] Nothing! Absolutely nothing!

[*Suddenly, thunder and lightning.* MARLEY *laughs and disappears. The room shakes and glows. There is suddenly springlike music.* SCROOGE *makes a run for the door.*]

---

astonish (ə stän´ ish) *v.* amaze

Literary Analysis
Characterization How do Marley's actions suggest that he can be mischievous?

✔**Reading Check**

How does Marley try to surprise Scrooge?

MARLEY. Scrooge!

SCROOGE. What?

MARLEY. Stay you put!

SCROOGE. Just checking to see if anyone is in here.

[*Lights and thunder again: more music.* MARLEY *is of a sudden gone. In his place sits the* GHOST OF CHRISTMAS PRESENT—*to be called in the stage directions of the play,* PRESENT—*center of room. Heaped up on the floor, to form a kind of throne, are turkeys, geese, game, poultry, brawn, great joints of meat, suckling pigs, long wreaths of sausages, mince-pies, plum puddings, barrels of oysters, red hot chestnuts, cherry-cheeked apples, juicy oranges, luscious pears, immense twelfth cakes, and seething bowls of punch, that make the chamber dim with their delicious steam. Upon this throne sits* PRESENT, *glorious to see. He bears a torch, shaped as a Horn of Plenty.*[1] SCROOGE *hops out of the door, and then peeks back again into his bedroom.* PRESENT *calls to* SCROOGE.]

PRESENT. Ebenezer Scrooge. Come in, come in! Come in and know me better!

SCROOGE. Hello. How should I call you?

PRESENT. I am the Ghost of Christmas Present. Look upon me.

[PRESENT *is wearing a simple green robe. The walls around the room are now covered in greenery, as well. The room seems to be a perfect grove now: leaves of holly, mistletoe and ivy reflect the stage lights. Suddenly, there is a mighty roar of flame in the fireplace and now the hearth burns with a lavish, warming fire. There is an ancient scabbard girdling the* GHOST'S *middle, but without sword. The sheath is gone to rust.*]

You have never seen the like of me before?

SCROOGE. Never.

PRESENT. You have never walked forth with younger members of my family; my elder brothers born on Christmases past.

SCROOGE. I don't think I have. I'm afraid I've not. Have you had many brothers, Spirit?

▼ **Critical Viewing**
Which details of this costume are identified in the stage directions? **[Analyze]**

PRESENT. More than eighteen hundred.

SCROOGE. A tremendous family to provide for! [PRESENT *stands*] Spirit, conduct me where you will. I went forth last night on <u>compulsion</u>, and learnt a lesson which is working now. Tonight, if you have aught to teach me, let me profit by it.

PRESENT. Touch my robe.

[SCROOGE *walks cautiously to* PRESENT *and touches his robe. When he does, lightning flashes, thunder claps, music plays. Blackout*]

Scene 2

[PROLOGUE: MARLEY *stands spotlit,* L. *He speaks directly to the audience.*]

MARLEY. My ghostly friend now leads my living partner through the city's streets.

[*Lights up on* SCROOGE *and* PRESENT]

See them there and hear the music people make when the weather is <u>severe</u>, as it is now.

[*Winter music. Choral group behind scrim, sings. When the song is done and the stage is re-set, the lights will fade up on a row of shops, behind the singers. The choral group will hum the song they have just completed now and mill about the streets,[2] carrying their dinners to the bakers' shops and restaurants. They will, perhaps, sing about being poor at Christmastime, whatever.*]

PRESENT. These revelers, Mr. Scrooge, carry their own dinners to their jobs, where they will work to bake the meals the rich men and women of this city will eat as their Christmas dinners. Generous people these . . . to care for the others, so . . .

[PRESENT *walks among the choral group and a sparkling incense[3] falls from his torch on to their baskets, as he pulls the covers off of the baskets. Some of the choral group become angry with each other.*]

MAN #1. Hey, you, watch where you're going.

MAN #2. Watch it yourself, mate!

[PRESENT *sprinkles them directly, they change.*]

MAN #1. I pray go in ahead of me. It's Christmas. You be first!

MAN #2. No, no, I must insist that YOU be first!

---

2. **mill about the streets** walk around aimlessly.
3. **incense** (in´ sens) *n.* any of various substances that produce a pleasant odor when burned.

compulsion (kəm pul´ shən) *n.* a driving, irresistible force

severe (sə vir´) *adj.* harsh

Reading Check

What does the Ghost of Christmas Present show Scrooge?

MAN #1. All right, I shall be, and gratefully so.

MAN #2. The pleasure is equally mine, for being able to watch you pass, smiling.

MAN #1. I would find it a shame to quarrel on Christmas Day . . .

MAN #2. As would I.

MAN #1. Merry Christmas then, friend!

MAN #2. And a Merry Christmas straight back to you!

[*Church bells toll. The choral group enter the buildings: the shops and restaurants; they exit the stage, shutting their doors closed behind them. All sound stops.* SCROOGE *and* PRESENT *are alone again.*]

SCROOGE. What is it you sprinkle from your torch?

PRESENT. Kindness.

SCROOGE. Do you sprinkle your kindness on any particular people or on all people?

PRESENT. To any person kindly given. And to the very poor most of all.

SCROOGE. Why to the very poor most?

PRESENT. Because the very poor need it most. Touch my heart . . . here, Mr. Scrooge. We have another journey.

[SCROOGE *touches the* GHOST'S *heart and music plays, lights change color, lightning flashes, thunder claps. A choral group appears on the street, singing Christmas carols.*]

Scene 3

[MARLEY *stands spotlit in front of a scrim on which is painted the exterior of* CRATCHIT'S *four-roomed house. There is a flash and a clap and* MARLEY *is gone. The lights shift color again, the scrim flies away, and we are in the interior of the* CRATCHIT *family home.* SCROOGE *is there, with the* SPIRIT (PRESENT), *watching* MRS. CRATCHIT *set the table, with the help of* BELINDA CRATCHIT *and* PETER CRATCHIT, *a baby, pokes a fork into the mashed potatoes on his highchair's tray. He also chews on his shirt collar.*]

SCROOGE. What is this place, Spirit?

PRESENT. This is the home of your employee, Mr. Scrooge. Don't you know it?

SCROOGE. Do you mean Cratchit, Spirit? Do you mean this is Cratchit's home?

> **Literary Analysis**
> **Characterization** What do Scrooge's questions and reactions reveal about how his character is changing?

PRESENT. None other.

SCROOGE. These children are his?

PRESENT. There are more to come presently.

SCROOGE. On his <u>meager</u> earnings! What foolishness!

PRESENT. Foolishness, is it?

SCROOGE. Wouldn't you say so? Fifteen shillings[4] a week's what he gets!

PRESENT. I would say that he gets the pleasure of his family, fifteen times a week times the number of hours a day! Wait, Mr. Scrooge. Wait, listen and watch. You might actually learn something . . .

MRS. CRATCHIT. What has ever got your precious father then? And your brother, Tiny Tim? And Martha warn't as late last Christmas by half an hour!

[MARTHA *opens the door, speaking to her mother as she does.*]

MARTHA. Here's Martha, now, Mother! [*She laughs. The* CRATCHIT CHILDREN *squeal with delight.*]

BELINDA. It's Martha, Mother! Here's Martha!

PETER. Marthmama, Marthmama! Hullo!

BELINDA. Hurrah! Martha! Martha! There's such an enormous goose for us, Martha!

MRS. CRATCHIT. Why, bless your heart alive, my dear, how late you are!

MARTHA. We'd a great deal of work to finish up last night, and had to clear away this morning, Mother.

MRS. CRATCHIT. Well, never mind so long as you are come. Sit ye down before the fire, my dear, and have a warm, Lord bless ye!

BELINDA. No, no! There's Father coming. Hide, Martha, hide!

[MARTHA *giggles and hides herself.*]

MARTHA. Where? Here?

PETER. *Hide, hide!*

BELINDA. Not there! *THERE!*

[MARTHA *is hidden.* BOB CRATCHIT *enters, carrying* TINY TIM *atop his shoulder. He wears a* <u>threadbare</u> *and fringeless comforter hanging down in front of him.* TINY TIM *carries small crutches and his small legs are bound in an iron frame brace.*]

---

4. **Fifteen shillings** a small amount of money for a week's work.

meager (mē´ gər) *adj.* of poor quality; small in amount

Literary Analysis
Characterization What details show that the Cratchits are a loving, happy family?

threadbare (thred´ ber´) *adj.* worn; shabby

**Reading Check**

Whose home do Scrooge and the Ghost of Christmas Present visit?

BOB AND TINY TIM. Merry Christmas.

BOB. Merry Christmas my love, Merry Christmas Peter, Merry Christmas Belinda. Why, where is Martha?

MRS. CRATCHIT. Not coming.

BOB. Not coming: Not coming upon Christmas Day?

MARTHA. [*Pokes head out*] Ohhh, poor Father. Don't be disappointed.

BOB. What's this?

MARTHA. 'Tis I!

BOB. Martha! [*They embrace.*]

TINY TIM. Martha! Martha!

MARTHA. Tiny Tim!

[TINY TIM *is placed in* MARTHA'S *arms.* BELINDA *and* PETER *rush him offstage.*]

BELINDA. Come, brother! You must come hear the pudding singing in the copper.

TINY TIM. The pudding? What flavor have we?

PETER. Plum! Plum!

TINY TIM. Oh, Mother! I love plum!

[*The children exit the stage, giggling.*]

MRS. CRATCHIT. And how did little Tim behave?

BOB. As good as gold, and even better. Somehow he gets thoughtful sitting by himself so much, and thinks the strangest things you ever heard. He told me, coming home, that he hoped people saw him in the church, because he was a cripple, and it might be pleasant to them to remember upon Christmas Day, who made lame beggars walk and blind men see. [*Pauses*] He has the oddest ideas sometimes, but he seems all the while to be growing stronger and more hearty . . . one would never know. [*Hears* TIM'S *crutch on floor outside door*]

PETER. The goose has arrived to be eaten!

BELINDA. Oh, mama, mama, it's beautiful.

MARTHA. It's a perfect goose, Mother!

TINY TIM. To this Christmas goose, Mother and Father I say . . . [*Yells*] Hurrah! Hurrah!

OTHER CHILDREN. [*Copying* TIM] Hurrah! Hurrah!

[*The family sits round the table.* BOB *and* MRS. CRATCHIT *serve the trimmings, quickly. All sit; all bow heads; all pray.*]

Literary Analysis
Characterization What personality traits do members of the Cratchit family share?

BOB. Thank you, dear Lord, for your many gifts . . . our dear children; our wonderful meal; our love for one another; and the warmth of our small fire—[*Looks up at all*] A merry Christmas to us, my dear. God bless us!

ALL. [*Except* TIM] Merry Christmas! God bless us!

TINY TIM. [*In a short silence*] God bless us every one.

[*All freeze. Spotlight on* PRESENT *and* SCROOGE]

SCROOGE. Spirit, tell me if Tiny Tim will live.

PRESENT. I see a vacant seat . . . in the poor chimney corner, and a crutch without an owner, carefully preserved. If these shadows remain unaltered by the future, the child will die.

✓ **Reading Check**

What is wrong with Tiny Tim?

▼ **Critical Viewing** Why might a director stage the scene this way, with Tiny Tim standing on the table? [**Interpret**]

SCROOGE. No, no, kind Spirit! Say he will be spared!

PRESENT. If these shadows remain unaltered by the future, none other of my race will find him here. What then? If he be like to die, he had better do it, and decrease the surplus population.

[SCROOGE *bows his head. We hear* BOB'S *voice speak* SCROOGE'S *name.*]

BOB. Mr. Scrooge . . .

SCROOGE. Huh? What's that? Who calls?

BOB. [*His glass raised in a toast*] I'll give you Mr. Scrooge, the Founder of the Feast!

SCROOGE. Me, Bob? You toast *me*?

PRESENT. Save your breath, Mr. Scrooge. You can't be seen or heard.

MRS. CRATCHIT. The Founder of the Feast, indeed! I wish I had him here, that miser Scrooge. I'd give him a piece of my mind to feast upon, and I hope he'd have a good appetite for it!

BOB. My dear! Christmas Day!

MRS. CRATCHIT. It should be Christmas Day, I am sure, on which one drinks the health of such an odious, stingy, unfeeling man as Mr. Scrooge . . .

SCROOGE. Oh, Spirit, must I? . . .

MRS. CRATCHIT. You know he is, Robert! Nobody knows it better than you do, poor fellow!

BOB. This is Christmas Day, and I should like to drink to the health of the man who employs me and allows me to earn my living and our support and that man is Ebenezer Scrooge . . .

MRS. CRATCHIT. I'll drink to his health for your sake and the day's, but not for his sake . . . a Merry Christmas and a Happy New Year to you, Mr. Scrooge, wherever you may be this day!

▼ **Critical Viewing**
Martha plays a lute like the one below while her family sings. If this play were set in contemporary times, what instrument would Martha probably play? **[Analyze]**

SCROOGE. Just here, kind madam . . . out of sight, out of sight . . .

BOB. Thank you, my dear. Thank you.

SCROOGE. Thank *you*, Bob . . . and Mrs. Cratchit, too. No one else is toasting me, . . . not now . . . not ever. Of that I am sure . . .

BOB. Children . . .

ALL. Merry Christmas to Mr. Scrooge.

BOB. I'll pay you sixpence, Tim, for my favorite song.

TINY TIM. Oh, Father, I'd so love to sing it, but not for pay. This Christmas goose—this feast—you and Mother, my brother and sisters close with me: that's my pay—

BOB. Martha, will you play the notes on the lute,[5] for Tiny Tim's song.

BELINDA. May I sing, too, Father?

BOB. We'll all sing.

[*They sing a song about a tiny child lost in the snow—probably from Wordsworth's poem.* TIM *sings the lead vocal; all chime in for the chorus. Their song fades under, as the* GHOST OF CHRISTMAS PRESENT *speaks.*]

PRESENT. Mark my words, Ebenezer Scrooge. I do not present the Cratchits to you because they are a handsome, or brilliant family. They are not handsome. They are not brilliant. They are not well-dressed, or tasteful to the times. Their shoes are not even waterproofed by virtue of money or cleverness spent. So when the pavement is wet, so are the insides of their shoes and the tops of their toes. These are the Cratchits, Mr. Scrooge. They are not highly special. They are happy, grateful, pleased with one another, contented with the time and how it passes. They don't sing very well, do they? But, nonetheless, they do sing . . . [*Pauses*] think of that, Scrooge. Fifteen shillings a week and they do sing . . . hear their song until its end.

SCROOGE. I am listening.

[*The chorus sings full volume now, until . . . the song ends here.*]

Spirit, it must be time for us to take our leave. I feel in my heart that it is . . . that I must think on that which I have seen here . . .

PRESENT. Touch my robe again . . .

[SCROOGE *touches* PRESENT'S *robe. The lights fade out on the* CRATCHITS, *who sit, frozen, at the table.* SCROOGE *and* PRESENT *in a spotlight now. Thunder, lightning, smoke. They are gone.*]

Reading Strategy
Ask Questions Ask yourself the question Scrooge is asking himself: Why do the Cratchits sing even though they are poor? What will Scrooge learn about the Cratchits when he figures out the answer?

Reading Check

What does Scrooge observe the Cratchits doing?

Scene 4

[MARLEY *appears* D.L. *in single spotlight. A storm brews. Thunder and lightning.* SCROOGE *and* PRESENT *"fly" past,* U. *The storm continues, furiously, and, now and again,* SCROOGE *and* PRESENT *will zip past in their travels.* MARLEY *will speak straight out to the audience.*]

MARLEY. The Ghost of Christmas Present, my co-worker in this attempt to turn a miser, flies about now with that very miser, Scrooge, from street to street, and he points out partygoers on their way to Christmas parties. If one were to judge from the numbers of people on their way to friendly gatherings, one might think that no one was left at home to give anyone welcome . . . but that's not the case, is it? Every home is expecting company and . . . [*He laughs.*] Scrooge is amazed.

[SCROOGE *and* PRESENT *zip past again. The lights fade up around them. We are in the* NEPHEW's *home, in the living room.* PRESENT *and* SCROOGE *stand watching the* NEPHEW: FRED *and his wife, fixing the fire.*]

SCROOGE. What is this place? We've moved from the mines!

PRESENT. You do not recognize them?

SCROOGE. It is my nephew! . . . and the one he married . . .

[MARLEY *waves his hand and there is a lightning flash. He disappears.*]

FRED. It strikes me as sooooo funny, to think of what he said . . . that Christmas was a humbug, as I live! He believed it!

WIFE. More shame for him, Fred!

FRED. Well, he's a comical old fellow, that's the truth.

WIFE. I have no patience with him.

FRED. Oh, I have! I am sorry for him; I couldn't be angry with him if I tried. Who suffers by his ill whims? Himself, always . . .

SCROOGE. It's me they talk of, isn't it, Spirit?

FRED. Here, wife, consider this. Uncle Scrooge takes it into his head to dislike us, and he won't come and dine with us. What's the consequence?

WIFE. Oh . . . you're sweet to say what I think you're about to say, too, Fred . . .

FRED. What's the consequence? He don't lose much of a dinner by it, I can tell you that!

WIFE. Ooooooo, Fred! Indeed, I think he loses a very good dinner . . . ask my sisters, or your bachelor friend, Topper . . . ask any of them. They'll tell you what old Scrooge, your uncle, missed: a dandy meal!

FRED. Well, that's something of a relief, wife. Glad to hear it! [*He hugs his wife. They laugh. They kiss.*] The truth is, he misses much yet. I mean to give him the same chance every year, whether he likes it or not, for I pity him. Nay, he is my only uncle and I feel for the old miser . . . but, I tell you, wife: I see my dear and perfect mother's face on his own wizened cheeks and brow: brother and sister they were, and I cannot erase that from each view of him I take . . .

WIFE. I understand what you say, Fred, and I am with you in your yearly asking. But he never will accept, you know. He never will.

FRED. Well, true, wife. Uncle may rail at Christmas till he dies. I think I shook him some with my visit yesterday . . . [*Laughing*] I refused to grow angry . . . no matter how nasty he became . . . [*Whoops*] It was HE who grew angry, wife! [*They both laugh now.*]

SCROOGE. What he says is true, Spirit . . .

FRED AND WIFE. Bah, humbug!

FRED. [*Embracing his wife*] There is much laughter in our marriage, wife. It pleases me. You please me . . .

WIFE. And you please me, Fred. You are a good man . . . [*They embrace.*] Come now. We must have a look at the meal . . . our guests will soon arrive . . . my sisters, Topper . . .

FRED. A toast first . . . [*He hands her a glass.*] A toast to Uncle Scrooge . . . [*Fills their glasses*]

WIFE. A toast to him?

FRED. Uncle Scrooge has given us plenty of merriment, I am sure, and it would be ungrateful not to drink to his health. And I say . . . Uncle Scrooge!

WIFE. [*Laughing*] You're a proper loon,[6] Fred . . . and I'm a proper wife to you . . . [*She raises her glass.*] Uncle Scrooge! [*They drink. They embrace. They kiss.*]

SCROOGE. Spirit, please, make me visible! Make me <u>audible</u>! I want to talk with my nephew and my niece!

[*Calls out to them. The lights that light the room and* FRED *and wife fade out.* SCROOGE *and* PRESENT *are alone, spotlit.*]

PRESENT. These shadows are gone to you now, Mr. Scrooge. You may return to them later tonight in your dreams. [*Pauses*] My time grows short, Ebenezer Scrooge. Look you on me! Do you see how I've aged?

SCROOGE. Your hair has gone gray! Your skin, wrinkled! Are spirits' lives so short?

---

6. **a proper loon** a silly person.

A Christmas Carol: Scrooge and Marley, Act II ◆ 637

Literary Analysis
Character and Motive
What is Fred's motive for inviting Scrooge every year?

Literary Analysis
Characterization What does the dialogue show about Fred's personality?

audible (ô′ də bəl) *adj.* loud enough to be heard

✔**Reading Check**
What scenes does Christmas Present show Scrooge?

PRESENT. My stay upon this globe is very brief. It ends tonight.

SCROOGE. Tonight?

PRESENT. At midnight. The time is drawing near!

[*Clock strikes 11:45.*]

Hear those chimes? In a quarter hour, my life will have been spent! Look, Scrooge, man. Look you here.

[*Two gnarled baby dolls are taken from* PRESENT'S *skirts.*]

SCROOGE. Who are they?

PRESENT. They are Man's children, and they cling to me, appealing from their fathers. The boy is Ignorance; the girl is Want. Beware them both, and all of their degree, but most of all beware this boy, for I see that written on his brow which is doom, unless the writing be erased. [*He stretches out his arm. His voice is now amplified: loudly and oddly.*]

SCROOGE. Have they no refuge or resource?

PRESENT. Are there no prisons? Are there no workhouses? [*Twelve chimes*] Are there no prisons? Are there no workhouses?

[*A* PHANTOM, *hooded, appears in dim light,* D., *opposite.*]

Are there no prisons? Are there no workhouses?

[PRESENT *begins to deliquesce.* SCROOGE *calls after him.*]

SCROOGE. Spirit, I'm frightened! Don't leave me! Spirit!

PRESENT. Prisons? Workhouses? Prisons? Workhouses . . .

[*He is gone.* SCROOGE *is alone now with the* PHANTOM, *who is, of course, the* GHOST OF CHRISTMAS FUTURE. *The* PHANTOM *is shrouded in black. Only its outstretched hand is visible from under his ghostly garment.*]

SCROOGE. Who are you, Phantom? Oh, yes, I think I know you! You are, are you not, the Spirit of Christmas Yet to Come? [*No reply*] And you are about to show me the shadows of the things that have not yet happened, but will happen in time before us. Is that not so, Spirit?

[*The* PHANTOM *allows* SCROOGE *a look at his face. No other reply wanted here. A nervous giggle here.*]

Oh, Ghost of the Future, I fear you more than any Specter I have seen! But, as I know that your purpose is to do me good and as I hope to live to be another man from what I was, I am prepared to bear you company.

[FUTURE *does not reply, but for a stiff arm, hand and finger set, pointing forward.*]

gnarled (närld) *adj.* knotty and twisted

Literary Analysis
Characterization and Motive How do Scrooge's motives for welcoming the spirit indicate a change in his character?

Lead on, then, lead on. The night is waning fast, and it is precious time to me. Lead on, Spirit!

[FUTURE *moves away from* SCROOGE *in the same rhythm and motion employed at its arrival.* SCROOGE *falls into the same pattern, a considerable space apart from the* SPIRIT. *In the space between them,* MARLEY *appears. He looks to* FUTURE *and then to* SCROOGE. *He claps his hands. Thunder and lightning. Three* BUSINESSMEN *appear, spotlighted singularly: One is* D.L.; *one is* D.R.; *one is* U.C. *Thus, six points of the stage should now be spotted in light.* MARLEY *will watch this scene from his position,* C. SCROOGE *and* FUTURE *are* R. *and* L. *of* C.]

FIRST BUSINESSMAN. Oh, no, I don't know much about it either way, I only know he's dead.

SECOND BUSINESSMAN. When did he die?

FIRST BUSINESSMAN. Last night, I believe.

SECOND BUSINESSMAN. Why, what was the matter with him? I thought he'd never die, really . . .

FIRST BUSINESSMAN. [*Yawning*] Goodness knows, goodness knows . . .

THIRD BUSINESSMAN. What has he done with his money?

SECOND BUSINESSMAN. I haven't heard. Have you?

FIRST BUSINESSMAN. Left it to his Company, perhaps. Money to money; you know the expression . . .

THIRD BUSINESSMAN. He hasn't left it to me. That's all I know . . .

FIRST BUSINESSMAN. [*Laughing*] Nor to me . . . [*Looks at* SECOND BUSINESSMAN] You, then? You got his money???

SECOND BUSINESSMAN. [*Laughing*] Me, me, his money? Nooooo! [*They all laugh.*]

THIRD BUSINESSMAN. It's likely to be a cheap funeral, for upon my life, I don't know of a living soul who'd care to venture to it. Suppose we make up a party and volunteer?

SECOND BUSINESSMAN. I don't mind going if a lunch is provided, but I must be fed, if I make one.

FIRST BUSINESSMAN. Well, I am the most disinterested among you, for I never wear black gloves, and I never eat lunch. But I'll offer to go, if anybody else will. When I come to think of it, I'm not all sure that I wasn't his most particular friend; for we used to stop and speak whenever we met. Well, then . . . bye, bye!

SECOND BUSINESSMAN. Bye, bye . . .

THIRD BUSINESSMAN. Bye, bye . . .

[*They glide offstage in three separate directions. Their lights follow them.*]

Literary Analysis
Characterization and Motive What is each character's motive for attending the funeral?

Reading Check

What warning does the Ghost of Christmas Present give Scrooge?

SCROOGE. Spirit, why did you show me this? Why do you show me businessmen from my streets as they take the death of Jacob Marley. That is a thing past. You are *future!*

[JACOB MARLEY *laughs a long, deep laugh. There is a thunder clap and lightning flash, and he is gone.* SCROOGE *faces* FUTURE, *alone on stage now.* FUTURE *wordlessly stretches out his arm-hand-and-finger-set, pointing into the distance,* U. *There, above them. Scoundrels "fly" by, half-dressed and slovenly. When this scene has passed, a woman enters the playing area. She is almost at once followed by a second woman; and then a man in faded black; and then, suddenly, an old man, who smokes a pipe. The old man scares the other three. They laugh, anxious.*]

FIRST WOMAN. Look here, old Joe, here's a chance! If we haven't all three met here without meaning it!

OLD JOE. You couldn't have met in a better place. Come into the parlor. You were made free of it long ago, you know; and the other two an't strangers [*He stands; shuts a door. Shrieking*] We're all suitable to our calling. We're well matched. Come into the parlor. Come into the parlor . . .

[*They follow him* D. SCROOGE *and* FUTURE *are now in their midst, watching; silent. A truck comes in on which is set a small wall with fireplace and a screen of rags, etc. All props for the scene.*]

Let me just rake this fire over a bit . . .

[*He does. He trims his lamp with the stem of his pipe. The* FIRST WOMAN *throws a large bundle on to the floor. She sits beside it crosslegged, defiantly.*]

FIRST WOMAN. What odds then? What odds, Mrs. Dilber? Every person has a right to take care of themselves. HE always did!

MRS. DILBER. That's true indeed! No man more so!

FIRST WOMAN. Why, then, don't stand staring as if you was afraid, woman! Who's the wiser? We're not going to pick holes in each other's coats, I suppose?

MRS. DILBER. No, indeed! We should hope not!

FIRST WOMAN. Very well, then! That's enough. Who's the worse for the loss of a few things like these? Not a dead man, I suppose?

MRS. DILBER. [*Laughing*] No, indeed!

FIRST WOMAN. If he wanted to keep 'em after he was dead, the wicked old screw, why wasn't he natural in his lifetime? If he had been, he'd have had somebody to look after him when he was struck with Death, instead of lying gasping out his last there, alone by himself.

MRS. DILBER. It's the truest word that was ever spoke. It's a judgment on him.

FIRST WOMAN. I wish it were a heavier one, and it should have been, you may depend on it, if I could have laid my hands on anything else. Open that bundle, old Joe, and let me know the value of it. Speak out plain. I'm not afraid to be the first, nor afraid for them to see it. We knew pretty well that we were helping ourselves, before we met here, I believe. It's no sin. Open the bundle, Joe.

FIRST MAN. No, no, my dear! I won't think of letting you being the first to show what you've . . . earned . . . earned from this. I throw in mine. [*He takes a bundle from his shoulder, turns it upside down, and empties its contents out on to the floor.*] It's not very extensive, see . . . seals . . . a pencil case . . . sleeve buttons . . .

MRS. DILBER. Nice sleeve buttons, though . . .

FIRST MAN. Not bad, not bad . . . a brooch there . . .

OLD JOE. Not really valuable, I'm afraid . . .

FIRST MAN. How much, old Joe?

OLD JOE. [*Writing on the wall with chalk*] A pitiful lot, really. Ten and six and not a sixpence more!

FIRST MAN. You're not serious!

OLD JOE. That's your account and I wouldn't give another sixpence if I was to be boiled for not doing it. Who's next?

MRS. DILBER. Me! [*Dumps out contents of her bundle*] Sheets, towels, silver spoons, silver sugar-tongs . . . some boots . . .

OLD JOE. [*Writing on wall*] I always give too much to the ladies. It's a weakness of mine and that's the way I ruin myself. Here's your total comin' up . . . two pounds-ten . . . if you asked me for another penny, and made it an open question, I'd repent of being so liberal and knock off half-a-crown.

FIRST WOMAN. And now do MY bundle, Joe.

OLD JOE. [*Kneeling to open knots on her bundle*] So many knots, madam . . . [*He drags out large curtains; dark*] What do you call this? Bed curtains!

FIRST WOMAN. [*Laughing*] Ah, yes, bed curtains!

OLD JOE. You don't mean to say you took 'em down, rings and all, with him lying there?

FIRST WOMAN. Yes, I did, why not?

OLD JOE. You were born to make your fortune and you'll certainly do it.

FIRST WOMAN. I certainly shan't hold my hand, when I can get anything in it by reaching it out, for the sake of such a man as he

Reading Strategy
Ask Questions Ask yourself why the characters are so cold and unfeeling toward the deceased. What answer do you think you will find?

Literary Analysis
Characterizations What details indicate that each character in this group is greedy?

Reading Check
What does Scrooge think the spirit is showing him?

was, I promise you, Joe. Don't drop that lamp oil on those blankets, now!

OLD JOE. His blankets?

FIRST WOMAN. Whose else's do you think? He isn't likely to catch cold without 'em, I daresay.

OLD JOE. I hope that he didn't die of anything catching? Eh?

FIRST WOMAN. Don't you be afraid of that. I ain't so fond of his company that I'd loiter about him for such things if he did. Ah! You may look through that shirt till your eyes ache, but you won't find a hole in it, nor a threadbare place. It's the best he had, and a fine one, too. They'd have wasted it, if it hadn't been for me.

OLD JOE. What do you mean 'They'd have wasted it?'

FIRST WOMAN. Putting it on him to be buried in, to be sure. Somebody was fool enough to do it, but I took it off again . . . [*She laughs, as do they all, nervously.*] If calico[7] ain't good enough for such a purpose, it isn't good enough then for anything. It's quite as becoming to the body. He can't look uglier than he did in that one!

SCROOGE. [*A low-pitched moan emits from his mouth; from the bones.*] OOOOOOOooooOOOOOooooOOOOOOOOooooOOOOOOooooOO!

OLD JOE. One pound six for the lot. [*He produces a small flannel bag filled with money. He divvies it out. He continues to pass around the money as he speaks. All are laughing.*] That's the end of it, you see! He frightened every one away from him while he was alive, to profit us when he was dead! Hah ha ha!

ALL. HAHAHAHAhahahahahahah!

SCROOGE. OOOoooOOOoooOOoooOOOooo OOoooOOoooOOOooo! [*He screams at them.*] Obscene demons! Why not market the corpse itself, as sell its trimming??? [*Suddenly*] Oh, Spirit, I see it, I see it! This unhappy man—this stripped-bare corpse . . . could very well be my own. My life holds parallel! My life ends that way now!

[SCROOGE *backs into something in the dark behind his spotlight.* SCROOGE *looks at* FUTURE, *who points to the corpse.* SCROOGE *pulls back the blanket. The corpse is, of course,* SCROOGE, *who screams. He falls aside the bed; weeping.*]

Spirit, this is a fearful place. In leaving it, I shall not leave its lesson, trust me. Let us go!

[FUTURE *points to the corpse.*]

Spirit, let me see some tenderness connected with a death, or that dark chamber, which we just left now, Spirit, will be forever present to me.

---

7. **calico** (kal′ ə kō) *n.* coarse and cheap cloth.

Literary Analysis
Characterization What do you learn about the character who has died from what these other characters say about him?

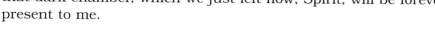

[FUTURE *spreads his robes again. Thunder and lightning. Lights up,* U., *in the* CRATCHIT *home setting.* MRS. CRATCHIT *and her daughters, sewing*]

TINY TIM'S VOICE. [*Off*] And He took a child and set him in the midst of them.

SCROOGE. [*Looking about the room; to* FUTURE] Huh? Who spoke? Who said that?

MRS. CRATCHIT. [*Puts down her sewing*] The color hurts my eyes. [*Rubs her eyes*] That's better. My eyes grow weak sewing by candlelight. I shouldn't want to show your father weak eyes when he comes home . . . not for the world! It must be near his time . . .

PETER. [*In corner, reading. Looks up from book*] Past it, rather. But I think he's been walking a bit slower than usual these last few evenings, Mother.

MRS. CRATCHIT. I have known him walk with . . . [*Pauses*] I have know him walk with Tiny Tim upon his shoulder and very fast indeed.

PETER. So have I, Mother! Often!

✔ **Reading Check**

Whose corpse does Scrooge see?

▼ **Critical Viewing** Why might a director choose to place the actors playing the Cratchits this way? What does their position reveal about their family? **[Analyze]**

DAUGHTER. So have I.

MRS. CRATCHIT. But he was very light to carry and his father loved him so, that it was not trouble—no trouble.

[BOB, *at door*]

And there is your father at the door.

[BOB CRATCHIT *enters. He wears a comforter. He is cold, forlorn.*]

PETER. Father!

BOB. Hello, wife, children . . .

[*The daughter weeps; turns away from* CRATCHIT.]

Children! How good to see you all! And you, wife. And look at this sewing! I've no doubt, with all your industry, we'll have a quilt to set down upon our knees in church on Sunday!

MRS. CRATCHIT. You made the arrangements today, then, Robert, for the . . . service . . . to be on Sunday.

BOB. The funeral. Oh, well, yes, yes, I did. I wish you could have gone. It would have done you good to see how green a place it is. But you'll see it often. I promised him that I would walk there on Sunday, after the service. [*Suddenly*] My little, little child! My little child!

ALL CHILDREN. [*Hugging him*] Oh, Father . . .

BOB. [*He stands*] Forgive me. I saw Mr. Scrooge's nephew, who you know I'd just met once before, and he was so wonderful to me, wife . . . he is the most pleasant-spoken gentleman I've ever met . . . he said "I am heartily sorry for it and heartily sorry for your good wife. If I can be of service to you in any way, here's where I live." And he gave me this card.

PETER. Let me see it!

BOB. And he looked me straight in the eye, wife, and said, meaningfully, "I pray you'll come to me, Mr. Cratchit, if you need some help. I pray you do." Now it wasn't for the sake of anything that he might be able to do for us, so much as for his kind way. It seemed as if he had known our Tiny Tim and felt with us.

MRS. CRATCHIT. I'm sure that he's a good soul.

BOB. You would be surer of it, my dear, if you saw and spoke to him. I shouldn't be at all surprised, if he got Peter a situation.

MRS. CRATCHIT. Only hear that, Peter!

MARTHA. And then, Peter will be keeping company with someone and setting up for himself!

PETER. Get along with you!

Literary Analysis
Characterization What do Bob Cratchit's words reveal about the character of Fred (Scrooge's nephew)?

BOB. It's just as likely as not, one of these days, though there's plenty of time for that, my dear. But however and whenever we part from one another, I am sure we shall none of us forget poor Tiny Tim—shall we?—or this first parting that was among us?

ALL CHILDREN. Never, Father, never!

BOB. And when we recollect how patient and mild he was, we shall not quarrel easily among ourselves, and forget poor Tiny Tim in doing it.

ALL CHILDREN. No, Father, never!

LITTLE BOB. I am very happy, I am, I am, I am very happy.

[BOB *kisses his little son, as does* MRS. CRATCHIT, *as do the other children. The family is set now in one sculptural embrace. The lighting fades to a gentle pool of light, tight on them.*]

SCROOGE. Specter, something informs me that our parting moment is at hand. I know it, but I know not how I know it.

[FUTURE *points to the other side of the stage. Lights out on* CRATCHITS. FUTURE *moves slowing, gliding.* SCROOGE *follows.* FUTURE *points opposite.* FUTURE *leads* SCROOGE *to a wall and a tombstone. He points to the stone.*]

Am *I* that man those ghoulish parasites[8] so gloated over? [*Pauses*] Before I draw nearer to that stone to which you point, answer me one question. Are these the shadows of things that will be, or the shadows of things that MAY be, only?

[FUTURE *points to the gravestone.* MARLEY *appears in light well* U. *He points to grave as well. Gravestone turns front and grows to ten feet high. Words upon it:* EBENEZER SCROOGE: *Much smoke billows now from the grave. Choral music here.* SCROOGE *stands looking up at gravestone.* FUTURE *does not at all reply in mortals' words, but points once more to the gravestone. The stone undulates and glows. Music plays, beckoning* SCROOGE. SCROOGE *reeling in terror*]

Oh, no. Spirit! Oh, no, no!

[FUTURE'S *finger still pointing*]

Spirit! Hear me! I am not the man I was. I will not be the man I would have been but for this intercourse. Why show me this, if I am past all hope?

[FUTURE *considers* SCROOGE'S *logic. His hand wavers.*]

Oh, Good Spirit, I see by your wavering hand that your good nature intercedes for me and pities me. Assure me that I yet may

8. **ghoulish parasites** (gōōl′ ish par′ ə sĭts) man and women who stole and divided Scrooge's goods after he died.

> **Literary Analysis**
> **Characterization** What do the characters' words reveal about Tiny Tim's character?

change these shadows that you have shown me by an altered life!

[FUTURE's *hand trembles; pointing has stopped.*]

I will honor Christmas in my heart and try to keep it all the year. I will live in the Past, the Present, and the Future. The Spirits of all Three shall strive within me. I will not shut out the lessons that they teach. Oh, tell me that I may sponge away the writing that is upon this stone!

Reading Strategy
Ask Questions What does Scrooge mean by this promise?

[SCROOGE *makes a desperate stab at grabbing* FUTURE'S *hand. He holds firm for a moment, but* FUTURE, *stronger than* SCROOGE, *pulls away.* SCROOGE *is on his knees, praying.*]

Spirit, dear Spirit, I am praying before you. Give me a sign that all is possible. Give me a sign that all hope for me is not lost. Oh, Spirit, kind Spirit, I beseech thee: give me a sign . . .

[FUTURE *deliquesces, slowly, gently. The* PHANTOM'S *hood and robe drop gracefully to the ground in a small heap. Music in. There is nothing in them. They are mortal cloth. The* SPIRIT *is elsewhere.* SCROOGE *has his sign.* SCROOGE *is alone. Tableau. The lights fade to black.*]

◀ **Critical Viewing** How does Scrooge's costume reveal the change in his character? [**Compare and Contrast**]

Scene 5

[*The end of it.* MARLEY, *spotlighted, opposite* SCROOGE, *in his bed, spotlighted.* MARLEY *speaks to audience, directly.*]

MARLEY. [*He smiles at* SCROOGE:] The firm of Scrooge and Marley is doubly blessed; two misers turned; one, alas, in Death, too late; but the other miser turned in Time's penultimate nick.[9] Look you on my friend, Ebenezer Scrooge . . .

SCROOGE. [*Scrambling out of bed; reeling in delight*] I will live in the Past, in the Present, and in the Future! The Spirits of all Three shall strive within me!

---

9. in Time's penultimate nick just at the last moment.

▲ **Critical Viewing**
How do the color and movement in this photo convey Scrooge's new attitude? [**Analyze Cause and Effect**]

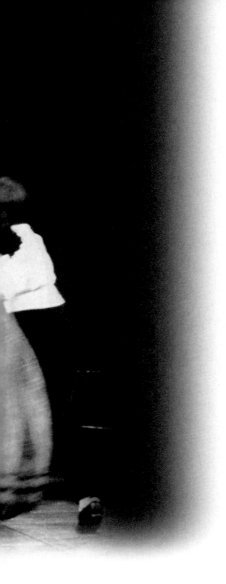

MARLEY. [*He points and moves closer to* SCROOGE'S *bed.*] Yes, Ebenezer, the bed-post is your own. Believe it! Yes, Ebenezer, the room is your own. Believe it!

SCROOGE. Oh, Jacob Marley! Wherever you are, Jacob, know ye that I praise you for this! I praise you . . . and heaven . . . and Christmastime! [*Kneels facing away from* MARLEY] I say it to ye on my knees, old Jacob, on my knees! [*He touches his bed curtains.*] Not torn down. My bed curtains are not at all torn down! Rings and all, here they are! They are here: I am here: the shadows of things that would have been, may now be <u>dispelled</u>. They will be, Jacob! I know they will be! [*He chooses clothing for the day. He tries different pieces of clothing and settles, perhaps on a dress suit, plus a cape of the bed clothing: something of color.*] I am light as a feather, I am happy as an angel, I am as merry as a schoolboy. [*Yells out window and then out to audience*] Merry Christmas to everybody! Merry Christmas to everybody! A Happy New Year to all the world! Hallo here! Whoop! Whoop! Hallo! Hallo! I don't know what day of the month it is! I don't care! I don't know anything! I'm quite a baby! I don't care! I don't care a fig! I'd much rather be a baby than be an old wreck like me or Marley! (Sorry, Jacob, wherever ye be!) Hallo! Hallo there!

[*Church bells chime in Christmas Day. A small boy, named* ADAM, *is seen now* D.R., *as a light fades up on him.*]

Hey, you boy! What's today? What day of the year is it?

ADAM. Today, sir? Why, it's Christmas Day!

SCROOGE. It's Christmas Day, is it? Whoop! Well, I haven't missed it after all, have I? The Spirits did all they did in one night. They can do anything they like, right? Of course they can! Of course they can!

ADAM. Excuse me, sir?

SCROOGE. Huh? Oh, yes, of course, what's your name, lad?

dispelled (dis peld') *v.* scattered and driven away; made to vanish

Reading Check

What promises does Scrooge make?

[SCROOGE *and* ADAM *will play their scene from their own spotlights.*]

ADAM. Adam, sir.

SCROOGE. Adam! What a fine, strong name! Do you know the poulterer's[10] in the next street but one, at the corner?

ADAM. I certainly should hope I know him, sir!

SCROOGE. A remarkable boy! An intelligent boy! Do you know whether the poulterer's have sold the prize turkey that was hanging up there? I don't mean the little prize turkey, Adam. I mean the big one!

ADAM. What, do you mean the one they've got that's as big as me?

SCROOGE. I mean, the turkey the size of Adam: that's the bird!

ADAM. It's hanging there now, sir.

SCROOGE. It is? Go and buy it! No, no, I am absolutely in earnest. Go and buy it and tell 'em to bring it here, so that I may give them the directions to where I want it delivered, as a gift. Come back here with the man, Adam, and I'll give you a shilling. Come back here with him in less than five minutes, and I'll give you half-a-crown!

ADAM. Oh, my sir! Don't let my brother in on this.

[ADAM *runs offstage.* MARLEY *smiles.*]

MARLEY. An act of kindness is like the first green grape of summer: one leads to another and another and another. It would take a queer man indeed to not follow an act of kindness with an act of kindness. One simply whets the tongue for more . . . the taste of kindness is too too sweet. Gifts—goods—are lifeless. But the gift of goodness one feels in the giving is full of life. It . . . is. . . a . . . wonder.

[*Pauses; moves closer to* SCROOGE, *who is totally occupied with his dressing and arranging of his room and his day. He is making lists, etc.* MARLEY *reaches out to* SCROOGE:]

ADAM. [*Calling, off*] I'm here! I'm here!

[ADAM *runs on with a man, who carries an enormous turkey.*]

Here I am, sir. Three minutes flat! A world record! I've got the poultryman and he's got the poultry! [*He pants, out of breath.*] I have earned my prize, sir, if I live . . .

[*He holds his heart, playacting.* SCROOGE *goes to him and embraces him.*]

SCROOGE. You are truly a champion, Adam . . .

Literary Analysis
Characterization Which actions reveal a change in Scrooge's character?

---

10. poulterer's (pōl′ tər ərz) *n.* British word for a store that sells chickens, turkeys, and geese.

MAN. Here's the bird you ordered, sir . . .

SCROOGE. *Oh, my, MY!!!* look at the size of that turkey, will you! He never could have stood upon his legs, that bird! He would have snapped them off in a minute, like sticks of sealingwax! Why you'll never be able to carry that bird to Camden-Town. I'll give you money for a cab . . .

MAN. Camden-Town's where it's goin', sir?

SCROOGE. Oh, I didn't tell you? Yes, I've written the precise address down just here on this . . . [*Hands paper to him*] Bob Cratchit's house. Now he's not to know who sends him this. Do you understand me? Not a word . . . [*Handing out money and chuckling*]

MAN. I understand, sir, not a word.

SCROOGE. Good. There you go then . . . this is for the turkey . . . [*Chuckle*] and this is for the taxi. [*Chuckle*] . . . and this is for your world-record run, Adam . . .

ADAM. But I don't have change for that, sir.

SCROOGE. Then keep it, my lad. It's Christmas!

ADAM. [*He kisses* SCROOGE'S *cheek, quickly.*] Thank you, sir. Merry, Merry Christmas! [*He runs off.*]

MAN. And you've given me a bit overmuch here, too, sir . . .

SCROOGE. Of course I have, sir. It's Christmas!

MAN. Oh, well, thanking you, sir. I'll have this bird to Mr. Cratchit and his family in no time, sir. Don't you worry none about that. Merry Christmas to you, sir, and a very happy New Year, too . . .

[*The man exits.* SCROOGE *walks in a large circle about the stage, which is now gently lit. A chorus sings Christmas music far in the distance. Bells chime as well, far in the distance. A gentlewoman enters and passes.* SCROOGE *is on the streets now.*]

SCROOGE. Merry Christmas, madam . . .

WOMAN. Merry Christmas, sir . . .

[*The portly businessman from the first act enters.*]

SCROOGE. Merry Christmas, sir.

PORTLY MAN. Merry Christmas, sir.

SCROOGE. Oh, you! My dear sir! How do you do? I do hope that you succeeded yesterday! It was very kind of you. A Merry Christmas.

Literary Analysis

Characterization and Motive What is Scrooge's motive for keeping his change of personality a secret from Cratchit?

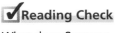

Reading Check

What does Scrooge instruct Adam to do?

PORTLY MAN. Mr. Scrooge?

SCROOGE. Yes, Scrooge is my name though I'm afraid you may not find it very pleasant. Allow me to ask your pardon. And will you have the goodness to—[*He whispers into the man's ear.*]

PORTLY MAN. Lord bless me! My dear Mr. Scrooge, are you *serious!?!*

SCROOGE. If you please. Not a farthing[11] less. A great many back payments are included in it, I assure you. Will you do me that favor?

PORTLY MAN. My dear sir, I don't know what to say to such munifi—

SCROOGE. [*Cutting him off*] Don't say anything, please. Come and see me. Will you?

PORTLY MAN. I will! I will! Oh I will, Mr. Scrooge! It will be my pleasure!

SCROOGE. Thank'ee, I am much obliged to you. I thank you fifty times. Bless you!

[*Portly man passes offstage, perhaps by moving backwards.* SCROOGE *now comes to the room of his* NEPHEW *and* NIECE. *He stops at the door, begins to knock on it, loses his courage, tries again, loses his courage again, tries again, fails again, and then backs off and runs at the door, causing a tremendous bump against it. The* NEPHEW *and* NIECE *are startled.* SCROOGE, *poking head into room*]

Fred!

NEPHEW. Why, bless my soul! Who's that?

NEPHEW AND NIECE. [*Together*] How now? Who goes?

SCROOGE. It's I. Your Uncle Scrooge.

NIECE. Dear heart alive!

SCROOGE. I have come to dinner. May I come in, Fred?

NEPHEW. *May you come in???!!!* With such pleasure for me you may, Uncle!!! What a treat!

NIECE. What a treat, Uncle Scrooge! Come in, come in!

[*They embrace a shocked and delighted* SCROOGE: FRED *calls into the other room.*]

---

11. **farthing** (fär thin) *n.* small British coin.

NEPHEW. Come in here, everybody, and meet my Uncle Scrooge! He's come for our Christmas party!

[*Music in. Lighting here indicates that day has gone to night and gone to day again. It is early, early morning.* SCROOGE *walks alone from the party, exhausted, to his offices, opposite side of the stage. He opens his offices. The offices are as they were at the start of the play.* SCROOGE *seats himself with his door wide open so that he can see into the tank, as he awaits* CRATCHIT, *who enters, head down, full of guilt.* CRATCHIT *starts writing almost before he sits.*]

SCROOGE. What do you mean by coming in here at this time of day, a full eighteen minutes late, Mr. Cratchit? Hallo, sir? Do you hear me?

BOB. I am very sorry, sir. I am behind my time.

SCROOGE. You are? Yes, I certainly think you are. Step this way, sir, if you please . . .

BOB. It's only but once a year, sir . . . it shall not be repeated. I was making rather merry yesterday and into the night . . .

SCROOGE. Now, I'll tell you what, Cratchit. I am not going to stand this sort of thing any longer. And therefore . . .

[*He stands and pokes his finger into* BOB'S *chest.*]

I am . . . about . . . to . . . raise . . . your salary.

BOB. Oh, no, sir, I . . . [*Realizes*] what did you say, sir?

SCROOGE. A Merry Christmas, Bob . . . [*He claps* BOB'S *back.*] A merrier Christmas, Bob, my good fellow! than I have given you for many a year. I'll raise your salary and endeavor to assist your struggling family and we will discuss your affairs this very afternoon over a bowl of smoking bishop.[12] Bob! Make up the fires and buy another coal scuttle before you dot another i, Bob. It's too cold in this place! We need warmth and cheer, Bob Cratchit! Do you hear me? DO . . . YOU . . . HEAR . . . ME?

[BOB CRATCHIT *stands, smiles at* SCROOGE: BOB CRATCHIT *faints. Blackout. As the main lights black out, a spotlight appears on* SCROOGE: C. *Another on* MARLEY: *He talks directly to the audience.*]

MARLEY. Scrooge was better than his word. He did it all and infinitely more; and to Tiny Tim, who did NOT die, he was a second

---

Literary Analysis
Characterization Why doesn't Cratchit realize that Scrooge's character has changed?

✔ **Reading Check**
Where does Scrooge go?

---

12. **smoking bishop** hot sweet orange-flavored drink.

A Christmas Carol: Scrooge and Marley, Act II ◆ 653

father. He became as good a friend, as good a master, as good a man, as the good old city knew, or any other good old city, town, or borough in the good old world. And it was always said of him that he knew how to keep Christmas well, if any man alive possessed the knowledge. [*Pauses*] May that be truly said of us, and all of us. And so, as Tiny Tim observed . . .

TINY TIM. [*Atop* SCROOGE'S *shoulder*] God Bless Us, Every One . . .

[*Lights up on chorus, singing final Christmas Song.* SCROOGE *and* MARLEY *and all spirits and other characters of the play join in. When the song is over, the lights fade to black.*]

Review and Assess

Thinking About the Literature

1. **Respond:** Do you believe that people can really change completely, as Scrooge does? Explain your answer.

Interpreting Meaning

2. **(a) Recall:** What does Scrooge find out about the Cratchits in Scene 3? **(b) Analyze:** Why does Scrooge care about the fate of Tiny Tim? **(c) Draw Conclusions:** In what way is Scrooge changing?

3. **(a) Recall:** What does the Ghost of Christmas Present show to Scrooge just before his departure? **(b) Analyze:** Why does the ghost repeat Scrooge's own words from Act l?
(c) Make a Judgment: What is the ghost urging Scrooge to do?

4. **(a) Recall:** What happens to Scrooge's belongings in Christmas Future? **(b) Infer:** Why does it bother Scrooge to see them handled that way? **(c) Generalize:** What does he learn from this experience?

5. **(a) Analyze:** Why is Scrooge happy at the end of the play?
(b) Evaluate: How well does he live up to his promise to learn his "lessons"?

6. **Take a Position:** Do you think Cratchit and Scrooge's nephew do the right thing in forgiving Scrooge immediately? Explain.

Review and Assess

Literary Analysis

Characterization

1. By the end of the play, how has the character Scrooge changed? Support your answer with three incidents that show this change.

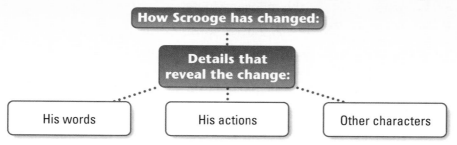

How Scrooge has changed:

Details that reveal the change:

His words | His actions | Other characters

2. Where does the dialogue show what Tiny Tim is like? Give at least two examples.
3. Where does an action or gesture show what Marley is like? Give two examples.

Connecting Literary Elements

4. Make a chart like the one below. Fill in motives and actions to complete the chart.

Scrooge			
Motive	Wants to help poor		
Action		Visits nephew	Gives Cratchit a raise

Reading Strategy

Asking Questions

5. What questions did you ask yourself about Scrooge's actions? Why?
6. What questions did you ask about other characters' actions? Why?
7. How did asking questions help you understand characters' actions, traits, and motives?

Extend Understanding

8. **Extend:** Find two passages that hint at ways in which Dickens thinks society should change.

Quick Review

Characterization is the act of creating and developing a character. To review characterization, see page 626.

 Take It to the Net
www.phschool.com
Take the interactive self-test online to check your understanding of the selection.

Integrate Language Skills

Vocabulary Development Lesson

Word Analysis: Latin Root -aud-

In a scene in Act II, Scrooge asks to be made audible—able to be heard. The Latin root -aud- means "hear." For each of the following words, write a sentence that contains both the word and the meaning of -aud-.

1. auditorium **2.** audition **3.** audiovisual

Spelling Strategy

Gnarled is one of a handful of words that start with the letters *gn*. The letter *g* is silent; the words start with the *n* sound. Add *gn* to each of the following groups of letters. Then, use each word in a sentence.

1. _____ome **3.** _____ash

2. _____at **4.** _____u

Fluency: Definitions

Identify the vocabulary word from the list on page 626 that is best suited to describe each of the following items.

1. frayed, worn-out clothing
2. ancient, twisted tree
3. loud stereo in the next room
4. amount of food on a dieter's plate
5. desire to do something
6. getting an A on an exam you thought you had failed
7. police sent away a curious crowd
8. strong allergic reaction

Grammar Lesson

Pronouns and Antecedents

A **pronoun** takes the place of a noun. An **antecedent** is the noun that a pronoun stands for. Pronouns should agree with their antecedents in number and gender. **Number** indicates whether a pronoun is singular (referring to one) or plural (referring to more than one). **Gender** indicates whether a pronoun refers to a male or a female.

PLURAL ANTECEDENT; PLURAL PRONOUN

The Cratchits enjoy their holiday meal.

SINGULAR, MASCULINE ANTECEDENT;
SINGLE, MASCULINE PRONOUN

Marley drags his chains.

▶ *For more practice, see page R33, Exercise D.*
Practice Complete each sentence with a pronoun that agrees with the antecedent.

1. Mrs. Cratchit made dinner for ___?___ family.
2. She cooked the goose and put ___?___ on the table.
3. Scrooge changed, and ___?___ helped the poor.
4. Scrooge and Cratchit enjoyed ___?___ friendship.
5. When Scrooge arrived, Fred welcomed ___?___.

Writing Application Use these words in a paragraph. Use a pronoun in place of each word at least once.

1. Marley **2.** the Cratchits **3.** Christmas

*W*G *Prentice Hall Writing and Grammar Connection: Chapter 24, Section 2*

Writing Lesson

Critical Response

Share your reaction to *A Christmas Carol* by writing a critical response, your evaluation of the play's strengths and weaknesses.

Prewriting On a two-column chart, list what you think are the play's strengths and weaknesses. Then, choose at least four points on which to focus.

Drafting Begin by stating your overall reaction in an introduction. Discuss each strength and weakness in a separate paragraph. State the point, explain your reaction, and give specific examples from the play as support.

Model: Supporting a Critical Opinion

The character of Marley is too exaggerated. His appearances include too many bangs, flashes of light, and other special effects. For example, Act II begins with a flame shooting from Marley's hand, thunder, lightning, ghostly music, and changing colors. These effects get tiresome because they are repeated so often.

> The writer provides an explanation of why the character of Marley seems too exaggerated. Then, the writer gives specific examples.

Revising Underline each strength and weakness you point out. Identify the support you provide. If you can't identify support, add some or eliminate the strength or weakness.

 Prentice Hall Writing and Grammar Connection: Chapter 12, Section 2

Extension Activities

Research and Technology With a group of classmates, create a **timeline** of the life of Charles Dickens. Use the Internet and library resources to gather information about the following:

- major events in Dickens's life
- his most important literary works
- his travels and speaking engagements

Include visuals, such as a picture of Dickens, or quotations from his work. [**Group Activity**]

Speaking and Listening Give an **oral summary** of one review of a performance of *A Christmas Carol*. Explain the main points and how the reviewer supports them. Make sure to use your own words, except where you quote from the review. (Read reviews of performances of *A Christmas Carol* on pp. 659–662.)

 Take It to the Net www.phschool.com

Go online for an additional research activity using the Internet.

READING INFORMATIONAL MATERIALS

Literary Criticism

About Literary Criticism

Literary criticism is writing that analyzes and makes a judgment about a work of literature. Note that the word *criticism* in this context can mean either a positive or a negative judgment. A piece of writing of this kind is often called a review, and the writer is called a critic.

Most literary criticism contains the following elements:

- a brief summary of the work
- a comparison or contrast to other works of literature
- a judgment or recommendation

Reading Strategy

Analyzing Responses to Literature

When reading literary criticism, it can be helpful to scan a review, looking for the critic's overall judgment of the work. You can then read about the details that led the critic to make that judgment. In particular, look for the critic's analysis of literary elements such as character, setting, and plot. When possible, you might compare different evaluations of the same work by reading the reviews of different critics. As you read the reviews of dramatic performances of Charles Dickens's *A Christmas Carol* on the following pages, use a chart like the one shown to record and compare each critic's impressions of the work.

Performance Reviews

Source	Overall Judgment	Details Leading to the Judgment
People Weekly (national)		
Variety (national)		
The Oakland Press (Pontiac, Michigan)		

A Christmas Carol TNT

(Sun., Dec. 5, 8 p.m. ET)

People Weekly, Dec 6, 1999
v52 i22 p31+ Tube.

Picks & Pans: Television

> The newspaper or magazine where a review appears tells you something about the audience of the criticism. In this case it's the TV viewers.

So you muttered "humbug" when you spied yet another version of *A Christmas Carol* on the TV schedule. Don't feel guilty. It doesn't take a spiritual descendant of Ebenezer Scrooge to notice that the Charles Dickens classic has been adapted nearly to death. (Two years ago, there was even a Ms. Scrooge.)

> This paragraph reveals what this critic thinks is the strongest aspect of this performance.

But TNT's *Carol* would be worth watching if only for the lead performance of Patrick Stewart. The ex-skipper of *Star Trek: The Next Generation* has been giving staged, one-man readings of *A Christmas Carol* for 10 years, and his approach to Scrooge is consistently interesting and intelligent. Early on, Stewart seems to be speaking the misanthropic diatribes straight from Scrooge's flinty heart, rather than reciting thoroughly familiar quotations. And when Scrooge offers a boy a one-shilling tip, Stewart has the reformed miser feel a pang of the old parsimony.

Filmed in England with a solid supporting cast (including

> ... this *Carol* feels more like Masterpiece Theatre than seasonal merchandise ...

Richard E. Grant as Bob Cratchit and Joel Grey as the Spirit of Christmas Past), this *Carol* feels more like Masterpiece Theatre than seasonal merchandise—except when the filmmakers embellish Scrooge's nocturnal visions with gratuitous special effects.

Bottom Line: *Old story well told.*

—Terry Kelleher

VARIETY

Variety, Nov 22, 1999   v377 i2 p36

A CHRISTMAS CAROL

Review: Television

Variety is a publication whose audience is professionals in the entertainment and media industries. Thus, reviews in *Variety* include information about the production staff and cast of each production.

MICHAEL SPEIER.

Filmed in England by Hallmark Entertainment. Executive producers, Robert Halmi Sr., Patrick Stewart. Producer Dyson Lovell; director, David Jones; writer, Peter Barnes, based on the novel by Charles Dickens; camera, Ian Wilson: production designer, Roger Hall; editor; David Martin; costume designer Charles Knode; music, Stephen Warbeck; casting, Joyce Gallie. 120 MIN.

Ebenezer Scrooge	Patrick Stewart
Bob Cratchit	Richard E. Grant
Christmas Past	Joel Grey
Albert Fezziwig	Ian McNeice
Mrs. Cratchit	Saskia Reeves
Christmas Present	Desmond Barrit
Jacob Marley	Bernard Lloyd
Christmas Future	Tim Potter
Tiny Tim	Ben Tibber

With: Dominic West, Trevor Peacock, Liz Smith, Elizabeth Spriggs, Kenny Doughty, Laura Fraser, Celia Imrie.

Only Ebenezer Scrooge would knock TNT's "A Christmas Carol." Handsome, wholesome and finely tuned, the cable web's take on Charles Dickens's 1843 masterwork is TV at its classiest. Treated to Hallmark touches at every turn, and Patrick Stewart's graceful performance, viewers who aren't yet in the holiday spirit will be ready for the tinsel and mistletoe as soon as the opening credits roll. Bah humbug? No way.

Oft-told tales are difficult to pull off, but there are many nifty strokes here that elevate the story above most interpretations. True to the novel but peppered with sharp special effects that don't encumber the narrative, this one gets it right. And from the wonderful set pieces to the wintry locales, "Carol" contains a beauty rarely captured in today's telepic arena. Director David Jones displays a smooth hand that adds mounds of style to the rendition, and his approach to Peter Barnes's script is a tribute to delicate staging.

This review includes a very simple sketch of the plot of the literary work.

The story is still ageless. Miserly Mr. Scrooge intimidates carolers, fends off charity workers and terrorizes his lone employee, Bob Cratchit (Richard E. Grant). But after the specter of ex-partner Jacob Marley (Bernard Lloyd) visits him, along with a parade of phantoms, Scrooge's hum gets de-bugged.

As Christmas Past, Joel Grey, decked out in silken white sheeting and a radiant tracking light, carries Scrooge back to relive the pain of

Stewart's Scrooge will be a tough act to follow in years to come.

bad Decembers gone by. Desmond Barrit's Christmas Present applies the guilt card, fairly questioning the reasons behind his client's blistering hatred of humanity. Christmas Future (Tim Potter) is hidden beneath a black robe, bearing two very menacing eyes as he proposes a humbling destiny. Stewart's Scrooge will be a tough act to follow in years

to come. For a decade, the thesp has toured with "Carol" across the country and the experience shows; his initial inflections are full of genuine antipathy, and his transformation to a goodhearted citizen is entirely believable. With a robust eloquence, he speaks Barnes's words with so much polish that even his bitterness is delightful.

The supporting actors are also first-rate. Grey and Barrit enjoy their flashy parts, but they're stately apparitions, trading in their rattles and chains for more pragmatic attributes. Grant's Cratchit is appropriately loving and sympathetic, doting on Tiny Tim (Ben Tibber).

But the strongest trait comes in the overall execution. Robert Halmi Sr.'s epics have always embraced razzle-dazzle visuals, some outstanding ("Merlin") and some mediocre ("Leprechauns"). "Carol" is one of the best so far, because its different parts are all solid; the allure is in the whole package and not just the tricks. And while walking through walls and fairy dust might not seem like the freshest use of technology, the restrained magic is very effective.

From Stephen Warbeck's score to the reproduction of 19th century architecture at the famed Ealing Studio, pic's tech credits are smashing.

Toned-down *Christmas Carol* has more spirit

By John Sousanis
Special to *The Oakland Press*

Director Debra Wicks has tinkered with Meadow Brook's recipe for *A Christmas Carol* just enough to make the old holiday fruitcake seem fresh. To be sure, Wicks's changes are subtle. Meadow Brook is still producing the Charles Nolte adaptation of Charles Dickens's Christmas classic that has been a mainstay of local theater for most of the last two decades.

The audience still is serenaded by a band of merry carolers in the lobby before the show. With its giant revolving set pieces and big bag of special effects, the production's script, set and costumes are unchanged from these many Christmases past.

But ironically, Wicks has infused the show with new energy by calming everything down a bit. In prior productions, the play's singing Londoners seemed positively hopped up on Christmas cheer to the point where one feared for the life of anyone not bubbling over with the spirit of the season.

Against this unebbing Yuletide, it was easy to forgive Scrooge of all his bah-humbugging. If only he had seen fit to give Tiny Tim a good spanking, we might all have enjoyed Christmas a little more. But Wicks has introduced a modicum of restraint into the Happy English populace, reducing the play's saccharine content considerably and making *A Christmas Carol* a more palatable holiday treat for adults and children.

Peter Hicks's set design for the show is, as always, enormous and gorgeous: Scrooge's storefront on a busy London street revolves to reveal the interior of the businessman's office and home, then opens on itself, providing the frame for scenes from Scrooge's boyhood, young adulthood and, of course, his potential end.

Meadow Brook's technical crew executes its stage magic without a hitch: Ghosts materialize and dematerialize in thick fogs and bolts of bright light, speaking to Scrooge in electronically altered voices and freezing the action onstage with a wave of their otherworldly hands.

The cast members take on multiple roles populating busy London in one scene, then visiting poor Scrooge in his dreams of Christmas Then, Now and Soon.

Standouts in the huge ensemble include John Biedenbach as Scrooge's put-upon assistant Bob Cratchit, Jodie Kuhn Ellison as Cratchit's fiercely loyal wife and Mark Rademacher, who pulls double duty as the Spirit of Christmas Present (the beefiest role in the play) and as a determined charity worker.

Scott Crownover, paying only passing attention to his English accent, takes an energetic turn as Scrooge's nephew, Fred, and Tom Mahard and Geoffrey Beauchamp have fun with a handful of roles they've been performing for years. Newcomer Sara Catheryn Wolf, fresh from three seasons at the Hilberry Theatre Company, provides an ethereal Spirit of Christmas Past.

The biggest change for longtime fans of the spectacle, however, is the replacement of Booth Coleman as Scrooge. Dennis Robertson's debut as the man in need of serious Christmas redemption is in perfect keeping with Wicks's toned-down production. If he's not quite as charismatic a miser as Coleman, Robertson is a much darker, even scarier Scrooge, which makes his ultimate transformation into an unabashed philanthropist that much more affecting.

All in all, *A Christmas Carol* is what it always has been: a well-produced, grand-scale event that is as much pageant as play. And like a beautifully wrapped gift under a well-decorated tree, it suits the season to a tee.

If you go, *A Christmas Carol* runs through December 24 at Meadow Brook Theatre, 127 Wilson Hall, Oakland University, Rochester Hills. Call 377-3300.

Check Your Comprehension

1. How does the *People Weekly* critic generally feel about adaptations of *A Christmas Carol?*
2. Do the *People Weekly* and *Variety* critics agree or disagree about their judgment of the special effects used in this production of *A Christmas Carol?* Explain.
3. Is the Meadow Brook Theatre producing *A Christmas Carol* for the first time? How do you know?
4. What is John Sousanis's overall judgment of the Meadow Brook performance?

Applying the Reading Strategy

Analyzing Responses to Literature

5. Identify one sentence from the *People Weekly* review that shows the critic's judgment of the character portrayal in *A Christmas Carol.*
6. Find one sentence from each review that supports this statement: All three reviewers seem to think the reader is already familiar with the plot of *A Christmas Carol.*
7. What does *The Oakland Press* critic have to say about the set (setting) of the Meadow Brook Theatre production?

Activity

Movie Review

Watch a video of one of the many versions of *A Christmas Carol*. Review the overall work and the actors based on the following elements:

- setting
- characterization
- plot
- performance

Contrasting Informational Materials

Literary Criticism and Summaries

Find one or two summaries of *A Christmas Carol* in books such as *The Oxford Companion to English Literature* and *Merriam-Webster's Encyclopedia of Literature* or on the Internet. In a chart like the one on this page, write the purpose of the summaries as well as their features. Then, write the purpose and features of the reviews on pages 659–662. Finally, explain the differences between the two types of writing.

	Summaries	Reviews
Purpose		
Features		

Prepare to Read

The Monsters Are Due on Maple Street

 Take It to the Net

Visit www.phschool.com for interactive activities and instruction related to "The Monsters Are Due on Maple Street," including:
- background
- graphic organizers
- literary elements
- reading strategies

Preview

Connecting to the Literature

Rumors can spread quickly and become increasingly distorted with each retelling. Sometimes, as in this screenplay, wild rumors have terrible effects.

Background

This screenplay was written during the Cold War, a period of intense rivalry between the United States and the communist Soviet Union that lasted from the mid-1940s through the 1980s. The two countries engaged in a dangerous nuclear arms race. Fear led to suspicion, and many people in the United States were accused of being communist spies. Few of those accused were spies, but many who were accused found their careers and lives ruined by the suspicion that followed an accusation.

Literary Analysis

Plot in Drama

Plot is the arrangement of events in a literary work. This screenplay—a drama written for television or the movies—has all the elements of a conventional plot:

- **Exposition:** The situation is explained.
- **Rising Action:** Events move toward a high point.
- **Conflict:** A struggle develops between two opposing forces.
- **Climax:** Events reach a turning point.
- **Falling Action:** The events following the climax lead to the ending.
- **Resolution:** The outcome of the conflict is settled.

Identify the details that set the plot in motion by asking yourself the following questions:

1. What makes the people fearful?
2. Why do they begin to suspect one another?

Connecting Literary Elements

Through **foreshadowing,** an author hints at upcoming events. A small event or comment may foreshadow an upcoming disaster. Look for hints in the beginning of the play that indicate the kind of trouble to come. In the example, the look Steve exchanges with Charlie hints at upcoming mysterious events.

> STEVE. It couldn't be a meteor. A meteor couldn't do this. [*He and* CHARLIE *exchange a look, then they start to walk away from the group.*]

Reading Strategy

Predicting

An author's use of foreshadowing gives hints on which readers can base **predictions,** or educated guesses, about where the story is headed. Base your predictions on clues that the author provides. Use a chart like the one shown to note the clues and your predictions, revising as you encounter new information.

Vocabulary Development

flustered (flus′ terd) *adj.* nervous; confused (p. 669)

sluggishly (slug′ ish lē) *adv.* as if lacking energy (p. 669)

assent (ə sent′) *n.* agreement (p. 670)

persistently (pər sist′ ənt lē) *adv.* firmly and steadily (p. 671)

defiant (dē fī′ ənt) *adj.* boldly resisting (p. 672)

metamorphosis (met′ ə môr′ fə sis) *n.* change of form (p. 673)

scapegoat (skāp′ gōt′) *n.* person or group blamed for the mistakes or crimes of others (p. 678)

The Monsters are Due on Maple Street

Rod Serling

CHARACTERS	RESIDENTS OF MAPLE STREET	
NARRATOR	STEVE BRAND	SALLY (*TOMMY'S*
FIGURE ONE	CHARLIE'S WIFE	*MOTHER*)
FIGURE TWO	MRS. GOODMAN	MAN ONE
	MRS. BRAND	MAN TWO
	TOMMY	PETE VAN HORN
	WOMAN	CHARLIE
	DON MARTIN	LES GOODMAN

ACT I

[*Fade in on a shot of the night sky. The various nebulae and planet bodies stand out in sharp, sparkling relief, and the camera begins a slow pan across the Heavens.*]

NARRATOR'S VOICE. There is a fifth dimension beyond that which is known to man. It is a dimension as vast as space, and as timeless as infinity. It is the middle ground between light and shadow—between science and superstition. And it lies between the pit of man's fears and the summit of his knowledge. This is the dimension of imagination. It is an area which we call The Twilight Zone.

[*The camera has begun to pan down until it passes the horizon and is on a sign which reads "Maple Street." Pan down until we are shooting down at an angle toward the street below. It's a tree-lined, quiet residential American street, very typical of the small town. The houses have front porches on which people sit and swing on gliders, conversing across from house to house. STEVE BRAND polishes his car parked in front of his house. His neighbor, DON MARTIN, leans against the fender watching him. A Good Humor man rides a bicycle and is just in the process of stopping to sell some ice cream to a couple of kids. Two women gossip on the front lawn. Another man waters his lawn.*]

Reading Check

What is the fifth dimension?

NARRATOR'S VOICE. Maple Street, U.S.A., late summer. A tree-lined little world of front porch gliders, hop scotch, the laughter of children, and the bell of an ice cream vendor.

[*There is a pause and the camera moves over to a shot of the Good Humor man and two small boys who are standing alongside, just buying ice cream.*]

NARRATOR'S VOICE. At the sound of the roar and the flash of light it will be precisely 6:43 P.M. on Maple Street.

[*At this moment one of the little boys,* TOMMY, *looks up to listen to a sound of a tremendous screeching roar from overhead. A flash of light plays on both their faces and then it moves down the street past lawns and porches and rooftops and then disappears.*

Various people leave their porches and stop what they're doing to stare up at the sky. STEVE BRAND, *the man who's been polishing his car, now stands there transfixed, staring upwards. He looks at* DON MARTIN, *his neighbor from across the street.*]

STEVE. What was that? A meteor?

DON. [*Nods*] That's what it looked like. I didn't hear any crash though, did you?

STEVE. [*Shakes his head*] Nope. I didn't hear anything except a roar.

MRS. BRAND. [*From her porch*] Steve? What was that?

STEVE. [*Raising his voice and looking toward porch*] Guess it was a meteor, honey. Came awful close, didn't it?

MRS. BRAND. Too close for my money! Much too close.

[*The camera pans across the various porches to people who stand there watching and talking in low tones.*]

NARRATOR'S VOICE. Maple Street. Six-forty-four P.M. on a late September evening. [*A pause*] Maple Street in the last calm and reflective moment . . . before the monsters came!

[*The camera slowly pans across the porches again. We see a man screwing a light bulb on a front porch, then getting down off the stool to flick the switch and finding that nothing happens.*

Another man is working on an electric power mower. He plugs in the plug, flicks on the switch of the power mower, off and on, with nothing happening.

Through the window of a front porch, we see a woman pushing her finger back and forth on the dial hook. Her voice is indistinct and distant, but intelligible and repetitive.]

WOMAN. Operator, operator, something's wrong on the phone, operator!

[MRS. BRAND *comes out on the porch and calls to* STEVE.]

MRS. BRAND. [*Calling*] Steve, the power's off. I had the soup on the

Reading Strategy
Making Predictions
What do you think the flash is? Predict what effect this event will have on the community.

Literary Analysis
Plot and Foreshadowing
Do you think the events described in the stage directions are included to move the action forward or to hint that something strange is happening? Explain.

stove and the stove just stopped working.

WOMAN. Same thing over here. I can't get anybody on the phone either. The phone seems to be dead.

[*We look down on the street as we hear the voices creep up from below, small, mildly disturbed voices highlighting these kinds of phrases:*]

VOICES.

Electricity's off.

Phone won't work.

Can't get a thing on the radio.

My power mower won't move, won't work at all.

Radio's gone dead!

[PETE VAN HORN, *a tall, thin man, is seen standing in front of his house.*]

VAN HORN. I'll cut through the back yard . . . See if the power's still on on Floral Street. I'll be right back!

[*He walks past the side of his house and disappears into the back yard.*

The camera pans down slowly until we're looking at ten or eleven people standing around the street and overflowing to the curb and sidewalk. In the background is STEVE BRAND'S *car.*]

STEVE. Doesn't make sense. Why should the power go off all of a sudden, and the phone line?

DON. Maybe some sort of an electrical storm or something.

CHARLIE. That don't seem likely. Sky's just as blue as anything. Not a cloud. No lightning. No thunder. No nothing. How could it be a storm?

WOMAN. I can't get a thing on the radio. Not even the portable.

[*The people again murmur softly in wonderment and question.*]

CHARLIE. Well, why don't you go downtown and check with the police, though they'll probably think we're crazy or something. A little power failure and right away we get all <u>flustered</u> and everything.

STEVE. It isn't just the power failure, Charlie. If it was, we'd still be able to get a broadcast on the portable.

[*There's a murmur of reaction to this.* STEVE *looks from face to face and then over to his car.*]

STEVE. I'll run downtown. We'll get this all straightened out.

[*He walks over to the car, gets in it, turns the key. Looking through the open car door, we see the crowd watching him from the other side.* STEVE *starts the engine. It turns over* <u>sluggishly</u> *and then just stops dead. He tries it again and this time he can't get it to turn*

Literary Analysis
Plot in Drama How does the playwright use dialogue as the exposition?

flustered (flus´ terd) *adj.* nervous; confused

sluggishly (slug´ ish lē) *adv.* as if lacking energy

Reading Check

What strange event occurs just before Maple Street loses electricity?

over. Then, very slowly and reflectively, he turns the key back to "off" and slowly gets out of the car.

The people stare at STEVE. *He stands for a moment by the car, then walks toward the group.*]

STEVE. I don't understand it. It was working fine before . . .

DON. Out of gas?

STEVE. [*Shakes his head*] I just had it filled up.

WOMAN. What's it mean?

CHARLIE. It's just as if . . . as if everything had stopped. [*Then he turns toward* STEVE.] We'd better walk downtown. [*Another murmur of* <u>assent</u> *at this.*]

STEVE. The two of us can go, Charlie. [*He turns to look back at the car.*] It couldn't be the meteor. A meteor couldn't do this.

[*He and* CHARLIE *exchange a look, then they start to walk away from the group.*

We see TOMMY, *a serious-faced fourteen-year-old in spectacles who stands a few feet away from the group. He is halfway between them and the two men, who start to walk down the sidewalk.*]

TOMMY. Mr. Brand . . . you better not!

STEVE. Why not?

TOMMY. They don't want you to.

[STEVE *and* CHARLIE *exchange a grin, and* STEVE *looks back toward the boy.*]

STEVE. Who doesn't want us to?

TOMMY. [*Jerks his head in the general direction of the distant horizon*] Them!

STEVE. Them?

CHARLIE. Who are them?

TOMMY. [*Very intently*] Whoever was in that thing that came by overhead.

[STEVE *knits his brows for a moment, cocking his head questioningly. His voice is intense.*]

STEVE. What?

Woman on telephone as seen through window, William Low, Courtesy of the artist.

▲ **Critical Viewing**
What impression does this illustration convey about life on Maple Street? **[Analyze]**

assent (ə sent´) *n.* agreement

TOMMY. Whoever was in that thing that came over. I don't think they want us to leave here.

[STEVE *leaves* CHARLIE *and walks over to the boy. He kneels down in front of him. He forces his voice to remain gentle. He reaches out and holds the boy.*]

STEVE. What do you mean? What are you talking about?

TOMMY. They don't want us to leave. That's why they shut everything off.

STEVE. What makes you say that? Whatever gave you that idea?

WOMAN. [*From the crowd*] Now isn't that the craziest thing you ever heard?

TOMMY. [*Persistently but a little intimidated by the crowd*] It's always that way, in every story I ever read about a ship landing from outer space.

WOMAN. [*To the boy's mother,* **SALLY***, who stands on the fringe of the crowd*] From outer space, yet! Sally, you better get that boy of yours up to bed. He's been reading too many comic books or seeing too many movies or something.

SALLY. Tommy, come over here and stop that kind of talk.

STEVE. Go ahead, Tommy. We'll be right back. And you'll see. That wasn't any ship or anything like it. That was just a . . . a meteor or something. Likely as not—[*He turns to the group, now trying to weight his words with an optimism he obviously doesn't feel but is desperately trying to instill in himself as well as the others.*] No doubt it did have something to do with all this power failure and the rest of it. Meteors can do some crazy things. Like sunspots.

DON. [*Picking up the cue*] Sure. That's the kind of thing—like sunspots. They raise Cain[1] with radio reception all over the world. And this thing being so close—why, there's no telling the sort of stuff it can do. [*He wets his lips, smiles nervously.*] Go ahead, Charlie. You and Steve go into town and see if that isn't what's causing it all.

[STEVE *and* CHARLIE *again walk away from the group down the sidewalk. The people watch silently.*

TOMMY *stares at them, biting his lips, and finally calling out again.*]

TOMMY. *Mr. Brand!*

[*The two men stop again.* TOMMY *takes a step toward them.*]

TOMMY. Mr. Brand . . . please don't leave here.

[STEVE *and* CHARLIE *stop once again and turn toward the boy. There's*

---

1. raise Cain badly disturb.

Literary Analysis
Plot in Drama How do Tommy's words intensify the uneasiness people are feeling?

persistently
(pər sist′ ənt lē) *adv.* firmly and steadily

**Reading Check**

What does Tommy tell Steve, Don, and Charlie?

a murmur in the crowd, a murmur of irritation and concern as if the boy were bringing up fears that shouldn't be brought up; words which carried with them a strange kind of validity that came without logic but nonetheless registered and had meaning and effect. Again we hear a murmur of reaction from the crowd.

TOMMY *is partly frightened and partly* defiant *as well.*]

TOMMY. You might not even be able to get to town. It was that way in the story. Nobody could leave. Nobody except—

STEVE. Except who?

TOMMY. Except the people they'd sent down ahead of them. They looked just like humans. And it wasn't until the ship landed that—

[*The boy suddenly stops again, conscious of the parents staring at them and of the sudden hush of the crowd.*]

SALLY. [*In a whisper, sensing the antagonism of the crowd*] Tommy, please son . . . honey, don't talk that way—

MAN ONE. That kid shouldn't talk that way . . . and we shouldn't stand here listening to him. Why this is the craziest thing I ever heard of. The kid tells us a comic book plot and here we stand listening—

[STEVE *walks toward the camera, stops by the boy.*]

STEVE. Go ahead, Tommy. What kind of story was this? What about the people that they sent out ahead?

TOMMY. That was the way they prepared things for the landing. They sent four people. A mother and a father and two kids who looked just like humans . . . but they weren't.

[*There's another silence as* STEVE *looks toward the crowd and then toward* TOMMY. *He wears a tight grin.*]

STEVE. Well, I guess what we'd better do then is to run a check on the neighborhood and see which ones of us are really human.

[*There's laughter at this, but it's a laughter that comes from a desperate attempt to lighten the atmosphere. It's a release kind of laugh. The people look at one another in the middle of their laughter.*]

CHARLIE. There must be somethin' better to do than stand around makin' bum jokes about it.

[*Rubs his jaw nervously*] I wonder if Floral Street's got the same deal we got. [*He looks past the houses.*] Where is Pete Van Horn anyway? Didn't he get back yet?

[*Suddenly there's the sound of a car's engine starting to turn over.*

We look across the street toward the driveway of LES GOODMAN'S *house. He's at the wheel trying to start the car.*]

SALLY. Can you get it started, Les? [*He gets out of the car, shaking his head.*]

defiant (dē fī′ ənt) *adj.* boldly resisting

Reading Strategy
Making Predictions
How do you think Tommy will fare in the face of the crowd's growing irritation with him?

Literary Analysis
Plot and Foreshadowing
What hint does Steve's comment give about how characters will react later in the play?

GOODMAN. No dice.

[*He walks toward the group. He stops suddenly as behind him, inexplicably and with a noise that inserts itself into the silence, the car engine starts up all by itself.* GOODMAN *whirls around to stare toward it.*

The car idles roughly, smoke coming from the exhaust, the frame shaking gently.

GOODMAN'S *eyes go wide, and he runs over to his car.*

The people stare toward the car.]

MAN ONE. He got the car started somehow. He got his car started!

[*The camera pans along the faces of the people as they stare, somehow caught up by this revelation and somehow, illogically, wildly, frightened.*]

WOMEN. How come his car just up and started like that?

SALLY. All by itself. He wasn't anywheres near it. It started all by itself.

[DON *approaches the group, stops a few feet away to look toward* GOODMAN'S *car and then back toward the group.*]

DON. And he never did come out to look at that thing that flew overhead. He wasn't even interested. [*He turns to the faces in the group, his face taut and serious.*] Why? Why didn't he come out with the rest of us to look?

CHARLIE. He always was an oddball. Him and his whole family. Real oddball.

DON. What do you say we ask him?

[*The group suddenly starts toward the house. In this brief fraction of a moment they take the first step toward performing a <u>metamorphosis</u> that changes people from a group into a mob. They begin to head purposefully across the street toward the house at the end.* STEVE *stands in front of them. For a moment their fear almost turns their walk into a wild stampede, but* STEVE'S *voice, loud, incisive, and commanding, makes them stop.*]

STEVE. Wait a minute . . . wait a minute! Let's not be a mob!

[*The people stop as a group, seem to pause for a moment, and then much more quietly and slowly start to walk across the street.* GOODMAN *stands alone facing the people.*]

GOODMAN. I just don't understand it. I tried to start it and it wouldn't start. You saw me. All of you saw me.

[*And now, just as suddenly as the engine started, it stops and there's a long silence that is gradually intruded upon by the frightened murmuring of the people.*]

GOODMAN. I don't understand. I swear . . . I don't understand. What's happening?

Literary Analysis
Plot in Drama and Conflict What forces are in conflict now? How has the nature of the conflict changed?

metamorphosis
(met′ ə môr′ fə sis) *n.* change of form

✔ **Reading Check**
What happens to Goodman's car?

The Monsters Are Due on Maple Street ◆ 673

Overview of family walking dog on the street, William Low, Courtesy of the artist

DON. Maybe you better tell us. Nothing's working on this street. Nothing. No lights, no power, no radio. [*And then meaningfully*] Nothing except one car—yours!

[*The people pick this up and now their murmuring becomes a loud chant filling the air with accusations and demands for action. Two of the men pass* DON *and head toward* GOODMAN, *who backs away, backing into his car and now at bay.*]

GOODMAN. Wait a minute now. You keep your distance—all of you. So I've got a car that starts by itself—well, that's a freak thing, I admit it. But does that make me some kind of a criminal or something? I don't know why the car works—it just does!

[*This stops the crowd momentarily and now* GOODMAN, *still backing away, goes toward his front porch. He goes up the steps and then stops to stand facing the mob.*

We see a long shot of STEVE *as he comes through the crowd.*]

STEVE. [*Quietly*] We're all on a monster kick, Les. Seems that the general impression holds that maybe one family isn't what we think

▲ Critical Viewing
How do the colors in this illustration contrast with the mood of the drama? Explain. [**Compare and Contrast**]

they are. Monsters from outer space or something. Different than us. Fifth columnists[2] from the vast beyond. [*He chuckles.*] You know anybody that might fit that description around here on Maple Street?

GOODMAN. What is this, a gag or something? This a practical joke or something?

[*We see a close-up of the porch light as it suddenly goes out. There's a murmur from the group.*]

GOODMAN. Now I suppose that's supposed to incriminate me! The light goes on and off. That really does it, doesn't it? [*He looks around the faces of the people.*] I just don't understand this— [*He wets his lips, looking from face to face.*] Look, you all know me. We've lived here five years. Right in this house. We're no different from any of the rest of you! We're no different at all. Really . . . this whole thing is just . . . just weird—

WOMAN. Well, if that's the case, Les Goodman, explain why— [*She stops suddenly, clamping her mouth shut.*]

GOODMAN. [*Softly*] Explain what?

STEVE. [*Interjecting*] Look, let's forget this—

CHARLIE. [*Overlapping him*] Go ahead, let her talk. What about it? Explain what?

WOMAN. [*A little reluctantly*] Well . . . sometimes I go to bed late at night. A couple of times . . . a couple of times I'd come out on the porch and I'd see Mr. Goodman here in the wee hours of the morning standing out in front of his house . . . looking up at the sky. [*She looks around the circle of faces.*] That's right, looking up at the sky as if . . . as if he were waiting for something. [*A pause*] As if he were looking for something.

[*There's a murmur of reaction from the crowd again.*

We cut suddenly to a group shot. As GOODMAN *starts toward them, they back away frightened.*]

GOODMAN. You know really . . . this is for laughs. You know what I'm guilty of? [*He laughs.*] I'm guilty of insomnia. Now what's the penalty for insomnia? [*At this point the laugh, the humor, leaves his voice.*] Did you hear what I said? I said it was insomnia. [*A pause as he looks around, then shouts.*] I said it was insomnia! You fools. You scared, frightened rabbits, you. You're sick people, do you know that? You're sick people—all of you! And you don't even know what you're starting because let me tell you . . . let me tell you—this thing you're starting— that should frighten you. As God is my witness . . . you're letting something begin here that's a nightmare!

Literary Analysis
Plot in Drama Why is the problem with Les Goodman considered part of the rising action of the plot?

✓ **Reading Check**

What does Charlie accuse Goodman of?

---

2. Fifth columnists people who help an invading enemy from within their own country.

ACT II

[*We see a medium shot of the* GOODMAN *entry hall at night. On the side table rests an unlit candle.* MRS. GOODMAN *walks into the scene, a glass of milk in hand. She sets the milk down on the table, lights the candle with a match from a box on the table, picks up the glass of milk, and starts out of scene.*

MRS. GOODMAN *comes through her porch door, glass of milk in hand. The entry hall, with table and lit candle, can be seen behind her.*

Outside, the camera slowly pans down the sidewalk, taking in little knots of people who stand around talking in low voices. At the end of each conversation they look toward LES GOODMAN'S *house. From the various houses we can see candlelight but no electricity, and there's an all-pervading quiet that blankets the whole area, disturbed only by the almost whispered voices of the people as they stand around. The camera pans over to one group where* CHARLIE *stands. He stares across at* GOODMAN'S *house.*

We see a long shot of the house. Two men stand across the street in almost sentry-like poses. Then we see a medium shot of a group of people.]

SALLY. [*A little timorously*] It just doesn't seem right, though, keeping watch on them. Why . . . he was right when he said he was one of our neighbors. Why, I've known Ethel Goodman ever since they moved in. We've been good friends—

CHARLIE. That don't prove a thing. Any guy who'd spend his time lookin' up at the sky early in the morning—well, there's something wrong with that kind of person. There's something that ain't legitimate. Maybe under normal circumstances we could let it go by, but these aren't normal circumstances. Why, look at this street! Nothin' but candles. Why, it's like goin' back into the dark ages or somethin'!

[STEVE *walks down the steps of his porch, walks down the street over to* LES GOODMAN'S *house, and then stops at the foot of the steps.* GOODMAN *stands there, his wife behind him, very frightened.*]

GOODMAN. Just stay right where you are, Steve. We don't want any trouble, but this time if anybody sets foot on my porch, that's what they're going to get—trouble!

STEVE. Look, Les—

GOODMAN. I've already explained to you people. I don't sleep very well at night sometimes. I get up and I take a walk and I look up at the sky. I look at the stars!

MRS. GOODMAN. That's exactly what he does. Why this whole thing, it's . . . it's some kind of madness or something.

STEVE. [*Nods grimly*] That's exactly what it is—some kind of madness.

Reading Strategy
Predicting Do you predict that the neighbors watching the Goodman house will or will not discover anything suspicious? Explain.

CHARLIE'S VOICE. [*Shrill, from across the street*] You best watch who you're seen with, Steve! Until we get this all straightened out, you ain't exactly above suspicion yourself.

STEVE. [*Whirling around toward him*] Or you, Charlie. Or any of us, it seems. From age eight on up!

WOMAN. What I'd like to know is—what are we gonna do? Just stand around here all night?

CHARLIE. There's nothin' else we can do! [*He turns back looking toward* STEVE *and* GOODMAN *again.*] One of 'em'll tip their hand. They got to.

STEVE. [*Raising his voice*] There's something you can do, Charlie. You could go home and keep your mouth shut. You could quit strutting around like a self-appointed hanging judge and just climb into bed and forget it.

CHARLIE. You sound real anxious to have that happen, Steve. I think we better keep our eye on you too!

DON. [*As if he were taking the bit in his teeth, takes a hesitant step to the front*] I think everything might as well come out now. [*He turns toward* STEVE.] Your wife's done plenty of talking, Steve, about how odd you are!

CHARLIE. [*Picking this up, his eyes widening*] Go ahead, tell us what she's said.

[*We see a long shot of* STEVE *as he walks toward them from across the street.*]

STEVE. Go ahead, what's my wife said? Let's get it all out. Let's pick out every idiosyncrasy of every single man, woman, and child on the street. And then we might as well set up some kind of kangaroo court.[3] How about a firing squad at dawn, Charlie, so we can get rid of all the suspects? Narrow them down. Make it easier for you.

DON. There's no need gettin' so upset, Steve. It's just that . . . well . . . Myra's talked about how there's been plenty of nights you spent hours down in your basement workin' on some kind of radio or something. Well, none of us have ever seen that radio—

[*By this time* STEVE *has reached the group. He stands there defiantly close to them.*]

CHARLIE. Go ahead, Steve. What kind of "radio set" you workin' on? I never seen it. Neither has anyone else. Who you talk to on that radio set? And who talks to you?

STEVE. I'm surprised at you, Charlie. How come you're so dense all of a sudden? [*A pause*] Who do I talk to? I talk to monsters from outer space. I talk to three-headed green men who fly over here in

Reading Strategy
Predicting Do you predict that the suspicion will end with Goodman? Why or why not?

Reading Check

What does Don reveal about Steve to their neighbors?

---

3. **kangaroo court** unofficial court that does not follow normal rules.

what look like meteors.

[STEVE'S *wife steps down from the porch, bites her lip, calls out.*]

MRS. BRAND. Steve! Steve, please. [*Then looking around, frightened, she walks toward the group.*] It's just a ham radio set, that's all. I bought him a book on it myself. It's just a ham radio set. A lot of people have them. I can show it to you. It's right down in the basement.

STEVE. [*Whirls around toward her*] Show them nothing! If they want to look inside our house—let them get a search warrant.

CHARLIE. Look, buddy, you can't afford to—

STEVE. [*Interrupting*] Charlie, don't tell me what I can afford! And stop telling me who's dangerous and who isn't and who's safe and who's a menace. [*He turns to the group and shouts.*] And you're with him, too—all of you! You're standing here all set to crucify—all set to find a <u>scapegoat</u>—all desperate to point some kind of a finger at a neighbor! Well now look, friends, the only thing that's gonna happen is that we'll eat each other up alive—

[*He stops abruptly as* CHARLIE *suddenly grabs his arm.*]

CHARLIE. [*In a hushed voice*] That's not the only thing that can happen to us.

[*Cut to a long shot looking down the street. A figure has suddenly materialized in the gloom and in the silence we can hear the clickety-clack of slow, measured footsteps on concrete as the figure walks slowly toward them. One of the women lets out a stifled cry. The young mother grabs her boy as do a couple of others.*]

TOMMY. [*Shouting, frightened*] It's the monster! It's the monster!

[*Another woman lets out a wail and the people fall back in a group, staring toward the darkness and the approaching figure.*

We see a medium group shot of the people as they stand in the shadows watching. DON MARTIN *joins them, carrying a shotgun. He holds it up.*]

DON. We may need this.

STEVE. A shotgun? [*He pulls it out of* DON'S *hand.*] Good Lord—will anybody think a thought around here? Will you people wise up? What good would a shotgun do against—

[*Now* CHARLIE *pulls the gun from* STEVE'S *hand.*]

CHARLIE. No more talk, Steve. You're going to talk us into a grave! You'd let whatever's out there walk right over us, wouldn't yuh? Well, some of us won't!

[*He swings the gun around to point it toward the sidewalk. The dark figure continues to walk toward them.*

Literary Analysis
Plot in Drama How do Don's actions advance the plot toward a climax?

Streetlight, 1930, Constance Coleman Richardson, Indianapolis Museum of Art

▲ **Critical Viewing** Why does night's darkness, shown in this illustration, make people more fearful? **[Hypothesize]**

The group stands there, fearful, apprehensive, mothers clutching children, men standing in front of wives. CHARLIE *slowly raises the gun. As the figure gets closer and closer he suddenly pulls the trigger. The sound of it explodes in the stillness. There is a long angle shot looking down at the figure, who suddenly lets out a small cry, stumbles forward onto his knees and then falls forward on his face.* DON, CHARLIE, *and* STEVE *race forward over to him.* STEVE *is there first and turns the man over. Now the crowd gathers around them.*]

STEVE. [*Slowly looks up*] It's Pete Van Horn.

DON. [*In a hushed voice*] Pete Van Horn! He was just gonna go over to the next block to see if the power was on—

WOMAN. You killed him, Charlie. You shot him dead!

✔**Reading Check**
What happens to the dark figure that is walking down Maple Street?

The Monsters Are Due on Maple Street ◆ 679

CHARLIE. [*Looks around at the circle of faces, his eyes frightened, his face contorted*] But . . . but I didn't know who he was. I certainly didn't know who he was. He comes walkin' out of the darkness—how am I supposed to know who he was? [*He grabs* STEVE.] Steve—you know why I shot! How was I supposed to know he wasn't a monster or something? [*He grabs* DON *now.*] We're all scared of the same thing. I was just tryin' to . . . tryin' to protect my home, that's all! Look, all of you, that's all I was tryin' to do. [*He looks down wildly at the body.*] I didn't know it was somebody we knew! I didn't know—

[*There's a sudden hush and then an intake of breath. We see a medium shot of the living room window of* CHARLIE'S *house. The window is not lit, but suddenly the house lights come on behind it.*]

WOMAN. [*In a very hushed voice*] Charlie . . . Charlie . . . the lights just went on in your house. Why did the lights just go on?

DON. What about it, Charlie? How come you're the only one with lights now?

GOODMAN. That's what I'd like to know.

[*A pause as they all stare toward* CHARLIE.]

GOODMAN. You were so quick to kill, Charlie, and you were so quick to tell us who we had to be careful of. Well, maybe you had to kill. Maybe Peter there was trying to tell us something. Maybe he'd found out something and came back to tell us who there was amongst us we should watch out for—

[CHARLIE *backs away from the group, his eyes wide with fright.*]

CHARLIE. No . . . no . . . it's nothing of the sort! I don't know why the lights are on. I swear I don't. Somebody's pulling a gag or something.

[*He bumps against* STEVE, *who grabs him and whirls him around.*]

STEVE. A gag? A gag? Charlie, there's a dead man on the sidewalk and you killed him! Does this thing look like a gag to you?

[CHARLIE *breaks away and screams as he runs toward his house.*]

CHARLIE. No! No! Please!

[*A man breaks away from the crowd to chase* CHARLIE.

   We see a long angle shot looking down as the man tackles CHARLIE *and lands on top of him. The other people start to run toward them.* CHARLIE *is up on his feet, breaks away from the other man's grasp, lands a couple of desperate punches that push the man aside. Then he forces his way, fighting, through the crowd to once again break free, jumps up on his front porch. A rock thrown from the group smashes a window alongside of him, the broken glass flying past him. A couple of pieces cut him. He stands there perspiring, rumpled, blood running down from a cut on the cheek. His wife breaks away*

Reading Strategy
Predicting Do you think the blackout will be resolved? How?

Literary Analysis
Plot in Drama What events are increasing the tension of the conflict?

from the group to throw herself into his arms. He buries his face against her. We can see the crowd converging on the porch now.]

VOICES.

It must have been him.

He's the one.

We got to get Charlie.

[*Another rock lands on the porch. Now* CHARLIE *pushes his wife behind him, facing the group.*]

CHARLIE. Look, look I swear to you . . . it isn't me . . . but I do know who it is . . . I swear to you, I do know who it is. I know who the monster is here. I know who it is that doesn't belong. I swear to you I know.

GOODMAN. [*Shouting*] What are you waiting for?

WOMAN. [*Shouting*] Come on, Charlie, come on.

MAN ONE. [*Shouting*] Who is it, Charlie, tell us!

DON. [*Pushing his way to the front of the crowd*] All right, Charlie, let's hear it!

[CHARLIE'S *eyes dart around wildly.*]

CHARLIE. It's . . . it's . . .

MAN TWO. [*Screaming*] Go ahead, Charlie, tell us.

CHARLIE. It's . . . it's the kid. It's Tommy. He's the one!

[*There's a gasp from the crowd as we cut to a shot of* SALLY *holding her son* TOMMY. *The boy at first doesn't understand and then, realizing the eyes are all on him, buries his face against his mother.*]

SALLY. [*Backs away*] That's crazy! That's crazy! He's a little boy.

WOMAN. But he knew! He was the only one who knew! He told us all about it. Well, how did he know? How could he have known?

[*The various people take this up and repeat the question aloud.*]

VOICES.

How could he know?

Who told him?

Make the kid answer.

DON. It was Charlie who killed old man Van Horn.

WOMAN. But it was the kid here who knew what was going to happen all the time. He was the one who knew!

[*We see a close-up of* STEVE.]

STEVE. Are you all gone crazy? [*Pause as he looks about*] Stop.

[*A fist crashes at* STEVE'S *face, staggering him back out of the frame of the picture.*

Reading Strategy
Predicting Who will Charlie name? Why?

**Reading Check**

According to Charlie, who is the monster?

The Monsters Are Due on Maple Street ◆ 681

There are several close camera shots suggesting the coming of violence. A hand fires a rifle. A fist clenches. A hand grabs the hammer from VAN HORN'S *body, etc. Meanwhile, we hear the following lines.*]

DON. Charlie has to be the one—Where's my rifle—

WOMAN. Les Goodman's the one. His car started! Let's wreck it.

MRS. GOODMAN. What about Steve's radio—He's the one that called them—

MRS. GOODMAN. Smash the radio. Get me a hammer. Get me something.

STEVE. Stop—Stop—

CHARLIE. Where's that kid—Let's get him.

MAN ONE. Get Steve—Get Charlie—They're working together.

[*The crowd starts to converge around the mother, who grabs the child and starts to run with him. The crowd starts to follow, at first walking fast, and then running after him.*

We see a full shot of the street as suddenly CHARLIE'S *lights go off and the lights in another house go on. They stay on for a moment, then from across the street other lights go on and then off again.*]

MAN ONE. [*Shouting*] It isn't the kid . . . it's Bob Weaver's house.

WOMAN. It isn't Bob Weaver's house. It's Don Martin's place.

Reading Strategy
Making Predictions What do you think will happen next on Maple Street?

CHARLIE. I tell you it's the kid.

DON. It's Charlie. He's the one.

[*We move into a series of close-ups of various people as they shout, accuse, scream, interspersing these shots with shots of houses as the lights go on and off, and then slowly in the middle of this nightmarish morass of sight and sound the camera starts to pull away, until once again we've reached the opening shot looking at the Maple Street sign from high above.*

The camera continues to move away until we dissolve to a shot looking toward the metal side of a space craft, which sits shrouded in darkness. An open door throws out a beam of light from the illuminated interior. Two figures silhouetted against the bright lights appear. We get only a vague feeling of form, but nothing more explicit than that.]

FIGURE ONE. Understand the procedure now? Just stop a few of their machines and radios and telephones and lawn mowers . . . throw them into darkness for a few hours, and then you just sit back and watch the pattern.

FIGURE TWO. And this pattern is always the same?

FIGURE ONE. With few variations. They pick the most dangerous enemy they can find . . . and it's themselves. And all we need do is sit back . . . and watch.

▲ Critic

How doe
manipula
help to c
ideas of t
[Connect

☑ Read

Who is w
happenir
Street? V
watching

FIGURE TWO. Then I take it this place . . . this Maple Street . . . is not unique.

FIGURE ONE. [*Shaking his head*] By no means. Their world is full of Maple Streets. And we'll go from one to the other and let them destroy themselves. One to the other . . . one to the other . . . one to the other—

[*Now the camera pans up for a shot of the starry sky and over this we hear the* NARRATOR'S *voice.*]

NARRATOR'S VOICE. The tools of conquest do not necessarily come with bombs and explosions and fallout. There are weapons that are simply thoughts, attitudes, prejudices—to be found only in the minds of men. For the record, prejudices can kill and suspicion can destroy and a thoughtless frightened search for a scapegoat has a fallout all its own for the children . . . and the children yet unborn. [A pause] And the pity of it is . . . that these things cannot be confined to . . . The Twilight Zone!

Review and Assess

Thinking About the Literature

1. **Respond:** If you were a resident of Maple Street, how would you have responded to the strange events?

2. **(a) Recall:** What are the first signs that something strange is happening on Maple Street? **(b) Analyze Cause and Effect:** How do these signs initiate the conflict on Maple Street?

3. **(a) Recall:** How do the people on Maple Street single out Les Goodman in Act I? **(b) Interpret:** What qualities of his cause the reaction? **(c) Deduce:** What does this suggest about what is really happening on Maple Street?

4. **(a) Recall:** Why does Charlie shoot Pete Van Horn? **(b) Infer:** What does the crowd's response to this shooting suggest about how well they are thinking?

5. **(a) Recall:** Who accuses Tommy after the shooting, and why? **(b) Connect:** Why are people prepared to believe such an accusation? **(c) Support:** How do the events of the play support this statement: "The tools of conquest do not necessarily come with bombs and explosions and fallout"?

6. **(a) Recall:** What causes the power fluctuations on Maple Street? **(b) Generalize:** What warning should people take from this play? **(c) Draw Conclusions:** Who are the monsters of Maple Street?

7. **Take a Position:** Do you believe that people are usually treated as if they are innocent until proved guilty? Explain.

Rod Serling

(1924–1975)

Rod Serling once said that he didn't have much imagination, an odd statement from a man who wrote more than 200 television scripts. Serling didn't become serious about writing until college, after he served as a paratrooper in World War II. Driven by a love for radio drama, Serling earned second place in a national script contest. Soon after, he landed his first staff job as a radio writer.

Serling branched out into writing for a new medium—television—and rocketed to fame. Just six years after the contest, everyone wanted to watch—and perform—Serling's work.

Review and Assess

Literary Analysis

Plot in Drama

1. What makes the people on Maple Street fearful?
2. Why do they begin to suspect one another?
3. Use a diagram similar to the one shown to outline the **plot.** Describe three events that are part of the rising action, the climax, two events that are part of the falling action, and the resolution.

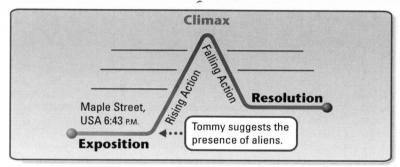

Connecting Literary Elements

4. What hints **foreshadow** that the people will begin to turn on one another?
5. Complete a chart like the one shown here to identify examples of foreshadowing.

Foreshadowing	"A little power failure and right away we get all flustered."		
Event		Charlie shoots Pete	Charlie accuses Tommy

Reading Strategy

Making Predictions

6. Based on Steve Brand's responses to Tommy, what role did you expect Brand to play in the story? Why?
7. How did you expect the play to end? Did you at any point think there might actually be aliens? Why or why not?

Extend Understanding

8. **Social Studies Connection:** Why do you think people's behaviors change when they are in a group?

Quick Review

Plot is the sequence of events in a literary work. To review plot, see page 665.

Foreshadowing is the use of hints to suggest upcoming events or situations. To review foreshadowing, see page 665.

A **prediction** is an educated guess about what will happen.

 Take It to the Net
www.phschool.com
Take the interactive self-test online to check your understanding of the selection.

Integrate Language Skills

Vocabulary Development Lesson

Word Analysis: Latin Word Root -sist-

The Latin word root -sist- means "stand." Complete these sentences with -sist- words:

consist   resist   assist

1. He begged them to ___?___ acting like a mob.
2. His wife tried to ___?___ him, pointing out that the rumors did not ___?___ of any real facts.

Spelling Strategy

The *f* sound is sometimes spelled *ph*, as in *metamorphosis*. Complete the words containing the *ph* spelling of the *f* sound.

1. Equipment used to listen to music: he___?___
2. A person's life story: bi___?___
3. Letters in ordered sequence: al___?___

Concept Development: Antonyms

Choose the word most opposite in meaning from the first word.

1. defiant: (a) agreeable, (b) angry, (c) curious
2. persistently: (a) quickly, (b) sadly, (c) occasionally
3. metamorphosis: (a) bloom, (b) choice, (c) stability
4. scapegoat: (a) hero, (b) victim, (c) director
5. flustered: (a) shy, (b) confident, (c) sleepy
6. sluggishly: (a) energetically, (b) newly, (c) dimly
7. assent: (a) confusion, (b) approval, (c) denial

Grammar Lesson

Pronoun and Antecedent Agreement

Pronouns should agree with their antecedents in number and gender. In this example, the plural pronoun *their* agrees in number with its plural antecedent *neighbors*.

The neighbors have lost their ability to think.

Here, the singular pronoun *his* agrees with its singular antecedent *Tommy*.

Tommy gave his opinion.

When revising your work, be especially careful to check for errors in pronoun-antecedent agreement.

▶ *For more practice, see page R32, Exercise D.*
Practice Fill in the blank in each item with an appropriate pronoun, taking care to avoid errors in pronoun-antecedent agreement.

1. The aliens had planned _____ game carefully.
2. Each woman did what _____ could.
3. Pete showed _____ fear.
4. Charlie became angry, while Steve tried to solve the puzzle with _____ mind.
5. The shooting shocked the crowd. _____ was unexpected.

Writing Application Write a summary of the play. Identify the pronouns and antecedents and check that they agree.

W/G Prentice Hall Writing and Grammar Connection: Chapter 24, Section 2

Writing Lesson

Sequel

Write the opening scene for a sequel that begins the morning after the events in the play. Include realistic dialogue and stage directions. (Use the plays in this unit as models.)

Prewriting Write a list of events. Put them in time order. Next to each event, briefly describe how the characters will respond.

Drafting Begin with stage directions that set the morning scene. Then, show how the events have moved forward since the previous night. Use script format, which identifies who is speaking, and include stage directions in brackets.

Model: Stage Directions

Act III

[*Curtain rises. In the background, a glowing dawn gradually lights the stage. A corpse is lying on the sidewalk next to a car with several dents and smashed windows. Tommy and Sally emerge from their house with suitcases and glance around cautiously. Tommy approaches the corpse.*]

Sally. [*In a sharp, fearful whisper.*] Tommy, come away! We must leave before the neighbors wake up.

> The writer uses stage directions to set the scene and to tell how characters talk.

Revising Review your scene to make sure characters' actions are consistent with their behavior earlier in the play.

W͞G Prentice Hall Writing and Grammar Connection: Chapter 5, Section 2

Extension Activities

Listening and Speaking Learn about conflict-resolution techniques from the library or a school counselor. Then, lead a **group discussion** on how these techniques might be used to resolve the conflicts on Maple Street. Consider the actions and positions of Steve, Charles, and Mr. Goodman in your resolution, and summarize your findings for the rest of the class.

Research and Technology Think of a science-fiction movie you have seen recently. Use the Internet to research special effects used in such films—visual effects, sound, and models. Write an **explanation** of how some of these special effects could be used to enhance a production of "The Monsters Are Due on Maple Street."

 **Take It to the Net** www.phschool.com

Go online for an additional research activity using the Internet.

From Jules Verne's *20,000 Leagues Under the Sea* to *Star Wars* and *The X-Files*, people have enjoyed science fiction. This type of fiction combines elements of fantasy and adventure with scientific fact. Some science fiction depends on violent action and weird space monsters. Most good science-fiction writing, however, creates settings and characters that are believable, even if some aspects are strange or alien. "The Monsters Are Due on Maple Street," for example, takes place in what seems to be an ordinary neighborhood whose residents are people whom you can recognize. Until the last scene, there are only a few hints about alien events. Science fiction also often deals with important themes and ideas—such as good versus evil, individuality, tolerance, and the power of love and friendship.

A Wrinkle in Time, an award-winning novel by Madeleine L'Engle, has these qualities. Meg Murry, her strange but brilliant younger brother, Charles Wallace, and their friend Calvin O'Keefe travel through time and space. The "wrinkle in time" is a "tesseract," which allows them to travel in the fifth dimension. Their goal is to rescue Meg's scientist father, whom an evil force has trapped on the planet Camazotz. In this scene, the three travelers get their first glimpse of the "dark planet." Although the neighborhood looks much like a neighborhood at home on Earth, they soon notice strange and sinister things about the way people behave.

As you read the excerpt from *A Wrinkle in Time*, look for attitudes and fears that are similar to and different from the ones in "The Monsters Are Due on Maple Street."

from

A Wrinkle in Time

MADELEINE L'ENGLE

Below them the town was laid out in harsh angular patterns. The houses in the outskirts were all exactly alike, small square boxes painted gray. Each had a small, rectangular plot of lawn in front, with a straight line of dull-looking flowers edging the path to the door. Meg had a feeling that if she could count the flowers there would be exactly the same number for each house. In front of all the houses children were playing. Some were skipping rope, some were bouncing balls. Meg felt vaguely that something was wrong with their play. It seemed exactly like children playing around any housing development at home, and yet there was something different about it. She looked at Calvin, and saw that he, too, was puzzled.

"Look!" Charles Wallace said suddenly. "They're skipping and bouncing in rhythm! Everyone's doing it at exactly the same moment."

This was so. As the skipping rope hit the pavement, so did the ball. As the rope curved over the head of the jumping child, the child with the ball caught the ball. Down came the ropes. Down came the balls. Over and over again. Up. Down. All in rhythm. All identical. Like the houses. Like the paths. Like the flowers.

Thematic Connection
What is the first strange thing that Meg and Charles Wallace notice about people on Camazotz?

Then the doors of all the houses opened <u>simultaneously</u>, and out came women like a row of paper dolls. The print of their dresses was different, but they all gave the appearance of being the same. Each woman stood on the steps of her house. Each clapped. Each child with the ball caught the ball. Each child with the skipping rope folded the rope. Each child turned and walked into the house. The doors clicked shut behind them.

"How can they do it?" Meg asked wonderingly. "We couldn't do it that way if we tried. What does it mean?"

"Let's go back." Calvin's voice was urgent.

"Back?" Charles Wallace asked. "Where?"

"I don't know. Anywhere. Back to the hill. Back to Mrs. Whatsit and Mrs. Who and Mrs. Which. I don't like this."

"But they aren't there. Do you think they'd come to us if we turned back now?"

"I don't like it," Calvin said again.

"Come *on*." Impatience made Meg squeak. "You know we can't go back. Mrs. Whatsit *said* to go into the town." She started on down the street, and the two boys followed her. The houses, all identical, continued, as far as the eye could reach.

Then, all at once, they saw the same thing, and stopped to watch. In front of one of the houses stood a little boy with a ball, and he was bouncing it. But he bounced it rather badly and with no particular rhythm, sometimes dropping it and running after it with awkward, furtive leaps, sometimes throwing it up into the air and trying to catch it. The door of his house opened and out ran one of the mother figures. She looked wildly up and down the street, saw the children and put her hand to her mouth as though to <u>stifle</u> a scream, grabbed the little boy and rushed indoors with him. The ball dropped from his fingers and rolled out into the street.

Charles Wallace ran after it and picked it up, holding it out for Meg and Calvin to see. It seemed like a perfectly ordinary, brown rubber ball.

"Let's take it in to him and see what happens," Charles Wallace suggested.

Meg pulled at him. "Mrs. Whatsit said for us to go on into the town."

"Well, we *are* in the town, aren't we? The outskirts anyhow. I want to know more about this. I have a hunch it may help us later. You go on if you don't want to come with me."

"No," Calvin said firmly. "We're going to stay together. Mrs. Whatsit said we weren't to let them separate us. But I'm with you on this. Let's knock and see what happens."

They went up the path to the house, Meg reluctant, eager to get on into the town. "Let's hurry," she begged, "*please!* Don't you want to find father?"

"Yes," Charles Wallace said, "but not blindly. How can we help him if we don't know what we're up against? And it's obvious we've been brought here

simultaneously
(sī məl tā´ nē əs) *adv.*
occurring at the same time

Thematic Connection
Why is the little boy's mother so upset?

stifle (stī´ fəl) *v.* to stop; inhibit

to help him, not just to find him." He walked briskly up the steps and knocked at the door. They waited. Nothing happened. Then Charles Wallace saw a bell, and this he rang. They could hear the bell buzzing in the house, and the sound of it echoed down the street. After a moment the mother figure opened the door. All up and down the street other doors opened, but only a crack, and eyes peered toward the three children and the woman looking fearfully out the door at them.

"What do you want?" she asked. "It isn't paper time yet; we've had milk time; we've had this month's Puller Prush Person; and I've given my Decency Donations regularly. All my papers are in order."

"I think your little boy dropped his ball," Charles Wallace said, holding it out.

The woman pushed the ball away. "Oh, no! The children in our section *never* drop balls! They're all perfectly trained. We haven't had an <u>Aberration</u> for three years."

All up and down the block, heads nodded in agreement.

Charles Wallace moved closer to the woman and looked past her into the house. Behind her in the shadows he could see the little boy, who must have been about his own age.

"You can't come in," the woman said. "You haven't shown me any papers. I don't have to let you in if you haven't any papers."

Charles Wallace held the ball out beyond the woman so that the little boy could see it. Quick as a flash the boy leaped forward and grabbed the ball from Charles Wallace's hand, then darted back into the shadows. The woman went very white, opened her mouth as though to say something, then slammed the door in their faces instead. All up and down the street doors slammed.

"What are they afraid of?" Charles Wallace asked. "What's the matter with them?"

"Don't *you* know?" Meg asked him. "Don't you know what all this is about, Charles?"

"Not yet," Charles Wallace said. "Not even an inkling. And I'm trying. But I didn't get through anywhere. Not even a chink. Let's go." He stumped down the steps.

Thematic Connection
What do you think Charles Wallace expects to discover in the house?

aberration (ab ə rā´ shən) *n.* a departure from what is normal or correct

Madeleine L'Engle

(b. 1918)

"Often the only way to look clearly at this extraordinary universe is through fantasy, fairy tale, myth," Madeleine L'Engle has said. Her more than 60 books of poetry, novels, plays, and essays follow this idea. Born in New York City in 1918, L'Engle began to write novels in the 1940s while working in the theater. At first, L'Engle had trouble finding a publisher for *A Wrinkle in Time*, but it won the 1963 Newbery Medal and made her a favorite with readers. Several sequels, beginning with *A Wind in the Door* (1973), trace the characters' later lives. L'Engle also has written about her home, Crosswicks, as well as a series of novels about another fictional family, the Austins.

Connecting Literature Past and Present

1. Some people on Maple Street believe that their "oddball" neighbors may be aliens. How is this attitude like the social "rules" that control the people of Camazotz?
2. Why do you think the children on Camazotz and the people of Maple Street are afraid of differences?
3. Would Meg and Charles Wallace be likely to side with Charlie and Don in suspecting their neighbors because they are "different"? Why or why not?

READING INFORMATIONAL MATERIALS

Responses to Literature

About Responses to Literature

A response to literature is an essay or other type of writing that discusses what is of value in a book, a short story, an essay, an article, or a poem. A response might retell the plot of a story to show why it is exciting, explain why a poem is beautiful, or show disappointment with a writer's latest play. When reading a response to literature critically, look for the following details:

- A strong, interesting focus
- A clear organization that groups related details
- Supporting details for each main idea
- A summary of important features of the work
- A judgment about the value of the work

Reading Strategy

Identifying Evidence

The writer of a response to literature or another piece of nonfiction should provide evidence to support each main point. A writer's evidence may not be provable facts but may consist instead of details that support the writer's opinion. In the following response to literature, the author makes many statements about her opinions of a famous author. By supplying evidence for her opinions, her response has a much stronger effect. As you read nonfiction critically, identify the evidence presented. Make a chart like the one below. In the left column are the author's main points; in the middle column is the evidence that supports those points. Find other points the author makes, supply the appropriate evidence, and then write explanations.

Author's Opinion	Evidence	Explanation
"The heroes and heroines are not stereotypes;"	". . . they live and breathe and become individuals, named or not."	The author follows with descriptions of a few characters in order to show how the characters are individuals.
". . . his genius for characterization . . ."	". . . so persuasive is Andersen's art that, in spite of the physical agony, we still agree with her that the prince is worth dying for."	The author uses an example from one of Andersen's stories to prove that his characters are so lifelike that the reader is persuaded to believe them to be real.

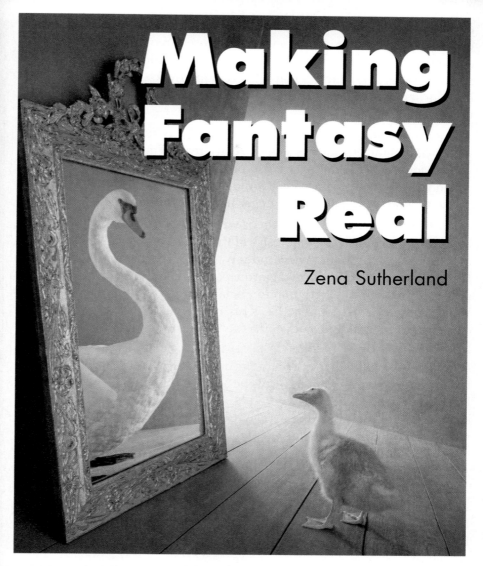

Making Fantasy Real

Zena Sutherland

A response to
literature often
gives the context
of the time period
in which the
author worked.

Hans Christian Andersen (1805–1875) was born in Odense, Denmark, of a peasant family. His . . . first book, a travel diary of a walking trip, appeared in 1829, published by himself, and his first volumes of *Fairy Tales, Told for Children* appeared in 1835 . . . . Andersen poured himself into his writing; it became the vehicle for expressing his emotions, flashes of humor, commentaries on life, and the follies of humankind. Some of his stories are retellings of folktales: "Little Claus and Big Claus," "The Princess and the Pea," and "The Emperor's New Clothes."

Specific literary
elements are
pointed out.

In these, Andersen took the traditional story and added to it his own interpretation of character, providing motivation for the action in the tale. The heroes and heroines are not stereotypes; they live and breathe and become individuals, named or not. The princess who can feel a pea under twenty mattresses can never be confused in our thinking with any other princess, sensitive though she may be. Andersen imparted such life to these characters that we feel empathy for the emperor and his courtiers, none of whom naturally wish to admit they are stupid or unfit for office.

But it is in Andersen's own creations, his literary fairy tales, that his genius for characterization is shown. As we read "The Little Mermaid," we shudder at the pain the mermaid must feel as she puts foot to ground[.A]nd yet, so persuasive is Andersen's art that, in spite of the physical agony, we still agree with her that the prince is worth dying for.

What literary element does the writer focus on most?

"The Ugly Duckling" is, rightly or wrongly, seen as symbolic of Andersen's own life. The animosity of the neighbors to the "different" one seems so natural that we wonder if we ourselves would have seen the promise implicit in the awkward creature. The conversations in the poultry-yard ring true both to human nature and to the human ear. What mother would not say, "He is my own child and, when you look closely at him, he's quite handsome . . ."? Because of Andersen, every "ugly duckling" promises a swan.

Connections between the author's life and the author's work may be called out in a literary response.

Andersen's ability to draw character does not rest on extensive description. In a few carefully chosen words he establishes important qualities, leaving our imaginations so stimulated that we supply the rest of the picture. Of the hero of "The Steadfast Tin Soldier" Andersen says, "he stood as firm and steadfast on his one leg as the others did on their two." The outward description is not important; what Andersen is emphasizing is the constancy of his character.

Andersen's fantasies do not lack supernatural beings or things, and many of them have otherworldly settings, talking animals, and personifications of inanimate objects. But his main contribution was to make us look more sharply at daily life through the window of his imagination.

Check Your Comprehension

1. What kind of book did Andersen first publish?
2. What are two folktales that Andersen retold?
3. In what ways did Andersen change the traditional story of the folktales?
4. What are two stories that are originally written by Andersen?

Applying the Reading Strategy

Identifying the Evidence

5. What evidence does the writer give to support her belief that Andersen's description of the mermaid is so persuasive?
6. What does the writer believe to be symbolic of Andersen's life?
7. What evidence does the writer give to support her belief that Andersen's characters do not rely on extensive description?

Activity

Response Evaluation

Find a literary response to a work you have read. Look in the following sources.

- books
- newspaper articles
- magazines
- brochures

Then, evaluate the response and how well the author supports his or her assertions with evidence from the text.

Information from Text	Evidence	Evaluation

Comparing Informational Materials

Different Types of Responses to Literature

In addition to a standard literary essay, there are other types of responses to literature. There are book reviews and letters to an author. A book review gives readers an impression of a book, encouraging them to either read it or to avoid reading it. Letters to an author let a writer know what a reader found enjoyable or disappointing in a work. Choose one of the previously mentioned responses to literature. Then, write about a story that you have recently read. When you are finished, share your response with the class.

Writing WORKSHOP

Response to Literature

A **response to literature** is a piece of writing that discusses what is of value in a book, a short story, a play, a poem, an essay, or an article. Using examples from the literature, you can explain *what, why,* and *how* a work affects you. In this workshop, you will choose a piece of literature you feel strongly about and write about what it means to you.

Assignment Criteria Your response to literature should have the following characteristics:

- A strong, interesting response based on some aspect of the literary work
- Your own interpretation based on careful reading, understanding, and insight
- A clear organization based on several ideas, premises, or images
- Examples and textual evidence that support and justify your interpretation
- An analysis of how the literary elements in the work shaped your responses

To preview the criteria on which your response to literature may be assessed, see the Rubric on page 699.

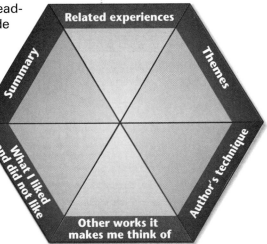

Prewriting

Choose a topic. Choose a piece of literature that you have a strong reaction to, either positive or negative. If you keep a reader's response journal, look back through it for works that made an impression on you. Select one of these works. As you reread it, record your thoughts and feelings. Keep track of specific quotations, images, or ideas that you can use later.

Use hexagonal writing. To gather details about various sides of your topic, use a hexagon. Cut out six large triangles of equal size from colored sheets of paper. Arrange the triangles, and label them as shown here. Then, look through the work to find details for each triangle.

Think about literary elements. To help plan your response, think about the various literary elements that are appropriate to the kind of literature you are analyzing.

Develop your own interpretation. Read through the literature several times. Each time, think of new ways to interpret the meaning of what you have read. Remember, you are not just summarizing the work.

Hexagonal Writing

Related experiences

Summary

Themes

What I liked and did not like

Author's technique

Other works it makes me think of

Student Model

Before you begin drafting your response to literature, read this student model and review the characteristics of a successful response.

Lan Le
Elk Grove, California

Response to Literature

In *A Christmas Carol* by Charles Dickens, Ebenezer Scrooge's personality alters for the better from the beginning of the play to the end—showing that people can change for the better. At first, Scrooge was heartless, but as the story progresses, a richer and fuller heart filled that empty space. How could someone's worthless heart become as rich as gold?

Scrooge cared only about working, earning, and saving money. While Scrooge prospered outside, he lost value inside. He wanted to remain in solitude and had a nasty attitude toward everyone around him. During the holidays, solicitors come to ask for donations from Scrooge for the needy, but Scrooge thinks he helps them enough through taxes. He maliciously remarks, "If they would rather die (than seek help), they had better do it, and decrease the surplus population." Scrooge's negative attitude attracts the spirit of his old partner, Marley, who sends three spirits (Past, Present, and Future) to help guide him. The Spirit of the Past teaches Scrooge that he had lost his beloved Belle by putting the "golden idol," money, above all else. The Spirit of the Present shows Scrooge that money is not needed to be able to enjoy life. The Cratchit family had a small turkey for supper, yet the whole family was joyous. The Spirit of the Future presents that there will be no love in store for Scrooge when he dies because he hasn't been thoughtful and generous to others. Scrooge's servants take his possessions while he lies dead on a bed. Nevertheless, in the end, Scrooge learns his lesson and has a positive attitude. He visits his nephew, gives Bob Cratchit a raise, and donates a large amount of money to charity. Scrooge does all this from the goodness of his heart.

The old Victorian England setting makes this timeless message even more powerful. Perhaps it's because of the hidden poverty of the time that Scrooge's kindness is so welcome and so wonderful.

Scrooge contributed riches but received everything back inside by knowing he made differences in someone's day and life. By giving time and assistance to others who need it, the community can advance knowing that people who needed help received it.

The writer applies the events in *A Christmas Carol* to a broader question about whether people can change their natures.

The response includes the writer's insights into the character's actions.

Citations from the text give strong support to the writer's comments.

The essay is organized with an introduction, a body, and a conclusion.

The writer ties literary elements into her response and comments on how they influenced her response.

Drafting

Define and develop your focus. Review your notes to find a main idea or focus for your response. The focus statement sums up your reaction to one aspect of the work. Answer questions like the ones shown here. Then, write one good sentence that states the focus and references a literary element.

Support interpretations with textual evidence and examples. Try not to stray from your topic—the literary work. Rely on examples from the work to support your interpretations. Refer to specific scenes, characters, images, and actions. Justify your interpretations with quotations from the text. Tie every sentence in your draft to the literature.

Conclude with an insight. A good response to literature provides insight into the work. You might evaluate a literary element in the work, interpret the theme, or analyze how the parts work together. Ask yourself

- What details of the work contributed to my reaction?
- How do these details fit with other details in the work?

My Main Response

What is my main response to my topic?

What Causes it

What features of the work cause my reaction?

My Focus

What conclusion can I draw about these features of the work?

Revising

Organize around your strongest idea. Review your draft to find places to support your main point.

1. Circle your strongest point—your most profound insight or a quotation that pulls your whole response together. Consider moving this point to the end.

2. If you move your strongest point to the end, add a transition sentence that clearly explains the connection between this point and your other ideas.

3. Then, go back to other paragraphs to add sentences that link each paragraph to your concluding point.

Scrooge contributed riches but received everything back inside by knowing he made differences in someone's day and life. By giving time and assistance to others who need it, the community can advance knowing that people who needed help received it.

> The writer concludes with a powerful statement that captures the combination of the other points in her essay.

Use correct capitalization. Use capital letters for the first word and all other key words in the titles of books, magazines, short stories, poems, and plays. Do not capitalize articles, short prepositions, and conjunctions.

Examples: *The Grapes of Wrath*
"A Narrow Fellow in the Grass"
National Geographic

Compare the nonmodel and the model. Why is the model more effective than the nonmodel?

Nonmodel	Model
In *A Christmas carol* by Charles Dickens, Ebenezer Scrooge's personality alters for the better. It reminds me of George Eliot's poem "Count that day lost."	In *A Christmas Carol* by Charles Dickens, Ebenezer Scrooge's personality alters for the better. It reminds me of George Eliot's poem "Count That Day Lost."

Publishing and Presenting

Choose one of these ways to share your writing with classmates or a larger audience.

Good Reading for Teens Work with your classmates to assemble your responses to literature in a book for your school or local library. Include a rating system and rate each work to which you have responded.

Electronic Recommendations Create a recommended reading list on a Web site on your school's server. Post your responses to literature. Invite others to share their opinions and reactions.

 *Prentice Hall Writing and Grammar Connection: Chapter 12, Section 2*

 **Listening Connection**
To practice evaluating how the media attempts to influence opinions and responses, see the **Listening and Speaking Workshop: Analyzing Media Messages,** page 700.

Rubric for Self-Assessment

Evaluate your response to literature using the following criteria and rating scale.

Criteria	Rating Scale				
	Not very				Very
How well is the response based on an interesting aspect of the literary work?	1	2	3	4	5
How well does the interpretation reflect careful reading, understanding, and insight?	1	2	3	4	5
How clearly is the response organized around several ideas, premises, or images?	1	2	3	4	5
How well does the writer justify the interpretation with supporting examples and textual evidence?	1	2	3	4	5
How effectively does the writer refer to literary elements to express the response?	1	2	3	4	5

Listening and Speaking WORKSHOP

Analyzing Media Messages

Every day, you are bombarded with media messages—commercials, news, announcements, game shows, talk shows, and music videos, to name just a few. It is important to **analyze media messages**—to actively and critically evaluate what you hear and see. Use these strategies in your analysis.

Analyze effects.

Even when you are sitting passively, the sounds, images, and words in media messages affect you. Be aware of these effects.

Analyze images. First, consider what you see. Is it realistic or imaginary? Colorful or muted? Fast- or slow-paced? Is the focus on people, places, or things? Look carefully at what you see, and ask yourself why it was created.

Analyze text. Consider what is not said, as well as what is. "Dentists recommend this toothpaste" does not tell you *how many* dentists recommend it.

Analyze sound. In addition to the words, what music or sound effects do you hear? What mood do they create?

> ### Evaluation Form for Media Messages
>
> **Effects**
> What are the key images?_____
> What are the key words in the text? _____
> What sound effects do you hear? _____
>
> **Techniques**
> Is there slant or bias?_____
> Is there a bandwagon approach?_____
> Who is the spokesperson?_____
> What is the purpose?_____
> How would you rate the credibility of this message?
> ____Excellent   ____Good   ____Fair   ____Poor
>
> Give a reason for your rating: _____

Identify techniques.

- **Slant and Bias** Beware of any message that presents only one side of an issue that has many different sides. Always look for the other perspective as you evaluate and analyze media messages.

- **Bandwagon** Watch out for any message that suggests that everyone is doing something and that you will be unpopular if you do not do it.

- **Spokespersons** Just because a celebrity or experts deliver a message does not make it believable. Ask yourself if the spokesperson really has the knowledge or background to make the advice significant.

- **Purpose** Identify the *goal* of what you are watching. Some messages are attempts to sell you something. Others are attempts to convince you of the value of participating in some activity—such as watching more television!

(Activity:)
Analyze a commercial With a partner, videotape a commercial aimed at young people. Together, write a short analysis of its message using the terms defined above as a guide. Present your analysis to your classmates.

Assessment WORKSHOP

Sentence Construction

The writing sections of some tests require you to read a passage and answer multiple-choice questions about sentence construction. Use the following strategies to help you answer such questions:

Recognize incomplete sentences and run-on sentences.
Sentences should express complete, unified thoughts. Incomplete sentences lack either a subject or a predicate. Run-on sentences include two or more sentences without proper punctuation between them. You can correct an incomplete sentence by adding to it or by combining it with a sentence or another incomplete sentence. Run-on sentences can be corrected by adding the proper punctuation.

Combine sentences. Sometimes two short sentences that are closely related sound better if they are combined to make a single sentence.

Test-Taking Strategy

When choosing a rewrite or correction, read your selection carefully to make sure it does not introduce a new error or problem.

Sample Test Item

Directions: Choose the best way to write the underlined section. If it needs no change, choose **D**.

(1) In 1984, two men were cutting peat. They were cutting it from a bog in Lindow Moss, England. Suddenly, they saw a human foot sticking up out of the peat. (2) The men called the police, but they needed an archaeologist instead. Lindow Man had been dead for about 2,300 years.

1. **A** In 1984, two men cutting peat from a bog in Lindow Moss, England.

   B In 1984, two men were cutting peat they were cutting it from a bog in Lindow Moss, England.

   C In 1984, two men were cutting peat from a bog in Lindow Moss, England.

   D Correct as is

Answer and Explanation

A is incomplete. **B** is a run-on sentence. *C* is correct because it properly combines two short, related sentences.

▶ Practice

Directions: Choose the best way to write each underlined section. If a section needs no change, choose **D**.

(1) When you eat breakfast cereal. You are actually getting muscle power. From the sun. (2) Plants absorb the sun's energy. They use it to produce glucose. Glucose is changed to starch, which gives humans energy when eaten.

1. **A** When you eat breakfast cereal, you are actually getting muscle power. From the sun.

   B When you eat breakfast. Cereal you are actually getting muscle power from the sun.

   C When you eat breakfast cereal, you are actually getting muscle power from the sun.

   D Correct as is

2. **A** Plants absorb the sun's energy and use it to produce glucose.

   B Plants absorb the sun's energy. Using it to produce glucose.

   C Plants absorbing the sun's energy. They using it to produce energy.

   D Correct as is

Phoebe Beasley

Exploring the Genre

Whether telling a story, capturing a single moment, or describing nature in a whole new way, poetry is the most musical of all literary forms. In this unit you will encounter the following types of poetry:

- **Narrative poetry,** which tells a story.
- **Lyric poetry,** which expresses thought and feelings.
- **Haiku,** which uses a few short lines to create a single vivid picture.
- **Concrete poetry,** which uses the arrangement of letters in the poem to suggest a shape.

◀ **Critical Viewing** Does this painting capture the artist's impressions of a single moment? **[Connect]**

Why Read Literature?

Reading poetry is a special experience. When you read poems, you put your mind, your voice, and all of your senses to work to get the full meaning. To help you understand and remember poems, set different purposes for your reading. Review the three purposes you might set before reading the poems in this unit.

1

Read for the love of literature.

The coldest temperature ever recorded on Earth was in Antarctica, −128.6°F! Read how the poet Robert Service takes this very serious subject and turns it into a humorous tale of two men in the freezing cold in **"The Cremation of Sam McGee,"** page 708.

Did you know that a seal is born already knowing how to swim? It's true! Read a description of how a seal swims in William Jay Smith's concrete poem **"Seal,"** page 720.

2

Read to be inspired.

Martin Luther King, Jr., inspired many people with his "I Have a Dream" speech. More than 250,000 people gathered near the steps of the Lincoln Memorial in Washington, D.C., to hear him speak. To read how one person was inspired by the life of Dr. King, read Raymond Richard Patterson's poem **"Martin Luther King,"** page 730.

Animals prepare for winter in a number of different ways. A single squirrel preparing for winter may gather up to 10 bushels (large baskets) of food. Also, a very rare type of tree frog actually spends the winter frozen on land, only to thaw when spring comes. Read about how one woman is inspired by animals to prepare for winter in **"Winter,"** page 714.

3

Read for information.

Babe Ruth is credited with the invention of the modern baseball bat. He was the first player to order a bat with a knob on the end of the handle. At that time, bats were always made from wood. Today, bats are made out of either wood or metal. To learn more about the differences between wooden and metal bats, read **"Bat Attacks?",** page 763.

 Take It to the Net

Visit the Web site for online instruction and activities related to each selection in this unit.

www.phschool.com

How to Read Literature

Use Strategies for Reading Poetry

Reading poetry is like solving a mystery. The poet provides you with clues in the form of words and phrases. Studying the clues carefully helps you put pieces together to form a complete picture. Use these strategies to help you in your poetic detective work.

1. Interpret figurative language.

Just as carpenters use special tools when they build, poets use figurative language to add meaning to poems. Figurative language is language that is not intended to be taken literally. It sets up comparisons that help readers see things in new ways or form a vivid mental picture of something. When you come across figurative language, think of what the writer is trying to show you through the comparison being presented. Notice how the figurative language below helps you experience the biting cold.

> Talk of your cold! through the parka's fold
> it stabbed like a driven nail.
> —from "The Cremation of Sam McGee"

2. Read lines according to punctuation.

Punctuation in poems indicates when to pause or stop reading:

- Keep reading when a line has no punctuation at the end.

- Pause at commas, dashes, and semicolons.

- Stop at end marks, like periods, question marks, or exclamation points. See the example on the right.

Read with Punctuation

Clad in silver tissue, I   *Pause/Keep going*

March magnificently by   *Stop*
— from "Washed in Silver"

3. Paraphrase

If you are unsure of the meaning of a line or passage in a poem, try putting it in your own words.

- Look up any words that you do not know and replace them with familiar synonyms.

- Use language you use in everyday speech in place of formal language.

- Reread the passage to see if your new interpretation makes sense when read with surrounding text.

4. Use your senses.

Poets often include details that appeal to your senses of sight, hearing, smell, touch, or taste. Use these descriptive words to paint a mental picture that helps you visualize the setting and action of a poem.

As you read the selections in this unit, review these strategies for reading poetry. Use the suggestions to help you interact with the text.

Prepare to Read

The Cremation of Sam McGee ◆ Washed in Silver ◆ Winter

 Take It to the Net

Visit www.phschool.com
for interactive activities
and instruction related to
these selections, including

- background
- graphic organizers
- literary elements
- reading strategies

Preview

Connecting to the Literature

Ice thickening on a pond, snow draping tree limbs—the natural forces of winter stir our emotions and imaginations. These poems capture the beauty and the cruelty of winter weather. As you read, think of the preparations that humans and animals make to deal with the cold.

Background

In "The Cremation of Sam McGee," by Robert Service, two men prospect for gold in Canada's Yukon Territory. Located just east of Alaska, the Yukon stretches north of the Arctic Circle. Though the temperature can reach –60°F, miners have long come to the area for its mineral wealth.

Literary Analysis

Types of Poetry

"The Cremation of Sam McGee" is an example of **narrative poetry**—poetry that tells a story. Like a story, a narrative poem has a plot, characters, and a setting. Unlike a story, a narrative poem makes use of sound devices, such as rhythm and repetition.

"Washed in Silver" and "Winter" are examples of **lyric poetry**—verse that expresses a poet's thoughts and feelings about a single image or idea. Lyric poetry is written in vivid, musical language.

Comparing Literary Works

As you read these poems, compare and contrast the features and effects of narrative and lyric poetry. Also look at the similarities and differences in how the three poets address a common topic: winter. Use these focus questions to guide you:

1. How do the poems illustrate features of lyric or narrative poetry?
2. What effects and characteristics of winter does each poet explore?

Reading Strategy

Interpreting Figures of Speech

A **figure of speech** is an expression that is not meant to be taken literally. Writers use figures of speech to express ideas in vivid and imaginative ways. Common figures of speech include the following:

- **Simile:** A comparison between two unlike things using *like* or *as*
- **Metaphor:** A comparison between two unlike things without using *like* or *as*
- **Hyperbole:** Exaggeration meant to produce a particular effect
- **Personification:** Giving human characteristics to a nonhuman subject

As you read, look for examples of these figures of speech. Make a chart like the one shown and add examples to each category.

Simile
cold . . . stabbed like a driven nail
Metaphor
a promise made is a debt unpaid
Hyperbole
chilled through to the bone
Personification
the stars . . . were dancing heel to toe

Vocabulary Development

cremated (krē′ māt id) *v.* burned to ashes (p. 709)

whimper (hwim′ pər) *v.* make low, crying sounds; complain (p. 709)

ghastly (gast′ lē) *adv.* ghostlike; frightful (p. 710)

loathed (lōthd) *v.* hated (p. 710)

stern (sturn) *adj.* strict; unyielding (p. 710)

grisly (griz′ lē) *adj.* horrible (p. 711)

radiance (rā′ dē əns) *n.* quality of shining brightly (p. 713)

burrow (bʉr′ ō) *v.* to dig a hole or tunnel, especially for shelter (p. 714)

The Cremation of Sam McGee

Robert Service

There are strange things done in the midnight sun[1]
　　By the men who moil[2] for gold;
The Arctic trails have their secret tales
　　That would make your blood run cold;
5　The Northern Lights have seen queer sights,
　　But the queerest they ever did see
Was that night on the marge[3] of Lake Lebarge
　　I <u>cremated</u> Sam McGee.

Now Sam McGee was from Tennessee,
　　where the cotton blooms and blows
10　Why he left his home in the South to roam
　　'round the Pole, God only knows.
He was always cold, but the land of gold
　　seemed to hold him like a spell;
Though he'd often say in his homely way
　　that "he'd sooner live in hell."

On a Christmas Day we were mushing[4] our way
　　over the Dawson trail.
Talk of your cold! through the parka's fold
　　it stabbed like a driven nail.
15　If our eyes we'd close, then the lashes froze
　　til sometimes we couldn't see;
It wasn't much fun, but the only one
　　to <u>whimper</u> was Sam McGee.

And that very night, as we lay packed tight
　　in our robes beneath the snow,
And the dogs were fed, and the stars o'erhead
　　were dancing heel and toe,
He turned to me, and "Cap," says he,
　　"I'll cash in[5] this trip, I guess;
20　And if I do, I'm asking that you
　　won't refuse my last request."

Well, he seemed so low that I couldn't say no;
　　then he says with a sort of moan:

cremated (krē´ māt id) *v.*
burned to ashes

Reading Strategy
**Interpreting Figures
of Speech** In what way is
the cold like a nail?

whimper (hwim´ pər) *v.*
make low, crying sounds;
complain

✔**Reading Check**

What is Sam McGee's
complaint?

---

1. **the midnight sun** the sun visible at midnight in the Arctic or Antarctic
regions during their summers.
2. **moil** (moil) *v.* to toil and slave.
3. **marge** (märj) *n.* poetic word for the shore of the lake.
4. **mushing** (mush´ in) *v.* traveling by foot over snow, usually with a dog sled.
"Mush" is a command to sled dogs to start or to go faster.
5. **cash in** slang expression meaning "die."

"It's the cursed cold, and it's got right hold
        till I'm chilled clean through to the bone.
Yet 'tain't being dead—it's my awful dread
        of the icy grave that pains;
So I want you to swear that, foul or fair,
        you'll cremate my last remains."

25 A pal's last need is a thing to heed,
        so I swore I would not fail;
And we started on at the streak of dawn;
        but God! he looked <u>ghastly</u> pale.
He crouched on the sleigh, and he raved all day
        of his home in Tennessee;
And before nightfall a corpse was all
        that was left of Sam McGee.

There wasn't a breath in that land of death,
        and I hurried, horror-driven,
30 With a corpse half hid that I couldn't get rid,
        because of a promise given;
It was lashed to the sleigh, and it seemed to say:
        "You may tax your brawn[6] and brains,
But you promised true, and it's up to you
        to cremate those last remains."

Now a promise made is a debt unpaid,
        and the trail has its own <u>stern</u> code.
In the days to come, though my lips were dumb,
        in my heart how I cursed that load.
35 In the long, long night, by the lone firelight,
        while the huskies,[7] round in a ring,
Howled out their woes to the homeless snows—
        O God! how I <u>loathed</u> the thing.

6. **brawn:** (brôn) *n.* physical strength.
7. **huskies** (hus′ kēs) *n.* strong dogs used for pulling sleds over the snow.

Literary Analysis
Types of Poetry In what ways is this poem like a story?

ghastly (gast′ lē) *adv.* ghostlike; frightful

stern (stʉrn) *adj.* strict; unyielding

loathed (lōthd) *v.* hated

And every day that quiet clay
    seemed to heavy and heavier grow;
And on I went, though the dogs were spent
    and the grub was getting low;
The trail was bad, and I felt half mad,
    but I swore I would not give in;
40 And I'd often sing to the hateful thing,
    and it hearkened with a grin.

Till I came to the marge of Lake Lebarge,
    and a derelict[8] there lay;
It was jammed in the ice, but I saw in a trice
    it was called the "Alice May."
And I looked at it, and I thought a bit,
    and I looked at my frozen chum;
Then "Here," said I, with a sudden cry,
    "is my cre-ma-tor-eum."

45 Some planks I tore from the cabin floor,
    and I lit the boiler fire;
Some coal I found that was lying around,
    and I heaped the fuel higher;
The flames just soared, and the furnace roared—
    such a blaze you seldom see;
And I burrowed a hole in the glowing coal,
    and I stuffed in Sam McGee.

Then I made a hike, for I didn't like
    to hear him sizzle so;
50 And the heavens scowled, and the huskies howled,
    and the wind began to blow.
It was icy cold, but the hot sweat rolled
    down my cheeks, and I don't know why;
And the greasy smoke in an inky cloak
    went streaking down the sky.

I do not know how long in the snow
    I wrestled with <u>grisly</u> fear;
But the stars came out and they danced about
    ere again I ventured near;

Literary Analysis
Types of Poetry What does the poet do in the last line of this stanza to maintain the strong rhythm of the poem?

grisly (griz´ lē) *adj.* horrible

✔**Reading Check**

What promise does the speaker keep?

---

8. derelict (der´ ə likt´) *n.* abandoned ship.

◀ **Critical Viewing** How well does this picture capture the desolate landscape described in the poem? **[Evaluate]**

55 I was sick with dread, but I bravely said:
        "I'll just take a peep inside.
    I guess he's cooked, and it's time I looked"; . . .
        then the door I opened wide.

    And there sat Sam, looking cool and calm,
        in the heart of the furnace roar;
    And he wore a smile you could see a mile,
        and he said: "Please close that door.
    It's fine in here, but I greatly fear
        you'll let in the cold and storm—
60 Since I left Plumtree, down in Tennessee,
        it's the first time I've been warm."

    There are strange things done in the midnight sun
        By the men who moil for gold;
    The Arctic trails have their secret tales
        That would make your blood run cold;
65 *The Northern Lights have seen queer sights,*
        But the queerest they ever did see
    Was that night on the marge of Lake Lebarge
        I cremated Sam McGee.

Review and Assess

Thinking About the Selection

1. **Respond:** What was your reaction to the ending of this poem? Why?

2. **(a) Recall:** What problem does Sam McGee have with his surroundings? **(b) Infer:** What do Sam's fears reveal about his personality? **(c) Deduce:** Why doesn't Sam go home?

3. **(a) Recall:** Who is the speaker, and what does he promise Sam? **(b) Interpret:** Why is the speaker so determined to keep his promise?

4. **(a) Recall:** How does the speaker behave toward the corpse before he can cremate it? **(b) Interpret:** What does this behavior reveal about the speaker's conflicting emotions about fulfilling his promise?

5. **(a) Recall:** What does the speaker find when he opens the furnace door? **(b) Infer:** What reaction does the poet expect you to have to this unexpected occurrence?

6. **Take a Stand:** Is the speaker obligated to cremate Sam McGee? Why or why not?

Robert Service

(1874–1958)

Born in England and raised in Scotland, Robert Service went to Canada at age twenty to work for a bank. Sent by the bank to the Yukon Territory, Service came face to face with the rough world of trappers and gold prospectors. Soon, he was writing poems about these lively characters.

It didn't take Service long to leave banking for a life of full-time writing. He traveled to the Yukon and other Arctic areas for eight years, recording his adventures. His most popular poem, "The Cremation of Sam McGee," grew out of his experiences in the Arctic.

Washed in Silver

James Stephens

Gleaming in silver are the hills!
Blazing in silver is the sea!

And a silvery <u>radiance</u> spills
Where the moon drives royally!

5 Clad in silver tissue, I
March magnificently by!

radiance (rā′ dē əns) *n.*
quality of shining brightly

James Stephens

(1880?–1950)

Growing up in
a poor neighbor-
hood in Dublin,
Ireland, James
Stephens read
everything he
could get his
hands on. He came
to love Ireland's
powerful legends and fairy
tales. Later, he began to
write poetry and novels.
"Washed in Silver" captures
the magical quality of
Irish legends.

Review and Assess

Thinking About the Selection

1. **Respond:** Do you find the scene described appealing? Why or why not?

2. **(a) Recall:** What natural scene is described in "Washed in Silver"? **(b) Interpret:** Who or what is "Clad in silver tissue"?

3. **(a) Interpret:** Explain what the title "Washed in Silver" means. **(b) Connect:** What word or words in the poem echo the word *washed* in the title?

Winter

Nikki Giovanni

Frogs <u>burrow</u> the mud
snails bury themselves
and I air my quilts
preparing for the cold

5   Dogs grow more hair
mothers make oatmeal
and little boys and girls
take Father John's Medicine[1]

Bears store fat
10 chipmunks gather nuts
and I collect books
For the coming winter

---

1. **Father John's Medicine** an old-fashioned cough syrup.

burrow (bʉr´ ō) *v.* to dig a hole or tunnel, especially for shelter

Review and Assess

Thinking About the Selections

1. **Respond:** Which poem do you like better—"Washed in Silver" or "Winter"? Why?

2. **(a) Recall:** What is the speaker doing? **(b) Connect:** How do these actions suggest the coming of winter?

3. **(a) Recall:** What are the animals doing? **(b) Compare:** In what ways does this poem suggest that people and animals are alike?

4. **Apply:** How might an acceptance of natural cycles, like the change of seasons, help people improve their lives?

Nikki Giovanni

(b. 1943)
Nikki Giovanni's poems share the major events in her life—working for civil rights, celebrating the birth of her son, and experiencing the joys of African American family life. In "Winter," she writes about a universal subject: the changing of the seasons.

Review and Assess

Literary Analysis

Types of Poetry

1. Like a short story, a narrative poem includes a plot, characters, and a setting. In a chart like the one below, write a brief explanation of each of these elements in "The Cremation of Sam McGee."

Plot	Characters	Setting

2. What is the central conflict, or struggle between opposing forces, that drives the story's plot?
3. In what ways is "The Cremation of Sam McGee" different from a short story?
4. Explain why both "Winter" and "Washed in Silver" are lyric poems.

Comparing Literary Works

5. What is similar about the topics explored and the feelings expressed in "Winter" and "Washed in Silver"?
6. Compare and contrast the features of narrative and lyric poetry by filling in a chart like this one. For each feature you list, include at least one example from one of the three poems you just read.

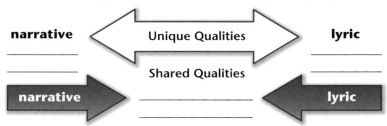

7. Explain which of these poems would be effective if set to music.

Reading Strategy

Interpreting Figures of Speech

8. Look at the list of figures of speech on page 707. Find at least one example of each in the poems you just read. Explain each example.
9. Which of the examples do you think is the most vivid? Why?

Extend Understanding

10. **Social Studies Connection:** What background would you give readers of these poems in countries without cold winters?

Quick Review

Narrative poetry is poetry that tells a story. To review narrative poetry, see page 707.

Lyric poetry is poetry that expresses the poet's thoughts and feelings in musical, sensory language. To review lyric poetry, see page 707.

Figures of speech are expressions that are not meant to be taken literally. To review figures of speech, see page 707.

 Take It to the Net
www.phschool.com
Take the interactive self-test online to check your understanding of these selections.

Integrate Language Skills

Vocabulary Development Lesson

Word Analysis: Latin Root -rad-

The Latin root -radi- means "branch" or "spoke." It usually indicates something spreading out from a center. *Radiance*, then, is "the quality of sending out rays of light." Define the following words.

1. radiator   2. radiation   3. radio

Spelling Strategy

The *hw* sound in *whimper* and other words is spelled *wh* and can be difficult to hear. Practice pronouncing the following words:

where   while   whine

Write the word for each clue.

1. question about location
2. at the same time
3. complain

Fluency: Definitions

On your paper, write the letter of the best definition for each word. To help you, review the vocabulary list on page 707.

1. loathed   a. strict
2. burrow   b. horrible
3. whimper   c. hated
4. stern   d. brightness
5. radiance   e. dig a hole
6. cremated   f. make low crying sounds
7. grisly   g. frightful; like a ghost
8. ghastly   h. burned into ashes

Read the above list of numbered words out loud. Make a note of any that you need to practice recognizing or pronouncing.

Grammar Lesson

Degrees of Comparison of Modifiers

Modifiers change the meanings of the words they modify. How much they change the meaning depends on the **degree,** or intensity. A modifier should be close to what it modifies.

Positive:	cold	scared
Comparative:	colder	more scared
Superlative:	coldest	most scared

A few modifiers, such as *good* and *bad*, are **irregular**—their comparative and superlative forms are not constructed in the same way as most other modifiers.

Irregular:	good
Comparative:	better
Superlative:	best

▶ *For more practice, see page R33, Exercise E.*
Practice Write the correct form of the modifier in parentheses.

1. This was the ____?____ trip ever. (*bad*)
2. We had ____?____ food than last time. (*little*)
3. ____?____ snow fell than last year. (*much*)
4. The ____?____ moment of the trip was when she finally reached the warm cabin. (*good*)
5. She slept ____?____ there than she had in weeks. (*well*)

Writing Application Describe your reactions to one of the poems. Use the comparative or superlative forms of at least three modifiers.

W̶G *Prentice Hall Writing and Grammar Connection: Chapter 25, Section 1*

Writing Lesson

Introduction to a Poetry Collection

Imagine that you are the editor of a poetry collection entitled *Voices of Winter*, which will include the three poems here. Write a brief introduction to the collection. Use the three poems to show how poetry can help readers share the many aspects of winter.

Prewriting Review the poems and take notes about what each conveys about winter. Then, list details from the poems that contribute to the impressions you have noted. For example, you might note images from Service's poem that capture the biting cold of winter.

Drafting Begin with an introductory paragraph that provides a general statement about the power of poetry to bring winter to life for readers. Follow with a paragraph about each poem, focusing on the aspect of winter that each captures. Support your points with examples.

Model: Providing Support Through Examples

In "Winter," Nikki Giovanni captures the idea of being warm and cozy inside during winter, when she writes, "I collect books/For the coming winter."

> The quotation from the poem provides support for the writer's ideas and interpretations.

Revising As you revise, look for places where you can include more examples to support the impressions of winter that you describe.

*W*G *Prentice Hall Writing and Grammar Connection: Chapter 12, Section 3*

Extension Activities

Listening and Speaking In a group, decide how you think Sam McGee and the speaker came to find themselves in the situation described in the poem. In other words, what happened *before* the events recounted by Robert Service? Develop this **background** as a story told from the speaker's point of view. Include the following plot elements:

- Exposition: an explanation of the situation
- Rising action: Events leading to the climax
- Climax: The turning point at which the conclusion of the story becomes clear

With your group, present your **background story** to your class. [**Group Activity**]

Research and Technology Use the Internet to gather information about the effects of Yukon weather on people's clothing, shelter, and means of travel. Write a brief **essay** contrasting the effects of the extremely cold winters of the Yukon with the heat of summers in places such as Texas or Florida. File your findings in your portfolio, in case you want to use them to write something at a later point.

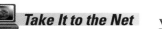 **Take It to the Net**   www.phschool.com

Go online for an additional research activity using the Internet.

Prepare to Read

Seal ◆ The Pasture ◆ Three Haiku

 Take It to the Net

Visit www.phschool.com for interactive activities and instruction related to these selections, including
- background
- graphic organizers
- literary elements
- reading strategies

Preview

Connecting to the Literature

Each day, we witness natural events, such as a rain shower or a sunset. Each of the following poems—"Seal," by William Jay Smith, "The Pasture," by Robert Frost, and three haiku by Matsuo Bashō—celebrates some aspect of nature. Reading them may help you appreciate the aspects of nature you encounter.

Background

As you will discover when you read the three haiku by Matsuo Bashō, Japanese poems are characterized by being short and simple. Such traditional poems present vivid images of nature that spark associations in the reader's mind. As you read Bashō's haiku, note the thoughts and emotions that each image sparks in your mind.

Literary Analysis

Form in Poetry

Poetry can take on many different forms. **Form** refers to the physical structure of the poem and the rules the poet follows to achieve a particular structure.

- A **stanza** is a group of lines that might be thought of as corresponding to a paragraph in prose. Most traditional English poems are divided into stanzas.
- A **concrete poem** is one in which the shape suggests its subject. The poet arranges the letters and lines to create a visual image.
- **Haiku** is a traditional form of Japanese poetry. A haiku always has three lines and seventeen syllables. There are five syllables in the first and third lines and seven syllables in the second line.

Comparing Literary Works

Although these poems use different forms, they all convey themes, or messages, related to nature. As you read, compare and contrast the ideas and feelings that the poems convey about nature. Use these focus questions to guide you:

1. How would you compare the attitude toward nature that each poem conveys?
2. Which poems capture the beauty of nature?
3. Which capture the soothing effect of nature?
4. Which convey a sense of wonder related to nature?

Reading Strategy

Reading According to Punctuation

Poets use **punctuation** the same way prose writers do: to show where thoughts begin and end and how they relate. Since poets do not always complete a sentence at the end of a line, remember to

- read in sentences.
- not make a full stop at the end of a line unless there is a period, colon, semicolon, or dash.

Keep Going

I'm going out to fetch the little calf
That's standing by the mother. It's so young

Full Stop   Keep Going

Vocabulary Development

swerve (swʉrv) *n.* curving motion (p. 720)

utter (ut′ ər) *v.* speak (p. 720)

pasture (pas′ chər) *adj., usually n.* in a field used by animals to graze (p. 721)

totters (tät′ ərz) *v.* rocks or shakes as if about to fall; is unsteady (p. 721)

Seal

William Jay Smith

See how he dives
From the rocks with a zoom!
See how he darts
Through his watery room
5   Past crabs and eels
And green seaweed,
Past fluffs of sandy
Minnow feed![1]
See how he swims
10   With a <u>swerve</u> and a twist,
A flip of the flipper,
A flick of the wrist!
Quicksilver-quick,
Softer than spray,
15   Down he plunges
And sweeps away;
Before you can think,
Before you can <u>utter</u>
Words like "Dill pickle"
20   Or "Apple butter,"
Back up he swims
Past Sting Ray and Shark,
Out with a zoom,
A whoop, a bark;
25   Before you can say
Whatever you wish,
He plops at your side
With a mouthful of fish!

---

1. feed (fēd) *n.* tiny particles that minnows feed on.

swerve (swʉrv) *n.* curving motion

utter (ut′ ər) *v.* speak

William Jay Smith

(b. 1918)
Smith was born in Winnfield, Louisiana, and has led a busy life—teaching college students, writing poetry and essays, translating Russian and French poetry, and even serving in the Vermont State Legislature for two years. His most successful writing has been his poetry for young people. Like "Seal," many of Smith's poems show that poetry can be pure and simple and fun.

The Pasture

ROBERT FROST

I'm going out to clean the <u>pasture</u> spring:
I'll only stop to rake the leaves away
(And wait to watch the water clear, I may):
I shan't be gone long.—You come too.

5 I'm going out to fetch the little calf
That's standing by the mother. It's so young
It <u>totters</u> when she licks it with her tongue.
I shan't be gone long.—You come too.

pasture (pas´ chər) *adj.,
usually n.* in a field used
by animals to graze

totters (tät´ ərz) *v.* rocks or
shakes as if about to fall;
is unsteady

Review and Assess

Thinking About the Selections

1. **Respond:** As you read "The Pasture," did you want to accept the speaker's invitation? Why or why not?

2. **(a) Infer:** How would you describe the mood of "Seal"?
   (b) Support: Find at least three words, phrases, or images that help create this mood.

3. **(a) Compare and Contrast:** Compare and contrast the behavior of the seal with that of the other animals mentioned in the poem. **(b) Hypothesize:** Suppose Smith had chosen to call his poem "Shark" and changed its shape accordingly. In what ways would he have had to change how the poem sounds?

4. **(a) Interpret:** Who do you think is being addressed as "you" in "Seal" and "The Pasture"? **(b) Support:** Name at least two details from each poem to support your interpretation.

5. **(a) Recall:** What activities is the speaker in "The Pasture" going out to do? **(b) Support:** What images make these activities sound attractive and inviting?

Robert Frost

(1874–1963)
   Born in San Francisco, Robert Frost spent most of his life in New England. At different times, he worked as a farmer and as a part-time teacher. He was not well known as a writer until his first book of poetry, *A Boy's Will* (1913), appeared in Great Britain. Then, almost overnight, he became famous for his poems about New England people and landscapes. Frost had a long and distinguished career as a poet, winning the Pulitzer Prize four times—more than any other poet.

Three Haiku

Matsuo Bashō

On sweet plum blossoms
The sun rises suddenly.
Look, a mountain path!

Has spring come indeed?
On that nameless mountain lie
Thin layers of mist.

Temple bells die out.
The fragrant blossoms remain.
A perfect evening!

Review and Assess

Thinking About the Selections

1. **Respond:** Of the three haiku, which do you like best? Why?
2. **(a) Recall:** Would you say the speaker in the first haiku is alarmed, discouraged, or surprised? **(b) Infer:** What causes this reaction in the speaker?
3. **(a) Recall:** What season is the subject of the second haiku? **(b) Interpret:** Why is the speaker uncertain whether that season has come?
4. **(a) Interpret:** In the third haiku, why do you think the speaker feels it is a perfect evening? **(b) Connect:** What effect would the silence of bells and the presence of fragrant blossoms have on you? Explain.
5. **(a) Analyze:** How would you describe Bashō's attitude toward nature? **(b) Speculate:** What do you think his favorite season was? Support your answer.
6. **Evaluate:** Do these poems have meaning and relevance for today's readers? Explain.

Matsuo Bashō

(1644–1694)

Matsuo Bashō was born near Kyoto, Japan. Regarded as one of the greatest Japanese poets, his three-line poems present a scene in which a momentary feature stands out against an unchanging background. Many of his best poems were inspired by travels in which he observed nature. He evokes a whole landscape or an entire season by describing just a few details.

Review and Assess

Literary Analysis

Form in Poetry

1. What is the effect of the repetitive words and lines in "The Pasture"?
2. (a) How can you tell that the three poems by Bashō are haiku? (b) For each haiku, choose one word that sums up the emotion expressed in the poem.
3. Create a curving diagram like the one shown. In each curve, write a word from "Seal" that suggests the motion of the poem.

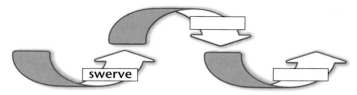

Comparing Literary Works

4. Using a chart like the one below, compare the attitude toward nature that each poem conveys.

Poem	Attitude	Words from the Poem that Convey the Attitude

5. (a) Which poems capture the beauty of nature? (b) Which capture the soothing effect of nature?
6. Which poems convey a sense of wonder related to nature?

Reading Strategy

Reading According to Punctuation

7. Read the second stanza of "The Pasture" aloud. Pause at the end of each line. Then, read it aloud according to punctuation. Which way makes more sense?
8. Does reading "Seal" according to the punctuation change your understanding of it? Explain.

Extend Understanding

9. **Literary Connection:** Choose two other poems in this unit, and describe the form of those poems.

Quick Review

Form refers to the physical structure of a poem. A **stanza** is a group of lines that might be thought of as corresponding to a paragraph in prose. A **concrete** poem is one with a shape that suggests its subject. **Haiku** is a traditional form of Japanese poetry made up of three lines—the first and third lines have five syllables and the second line has seven syllables. To review form, see page 719.

Punctuation shows readers where thoughts begin and end. To review punctuation, see page 719.

 Take It to the Net
www.phschool.com
Take the interactive self-test online to check your understanding of these selections.

Integrate Language Skills

Vocabulary Development Lesson

Word Analysis: The Suffix -less

When the Anglo-Saxon suffix -less is added to a word, it means "without," "lacking," or "not able to." Note this meaning in these words:

endless   flawless
harmless   tireless

Identify the word that completes each sentence.

1. If something is ___?___, it seems to have no *end*.
2. A person who is ___?___ seems never to get *tired*.
3. Something that is ___?___ has no *flaws*.
4. An animal is ___?___ if it causes no *harm*.

Fluency: Synonyms

Choose the best **synonym**, or word with almost the same meaning, for each of the following words.

1. swerve: **(a)** turn, **(b)** somersault, **(c)** reversal
2. utter: **(a)** shout, **(b)** murmur, **(c)** speak
3. pasture: **(a)** field, **(b)** lot, **(c)** yard
4. totters: **(a)** falls, **(b)** sways, **(c)** grows

Spelling Strategy

The *cher* sound at the end of a word is often spelled *ture*. After each definition, write a word that fits the definition and contains the *ture* spelling of the *cher* sound.

1. handwritten name: signa___?___
2. government body that makes laws: legisla___?___
3. framework: struc___?___

Grammar Lesson

Placement of *only*

The placement of certain words in a sentence can be very important to the meaning of the sentence. The position of the adverb *only* can affect the entire meaning of a sentence. Place *only* directly before the word or phrase it modifies. For example, in "The Pasture," Frost says:

I'll *only* stop to rake the leaves away

Notice how the meaning would change if he had written:

I'll stop to rake *only* the leaves away

▶ For more practice, see page R33, Exercise F.

Practice Explain how the placement of *only* changes meaning in each of these sentence pairs.

1. **(a)** He wished *only* to watch the snow fall.
   (b) *Only* he wished to watch the snow fall.
2. **(a)** Matsuo Bashō wrote *only* haiku.
   (b) *Only* Matsuo Bashō wrote haiku.
3. **(a)** The seal plops *only* at your side.
   (b) *Only* the seal plops at your side.
4. **(a)** He *only* taps the table.
   (b) He taps *only* the table.
5. **(a)** *Only* he dives from the rocks.
   (b) He *only* dives from the rocks.

Writing Application Write five original sentences using *only* as a modifier.

W̶G Prentice Hall Writing and Grammar Connection: Chapter 25, Section 2

Writing Lesson

Poem in a Particular Form

Review the form of each poem in this section. Then, write a poem in one of the forms—traditional stanza style, concrete, or haiku.

Prewriting Make a list of the qualities you like best about each form. Based on your list, decide which form would be the most fun or interesting to use.

Drafting As you draft, adjust your details to fit your chosen form. For example, if you are writing a concrete poem, sketch the shape you want to create and then add or delete words to fit the shape.

Revising Read the poem aloud. Circle vague words that do not convey a clear picture, and replace them with more precise, lively words.

Model: Revising Word Choice

crouches
She ~~sits~~ by the kitchen window
         ∧ _guards_
She ~~watches~~ the little patch of sun
         ∧
As if she thinks there's only one
Ray of warmth and light in the world.

> Replacing vague words like *sits* and *watches* with precise words like *crouches* and *guards* makes the image more vivid.

WG *Prentice Hall Writing and Grammar Connection: Chapter 6, Section 4*

Extension Activities

Listening and Speaking Work with a group of classmates to **read aloud selected poems** by Robert Frost. Choose poems that you like from a collection of Frost's works.

- Rehearse your readings alone and with the group.
- Practice reading slowly and with expression in your voice.
- Speak clearly, and make eye contact periodically with your audience.

After you have finished rehearsing, hold a reading for the class. **[Group Activity]**

Research and Technology Use library resources to find out more about Japan during the time of Matsuo Bashō. Topics for research can include Japanese government, society, and culture during this period. Present your findings in an **oral report.**

Writing Write a **personal letter** responding to the invitation in "The Pasture." Explain why you will or will not accept the invitation.

 *Take It to the Net*   www.phschool.com

Go online for an additional research activity using the Internet.

Prepare to Read

Annabel Lee ◆ Martin Luther King

 Take It to the Net

Preview

Connecting to the Literature

One role of poetry is to keep important memories alive. In "Martin Luther King," Raymond Richard Patterson honors a beloved national hero. In "Annabel Lee," Edgar Allan Poe pays tribute to a woman or women he loved. As you read these poems, think about memories that you wish to keep alive.

Background

Martin Luther King, Jr. (1929–1968), was a great civil rights leader. Using nonviolent methods, he helped end legal discrimination against African Americans in the South and elsewhere in the United States. In 1968, he was shot and killed by an assassin in Memphis, Tennessee.

Literary Analysis

Rhythm and Rhyme

One of the first things readers of poetry respond to is its pattern of sound. **Rhythm** is a poem's pattern of stressed (´) and unstressed (˘) syllables. Notice the drumbeat rhythm here:

> Hĕ cáme ŭpón ăn áge

The **meter** of a poem is its rhythmical pattern. Meter is measured in **feet**, or single units of stressed and unstressed syllables. You can describe a poem's meter by stating what kind of feet are used and how many feet are in each line. The line below has three feet. Each foot has two syllables: an unstressed one followed by a stressed one. Slashes separate the feet.

> Bĕsét / bў gríef, / bў ráge—

Rhyme is the repetition of a sound at the ends of nearby words—*age/rage*, for example. These poems have end rhymes—the rhyming words appear at the ends of lines. The arrangement of rhyming lines varies from poem to poem.

Comparing Literary Works

Both of these poems have a regular rhythm, but the number of feet in the lines creates a different effect in each poem. Similarly, both poems use pairs of rhyming words at the ends of lines, but the arrangement of rhymes is different. Compare and contrast these poems based on their rhythm and their rhyme. Use the following focus questions to guide you.

1. How do the rhythm and rhyme schemes differ?
2. How do the rhythm and rhyme give both poems a musical quality?
3. Which poem's "sound" is more appealing to you? Why?

Reading Strategy

Paraphrasing

To help you grasp the meaning of a poem, you might **paraphrase**, or restate in your own words, some or all of it. Though it cannot replace the unique music or phrasing of a poem, a paraphrase can get to the heart of its meaning. As you read, use a chart like this one to paraphrase portions of the poems.

Stanza	Paraphrase
1. He came upon an age/ Beset by grief, by rage—	King was born in a troubled time.
2.	
3.	

Vocabulary Development

coveted (kuv´ it id) *v.*: wanted greatly (p. 728)

beset (bē set´) *adj.*: covered; set thickly with (p. 730)

profound (prō found´) *adj.*: deeply or intensely felt (p. 730)

Annabel Lee

Edgar Allan Poe

It was many and many a year ago,
    In a kingdom by the sea.
That a maiden there lived whom you may know
    By the name of Annabel Lee;—
And this maiden she lived with no other thought
    Than to love and be loved by me.

She was a child and *I* was a child,
    In this kingdom by the sea.
5 But we loved with a love that was more than love—
    I and my Annabel Lee—
With a love that the wingèd seraphs of Heaven
    <u>Coveted</u> her and me.

And this was the reason that, long ago,
    In this kingdom by the sea,
A wind blew out of a cloud by night
    Chilling my Annabel Lee;
So that her highborn kinsmen came
    And bore her away from me,
10 To shut her up in a sepulcher
    In this kingdom by the sea.

The angels, not half so happy in Heaven,
    Went envying her and me:—
Yes! that was the reason (as all men know,
    In this kingdom by the sea)
That the wind came out of a cloud, chilling
    And killing my Annabel Lee.

But our love it was stronger by far than the love
    Of those who were older than we—
    Of many far wiser than we—
15 And neither the angels in Heaven above
    Nor the demons down under the sea,
Can ever dissever my soul from the soul
    Of the beautiful Annabel Lee:—

Literary Analysis
Rhythm and Rhyme
What is the pattern of stressed and unstressed syllables in line 2?

coveted (kuv´ it id) *v.* wanted greatly

Reading Strategy
Paraphrase
Paraphrase lines 10–13.

For the moon never beams without bringing
    me dreams
Of the beautiful Annabel Lee;
And the stars never rise but I see the bright eyes
    Of the beautiful Annabel Lee;
20 And so, all the nighttide, I lie down by the side
    Of my darling, my darling, my life and my bride,
        In her sepulcher there by the sea—
        In her tomb by the side of the sea.

Review and Assess

Thinking About the Selection

1. **Respond:** Do you think this poem would make a good song? Why or why not?

2. **(a) Recall:** At what stage in life did the speaker in the poem fall in love? **(b) Interpret:** In your own words, describe the love between the speaker and Annabel Lee. **(c) Support:** What words and images in the poem support your description?

3. **(a) Recall:** Tell three ways in which Poe makes the setting of the poem seem distant, as if in a fairy tale. **(b) Speculate:** What was Poe's purpose in making the poem seem distant? **(c) Compare and Contrast:** What parts of the poem seem realistic?

4. **(a) Recall:** How do the angels feel about the love between the speaker and Annabel Lee? **(b) Infer:** What caused the death of Annabel Lee?

5. **(a) Recall:** How does the speaker react to Annabel Lee's death? **(b) Infer:** Why will nothing be able to separate the speaker's soul from the soul of Annabel Lee? **(c) Analyze:** How does the last stanza make the sense of sadness in the poem seem immediate and never-ending?

Edgar Allan Poe

(1809–1849)

Edgar Allan Poe's life is a story of great literary achievement and much personal loss. His parents were impoverished traveling actors. When Poe was not yet three, his mother died, and he went to live with the Allans of Richmond, Virginia.

Although his writing won recognition, it did not bring financial success. Two years after the death of his beloved wife, Virginia, Poe died poor and alone.

Poe's biographer Kenneth Silverman believes that the heroine of "Annabel Lee" "represents all of the women he loved and lost." Poe finished the poem about a year after his wife's death. He had a special feeling for the poem, which he distributed among his friends a few months before his own death.

Martin Luther King

Raymond Richard Patterson

He came upon an age
<u>Beset</u> by grief, by rage—

His love so deep, so wide,
He could not turn aside.

5 His passion, so <u>profound</u>,
He would not turn around.

He taught this suffering Earth
The measure of Man's worth.

He showed what Man can be
10 Before death sets him free.

beset (bē set´) *adj.*
covered; set thickly with

profound (prō found´) *adj.*
deeply or intensely felt

Review and Assess

Thinking About the Selection

1. **Respond:** Do you think this poem captures the spirit of Martin Luther King, Jr.? Why or why not?

2. **(a) Recall:** Describe the "age" into which King was born.
   (b) Apply: What two personal qualities did King bring to this age? **(c) Analyze Cause and Effect:** What kinds of actions resulted from these personal qualities?

3. **(a) Interpret:** What does the poet mean by King's "passion, so profound"? **(b) Synthesize:** Using ideas from the poem, name two qualities that are important in a leader. Explain your answer.

4. **(a) Recall:** What did King teach "this suffering Earth"?
   (b) Interpret: In your own words, explain the phrases in lines 7–10 that describe King's achievements. **(c) Assess:** Overall, how did King's actions affect other people?

5. **Make a Judgment:** If King were alive today, would he feel his civil rights goals have been achieved? Explain.

Raymond Richard Patterson

(b. 1929)

Raymond Patterson's poetry appears in many anthologies, as well as in individual collections such as *Elemental Blues*. Patterson's passion for sharing his knowledge of African American history is shown in his newspaper column, "From Our Past," and in poems such as "Martin Luther King."

Review and Assess

Literary Analysis
Rhythm and Rhyme

1. Use a chart like this one to mark the meter of the first two stanzas of each poem. Use slashes to separate the feet.

Stanza 1	Hĕ cáme / ŭpón / ăn agé / Beset by grief, by rage—
Stanza 2	

2. Is the rhythm in "Annabel Lee" structured or unstructured? Explain your answer.
3. Describe the rhyme scheme used at the end of lines in the first four stanzas of "Annabel Lee."

Comparing Literary Works

4. Why can both poems be described as having a regular rhyme scheme?
5. How do the rhyme schemes differ?
6. How do the rhythms of the two poems differ?
7. Explain how rhythm and rhyme give both poems a musical quality.
8. Which poem's "sound" is more appealing to you? Why?

Reading Strategy
Paraphrasing

9. Paraphrase the first stanza of "Annabel Lee."
10. Paraphrase the following lines from Richard Patterson's poem "Martin Luther King."

    > He taught this suffering Earth
    > The measure of man's worth.

11. Tell two ways in which a paraphrase differs from the actual text of a poem.

Extend Understanding

12. **Community Connection:** If he were alive today, what causes might Martin Luther King, Jr., support? Why?

Quick Review

Rhythm is a poem's pattern of stressed and unstressed syllables. To review rhythm, see page 727.

Rhyme is the repetition of a sound at the ends of nearby words. To review rhyme, see page 727. The **meter** of a poem is its rhythmical pattern. To review meter, see page 727.

To **paraphrase,** restate a difficult passage using your own words. To review paraphrasing, see page 727.

 Take It to the Net
www.phschool.com
Take the interactive self-test online to check your understanding of these selections.

Integrate Language Skills

Vocabulary Development Lesson

Word Analysis: Latin Root -found-

The Latin root -found- means "bottom," and often refers to something deep. Patterson calls King's passion "profound," which means "deeply felt."

Use your knowledge of this Latin root to match each numbered word with its definition:

1. profound   2. foundation   3. founder

a. one who builds something from the bottom up
b. deeply or intensely felt
c. a structure's support at the bottom

Fluency: Synonyms

Choose the lettered word or phrase that is closest in meaning to the numbered word.

1. beset: a. placed in   b. surrounded by   c. set again
2. profound: a. strongly felt   b. hardly felt   c. quietly felt
3. coveted: a. chilled   b. refused   c. envied

Spelling Strategy

In the word *coveted*, the *o* sounds like a short *u*. This is true for many words in which *o* is followed by *v*. Complete the following definitions to form a list of words in which *o* sounds like short *u*.

1. What the speaker in "Annabel Lee" feels for her: ____?____
2. What you put on a pot to keep food hot: ____?____
3. The bird that symbolizes peace: ____?____
4. To fly slowly above something: ____?____

Grammar Lesson

Capitalization

Capital letters are used to signal the beginning of a sentence or quotation and to identify proper nouns and adjectives. Proper nouns include the names of people, geographical locations, specific events and time periods, organizations, languages, and religions. Proper adjectives are derived from proper nouns (such as *France/French*, *Canada/Canadian*).

> **Proper Nouns:** Canada, Thanksgiving, Friday, Lynch Park
>
> **Proper Adjectives:** Canadian, Jeffersonian

▶ *For more practice, see page R35, Exercise D.*

Practice Rewrite the following paragraph on your paper. Correct ten errors in capitalization.

Edgar allan Poe was born on january 19, 1809, in boston, Massachusetts. He began writing poetry in his youth, influenced by english poets such as John Keats. he studied for a while at the U.S. Military Academy at west point, but writing was His true interest. poe wrote the earliest detective stories, as well as other stories and poetry. He died in Baltimore, maryland.

Writing Application Write a summary of each poem. Make sure you have capitalized all titles and all author's names.

Writing Lesson

Response to Poetry

Write a brief essay in which you respond to and analyze an element of "Martin Luther King" or "Annabel Lee." Focus on rhythm, rhyme, or meaning. Explain how the poet uses the element you choose and how the element shapes your reaction to the poem.

Prewriting   First, jot down the meaning behind each poem. Then, make a list of the ways you see rhyme and rhythm used in the poem. Decide which aspect you would like to focus on in your essay.

Drafting   Draft your essay, drawing on ideas from your prewriting notes. Use specific examples to expand on the points you make. End with what you thought of the poem overall.

Model: Using Examples From Literature

Poe's singsong rhythm often makes use of repeated words. "It was many and many a year ago" and "She was a child and I was a child" are just two examples.

> Use examples to support your main points, quoting the words exactly and using correct capitalization and punctuation.

Revising   Reread your draft. Combine short sentences, using words such as *because* and *when* to show how ideas are related.

Prentice Hall Writing and Grammar Connection: Chapter 12, Section 3

Extension Activities

Listening and Speaking Listen to a recording of Martin Luther King, Jr.'s, "I Have a Dream" speech. Identify the main topic of the speech. Then, summarize King's attitude toward his topic by considering the following points.

1. the support he provides for his main point
2. the way he appeals to people's sense of right and wrong
3. the emotion that comes through in his voice

After taking notes, write a **summary.** Read it aloud to your class.

Research and Technology In a group, use library resources including the Internet to find three critical responses to "Annabel Lee." Read each response, and then provide an **evaluation** of the responses. Determine if the writers of the responses focused on the meaning of the poem or on the literary elements like rhythm, rhyme, or figures of speech. Finally, explain whether the responses were favorable toward the poem or not. **[Group Activity]**

 **Take It to the Net**   www.phschool.com

Go online for an additional research activity using the Internet.

Prepare to Read

Full Fathom Five ◆ Onomatopoeia ◆ Maestro

Take It to the Net

Visit www.phschool.com
for interactive activities
and instruction related to
these selections, including
• background
• graphic organizers
• literary elements
• reading strategies

Preview

Connecting to the Literature

When you listen to your favorite song on the radio, you respond as much, if not more, to the sound of the music as you do to the meaning. Sound is also very important in poetry. In "Full Fathom Five," by William Shakespeare, "Onomatopoeia," by Eve Merriam, and "Maestro," by Pat Mora, you will discover words that were chosen for their musical effect as much as for their meaning.

Background

"Full Fathom Five" is from Shakespeare's *The Tempest*. A spirit named Ariel sings it to Prince Ferdinand, whose father, King Alonso, is thought lost in a shipwreck. Ariel sings of the king's death, though later it is revealed that the king is still alive.

Literary Analysis

Sound Devices

Sound devices make a poem appeal to the ear. One device is **onomatopoeia**—the use of words whose sounds suggest their meaning, like *sputter.* Another device is **alliteration,** in which sounds at the beginning of words are repeated, as in this line from Shakespeare's song:

> Full *f*athom *f*ive thy *f*ather lies

Assonance is the repetition of the same vowel sound in different words, as in the words, "would blend again and again." **Consonance** is the repetition of similar final consonant sounds at the ends of words or accented syllables. For example, the words *splatters, scatters,* and *spurts* in "Onomatopoeia" share the final *s* sound.

As you read, think about the following focus questions:

1. Which sound devices stand out to you the most in each poem?
2. How do they give the poems a musical sound?

Comparing Literary Works

Each of the poets in this group uses sound devices. While one poet uses onomatopoeia to create the effect of water pouring out of a faucet, another poet uses onomatopoeia to create the effect of an applauding crowd. Compare and contrast which sound devices are used and the effects they produce.

Reading Strategy

Clarifying Word Meanings

In some poems, you may encounter an unfamiliar word or a word you think you know but about which you are not sure. Follow these steps to help you **clarify word meanings:**

- Pause when you come to a difficult word.
- Think about a familiar word that might mean the same as the difficult word.
- Reread the sentence, replacing the difficult word with your familiar word to see if it makes sense.
- If you are still unsure of the meaning, check a dictionary.

As you read, use a chart like the one shown to help you as you clarify word meanings.

Word	Hark! Now I hear them
Replaced	"Listen!" Now I hear them
Makes sense?	yes
Checked in Dictionary	✔

Vocabulary Development

knell (nel) *n.* funeral bell (p. 736)

sputters (sput′ ərz) *v.* makes hissing or spitting sounds (p. 737)

maestro (mīs′ trō) *n.* master musician (p. 738)

snare (snar) *v.* catch or trap (p. 738)

Full Fathom Five

WILLIAM SHAKESPEARE

Full fathom[1] five thy father lies;
  Of his bones are coral made;
Those are pearls that were his eyes;
  Nothing of him that doth fade
5 But doth suffer a sea change
Into something rich and strange.
Sea nymphs hourly ring his <u>knell</u>;
                Ding-dong.
Hark! Now I hear them—ding-dong bell.

knell (nel) *n.* funeral bell

---

1. fathom (fath´ əm) *n.* length of six feet used to measure water depth.

William Shakespeare

(1564–1616)

Many people regard William Shakespeare as the greatest writer in the English language. He wrote thirty-seven plays, many of which are performed frequently today. They include *Romeo and Juliet, Hamlet,* and other classics. *The Tempest,* from which "Full Fathom Five" is taken, was among Shakespeare's last plays.

ONOMATOPOEIA

Eve Merriam

The rusty spigot
sputters,
utters
a splutter,
5   spatters a smattering of drops,
gashes wider;
slash,
splatters,
scatters,
10   spurts,
finally stops sputtering
and plash!
gushes rushes splashes
clear water dashes.

sputters (sput´ ərz) *v.*
makes hissing or spitting
sounds

Review and Assess
Thinking About the Selections

1. **Respond:** Which poem seemed more unusual to you? Explain your answer.
2. **(a) Recall:** Name two changes that the speaker describes happening to the father in "Full Fathom Five." **(b) Interpret:** Why do you think the poet calls these changes "rich and strange"? **(c) Generalize:** In one sentence, state what is happening to the father underwater.
3. **(a) Recall:** Describe the length of lines in "Onomatopoeia." **(b) Analyze:** How do the line lengths contribute to the effect of the poem on the reader?
4. **(a) Recall:** Name three verbs from "Onomatopoeia" that sound like falling water. **(b) Apply:** Brainstorm for three verbs not used in the poem that sound like falling water.
5. **(a) Recall:** How does each of the two poems involve water? **(b) Infer:** What happens in each poem? **(c) Support:** Name one similarity and one difference between the two poems.

Eve Merriam

(1916–1992)
Eve Merriam's fascination with words began at an early age. "I remember being enthralled by the sound of words," she said. This love, which led her to write poetry, fiction, nonfiction, and drama, is reflected in the poem "Onomatopoeia."

MAESTRO

Pat Mora

He hears her
when he bows.
Rows of hands clap
again and again he bows
5 to stage lights and upturned faces
but he hears only his mother's voice

years ago in their small home
singing Mexican songs
one phrase at a time
10 while his father strummed the guitar
or picked the melody with quick fingertips.
Both cast their music in the air
for him to <u>snare</u> with his strings,
songs of *lunas*[1] and *amor*[2]
15 learned bit by bit.
She'd nod, smile, as his bow slid
note to note, then the trio
    voz,[3] *guitarra*,[4] *violín*[5]
would blend again and again
20 to the last pure note
sweet on the tongue.

---

1. **lunas** (lōō′ näs) *n.* Spanish for "moons."
2. **amor** (ä môr′) *n.* Spanish for "love."
3. **voz** (vōs) *n.* Spanish for "voice."
4. **guitarra** (gē tär′ rä) *n.* Spanish for "guitar."
5. **violín** (vē ō lēn′) Spanish for "violin."

maestro (mīs′ trō) *n.* great musician

snare (snar) *v.* catch or trap

Review and Assess

Thinking About the Selection

1. **Respond:** Would you like to know the family described in "Maestro"? Why or why not?
2. **(a) Recall:** Which Spanish words are used in the poem?
   (b) Analyze: What do they add to the poem?
3. **(a) Recall:** How does the maestro react to the applause?
   (b) Interpret: What does this say about his feelings about his family?

Pat Mora

(b. 1942)
Pat Mora grew up in El Paso, Texas, on the border between the United States and Mexico. Many of her writings speak of her experience as a Mexican American. She has won many awards for her stories and poetry.

Review and Assess

Literary Analysis

Sound Devices

1. Give three examples of **sound devices** in "Onomatopoeia." Explain which sound device is being used for each.

2. Give one example of onomatopoeia found in "Maestro."

3. Using a chart like this, add an alliterative word to go with each of these onomatopoeic words from the poems: ring, dashes, strummed.

Onomatopoeia	With Alliteration Added
Sputter	Spattering Sputter

Comparing Literary Works

4. Using a chart like the one below, compare the sound devices used in each poem by providing examples of sound devices and the effect created.

Poem	...▶	Type of Sound Device	...▶	Effect

5. Which poem uses sound devices most effectively? Explain.

Reading Strategy

Clarify Word Meanings

6. Rewrite each sentence below, replacing each underlined word with a familiar word.

   a. The rusty <u>spigot</u> sputters.

   b. The <u>maestro</u> stepped onto the stage and the music began.

   c. He tries to <u>snare</u> the music with his fingers and capture the beauty in the sound.

Extend Understanding

7. **Social Studies Connection:** Why would writers of Shakespeare's time be concerned with shipwrecks and sea travel?

8. **Take a Position:** Today, explorers seek new adventures in space rather than on the sea. Do you think space exploration is a worthwhile activity? Explain.

Quick Review

Alliteration is the repetition of a sound at the beginnings of nearby words.

Onomatopoeia is the use of words that sound like, or mimic, the things they describe.

Assonance is the repetition of vowel sounds in nearby words.

Consonance is the repetition of a similar final consonant sound at the ends of words or accented syllables. To review these sound devices, see page 735.

To **clarify word meanings,** replace difficult words with familiar words. To review clarifying word meanings, see page 735.

 Take It to the Net

www.phschool.com

Take the interactive self-test online to check your understanding of these selections.

Integrate Language Skills

Vocabulary Development Lesson

Concept Development: Using Words Based on Onomatopoeia

Onomatopoeia is the use of words that sound like the things they describe. For each of these words, fill in a type of sound that it imitates (the first has been done for you).

1. sputter   water being coughed
   from a faucet
2. sizzle   _____

3. hiss   _____

4. zing   _____

5. jingle   _____

Fluency: Word Choice

On your paper, answer each question with *yes* or *no*. Then, explain your answer.

1. Could a *maestro* supervise an orchestra?
2. Does a *knell* usually sound joyful?
3. Would you call a plumber to fix a faucet that *sputters*?
4. Could you use cheese to *snare* a mouse?

Spelling Strategy

In some words, an initial *n* sound is spelled *kn*, as in *knell*. Other words with this silent *k* before an *n* include *knowledge*, *knight*, and *knuckle*. On your paper, write the words with initial *kn* that fit these definitions.

1. A rap, as on a door: _____?_____
2. A tool for cutting food: _____?_____
3. A handle on a door: _____?_____

Grammar Lesson

Interjections

In "Full Fathom Five," though the word *hark!* simply means "listen," the speaker calls it out to show excitement. The word is used as an interjection. An **interjection** is a part of speech that exclaims and expresses a feeling, such as pain or uncertainty. An interjection may be set off with commas or an exclamation point.

> **Pain:** *Ouch!* I hit my arm.
> **Excitement:** *Wow*, Melissa can certainly run fast.
> **Uncertainty:** I thought, *um*, that I knew the answer.

▶ *For more practice, see page R29, Exercise G.*
Practice On your paper, identify the interjection in each of these sentences.

1. Boy, that violinist plays well!
2. Huh! I'd never heard her before.
3. Yikes, Jim, you almost fell!
4. Ugh, the cake tastes burnt.
5. Hey, Gina, come here!

Writing Application Add an interjection to each sentence that helps express the feeling noted.

1. (fear) I heard a strange noise.
2. (joy) Manuel won the prize!
3. (disappointment) Cathy had hoped to win.

$\mathcal{W}_{G}$ *Prentice Hall Writing and Grammar Connection: Chapter 18, Section 2*

Writing Lesson

Analysis of a Poem

Dig deeper into one of the poems in this section by analyzing two of its features, such as sound devices, rhyme, word choice, or images.

Prewriting Choose the poem and the elements you'll discuss. Jot down your ideas, focusing on how the elements work in the poem and what they contribute to it. Note specific details to support your ideas.

Drafting Draft an introduction, body, and conclusion for your paper. In the body, focus on each literary element in turn. State clearly how the poet uses the element, and back up your statement with evidence from the poem.

Model: Clear Interpretive Statements

[statement of idea about word choice] The musical terms in "Maestro" help show how music is at the heart of the family's life together. [supporting details] Word choice such as "melody," "note," "strings," and "trio" create a strong picture of the father, mother, and son making music together.

> Make a clear statement of your ideas, and support it with specific details.

Revising Check that your introduction interests the reader and your conclusion sums up your ideas. Revise as needed.

𝒲𝒢 *Prentice Hall Writing and Grammar Connection: Chapter 12, Section 3*

Extension Activities

Speaking and Listening Prepare a group **oral report** about Shakespeare. When assigning subtopics to group members, include the following:

1. Main events in his life
2. The scope or range of topics in his writing
3. Background about the time in which he lived

Each person should study one subtopic in depth. During the presentation, use your own words to show what you have learned. [**Group Activity**]

Research and Technology With classmates, create an "onomatopoeia factory." Build an **inventory** of sound words to imitate sounds such as heavy scraping or hearty laughing. Compile your inventory in a computer file. [**Group Activity**]

Writing Just as Merriam wrote a poem entitled "Onomatopoeia," write a poem called "Alliteration" that includes examples of alliteration.

 **Take It to the Net** www.phschool.com

Go online for an additional research activity using the Internet.

Both "Full Fathom Five" and the following interview with Navy diver Carl Brashear involve the sea. Throughout history, humans have had a complex relationship with the sea. Those who depend on the sea for their livelihood sometimes regard it as a living creature, with its own changeable moods. The sea is often generous, sustaining people with the food it provides. But there is another side to the sea, where danger never lies far from the surface. This is the angry sea, which does not hesitate to take away as freely as it gives.

The speaker in Shakespeare's "Full Fathom Five" comments on a man's loss of his father to the powerful sea. As you read the interview with Brashear, compare his determined attitude to not let the sea take away something precious to him with the indifferent attitude of the speaker in Shakespeare's poem. You will see why the naval officer's heroic struggle inspired a major Hollywood movie, "Men of Honor," starring Robert De Niro and Cuba Gooding, Jr.

Men of Honor

Interview With
Carl M. Brashear, Navy Diver
Paul Stillwell

In an interview with Paul Stillwell for the Navy's Oral History Program, Master Chief Boatswain's Mate Carl M. Brashear discusses how he lost his leg in a Navy diving accident and how his determination allowed him to continue in his career, becoming the first amputee in Navy history to be a diver.

Master Chief Brashear: In 1966, the Air Force lost a nuclear bomb off the coast of Palomares, Spain. The Air Force asked the Navy to recover that bomb, and, of course, the Navy said yes. Admiral Guest formed the task force, and we started searching for that bomb in January of 1966.

The reason the bomb dropped in the water was that two airplanes were maneuvering, and the fuel plane was fueling a B-52. According to what the people said, it gained on the B-52 too fast, and they collided in midair. Three of the bombs' parachutes opened and landed over on the land in Spain. One of the parachutes didn't open, and it fell in the water. So we searched for the bomb close to the shoreline for about two and a half months, and all we were getting was pings on beer cans, coral heads, and other contacts.

Paul Stillwell: This is with your sonar?

Master Chief Brashear: Yes. But every time we would get a contact, we would dive on it. And we dove around the clock for two months. So the fisherman that saw the bomb go into the water kept telling the officials, "You're too close! Too close! Out there! Out there!" He'd take his fingers and measure. So one day Admiral Guest said we would try it. So they made a <u>replica</u> of the bomb on the tender and then dropped it to see how it would show up on the screen, same dimension, same length, same diameter. Then we went out six miles, and the first pass, there the bomb was, six miles in 2,600 feet of water.

So we rigged to pick this thing up. The CURV, out of Woods Hole was going down to hook this thing up. Stillwell, I rigged up what I call a spider. It was a three-legged contraption that I was going to

replica *n.* an exact copy, or duplicate

▲ **Critical Viewing** What clues tell you that these men are preparing for a dive? **[Deduce]**

drop for this bomb to be hooked up to. I had my grapnel hooks and everything, you know. So the Hoist had a very good skipper. Doggone, he was nice!

We dropped that equipment in 2,600 feet of water, and it landed 15 feet from the bomb. The crew of Alvin said it was amazing. The parachute on the bomb hadn't opened, so the Alvin went down and put the parachute shrouds in the grapnel hooks that I had on each leg of the spider. But the Alvin ran out of batteries and had to surface.

So Admiral Guest, through the radio conversation with our skipper, said to pick it up. So we picked it up to a certain depth. Then we brought a boat alongside to pick the crate up out of the boat and set it on the deck so when I picked that bomb up I'd put it in this crate. I was picking the bomb up with the capstan. I got the crate, picking it up, and the boat broke loose. It was a Mike-8. The engineer was revving up the engines, and it parted the line. I was trying to get my sailors out of the way, and I ran back down to grab a sailor, just manhandling him out of the way. Just as I started to leave, the boat pulled on the pipe that had the mooring line tied to it. That pipe came loose, flew across the deck, and it struck my leg below the knee. They said I was way up in the air just turning flips. I landed about two foot inside of that freeboard. They said if I'd been two feet farther over, I'd have gone over the side. I jumped up and started to run and fell over. That's when I knew how bad my leg was.

Paul Stillwell: Was it taken off by the mooring line?
Master Chief Brashear: Taken off by a pipe and the boat's mooring line that parted.

Then we dropped the bomb back down into 2,600 feet of water. So there I was on the ship with my leg torn off—no doctor, no morphine, six and a half miles from the Albany. So the corpsmen placed two tourniquets on my leg. He was interviewed for a program in the "Comeback" TV series, and he said that the reason he couldn't stop the bleeding with two tourniquets was because I was in such good physical condition and my leg was such a mass of muscle. . . .

I came down to Portsmouth Naval Hospital. . . . Dr. O'Neill was the major surgeon there. He said he could have me fixed in 30 months or four years or something like that, have me walking on a brace. He told me all the different types of pins he could put on there. So I said, "Well, I can't stay here that long." I said, "I've got to get out of here." I said, "Go ahead and amputate."

So he said, "Chief! Anybody could amputate. It takes a good doctor to fix it."

grapnel *n.* an iron bar with claws at one end for grasping and holding things

shrouds *n.* lines, or ropes, on a parachute

Thematic Connection

What actions in this paragraph are those of a hero?

mooring *n.* the lines and cables that hold a boat to a pier or anchor

freeboard *n.* the distance from the main deck to the waterline of a ship

tourniquets *n.* devices used to stop bleeding

amputate *v.* to cut off an arm or leg by surgery

I said, "Yeah, but I can't stay here three years. I can't be tied up that long. I've got to go back to diving." They just laughed, "The fool's crazy! He doesn't have a . . . chance of staying in the Navy. And a diver? No way! Impossible!" . . .

After that I kept saying, "I'm going to be a deep-sea diver, doggone it!" By this time, I was reading some books about a Canadian Air Force pilot that flew airplanes with no legs. I had also read books that said a prosthesis can support any amount of weight. I also read you've got to develop an attitude that, "Hey, look, I'm going to accept this. I'm going to make it work." I worked towards it. . . .

Brashear did choose amputation and learned to walk with a prosthetic leg, unassisted by crutches or a cane. Soon he was eager to take on an even bigger challenge—returning to the sea to dive again.

I had to spend a week at the deep-sea diving school diving with a captain and a commander. Quite a few people from BuMed came over and watched me. They watched me dive for a week as an amputee and run around the building, do physical fitness every morning, lead the calisthenics. . . .

Captain Jacks . . . said, "Most of the people in your position want to get a medical disability, get out of the Navy, and do the least they can and draw as much pay as they can. And then you're asking for full duty. I don't know how to handle it." He said, "Suppose you would be diving and tear your leg off?"

I said, "Well, Captain, it wouldn't bleed."

He said, "Get out of here. Get out." He ran me off.

So finally they called me back in. I reported back to the diving school. . . . At the end of that year he wrote the most beautiful letter. Boy, that was something. I was returned to full duty and full diving—the first time in naval history for an amputee.

Thematic Connection

What do the doctors think of Brashear's chances of continuing to dive? What does Brashear think?

▼ **Critical Viewing**

What details from this picture and from the interview suggest that Carl Brashear is a "man of honor"? [**Synthesize**]

Connecting Literature Past and Present

1. What qualities make Brashear a good naval officer?
2. How does Brashear's attitude about death and injury differ from that of the speaker in "Full Fathom Five"?
3. If you had the same choice as Brashear between amputation and a long recovery and less mobility with your leg intact, which would you choose? Why?

Prepare to Read

The Village Blacksmith ◆ Fog ◆ Life ◆ Loo-Wit

Take It to the Net

Visit www.phschool.com for interactive activities and instruction related to these selections, including
- background
- graphic organizers
- literary elements
- reading strategies

Preview

Connecting to the Literature

Both nature and human life move in cycles through different seasons and moods. As you read the poems by Henry Wadsworth Longfellow, Carl Sandburg, Naomi Long Madgett, and Wendy Rose, notice the cycles and patterns they describe and connect to cycles you have experienced and witnessed.

Background

"Loo-Wit" describes the eruption of the Mount St. Helens volcano in Washington State on May 18, 1980. A volcano is an opening in the Earth's crust through which rocks, dust, and ash, or hot liquid rock, can shoot out. The Mount St. Helens eruption killed about sixty people and destroyed about six million trees. Volcanic ash rained down on cities hundreds of miles away.

Literary Analysis

Figurative Language

Poetry often includes **figurative language,** writing or speaking that is not meant to be interpreted literally. Three common uses of figurative language are simile, metaphor, and personification.

- A **simile** uses *like* or *as* to compare two apparently unlike items. Longfellow uses a simile in "The Village Blacksmith" when he says "his brawny arms / Are strong as iron bands."
- A **metaphor** compares one thing to another without using *like* or *as*. Madgett uses a metaphor in "Life" when she says "Life is but a toy."
- An **extended metaphor** is a metaphor that continues past a phrase or sentence. The poem "Fog" develops an extended metaphor.
- **Personification** uses language that gives human traits to an animal, object, or idea. In the poem "Loo-Wit," a volcano is personified as a woman.

Comparing Literary Works

These poets use figurative language in their poems to convey a larger idea or to create a vivid image. Compare and contrast the types of figurative language that are used and the effects they produce. Use these focus questions to guide you:

1. Which examples of figurative language are most striking or unusual?
2. What is similar and different about the overall feeling that each poem creates?

Reading Strategy

Using Your Senses

You can experience a poem more fully if you use your senses. Use your imagination to put yourself in the scene, and think about what you can taste, touch, see, smell, and hear.

In the following example, details that appeal to the senses are italicized.

> Life is but a toy that swings on a *bright gold chain*
> *Ticking* for a little while . . .

Vocabulary Development

brawny (brôn´ ē) *adj.* strong and muscular (p. 748)

haunches (hônch´ iz) *n.* an animal's legs (p. 752)

buttes (byo͞ots) *n.* steep hills standing in flat land (p. 753)

crouches (krouch´ iz) *v.* stoops or bends low (p. 753)

unravel (un rav´ əl) *v.* become untangled or separated (p. 753)

dislodge (dis läj´) *v.* leave a resting place (p. 753)

The Village Blacksmith

Henry Wadsworth Longfellow

Under a spreading chestnut tree
    The village smithy[1] stands;
The smith, a mighty man is he,
    With large and sinewy[2] hands;
5 And the muscles of his <u>brawny</u> arms
    Are strong as iron bands.

His hair is crisp,[3] and black, and long,
    His face is like the tan;
His brow is wet with honest sweat,
10   He earns whate'er he can,
And looks the whole world in the face,
    For he owes not any man.

Week in, week out, from morn till night,
    You can hear his bellows[4] blow;
15 You can hear him swing his heavy sledge,[5]
    With measured beat and slow,
Like a sexton[6] ringing the village bell,
    When the evening sun is low.

And children coming home from school
20   Look in at the open door;
They love to see the flaming forge,
    And hear the bellows roar,
And catch the burning sparks that fly
    Like chaff from a threshing floor.

---

1. smithy (smith´ ē) *n.* workshop of a blacksmith.
2. sinewy (sin´ yōō wē) *adj.* tough and strong.
3. crisp (krisp) *adj.* closely curled and wiry.
4. bellows (bel´ ōz) *n.* device for quickening the fire by blowing air on it.
5. sledge (slej) *n.* sledgehammer; a long, heavy hammer, usually held with both hands.
6. sexton (seks´ tən) *n.* person who cares for church property and rings church bells.

brawny (brôn´ ē) *adj.*
strong and muscular

Literary Analysis
Figurative Language
What simile does
Longfellow use here?
What is its effect?

25 He goes on Sunday to the church,
        And sits among his boys;
    He hears the parson pray and preach,
        He hears his daughter's voice,
    Singing in the village choir,
30   And it makes his heart rejoice.

    It sounds to him like her mother's voice,
        Singing in Paradise!
    He needs must think of her once more,
        How in the grave she lies;
35 And with his hard, rough hand he wipes
        A tear out of his eyes.

    Toiling—rejoicing—sorrowing,
        Onward through life he goes;
    Each morning sees some task begin,
40   Each evening sees it close;
    Something attempted, something done,
        Has earned a night's repose.

    Thanks, thanks to thee, my worthy friend,
        For the lesson thou hast taught!
45 Thus at the flaming forge of life
        Our fortunes must be wrought;
    Thus on its sounding anvil shaped
        Each burning deed and thought.

Reading Strategy
Use Your Senses
Which images appeal to the sense of hearing? How do the images help you share the blacksmith's experiences?

Review and Assess

Thinking About the Selection

1. **Respond:** Do you admire the blacksmith? Explain your answer.

2. **(a) Recall:** Find three details that show how hard the blacksmith works. **(b) Distinguish:** Does the poet present hard work as a positive or a negative thing? Give evidence to support your answer. **(c) Generalize:** Based on this poem, what is Longfellow's attitude toward work?

3. **(a) Recall:** Where does the poet show how the blacksmith relates to his children? **(b) Infer:** What does the tear in his eye reveal about the blacksmith? **(c) Assess:** How does the blacksmith set an example for his family? State at least two ways.

Henry Wadsworth Longfellow

(1807–1882)
During his lifetime, Henry Wadsworth Longfellow's poems were as popular as are the best-loved television programs today. A professor of modern languages, Longfellow wrote many poems that have become American classics. Longfellow was part of a group called the Fireside poets because their family audiences would read poems, including "The Village Blacksmith," aloud in front of their fireplaces.

FOG

Carl Sandburg

The fog comes
on little cat feet.

It sits looking
over harbor and city
5   on silent <u>haunches</u>
and then moves on.

haunches (hônch′ iz) *n.*
upper legs and hips
of an animal

Carl Sandburg

(1878–1967)
The son of Swedish immigrants, Carl Sandburg was born in Illinois. Although he won the Pulitzer Prize in both poetry and history, he was not a typical scholar. By the time his first book appeared, he had been a farm worker, a stage-hand, a railroad worker, a soldier, and a cook, among other things. Sandburg was working as a reporter when he jotted down the poem "Fog."

Life

Naomi Long Madgett

Life is but a toy that swings on a bright gold chain
Ticking for a little while
To amuse a fascinated infant,
Until the keeper, a very old man,
5   Becomes tired of the game
And lets the watch run down.

Review and Assess

Thinking About the Selections

1. **Respond:** Do you agree with the statement in "Life" that "Life is but a toy"? Explain your answer.

2. **(a) Recall:** Describe the setting of "Fog." **(b) Modify:** How would your experience of the poem differ if Sandburg had given more details about the setting? **(c) Generalize:** What is the overall effect of using so few words?

3. **(a) Recall:** Identify three things the fog does. **(b) Speculate:** What qualities of fog make it a good subject for a poem?

4. **(a) Recall:** What image does Madgett use to describe life? **(b) Interpret:** What does this image suggest about life? **(c) Evaluate:** Is it a good image for life? Why or why not?

5. **(a) Synthesize:** What overall feeling does "Fog" convey about fog? **(b) Synthesize:** What overall feeling does "Life" convey about life? **(c) Compare and Contrast:** What is similar and different about the mood of the two poems?

Naomi Long Madgett

(b. 1923)

Naomi Long Madgett retired from Eastern Michigan University in 1984 after sixteen years of teaching in the English department. She once said, "I would rather be a good poet than anything else." Her ambition to write good poetry has led to more than seven collections of poetry and the inclusion of her poems in hundreds of anthologies.

LOO-WIT[1]

Wendy Rose

The way they do
this old woman
no longer cares
what others think
5   but spits her black tobacco
any which way
stretching full length
from her bumpy bed.
Finally up
10 she sprinkles ashes
on the snow,
cold <u>buttes</u>
promise nothing
but the walk
15 of winter.
Centuries of cedar
have bound her
to earth,
huckleberry ropes

▶ **Critical Viewing** Which lines of the poem best capture the action of this photograph? Explain. **[Assess]**

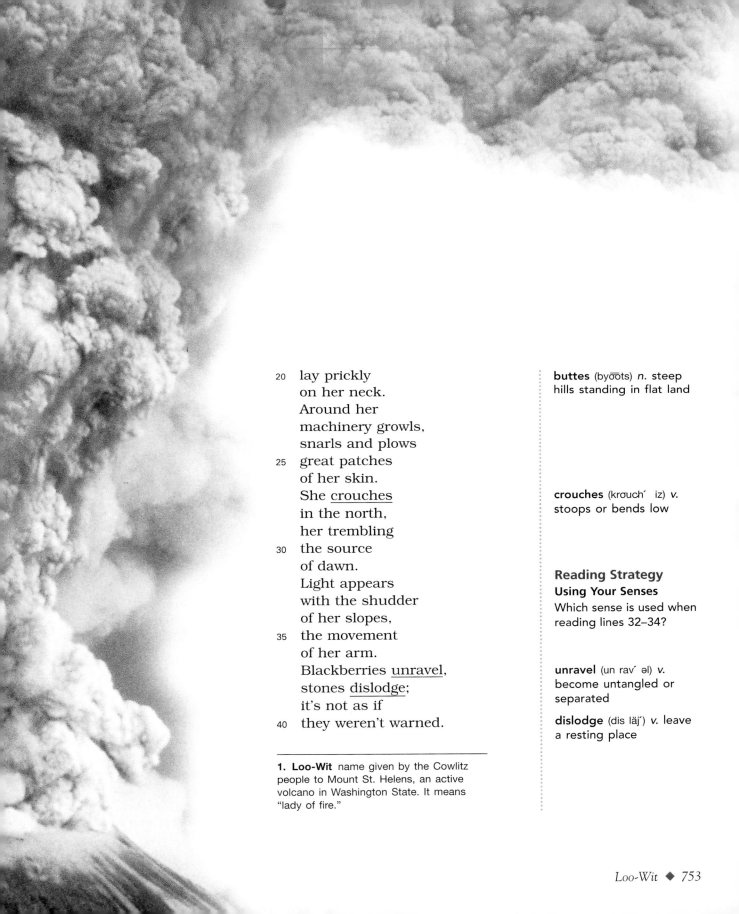

20 lay prickly
on her neck.
Around her
machinery growls,
snarls and plows
25 great patches
of her skin.
She <u>crouches</u>
in the north,
her trembling
30 the source
of dawn.
Light appears
with the shudder
of her slopes,
35 the movement
of her arm.
Blackberries <u>unravel</u>,
stones <u>dislodge</u>;
it's not as if
40 they weren't warned.

---

1. Loo-Wit name given by the Cowlitz people to Mount St. Helens, an active volcano in Washington State. It means "lady of fire."

buttes (byo͞ots) *n.* steep hills standing in flat land

crouches (krouch´ iz) *v.* stoops or bends low

Reading Strategy
Using Your Senses
Which sense is used when reading lines 32–34?

unravel (un rav´ əl) *v.* become untangled or separated

dislodge (dis läj´) *v.* leave a resting place

She was sleeping
but she heard the boot
        scrape,
45   the creaking floor,
felt the pull of the blanket
from her thin
        shoulder.
With one free hand
50   she finds her weapons
and raises them high;
clearing the twigs from her
        throat
she sings, she
55   sings,
shaking the sky
like a blanket about her
Loo-wit sings and sings and
        sings!

Review and Assess

Thinking About the Selection

1. **Respond:** When have you thought of nature—or something in it—as having a personality? Explain.

2. **(a) Recall:** To what kind of person does the poet compare Loo-Wit? **(b) Infer:** How does Loo-Wit show that she doesn't care what others think of her? **(c) Speculate:** Why did the poet choose to compare the volcano to this type of person?

3. **(a) Recall:** In which line does the poem point to the presence of humans? **(b) Infer:** What does Loo-Wit feel about humans and their activities? **(c) Support:** How do Loo-Wit's actions reveal her feelings?

4. **(a) Recall:** What details describe the eruption of the volcano? **(b) Analyze Causes and Effects:** According to the poem, what caused the eruption? **(c) Deduce:** Does the poet give the scientific causes of a volcano? Explain your answer.

5. **(a) Synthesize:** What does the poem say about the relationship between nature and humans? **(b) Speculate:** Why do you think people speak of volcanoes and other natural forces as if they were people?

Wendy Rose

(b. 1948)
Wendy Rose was born in Oakland, California to a Hopi father and a Scots-Irish-Miwok mother. Besides writing poetry, Rose is also an anthropologist who has worked to protect Native American burial sites from developers and a painter who has illustrated some of her own books. "Loo-Wit" is based on legends of the Cowlitz people of Washington State.

Review and Assess

Literary Analysis

Figurative Language

1. What is the comparison that extends throughout the poem "Fog"?
2. What metaphor at the end of "The Village Blacksmith" expresses Longfellow's view of life?
3. Give three examples that show how "Loo-Wit" employs personification. Organize each example and explanation on an organizer like the one shown.

Personification		Actual Detail
Spits her black tobacco	The early volcanic activity is unattractive but seems harmless	Ash and rock fly out of volcano
	Explanation	

Comparing Literary Works

4. Which examples of figurative language are most striking? Explain.
5. What is similar and different about the overall feeling that each poem creates?

Reading Strategy

Using Your Senses

6. On a chart like this one, record examples of details that appealed to your senses. Identify the overall impression in each poem.

Poem	Sound	Sight	Touch	Smell	Taste
Blacksmith					
Fog					
Life					
Loo-Wit					

Extend Understanding

7. **Science Connection:** What are the differences in the ways poets and scientists approach nature?

Quick Review

Figurative language is vivid, imaginative language that is not meant to be interpreted literally. To review **figurative language,** see page 747.

Sensory details are details that appeal to the five senses. To review sensory details, see page 747.

 Take It to the Net

www.phschool.com

Take the interactive self-test online to check your understanding of these selections.

Integrate Language Skills

Vocabulary Development Lesson

Word Analysis: Latin Prefix *dis-*

The Latin prefix *dis-* means "away, apart, not," or "the opposite." Add *dis-* to the following words, and explain the meaning of each word that results.

   1. respect   **2.** honor   **3.** similar

Spelling Strategy

If the last syllable of a word ending with a consonant-vowel-consonant pattern is not stressed, you usually don't double the final consonant when adding an ending:

   un rav´ el + -ing = *unraveling*
   ben´ e fit + -ed = *benefited*

Correctly spell these combinations.

   1. benefit + -ing =   **2.** unravel + -ed =

Fluency: Context

On your paper, fill in each blank with an appropriate word. Do not use any word more than once. To help you, review the vocabulary list on page 747.

I am a proud thunderstorm. I'm not a storm that ___?___, hiding behind the ___?___ so that its steep hill can block me, squatting on my ___?___. I approach boldly, with my ___?___ strength wanting to ___?___ everything you've tied together. Even boulders will ___?___ when they hear my thunder-footsteps.

Grammar Lesson

Semicolons

A **semicolon** signals a pause that is less final than that of a period but stronger than that of a comma. Semicolons can be used to join independent clauses (groups of words with a subject and a verb that can stand on their own). To be joined by a semicolon, the independent clauses should be closely related in meaning.

Example: Carmen told us about his cake recipe; we simply had to try it.

A semicolon can also be used to avoid confusion when items in a series already contain commas.

Example: Caitlin brought apples, oranges, and lemons; Al brought flour, sugar, and spices; and Carmen brought a mixing bowl.

▶ *For more practice, see page R34, Exercise A.*
Practice Revise the punctuation in each sentence, using semicolons. If a sentence needs no revision, write *correct*.

   1. I walked through the park, the leaves were falling.
   2. I saw birch trees, maples, and oaks, young children, babies, and adults, and squirrels, chipmunks, and rabbits.
   3. Everyone was enjoying the park and the change of seasons.
   4. Soon the pond would freeze, I couldn't wait to go skating.
   5. I like skating, skiing, bobsledding, and making ice sculptures.

Writing Application Write three sentences about nature. Use a semicolon in each sentence.

W̶G̶ Prentice Hall Writing and Grammar Connection: Chapter 26, Section 3

Writing Lesson

Composition About Life

Write a composition responding to the poem "Life," explaining whether or not you agree with the view of life presented in the poem.

Prewriting Using a two-column chart, list the ideas about life found in the poem. Highlight your most important points.

Drafting Refer to your notes to write your first paragraph, which should state the main idea or point of your composition—whether you agree or disagree with the ideas in the poem. Devote the second paragraph to the ideas about life found in the poem. In your third paragraph, explain the similarities and differences between the poem's view of life and your own view. Finally, write a concluding paragraph that restates the main point of your composition.

Revising Reread your draft. If the relationship between sentences is not clear, add transition words like *since*, *therefore*, and *so*.

Model: Use Transitions Between Sentences

I agree that life is like a pocket watch because life does tick

However,

just "for a little while." ʌI don't agree with the idea that life

First,

is meant to just "amuse" us. ʌLife is meaningful. . . .

> Transition words like *however* and *first* show the connection between sentences.

𝒲G *Prentice Hall Writing and Grammar Connection: Chapter 9, Section 3*

Extension Activities

Research and Technology Research and present a **report** about fog or Mount St. Helens. Find information in the library and on the Internet. Include quotations in your report, making sure that they convey a clear and accurate perspective on your subject. Also, include a visual aid, such as the following:

- a diagram showing how volcanos erupt
- photographs of the results of well-known volcanic eruptions
- an illustration of how fog is formed

Speaking and Listening Have a classroom **figurative-language contest.** Choose your favorite simile, metaphor, or personification from one of the poems, read it to the class, and explain why it works so well.

Ask the class to select a winner based on the best reading and the most convincing explanation. [**Group Activity**]

 **Take It to the Net**   www.phschool.com

Go online for an additional research activity using the Internet.

READING INFORMATIONAL MATERIALS

Technical Directions

About Technical Directions

To find out what that mysterious button on your stereo was—or to learn how to fix a loose wheel on your bike, you may have consulted **technical directions.** Technical directions offer step-by-step instruction on how to assemble, operate, or repair a product. You might find technical directions accompanying a new VCR, model airplane kit, camera, or car. Regardless of the type or size of the product, technical directions often share these features:

- A diagram of the device with the parts listed and labeled
- Safety warnings that describe "do's" and "don'ts"
- Numbered steps to follow, or steps grouped by function and feature
- A troubleshooting guide that explains how to fix common problems
- A customer support contact number, in case you need the manufacturer's help with problems

Reading Strategy

Understanding and Explaining Directions

Understanding directions is a basic, rational process:

1. Check if any parts are missing and you have all the tools required.
2. Read through the entire set of directions, visualizing each step.
3. Pay attention to safety warnings as you proceed, step-by-step, to build or operate your product. Follow instructions in the proper order, matching the numbers and labels on the diagrams with the actual parts.
4. If you encounter any difficulties, reread the directions and consult the troubleshooting guide for help. If all else fails, contact the manufacturer.

Once you can understand and carry out a set of technical directions, you can *demonstrate* how that product is assembled or operated to others without that knowledge. When you take on the role of teacher, you are not only passing on information. As you explain, you also learn the skill more completely yourself. Consult the chart for tips on how to conduct a successful demonstration.

Demonstration Tips

To conduct a successful demonstration:

- Do a "dry run," in which you practice your demonstration beforehand
- Speak slowly, keeping in mind your audience's level of knowledge
- Follow all steps in order, without skipping any steps
- Explain any problems the audience might have in use or assembly, and offer solutions
- Leave time for questions

How to Use Your New Alarm Chronograph Timer

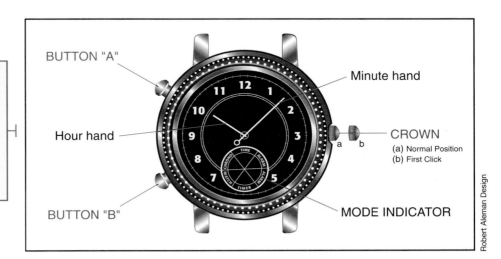

Robert Aleman Design

BUTTON "A"

Minute hand

Hour hand

CROWN
(a) Normal Position
(b) First Click

BUTTON "B"

MODE INDICATOR

Features

Time: Analog display with hour and minute hands
Alarm: Can be set up to 12 hours ahead
Countdown Timer: Can set for up to 60 minutes
Chronograph: Can measure up to 60 seconds in 1/5 seconds
Zero Match: To set both hands in the 12 o'clock position

Time
Time setting

Crown:	**1.** Turn to set function to TIME.
	2. Pull out to First Click.
Button A:	Press repeatedly to set minute hand.
Button B:	Press repeatedly to set hour hand.
Crown:	Push back into Normal position.

Alarm
Alarm time setting

Crown:	Turn to set function to ALARM.
Button A:	Press repeatedly to set minute hand.
Button B:	Press repeatedly to set hour hand.

Alarm on/off

Crown: To turn alarm on, turn to set function to ALARM.

- Alarm rings at the designated time for 20 seconds.
- To stop it, press Button A or B.
- To turn alarm off, turn to set function to TIME.

Chronograph

Crown:	Turn to set function to CHRONO.
Button A:	Start/Stop/Restart
Button B:	Split/Split release/Reset

These directions describe the functions of each button in the chronograph mode.

Zero match

Crown:	1. Turn at Normal position to set function to 0 MATCH.
	2. Pull out to First Click.
Button A:	Press repeatedly to reset minute hand to the 12 o'clock position.
Button B:	Press repeatedly to reset hour hand to the 12 o'clock position.

Countdown Timer

Timer setting

Crown:	1. Turn to set function to TIMER.
Button B:	Press repeatedly to set minute hand for the desired minutes.

Timer operation

Button A:	Start/Stop/Restart
Button B:	Reset

- Warning beep: Beeps for 5 seconds when the time is up.
- To stop it, press Button A or B.

Operation After Battery Change

Crown:	1. Turn to set function to 0 MATCH.
	2. Pull out to First Click.
Button A & Button B:	Press continuously at the same time for 3 seconds. A beep sounds when the buttons are released and the hands start to move automatically.
Button A or Button B:	Press to stop the hands.
Button A:	Press to reset minute hand to 12 o'clock.
Button B:	Press to reset hour hand to 12 o'clock. *
Crown:	Push back into Normal position. Then, set the time following the procedure in Time setting.

*Hand moves quickly if the button is kept pressed.

Certain functions require multiple steps to carry out, and may be confusing to new users. Speak slowly when demonstrating and explaining complex functions.

When an asterisk or other symbol follows a sentence, match the symbol with the information at the bottom of the page next to the asterisk.

Check Your Comprehension

1. How far in advance can you set the alarm feature of the alarm chronograph timer?
2. For which features do you have to pull out the crown of the alarm chronograph timer?
3. When the alarm rings, how do you stop it?

Apply the Reading Strategy

Understanding and Explaining Directions

4. Describe the parts of the alarm chronograph timer.
5. What feature should you use if you want to time a friend who is running the 200-meter dash?
6. Explain what to do after you change the battery of the alarm chronograph timer.

Activity

Use Technical Directions

With a partner, obtain technical directions for a device that you have available.

- Read the directions thoroughly, and then carry them out.
- When you have successfully completed the task, demonstrate it to your partner.
- At the end of the demonstration, ask your partner to carry out the instructions without assistance.
- Discuss the difficulties your partner encounters in following your instructions.
- Note the strong and weak points and how you could improve your demonstrations in the future.

Contrasting Informational Materials

Technical Directions and Warranties

Warranties are frequently packaged with technical directions when you buy a new product. A warranty includes information that explains a manufacturer's responsibility if a product is defective. Look at a warranty and a set of directions for the same product. Use a chart like the one shown to contrast these two types of informational materials.

	Technical Directions	Warranties
Description		
Intended Audience		
Purpose		
Features		

Comparison-and-Contrast Essays

About Comparison-and-Contrast Essays

A comparison-and-contrast essay analyzes the similarities and differences between two or more things. A good comparison-and-contrast essay can help you make decisions or give you new insight into an experience you may have already had. For instance, when a movie critic compares a recent hit movie to an older movie, you might see both movies in a completely new light. In order to read a comparison-and-contrast essay critically, you should look for the following:

- A topic that involves two or more subjects that are well suited for comparison
- Details that illustrate both the similarities and the differences
- A clear organization that highlights the points of comparison

Reading Strategy

Identifying the Author's Main Points

By identifying an author's main points—the points he or she wants you to remember—you can better understand the information presented. To help you read critically, follow these points:

- Ask yourself what the author wants you to discover or think as you read.
- Identify the main points of individual paragraphs.
- Look in the introductory opening paragraph and in the concluding final paragraph.

Use a chart like this to help you identify the author's point in each paragraph. Then, state the author's main point of the selection.

Essay	Individual Paragraph
Is a main point mentioned in the introduction and conclusion?	What is the main point of each paragraph?
Is this main point supported throughout the essay?	Do these main points support the main point of the whole story?

"Bat Attacks?"

Laura Allen

In this paragraph, the author introduces her subject for comparison—aluminum versus wooden baseball bats.

If you play baseball, you may swing an aluminum bat. Metal bats make balls fly faster than wooden bats, and that has some baseball officials worried. They say metal bats just might seriously injure players.

Slugging a ball gives it *kinetic energy*—the energy of motion. The more kinetic energy a ball has, the harder it strikes a player who misses a catch!

If you use a wooden bat, the baseball compresses briefly. (The bat does too, but only slightly.) The compression causes friction in the ball, transforming some kinetic energy into heat. That means less kinetic energy for a fast hit.

But an aluminum bat compresses much more than the baseball does. "That's because metal bats are more elastic (springy) than wooden bats," says Yale University baseball physicist Robert Adair. Unlike a solid wooden bat, aluminum bats are hollow inside. The compressed bat bounces back like a trampoline, giving the ball an added thrust forward. That's why pro players don't use aluminum—there'd be too many home runs!

[Both a metal bat and a wooden bat have "sweet spots."] A metal bat [though] sports larger sweet spots than wooden bats. That's another reason metal bats slug balls so fast. Sweet spots are areas on a bat that drive the farthest hits.

Any bat vibrates along its length when struck, says Adair. But at the sweet spots, there are no energy-sucking vibrations. That leaves more energy to send the ball sailing.

But a metal bat is stiffer (lengthwise) than a wooden bat. Stiff bats vibrate less *overall*. So aluminum bats may guarantee you a home run, but there's a tradeoff—if the ball hits a player, you've struck him or her out. Most coaches haven't noticed an increase in injuries. But batter beware!

> Each paragraph illustrates a key difference between the bats on a point-by-point basis.

> The author offers details that support her main point

Check Your Comprehension

1. Why does the author believe aluminum bats are more dangerous than wooden ones?
2. Why do aluminum bats compress more than wooden bats?
3. Why don't professional baseball players use aluminum bats?

Applying the Reading Strategy

Identifying the Author's Main Purpose

4. What is the main point of the essay?
5. What is the author's reason for including information about wooden bats?
6. Do you think the author proves her overall point throughout the essay? Why or why not?

Activity

Investigating Differences in Products

"Bat Attacks?" is an essay that is based on research results from a new "field" of science—sports physics. Sports physics is the study of the laws of motion as they apply to the actions of objects and materials in sports. With a partner, do your own sports physics test by comparing two different kinds of balls. Then, write an explanation of your findings. Make sure to include details about:

- the kinds of balls you use
- what material they are made of
- how well they bounce
- their cost and quality

Contrasting Informational Materials

Product Comparisons and Product Advertisements

Another type of comparison you commonly encounter is a product comparison. A product comparison compares two or more products by providing current information on each one. It also discusses the advantages and disadvantages of purchasing each one. Product comparisons differ from another type of informational material, product advertisements. Product advertisements provide details about a product's positive features so that people will want to buy the product. Complete a chart like the one shown to discover their differences.

	Product Comparisons	Product Advertisements
Description		
Intended Audience		
Features		
Purpose		

Writing WORKSHOP

Exposition: Comparison-and-Contrast Essay

A **comparison-and-contrast essay** analyzes the similarities and differences between two or more related subjects. In this workshop, you will write a comparison-and-contrast essay that will help readers make a decision or see old things in a fresh way.

Assignment Criteria. Your comparison-and-contrast essay should have the following characteristics:

- A topic involving related subjects that are similar in some ways and different in others
- Supporting details (anecdotes, descriptions, facts, statistics, and examples) that show both similarities and differences
- A clear organization that highlights the points of comparison
- An introduction that grabs a reader's interest and a strong, memorable conclusion

To preview the criteria on which your comparison-and-contrast essay may be assessed, see the Rubric on page 769.

Prewriting

Choose a topic. Fold a piece of paper in thirds lengthwise. In the first column, write a list of recent choices you have made—for instance, products you have bought. In the second column, next to each choice, write a descriptive phrase. In the third column, give an alternative to your choice. Review your list, and choose the most interesting topic. Use the chart shown here to help you.

Choice:
I voted for Eliza for class president.

Description:
Eliza promised to boost school spirit.

Alternative:
Julio, the other candidate, focused more on fund-raising ideas.

Consider your audience. It's important to know the audience, or readers, you are targeting. Decide which details and vocabulary will best suit your readers' level of knowledge.

Analyze your purpose. It is always a good idea to determine your purpose, or reason, before writing. Ask yourself these questions:

- Am I trying to **persuade** my readers?
- Is it my purpose to **inform** my audience?
- Will my essay attempt to **entertain** readers?

Choose details in your writing that support one or more of the purposes above.

Organize your thoughts. Keep your organization clear with:

- a brief introduction outlining your thesis
- a body presenting supporting arguments along with key evidence
- a summary of your main argument

Student Model

Before you begin drafting your comparison-and-contrast essay, read this student model and review the characteristics of a successful comparison-and-contrast essay.

Mackenzie Ames
Daytona Beach, Florida

Stage vs. Set

Theater or television? If you are under eighteen, you more than likely said "television." Have you ever stopped to consider what the magical world of theater has to offer?

Anyone who has been to the theater can tell you that there is nothing like the feeling of sitting and watching people perform. Actors get something special out of theater too. Knowing that hundreds of people are watching your every move creates a special kind of excitement.

There's also variety. Every show is different. When you watch a rerun on television, it's the exact same thing every time. With theater, you get a different experience every night. You can go to see the same show with a different cast or director and the performance will be totally different. Even if you go to a show with the same cast and director, it will be different. An actor might forget a line and improvise or suddenly decide to change the way he or she is playing a character in a scene.

Theater is also larger than the drama you see on television. I don't care how big a screen your television has, theater will always be BIGGER—the emotion more passionate, the voices louder, and the effect more profound. In theater, you have to project your voice and movements so that they carry to the back rows of the audience. In television, actors just need to be seen and heard by the cameras and microphones.

Lastly, the best thing about theater is it's human and real. What I mean is you see when people make mistakes. On television, everything has to be perfect or they do a retake. You never see television actors miss a line or trip over their feet. Since there is no second chance in theater, everything is more spontaneous.

In conclusion, next time you're channel surfing and there's nothing good on, why not take some time to check out what's playing in your community playhouse? Who knows? Maybe you'll discover a rising talent. Even better, maybe you'll decide you want to become an actor or actress after you see how thrilling a live production really is.

In the first paragraph, Mackenzie introduces the comparison in a way that grabs the reader's attention.

The author develops her argument by including examples and explanations, using the point-by-point method of organization.

In the final paragraph, Mackenzie offers a strong conclusion that challenges the reader to accept her point of view.

Drafting

Select an appropriate method of organization. There are two main ways to organize a comparison-and-contrast essay. Choose the one that is most appropriate to your topic and purpose.

● **Block Method** Present details about one of your subjects, then details about your next subject, and so on. This method works well if you are writing about more than two subjects or if your topic is complex.

● **Point-by-Point Method** Discuss one aspect of both subjects, then another aspect of both subjects, and so on.

Layer ideas. Often, the most interesting parts of an essay are the details and anecdotes you offer to support your main ideas. To make sure you stay on topic, *state* your main idea in every paragraph. Then, *extend* the idea by offering a specific example that proves the main idea. Finally, *elaborate* by offering further details to describe your example.

Revising

Revise to heighten interest. Check your essay to make sure it grabs and holds your reader's attention.

● Sharpen your introduction to intrigue readers, teasing them into reading further and finding out more.

● Add details that are surprising, colorful, and important.

● Add language to emphasize similarities or differences.

● Rework your conclusion to add impact or leave readers with a lingering question.

Methods of Organization

Block Method

A. Theater
  1. Amount of Variety
  2. Intensity
  3. Realism
B. Television
  1. Amount of Variety
  2. Intensity
  3. Realism

Point-by-Point Comparison

A. Amount of Variety
  1. Theater
  2. Television
B. Intensity
  1. Theater
  2. Television
C. Realism
  1. Theater
  2. Television

Model: Heightening Interest

You never see television actors miss a line or trip over their feet.

On television, everything has to be perfect or they do a retake. Since there is no second chance in theater, everything is more spontaneous.

Mackenzie uses strong language and interesting detail to point out a key difference.

Revise to avoid repetition. Check your writing for unnecessary repetition. Sometimes writers will repeat a point but add something slightly different the second time. If this is the case, consider combining the two sentences to preserve your additional material while avoiding repetition.

Compare the nonmodel and the model. Why is the model more effective than the nonmodel?

Nonmodel	Model
Lastly, the best thing about theater is it's real. What I mean is you see when people make mistakes. You see people being human by making mistakes every so often.	Lastly, the best thing about theater is it's human and real. What I mean is you see when people make mistakes.

Publishing and Presenting

Choose one of the following ways to share your writing with classmates or a larger audience.

Be a consumer watchdog. If your essay contains information useful to consumers, form a Consumer Information Panel with classmates. Read your essays to the class, using visual aids to enhance your presentation.

Share it with your family. If you wrote about something in your own life, arrange to read your essay aloud to family members or friends. Ask audience members to share their reactions.

Submit it to a magazine. Submit a copy of your essay to a magazine that specializes in the subject you've chosen. Near the magazine's table of contents, you can find publishing information and an address. Send them your essay to see if they will publish it.

W̶G Prentice Hall Writing and Grammar Connection: Chapter 8, Section 4

Speaking Connection
To learn more about presenting comparisons in a speech, see the **Listening and Speaking Workshop: Presenting Pros and Cons,** page 770.

Rubric for Self-Assessment

Evaluate your persuasive composition using the following criteria and rating scale:

Criteria	Rating Scale				
	Not very				Very
How clearly does the essay address two or more related subjects?	1	2	3	4	5
How well do the supporting details show both similarities and differences?	1	2	3	4	5
How clear, consistent, and appropriate is the method of organization?	1	2	3	4	5
How strong and memorable are the introduction and the conclusion?	1	2	3	4	5

Listening and Speaking WORKSHOP

Presenting Pros and Cons

Suppose you and your classmates faced a difficult decision: Should we use money from a bake sale for a school dance or a field trip? One way to make the decision is to explore all the reasons for it (the pros) and against it (the cons). The following strategies will help you evaluate a decision and **present pros and cons**.

Evaluate your decision

Pose a question. A good analysis of pros and cons begins with a clear question. For example, you might ask, "Should our class take a field trip to New York?"

Find evidence for each side. Conduct research to collect solid evidence for both sides. For example, you might determine the cost of the field trip in order to argue that it would be too expensive. Arrange your evidence according to the categories, pro or con.

State each position clearly. Write your initial question on the chalkboard or a poster so your audience can look at it while you speak. Explain the pros and cons thoroughly, and try to give an equal amount of support to each. As presenter, remain neutral by sticking to the facts. Let your listeners make up their minds based on the evidence.

Present pros and cons

Be dynamic. Try using the following techniques to make your presentation lively and interesting:

- **Visual aids** If possible, use visual aids to help the audience keep track of information. Consider using charts, posters, diagrams, photographs, videos, slides, models, or maps.
- **Effective speaking techniques** Speak each word clearly so listeners can hear and understand you. At key points in your speech, slow down and make eye contact with your audience.

Find evidence

Question: Should our class take a field trip to New York City?	
Pros	**Cons**
• Idea is popular with students	• Too expensive
• Would be educational	• Too time-consuming

(Activity:)
Debate and Decision With a partner, choose one of the questions below. One of you should prepare the *pro* presentation and the other should prepare the *con* presentation. Present both to your classmates, and then cast votes to determine the outcome.

- Should the voting age be lowered to sixteen?
- Should our town build a new soccer field?
- Should our school require school uniforms?

Assessment WORKSHOP

Distinguishing Between Fact and Opinion

The writing sections of some tests require you to read a passage and answer multiple-choice questions that ask you to distinguish between fact and opinion. Use the following strategies to help you answer such questions:

- A **fact** is something that can be seen or proved.
- An **opinion** is a belief or judgment about a subject.
- Determine if the statement is objective, or neutral. If the statement could be expressed from a different viewpoint, then it is an opinion.
- Remember that some statements include both facts and opinions.

Test-Taking Strategies

- Look for words like "think" and "believe" that signify an opinion.
- If a statement could be proved true, then the author is <u>not</u> offering an opinion.

Sample Test Item

Directions: Read the following passage, and then choose the letter of the best possible answer.

Heavy rains flooded the downtown area last night, damaging 12 stores and 26 residences. A 50-person work crew tried to stop the flooding but was probably too tired to build a protective wall. Yesterday was the fifth rainy day in a row. The rain is supposed to end tomorrow.

1. The first sentence in the passage is ___?___ .

   A opinion

   B fact

   C both fact and opinion

   D neither fact nor opinion

Answer and Explanation

The correct answer is **B.** You could verify the flood damage by consulting a news report. The statement is objective fact, not opinion, so **A, C,** and **D** are incorrect.

▶ Practice

Directions: Read the following statements, and then choose the letter of the best possible answer.

I. Mary won the essay contest.
II. Mary is a good writer.
1. Which of these statements represents an *opinion?*

   A I

   B II

   C Both I and II

   D Neither statement

I. The dance was held on Tuesday.
II. It was a very fun theme party.
1. Which of these statements represents a fact?

   A I

   B II

   C Both I and II

   D Neither statement

Legends, Folk Tales, and Myths

Sleeping Beauty, John Dixon Batten, Christie's Images, London

Exploring the Genre

Gods and goddesses, talking animals, strange and wondrous events—these are some of the elements of legends, folk tales, and myths. The stories, passed down orally from generation to generation, reveal important truths about the way people once lived and what they valued. They also present important messages to today's generation.

◀ **Critical Viewing** Recall the story of Sleeping Beauty. What do you think is going to happen next to the girl in the painting? **[Predict]**

Why Read Literature?

The legends, folk tales, and myths in this unit are old and new at the same time. Most of the stories are hundreds of years old and were shared orally long before being captured in print. They provide a picture of how people once lived, but they also present values that are still important today. When you read these stories, set a purpose for yourself—such as the three purposes discussed below—to help you enjoy your reading more, learn new ideas, and be inspired by what you read.

1 Read for the love of literature.

Did you know that the ancient Greeks believed the sun was dragged across the sky by the god Apollo? Read what happens when his son wants the job in **"Phaethon, Son of Apollo,"** page 814.

We usually think of volcanoes as destructive, but did you know that they also create? It's true. In 1965, the Island of Surtsey achieved permanence when volcano lava spread over its surface. Read about the mythological creation of a volcano in **"Popocatepetl and Ixtlaccihuatl,"** page 778.

In the mid-nineteenth century, a new form of literature was created: the novella. A novella was originally grouped with several ancient myths that shared a common theme. Read an excerpt from a novella by Edith Wharton, **"False Dawn,"** page 829.

2 Read for information.

Did you know that chocolate was the favorite drink of Montezuma, the emperor of the Aztecs? It wasn't until the 1500s, after Hernando Cortés conquered the Aztec capital, Tenochtitlan, that chocolate was first introduced to Europeans. To learn more about this incredible people, read **"Tenochtitlan,"** page 789.

3 Read to be inspired.

Every political leader or sports coach knows the value of an inspirational proverb, such as "look before you leap," "slow and steady wins the race," or "deeds speak louder than words." These proverbs originated as morals of ancient fables by Aesop. For more inspiration, read Aesop's **"The Lion and the Statue"** and **"The Fox and the Crow,"** pages 802 and 803.

Take It to the Net

Visit the Web site for online instruction and activities related to each selection in this unit.

www.phschool.com

How to Read Literature

Use Strategies for Reading Legends, Folk Tales, and Myths

When you read legends, folk tales, and myths, you are really exploring the history of a culture. Like an explorer, you want to discover all you can about the people and events in your reading. You ask yourself: Who was important in the culture? What did they value? Where and when did they live? Why do the events in the story matter? The following strategies may help you discover the meaning in a legend, folk tale, or myth.

1. Reread or read ahead.

- Different cultures may have unfamiliar-sounding names. Skim the story, noting names of places and characters. Make a list with brief descriptions or notes to help you remember the names.

- If you do not understand a passage, reread it to look for connections among the words and sentences. It may also help to read ahead, because a word or idea may be clarified later in the story.

Names and Notes

Set in Mexico
Near old capital city–Tenochtitlan

Two Mountains
Ixtlaccihuatl (Ixtla)–"The White
Woman" because snow-capped
Popocatepetl (Popo)–"Smoking
Mountain" because smokes
and erupts

2. Identify the cultural context.

- Read any background information or side notes that are provided to learn more about the culture from which the work originated.

- Look for details in the story that suggest how the people in the culture lived or what they found important. Notice, for example, how the importance of being free is suggested in this passage from a folk tale told by African American slaves:

  > Say the people who could fly kept their power, although they shed their wings. They kept their secret magic in the land of slavery.
  >
  > —from "The People Could Fly"

3. Make predictions.

- Keep actively involved in the reading by following the action and predicting what might happen next.

- While you read, you may want to revise your predictions as you encounter new information.

As you read the selections in this unit, review the strategies for reading legends, folk tales, and myths and look at the example in the side column. Use the suggestions to help you interact with the text.

Prepare to Read

Popocatepetl and Ixtlaccihuatl

 Take It to the Net

Visit www.phschool.com for interactive activities and instruction related to "Popocatepetl and Ixtlaccihuatl," including

- background
- graphic organizers
- literary elements
- reading strategies

Preview

Connecting to the Literature

Even with modern technology, humans do not have a full understanding of natural events. We cannot predict just when a volcano will erupt or an earthquake will strike. Imagine how hard it was to understand natural events in ancient times. In their efforts to understand and explain them, people created stories like the one you are about to read.

Background

The legend of "Popocatepetl and Ixtlaccihuatl" comes to us from the Aztec Indians. They were great builders and engineers—their capital city of Tenochtitlan (tā nôch′ tēt län′), built on a lake, had a complex system of canals for transportation and floating gardens for crops. The influence of Aztec culture continues in Mexico's art, language, and food.

Literary Analysis

Legends

Legends are part of the oral tradition—they were passed down by word of mouth from generation to generation. Although people or events in many legends may have a basis in real people or events of the past, details become exaggerated over time. As a result, legends often contain fantastic details and involve larger-than-life characters. The qualities of the characters often reveal the values and attitudes of the cultures from which they come. Use the following focus questions as you read the legend:

1. Which events might have been based on historical events?
2. Which exaggerated qualities or outcomes reflect values or attitudes?

Connecting Literary Elements

The **oral tradition** is the passing of songs, stories, and poems from generation to generation by word of mouth. People used the traditional stories to communicate shared beliefs and to explain their world. No one knows who first created these stories and poems. As the legend unfolds, notice how the storyteller shares Aztec attitudes and beliefs.

Reading Strategy

Rereading or Reading Ahead

Rereading and **reading ahead** are problem-solving reading strategies that can help you to understand the authors' words and ideas. If you do not understand a certain passage, reread it to look for connections among the words and sentences. It might also help to read ahead, because a word or idea may be clarified further on. Use a chart like the one shown to record your notes. In the left column, write questions. In the right column, take notes on answers you find as you reread or read ahead.

Reading Ahead Chart

Questions	Explanation
What is Tenochtitlan?	Once the Aztec capital, now Mexico City
Why do some people think the emperor is wise and others don't?	

Vocabulary Development

besieged (bi sējd´) *adj.* surrounded by enemies (p. 780)

decreed (di krēd´) *v.* officially ordered (p. 780)

relished (rel´ isht) *v.* especially enjoyed (p. 781)

brandishing (bran´ dish iŋ) *adj.* waving in a menacing way (p. 781)

unanimous (yo͞o nan´ ə məs) *adj.* based on complete agreement (p. 782)

refute (ri fyo͞ot´) *v.* prove someone wrong (p. 782)

routed (rout´ əd) *v.* completely defeated (p. 783)

edifice (ed´ ə fis) *n.* large structure (p. 783)

Popocatepetl and Ixtlaccihuatl

MEXICAN LEGEND

Juliet Piggott

Before the Spaniards came to Mexico and marched on the Aztec capital of Tenochtitlan[1] there were two volcanoes to the southeast of that city. The Spaniards destroyed much of Tenochtitlan and built another city in its place and called it Mexico City. It is known by that name still, and the pass through which the Spaniards came to the ancient Tenochtitlan is still there, as are the volcanoes on each side of that pass. Their names have not been changed. The one to the north is Ixtlaccihuatl [ēs′ tlä sē′ wät′ əl] and the one on the south of the pass is Popocatepetl [pô pô kä tē′ peť əl]. Both are snowcapped and beautiful, Popocatepetl being the taller of the two. That name means Smoking Mountain. In Aztec days it gushed forth smoke and, on occasion, it does so still. It erupted too in Aztec days and has done so again since the Spaniards came. Ixtlaccihuatl means The White Woman, for its peak was, and still is, white.

Perhaps Ixtlaccihuatl and Popocatepetl were there in the highest part of the Valley of Mexico in the days when the earth was very young, in the days when the new people were just learning to eat and grow corn. The Aztecs claimed the volcanoes as their own, for they possessed a legend about them and their creation, and they believed that legend to be true.

There was once an Aztec Emperor in Tenochtitlan. He was very powerful. Some thought he was wise as well, whilst others doubted his wisdom. He was both a ruler and a warrior and he kept at bay those tribes living in and beyond the mountains surrounding the Valley of Mexico, with its huge lake called Texcoco [tā skō′ kō] in which Tenochtitlan was built. His power was absolute and the splendor in which he lived was very great.

It is not known for how many years the Emperor ruled in Tenochtitlan, but it is known that he lived to a great age. However, it was not until he was in his middle years that his wife gave him an heir, a girl. The Emperor and Empress loved the princess very much and she was their only child. She was a dutiful daughter and learned all she could from her father about the art of ruling, for she knew that when he died she would reign in his stead in Tenochtitlan.

Her name was Ixtlaccihuatl. Her parents and her friends called her Ixtla. She had a pleasant disposition and, as a result, she had many friends. The great palace where she lived with the Emperor and Empress rang with their laughter when they came to the parties her parents gave for her. As well as being a delightful companion Ixtla was also very pretty, even beautiful.

Her childhood was happy and she was content enough when she became a young woman. But by then she was fully aware of the great responsibilities which would be hers when her father died and she became serious and studious and did not enjoy parties as much as she had done when younger.

Another reason for her being so serious was that she was in love. This in itself was a joyous thing, but the Emperor forbade her to marry. He wanted her to reign and rule alone when he died, for he trusted no one, not even his wife, to rule as he did except his much loved only child, Ixtla. This was why there were some who doubted the wisdom of the Emperor for, by not allowing his heiress to marry, he showed a selfishness and shortsightedness towards his daughter and his empire which many considered was not truly wise. An emperor, they felt, who was not truly wise could not also be truly great. Or even truly powerful.

Reading Strategy
Reading Ahead and Rereading Read ahead to see if the emperor makes wise decisions.

✔**Reading Check**

What does the Emperor forbid Ixtla to do?

---

1. **Tenochtitlan** (tā nôch′ tēt län′) The Spanish conquered the Aztec capital in 1521.

The man with whom Ixtla was in love was also in love with her. Had they been allowed to marry their state could have been doubly joyous. His name was Popocatepetl and Ixtla and his friends all called him Popo. He was a warrior in the service of the Emperor, tall and strong, with a capacity for gentleness, and very brave. He and Ixtla loved each other very much and while they were content and even happy when they were together, true joy was not theirs because the Emperor continued to insist that Ixtla should not be married when the time came for her to take on her father's responsibilities.

This unfortunate but moderately happy relationship between Ixtla and Popo continued for several years, the couple pleading with the Emperor at regular intervals and the Emperor remaining constantly adamant. Popo loved Ixtla no less for her father's stubbornness and she loved him no less while she studied, as her father demanded she should do, the art of ruling in preparation for her reign.

When the Emperor became very old he also became ill. In his feebleness he channeled all his failing energies towards instructing Ixtla in statecraft, for he was no longer able to exercise that craft himself. So it was that his enemies, the tribes who lived in the mountains and beyond, realized that the great Emperor in Tenochtitlan was great no longer, for he was only teaching his daughter to rule and not ruling himself.

The tribesmen came nearer and nearer to Tenochtitlan until the city was <u>besieged</u>. At last the Emperor realized himself that he was great no longer, that his power was nearly gone and that his domain was in dire peril.

Warrior though he long had been, he was now too old and too ill to lead his fighting men into battle. At last he understood that, unless his enemies were frustrated in their efforts to enter and lay waste to Tenochtitlan, not only would he no longer be Emperor but his daughter would never be Empress.

Instead of appointing one of his warriors to lead the rest into battle on his behalf, he offered a bribe to all of them. Perhaps it was that his wisdom, if wisdom he had, had forsaken him, or perhaps he acted from fear. Or perhaps he simply changed his mind. But the bribe he offered to whichever warrior succeeded in lifting the siege of Tenochtitlan and defeating the enemies in and around the Valley of Mexico was both the hand of his daughter and the equal right to reign and rule, with her, in Tenochtitlan. Furthermore, he <u>decreed</u> that directly he learned that his enemies

Literature in context   Social Studies Connection

Tenochtitlan

Archaeologists believe that at one time, 300,000 people lived in Tenochtitlan, the Aztec capital city in the middle of the giant lake Texcoco. Approximately one half of the population were farmers. The rest of the population was made up of nobility, craftspeople, and others. Tenochtitlan depended on food the farmers grew outside the city to feed its population. It also depended on water from outside the city, carried by a system of aqueducts.

Because of its location and dependence on outside food and water sources, Tenochtitlan would be helpless in the face of a siege. With no way to get in or out to get food, a siege would soon lead to a starving population who would grow increasingly weaker and less able to fight. The extravagant rewards offered by the Emperor in the folk tale are appropriate when weighed against the life-or-death necessity of breaking a siege quickly, before food supplies began to dwindle.

To learn more about Tenochtitlan, see page 789.

Ruins of Tenochtitlan

besieged (bi sējd´) *adj.* surrounded by enemies

had been defeated he would instantly cease to be Emperor himself. Ixtla would not have to wait until her father died to become Empress and, if her father should die of his illness or old age before his enemies were vanquished, he further decreed that he who overcame the surrounding enemies should marry the princess whether he, the Emperor, lived or not.

Ixtla was fearful when she heard of her father's bribe to his warriors, for the only one whom she had any wish to marry was Popo and she wanted to marry him, and only him, very much indeed.

The warriors, however, were glad when they heard of the decree: there was not one of them who would not have been glad to have the princess as his wife and they all <u>relished</u> the chance of becoming Emperor.

And so the warriors went to war at their ruler's behest, and each fought trebly[2] hard for each was fighting not only for the safety of Tenochtitlan and the surrounding valley, but for the delightful bride and for the right to be the Emperor himself.

Even though the warriors fought with great skill and even though each one exhibited a courage he did not know he possessed, the war was a long one. The Emperor's enemies were firmly entrenched around Lake Texcoco and Tenochtitlan by the time the warriors were sent to war, and as battle followed battle the final outcome was uncertain.

The warriors took a variety of weapons with them; wooden clubs edged with sharp blades of obsidian,[3] obsidian machetes,[4] javelins which they hurled at their enemies from troughed throwing boards, bows and arrows, slings and spears set with obsidian fragments, and lances, too. Many of them carried shields woven from wicker[5] and covered in tough hide and most wore armor made of thick quilted cotton soaked in brine.

The war was long and fierce. Most of the warriors fought together and in unison, but some fought alone. As time went on natural leaders emerged and, of these, undoubtedly Popo was the best. Finally it was he, <u>brandishing</u> his club and shield, who led the great charge of running warriors across the valley, with their enemies fleeing before them to the safety of the coastal plains and jungles beyond the mountains.

The warriors acclaimed Popo as the man most responsible for the victory and, weary though they all were, they set off for Tenochtitlan to report to the Emperor and for Popo to claim Ixtla as his wife at last.

But a few of those warriors were jealous of Popo. Since they knew none of them could rightly claim the victory for himself (the decision

---

2. **trebly** (treʹ blē) *adv.* three times as much; triply.
3. **obsidian** (əb sidʹ ē ən) *n.* hard, usually dark-colored or black, volcanic glass.
4. **machetes** (mə shetʹ ēs) *n.* large, heavy-bladed knives.
5. **wicker** (wikʹ ər) *n.* thin, flexible twig.

decreed (di krēdʹ) *v.* officially ordered

relished (relʹ isht) *v.* especially enjoyed

Literary Analysis
Legend What does the account of the battle suggest about the Aztec's attitudes about war?

brandishing (branʹ dish iŋ) *adj.* waving in a menacing way

**Reading Check**

What is the reward for lifting the siege?

▲ **Critical Viewing**
Use the descriptions at the beginning of the legend to identify which volcano is which in this painting of Popocatepetl and Ixtlaccihuatl. **[Connect]**

among the Emperor's fighting men that Popo was responsible for the victory had been <u>unanimous</u>), they wanted to spoil for him and for Ixtla the delights which the Emperor had promised.

These few men slipped away from the rest at night and made their way to Tenochtitlan ahead of all the others. They reached the capital two days later, having traveled without sleep all the way, and quickly let it be known that, although the Emperor's warriors had been successful against his enemies, the warrior Popo had been killed in battle.

It was a foolish and cruel lie which those warriors told their Emperor, and they told it for no reason other than that they were jealous of Popo.

When the Emperor heard this he demanded that Popo's body be brought to him so that he might arrange a fitting burial. He knew the man his daughter had loved would have died courageously. The jealous warriors looked at one another and said nothing. Then one of them told the Emperor that Popo had been killed on the edge of Lake Texcoco and that his body had fallen into the water and no man had been able to retrieve it. The Emperor was saddened to hear this.

After a little while he demanded to be told which of his warriors had been responsible for the victory but none of the fighting men before him dared claim the successful outcome of the war for himself, for each knew the others would <u>refute</u> him. So they were silent. This puzzled the Emperor and he decided to wait for the main body of his warriors to return and not to press the few who had brought the news of the victory and of Popo's death.

unanimous
(yōō nan´ ə məs) *adj.* based on complete agreement

refute (ri fyōōt´) *v.* prove someone wrong

Then the Emperor sent for his wife and his daughter and told them their enemies had been overcome. The Empress was thoroughly excited and relieved at the news. Ixtla was only apprehensive. The Emperor, seeing her anxious face, told her quickly that Popo was dead. He went on to say that the warrior's body had been lost in the waters of Lake Texcoco, and again it was as though his wisdom had left him, for he spoke at some length of his not being able to tell Ixtla who her husband would be and who would become Emperor when the main body of warriors returned to Tenochtitlan.

But Ixtla heard nothing of what he told her, only that her beloved Popo was dead. She went to her room and lay down. Her mother followed her and saw at once she was very ill. Witch doctors were sent for, but they could not help the princess, and neither could her parents. Her illness had no name, unless it was the illness of a broken heart. Princess Ixtlaccihuatl did not wish to live if Popocatepetl was dead, and so she died herself.

The day after her death Popo returned to Tenochtitlan with all the other surviving warriors. They went straight to the palace and, with much cheering, told the Emperor that his enemies had been <u>routed</u> and that Popo was the undoubted victor of the conflict.

routed (rout´ əd) v. completely defeated

The Emperor praised his warriors and pronounced Popo to be the new Emperor in his place. When the young man asked first to see Ixtla, begging that they should be married at once before being jointly proclaimed Emperor and Empress, the Emperor had to tell Popo of Ixtla's death, and how it had happened.

Popo spoke not a word.

He gestured the assembled warriors to follow him and together they sought out the few jealous men who had given the false news of his death to the Emperor. With the army of warriors watching, Popo killed each one of them in single combat with his obsidian studded club. No one tried to stop him.

That task accomplished Popo returned to the palace and, still without speaking and still wearing his stiff cotton armor, went to Ixtla's room. He gently lifted her body and carried it out of the palace and out of the city, and no one tried to stop him doing that either. All the warriors followed him in silence.

Reading Strategy
Reading Ahead or Rereading What details about Popo make him larger-than-life? Read ahead to find out.

When he had walked some miles he gestured to them again and they built a huge pile of stones in the shape of a pyramid. They all worked together and they worked fast while Popo stood and watched, holding the body of the princess in his arms. By sunset the mighty <u>edifice</u> was finished. Popo climbed it alone, carrying Ixtla's corpse with him. There, at the very top, under a heap of stones, he buried the young woman he had loved so well and for so long, and who had died for the love of him.

edifice (ed´ ə fis) n. large structure

That night Popo slept alone at the top of the pyramid by Ixtla's grave. In the morning he came down and spoke for the first time

✔**Reading Check**

Why does Ixtla die?

since the Emperor had told him the princess was dead. He told the warriors to build another pyramid, a little to the southeast of the one which held Ixtla's body and to build it higher than the other.

He told them too to tell the Emperor on his behalf that he, Popocatepetl, would never reign and rule in Tenochtitlan. He would keep watch over the grave of the Princess Ixtlaccihuatl for the rest of his life.

The messages to the Emperor were the last words Popo ever spoke. Well before the evening the second mighty pile of stones was built. Popo climbed it and stood at the top, taking a torch of resinous pine wood with him.

And when he reached the top he lit the torch and the warriors below saw the white smoke rise against the blue sky, and they watched as the sun began to set and the smoke turned pink and then a deep red, the color of blood.

So Popocatepetl stood there, holding the torch in memory of Ixtlaccihuatl, for the rest of his days.

The snows came and, as the years went by, the pyramids of stone became high white-capped mountains. Even now the one called Popocatepetl emits smoke in memory of the princess whose body lies in the mountain which bears her name.

Literary Analysis
Legend What details in the explanation for the origin of the volcanoes fulfill the characteristics of a legend?

Juliet Piggott

(1924–1996)
Juliet Piggott found her love for learning about different cultures while living in Japan. Her grandfather was a legal advisor to Japan's Prince Ito—a position that probably gave Piggott a close view of Japanese culture. Piggott's interest in Japan inspired her to produce several books on Japanese history and folklore.

Piggott's interest in folklore was not limited to Japan. The tale you are about to read, retold by Piggott, appeared first in her book *Mexican Folk Tales.* Her own experiences may have influenced her interest in Aztec military battles. She knew a great deal about war from her own World War II service in England in the Women's Royal Naval Service.

Review and Assess

Thinking About the Literature

1. **Respond:** If you were either Ixtla or Popo, how would you have responded to the news of the other's death?

2. **(a) Recall:** Why are Ixtla and Popo unable to marry?
   (b) Analyze: What qualities make the two well-matched?

3. **(a) Recall:** What effect does the emperor's selfishness have on the safety of his kingdom? **(b) Connect:** In what way are events caused by the characters' selfishness, jealousy, and love?

4. **(a) Recall:** What leads to Ixtla's death at the end of the war?
   (b) Interpret: How does this story turn tragedy into something positive?

5. **(a) Recall:** Why does Popo refuse to become emperor and rule in Tenochtitlan? **(b) Draw Conclusions:** Based on this legend, what traits do you think the Aztecs admired?

6. **(a) Interpret:** What lesson does the story suggest?
   (b) Evaluate: Can this lesson be applied in modern times? Explain.

7. **Take a Position:** What do you think would be the appropriate punishment for the men who lied about Popo's death? Explain.

Review and Assess

Literary Analysis

Legends

1. Which events in this **legend** might have been based on historical events?
2. Which exaggerated qualities or outcomes seem to reflect values or attitudes? What are those values?
3. Use a chart like the one shown to provide at least one example of each of the features most often found in legends.

"Popocatepetl and Ixtlaccihuatl"		
Fantastic Elements	**Larger-Than-Life Characters**	**Rooted in History**
• burial pyramids •	• Popocatepetl •	• Siege •

Connecting Literary Elements

4. Which event in this legend probably has a basis in history?
5. What does the story reveal about Aztec values and beliefs based on this legend? Use a web like the one shown to report your answer.

Reading Strategy

Rereading or Reading Ahead

6. How did **reading ahead** help you clarify statements made about the emperor at the beginning of the story?
7. Why might someone **reread** the conditions of the emperor's reward?

Extend Understanding

8. **Social Studies Connection:** Why might archaeologists be interested in the legends of ancient places like Tenochtitlan?

Quick Review

A **legend** is a traditional story about the past passed down by word of mouth from generation to generation. To review legends, see page 777.

The **oral tradition** is the passing of songs, stories, and poems from generation to generation by word of mouth. To review the oral tradition, see page 777.

Rereading and reading ahead are problem-solving reading strategies that can help you understand the authors' words and ideas.

 Take It to the Net
www.phschool.com
Take the interactive self-test online to check your understanding of the selection.

Integrate Language Skills

Vocabulary Development Lesson

Word Analysis: Anglo-Saxon Prefix *be-*

Words that start with the prefix *be-* are usually action verbs. They tell you something has been "made" to happen. With this information in mind, work with a partner (and a dictionary, if necessary) to define these words.

1. becalm
2. befriend
3. bewitch
4. belittle

Spelling Strategy

Use *i* before *e* except after *c* in words containing the long *e* sound: *besiege*. Complete the spelling of these words.

1. bel___?___ve
2. f___?___ld
3. th___?___f
4. p___?___ce

Fluency: Definitions

Write the letter of the definition that best matches each vocabulary word from the list on page 777.

1. besieged
2. decreed
3. relished
4. brandishing
5. unanimous

6. refute
7. routed
8. edifice

a. all in agreement
b. prove wrong
c. large structure
d. surrounded
e. waving in a menacing way
f. especially enjoyed
g. completely defeated
h. officially ordered

Grammar Lesson

Parentheses and Brackets

Parentheses and **brackets** are sometimes used to set off certain words or groups of words from a sentence.

Use parentheses to set off additional information—such as dates, a definition, or an explanation—that is not needed in a sentence.

> I just read a legend about those two volcanoes (the ones south of Mexico City) that will amaze you!

Brackets are used to enclose comments or explanations not written by the original writer.

> "These few men [warriors jealous of Popo] slipped away from the rest at night and made their way to Tenochtitlan ahead of all the others."

▶ *For more practice, see page R35, Exercise C.*
Practice Write the following sentences, adding parentheses or brackets where necessary.

1. The author Juliet Piggott 1924–1996 published a book of Mexican folk tales.
2. The legend reads, "she Ixtla the daughter was so serious because she was in love."
3. The Emperor demanded the body of Popo from the name Popocatepetl so he could arrange a fitting burial.
4. Piggott wrote, "The war the one the warriors fought without an assigned leader was long and fierce."
5. The legend explains that two lovers' tombs pyramids grew into two mountains.

Writing Application Write a paragraph explaining the story. Use at least one pair of parentheses and one quotation with a bracketed comment.

 Prentice Hall Writing and Grammar Connection: Chapter 26

Writing Lesson

Research Summary

Read two or three articles on how mountains are formed. Then, write a summary that can be used to contrast the explanation in the legend to the actual process.

Prewriting   First, retell the events or steps that occur in the formation of a mountain. Then, choose only the steps that cause or lead to another part of the process.

Drafting   Begin by stating the process you will summarize. As you draft, keep your purpose in mind: to prepare a summary, not a detailed research report. Include only details that provide important information. Use transitional words to show time order or cause and effect.

Revising   Add introductory or transitional words to sentences to clarify relationships between events. Look at the example below.

Model: Revising Sequence of Events

A volcano is an opening in Earth's crust called a vent. *First,* Heat inside

> *First* indicates the initial event.

Earth causes the vent to discharge gas, lava, solid fragments, and

ash. *Periodically,* The vent ejects the material, and *over time* the ejected rock material builds

up as a conical mountain around the vent.

> *Periodically* and *over time* indicate that a type of event occurs several times at different points.

 Prentice Hall Writing and Grammar Connection: Chapter 11

Extension Activities

Listening and Speaking Prepare a **news report** on the siege and the battle. Research the warfare of the Aztec period. Organize your information to make the report straightforward and factual. Include details that will appeal to an audience looking for news, not excitement.

Writing Write a brief **essay** in which you **compare and contrast** the legend of Popacatepetl and Ixtlaccihuatl with another legend you have read.

Research and Technology Use the Internet or a library to conduct research on what the Aztec city of Tenochtitlan looked like. Then, draw a **map,** showing the arrangement of the buildings and the floating gardens. Label the canals and buildings so that the plan is clear. Share your findings with the class.

 **Take It to the Net**   www.phschool.com

Go online for an additional research activity using the Internet.

READING INFORMATIONAL MATERIALS

Social Studies Articles

About Social Studies Articles

Social studies articles are short works of nonfiction that present factual information about people and places—both past and current. In school, you study different types of social studies texts—history, civics, geography, world cultures, and economics. These textbooks include different aspects of the human world and the people who live in it. However, social studies is not just a subject for school textbooks. The writers of social studies articles convey informational materials in various publications, including

- history magazines.
- travel magazines and newspaper travel sections.
- magazines about politics, current events, and economics.
- books by scientists and explorers.

Reading Strategy

Locating Information

The main purpose of a social studies article is to inform—to share information. Often writers also include descriptive passages to entertain the reader. Information may be provided visually in one or more of the following features.

- photographs • illustrations • diagrams • charts • maps

These art forms make the article more enjoyable and provide different types of supporting information. Unlike almanacs and encyclopedias that focus mainly on facts and statistics, social studies articles offer insights into and interpretations of information.

When reading a social studies article, review the overall structure to figure out where to find information. Look at how the written text is organized and what visual or graphic features are used.

K	W	L
What do I **know** about the subject?	What do I **want** to know about it?	What have I **learned** about it?

- The structure of heads and subheads point out the main ideas and themes.
- The graphic features support the text by elaborating on main points.

To guide you in locating information, use a K-W-L chart like the one shown. Fill in the first and second sections before you read. As you read, add more questions in the "want to know" section.

TENOCHTITLAN: Inside the Aztec Capital

Jacqueline Dineen

An article usually contains heads like this. Heads break up the text and help you find information on specific topics

The Lake City of Tenochtitlan[1]

The city of Tenochtitlan began on an island in the middle of a swampy lake. There the Aztecs built their first temple to Huitzilopochtli.[2] The place was given the name Tenochtitlan, which means "The Place of the Fruit of the Prickly Pear Cactus." Later on the name was given to the city that grew up around the temple. The Aztecs rebuilt their temples on the same site every 52 years, so the first temple eventually became the great Temple Mayor[3] that stood at the center of the city.

The article begins with a short history, which gives you background for the information to come.

from THE AZTECS by Jacqueline Dineen (Words of the Past), Heineman Educational Books Ltd, an Import of Reed Educational and professional Publishing

How does this city map compare and contrast with modern maps? **[Compare and Contrast]**

The Lake City of Tenochtitlan
Each grouping of houses in Tenochtitlan was planned so that the houses could be reached through the many waterways. These canals crisscrossed the city, and some are still in and around Mexico City today.

---

1. Tenochtitlan (tä nôch′ tēt län′) *n.* ancient Aztec capital located in what is now Mexico City.
2. Huitzilopochtli (wēt sē pōch′ tlē)
3. Mayor (mä yōr′) *adj.* (Sp.) main

Why do you think the Aztecs found so many uses for the cactus plants, like those in this photograph? [Infer]

The photograph shows you the vegetation of the area. The caption provides further interesting information.

Maguey cactus plants, like these in front of a rebuilt Aztec temple, had many uses. Parts of the plants were used to make medicines. The thorns were used as sewing needles, and fibers of the maguey were spun together and woven into coarse cloth. Pulque, a popular drink, comes from the plant. The maguey even had its own goddess—Mayahuel!

The city started as a collection of huts. It began to grow after 1385, while Acamapichtli[4] was king. The Aztecs were excellent engineers. They built three causeways over the swamp to link the city with the mainland. These were raised roads made of stone supported on wooden pillars. Parts of the causeways were bridges. These bridges could be removed to leave gaps and this prevented enemies from getting to the city. Fresh water was brought from the mainland to the city along stone aqueducts.[5]

---

4. **Acamapichtli** (ä kä mä pēch´ tlē)
5. **aqueducts** (ak´ wə dukts´) *n.* Large pipes made for bringing water from a distant source.

Inside the City

The Spaniards' first view of Tenochtitlan was described by one of Cortés's[6] soldiers, Bernal Diaz: "And when we saw all those towns and level causeway leading into Mexico, we were astounded. These great towns and buildings rising from the water, all made of stone, seemed like an enchanted vision."

By that time Tenochtitlan was the largest city in Mexico. About 200,000 people lived there. The houses were one story high and had flat roofs. In the center of the city was a large square. The twin temple stood on one side, and the king's palace on another. Officials' houses

---

6. **Hernando Cortés** (er nän´ dō kōr tes´) Spanish adventurer (1485–1547) who conquered what is now central and southern Mexico.

This Aztec codex (the first manuscript presented in modern book form) shows the life of a corn plant over four years. Corn was so precious to the Aztecs that special gods and goddesses were in charge of it. Tlaloc, the God of Rain; Xipe Totec, the God of Planting and Spring; and the Storm Goddess are all featured with the corn in this codex.

Codex Fejervary-Mayer (detail) The life of a corn plant over four years, Werner Forman Archive, Liverpool Museum, Liverpool

What does seeing a codex like this one add to your understanding of Aztec culture? **[Connect]**

What details in the drawing suggest the emperor's importance? **[Analyze]**

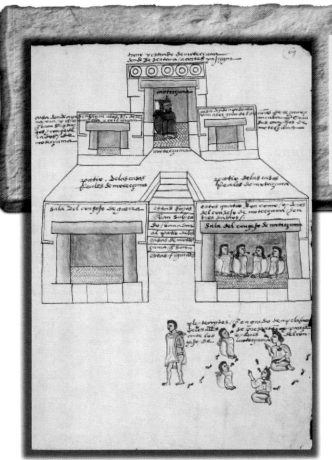

Drawing of the King's Palace from the Codex Mendoza,
The Bodleian Library, Oxford

This drawing from the Codex Mendoza shows what the Aztec emperor Montezuma's palace looked like. Practically a small town, it had a main palace and smaller surrounding palaces, council offices, courts of law, and storerooms.

made of white stone also lined the square. There were few roads. People traveled in canoes along canals.

Floating Gardens

Tenochtitlan was built in a huge valley, the Valley of Mexico, which was surrounded by mountains. Rivers flowed from the mountains into Lake Texcoco, where Tenochtitlan stood.

The lake was linked to four other shallow, swampy lakes. The land around the lakes was dry because there was very little rain. The Aztecs dug ditches and piled up the earth to make islands in the shallow parts of the lake. These chinampas, or swamp gardens, could be farmed. The ditches carried water into larger canals that were used for irrigation[7] and as waterways to the city.

Texcoco and the lake to the south contained fresh water, but the northern lakes contained salt water, which was no good for irrigation. The Aztecs built an embankment[8] 10 miles long to keep out the salt water and also to protect the city from flooding.

---

7. **irrigation** (ir′ ə gā′ shən) *n.* act of supplying water by means of ditches, canals, or sprinklers.
8. **embankment** (em bank′ mənt) *n.* bank of earth to keep water back.

Feeding the People

Archaeologists think that when Tenochtitlan was at its greatest, about one million people lived in the Valley of Mexico. That included Tenochtitlan and the 50 or 60 city-states on the mainland surrounding the lakes. Food for all these people had to come from farming.

Historians are not sure how many people in Tenochtitlan were farmers, but they think it may have been between one third and one half of the population. The rest were the nobility, craftspeople, and others. Each chinampa was only big enough to grow food for one family. Most people in Tenochtitlan depended on food from outside the city.

As the city grew, more and more land was drained for farming and for building. Farmers had no tools except simple hoes and digging sticks, but the loose soil was fertile and easy to turn. The main crop was corn, but farmers also grew tomatoes, beans, chili peppers, and prickly pears. They grew maguey cactus for its fibers and to make a drink called pulque. Cacao trees were grown in the hottest areas. The seeds were used for trading and to make a chocolate drink.

Writers of social studies articles often draw on information and evidence from archaeologists, historians, and other specialists to explain the past.

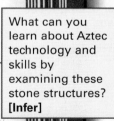

What can you learn about Aztec technology and skills by examining these stone structures? [Infer]

The priest's house is located at Teotihuacan, an Aztec ruin site outside Mexico City. It is probably similar to the homes of Aztec nobles. A doorway opened onto a central courtyard, and the outside walls are decorated with carvings. The houses had flat roofs that were often decorated with flower gardens.

Inside an Aztec Home

There were big differences between a rich Aztec home and a poor one. The nobles' houses were like palaces. They were one story high and built around a courtyard. Each of the four sides contained four or five large rooms. The courtyards were planted with flower and vegetable gardens. Some houses on the island in the center of the city were built of adobe—bricks made from mud and dried in the sun. Adobe is still used for building in Mexico today. These grand houses and palaces were white-washed so that they shone in the sun. The Spanish soldier Bernal Diaz described buildings that looked like "gleaming white towers and castles: a marvelous sight."

There is very little evidence about the buildings in Tenochtitlan and hardly any about the poor people's houses. What we do know has been pieced together from scattered historical records such as documents that record the sale of building sites on the chinampa gardens. All of the poorer people's homes were built on the chinampas on the outskirts of the city. Because the chinampas would not take the weight of stone, houses had to be built of lighter materials such as wattle-and-daub. This was made by weaving reeds together and then plastering them with mud. We know that the outskirts of the city were divided into groups of houses inside walled areas, or compounds. A whole family lived in each compound. The family consisted of a couple, their married children, and their grandchildren. Every married couple in the family had a separate house of one or two rooms. All the houses opened onto an outdoor patio that belonged to the whole family.

Outside the house, the families often kept turkeys in pens. The turkeys provided eggs and meat. There was also a beehive for honey. Most families had a bathhouse in the garden.

Furniture and Decoration

Aztec houses were very plain inside. Everyone slept on mats of reeds that were spread on the dirt floor at night. Families had cooking pots and utensils made of clay. There were goblets for pulque and other drinks, graters for grinding chilis, and storage pots of various designs. Reed baskets were also used for storage. Households had grinding stones for grinding corn into flour. There was also a household shrine with statues of the gods.

The houses had no windows or chimneys, so they must have been dark and smoky from the cooking fire. There were no doors, just an open doorway. Even the palaces had open doorways with cloths hanging over them.

Check Your Comprehension

1. Describe the setting of the city of Tenochtitlan.
2. Where did both wealthy and poor Aztec people live?
3. Identify three problems the Aztecs faced and explain how they solved them.

Applying the Reading Strategy

Locating Information

Use the text and visual features of the article "Tenochtitlan: Inside the Aztec Capital" to help you locate information. Remember to use heads, subheads, photos, and other graphic devices. Answer each of the following questions. Then explain how text and visual features helped you locate the information.

4. What kinds of building materials did the Aztecs use?
5. What was life like inside an average Aztec family's home?
6. What two plants were very important to the Aztecs?

Activity

Research Ancient American Civilizations

Use a variety of research sources to locate information about at least two other early cultures in the Americas, such as the Maya or Olmec in Mesoamerica (Mexico and Central America) and the Incas in the Andes. Compare their governments, social structure, geography, economies, and religious beliefs. Look for information in magazines, standard and online encyclopedias, and books by specialists and historians. Notice differences in how each source organizes and presents information. Finally, prepare a spreadsheet to display the information you have found.

Contrasting Informational Materials

Articles and Almanacs

Using library resources, find articles with information on "Cities." Look in an almanac. Compare the article in the almanac with "Tenochtitlan: Inside the Aztec Capital." Compare text organization, text features (heads and subheads), and graphics (photographs, drawings, and maps). Compare the writer's purpose in each article—is it to inform and engage the reader or is it purely to inform by focusing mainly on data and statistics? Present your information in a chart like this one.

	Almanac	Tenochtitlan Article
Purpose		
Structure		

Prepare to Read

The People Could Fly ◆ All Stories Are Anansi's ◆ The Lion and the Statue ◆ The Fox and the Crow

The Ride for Liberty - the Fugitive Slaves, Eastman Johnson

Preview

Connecting to the Literature

Stories that live on often tell about people who look within themselves and find reserves of strength they did not know they had. Other stories tell of experiences we can all understand. The special qualities of these stories have compelled people to pass them on, generation after generation.

Background

One way that enslaved Africans kept their hopes alive despite the tremendous hardships they faced was to tell freedom tales—folk tales about the fight for freedom. These tales served an important function: They helped people to believe that they would eventually find freedom from slavery and injustice. As you'll notice in the freedom tale "The People Could Fly," these stories are full of references to the storytellers' native Africa.

Literary Analysis

Folk Tales and Fables

The stories you are about to read are examples of two types of traditional literature that continue to inspire, teach, and entertain people from generation to generation.

- A **folk tale** is an entertaining story composed orally and then passed along by word of mouth.
- A **fable** is a brief story or poem, usually with animal characters, that teaches a lesson.

As you read the works in this group, think about the reasons they continue to be told and retold.

Comparing Literary Works

The **theme** of a folk tale—the message or insight about life it suggests—often reflects a belief, attitude, or value of the culture from which the folk tale comes. In fables, the message is called a **moral,** a wise saying at the end of the story that states the lesson. Compare and contrast the works by thinking about the focus questions:

1. What are the similarities and differences in the way these tales encourage people to behave?
2. How much or how little does each story's message apply to contemporary life?

Reading Strategy

Recognizing Cultural Context

When you encounter characters that act in ways you don't expect or details that seem strange to you, consider that these details may be influenced by the **cultural context**—the background, customs, and beliefs of the people who originally told the story. Keep track of the cultural context of each story by making a chart like the one shown. It will provide a window of understanding into what you read.

Vocabulary Development

croon (krōōn) v. sing or hum quietly, soothingly (p. 799)

shuffle (shuf′ əl) v. walk with dragging feet (p. 801)

glossy (glôs′ ē) adj. smooth and shiny (p. 803)

surpass (sər pas′) v. be superior to (p. 803)

flatterers (flat′ ər ərz) n. those who praise a person insincerely (p. 803)

yearned (yərnd) v. wanted very much (p. 804)

gourd (gôrd) n. a fruit; the dried shell is used as a cup (p. 804)

acknowledge (ak näl′ ij) v. recognize and admit (p. 808)

▲ Critical Viewing How does the folk tale explain the unique way the people in this illustration fly? [Interpret]

THE PEOPLE COULD FLY

African American Folk Tale
VIRGINIA HAMILTON

From THE PEOPLE COULD FLY by Virginia Hamilton, illustrated by Leo and Diane Dillon

They say the people could fly. Say that long ago in Africa, some of the people knew magic. And they would walk up on the air like climbin up on a gate. And they flew like blackbirds over the fields. Black, shiny wings flappin against the blue up there.

Then, many of the people were captured for Slavery. The ones that could fly shed their wings. They couldn't take their wings across the water on the slave ships. Too crowded, don't you know.

The folks were full of misery, then. Got sick with the up and down of the sea. So they forgot about flyin when they could no longer breathe the sweet scent of Africa.

Say the people who could fly kept their power, although they shed their wings. They kept their secret magic in the land of slavery. They looked the same as the other people from Africa who had been coming over, who had dark skin. Say you couldn't tell anymore one who could fly from one who couldn't.

One such who could was an old man, call him Toby. And standin tall, yet afraid, was a young woman who once had wings. Call her Sarah. Now Sarah carried a babe tied to her back. She trembled to be so hard worked and scorned.

The slaves labored in the fields from sunup to sundown. The owner of the slaves callin himself their Master. Say he was a hard lump of clay. A hard, glinty[1] coal. A hard rock pile, wouldn't be moved. His Overseer[2] on horseback pointed out the slaves who were slowin down. So the one called Driver[3] cracked his whip over the slow ones to make them move faster. That whip was a slice-open cut of pain. So they did move faster. Had to.

Sarah hoed and chopped the row as the babe on her back slept.

Say the child grew hungry. That babe started up bawling too loud. Sarah couldn't stop to feed it. Couldn't stop to soothe and quiet it down. She let it cry. She didn't want to. She had no heart to <u>croon</u> to it.

"Keep that thing quiet," called the Overseer. He pointed his finger at the babe. The woman scrunched low. The Driver cracked his whip across the babe anyhow. The babe hollered like any hurt child, and the woman fell to the earth.

The old man that was there, Toby, came and helped her to her feet.

Literary Analysis
Folk Tales and Fables
How does the use of language in this retelling suggest that this story has been passed on orally?

croon (kro͞on) v. sing or hum quietly, soothingly

 **Reading Check**

What special gift do some of the people have?

---

1. **glinty** (glint′ ē) adj. shiny; reflecting light.
2. **Overseer** (ō′ vər sir′) n. someone who watches over and directs the work of others.
3. **Driver** n. someone who forced (drove) the slaves to work harder.

"I must go soon," she told him.

"Soon," he said.

Sarah couldn't stand up straight any longer. She was too weak. The sun burned her face. The babe cried and cried, "Pity me, oh, pity me," say it sounded like. Sarah was so sad and starvin, she sat down in the row.

"Get up, you black cow," called the Overseer. He pointed his hand, and the Driver's whip snarled around Sarah's legs. Her sack dress tore into rags. Her legs bled onto the earth. She couldn't get up.

Toby was there where there was no one to help her and the babe.

"Now, before it's too late," panted Sarah. "Now, Father!"

"Yes, Daughter, the time is come," Toby answered. "Go, as you know how to go!"

He raised his arms, holding them out to her. "*Kum . . . yali, kum buba tambe*," and more magic words, said so quickly, they sounded like whispers and sighs.

The young woman lifted one foot on the air. Then the other. She flew clumsily at first, with the child now held tightly in her arms. Then she felt the magic, the African mystery. Say she rose just as free as a bird. As light as a feather.

The Overseer rode after her, hollerin. Sarah flew over the fences. She flew over the woods. Tall trees could not snag her. Nor could the Overseer. She flew like an eagle now, until she was gone from sight. No one dared speak about it. Couldn't believe it. But it was, because they that was there saw that it was.

Say the next day was dead hot in the fields. A young man slave fell from the heat. The Driver come and whipped him. Toby come over and spoke words to the fallen one. The words of ancient Africa once heard are never remembered completely. The young man forgot them as soon as he heard them. They went way inside him. He got up and rolled over on the air. He rode it awhile. And he flew away.

Another and another fell from the heat. Toby was there. He cried out to the fallen and reached his arms out to them. "*Kum kunka yali, kum . . . tambe!*" Whispers and sighs. And they too rose on the air. They rode the hot breezes. The ones flyin were black and shinin sticks, wheelin above the head of the Overseer. They crossed the rows, the fields, the fences, the streams, and were away.

"Seize the old man!" cried the Overseer. "I heard him say the magic *words*. Seize him!"

The one callin himself Master come runnin. The Driver got his whip ready to curl around old Toby and tie him up. The slaveowner took his hip gun from its place. He meant to kill old, black Toby.

But Toby just laughed. Say he threw back his head and said, "Hee, hee! Don't you know who I am? Don't you know some of us in this field?" He said it to their faces. "We are ones who fly!"

And he sighed the ancient words that were a dark promise. He said them all around to the others in the field under the whip,

Reading Strategy
Recognizing Cultural Context What negative attitudes and injustices are part of the cultural context from which this story comes?

Literary Analysis
Folk Tales and Fables What do you think the message of this story was to enslaved Africans?

"... *buba yali ... buba tambe.* ..."

There was a great outcryin. The bent backs straightened up. Old and young who were called slaves and could fly joined hands. Say like they would ring-sing.[4] But they didn't <u>shuffle</u> in a circle. They didn't sing. They rose on the air. They flew in a flock that was black against the heavenly blue. Black crows or black shadows. It didn't matter, they went so high. Way above the plantation, way over the slavery land. Say they flew away to *Free-dom.*

And the old man, old Toby, flew behind them, takin care of them. He wasn't cryin. He wasn't laughin. He was the seer.[5] His gaze fell on the plantation where the slaves who could not fly waited.

"Take us with you!" Their looks spoke it but they were afraid to shout it. Toby couldn't take them with him. Hadn't the time to teach them to fly. They must wait for a chance to run.

"Goodie-bye!" The old man called Toby spoke to them, poor souls! And he was flyin gone.

So they say. The Overseer told it. The one called Master said it was a lie, a trick of the light. The Driver kept his mouth shut.

The slaves who could not fly told about the people who could fly to their children. When they were free. When they sat close before the fire in the free land, they told it. They did so love firelight and *Free-dom,* and tellin.

They say that the children of the ones who could not fly told their children. And now, me, I have told it to you.

---

4. **ring-sing** joining hands in a circle to sing and dance.
5. **seer** (sē´ ər) *n.* one who has supposed power to see the future; prophet.

shuffle (shuf´ əl) *v.* walk with dragging feet

Review and Assess

Thinking About the Literature

1. **Respond:** Who do you think is the most important character in the story, Toby or the narrator? Why?

2. **(a) Describe:** What words would you use to communicate the living conditions of African Americans during the time this story originated? **(b) Support:** Describe three details that help you understand these living conditions.

3. **(a) Infer:** What are the "magic words" Toby says? **(b) Interpret:** Why do you think the author includes these words in the story?

4. **(a) Recall:** What happens when Toby says the "magic words"? **(b) Draw Conclusions:** To what do you think "flying" really refers?

5. **(a) Recall:** Who is called Master? **(b) Contrast:** Who is the real "master" in the story? **(c) Evaluate:** Do you think this folk tale effectively inspires hope? Explain.

Virginia Hamilton

(b. 1936)

In her many award-winning novels for young readers, Virginia Hamilton uses elements of history, myth, folklore, legend, and dream to bring to life her African American heritage. As she puts it, writing "is my way of exploring the known, the remembered, and the imagined, the literary triad of which all stories are made."

THE LION AND THE STATUE AESOP

A Man and a Lion were discussing the relative[1] strength of men and lions in general. The Man contended[2] that he and his fellows were stronger than lions by reason of their greater intelligence. "Come now with me," he cried, "and I will soon prove that I am right." So he took him into the public gardens and showed him a statue of Hercules[3] overcoming the Lion and tearing his mouth in two.

"That is all very well," said the Lion, "but proves nothing, for it was a man who made the statue."

We can easily represent things as we wish them to be.

___

1. **relative** (rel′ ə tiv) *adj.* related to another; comparative.
2. **contended** (kən tend′ id) *v.* argued.
3. **Hercules** (hʉr′ kyo͞o lēz′) hero of Ancient Greek mythology known for his strength.

▲ **Critical Viewing**
Why would the Lion be bothered by his species' portrayal in the statue shown here? **[Speculate]**

Literary Analysis
Folk Tales and Fables
How can you tell that this story is a fable?

THE FOX AND THE CROW

AESOP

A Fox once saw a Crow fly off with a piece of cheese in its beak and settle on a branch of a tree. "That's for me, as I am a Fox," said Master Reynard,[1] and he walked up to the foot of the tree.

"Good day, Mistress Crow," he cried. "How well you are looking today: how <u>glossy</u> your feathers; how bright your eye. I feel sure your voice must <u>surpass</u> that of other birds, just as your figure does; let me hear but one song from you that I may greet you as the Queen of Birds."

The Crow lifted up her head and began to caw her best, but the moment she opened her mouth the piece of cheese fell to the ground, only to be snapped up by Master Fox. "That will do," said he. "That was all I wanted. In exchange for your cheese I will give you a piece of advice for the future—

Do not trust <u>flatterers</u>."

---

1. **Master Reynard** (ren′ ərd) the fox in the medieval beast epic *Reynard the Fox;* therefore, a proper name for the fox in other stories.

glossy (glôs′ ē) *adj.* smooth and shiny

surpass (sər pas′) *v.* be superior to

flatterers (flat′ ər ərz) *n.* those who praise a person insincerely

Review and Assess

Thinking About the Literature

1. **Respond:** What is your reaction to the moral of each fable? Explain.

2. **(a) Interpret:** When the lion in "The Lion and the Statue" speaks to the man, what point is he trying to make? **(b) Deduce:** What might the statue look like if it were created by a lion?

3. **(a) Recall:** In "The Fox and the Crow," how does the fox induce the crow to drop the piece of cheese? **(b) Infer:** How does the fox's attitude change when he gets the cheese?

4. **(a) Draw Conclusions:** What human character traits do the characters in these fables represent? **(b) Support:** What details in the fables support your answers?

5. **(a) Recall:** What is the moral of each fable? **(b) Connect:** How do the actions of the characters support each of these morals? **(c) Evaluate:** Are the morals of Aesop's fables useful or relevant to today's world? Explain.

Aesop

(about 620–560 B.C.)

Aesop's fables have been enjoyed for centuries. However, we know very little about their origin—including who actually wrote them.

Aesop may have been a slave who lived on the Greek island of Samos, or a spokesman who defended criminals in court, or an advisor or a riddle solver for one of the Greek kings. The most widely held theory, however, is that Aesop wasn't an actual person at all. Rather, because certain stories in ancient Greece were told over and over, people invented an imaginary author for them.

ALL STORIES ARE ANANSI'S

AFRICAN FOLK TALE
Harold Courlander

In the beginning, all tales and stories belonged to Nyame (nē ä´ mē), the Sky God. But Kwaku Anansi (kwä´ kōō ə nän´ sē), the spider, yearned to be the owner of all the stories known in the world, and he went to Nyame and offered to buy them.

The Sky God said: "I am willing to sell the stories, but the price is high. Many people have come to me offering to buy, but the price was too high for them. Rich and powerful families have not been able to pay. Do you think you can do it?"

Anansi replied to the Sky God: "I can do it. What is the price?"

"My price is three things," the Sky God said. "I must first have Mmoboro (mō bô´ rō), the hornets. I must then have Onini (ō nē´ nē), the great python. I must then have Osebo (ō sā´ bō), the leopard. For these things I will sell you the right to tell all stories."

Anansi said: "I will bring them."

He went home and made his plans. He first cut a gourd from a vine and made a small hole in it. He took a large calabash[1] and

> **yearned** (yɐrnd) v. wanted very much

> **gourd** (gôrd) n. a fruit; the dried shell is used as a cup

---

1. calabash (kal´ ə bash´) n. large fruit that is dried and made into a bowl or cup.

▲ **Critical Viewing**
Why might storytelling be a popular pasttime in a landscape such as this?

filled it with water. He went to the tree where the hornets lived. He poured some of the water over himself, so that he was dripping. He threw some water over the hornets, so that they too were dripping. Then he put the calabash on his head, as though to protect himself from a storm, and called out to the hornets: "Are you foolish people? Why do you stay in the rain that is falling?"

The hornets answered: "Where shall we go?"

"Go here, in this dry gourd," Anansi told them.

The hornets thanked him and flew into the gourd through the small hole. When the last of them had entered, Anansi plugged the hole with a ball of grass, saying: "Oh, yes, but you are really foolish people!"

He took the gourd full of hornets to Nyame, the Sky God. The Sky God accepted them. He said: "There are two more things."

Anansi returned to the forest and cut a long bamboo pole and some strong vines. Then he walked toward the house of Onini, the python, talking to himself. He said: "My wife is stupid. I say he is longer and stronger. My wife says he is shorter and weaker.

✔**Reading Check**

Who is Anansi and what does he have to bring to the Sky God?

I give him more respect. She gives him less respect. Is she right or am I right? I am right, he is longer. I am right, he is stronger."

When Onini, the python, heard Anansi talking to himself, he said: "Why are you arguing this way with yourself?"

The spider replied: "Ah, I have had a dispute with my wife. She says you are shorter and weaker than this bamboo pole. I say you are longer and stronger."

Onini said: "It's useless and silly to argue when you can find out the truth. Bring the pole and we will measure."

So Anansi laid the pole on the ground, and the python came and stretched himself out beside it.

"You seem a little short," Anansi said.

The python stretched further.

"A little more," Anansi said.

"I can stretch no more," Onini said.

"When you stretch at one end, you get shorter at the other end," Anansi said. "Let me tie you at the front so you don't slip."

He tied Onini's head to the pole. Then he went to the other end and tied the tail to the pole. He wrapped the vine all around Onini, until the python couldn't move.

"Onini," Anansi said, "it turns out that my wife was right and I was wrong. You are shorter than the pole and weaker. My opinion wasn't as good as my wife's. But you were even more foolish than I, and you are now my prisoner."

Anansi carried the python to Nyame, the Sky God, who said: "There is one thing more."Osebo, the leopard, was next. Anansi went into the forest and dug a deep pit where the leopard was accustomed to walk. He covered it with small branches and leaves and put dust on it, so that it was impossible to tell where the pit was. Anansi went away and hid. When Osebo came prowling in the black of night, he stepped into the

▶Critical Viewing What characteristic of the leopard does Anansi use in his trick? [Connect]

trap Anansi had prepared and fell to the bottom. Anansi heard the sound of the leopard falling, and he said: "Ah, Osebo, you are half-foolish!"

When morning came, Anansi went to the pit and saw the leopard there.

"Osebo," he asked, "what are you doing in this hole?"

"I have fallen into a trap," Osebo said. "Help me out."

"I would gladly help you," Anansi said. "But I'm sure that if I bring you out, I will have no thanks for it. You will get hungry, and later on you will be wanting to eat me and my children."

"I swear it won't happen!" Osebo said.

"Very well. Since you swear it, I will take you out," Anansi said.

He bent a tall green tree toward the ground, so that its top was over the pit, and he tied it that way. Then he tied a rope to the top of the tree and dropped the other end of it into the pit.

"Tie this to your tail," he said.

Osebo tied the rope to his tail.

"Is it well tied?" Anansi asked.

"Yes, it is well tied," the leopard said.

"In that case," Anansi said, "you are not merely half-foolish, you are all-foolish." And he took his knife and cut the other rope, the one that held the tree bowed to the ground. The tree straightened up with a snap, pulling Osebo out of

Reading Strategy
Recognizing Cultural Context Several times in the story, Anansi calls others foolish. What did the Ashanti consider foolish behavior?

✓Reading Check

How does Anansi catch the python and the leopard?

the hole. He hung in the air head down-ward, twisting and turning. And while he hung this way, Anansi killed him with his weapons.

Then he took the body of the leopard and carried it to Nyame, the Sky God, saying: "Here is the third thing. Now I have paid the price."

Nyame said to him: "Kwaku Anansi, great warriors and chiefs have tried, but they have been unable to do it. You have done it. Therefore, I will give you the stories. From this day onward, all stories belong to you. Whenever a man tells a story, he must acknowledge that it is Anansi's tale."

In this way Anansi, the spider, became the owner of all stories that are told. To Anansi all these tales belong.

▼ Critical Viewing
Anansi, the spider, is the clever one in this folk tale. What traits of a spider lend themselves to this characterization? [Defend]

acknowledge (ak näl´ ij) v. recognize and admit

Review and Assess

Thinking About the Literature

1. **Respond:** Which of Anansi's accomplishments impressed you the most? Why?

2. **(a) Infer:** What can you infer about the hornets, the python, and the leopard from the fact that they listen to Anansi?
   (b) Interpret: In what way do these animals resemble humans in their behavior?

3. **(a) Infer:** What is Anansi's attitude toward the other animals? **(b) Support:** What details reveal this attitude?

4. **(a) Recall:** What does the Sky God ask Anansi to do?
   (b) Draw Conclusions: Why is Anansi able to do what warriors and chiefs have failed to do?
   (c) Apply: What qualities or characteristics are revealed by his success?

5. **(a) Interpret:** How would you describe Anansi's personal code of behavior? **(b) Make a Judgment:** Do you approve or disapprove of Anansi's behavior? Explain.

Harold Courlander

(1908–1996)

Harold Courlander studied and wrote about African, West Indian, Native American, and African American cultures. His books include works on literature and music, novels, and several collections of folk tales from around the world. Courlander was interested in those folk tales, he said, that "convey human values, philosophical outlook, and cultural heritage."

Review and Assess

Literary Analysis
Folk Tales and Fables

1. Which of these works are **folk tales** and which are **fables**?
2. In a chart like the one shown here, record one or more examples of language and expressions that reflect that these works are usually told orally, or aloud.

Story	Examples

Comparing Literary Works

3. Identify the **theme** or **moral** of each story on a chart like the one shown here.

Tale	Theme or Moral
"The People Could Fly"	
"All Stories Are Anansi's"	
"The Lion and the Statue"	
"The Fox and the Crow"	

4. What similarities can you find in each work's theme relating to how people should behave?
5. How much or how little does each story's message apply to contemporary life?

Reading Strategy
Recognizing Cultural Context

6. Why do you think that freedom tales were still told after the abolition of slavery?
7. Why might cleverness and resourcefulness have been important to the Ashanti who told "All Stories Are Anansi's"?
8. To what degree do the values of Aesop's ancient Greece resemble values of your community today? Explain.

Extend Understanding

9. **Cultural Connection:** Different cultures have focused on different animals in the trickster role. The Ashanti chose a spider. What animal do you think would make a good trickster? Why?

Quick Review

Folk tales are stories about ordinary people that are passed down by word of mouth. To review folk tales, see page 797.
Fables are very brief stories that often feature animals and that often have a moral. To review fables, see page 797.

A **theme** is a message or insight about life.
A **moral** is the wise saying at the end of a fable.
To review theme and moral, see page 797.

 Take It to the Net
www.phschool.com
Take the interactive self-test online to check your understanding of these selections.

Integrate Language Skills

Vocabulary Development Lesson

Word Analysis: Latin Prefix sur-

The Latin prefix *sur-* means "over, upon, above, or beyond." *Surpass* means "to pass above," or "to be superior to." Explain how the meaning of the prefix contributes to the meaning of the following words:

1. surplus   2. surround   3. surreal

Spelling Strategy

The *ur* sound can be spelled *ur*, *er*, and *ear*. Write the correctly spelled word in each set.

1. earth   erth   urth
2. searface   serface   surface
3. tearm   term   turm

Concept Development: Analogies

In your notebook, write down the vocabulary word that best completes each analogy.

1. *Slur* is to *talk* as ____?____ is to *walk*.
2. *Pumpkin* is to *jack-o'-lantern* as ____?____ is to *cup*.
3. *Athletes* is to *disciplined* as ____?____ is to *insincere*.
4. *Stroke* is to *scratch* as ____?____ is to *screech*.
5. *Nurse* is to *neglect* as ____?____ is to *disappoint*.
6. *Participate* is to *quit* as ____?____ is to *deny*.
7. *Imaginary* is to *fantastic* as ____?____ is to *shiny*.
8. *Pitch* is to *throw* as ____?____ is to *desired*.

Grammar Lesson

Quotation Marks

Quotation marks are punctuation marks that can be used to set off someone else's exact words. Writers use quotation marks to set off dialogue, or conversations between characters. When the dialogue appears inside a sentence, commas are used to separate the quotation from the rest of the sentence, unless the quotation ends in a question mark or an exclamation point. These punctuation marks are left as they are, not changed to commas. Notice how Aesop uses quotation marks to indicate that the Fox is speaking:

Quotation marks enclose the Fox's words.
"Good day, Mistress Crow," he cried.

A comma separates the Fox's words from the rest of the sentence.

▶ *For more practice, see page R35, Exercise E.*

Practice Rewrite each sentence with correctly placed quotation marks and commas.

1. What fables have you read? he asked.
2. I've read some modern fables by James Thurber she said. They were very funny.
3. I like folk tales with magical objects he said.
4. My favorites he said are the ones featuring the trickster Coyote.
5. I like those too she said. I have learned a lot about other cultures from their tales.

Writing Application Write a continuation of a conversation between the characters from one of the fables. Use quotation marks correctly.

𝓦𝓖 *Prentice Hall Writing and Grammar Connection: Chapter 26, Section 4*

Writing Lesson

Essay on Cultural Context

Write an essay about the cultural context that influences one of the stories. Include facts about the culture from which the story comes and cultural details from the story. Your essay can also include your own reactions to the tale.

Prewriting Choose a folk tale or fable. Use reference sources to find out more about the culture from which it comes. Group your details into categories, such as customs, beliefs, place, and time.

Drafting Write an introduction in which you identify the work you chose and the culture from which it comes. As you draft, develop your main points based on your research. Begin each paragraph by clearly stating a main idea. In the body of the paragraph, support this statement with specific details from the story and your research.

Model: Supporting Ideas

Aesop's "The Lion and the Statue" shows that people in <u>ancient Greece valued intelligence highly</u>. The Man and the Lion debate the intelligence of both species throughout the story. Also, in making his point at the end of the story, the Lion shows that he is more intelligent than the Man.

> The underlined sentence is followed by two details from the story as supporting ideas.

Revising As you revise, look for ideas that can be further supported with examples.

WG Prentice Hall Writing and Grammar Connection: Chapter 12, Section 3

Extension Activities

Research and Technology Hold a class **story-telling festival.** With a small group, use the Internet and other resources to locate stories from a wide variety of cultures. Each team can prepare stories to share with the group. Make sure the stories have a clear plot line with a beginning, a conflict, rising action, a climax, and a resolution.

Writing Write a **response** to one of the works in which you interpret the theme and explain how it applies to a specific situation in today's world.

Listening and Speaking In your own words, **retell** one of these stories. Review the story to remember the most important events. Use vivid language that appeals to the senses to describe the setting—the time and place of the story—and the characters—the "actors" in the story.

 **Take It to the Net**   www.phschool.com

Go online for an additional research activity using the Internet.

Prepare to Read

Phaëthon, Son of Apollo ◆
Demeter and Persephone ◆ Icarus and Daedalus

Le Char D'Apollon (Apollo's Chariot) (detail), Odilon Redon, Musee D'Orsay, Paris/Giraudon, Paris

Take It to the Net

Visit www.phschool.com for interactive activities and instruction related to these selections, including

- background
- graphic organizers
- literary elements
- reading strategies

Preview

Connecting to the Literature

You may know stories—either true or invented—about people who suffered the consequences of thinking too much of themselves. As you will learn from these myths, the ancient Greeks believed that people were punished for being too proud or arrogant.

Background

The works in this group are all retellings of Greek myths. The ancient Greeks believed in a complex collection of gods and goddesses, ruled by Zeus. Beneath Zeus in rank were many lesser gods and goddesses, each linked to different ideas or qualities. For example, Apollo was linked to poetry, music, and the sun.

Literary Analysis
Myths
Since time began, people have tried to understand the world around them. Ancient peoples created **myths**—stories that explain natural occurrences and express beliefs about right and wrong. Built on an imaginative understanding of nature, myths make sense to us because they explain the world in human terms. Use these focus questions to guide you as you read.

1. What lesson does each myth teach?
2. What natural occurrences does each myth explain?

Comparing Literary Works
Characterization is how a writer creates and develops characters. In these retellings, characters are not created, since they have long existed in the Greek oral tradition. However, all three writers make their characters come alive in several ways. In each tale, the writer has the narrator

- describe a character's traits, or characteristics.
- reveal a character's personality through his or her appearance, words, and actions.
- describe what others in the story think about the character.

As you read each myth, compare and contrast the characters and the methods used to bring the characters to life.

Reading Strategy
Making Predictions
A **prediction** is an educated guess, based on hints or clues, about what will happen. In some myths, characters get into trouble because they happen to be in the wrong place at the wrong time. Most of the time, however, characters' troubles are the result of their own actions. As you read, predict when a character's actions may lead to trouble. Then, read on to see if your predictions were correct. Use a chart like the one shown to record clues and your predictions based on these clues.

Prediction Chart

Clue	Prediction
Phaëthon boasts about his father.	

Vocabulary Development
mortal (môr´ təl) *n.* being who must eventually die (p. 814)

dissuade (di swād´) *v.* persuade someone against an action (p. 816)

dominions (də min´ yənz) *n.* regions ruled by someone (p. 819)

vacancy (vā´ kən sē) *n.* emptiness (p. 823)

sustained (sə stānd´) *adj.* supported (p. 824)

Phaëthon, Son of Apollo

retold by Olivia E. Coolidge

Though Apollo always honored the memory of Daphne she was not his only love. Another was a <u>mortal</u>, Clymene (klim′ ə nē), by whom he had a son named Phaëthon (fā′ ə tän). Phaëthon grew up with his mother, who, since she was mortal, could not dwell in the halls of Olympus[1] or in the palace of the sun. She lived not far from the East in the land of Ethiopia, and as her son grew up, she would point to the place where Eos (ē′ äs), goddess of the dawn, lighted up the sky and tell him that there his father dwelt. Phaëthon loved to boast of his divine father as he saw the golden chariot riding high through the air. He would remind his comrades of other sons of gods and mortal women who, by virtue of their great deeds, had themselves become gods at last. He must always be first in everything, and in most things this was easy, since he was in truth stronger, swifter, and more daring than the others. Even if he were not victorious, Phaëthon always claimed to be first in honor. He could never bear to be beaten, even if he must risk his life in some rash way to win.

Most of the princes of Ethiopia willingly paid Phaëthon honor, since they admired him greatly for his fire and beauty. There was one boy, however, Epaphos (ep′ ə fəs), who was rumored to be a child of Zeus himself. Since this was not certainly proved, Phaëthon chose to disbelieve it and to demand from Epaphos the deference that he obtained from all others. Epaphos was proud too, and one day he lost his temper with Phaëthon and turned on him, saying, "You are a fool to believe all that your mother tells you. You are all swelled up with false ideas about your father."

Crimson with rage, the lad rushed home to his mother and demanded that she prove to him the truth of the story that she had often told. "Give me some proof," he implored her, "with which I can answer this insult of Epaphos. It is a matter of life and death to me, for if I cannot, I shall die of shame."

mortal (môr′ təl) *n.* being who must eventually die

---

1. Olympus (ō lim′ pəs) mountain in northern Greece that was known as the home of the gods.

The Chariot of Phaëthon racing through the skies, Copper engraving, 1606

◄ **Critical Viewing**
What clues of the settings, characters, and events do you find in this picture?
[Analyze]

"I swear to you," replied his mother solemnly, "by the bright orb of the sun itself that you are his son. If I swear falsely, may I never look on the sun again, but die before the next time he mounts the heavens. More than this I cannot do, but you, my child, can go to the eastern palace of Phoebus[2] Apollo—it lies not far away—and there speak with the god himself."

The son of Clymene leaped up with joy at his mother's words. The palace of Apollo was indeed not far. It stood just below the eastern horizon, its tall pillars glistening with bronze and gold. Above these it was white with gleaming ivory, and the great doors were flashing silver, embossed with pictures of earth, sky, and sea, and the gods that dwelt therein. Up the steep hill and the bright steps climbed Phaëthon, passing unafraid through the silver doors, and stood in the presence of the sun. Here at last he was forced to turn away his face, for Phoebus sat in state on his golden throne. It gleamed with emeralds and precious stones, while on the head of the god was a brilliant diamond crown upon which no eye could look undazzled.

Phaëthon hid his face, but the god had recognized his son, and he spoke kindly, asking him why he had come. Then Phaëthon plucked up courage and said, "I come to ask you if you are indeed my father. If you are so, I beg you to give me some proof of it so that all may recognize me as Phoebus' son."

The god smiled, being well pleased with his son's beauty and daring. He took off his crown so that Phaëthon could look at him,

Reading Strategy
Making Predictions
Because of his arrogance and pride, what can you predict will happen to Phaëthon?

✔**Reading Check**

What does Phaëthon want?

---

2. **Phoebus** (fē´ bəs) means "bright one" in Greek.

and coming down from his throne, he put his arms around the boy, and said, "You are indeed my son and Clymene's, and worthy to be called so. Ask of me whatever thing you wish to prove your origin to men, and you shall have it."

Phaëthon swayed for a moment and was dizzy with excitement at the touch of the god. His heart leaped; the blood rushed into his face. Now he felt that he was truly divine, unlike other men, and he did not wish to be counted with men any more. He looked up for a moment at his radiant father. "Let me drive the chariot of the sun across the heavens for one day," he said.

Apollo frowned and shook his head. "I cannot break my promise, but I will dissuade you if I can," he answered. "How can you drive my chariot, whose horses need a strong hand on the reins? The climb is too steep for you. The immense height will make you dizzy. The swift streams of air in the upper heaven will sweep you off your course. Even the immortal gods could not drive my chariot. How then can you? Be wise and make some other choice."

The pride of Phaëthon was stubborn, for he thought the god was merely trying to frighten him. Besides, if he could guide the sun's chariot, would he not have proved his right to be divine rather than mortal? For that he would risk his life. Indeed, once he had seen Apollo's splendor, he did not wish to go back and live among men. Therefore, he insisted on his right until Apollo had to give way.

When the father saw that nothing else would satisfy the boy, he bade the Hours bring forth his chariot and yoke the horses. The chariot was of gold and had two gold-rimmed wheels with spokes of silver. In it there was room for one man to stand and hold the reins. Around the front and sides of it ran a rail, but the back was open. At the end of a long pole there were yokes for the four horses. The pole was of gold and shone with precious jewels: the golden topaz, the bright diamond, the green emerald, and the flashing ruby. While the Hours were yoking the swift, pawing horses, rosy-fingered Dawn hastened to the gates of heaven to draw them open. Meanwhile Apollo anointed his son's face with a magic ointment, that he might be able to bear the heat of the fire-breathing horses and the golden chariot. At last Phaëthon mounted the chariot and grasped the reins, the barriers were let down, and the horses shot up into the air.

At first the fiery horses sped forward up the accustomed trail, but behind them the chariot was too light without the weight of the immortal god. It bounded from side to side and was dashed up and down. Phaëthon was too frightened and too dizzy to pull the reins, nor would he have known anyway whether he was on the usual path. As soon as the horses felt that there was no hand controlling them, they soared up, up with fiery speed into the heavens till the earth grew pale and cold beneath them. Phaëthon shut his eyes, trembling at the dizzy, precipitous height. Then the horses dropped down, more swiftly than a falling stone, flinging themselves madly

dissuade (di swād´) v. persuade someone against an action

from side to side in panic because they were masterless. Phaëthon dropped the reins entirely and clung with all his might to the chariot rail. Meanwhile as they came near the earth, it dried up and cracked apart. Meadows were reduced to white ashes, cornfields smoked and shriveled, cities perished in flame. Far and wide on the wooded mountains the forests were ablaze, and even the snowclad Alps were bare and dry. Rivers steamed and dried to dust. The great North African plain was scorched until it became the desert that it is today. Even the sea shrank back to pools and caves, until dried fishes were left baking upon the white-hot sands. At last the great earth mother called upon Zeus to save her from utter destruction, and Zeus hurled a mighty thunderbolt at the unhappy Phaëthon, who was still crouched in the chariot, clinging desperately to the rail. The dart cast him out, and he fell flaming in a long trail through the air. The chariot broke in pieces at the mighty blow, and the maddened horses rushed snorting back to the stable of their master, Apollo.

Unhappy Clymene and her daughters wandered over the whole earth seeking the body of the boy they loved so well. When they found him, they took him and buried him. Over his grave they wept and could not be comforted. At last the gods in pity for their grief changed them into poplar trees, which weep with tears of amber in memory of Phaëthon.

Review and Assess

Thinking About the Literature

1. **Respond:** Have you ever regretted that you did not take someone's advice? Explain.

2. **(a) Recall:** Why does Phaëthon go to Apollo's palace?
   (b) Infer: What does Phaëthon's need to "always be first in everything" reveal about his character?

3. **(a) Recall:** What is Phaëthon's reason for his request?
   (b) Connect: Describe two ways that Phaëthon displays too much pride.

4. **(a) Recall:** What is the result of Phaëthon's request?
   (b) Speculate: Besides refusing to grant Phaëthon's request, how might Apollo have avoided his son's tragic end?

5. **(a) Recall:** What natural forces are explained in the myth?
   (b) Draw Conclusions: What lessons does this myth teach?
   (c) Apply: To what specific situation in modern times could you apply this lesson?

6. **Distinguish:** Based on Phaëthon's experience and examples from life and other literature, what is the difference between confidence and overconfidence?

Olivia E. Coolidge

(b. 1908)
Olivia Coolidge was born in London, England. Her father, Sir Robert Charles Kirkwood, was a historian and journalist. After attending high school and college in England, Coolidge taught English in Germany and then Latin and Greek at Wimbledon High School in Wimbledon, England. She then moved to the United States and taught English in high schools in Connecticut and Massachusetts. In 1946, Coolidge married, had four children, and published her first book in 1949. She has since published twenty-seven additional books. Besides her books of myths from ancient Greece, Rome, and Egypt, she has also written a number of biographies.

Demeter and Persephone

ANNE TERRY WHITE

Demeter Mourning for Persephone, 1906, Evelyn de Morgan, The De Morgan Foundation, London

◄ Critical Viewing
What symbols in this painting convey Demeter's role as goddess of the harvest? **[Analyze]**

Deep under Mt. Aetna, the gods had buried alive a number of fearful, fire-breathing giants. The monsters heaved and struggled to get free. And so mightily did they shake the earth that Pluto, the king of the underworld, was alarmed.

"They may tear the rocks asunder and leave the realm of the dead open to the light of day," he thought. And mounting his golden chariot, he went up to see what damage had been done.

Literary Analysis
Myth How do the Greeks explain how love happens?

Now the goddess of love and beauty, fair Aphrodite (af rə dīt´ ē), was sitting on a mountainside playing with her son, Eros.[1] She saw Pluto as he drove around with his coal-black horses and she said:

"My son, there is one who defies your power and mine. Quick! Take up your darts! Send an arrow into the breast of that dark monarch. Let him, too, feel the pangs of love. Why should he alone escape them?"

At his mother's words, Eros leaped lightly to his feet. He chose from his quiver[2] his sharpest and truest arrow, fitted it to his bow, drew the string, and shot straight into Pluto's heart.

The grim King had seen fair maids enough in the gloomy under-world over which he ruled. But never had his heart been touched. Now an unaccustomed warmth stole through his veins. His stern eyes softened. Before him was a blossoming valley, and along its edge a charming girl was gathering flowers. She was Persephone (pər sef´ ə nē), daughter of Demeter (di mēt´ ər), goddess of the harvest. She had strayed from her companions, and now that her basket overflowed with blossoms, she was filling her apron with lilies and violets. The god looked at Persephone and loved her at once. With one sweep of his arm he caught her up and drove swiftly away.

"Mother!" she screamed, while the flowers fell from her apron and strewed the ground. "Mother!"

And she called on her companions by name. But already they were out of sight, so fast did Pluto urge the horses on. In a few moments they were at the River Cyane.[3] Persephone struggled, her loosened girdle[4] fell to the ground, but the god held her tight. He struck the bank with his trident.[5] The earth opened, and darkness swallowed them all—horses, chariot, Pluto, and weeping Persephone.

From end to end of the earth Demeter sought her daughter. But none could tell her where Persephone was. At last, worn out and despairing, the goddess returned to Sicily. She stood by the River Cyane, where Pluto had cleft[6] the earth and gone down into his own <u>dominions</u>.

dominions (də min´ yənz) *n.* regions ruled by someone

Reading Check

Whose daughter is Persephone, and who kidnaps Persephone?

---

1. **Eros** (er´ äs) in Greek mythology, the god of love; identified by the Romans with Cupid.
2. **quiver** (kwiv´ ər) *n.* case for arrows.
3. **River Cyane** (sī´ an) a river in Sicily, an island just south of Italy.
4. **girdle** (gər´ dəl) *n.* belt or sash for the waist.
5. **trident** (trīd´ ənt) *n.* spear with three points.
6. **cleft** (kleft) *v.* split or opened.

Now a river nymph[7] had seen him carry off his prize. She wanted to tell Demeter where her daughter was, but fear of Pluto kept her dumb. Yet she had picked up the girdle Persephone had dropped, and this the nymph wafted[8] on the waves to the feet of Demeter.

The goddess knew then that her daughter was gone indeed, but she did not suspect Pluto of carrying her off. She laid the blame on the innocent land.

"Ungrateful soil!" she said. "I made you fertile. I clothed you in grass and nourishing grain, and this is how you reward me. No more shall you enjoy my favors!"

That year was the most cruel mankind had ever known. Nothing prospered, nothing grew. The cattle died, the seed would not come up, men and oxen toiled in vain. There was too much sun. There was too much rain. Thistles[9] and weeds were the only things that grew. It seemed that all mankind would die of hunger.

"This cannot go on," said mighty Zeus. "I see that I must intervene." And one by one he sent the gods and goddesses to plead with Demeter.

But she had the same answer for all: "Not till I see my daughter shall the earth bear fruit again."

Zeus, of course, knew well where Persephone was. He did not like to take from his brother the one joyful thing in his life, but he saw that he must if the race of man was to be preserved. So he called Hermes[10] to him and said:

"Descend to the underworld, my son. Bid Pluto release his bride. Provided she has not tasted food in the realm of the dead, she may return to her mother forever."

Down sped Hermes on his winged feet, and there in the dim palace of the king, he found Persephone by Pluto's side. She was pale and joyless. Not all the glittering treasures of the underworld could bring a smile to her lips.

"You have no flowers here," she would say to her husband when he pressed gems upon her. "Jewels have no fragrance. I do not want them."

When she saw Hermes and heard his message, her heart leaped within her. Her cheeks grew rosy and her eyes sparkled, for she knew that Pluto would not dare to disobey his brother's command. She sprang up, ready to go at once. Only one thing troubled her— that she could not leave the underworld forever. For she had

---

7. **river nymph** (nimf) goddess living in a river.
8. **wafted** (wäft' əd) v. carried.
9. **thistles** (this' əlz) n. stubborn, weedy plants with sharp leaves and usually purplish flowers.
10. **Hermes** (hʉr' mēz) a god who served as a messenger.

accepted a pomegranate[11] from Pluto and sucked the sweet pulp from four of the seeds.

With a heavy heart Pluto made ready his golden car.[12] He helped Persephone in while Hermes took up the reins.

"Dear wife," said the King, and his voice trembled as he spoke, "think kindly of me, I pray you. For indeed I love you truly. It will be lonely here these eight months you are away. And if you think mine is a gloomy palace to return to, at least remember that your husband is great among the immortals. So fare you well—and get your fill of flowers!"

Straight to the temple of Demeter at Eleusis, Hermes drove the black horses. The goddess heard the chariot wheels and, as a deer bounds over the hills, she ran out swiftly to meet her daughter. Persephone flew to her mother's arms. And the sad tale of each turned into joy in the telling.

So it is to this day. One third of the year Persephone spends in the gloomy abode of Pluto—one month for each seed that she tasted. Then Nature dies, the leaves fall, the earth stops bringing forth. In spring Persephone returns, and with her come the flowers, followed by summer's fruitfulness and the rich harvest of fall.

---

11. **pomegranate** (päm´ gran´ it) *n.* round fruit with a red leathery rind and many seeds.
12. **car** (kär) *n.* chariot.

Review and Assess

Thinking About the Literature

1. **Respond:** For whom do you feel sorrier—Persephone or Pluto? Explain.

2. **(a) Recall:** Why did Pluto take Persephone to his kingdom? **(b) Analyze:** What does Pluto's nickname, "the grim King," suggest about his emotional outlook on the world?

3. **(a) Recall:** What does Demeter do when she discovers her daughter is lost? **(b) Make a Judgment:** Do you think her actions were justifiable?

4. **(a) Recall:** How is Persephone reunited with her mother? **(b) Speculate:** How might their experiences in this myth change each of the three main characters?

5. **(a) Recall:** How does nature change as Persephone moves between Earth and the underworld? **(b) Synthesize:** How do the powerful emotions of the main characters account for the changing of the seasons?

Anne Terry White

(1896–1980)

Anne Terry White was born in Ukraine (then part of Russia) and became an editor, translator, and author. In order to introduce her young children to great works of literature, White wrote her first two books: *Heroes of the Five Books*, a look at figures of the Old Testament, and *Three Children and Shakespeare*, a family discussion of four of Shakespeare's plays. White was also an authority on ancient Greece. She shares this knowledge in retelling the myth "Demeter and Persephone." White also explored science, biography, and other topics in her many books for children and young adults.

ICARUS
AND
DAEDALUS

JOSEPHINE PRESTON PEABODY

Among all those mortals who grew so wise that they learned the secrets of the gods, none was more cunning[1] than Daedalus (ded´ əl əs).

He once built, for King Minos of Crete,[2] a wonderful Labyrinth[3] of winding ways so cunningly tangled up and twisted around that, once inside, you could never find your way out again without a magic clue. But the king's favor veered[4] with the wind, and one day he had his master architect imprisoned in a tower. Daedalus managed to escape from his cell; but it seemed impossible to leave the island, since every ship that came or went was well guarded by order of the king.

At length, watching the sea-gulls in the air—the only creatures that were sure of liberty—he thought of a plan for himself and his young son Icarus (ik´ ə rəs), who was captive with him.

Little by little, he gathered a store of feathers great and small. He fastened these together with thread, molded them in with wax, and so fashioned two great wings like those of a bird. When they were done, Daedalus fitted them to his own shoulders, and after one or two efforts, he found that by waving his arms he could winnow[5] the air and cleave it, as a swimmer does the sea. He held himself aloft, wavered this way and that with the wind, and at last, like a great fledgling,[6] he learned to fly.

Reading Strategy
Making Predictions From Daedalus' observation of the sea-gulls, what can you predict his plan might be?

---

1. **cunning** (kun´ iŋ) *adj.* skillful; clever.
2. **King Minos** (mī´ nəs) **of Crete** King Minos was a son of the god Zeus. Crete is a Greek island in the eastern Mediterranean Sea, southeast of Greece.
3. **Labyrinth** (lab´ ə rinth´) *n.* maze.
4. **veered** (vird) *v.* changed directions.
5. **winnow** (win´ ō) *v.* beat as with wings.
6. **fledgling** (flej´ liŋ) *n.* young bird.

Without delay, he fell to work on a pair of wings for the boy Icarus, and taught him carefully how to use them, bidding him beware of rash adventures among the stars. "Remember," said the father, "never to fly very low or very high, for the fogs about the earth would weigh you down, but the blaze of the sun will surely melt your feathers apart if you go too near."

For Icarus, these cautions went in at one ear and out by the other. Who could remember to be careful when he was to fly for the first time? Are birds careful? Not they! And not an idea remained in the boy's head but the one joy of escape.

The day came, and the fair wind that was to set them free. The father bird put on his wings, and, while the light urged them to be gone, he waited to see that all was well with Icarus, for the two could not fly hand in hand. Up they rose, the boy after his father. The hateful ground of Crete sank beneath them; and the country folk, who caught a glimpse of them when they were high above the treetops, took it for a vision of the gods—Apollo, perhaps, with Cupid after him.

At first there was a terror in the joy. The wide <u>vacancy</u> of the air dazed them—a glance downward made their brains reel.

Literary Analysis
Myth What lesson does Daedalus try to teach Icarus?

vacancy (vā´ kən sē) *n.* emptiness

✔**Reading Check**

What is Daedalus' escape plan?

Daedalus and Icarus, French colored engraving, 1660

◀**Critical Viewing**
Use the title of this myth, your knowledge of Greek mythology, and this illustration to predict what will happen to the two mortals in the story.
[Predict]

But when a great wind filled their wings, and Icarus felt himself sustained, like a halcyon bird[7] in the hollow of a wave, like a child uplifted by his mother, he forgot everything in the world but joy. He forgot Crete and the other islands that he had passed over: he saw but vaguely that wingèd thing in the distance before him that was his father Daedalus. He longed for one draft of flight to quench the thirst of his captivity: he stretched out his arms to the sky and made towards the highest heavens.

Alas for him! Warmer and warmer grew the air. Those arms, that had seemed to uphold him, relaxed. His wings wavered, drooped. He fluttered his young hands vainly—he was falling—and in that terror he remembered. The heat of the sun had melted the wax from his wings; the feathers were falling, one by one, like snowflakes; and there was none to help.

He fell like a leaf tossed down the wind, down, down, with one cry that overtook Daedalus far away. When he returned, and sought high and low for his poor boy, he saw nothing but the birdlike feathers afloat on the water, and he knew that Icarus was drowned.

The nearest island he named Icaria, in memory of the child; but he, in heavy grief, went to the temple of Apollo in Sicily, and there hung up his wings as an offering. Never again did he attempt to fly.

sustained (sə stānd′) *adj.* supported

---

7. **halcyon** (hal′ sē ən) **bird** *n.* legendary bird, identified with the kingfisher, which could calm the sea by resting on it.

Review and Assess

Thinking About the Literature

1. **Respond:** Do you think Icarus deserved his fate? Why or why not?

2. **(a) Recall:** Where is Daedalus when the story begins? **(b) Analyze:** In what ways does Daedalus show his "cunning"?

3. **(a) Recall:** Who is Icarus? **(b) Infer:** What does Daedalus reveal about himself in his words to his son?

4. **(a) Recall:** Summarize the warning Daedalus gives to Icarus. **(b) Infer:** What do Icarus' actions reveal about his character?

5. **(a) Recall:** What happens to Icarus at the end of the myth? **(b) Draw Conclusions:** What lesson does this myth teach? **(c) Evaluate:** Do you think this is a useful or valuable lesson in today's society?

6. **Take a Position:** Does Daedalus share any responsibility for Icarus' fall? Why or why not?

Josephine Preston Peabody

(1874–1922)

Josephine Preston Peabody was a quick starter. She began writing at thirteen and published her first book—*Old Greek Folk-Stories Told Anew*—when she was twenty-three. "Icarus and Daedalus" is from this collection. Peabody went on to write many poems and plays.

Review and Assess

Literary Analysis

Myths

1. What lesson does each **myth** teach, or what natural event does it explain? Use a chart like the one shown to report your answers.

Myth	Lesson or Explanation
"Phaëthon, Son of Apollo"	
"Demeter and Persephone"	
"Icarus and Daedalus"	

2. What beliefs about the relationship between humans and gods are expressed in these myths?

Comparing Literary Works

3. Which character or characters in each myth would you describe as powerful or wise? How are these qualities revealed?
4. Which characters in each myth would you describe as weak or foolish? How are these qualities revealed?
5. On a Venn diagram like the one shown here, compare and contrast the **characterization** of Phaëthon and Icarus.

Reading Strategy

Making Predictions

6. What **predictions** did you make based on characters' actions?
7. What predictions did you make based on characters' words?
8. How does Daedalus' warning to Icarus provide a clue about Icarus' fate?

Extend Understanding

9. **Career Connection:** To what modern-day professions would Icarus and Daedalus be well-suited?

Quick Review

A **myth** is a story about gods and heroes that explains natural occurrences and expresses beliefs about right and wrong. To review myths, see page 813.

Characterization is the process by which writers create and develop a character. To review characterization, see page 813.

A **prediction** is an educated guess, based on hints or clues.

 Take It to the Net
www.phschool.com
Take the interactive self-test online to check your understanding of these selections.

Integrate Language Skills

Vocabulary Development Lesson

Word Analysis: Using Latin Word Root *-domin-*

Complete the paragraph with the listed words containing the Latin root *-domin-*, meaning "master."

dominates   domain   dominant

Zeus is the ___?___ Greek god. He rules a ___?___ of lesser gods and goddesses. Each of them ___?___ a part of nature or human life.

Spelling Strategy

In some words, like *dissuade*, the *sw* sound is spelled *su*. Spell each defined word.

1. soft and fuzzy type of leather: s __ de
2. to convince: pers __ de
3. two or more connected rooms: s __ te

Concept Development: Context

Write sentences using each word in the specified context. **Context** is the situation in which a word is used.

1. Use *mortal* to explain the difference between the Greek gods and people.
2. Use *dissuade* in a sentence about Daedalus' warning to Icarus.
3. Use *dominion* in a sentence about Pluto's kingdom.
4. Use *vacancy* in a sentence about how Persephone looked at Pluto.
5. Use *sustained* in a sentence about what supported Persephone in the months she had to return to Pluto.

Grammar Lesson

Using Commas

Use a **comma after introductory words and phrases** in a sentence—words or phrases that come before the main clause (the part of the sentence that contains the subject and the verb). In the following examples, notice the commas after the word and phrase shown in italics:

Example: *Actually,* Apollo was well pleased with his son Phaëthon. *Up in the heavens,* Phaëthon became afraid.

Three or more similar **items in a series** need commas to separate them. Thus, four items are separated by three commas.

The seasons—*spring, summer, fall,* and *winter*—are explained in one of the myths.

▶ *For more practice, see page R34, Exercise A.*
Practice Copy the sentences, placing commas where needed.

1. Crimson with rage the lad rushed home.
2. At his mother's words Eros leaped up.
3. Suddenly the grim King's heart was filled with warmth.
4. The earth opened, and darkness swallowed them all—horses chariot Pluto and weeping Persephone.
5. Excited by the flight Icarus forgot his father's warnings.

Writing Application Write a paragraph about Icarus' adventure. Use commas as needed.

W͞G Prentice Hall Writing and Grammar Connection: Chapter 26

Writing Lesson

Myth

Choose a natural event or condition, such as an earthquake or the appearance of dew on the grass. Write a "myth" that offers an explanation. Use the myths you have just read as examples of style and of the type of details to include.

Prewriting   Decide on the situation that causes your event. Invent characters who will "act out" the situation. Prepare an outline like the one shown to help you organize details and events in your myth.

Model: Outline

I. Chlammy, Goddess of Dew

    A. Daughter of the Sunrise and the Chill of Dawn

        1. Father a god

        2. Mother a nymph

    B. Always absent-minded

        1. Gets lost at night

Drafting   Write the myth in clear time order. Use appropriate transition words such as *first*, *next*, and *finally*.

Revising   Look for places where you can make the move from one event to the next clearer. Add words or phrases such as *then* or *after a while* to show the connection.

Prentice Hall Writing and Grammar Connection: Chapter 5, Section 3

Extension Activities

Listening and Speaking In a small group, give a **dramatic reading** of a portion of one of the myths. After assigning roles, practice reading aloud the passages you have chosen. As you rehearse, act as dramatic coaches for one another and provide feedback about each person's delivery. Try to be helpful in your comments about such elements as establishing eye contact with the audience and using voice inflections and realistic gestures.

Writing Write a **summary** of each myth. Include characters' names and relationships as well as main events.

Research and Technology Conduct research on the scientific explanation for one of the events explained in the myths. Prepare a **chart** using both text and pictures to compare and contrast the two explanations.

 **Take It to the Net**   www.phschool.com

Go online for an additional research activity using the Internet.

CONNECTIONS
Novellas and Myths

Themes of Independence

The following selection is an excerpt from a novella by Edith Wharton entitled *False Dawn*. A modern description of a novella is a book that is shorter than a novel but longer than a short story. Historically, novellas were grouped in collections with legends from ancient and modern history. For example, in the past, a novella might have contained a story like *False Dawn* as well as an ancient myth like *Icarus and Daedalus* because the stories share a common theme: Testing the limits of independence.

Today, authors group a novella with several short stories or with other novellas that have similar topics or themes. *False Dawn* is from the collection *Old New York*.

from

False Dawn

Edith Wharton

In False Dawn, *Lewis's sister visits the wife of the poet Edgar Allan Poe in order to bring them food and other necessary items. Lewis himself, sailing to meet the woman he loves, sails into a beautiful dawn.*

Lewis Raycie was up the next morning before sunrise.

Unlatching his shutters without noise, he looked forth over the wet lawn merged in a blur of shrubberies, and the waters of the Sound dimly seen beneath a sky full of stars. His head ached but his heart glowed; what was before him was thrilling enough to clear a heavier brain than his.

He dressed quickly and completely (save for his shoes), and then, stripping the flowered quilt from his high mahogany bed, rolled it in a tight bundle under his arm. Thus enigmatically equipped he was feeling his way, shoes in hand, through the darkness of the upper story to the slippery oak stairs, when he was startled by a candle-gleam in the pitch-blackness of the hall below. He held his breath, and leaning over the stair-rail saw with amazement his sister Mary Adeline come forth, cloaked and bonneted, but also in stocking-feet, from the passage leading to the pantry. She too carried a double burden: her shoes and the candle in one hand, in the other a large covered basket that weighed down her bare arm.

Brother and sister stopped and stared at each other in the blue dusk: the upward slant of the candle-light distorted Mary Adeline's mild features, twisted them into a frightened grin as Lewis stole down to join her.

"Oh—" she whispered. "What in the world are you doing here? I was just getting together a few things for that poor young Mrs. Poe down the lane, who's so ill—before mother goes to the storeroom. You won't tell, will you?"

Lewis signaled his complicity, and cautiously slid open the bolt of the front door. They durst not say more till they were out of ear-shot. On the doorstep they sat down to put on their shoes; then they hastened on without a word through the ghostly shrubberies till they reached the gate into the lane.

"But you, Lewis?" the sister suddenly questioned, with an astonished stare at the rolled-up quilt under her brother's arm.

"Oh, I—. Look here, Addy—" he broke off and began to grope in his pocket— "I haven't much about me . . . the old gentleman keeps me as close as ever . . . but here's a dollar, if you think that poor Mrs. Poe could use it . . . I'd be too happy . . . considering it a privilege . . . "

"Oh Lewis, Lewis, how noble, how generous of you! Of course I can buy a few extra things with it . . . they never see meat unless I can bring them a bit, you know . . . and I fear she's dying of a decline . . . and she and her mother are so fiery proud. . . . " She wept with gratitude, and Lewis drew a breath of relief. He had diverted her attention from the bed-quilt.

"Ah, there's the breeze," he murmured, sniffing the suddenly chilled air.

"Yes, I must be off; I must be back before the sun is up," said Mary Adeline anxiously, "and it would never do if mother knew—"

"She doesn't know of your visits to Mrs. Poe?"

A look of childish guile sharpened Mary Adeline's undeveloped face. "She *does*, of course; but yet she doesn't . . . we've arranged it so. You see, Mr. Poe's an Atheist; and so father—"

"I see," Lewis nodded. "Well, we part here; I'm off for a swim," he said glibly. But abruptly, turned back and caught his sister's arm. "Sister, tell Mrs. Poe, please, that I heard her husband give a reading from his poems in New York two nights ago—"

("Oh, Lewis—*you*? But father says he's a blasphemer!")

"—And he's a great poet—a Great Poet. Tell her that from me, will you, please, Mary Adeline?"

"Oh, brother, I couldn't . . . we never speak of him," the startled girl faltered, hurrying away.

In the cove where the Commodore's sloop had ridden a few hours earlier a biggish rowing-boat took the waking ripples. Young Racie paddled out to her, fastened his skiff to the moorings, and hastily clambered into the boat.

From various recesses of his pockets he produced rope, string, a carpet-layer's needle, and other unexpected and incongruous tackle; then, lashing one of the oars across the top of the other, and jamming the latter upright between the forward thwart and the bow, he rigged the flowered bed-quilt on this mast, knotted a rope to the free end of the quilt, and sat down in the stern, one hand on the rudder, the other on his improvised sheet.

Venus, brooding silvery above a line of pale green sky, made a pool of glory in the sea as the dawn-breeze plumped the lover's sail. . . .

EDITH WHARTON

Old New York

FOUR NOVELLAS

Connecting Novellas and Myths

1. Why do you think Lewis and his sister are trying to be very quiet as they leave the house?
2. What feelings do Lewis and Icarus share?
3. How do Lewis and Icarus try to gain independence?

Edith Wharton

(1862–1937)

Edith Wharton became the first woman to win a Pulitzer Prize, in 1921, with her critically acclaimed novel *The Age of Innocence*. She was born in New York in the 1860s. A major theme throughout her work is the wealthy society of New York that she was a part of. Her works include *Ethan Frome*, *The House of Mirth*, and *The Custom of the Country*.

READING INFORMATIONAL MATERIALS

How-to Essays

About How-to Essays

Writing that explains or informs is called expository writing. One of the most common types of expository writing is the how-to essay. In a how-to essay, the writer explains how to do or make something. The writer breaks down the process into a series of logical steps in the order in which the reader should do them. When reading how-to essays critically, you must look for the following characteristics:

- A list of materials needed
- A series of logical steps explained in chronological order
- Details that tell *when, how much, how often,* or *to what extent*
- An introduction, a body, and a conclusion

Reading Strategy

Identifying Cause-and-Effect Relationships

A cause is an event, or a situation that produces a result; an effect is the result produced. When reading a story or an essay critically, you should understand that each effect may eventually become a cause for the next event, thereby linking causes and effects and propelling the action forward. Cause-and-effect relationships are especially important in the following types of texts:

- Science books
- Social studies books
- Instruction manuals

Look at the following diagram. It shows how each event in the essay is both a cause and an effect.

Cause	Effect/Cause	Effect/Cause	Effect/Cause
The glaciers on the mountains are grinding down rock into gravel and silt.	The gravel and silt are washed away by streams and rivers.	The Himalayas are losing mass.	They change position.

Moving Mountains

Janice VanCleave

The Himalayas, the highest mountain system in the world, lie just south of the Tibetan Plateau, where the Yangtze River originates. According to Professor Douglas Burbank of the University of Southern California, the normal process of erosion is affecting the Himalayas in two major ways. First, the enormous glaciers on the mountains are grinding down rock into huge amounts of gravel and silt, which are then washed away by streams and rivers. The Himalayas are gradually losing mass.

Second, the loss of mass is affecting the Himalayas' position on Earth's surface. Mountains are part of Earth's crust, or rigid outer layer. The crust floats on the mantle, a layer of molten rock, in the same way that a boat floats on an ocean.

> The cause-and-effect relationship is illustrated with a comparison.

How does the Himalayas' loss of mass affect its position on Earth's mantle? Try this demonstration to find out.

What You Need

How-to essays usually include a list of materials

- a lightweight wooden block measuring 5 centimeters by 10 centimeters by 5 centimeters (roughly 2 inches by 4 inches by 2 inches)
- a black marking pen
- a red marking pen
- masking tape
- sand
- a clear container twice as large as the wooden block
- a pencil and paper
- a tablespoon
- a ruler

What to Do

1. Fill the container about half full with water, and place a piece of masking tape down the outside of the container.
2. Starting at the top of the tape, mark it off in centimeters with the black pen. Mark the level that the water comes to with the red pen.
3. Place a piece of masking tape down one side of the wooden block and mark it off in centimeters with the black pen.
4. Float the wooden block in the container of water, and pour several spoonfuls of sand on top of the block. Using the red pen, record the level that the water comes to on the block and the level that the water now comes to in the container.
5. Use the spoon to scrape some sand from the top of the block into the water. Record the water level on the block and in the container again.
6. Scrape off some more sand and again record the water levels.

Procedures are usually outlined in numbered steps

What Happens?

After you have completed the experiment, you have the information you need to understand the effect of erosion on the Himalayas. Interpret the experiment by answering these questions:

The expected result is described.

- What happens to the block as it loses sand to the water?
- How do the objects in this experiment compare to the Himalayas and Earth's mantle?
- What conclusions can you draw about the effect of erosion on the Himalayas?

Check Your Comprehension

1. How is erosion affecting the Himalayas?
2. What is Earth's crust?
3. What does the essay instruct you to do in order to understand the erosion of the Himalayas?

Applying the Reading Strategy

Identifying Cause-and-Effect Relationships

4. What do you think the effect of removing sand from the box will have on the water level?
5. What causes the Himalayas to erode?
6. How does the experiment affect your understanding of erosion?

Activity

How-to Essay

Reading a how-to essay will give you instructions on how to do or make something. Some may even instruct you on how to improve a skill or how to achieve a desired effect.

Choose one of the following: cleaning your bike, playing your favorite game, or making microwave popcorn. Then, write a brief how-to essay explaining how to do it.

Contrasting Informational Materials

How-to Essays and Recipes

You read "how-to's" all the time. The instruction booklet for a computer game, the directions for making brownies, safety warnings, repair instructions, guidelines for washing your clothes—these are all forms of writing that explain how to do something. Although they are all similar to a how-to essay, they all differ in format. Look at the following chart. Explain the differences between the two different types of "how-to's."

	How-to Essay	**Recipe**
Description	• Tells how to do or make something	• Tells how to make food or a meal
Contents	• An essay format with an introduction, a body, and a conclusion • A list of materials needed • A series of logical steps in sequential order • Details that tell *when, how much, how often,* or *to what extent*	• List format • A list of ingredients and materials needed • A series of logical steps in sequential order • Details that tell *when, how much, how often,* or *to what extent*

Writing WORKSHOP

Research: Multimedia Report

A **multimedia report** presents information gathered from a variety of reliable sources, both print and non-print. You have a wide range of materials at your finger-tips—tape recorders, video cameras, slides, photographs, overhead projectors, prerecorded music and sound effects, digital imaging, graphics software, computers, spreadsheets, databases, electronic resources, and Web sites. In this workshop, you will create a multimedia report using a few of these kinds of media.

Assignment Criteria. Your multimedia report should have the following characteristics:

● One topic that can be thoroughly covered in the time and space alloted

● Supporting facts, details, examples, and explanations from multiple authoritative sources

● Appropriate formatting using a word processor and principles of design

● A bibliography that lists all sources using a consistent and sanctioned format

● Appropriate and dramatic visual and audio components

See the Rubric on page 839 for the criteria on which your multimedia report may be assessed.

Prewriting

Choose a topic. Choose a topic for which you can locate (or create) visual support, such as photographs, maps, or charts, and audio support, such as tapes or digital recordings. Also, choose a topic that will benefit from a simple spreadsheet or database, such as one that involves a lot of statistics.

Examples:

● How a population has changed over time

● The growth of a certain product or service

● The gradual movement of a landmass

Gather details from multiple sources. Expand your research to include nonprint materials. Use multimedia sources such as the Internet, videotaped documentaries, slides, charts, maps, photographs, music, and sound effects. You might want to tape-record and/or videotape portions of your report as a means of presenting information.

Engage your audience. Think about creative ways to present information and to grab the audience's attention. Use some of the suggestions shown here.

> **Creative Ways to Present Information**
>
> • Build a model
> • Draw on a transparency
> • Tape-record a reading of a piece of literature
> • Create your own animation
> • Make your report interactive
> • Project slides on a wall
> • Play music that creates a mood
> • Print images from the Internet

Student Model

Before you begin drafting your multimedia report, read this portion of a student model and review the characteristics of a successful multimedia report. To see the full report, go to www.phschool.com.

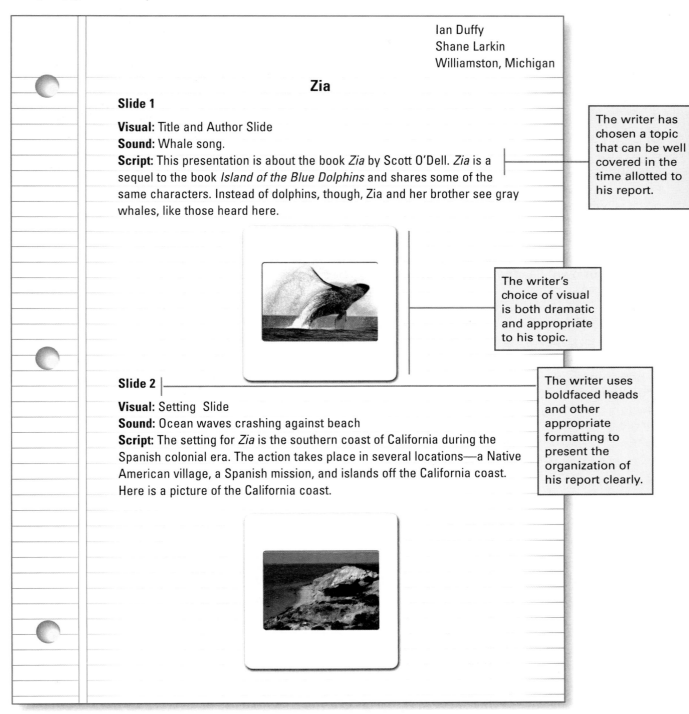

Ian Duffy
Shane Larkin
Williamston, Michigan

Zia

Slide 1

Visual: Title and Author Slide
Sound: Whale song.
Script: This presentation is about the book *Zia* by Scott O'Dell. *Zia* is a sequel to the book *Island of the Blue Dolphins* and shares some of the same characters. Instead of dolphins, though, Zia and her brother see gray whales, like those heard here.

> The writer has chosen a topic that can be well covered in the time allotted to his report.

> The writer's choice of visual is both dramatic and appropriate to his topic.

Slide 2

Visual: Setting Slide
Sound: Ocean waves crashing against beach
Script: The setting for *Zia* is the southern coast of California during the Spanish colonial era. The action takes place in several locations—a Native American village, a Spanish mission, and islands off the California coast. Here is a picture of the California coast.

> The writer uses boldfaced heads and other appropriate formatting to present the organization of his report clearly.

Drafting

Write a script. Plan every word and action in your multimedia presentation by writing a script. Include any words that you will speak and any stage directions that make actions and effects clear. Use a format similar to this one:

Example: (*Display the spreadsheet on the overhead projector.*)
"Take a few minutes to study the growth patterns in the wolf population."
(*Play background tape of wolf sounds while class studies spreadsheet.*)

Plan databases and spreadsheets. Examine samples of databases and spreadsheets used for managing large amounts of information, and design yours to meet the needs of your topic. Format them so they are easy to read. You can display them as posters, with overhead projectors, on computer monitors, or as handouts for your audience.

Give credit. In a research report, you must cite the sources for quotations, facts that are not common knowledge, and ideas that are not your own. See the chart for a commonly used method of citing sources.

Focusing on Citations

Internal Citations A basic form of citation is an internal citation in parentheses. An internal citation directly follows the information that came from the source cited. It includes the author's last name and the page number on which the information appears.

"I tell my students that the American Indian has a unique investment in the American landscape" (Momaday 33).

Works Cited List Provide full information about the sources in an alphabetical "Works Cited List" at the end of your report. The following is an example of the correct form:

Momaday, N. Scott. *The Man Made of Words.* New York: St. Martin's Press, 1997.

Revising

Find the glue between paragraphs. Read the final sentence of each paragraph. Then, read the opening sentence of the next paragraph. If one or both sentences clearly show the relationship between paragraphs, underline them in blue pencil. If you do not find a transition, draw a squiggly red line in the space between the paragraphs and add a word, phrase, or sentence to "glue" them together.

Finding the Glue Between Paragraphs

Several of the toothed whales shoot a jet of water at the ocean floor. They use this jet to stir up prey hiding in the sand. These whales include the beluga and the narwhal. These whales also have very flexible necks that help them scan the ocean floor for food. *Other characteristics can help a whale live in a harsh environment.*
, for instance,
The bowhead has several interesting physical features that allow it to live in the Arctic all the time.

Jamie found a few places where he needed transitions. He added words and phrases there to glue his paragraphs together.

Check spelling. Run a spelling and grammar check. Be careful, however, because spell checkers do not catch mistakes in homophones (*there, their, they're*). You must catch these errors yourself.

Remember, a mistake in spelling is magnified in a multimedia report. Each slide or display is on view for some time—enough time for your audience to notice and be distracted by the mistake.

Compare the nonmodel and the model. Why is the model more effective than the nonmodel?

Nonmodel	Model
They're length is about five and one-half feet, and they way about 135 pounds.	Their length is about five and one-half feet, and they weigh about 135 pounds.

Publishing and Presenting

Choose one of these ways to share your writing with classmates or a larger audience.

Report to a small audience. Perform your multimedia report for a few of your classmates. Ask them to evaluate what they see and hear.

Take it on the road. Take your report "on the road" outside your school. Contact a local library or club that might be interested in your report, or share it with a local elementary school class who may enjoy it.

WG *Prentice Hall Writing and Grammar Connection: Chapter 28, Section 2*

Speaking Connection
To learn more about hearing and evaluating a multimedia report, see the **Listening and Speaking Workshop: Evaluating a Media Presentation,** page 840.

Rubric for Self-Assessment

Evaluate your multimedia report using the following criteria and rating scale:

Criteria	Rating Scale				
	Not very				Very
How well does the report focus on one clear topic?	1	2	3	4	5
How well is the topic supported by evidence from a variety of sources?	1	2	3	4	5
How appropriate is the format and design?	1	2	3	4	5
How varied are the sources listed in the bibliography?	1	2	3	4	5
How effectively are the visual and audio components used?	1	2	3	4	5

Listening and Speaking WORKSHOP

Evaluating a Media Presentation

When watching a **media presentation,** think critically about what you see and hear. Use what you know about creating a successful multimedia presentation (see the Writing Workshop, pp. 836–839) to make insightful observations.

Evaluate the Presentation

Analyze the effects of images, text, and sound. Consider the following questions: Does the presenter use a variety of media to convey ideas? What is the effect of each medium on the viewer? Do they all add depth to the presentation, or do any of them seem distracting or tacked on?

Identify techniques used to achieve effects. Ask yourself how the presenter achieved the effects he or she created. Are images, text, and sound clear and easy to understand? Does the use of media present a well-rounded and unbiased view of the topic?

Evaluate the logic of the content and delivery. Did the presenter make wise decisions regarding when and how to use each medium? Or could images, text, and sound have been used in more logical ways?

Evaluate the Presenter

Consider whether the presenter covers his or her topic in a thorough, engaging, and logical manner. When the presentation is over, offer constructive feedback in the following ways:

- If there is something you do not understand, ask specific **questions.**

- If you disagree with an opinion or a judgment, **challenge** the ideas—not the presenter. Offer evidence that shows why you disagree.

- **Affirm,** or show your agreement with, points by sharing related information or experiences that support the same point.

Activity:
Presentation and Feedback In a small group, attend a media presentation in your school or community. Use the feedback form to evaluate what you see and hear based on the criteria above. Discuss your evaluation with your group and, if appropriate, share it with the presenter.

Feedback Form for Media Presentation

Rating System
+ = Excellent ✔ = Average – = Weak

Presentation
Variety of media _____
Effects of media _____
Techniques used to create effects _____
Logic of content and delivery _____

Feedback for presenter
Ask one question. _____
_____
Challenge one idea. _____
_____
Make one affirmation. _____
_____

Assessment WORKSHOP

Spelling, Capitalization, and Punctuation

The writing sections of some tests require you to read a passage and answer multiple-choice questions about spelling, capitalization, and punctuation. Use what you have learned in this unit to help you answer such questions.

Test-Taking Strategy

Before selecting a type of error, use scrap paper to write the word or sentence correctly. If you can't make a correction, there might not be an error.

Sample Test Item

Directions: Read the passage and decide which type of error, if any, appears in each underlined section.

(1) What's it like <u>two hundred miles above Earth</u> (2) <u>Astronaut and Senator John glenn says,</u> (3) <u>"Space is completely black, even when the son is shining."</u> Glenn was the first American to orbit Earth in 1962. Thirty-six years later, he went back into space on the space shuttle.

1. **A** Spelling error
    B Capitalization error
    C Punctuation error
    D No error

2. **A** Spelling error
    B Capitalization error
    C Punctuation error
    D No error

3. **A** Spelling error
    B Capitalization error
    C Punctuation error
    D No error

Answers and Explanations

For section 1: The sentence has no end punctuation, so **C** is correct.

For section 2: Glenn is a proper noun and should be capitalized, so **B** is correct.

For section 3: *Son* is a homophone for *sun,* so **A** is correct.

Practice

Directions: Read the passage and decide which type of error, if any, appears in each section.

(1) <u>If you are looking for extreme weather, here's a gide for where to go.</u> (2) <u>In Death Valley California</u>, the temperature has been known to reach 134 degrees Fahrenheit. (3) <u>To cool off, try Prospect Creek Camp, Alaska, where it can go down to eighty degrees below zero.</u> (4) For high winds, <u>climb Mount Washington, new Hampshire,</u> where winds have reached 231 miles per hour.

1. **A** Spelling error
    B Capitalization error
    C Punctuation error
    D No error

2. **A** Spelling error
    B Capitalization error
    C Punctuation error
    D No error

3. **A** Spelling error
    B Capitalization error
    C Punctuation error
    D No error

4. **A** Spelling error
    B Capitalization error
    C Punctuation error
    D No error

Suggested Works and Connections to Unit Themes

Following are some suggestions for longer works that will give you the opportunity to experience the fun of sustained reading. Each of the suggestions further explores one of the themes in this book. Many of the titles are included in the Prentice Hall Literature Library.

Unit One

Child of the Owl
Laurence Yep

When Casey is sent to live with her grandmother in San Francisco's Chinatown, she learns about her family's history and Chinese heritage.

Bearstone
Will Hobbs

Knowledge of his ancestors—and a helpful stranger—aid Cloyd, a Native American boy, in his struggle to build a future for himself.

Unit Two

The House on Mango Street
Sandra Cisneros

Through her Mango Street neighbors, Esperanza discovers that there are many different kinds of people, and each has something to give.

It's Our World, Too!
Phillip Hoose

In this book, young people take stands against racism and crime, work to save the environment, and help to create a world of peace.

Unit Three

The Giver
Lois Lowry

Jonas lives in a world of Sameness where everything is the same day after day. When he is given a special job, Jonas must decide what is most important in his life.

Amos Fortune, Free Man
Elizabeth Yates

Amos Fortune was born the son of an African king, but at fifteen years of age, Amos was captured by slave traders. This is his gripping story.

Unit Four

Words by Heart
Ouida Sebestyen

In this moving novel, a twelve-year-old girl struggles against racism in a small town.

Julie of the Wolves
Jean Craighead George

At the age of thirteen, Julie gets lost in the wilderness and relies on wolves and other animals to help her.

Unit Five

Squashed
Joan Bauer

In this witty and amusing book, Ellie Morgan sets a huge goal for herself—to grow the largest pumpkin in Iowa!

Pun and Games
Richard Lederer

Who would have IOPER8 for a license plate? A surgeon! Reading this book is a "punny" way to spend an afternoon.

absurdity (ab sur´ də tē) *n.* nonsense; foolishness

abundant (ə bun´ dənt) *adj.* plentiful

acknowledge (ak näl´ ij) *v.* recognize and admit

afflicted (ə flik´ tid) *v.* received pain or suffering

ajar (ə jär´) *adj.* open

allay (a lā´) *v.* put to rest; calm

anguish (aŋ´ gwish) *n.* great suffering; agony

anonymous (ə nän´ ə məs) *adj.* unsigned; written by a person whose name is unknown

apprehensions (ap´ rē hen´ shənz) *n.* fears; anxious feelings

aptitude (ap´ tə tōōd´) *n.* talent; ability

arched (ärcht) *adj.* curved

assent (ə sent´) *n.* agreement

assume (ə sōōm´) *v.* believe to be a fact

astonish (ə stän´ ish) *v.* amaze

audible (ô´ də bəl) *adj.* loud enough to be heard

automatically (ôt´ ə mat´ ik lē) *adv.* without thought; by reflex

awe (ô) *n.* mixed feelings of fear and wonder

balmy (bäm´ ē) *adj.* soothing; mild; pleasant

banish (ban´ ish) *v.* send away; exile

base (bās) *adj.* lowly; inferior

benevolence (bə nev´ ə ləns) *n.* kindliness

beset (bē set´) *adj.* covered; set thickly with

besieged (bi sējd´) *adj.* surrounded

bewilderment (bē wil´ dər mənt) *n.* state of confusion

bigots (big´ əts) *n.* narrow-minded, prejudiced people

blundered (blun´ dərd) *v.* made a foolish mistake

bog (bäg) *n.* small marsh or swamp

bound (bound) *v.* tied

brandished (bran´ disht) *v., used as adj.* waved in a threatening way

brandishing (bran´ dish iŋ) *adj.* waving in a menacing way

brawny (brôn´ ē) *adj.* strong and muscular

brooch (brōch) *n.* large ornamental pin worn on a blouse or dress

burrow (bur´ ō) *v.* to dig a hole or tunnel, especially for shelter

buttes (byōōts) *n.* steep hills standing in flat land

cascade (kas kād´) *n.* waterfall or anything tumbling like water

cherished (cher´ isht) *adj.* beloved; valued

cluster (klus´ tər) *n.* a set of similar items grouped together

coalition (kō ə lish´ ən) *n.* association or organization formed for a specific purpose

coax (kōks) *v.* use gentle persuasion

communal (kə myōō´ nəl) *adj.* shared by all

compelled (kəm peld´) *v.* forced

composure (kəm pō´ zhər) *n.* calmness of mind

compulsion (kəm pul´ shən) *n.* a driving, irresistible force

concussion (kən kush´ ən) *n.* violent shaking

confidential (kän fə den´ shəl) *adj.* entrusted with private or secret matters

consolation (kän´ sə lā´ shən) *n.* something that makes you feel better

console (kən sōl´) *v.* comfort; make less sad

conspired (kən spīrd´) *v.* planned together secretly

content (kən tent´) *adj.* happy enough

conviction (kən vik´ shən) *n.* belief

correspondent (kôr´ ə spän´ dənt) *n.* person hired by a news organization to provide news from a distant place

coveted (kuv´ it id) *v.* wanted greatly

cremated (krē´ māt id) *v.* burned to ashes

croon (krōōn) *v.* sing or hum quietly, soothingly

crouches (krouch´ iz) *v.* stoops or bends low

crucial (krōō´ shəl) *adj.* of great importance

culprit (kul´ prit) *n.* guilty person

cunningly (kun´ iŋ lē) *adv.* cleverly

curdled (kur´ dəld) *adj.* thickened; clotted

currency (kur´ ən sē) *n.* money

debut (dā byōō´) *n.* first performance in public

decreed (dē krēd´) *v.* officially ordered

defiant (dē fī´ ənt) *adj.* boldly resisting

dejectedly (dē jek´ tid lē) *adv.* sadly; showing discouragement

delicacies (del´ i kə sēz) *n.* foods that are rare and tasty

deluge (del´ yōōj) *n.* great flood or rush of anything

denigrate (den´ ə grāt´) *n.* discredit; put down; belittle

desolate (des´ ə lit) *adj.* lonely; solitary

desolation (des´ ə lā´ shən) *n.* loneliness; emptiness; misery

despondent (di spän´ dənt) *adj.* lacking hope; depressed

destination (des´ tə nā´ shən) *n.* the place to which something is being sent

destiny (des´ tə nē) *n.* what will necessarily happen to any person or thing; fate

destitute (des´ tə tōōt´) *adj.* living in complete poverty

devastated (dev´ ə stā tid) *v.* destroyed; completely upset

devastating (dev´ əs tāt´ iŋ) *adj.* destructive; overwhelming

dislodge (dis läj´) *v.* leave a resting place

dismally (diz´ məl lē) *adv.* gloomily; miserably

dismayed (dis mād´) *adj.* afraid; without confidence

dispelled (dis peld´) *v.* scattered and driven away; made to vanish

dissuade (di swād´) *v.* advise someone against an action

distinct (di stiŋkt´) *adj.* separate and different

distraught (dis trôt´) *adj.* extremely upset

domestic (dō mes´ tik) *n.* of the home and family

dominions (də min´ yənz) *n.* regions over which someone rules

downy (doun´ ē) *adj.* soft and fluffy

draggled (drag´ əld) *adj.* wet and dirty

ecstasy (ek´ stə sē) *n.* overpowering joy

edifice (ed´ ə fis) *n.* large structure

elective (ē lek´ tiv) *n.* optional course or subject in a school or college curriculum

emaciated (ē mā´ shē āt´ id) *adj.* extremely thin; starving

emblems (em´ bləmz) *n.* symbols, signs, or badges

eminent (em´ ə nənt) *adj.* distinguished or outstanding

endorsements (en dôrs´ mənts) *n.* acts of giving approval to something

enthralled (en thrôld´) *v.* fascinated; charmed

epidemic (ep´ ə dem´ ik) *n.* outbreak of a contagious disease

equal (ē´ kwəl) *adj.* of the same amount

evading (ē vād´ iŋ) *adj.* keeping away from or avoiding

evidently (ev´ ə dent´ lē) *adv.* clearly; obviously

exertion (eg zur´ shən) *n.* physical work

exquisite (eks kwi´ zit) *adj.* very beautiful, especially in a delicate way

extricate (eks´ tri kāt´) v. to set free; disentangle

ferocious (fə rō´ shəs) adj. fierce; savage

ferocity (fə räs´ ə tē) n. fierceness; wild force

fiasco (fē as´ cō) n. complete failure

flatterers (flat´ ər ərz) n. those who praise a person insincerely in order to gain something for themselves

flinched (flincht) v. moved back, as if away from a blow

fluent (flōō´ ənt) adj. able to write or speak easily and smoothly

flustered (flus´ tərd) adj. nervous; confused

forlorn (fôr lôrn´) adj. alone and miserable

formidable (fôr´ mi də bəl) adj. impressive

fortitude (fôrt´ ə tōōd´) n. firm courage

furtive (fur´ tiv) adj. sneaky

ghastly (gast´ lē) adv. ghostlike; frightful

glossy (glôs´ ē) adj. smooth and shiny

gnarled (närld) adj. knotty and twisted

goblets (gäb´ lits) n. bowl-shaped drinking containers without handles

gourd (gôrd) n. fruit of a certain kind of plant; the dried, hollowed shell of this fruit is used as a drinking cup or dipper

gratify (grat´ i fī´) v. to please

grisly (griz´ lē) adj. horrible

grotesquely (grō tesk´ le) adv. in a strange or distorted way

gumption (gump´ shən) n. courage; enterprise

haunches (hônch´ iz) n. an animal's legs

hindered (hin´ dərd) adj. held back

hissing (his´ iŋ) adj. making a sound like a prolonged s

hostility (häs til´ ə tē) n. anger; unfriendliness

humiliation (hyōō mil´ ē ā´ shən) n. embarrassment; feeling of hurt pride

illuminates (i lōō´ mə nāts´) v. brightens; sheds light on

immensity (i men´ si tē) n. something extremely large or immeasurably vast

implored (im plôrd´) v. asked or begged earnestly

impostors (im päs´ terz) n. people who trick or deceive others by pretending to be what they are not

impromptu (im prämp´ tōō) adj. unscheduled; unplanned

incessantly (in ses´ ənt lē) adv. without stopping

incorporate (in kôr´ pôr āt) v. form into a legal business

inevitability (in ev´ ə tə bil´ i tē) n. certainty

inevitable (in ev´ ə tə bəl) adj. certain to happen

inflammatory (in flam´ ə tôr´ ē) adj. characterized by pain and swelling

interacts (in´ tər akts´) v. affects and is affected by

interloper (in´ tər lō´ pər) n. person who intrudes on another's rights or territory

interplanetary (in´ tər plan´ ə ter´ ē) adj. between planets

intricate (in´ tri kit) adj. complex; full of complicated detail

intrigue (in´ trēg´) n. curiosity and interest

intrigued (in trēgd´) v. fascinated

knell (nel) n. funeral bell

kosher (kō´ shər) adj. fit to eat according to Jewish dietary laws

laborious (la bôr´ ē əs) adj. taking much work or effort; difficult

landlord (land´ lôrd) n. person who keeps a rooming house, inn, etc.

loaf (lōf) v. spend time idly

loathed (lōthd) v. hated

maestro (mīs´ trō) n. great musician

malevolent (mə lev´ ə lənt) adj. wishing evil or harm to others

malicious (mə lish´ əs) adj. spiteful; hateful

meager (mē´ gər) adj. of poor quality; small in amount

meek (mēk) adj. timid; humble; not showing anger

mesmerizing (mez´ mər īz´ iŋ) adj. hypnotizing

metamorphosis (met´ ə môr´ fə sis) n. change of form

misanthrope (mis´ ən throp´) n. person who hates or distrusts everyone

morose (mə rōs´) adj. gloomy; ill-tempered

mortal (môr´ təl) n. being who must eventually die

mortality (môr tal´ ə tē) n. the condition of being mortal; having to die eventually

mourning (môrn´ iŋ) adj. feeling sorrow for the death of a loved one

mutilated (myōōt´ əl āt´ id) adj. damaged or injured

obscure (əb skyoor´) adj. not well-known

ominous (äm´ ə nəs) adj. threatening

outskirts (out´ skurts´) n. part of a district far from the center of a city

pasture (pas´ chər) n. a field used by animals to graze in

pathetic (pə thet´ ik) adj. arousing pity, sorrow, and sympathy

pauper (pô´ pər) n. extremely poor person

perfunctorily (pər fuŋk´ tə rə lē) adv. without enthusiasm; routinely

perilous (per´ ə ləs) adj. dangerous

permanent (pur´ mə nənt) adj. lasting

perpetual (pər pech´ ōō əl) adj. constant; unending

persistently (pər sist´ ənt lē) adv. firmly and steadily

pinafore (pin´ ə fôr´) n. sleeveless, apron-like garment

ponderous (pän´ dər əs) adj. very heavy; bulky

porridge (pôr´ ij) n. soft food made of cereal boiled in water or milk

predecessors (pred´ ə ses´ ərz) n. those who came before

preen (prēn) v. dress up; show pride in one's appearance

premium (prē´ mē əm) n. additional charge

presumptuous (prē zump´ chōō əs) adj. overconfident; arrogant

prodigy (präd´ ə jē) n. child of unusually high talent

profound (prō found´) adj. deeply or intensely felt

profusely (prō fyōōs´ lē) adv. freely or plentifully

prone (prōn) adj. lying face downward

prose (prōz) n. nonpoetic language

protruded (prō trōōd´ id) v. stuck out; extended

psychiatrist (sī kī´ ə trist) n. medical doctor specializing in illnesses of the mind

pummeled (pum´ əld) v. beat

pungent (pun´ jənt) adj. sharp-smelling

queried (kwir´ ēd) v. asked

radiance (rā´ dē əns) n. quality of shining brightly

radiant (rā´ dē ənt) adj. filled with light; shining brightly

rancid (ran´ sid) adj. spoiled and smelling bad

rash (rash) adj. thoughtless

realign (rē´ ə līn´) v. readjust into a straight line or into proper coordination

reconnoiter (rē kə noit´ ər) v. look around

reeds (rēdz) n. tall, slender grasses that grow in marshy land

reeled (rēld) v. fell back from a blow

refugee (ref′ yŏŏ jē) *n.* person who flees home or country to seek shelter from war or cruelty

refute (ri fyŏŏt′) *v.* prove someone wrong

regime (rə zhēm′) *n.* system or rule of government

relished (rel′ isht) *v.* especially enjoyed

reluctance (ri luk′ təns) *n.* unwillingness

remote (ri mōt′) *adj.* far away from everything else

reproach (ri prōch′) *n.* disgrace; blame

resilient (ri zil′ yənt) *adj.* springing back into shape

resumed (ri zŏŏmd′) *v.* began again; continued

retrospective (re′ trə spek′ tiv) *n.* look on the past

revived (ri vīvd′) *v.* came back to consciousness

rheumatism (rŏŏ′ mə tiz′ əm) *n.* painful condition of the joints and muscles

rouge (rŏŏzh) *n.* reddish cosmetic used to color cheeks

routed (rout′ əd) *v.* completely defeated

sage (sāj) *n.* very wise person

sauciness (sô′ sē nes) *n.* liveliness; boldness; spirit

saunter (sôn′ tər) *v.* walk about idly; stroll

savored (sā′ vərd) *v.* enjoyed

scapegoat (skāp′ gōt′) *n.* person or group blamed for the mistakes or crimes of others

scowl (skoul) *v.* lower eyebrows and corners of the mouth; look angry or irritated

sensitive (sen′ sə tiv) *adj.* easily hurt or irritated; touchy

severe (sə vir′) *adj.* harsh

sheepishly (shēp′ ish lē) *adv.* in a shy or embarrassed way

shipment (ship′ mənt) *n.* a set of goods or cargo shipped together

shuffle (shuf′ əl) *v.* walk with dragging feet

simultaneously (sī məl tā′ nē əs lē) *adv.* at the same time

slackening (slak′ ən iŋ) *v.* easing; becoming less active

sluggishly (slug′ ish lē) *adv.* as if lacking energy

snare (snar) *v.* catch or trap

solemn (säl′ əm) *adj.* serious; somber

spectators (spek′ tāt′ ərz) *n.* people who watch something without taking part; onlookers

spry (sprī) *adj.* full of life; active; nimble

sputters (sput′ ərz) *v.* makes hissing or spitting sounds

stern (sturn) *adj.* strict; unyielding

strife (strīf) *n.* trouble; conflict; struggle

strive (strīv) *v.* struggle

sundered (sun′ dərd) *v.* broken apart

superimposed (sŏŏ′ pər im pōzd′) *adj.* put or stacked on top of something else

supple (sup′ əl) *adj.* flexible

surged (surjd) *v.* moved in a violent, swelling motion

surpass (sər pas′) *v.* be superior to

surreptitiously (sur′ əp tish′ əs lē) *adv.* secretly

sustained (sə stānd′) *adj.* supported

swarmed (swôrmd) *v.* came together in a large group

swerve (swurv) *n.* curving motion

taut (tôt) *adj.* tightly stretched

tawdry (tô′ drē) *adj.* cheap and showy; gaudy

tawny (tô′ nē) *adj.* tan; yellowish brown

tentatively (ten′ tə tiv lē) *adv.* hesitantly; with uncertainty

threadbare (*th*red′ ber) *adj.* worn; shabby

tiered (tird) *adj.* stacked in rows

tolerant (täl′ ər ənt) *adj.* free from bigotry or prejudice

torrent (tôr′ ənt) *n.* flood

totters (tät′ ərz) *v.* rocks or shakes as if about to fall; is unsteady

tourniquets (tur′ ni kits) *n.* devices used to stop bleeding in an emergency, as a bandage tightly twisted to stop the flow of blood.

transformation (trans′ fər mā′ shən) *n.* change in condition or outward appearance

translucent (trans lŏŏ′ sənt) *adj.* able to transmit light but no detail of that light

tumultuously (tŏŏ mul′ chŏŏ əs lē) *adv.* noisily and violently

unanimous (yŏŏ nan′ ə məs) *adj.* based on complete agreement

uncanny (un kan′ ē) *adj.* strange; eerie

unique (yŏŏ nēk′) *adj.* unlike any other; singular

unravel (un rav′ əl) *v.* become untangled or separated

utter (ut′ ər) *v.* speak

vacancy (vā′ kən sē) *n.* emptiness

vanity (van′ ə tē) *n.* the quality of being very proud of one's appearance

vibrant (vī′ brənt) *adj.* lively and energetic

virtue (vur′ chŏŏ) *n.* moral goodness

vital (vīt′ əl) *adj.* necessary to life; critically important

void (void) *n.* total emptiness

volleyed (väl′ ēd) *v.* fired together

whimper (hwim′ pər) *v.* make low, crying sounds; complain

wholesome (hōl′ səm) *adj.* promoting health; healthful

wielding (wēld′ iŋ) *v.* using with skill

withered (with′ ərd) *adj.* dried up

wonderment (wun′ dər ment) *n.* astonishment

yearned (yurnd) *v.* wanted very much

yield (yēld) *v.* give way to pressure or force

Approximately fifty percent of the words you read will be the same one hundred words. Learning to instantly recognize **high-frequency words**—words that are used often in print—will greatly improve your reading fluency. Learn to instantly recognize the words on this page. Practice any that give you trouble.

the	said	could	things	large	still	seemed	second
of	there	people	our	must	learn	next	later
and	use	my	just	big	should	hard	miss
a	an	than	name	even	American	open	idea
to	each	first	good	such	world	example	enough
in	which	water	sentence	because	high	beginning	eat
is	she	been	man	turned	ever	life	face
you	do	called	think	here	near	always	watch
that	how	who	say	why	add	those	far
it	their	oil	great	asked	food	both	Indians
he	if	sit	where	went	between	paper	rally
was	will	now	help	men	own	together	almost
for	up	find	through	read	below	got	let
on	other	long	much	need	country	group	above
are	about	down	before	land	plants	often	girl
as	out	day	line	different	last	run	sometimes
with	many	did	right	home	school	important	mountains
his	then	get	too	us	father	until	cut
they	them	come	means	move	keep	children	young
I	these	made	old	try	trees	side	talk
at	so	may	any	kind	never	feet	soon
be	some	part	same	hand	started	car	list
this	her	over	tell	picture	city	miles	song
have	would	new	boy	again	earth	night	being
from	make	sound	following	change	eyes	walked	leave
or	like	take	came	off	light	white	family
one	him	only	want	play	thought	sea	it's
had	into	little	show	spell	head	began	
by	time	work	also	air	under	grow	
words	has	know	around	away	story	took	
but	look	place	form	animals	saw	river	
not	two	years	three	house	left	four	
what	more	live	small	point	don't	carry	
all	write	me	set	page	few	state	
were	go	back	put	letters	while	once	
we	see	give	end	mother	along	book	
when	number	most	does	answer	might	hear	
your	no	very	another	found	close	stop	
can	way	after	well	study	something	without	

LITERARY TERMS HANDBOOK

ALLITERATION *Alliteration* is the repetition of initial consonant sounds. Writers use alliteration to draw attention to certain words or ideas, to imitate sounds, and to create musical effects.

ALLUSION An *allusion* is a reference to a well-known person, place, event, literary work, or work of art. Understanding what a writer is saying often depends on recognizing allusions.

ANALOGY An *analogy* makes a comparison between two or more things that are similar in some ways but otherwise unalike.

ANECDOTE An *anecdote* is a brief story about an interesting, amusing, or strange event. Writers tell anecdotes to entertain or to make a point.

ANTAGONIST An *antagonist* is a character or a force in conflict with a main character, or protagonist.

See *Conflict* and *Protagonist*.

ATMOSPHERE *Atmosphere*, or *mood*, is the feeling created in the reader by a literary work or passage.

AUTHOR'S ARGUMENT An *author's argument* is the position he or she puts forward, supported by reasons.

AUTOBIOGRAPHY An *autobiography* is the story of the writer's own life, told by the writer. Autobiographical writing may tell about the person's whole life or only a part of it.

Because autobiographies are about real people and events, they are a form of nonfiction. Most autobiographies are written in the first person.

See *Biography, Nonfiction,* and *Point of View*.

BALLAD A *ballad* is a songlike poem that tells a story, often one dealing with adventure and romance. Most ballads are written in four- to six-line stanzas and have regular rhythms and rhyme schemes. A ballad often features a refrain—a regularly repeated line or group of lines.

See *Oral Tradition* and *Refrain*.

BIOGRAPHY A *biography* is a form of nonfiction in which a writer tells the life story of another person. Most biographies are written about famous or admirable people. Although biographies are nonfiction, the most effective ones share the qualities of good narrative writing.

See *Autobiography* and *Nonfiction*.

CHARACTER A *character* is a person or an animal that takes part in the action of a literary work. The main, or *major*, character is the most important character in a story, poem, or play. A *minor*

character is one who takes part in the action but is not the focus of attention.

Characters are sometimes classified as flat or round. A *flat character* is one-sided and often stereotypical. A *round character,* on the other hand, is fully developed and exhibits many traits—often both faults and virtues. Characters can also be classified as dynamic or static. A *dynamic character* is one who changes or grows during the course of the work. A *static character* is one who does not change.

See *Characterization, Hero/Heroine,* and *Motive*.

CHARACTERIZATION *Characterization* is the act of creating and developing a character. Authors use two major methods of characterization—*direct* and *indirect*. When using *direct* characterization, a writer states the *characters' traits,* or characteristics.

When describing a character indirectly, a writer depends on the reader to draw conclusions about the character's traits. Sometimes the writer tells what other participants in the story say and think about the character.

See *Character* and *Motive*.

CLIMAX The climax, also called the turning point, is the high point in the action of the plot. It is the moment of greatest tension, when the outcome of the plot hangs in the balance.

See *Plot*.

COMEDY A *comedy* is a literary work, especially a play, which is light, often humorous or satirical, and ends happily. Comedies frequently depict ordinary characters faced with temporary difficulties and conflicts. Types of comedy include *romantic comedy,* which involves problems among lovers, and the *comedy of manners,* which satirically challenges social customs of a society.

CONCRETE POEM A *concrete poem* is one with a shape that suggests its subject. The poet arranges the letters, punctuation, and lines to create an image, or picture, on the page.

CONFLICT A *conflict* is a struggle between opposing forces. Conflict is one of the most important elements of stories, novels, and plays because it causes the action. There are two kinds of conflict: external and internal. An *external conflict* is one in which a character struggles against some outside force, such as another person. Another kind of external conflict may occur between a character and some force in nature.

An *internal conflict* takes place within the mind of a character. The character struggles to make a decision, take an action, or overcome a feeling.

See *Plot*.

CONNOTATIONS The *connotation* of a word is the set of ideas associated with it in addition to its explicit meaning. The connotation of a word can be personal, based on individual experiences. More often, cultural connotations—those recognizable by most people in a group—determine a writer's word choices.

See also *Denotation*.

COUPLET A *couplet* is two consecutive lines of verse with end rhymes. Often, a couplet functions as a stanza.

DENOTATION The *denotation* of a word is its dictionary meaning, independent of other associations that the word may have. The denotation of the word *lake*, for example, is "an inland body of water." "Vacation spot" and "place where the fishing is good" are connotations of the word *lake*.

See also *Connotation*.

DESCRIPTION A *description* is a portrait, in words, of a person, place, or object. Descriptive writing uses images that appeal to the five senses—sight, hearing, touch, taste, and smell.

See *Image*.

DEVELOPMENT See *Plot*.

DIALECT *Dialect* is the form of a language spoken by people in a particular region or group. Dialects differ in pronunciation, grammar, and word choice. The English language is divided into many dialects. British English differs from American English.

DIALOGUE A *dialogue* is a conversation between characters. In poems, novels, and short stories, dialogue is usually set off by quotation marks to indicate a speaker's exact words.

In a play, dialogue follows the names of the characters, and no quotation marks are used.

DRAMA A *drama* is a story written to be performed by actors. Although a drama is meant to be performed, one can also read the script, or written version, and imagine the action. The *script* of a drama is made up of dialogue and stage directions. The *dialogue* are the words spoken by the actors. The *stage directions,* usually printed in italics, tell how the actors should look, move, and speak. They also describe the setting, sound effects, and lighting.

Dramas are often divided into parts called *acts*. The acts are often divided into smaller parts called *scenes*.

DYNAMIC CHARACTER See *Character*.

ELEGY An *elegy* is a solemn and formal lyric poem about death. It may mourn a particular person or reflect on a serious or tragic theme, such as the passing of youth, beauty, or a way of life.

See *Lyric Poem*.

EPIC POEM An *epic* is a long narrative poem about the adventures of gods or a hero. An epic is serious in tone and broad in theme. It offers a portrait of the culture in which it was produced. The earliest known epics were created in ancient Greece and Rome and are part of the oral tradition.

Epic conventions are traditional characeristics of epic poems, including an opening statement of the theme; an appeal for supernatural help in telling the story (an invocation); a beginning "in the middle of things"; long lists of people and things; accounts of past events; and repeated epithets.

See *Oral Tradition* and *Epithets*.

EPITHET An *epithet* is a word or phrase that states a characteristic quality of a person or thing.

ESSAY An *essay* is a short nonfiction work about a particular subject. Most essays have a single major focus and a clear introduction, body, and conclusion.

There are many types of essays. An *informal essay* uses casual, conversational language. A *historical essay* gives facts, explanations, and insights about historical events. An *expository essay* explains an idea by breaking it down. A *narrative essay* tells a story about a real-life experience. An *informational essay* explains a process. A *persuasive essay* offers an opinion and supports it.

See *Exposition, Narration,* and *Persuasion*.

EXPOSITION In the plot of a story or a drama, the *exposition,* or introduction, is the part of the work that introduces the characters, setting, and basic situation.

See *Plot*.

EXPOSITORY WRITING *Expository writing* is writing that explains or informs.

EXTENDED METAPHOR In an *extended metaphor,* as in a regular metaphor, a subject is spoken or written of as though it were something else. However, extended metaphor differs from regular metaphor in that several connected comparisons are made.

See *Metaphor*.

EXTERNAL CONFLICT See *Conflict*.

FABLE A *fable* is a brief story or poem, usually with animal characters, that teaches a lesson, or moral. The moral is usually stated at the end of the fable.

See *Irony* and *Moral*.

FANTASY A *fantasy* is highly imaginative writing that contains elements not found in real life. Examples of fantasy include stories that involve supernatural elements, stories that resemble fairy tales, stories that deal with imaginary places and creatures, and science-fiction stories.

See *Science Fiction*.

FICTION *Fiction* is prose writing that tells about imaginary characters and events. Short stories and novels are works of fiction. Some writers base their fiction on actual events and people, adding invented characters, dialogue, settings, and plots. Other writers rely on imagination alone.

See *Narration, Nonfiction,* and *Prose.*

FIGURATIVE LANGUAGE *Figurative language* is writing or speech that is not meant to be taken literally. The many types of figurative language are known as *figures of speech.* Common figures of speech include metaphor, personification, and simile. Writers use figurative language to state ideas in vivid and imaginative ways.

See *Metaphor, Personification, Simile,* and *Symbol.*

FIGURE OF SPEECH See *Figurative Language.*

FLASHBACK A *flashback* is a scene within a story that interrupts the sequence of events to relate events that occurred in the past.

FLAT CHARACTER See *Character.*

FOLK TALE A *folk tale* is a story composed orally and then passed from person to person by word of mouth. Folk tales originated among people who could neither read nor write. These people entertained one another by telling stories aloud—often dealing with heroes, adventure, magic, or romance. Eventually, modern scholars collected these stories and wrote them down. Folk tales reflect the cultural beliefs and environments from which they come.
See *Fable, Legend, Myth,* and *Oral Tradition.*

FOOT See *Meter.*

FORESHADOWING *Foreshadowing* is the author's use of clues to hint at what might happen later in the story. Writers use foreshadowing to build their readers' expectations and to create suspense.

FREE VERSE *Free verse* is poetry not written in a regular, rhythmical pattern, or meter. The poet is free to write lines of any length or with any number of stresses, or beats. Free verse is therefore less constraining than *metrical verse,* in which every line must have a certain length and a certain number of stresses.
See *Meter.*

GENRE A *genre* is a division or type of literature. Literature is commonly divided into three major genres: poetry, prose, and drama. Each major genre is, in turn, divided into lesser genres, as follows:
1. *Poetry:* lyric poetry, concrete poetry, dramatic poetry, narrative poetry, epic poetry

2. *Prose:* fiction (novels and short stories) and nonfiction (biography, autobiography, letters, essays, and reports)
3. *Drama:* serious drama and tragedy, comic drama, melodrama, and farce

See *Drama, Poetry,* and *Prose.*

HAIKU The *haiku* is a three-line Japanese verse form. The first and third lines of a haiku each have five syllables. The second line has seven syllables. A writer of haiku uses images to create a single, vivid picture, generally of a scene from nature.

HERO/HEROINE A *hero* or *heroine* is a character whose actions are inspiring, or noble. Often heroes and heroines struggle to overcome the obstacles and problems that stand in their way. Note that the term *hero* was originally used only for male characters, while heroic female characters were always called *heroines*. However, it is now acceptable to use *hero* to refer to females as well as to males.

HISTORICAL FICTION In *historical fiction,* real events, places, or people are incorporated into a fictional, or made-up, story.

IDIOM An *idiom* is an expression that has a meaning particular to a language or region. For example, in "Seventh Grade," Gary Soto uses the idiom "making a face," which means to contort one's face in an unusual, usually unattractive, way.

IMAGE *Images* are words or phrases that appeal to one or more of the five senses. Writers use images to describe how their subjects look, sound, feel, taste, and smell. Poets often paint images, or word pictures, that appeal to your senses. These pictures help you to experience the poem fully.

IMAGERY See *Image.*

INTERNAL CONFLICT See *Conflict.*

IRONY *Irony* is the general name given to literary techniques that involve surprising, interesting, or amusing contradictions.

JOURNAL A *journal* is a daily, or periodic, account of events and the writer's thoughts and feelings about those events. Personal journals are not normally written for publication, but sometimes they do get published later with permission from the author or the author's family.

LEGEND A *legend* is a widely told story about the past—one that may or may not have a foundation in fact. Every culture has its own legends—its familiar, traditional stories.

See *Folk Tale, Myth,* and *Oral Tradition.*

LETTERS A *letter* is a written communication from one person to another. In personal letters, the writer shares information and his or her thoughts and feelings with one other person or group. Although letters are not normally written for publication, they sometimes do get published later with the permission of the author or the author's family.

LIMERICK A *limerick* is a humorous, rhyming, five-line poem with a specific meter and rhyme scheme. Most limericks have three strong stresses in lines 1, 2, and 5 and two strong stresses in lines 3 and 4. Most follow the rhyme scheme *aabba*.

LYRIC POEM A *lyric poem* is a highly musical verse that expresses the observations and feelings of a single speaker. It creates a single, unified impression.

MAIN CHARACTER See *Character*.

MEDIA ACCOUNTS *Media Accounts* are reports, explanations, opinions, or descriptions written for television, radio, newspapers, and magazines. While some media accounts report only facts, others include the writer's thoughts and reflections.

METAPHOR A *metaphor* is a figure of speech in which something is described as though it were something else. A metaphor, like a simile, works by pointing out a similarity between two unlike things.
See *Extended Metaphor* and *Simile*.

METER The *meter* of a poem is its rhythmical pattern. This pattern is determined by the number of *stresses*, or beats, in each line. To describe the meter of a poem, read it emphasizing the beats in each line. Then, mark the stressed and unstressed syllables, as follows:

My fath | er was | the first | to hear |

As you can see, each strong stress is marked with a slanted line (´) and each unstressed syllable with a horseshoe symbol (˘). The weak and strong stresses are then divided by vertical lines (|) into groups called *feet*.

MINOR CHARACTER See *Character*.

MOOD *Mood*, or *atmosphere*, is the feeling created by a literary work or passage. Writers use many devices to create mood, including images, dialogue, setting, and plot. Often, a writer creates a mood at the beginning of a work that he or she sustains throughout. Sometimes, however, the mood of the work changes dramatically.

MORAL A *moral* is a lesson taught by a literary work. A fable usually ends with a moral that is directly stated. A poem, novel, short story, or essay often suggests a moral that is not directly stated. The moral must be drawn by the reader, based on other elements in the work.
See *Fable*.

MOTIVATION See *Motive*.

MOTIVE A *motive* is a reason that explains or partially explains a character's thoughts, feelings, actions, or speech. Writers try to make their characters' motives, or motivations, as clear as possible. If the motives of a main character are not clear, then the character will not be believable.

Characters are often motivated by needs, such as food and shelter. They are also motivated by feelings, such as fear, love, and pride. Motives may be obvious or hidden.

MYTH A *myth* is a fictional tale that explains the actions of gods or heroes or the origins of elements of nature. Myths are part of the oral tradition. They are composed orally and then passed from generation to generation by word of mouth. Every ancient culture has its own mythology, or collection of myths. Greek and Roman myths are known collectively as *classical mythology*.
See *Oral Tradition*.

NARRATION *Narration* is writing that tells a story. The act of telling a story is also called narration. Each piece is a *narrative*. A story told in fiction, nonfiction, poetry, or even in drama is called a narrative.
See *Narrative, Narrative Poem,* and *Narrator*.

NARRATIVE A *narrative* is a story. A narrative can be either fiction or nonfiction. Novels and short stories are types of fictional narratives. Biographies and autobiographies are nonfiction narratives. Poems that tell stories are also narratives.
See *Narration* and *Narrative Poem*.

NARRATIVE POEM A *narrative poem* is a story told in verse. Narrative poems often have all the elements of short stories, including characters, conflict, and plot.

NARRATOR A *narrator* is a speaker or a character who tells a story. The narrator's perspective is the way he or she sees things. A *third-person narrator* is one who stands outside the action and speaks about it. A *first-person narrator* is one who tells a story and participates in its action.
See *Point of View*.

NONFICTION *Nonfiction* is prose writing that presents and explains ideas or that tells about real people, places, objects, or events. Autobiographies, biographies, essays, reports, letters, memos, and newspaper articles are all types of nonfiction.
See *Fiction*.

NOVEL A *novel* is a long work of fiction. Novels contain such elements as characters, plot, conflict, and setting. The writer of novels, or novelist, develops these elements. In addition to its main plot, a novel may contain one or more subplots, or independent, related stories. A novel may also have several themes.

See *Fiction* and *Short Story*.

NOVELLA A *novella* is a work of fiction that is longer than a short story but shorter than a novel.

ODE An *ode* is a formal lyric poem with a serious theme. It is usually long and may be written for a private occasion or a public ceremony. Odes often honor people, commemorate events, or respond to natural scenes.

See *Lyric Poem*.

ONOMATOPOEIA *Onomatopoeia* is the use of words that imitate sounds. *Crash, buzz, screech, hiss, neigh, jingle,* and *cluck* are examples of onomatopoeia. *Chickadee, towhee,* and *whippoorwill* are onomatopoeic names of birds.

Onomatopoeia can help put the reader in the activity of a poem.

ORAL TRADITION *Oral tradition* is the passing of songs, stories, and poems from generation to generation by word of mouth. Folk songs, folk tales, legends, and myths all come from the oral tradition. No one knows who first created these stories and poems.

See *Folk Tale, Legend,* and *Myth*.

PERSONIFICATION *Personification* is a type of figurative language in which a nonhuman subject is given human characteristics.

PERSPECTIVE See *Narrator* and *Point of View*.

PERSUASION *Persuasion* is used in writing or speech that attempts to convince the reader or listener to adopt a particular opinion or course of action. Newspaper editorials and letters to the editor use persuasion, as do advertisements and campaign speeches given by political candidates.

See *Essay*.

PLAYWRIGHT A *playwright* is a person who writes plays. William Shakespeare is regarded as the greatest playwright in English literature.

PLOT *Plot* is the sequence of events in which each event results from a previous one and causes the next. In most novels, dramas, short stories, and narrative poems, the plot involves both characters and a central conflict. The plot usually begins with an *exposition* that introduces the setting, the characters, and the basic situation. This is followed by the *inciting incident,* which

introduces the central conflict. The conflict then increases during the *development* until it reaches a high point of interest or suspense, the *climax*. The climax is followed by the *falling action,* or end, of the central conflict. Any events that occur during the falling action make up the *resolution,* or *denouement*.

Some plots do not have all of these parts. Some stories begin with the inciting incident and end with the resolution.

See *Conflict*.

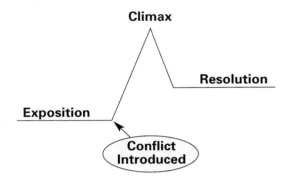

POETRY *Poetry* is one of the three major types of literature, the others being prose and drama. Most poems make use of highly concise, musical, and emotionally charged language. Many also make use of imagery, figurative language, and special devices of sound such as rhyme. Major types of poetry include *lyric poetry, narrative poetry,* and *concrete poetry*.

See *Concrete Poem, Genre, Lyric Poem,* and *Narrative Poem*.

POINT OF VIEW Point of view is the perspective, or vantage point, from which a story is told. It is either a narrator outside the story or a character in the story. *First-person point of view* is told by a character who uses the first person pronoun "I."

The two kinds of *third-person point of view,* limited and omniscient, are called "third person" because the narrator uses third-person pronouns, such as *he* and *she,* to refer to the characters. There is no "I" telling the story.

In stories told from the *omniscient third-person point of view,* the narrator knows and tells about what each character feels and thinks.

In stories told from the *limited third-person point of view,* the narrator relates the inner thoughts and feelings of only one character, and everything is viewed from this character's perspective.

In works written from a *subjective* point of view, the writer includes opinions and feelings. A work written from an *objective* point of view includes only facts, or an account of events.

See *Narrator*.

PROBLEM See *Conflict*.

PROSE *Prose* is the ordinary form of written language. Most writing that is not poetry, drama, or song is considered prose.

Prose is one of the major genres of literature and occurs in two forms—fiction and nonfiction.

See *Fiction, Genre,* and *Nonfiction.*

PROTAGONIST The *protagonist* is the main character in a literary work. Often, the protagonist is a person, but sometimes it can be an animal.

See *Antagonist* and *Character.*

REFRAIN A *refrain* is a regularly repeated line or group of lines in a poem or a song.

REPETITION *Repetition* is the use, more than once, of any element of language—a sound, word, phrase, clause, or sentence. Repetition is used in both prose and poetry.

See *Alliteration, Meter, Plot, Rhyme,* and *Rhyme Scheme.*

RESOLUTION The *resolution* is the outcome of the conflict in a plot.

See *Plot.*

RHYME *Rhyme* is the repetition of sounds at the ends of words. Poets use rhyme to lend a songlike quality to their verses and to emphasize certain words and ideas. Many traditional poems contain *end rhymes,* or rhyming words at the ends of lines.

Another common device is the use of *internal rhymes,* or rhyming words within lines. Internal rhyme also emphasizes the flowing nature of a poem.

See *Rhyme Scheme.*

RHYME SCHEME A *rhyme scheme* is a regular pattern of rhyming words in a poem. To indicate the rhyme scheme of a poem, one uses lowercase letters. Each rhyme is assigned a different letter, as follows in the first stanza of "Dust of Snow," by Robert Frost:

The way a crow	*a*
Shook down on me	*b*
The dust of snow	*a*
From a hemlock tree	*b*

Thus, the stanza has the rhyme scheme *abab.*

RHYTHM *Rhythm* is the pattern of stressed and unstressed syllables in spoken or written language.

See *Meter.*

ROUND CHARACTER See *Character.*

SCENE A *scene* is a section of uninterrupted action in the act of a drama.

See *Drama.*

SCIENCE FICTION *Science fiction* combines elements of fiction and fantasy with scientific fact. Many science-fiction stories are set in the future.

SENSORY LANGUAGE *Sensory language* is writing or speech that appeals to one or more of the five senses.

See *Image.*

SETTING The *setting* of a literary work is the time and place of the action. The setting includes all the details of a place and time—the year, the time of day, even the weather. The place may be a specific country, state, region, community, neighborhood, building, institution, or home. Details such as dialects, clothing, customs, and modes of transportation are often used to establish setting. In most stories, the setting serves as a backdrop—a context in which the characters interact. Setting can also help to create a feeling, or atmosphere.

See *Atmosphere.*

SHORT STORY A *short story* is a brief work of fiction. Like a novel, a short story presents a sequence of events, or plot. The plot usually deals with a central conflict faced by a main character, or protagonist. The events in a short story usually communicate a message about life or human nature. This message, or central idea, is the story's theme.

See *Conflict, Plot,* and *Theme.*

SIMILE A *simile* is a figure of speech that uses *like* or *as* to make a direct comparison between two unlike ideas. Everyday speech often contains similes, such as "pale as a ghost," "good as gold," "spread like wildfire," and "clever as a fox."

SOLILOQUY A *soliloquy* is a long speech, in a play or in a prose work, made by a character who is alone. The character reveals his or her private thoughts and feelings to the audience or reader.

SONNET A *sonnet* is a fourteen-line lyric poem with a single theme. Sonnets vary, but they are usually written in iambic pentameter, following one of two traditional patterns.

The *Petrarchan,* or *Italian, sonnet* is divided into two parts: an eight-line octave and six-line sestet. The octave rhymes *abba abba,* while the sestet usually rhymes *cde cde.* The two parts of this sonnet work together. The octave raises a question, states a problem, or presents a brief narrative, and the sestet answers the question, solves the problem, or comments on the narrative.

The *Shakespearean,* or *English, sonnet* has three four-line quatrains plus a concluding two-line couplet. The rhyme scheme is usually *abab cdcd efef gg.* Usually, each of the three quatrains explores a different variation of the main theme. Then, the couplet presents a summarizing or concluding statement.

See *Lyric Poem* and *Stanza.*

SPEAKER The *speaker* is the imaginary voice a poet uses when writing a poem. The speaker is the character who tells the poem. This character, or voice, often is not identified by name. There can be important differences between the poet and the poem's speaker.

See *Narrator.*

STAGE DIRECTIONS *Stage directions* are notes included in a drama to describe how the work is to be performed or staged. Stage directions are usually printed in italics and enclosed within parentheses or brackets. Some stage directions describe the movements, costumes, emotional states, and ways of speaking of the characters.

STAGING *Staging* includes the setting, the lighting, the costumes, special effects, music, dance, and so on that go into putting on a stage performance of a drama.

See *Drama.*

STANZA A *stanza* is a formal division of lines in a poem and is considered as a unit. Many poems are divided into stanzas that are separated by spaces. Stanzas often function just as paragraphs do in prose. Each stanza states and develops a single main idea.

Stanzas are commonly named according to the number of lines found in them, as follows:

- *Couplet:* two-line stanza
- *Tercet:* three-line stanza
- *Quatrain:* four-line stanza
- *Cinquain:* five-line stanza
- *Sestet:* six-line stanza
- *Heptastich:* seven-line stanza
- *Octave:* eight-line stanza

STATIC CHARACTER See *Character.*

SUBPLOT A *subplot* is a secondary story line that complicates or adds depth to the main plot.

SURPRISE ENDING A *surprise ending* is a conclusion that is unexpected. The reader has certain expectations about the ending based on details in the story. Often, a surprise ending is *foreshadowed,* or subtly hinted at, in the course of the work.

See *Foreshadowing* and *Plot.*

SUSPENSE *Suspense* is a feeling of anxious uncertainty about the outcome of events in a literary work. Writers create suspense by raising questions in the minds of their readers.

SYMBOL A *symbol* is anything that stands for or represents something else. Symbols are common in everyday life. A dove with an olive branch in its beak is a symbol of peace. A blindfolded woman holding a balanced scale is a symbol of justice. A crown is a symbol of a king's status and authority.

TALL TALE Most *tall tales* come out of the oral tradition of the American frontier. They typically involve characters with highly exaggerated abilities and qualities.

See *Legend, Myth, Oral Tradition,* and *Yarn.*

THEME The *theme* is a central message, concern, or purpose in a literary work. A theme can usually be expressed as a generalization, or a general statement, about human beings or about life. The theme of a work is not a summary of its plot. The theme is the writer's central idea.

Although a theme may be stated directly in the text, it is more often presented indirectly. When the theme is stated indirectly, or implied, the reader must figure out what the theme is by looking carefully at what the work reveals about people or about life.

TONE The *tone* of a literary work is the writer's attitude toward his or her audience and subject. The tone can often be described by a single adjective, such as *formal* or *informal, serious* or *playful, bitter,* or *ironic.* Factors that contribute to the tone are word choice, sentence structure, line length, rhyme, rhythm, and repetition.

TRAGEDY A *tragedy* is a work of literature, especially a play, that results in a catastrophe for the main character. In ancient Greek drama, the main character was always a significant person—a king or a hero—and the cause of the tragedy was a tragic flaw, or weakness, in his or her character. In modern drama, the main character can be an ordinary person, and the cause of the tragedy can be some evil in society itself. The purpose of tragedy is not only to arouse fear and pity in the audience, but also, in some cases, to convey a sense of the grandeur and nobility of the human spirit.

TURNING POINT See *Climax.*

VIGNETTE A *vignette* is a vivid literary sketch or brief narrative of a scene or an event that was memorable to the writer. It may be part of a longer work.

YARN A *yarn* is a folk tale—usually, a tall tale—about far-fetched characters and events.

See *Tall Tale.*

TYPES OF WRITING

NARRATION

Whenever writers tell any type of story, they are using **narration.** While there are many kinds of narration, most narratives share certain elements, such as characters, a setting, a sequence of events, and, often, a theme.

Autobiographical writing tells the story of an event or a person in the writer's life.

Biographical writing is a writer's account of another person's life.

Short story A short story is a brief, creative narrative—a retelling of events arranged to hold a reader's attention.

A few types of short stories are realistic stories, fantasy, science-fiction stories, and adventure stories.

DESCRIPTION

Descriptive writing is writing that creates a vivid picture of a person, a place, a thing, or an event. Descriptive writing can stand on its own or be part of a longer work, such as a short story.

Descriptive writing includes descriptions of people or places, remembrances, observations, vignettes, and character profiles.

PERSUASION

Persuasion is writing or speaking that attempts to convince people to accept a position or take a desired action. When used effectively, persuasive writing has the power to change people's lives. As a reader and a writer, you will find yourself engaged in many forms of persuasion.

Forms of persuasive writing include persuasive essays, advertisements, persuasive letters, editorials, persuasive speeches, and public-service announcements.

EXPOSITORY WRITING

Expository writing is writing that informs or explains. The information you include in expository writing is factual or based on fact. Effective expository writing reflects a well-thought-out organization—one that includes a clear introduction, body, and conclusion. The organization should be appropriate for the type of exposition you are writing. Here are some types of exposition:

Comparison-and-contrast essay A comparison-and-contrast essay analyzes the similarities and differences between two or more things.

Cause-and-effect essay A cause-and-effect essay is expository writing that explains the reasons that something happened or the results that an event or a situation will probably produce. You may examine several causes of a single effect or several effects of a single cause.

Problem-and-solution essay The purpose of a problem-and-solution essay is to describe a problem and offer one or more solutions to it. It describes a clear set of steps to achieve a result.

How-to essay A how-to essay explains how to do or make something. You break the process down into a series of logical steps and explain the steps in order.

Summary A summary is a brief statement of the main ideas and significant supporting details presented in a piece of writing. A summary should include

- main events, ideas, or images.
- connections among significant details.
- your own words.
- the underlying meaning rather than superficial details.
- background information, such as setting or characters.

RESEARCH WRITING

Writers often use outside research to gather information and explore subjects of interest. The product of that research is called **research writing.** Good research writing does not simply repeat information. It guides readers through a topic, showing them why each fact matters and creating an overall picture of the subject. Here are some types of research writing:

Research report A research report presents information gathered from reference books, observations, interviews, or other sources.

Biographical report A biographical report examines the high points and achievements in the life of a notable person. It includes dates, details, and main events in the person's life as well as background on the period in which the person lived. The writer may also make educated guesses about the reasons behind events in the person's life.

Multimedia report A multimedia report presents information gathered from a variety of reliable sources, both print and nonprint. A wide range of materials are available, such as tape recorders, videocameras, slides, photographs, overhead projectors, prerecorded music and sound effects, digital imaging, graphics software, computers, spreadsheets, databases, electronic resources, and Web sites.

I-Search report An I-Search report begins with a topic of immediate concern to you and provides well-researched information on that topic. Unlike a research report, it tells the story of your exploration of the topic, using the pronoun *I*. It explains

- your purpose in learning about the topic.
- the story of how you researched it.
- an account of what you learned.

RESPONSE TO LITERATURE

A **response to literature** is an essay or other type of writing that discusses and interprets what is of value in a book, short story, essay, article, or poem. You take a careful, critical look at various important elements in the work.

In addition to the standard literary essay, here are some other types of responses to literature:

Literary criticism Literary criticism is the result of literary analysis—the examination of a literary work or a body of literature. In literary criticism, you make a judgment or evaluation by looking carefully and critically at various important elements in the work. You then attempt to explain how the author has used those elements and how effectively they work together to convey the author's message.

Book or movie reviews A book review gives readers an impression of a book, encouraging them either to read it or to avoid reading it. A movie review begins with a basic response to whether or not you enjoyed the movie and then explains the reasons why or why not.

Letter to an author People sometimes respond to a work of literature by writing a letter to the writer. It lets the writer know what a reader found enjoyable or disappointing in a work. You can praise the work, ask questions, or offer constructive criticism.

Comparisons of works A comparison of works highlights specific features of two or more works by comparing them.

CREATIVE WRITING

Creative writing blends imagination, ideas, and emotions and allows you to present your own unique view of the world. Poems, plays, short stories, dramas, and even some cartoons are examples of creative writing. Here are some types of creative writing:

Lyric poem A lyric poem uses sensory images, figurative language, and sound devices to express deep thoughts and feelings about a subject. Writers give lyric poems a musical quality by employing sound devices, such as rhyme, rhythm, alliteration, and onomatopoeia.

Narrative poem A narrative poem is similar to a short story in that it has a plot, characters, and a theme. However, a writer divides a narrative poem into stanzas, usually composed of rhyming lines that have a definite rhythm, or beat.

Song lyrics Song lyrics, or words set to a tune, contain many elements of poetry—rhyme, rhythm, repetition, and imagery. In addition, song lyrics convey emotions, as well as interesting ideas.

Drama A drama or a dramatic scene is a story that is intended to be performed. The story is told mostly through what the actors say (dialogue) and what they do (action).

PRACTICAL AND TECHNICAL DOCUMENTS

Practical writing is fact-based writing that people do in the workplace or in their day-to-day lives. A business letter, memorandum, school form, job application, and a letter of inquiry are a few examples of practical writing.

Technical documents are fact-based documents that identify the sequence of activities needed to design a system, operate a tool, follow a procedure, or explain the bylaws of an organization. You encounter technical writing every time you read a manual or a set of instructions.

In the following descriptions, you'll find tips for tackling several types of practical and technical writing.

Business letter A business letter is a formal letter that follows one of several specific formats. (See page R16).

News release A news release, also called a press release, announces factual information about upcoming events. A writer might send a news release to a local newspaper, local radio station, TV station, or other media that will publicize the information.

Guidelines Guidelines give information about how people should act or provide tips on how to do something.

Process explanation A process explanation is a step-by-step explanation of how to do something. Your explanation should be clear and specific and might include diagrams or other illustrations to further clarify the process.

Proofreading and Preparing Manuscript

Before preparing a final copy, proofread your manuscript. The chart shows the standard symbols for marking corrections to be made.

Proofreading Symbols	
insert	∧
delete	ꝺ
close space	⌒
new paragraph	¶
add comma	∧
add period	⊙
transpose (switch)	∩
change to cap	a
change to lowercase	A

- Choose a standard, easy-to-read font.
- Type or print on one side of unlined 8 1/2" x 11" paper.
- Set the margins for the side, top, and bottom of your paper at approximately one inch. Most word-processing programs have a default setting that is appropriate.
- Double-space the document.
- Indent the first line of each paragraph.
- Number the pages in the upper right corner.

Follow your teacher's directions for formatting formal research papers. Most papers will have the following features:

- Title page
- Table of Contents or Outline
- Works-Cited List

Avoiding Plagiarism

Whether you are presenting a formal research paper or an opinion paper on a current event, you must be careful to give credit for any ideas or opinions that are not your own. Presenting someone else's ideas, research, or opinion as your own—even if you have rephrased it in different words—is *plagiarism*, the equivalent of academic stealing, or fraud.

Do not use the ideas or research of others in place of your own. Read from several sources to draw your own conclusions and form your own opinions. Incorporate the ideas and research of others to support your points. Credit the source of the following types of support:

- Statistics
- Direct quotations
- Indirectly quoted statements of opinions
- Conclusions presented by an expert
- Facts available in only one or two sources

Crediting Sources

When you credit a source, you acknowledge where you found your information and you give your readers the details necessary for locating the source themselves. Within the body of the paper, you provide a short citation, a footnote number linked to a footnote or an endnote number linked to an endnote reference. These brief references show the page numbers on which you found the information. Prepare a reference list at the end of the paper to provide full bibliographic information on your sources. These are two common types of reference lists:

- A **bibliography** provides a listing of all the resources you consulted during your research.
- A **works-cited list** indicates the works you have referenced in your paper.

The chart on the next page shows the Modern Language Association format for crediting sources. This is the most common format for papers written in the content areas in middle school and high school. Unless instructed otherwise by your teacher, use this format for crediting sources.

MLA Style for Listing Sources

Book with one author	Pyles, Thomas. *The Origins and Development of the English Language.* 2nd ed. New York: Harcourt Brace Jovanovich, Inc., 1971.
Book with two or three authors	McCrum, Robert, William Cran, and Robert MacNeil. *The Story of English.* New York: Penguin Books, 1987.
Book with an editor	Truth, Sojourner. *Narrative of Sojourner Truth.* Ed. Margaret Washington. New York: Vintage Books, 1993.
Book with more than three authors or editors	Donald, Robert B., et al. *Writing Clear Essays.* Upper Saddle River, NJ: Prentice-Hall, Inc., 1996.
A single work from an anthology	Hawthorne, Nathaniel. "Young Goodman Brown." *Literature: An Introduction to Reading and Writing.* Ed. Edgar V. Roberts and Henry E. Jacobs. Upper Saddle River, NJ: Prentice-Hall, Inc., 1998. 376–385. [Indicate pages for the entire selection.]
Introduction in a published edition	Washington, Margaret. Introduction. *Narrative of Sojourner Truth.* By Sojourner Truth. New York: Vintage Books, 1993, pp. v–xi.
Signed article in a weekly magazine	Wallace, Charles. "A Vodacious Deal." *Time* 14 Feb. 2000: 63.
Signed article in a monthly magazine	Gustaitis, Joseph. "The Sticky History of Chewing Gum." *American History* Oct. 1998: 30–38.
Unsigned editorial or story	"Selective Silence." Editorial. *Wall Street Journal* 11 Feb. 2000: A14. [If the editorial or story is signed, begin with the author's name.]
Signed pamphlet	[Treat the pamphlet as though it were a book.]
Pamphlet with no author, publisher, or date	*Are You at Risk of Heart Attack?* n.p. n.d. [n.p. n.d. indicates that there is no known publisher or date]
Filmstrip, slide program, or videotape	*The Diary of Anne Frank.* Dir. George Stevens. Perf. Millie Perkins, Shelley Winters, Joseph Schildkraut, Lou Jacobi, and Richard Beymer. Twentieth Century Fox, 1959.
Radio or television program transcript	"The First Immortal Generation." *Ockham's Razor.* Host Robyn Williams. Guest Damien Broderick. National Public Radio. 23 May 1999. Transcript.
Internet	*National Association of Chewing Gum Manufacturers.* 19 Dec. 1999 <http://www.nacgm.org/consumer/funfacts.html> [Indicate the date you accessed the information. Content and addresses at Web sites change frequently.]
Newspaper article	Thurow, Roger. "South Africans Who Fought for Sanctions Now Scrap for Investors." *Wall Street Journal* 11 Feb. 2000: A1+ [For a multipage article, write only the first page number on which it appears, followed by a plus sign.]
Personal interview	Smith, Jane. Personal interview. 10 Feb. 2000.
CD (with multiple publishers)	Simms, James, ed. *Romeo and Juliet.* By William Shakespeare. CD-ROM. Oxford: Attica Cybernetics Ltd.; London: BBC Education; London: HarperCollins Publishers, 1995.
Article from an encyclopedia	Askeland, Donald R. (1991). "Welding." *World Book Encyclopedia.* 1991 ed.

Formatting Business Letters

Business letters follow one of several acceptable formats. In **block format,** each part of the letter begins at the left margin. A double space is used between paragraphs. In **modified block format,** some parts of the letter are indented to the center of the page. No matter which format is used, all letters in business format have a heading, an inside address, a salutation or greeting, a body, a closing, and a signature.

These parts are shown and annotated on the model business letter below, formatted in modified block style.

Model Business Letter

In this letter, Yolanda Dodson uses modified block format to request information.

<table>
<tr>
<td>

The **inside address** indicates where the letter will be sent.

</td>
<td rowspan="5">

Students for a Cleaner Planet
c/o Memorial High School
333 Veterans' Drive
Denver, Colorado 80211

January 25, 20--

Steven Wilson, Director
Resource Recovery Really Works
300 Oak Street
Denver, Colorado 80216

Dear Mr. Wilson:

Memorial High School would like to start a branch of your successful recycling program. We share your commitment to reclaiming as much reusable material as we can. Because your program has been successful in other neighborhoods, we're sure that it can work in our community. Our school includes grades 9–12 and has about 800 students.

Would you send us some information about your community recycling program? For example, we need to know what materials can be recycled and how we can implement the program.

At least fifty students have already expressed an interest in getting involved, so I know we'll have the people power to make the program work. Please help us get started.

Thank you in advance for your time and consideration.

                            Sincerely,
                            Yolanda Dodson
                            Yolanda Dodson

</td>
</tr>
<tr>
<td>

The **salutation** is punctuated by a colon. When the specific addressee is not known, use a general greeting, such as "To whom it may

</td>
</tr>
<tr>
<td>

The **body** of the letter states the writer's purpose. In this case, the writer requests information.

</td>
</tr>
<tr>
<td>

The **closing** "Sincerely" is common, but "Yours truly" or "Respectfully yours" are also acceptable. To end the letter, the writer types her name and provides a **signature.**

</td>
</tr>
</table>

Key Word Search

Before you begin a search, you should identify your specific topic. To make searching easier, narrow your subject to a key word or a group of **key words.** These are your search terms, and they should be as specific as possible. For example, if you are looking for information about your favorite musical group, you might use the band's name as a key word. You might locate such information as band member biographies, the group's history, fan reviews of concerts, and hundreds of sites with related names containing information that is irrelevant to your search. Depending on your research needs you might need to narrow your search.

How to Narrow Your Search

If you have a large group of key words and still don't know which ones to use, write out a list of all the words you are considering. Once you have completed the list, scrutinize it. Then, delete the words that are least important to your search, and highlight those that are most important.

These **key search connectors** can help you fine-tune your search:

AND: narrows a search by retrieving documents that include both terms. For example: *baseball AND playoffs*

OR: broadens a search by retrieving documents including any of the terms. For example: *playoffs OR championships*

NOT: narrows a search by excluding documents containing certain words. For example: *baseball NOT history*

Tips for an Effective Search

1. Keep in mind that search engines can be case-sensitive. If your first attempt at searching fails, check your search terms for misspellings and try again.

2. If you are entering a group of key words, present them in order, from the most important to the least important key word.

3. Avoid opening the link to every single page in your results list. Search engines present pages in descending order of relevancy. The most useful pages will be located at the top of the list. However, read the description of each link before you open the page.

4. When you use some search engines, you can find helpful tips for specializing your search. Take the opportunity to learn more about effective searching.

Tips for Evaluating Internet Sources

Consider who constructed and who now maintains the Web page. Determine whether this author is a reputable source. Often, the URL endings indicate a source.

- Sites ending in *.edu* are maintained by educational institutions.
- Sites ending in *.gov* are maintained by government agencies (federal, state, or local).
- Sites ending in *.org* are normally maintained by nonprofit organizations and agencies.
- Sites with a *.com* ending are commercially or personally maintained.

Other Ways to Search

How you search should be tailored to what you are hoping to find. If you are looking for data and facts, use reference sites before you jump onto a simple search engine. For example, you can find reference sites to provide definitions of words, statistics about almost any subject, biographies, maps, and concise information on many topics. Some useful online reference sites:

Online libraries

Online periodicals

Almanacs

Encyclopedias

You can also use other electronic sources such as CD-ROMs. Ask a reference librarian to help you locate and use the full range of electronic resources.

Respecting Copyrighted Material

Because the Internet is a relatively new and quickly growing medium, issues of copyright and ownership arise almost daily. As laws begin to govern the use and reuse of material posted online, they may change the way that people can access or reprint material.

Text, photographs, music, and fine art printed online may not be reproduced without acknowledged permission of the copyright owner.

Applying Spelling Rules

Choosing Between *ie* and *ei*

When a word has a long *e* sound, use *ie*. When a word has a long *a* sound, use *ei*. When a word has a long *e* sound preceded by the letter *c,* use *ei*.

Long *e* Sound	Long *a* Sound	Long *e* Sound Preceded by *c*
believe	freight	deceive
grief	reign	receive

Exceptions: either, neither, seize, weird

Choosing the Ending *-cede, -ceed,* or *-sede*

There are ten words that end with this sound. You will need to memorize their spellings.

-cede Words	*-ceed* Words	*-sede* Words
accede	exceed	supersede
concede	proceed	
intercede	succeed	
precede		
recede		
secede		

Adding Prefixes

A *prefix* is one or more syllables added at the beginning of a word to form a new word. Adding a prefix to a word does not usually change the spelling of the original word.

re- + place = replace

un- + fair = unfair

mis- + spell = misspell

dis- + appear = disappear

il- + legal = illegal

Adding Suffixes

A *suffix* is one or more syllables added at the end of a word to form a new word. Adding a suffix often involves a spelling change in the original word.

Adding Suffixes That Begin With a Consonant

When adding a suffix that begins with a consonant—such as *-ly, -ness, -less, -ment,* and *-ful*—you usually do not change the spelling of the original word.

calm + *-ly* = calmly

open + *-ness* = openness

time + *-less* = timeless

employ + *-ment* = employment

help + *-ful* = helpful

Except for *truly, argument, judgment, daily*

Exceptions: If a word ends in *y* preceded by a consonant, change the *y* to *i* before adding these suffixes:

ready + *-ly* = readily

busy + *-ness* = business

Except for *shyness, slyly, spryness*

Adding Suffixes to Words That End in Silent *e*

If a word ends in a silent *e,* drop the *e* before adding a suffix that begins with a vowel.

love + *-able* = lovable

Except for *changeable, agreeable, useable*

Adding Suffixes That Begin With a Vowel to Words That End in *y*

When adding a suffix that begins with a vowel to a word that ends in *y* preceded by a consonant, change the *y* to *i* before adding the suffix.

greedy + *-er* = greedier

worry + *-ed* = worried

Exceptions: Do not change the *y* to *i* if the suffix begins with *i*—*carrying, babyish*

When adding a suffix that begins with a vowel to a word that ends in *y* preceded by a vowel, keep the *y* before adding the suffix.

portray + *-al* = portrayal

obey + *-ed* = obeyed

Exceptions: paid (not *payed*), said (not *sayed*), laid (not *layed*), gaiety (not *gayety*)

Doubling the Final Consonant Before Adding a Suffix
If a one-syllable word ends in a single consonant preceded by a single vowel, double the final consonant before adding a suffix that begins with a vowel.

stop + -ed = stopped

dim + -ing = dimming

Exceptions: Words that end in *x, y,* or *w* (*mixer, prayed, flowing*)

If a word of more than one syllable ends in a single consonant preceded by a single vowel and the accent is on the final syllable, double the final consonant before adding a suffix that begins with a vowel.

omit + -ed = omitted

occur + -ence = occurrence

Exceptions: Words in which the accent shifts when the suffix is added (*prefer—preference*)

Do not double the final consonant if the accent is not on the last syllable.

travel + -ing = traveling

endanger + -ed = endangered

Forming the Plurals of Nouns

Forming Regular Plurals The rules below apply to most nouns whose plurals are formed in regular ways.

Noun Ending	Rule	Examples
s, ss, x, z, zz, sh, ch	Add -es	circus, circuses
		lass, lasses
		fox, foxes
		waltz, waltzes
		buzz, buzzes
		bush, bushes
		church, churches
o preceded by a consonant	Add -es	potato, potatoes
		hero, heroes
		Exceptions:
		Musical terms—
		solo, solos
		piano, pianos

Noun Ending	Rule	Examples
o preceded by a vowel	Add -s	radio, radios
		patio, patios
y preceded by a consonant	Change y to i and add -es	party, parties
		enemy, enemies
y preceded by a vowel	Add -s	key, keys
		convoy, convoys
ff	Add -s	staff, staffs
		sheriff, sheriffs
fe	Change f to v and add -es	life, lives
		knife, knives
f	Add -s	chief, chiefs
		roof, roofs
	OR	
	Change f to v and add -es	leaf, leaves
		shelf, shelves

Forming Irregular Plurals The plurals of some nouns are formed in irregular ways. You will need to memorize these:

goose, geese	foot, feet
man, men	woman, women
ox, oxen	child, children
tooth, teeth	mouse, mice
deer, deer	sheep, sheep

Forming Plurals of Compound Nouns Most one-word compound nouns have regular plural forms. If one part of a compound word is irregular, the plural form will also be irregular.

flashlight, flashlights (regular)

handful, handfuls (regular)

stepchild, stepchildren (irregular)

The plurals of most compound nouns written with hyphens or as separate words are formed by making the modified word—the word being described—plural.

mother-in-law, mothers-in-law

Web site, Web sites

Forming Plurals of Proper Nouns To form the plurals of proper nouns, follow the same rules as with common nouns. In most cases, simply add -s to the proper noun. Add -es if the name ends in s, ss, x, z, sh, or ch.

> There are two Anns in our class.
>
> All of the Coxes arrived in one car.

For proper nouns ending in y, just add -s. Do not change the y to i and add -es.

> The Kennedys live in the house on the corner.
>
> There are two Kansas Citys; one in Missouri and one in Kansas.

Forming Plurals of Signs and Symbols Use an apostrophe and an -s to write the plurals of numbers, symbols, letters, and words used to name themselves.

> Business names often include &'s.
>
> All of the 6's were written as 9's.
>
> She received only A's and B's.
>
> You used too many and's in this sentence.

Writing Numbers

Spelling Out Numbers If a number begins a sentence, spell it out.

> *Twenty-two* players are on the field during a football game.

Within a sentence, spell out numbers that can be written in one or two words.

> There are *fifty-two* weeks in a year.

Spell out numbers used to indicate place or order.

> Shelley came in *second* in the race.
>
> This is the *fifth* day in a row that it has rained.

Using Numerals Use numerals for longer numbers that come within a sentence.

> Approximately *875* people attended the game.

If you include both small and large numbers in the same sentence, write them in the same way. It is best to use numerals.

> During a *12*-hour period, we counted *680* cars crossing the intersection.

Suggestions for Improving Your Spelling

Start a Personal Spelling List

Select the words that you have difficulty spelling, enter them in a special area in your notebook, and study them regularly. Add new words to your list, and cross out words you have mastered. You may find many of the words on your list among the Commonly Misspelled Words on the next page of this textbook.

Sound Out Difficult Words

Say the words aloud. Then, sound them out syllable by syllable as you study how to spell them.

Devise Memory Aids

Underline the part of a word that gives you the most trouble. Then, develop a memory device to help you remember the correct spelling.

Word	Memory Aid
des<u>s</u>ert	My des<u>s</u>ert is me<u>ss</u>y.
lib<u>ra</u>ry	lib<u>ra</u>ry b<u>ra</u>nch
ne<u>c</u>essary	Only one <u>c</u> is ne<u>c</u>essary.

Look for Roots and Derivatives

Many words have common *roots*. Look for the root inside a word to help you focus on its spelling. Then, use the root to help you spell related words.

> <u>bene</u>fit, <u>bene</u>ficial, <u>bene</u>factor
>
> pre<u>fer</u>red, re<u>fer</u>red, in<u>fer</u>red
>
> de<u>cide</u>, in<u>cid</u>ent, ac<u>cid</u>ent
>
> trans<u>mit</u>, trans<u>miss</u>ion, ad<u>mit</u>, ad<u>miss</u>ion

A *derivative* is a word that is formed from another word. Once you know how to spell a base word—the word from which the others are formed—you can more easily learn to spell its derivatives.

> de<u>cide</u>, de<u>cis</u>ion, de<u>cis</u>ive
>
> <u>caut</u>ion, <u>caut</u>ious, pre<u>caut</u>ion
>
> regu<u>lar</u>, regu<u>la</u>tion, regu<u>late</u>
>
> stro<u>ng</u>, stre<u>ng</u>th, stre<u>ng</u>then

Commonly Misspelled Words

The list of words on this page are words that cause spelling problems for many people. As you review the list, check to see how many of the words give you trouble in your own writing. Then, try some of the suggestions for improving your spelling discussed on the previous page to help you conquer these "spelling demons."

abbreviate	bicycle	criticize	grammar	naturally	realize
absence	bookkeeper	cylinder	grievance	necessary	really
absolutely	boulevard	deceive	guarantee	negotiate	receipt
accelerate	brief	decision	guard	neighbor	recipe
accidentally	brilliant	defendant	guidance	neutral	recognize
accurate	bruise	definitely	handkerchief	nickel	recommend
ache	bulletin	delinquent	harass	niece	rehearse
achievement	buoy	dependent	height	ninety	relevant
acquaintance	bureau	descendant	humorous	noticeable	reminiscence
adequate	bury	description	hygiene	nuclear	renowned
advertisement	buses	desirable	immediately	nuisance	repetition
aerial	business	dessert	immigrant	obstacle	restaurant
aggravate	cafeteria	dining	independent	occasion	rhythm
agreeable	calendar	disappoint	individual	occurrence	ridiculous
aisle	campaign	disastrous	inflammable	omitted	sandwich
all right	canceled	discipline	interfere	opinion	satellite
aluminum	candidate	eighth	irritable	opportunity	schedule
amateur	captain	eligible	jewelry	optimistic	scissors
analysis	career	embarrass	judgment	outrageous	secretary
analyze	carriage	enthusiastic	knowledge	pamphlet	siege
ancient	cashier	entrepreneur	laboratory	parallel	sincerely
anecdote	category	envelope	lawyer	paralyze	solely
anniversary	ceiling	environment	legible	parentheses	sponsor
anonymous	cemetery	equipped	legislature	particularly	subtle
answer	census	equivalent	leisure	patience	superintendent
anxiety	certain	especially	liable	permanent	surveillance
apologize	characteristic	exaggerate	library	permissible	susceptible
appall	chauffeur	excel	license	perseverance	tariff
appearance	clothes	excellent	lieutenant	persistent	temperamental
appreciate	colonel	exercise	lightning	perspiration	theater
appropriate	column	existence	likable	persuade	threshold
architecture	commercial	extraordinary	liquefy	phenomenon	truly
argument	commitment	familiar	literature	physician	unmanageable
associate	committee	fascinating	maintenance	pneumonia	unwieldy
athletic	competitor	February	marriage	possession	usage
attendance	condemn	fiery	mathematics	prairie	usually
awkward	congratulate	financial	maximum	preferable	valuable
banquet	conscience	fluorescent	meanness	prejudice	various
bargain	conscious	foreign	mediocre	prerogative	vegetable
barrel	convenience	forfeit	mileage	privilege	voluntary
battery	cooperate	fourth	millionaire	probably	volunteer
beautiful	correspondence	fragile	minuscule	procedure	weight
beggar	counterfeit	gauge	miscellaneous	pronunciation	weird
beginning	courageous	genius	mischievous	psychology	whale
behavior	courteous	genuine	misspell	pursue	wield
benefit	criticism	government	mortgage	questionnaire	yield

GRAMMAR AND MECHANICS HANDBOOK

Parts of Speech

Nouns A **noun** is the name of a person, place, or thing. A **common noun** names any one of a class of people, places, or things. A **proper noun** names a specific person, place, or thing.

Common Nouns	Proper Nouns
writer	Francisco Jiménez
city	Los Angeles

Pronouns A **pronoun** is a word that stands for a noun or for a word that takes the place of a noun.

A **personal pronoun** refers to (1) the person speaking, (2) the person spoken to, or (3) the person, place, or thing spoken about.

	Singular	Plural
First Person	I, me, my, mine	we, us, our, ours
Second Person	you, your, yours	you, your, yours
Third Person	he, him, his, she, her, hers, it, its	they, them, their, theirs

A **demonstrative pronoun** directs attention to a specific person, place, or thing.

this lamp	these rugs
that chair	those tables

An **interrogative pronoun** is used to begin a question.

Who is the author of "Jeremiah's Song"?

An **indefinite pronoun** refers to a person, place, or thing, often without specifying which one.

Many of the players were tired.

Everyone bought something.

Verbs A **verb** is a word that expresses time while showing an action, a condition, or the fact that something exists.

An **action verb** indicates the action of someone or something.

A **linking verb** connects the subject of a sentence with a noun or a pronoun that renames or describes the subject.

A **helping verb** can be added to another verb to make a single verb phrase.

Adjectives An **adjective** describes a noun or a pronoun or gives a noun or a pronoun a more specific meaning. Adjectives answer the questions *what kind, which one, how many,* or *how much.*

The articles *the, a,* and *an* are adjectives. *An* is used before a word beginning with a vowel sound.

A noun may sometimes be used as an adjective.

family home	*science* fiction

Adverbs An **adverb** modifies a verb, an adjective, or another adverb. Adverbs answer the questions *where, when, in what way,* or *to what extent.*

Prepositions A **preposition** relates a noun or a pronoun following it to another word in the sentence.

Conjunctions A **conjunction** connects other words or groups of words.

A **coordinating conjunction** connects similar kinds or groups of words.

Correlative conjunctions are used in pairs to connect similar words or groups of words.

both Grandpa *and* Dad	*neither* they *nor* I

Interjections An **interjection** is a word that expresses feeling or emotion and functions independently of a sentence.

"Ah!" says he—

Phrases, Clauses, and Sentences

Sentences A **sentence** is a group of words with two main parts: a complete subject and a complete predicate. Together, these parts express a complete thought.

We read that story last year.

A **fragment** is a group of words that does not express a complete thought.

"Not right away."

Subject The **subject** of a sentence is the word or group of words that tells whom or what the sentence is about. The **simple subject** is the essential noun, pronoun, or group of words acting as a noun that cannot be left out of the complete subject. A **complete subject** is the simple subject plus any modifiers. In the following example, the complete subject is underlined. The simple subject is italicized.

Pony express *riders* carried packages more than 2,000 miles.

A **compound subject** is two or more subjects that have the same verb and are joined by a conjunction.

> Neither the *horse nor the driver* looked tired.

Predicate The **predicate** of a sentence is the verb or verb phrase that tells what the complete subject of the sentence does or is. The **simple predicate** is the essential verb or verb phrase that cannot be left out of the complete predicate. A **complete predicate** is the simple predicate plus any modifiers or complements. In the following example, the complete predicate is underlined. The simple predicate is italicized.

> Pony express riders *carried* packages more than 2,000 miles.

A **compound predicate** is two or more verbs that have the same subject and are joined by a conjunction.

> She *sneezed and coughed* throughout the trip.

Complement A **complement** is a word or group of words that completes the meaning of the predicate of a sentence. Five different kinds of complements can be found in English sentences: *direct objects, indirect objects, objective complements, predicate nominatives* and *predicate adjectives.*

A **direct object** is a noun, pronoun, or group of words acting as a noun that receives the action of a transitive verb.

> We watched the *liftoff.*

An **indirect object** is a noun, pronoun, or group of words that appears with a direct object and names the person or thing that something is given to or done for.

> He sold the *family* a mirror.

An **objective complement** is an adjective or noun that appears with a direct object and describes or renames it.

> I called Meg my *friend.*

A **subject complement** is a noun, pronoun, or adjective that appears with a linking verb and tells something about the subject. A subject complement may be a *predicate nominative* or a *predicate adjective.*

A **predicate nominative** is a noun or pronoun that appears with a linking verb and renames, identifies, or explains the subject.

> Kiglo was the *leader.*

A **predicate adjective** is an adjective that appears with a linking verb and describes the subject of a sentence.

> Roko became *tired.*

Simple Sentence A **simple sentence** consists of a single independent clause.

Compound Sentence A **compound sentence** consists of two or more independent clauses joined by a comma and a coordinating conjunction or by a semicolon.

Complex Sentence A **complex sentence** consists of one independent clause and one or more subordinate clauses.

Compound-Complex Sentence A **compound-complex sentence** consists of two or more independent clauses and one or more subordinate clauses.

Declarative Sentence A **declarative sentence** states an idea and ends with a period.

Interrogative Sentence An **interrogative sentence** asks a question and ends with a question mark.

Imperative Sentence An **imperative sentence** gives an order or a direction and ends with either a period or an exclamation mark.

Exclamatory Sentence An **exclamatory sentence** conveys a strong emotion and ends with an exclamation mark.

Phrases A **phrase** is a group of words, without a subject and a verb, that functions in a sentence as one part of speech.

A **prepositional phrase** is a group of words that includes a preposition and a noun or a pronoun that is the object of the preposition.

> near the town   with them

An **adjective phrase** is a prepositional phrase that modifies a noun or a pronoun by telling *what kind* or *which one.*

> Mr. Sanderson brushed his hands over the shoes in the window . . . .

An **adverb phrase** is a prepositional phrase that modifies a verb, an adjective, or an adverb by pointing out *where, when, in what manner,* or *to what extent.*

> The trees were black where the bark was wet.

An **appositive phrase** is a noun or a pronoun with modifiers, placed next to a noun or a pronoun to add information and details.

> The story, *a tale of adventure,* takes place in the Yukon.

A **participial phrase** is a participle modified by an adjective or an adverb phrase or accompanied by a complement. The entire phrase acts as an adjective.

> *Running at top speed,* he soon caught up with them.

An **infinitive phrase** is an infinitive with modifiers, complements, or a subject, all acting together as a single part of speech.

> At first I was too busy enjoying my food *to notice how the guests were doing.*

Clauses A **clause** is a group of words with its own subject and verb.

An **independent clause** can stand by itself as a complete sentence.

> "I think it belongs to Rachel."

A **subordinate clause** has a subject and a verb but cannot stand by itself as a complete sentence; it can only be part of a sentence.

> "Although it was late"

Using Verbs and Pronouns

Principal Parts A verb has four **principal parts**: the *present,* the *present participle,* the *past,* and the *past participle.*

Regular verbs form the past and past participle by adding -ed to the present form.

> **Present**: walk
> **Present Participle**: (am) walking
> **Past**: walked
> **Past Participle**: (have) walked

Irregular verbs form the past and past participle by changing form rather than by adding -ed.

> **Present**: go
> **Present Participle**: (am) going
> **Past**: went
> **Past Participle**: (have) gone

Verb Tense A **verb tense** tells whether the time of an action or a condition is in the past, the present, or the future. Every verb has six tenses: *present, past, future, present perfect, past perfect,* and *future perfect.*

The **present tense** shows actions that happen in the present.

The **past tense** shows actions that have already happened.

The **future tense** shows actions that will happen.

The **present perfect tense** shows actions that begin in the past and continue to the present.

The **past perfect tense** shows a past action or condition that ended before another past action.

The **future perfect tense** shows a future action or condition that will have ended before another begins.

Pronoun Case The **case** of a pronoun is the form it takes to show its use in a sentence. There are three pronoun cases: *nominative, objective,* and *possessive.*

The **nominative case** is used to name or rename the subject of the sentence. The nominative case pronouns are *I, you, he, she, it, we, you, they.*

> **As the subject:** *She* is brave.
> **Renaming the subject:** The leader is *she.*

The **objective case** is used as the direct object, indirect object, or object of a preposition. The objective case pronouns are *me, you, him, her, it, us, you, them.*

> **As a direct object:** Tom called *me.*
> **As an indirect object:** My friend gave *me* advice.
> **As an object of a preposition:** The coach gave pointers to *me.*

The **possessive case** is used to show ownership. The possessive pronouns are *my, your, his, her, its, our, their, mine, yours, his, hers, its, ours, theirs.*

Subject-Verb Agreement To make a subject and a verb agree, make sure that both are singular or both are plural. Two or more singular subjects joined by *or* or *nor* must have a singular verb. When singular and plural subjects are joined by *or* or *nor,* the verb must agree with the closest subject.

> *He is* at the door.
> *They drive* home every day.
> Both *pets are* hungry.
> Either the *chairs* or the *table is* on sale.

Pronoun-Antecedent Agreement Pronouns must agree with their antecedents in number and gender. Use singular pronouns with singular antecedents and plural pronouns with plural antecedents. Many errors in pronoun-antecedent agreement occur when a plural pronoun is used to refer to a singular antecedent for which the gender is not specified.

>Incorrect: Everyone did their best.
>Correct: Everyone did his or her best.

The following indefinite pronouns are singular: *anybody, anyone, each, either, everybody, everyone, neither, nobody, no one, one, somebody, someone.*

The following indefinite pronouns are plural: *both, few, many, several.*

The following indefinite pronouns may be either singular or plural: *all, any, most, none, some.*

Glossary of Common Usage

accept, except *Accept* is a verb that means "to receive" or "to agree to." *Except* is a preposition that means "other than" or "leaving out." Do not confuse these two words.

>Aaron sadly *accepted* his father's decision to sell Zlateh.

>Everyone *except* the fisherman and his wife had children.

affect, effect *Affect* is normally a verb meaning "to influence" or "to bring about a change in." *Effect* is usually a noun, meaning "result."

among, between *Among* is usually used with three or more items. *Between* is generally used with only two items.

bad, badly Use the predicate adjective *bad* after linking verbs such as *feel, look,* and *seem.* Use *badly* whenever an adverb is required.

>Mouse does not feel *bad* about tricking Coyote.

>In the myth, Athene treats Arachne *badly.*

beside, besides *Beside* means "at the side of" or "close to." *Besides* means "in addition to."

can, may The verb *can* generally refers to the ability to do something. The verb *may* generally refers to permission to do something.

different from, different than *Different from* is generally preferred over *different than.*

farther, further Use *farther* when you refer to distance. Use *further* when you mean "to a greater degree or extent" or "additional."

fewer, less Use *fewer* for things that can be counted. Use *less* for amounts or quantities that cannot be counted.

good, well Use the predicate adjective *good* after linking verbs such as *feel, look, smell, taste,* and *seem.* Use *well* whenever you need an adverb.

hopefully You should not loosely attach this adverb to a sentence, as in "*Hopefully,* the rain will stop by noon." Rewrite the sentence so *hopefully* modifies a specific verb. Other possible ways of revising such sentences include using the adjective *hopeful* or a phrase like "everyone *hopes* that."

its, it's The word *its* with no apostrophe is a possessive pronoun. The word *it's* is a contraction for *it is.* Do not confuse the possessive pronoun *its* with the contraction *it's,* standing for "it is" or "it has."

lay, lie Do not confuse these verbs. *Lay* is a transitive verb meaning "to set or put something down." Its principal parts are *lay, laying, laid, laid. Lie* is an intransitive verb meaning "to recline." Its principal parts are *lie, lying, lay, lain.*

leave, let Be careful not to confuse these verbs. *Leave* means "to go away" or "to allow to remain." *Let* means "to permit."

like, as *Like* is a preposition that usually means "similar to" or "in the same way as." *Like* should always be followed by an object. Do not use *like* before a subject and a verb. Use *as* or *that* instead.

loose, lose *Loose* can be either an adjective (meaning "unattached") or a verb (meaning "to untie"). *Lose* is always a verb (meaning "to fail to keep, have, or win").

many, much Use *many* to refer to a specific quantity. Use *much* for an indefinite amount or for an abstract concept.

of, have Do not use *of* in place of *have* after auxiliary verbs like *would, could, should, may, might,* or *must.*

raise, rise *Raise* is a transitive verb that usually takes a direct object. *Rise* is intransitive and never takes a direct object.

set, sit *Set* is a transitive verb meaning "to put (something) in a certain place." Its principal parts are *set, setting, set, set*. *Sit* is an intransitive verb meaning "to be seated." Its principal parts are *sit, sitting, sat, sat*.

than, then The conjunction *than* is used to connect the two parts of a comparison. Do not confuse *than* with the adverb *then,* which usually refers to time.

that, which, who Use the relative pronoun *that* to refer to things or people. Use *which* only for things and *who* only for people.

their, there, they're *Their* is a possessive adjective and always modifies a noun. *There* is usually used either at the beginning of a sentence or as an adverb. *They're* is a contraction for "they are."

to, too, two *To* is a preposition that begins a prepositional phrase or an infinitive. *Too*, with two *o*'s, is an adverb and modifies adjectives and other adverbs. *Two* is a number.

when, where, why Do not use *when, where,* or *why* directly after a linking verb such as *is*. Reword the sentence.

Faulty:	Suspense is *when* an author increases the reader's tension.
Revised:	An author uses suspense to increase the reader's tension.
Faulty:	A biography is *where* a writer tells the life story of another person.
Revised:	In a biography, a writer tells the life story of another person.

who, whom In formal writing, remember to use *who* only as a subject in clauses and sentences and *whom* only as an object.

Capitalization and Punctuation Rules

Capitalization

1. Capitalize the first word of a sentence.

   Young Roko glances down the valley.
2. Capitalize all proper nouns and adjectives.

   Mark Twain   Amazon River   Thanksgiving Day
   Montana   October   Italian

3. Capitalize a person's title when it is followed by the person's name or when it is used in direct address.

   Doctor   General Khokhotov   Mrs. Price
4. Capitalize titles showing family relationships when they refer to a specific person, unless they are preceded by a possessive noun or pronoun.

   Granny-Liz   Margie's mother
5. Capitalize the first word and all other key words in the titles of books, periodicals, poems, stories, plays, paintings, and other works of art.

   from *Tom Sawyer*   "Grandpa and the Statue"
   "Breaker's Bridge"   "The Spring and the Fall"
6. Capitalize the first word and all nouns in letter salutations and the first word in letter closings.

   Dear Willis,   Yours truly,

Punctuation

End Marks

1. Use a **period** to end a declarative sentence, an imperative sentence, and most abbreviations.
2. Use a **question mark** to end a direct question or an incomplete question in which the rest of the question is understood.
3. Use an **exclamation mark** after a statement showing strong emotion, an urgent imperative sentence, or an interjection expressing strong emotion.

Commas

1. Use a comma before the conjunction to separate two independent clauses in a compound sentence.
2. Use commas to separate three or more words, phrases, or clauses in a series.
3. Use commas to separate adjectives of equal rank. Do not use commas to separate adjectives that must stay in a specific order.
4. Use a comma after an introductory word, phrase, or clause.
5. Use commas to set off parenthetical and nonessential expressions.
6. Use commas with places and dates made up of two or more parts.
7. Use commas after items in addresses, after the salutation in a personal letter, after the closing in all letters, and in numbers of more than three digits.

Semicolons

1. Use a semicolon to join independent clauses that are not already joined by a conjunction.

2. Use a semicolon to join independent clauses or items in a series that already contain commas.

> The Pengelly family had no say in the choosing of Lob; he came to them in the second way. . . .

Colons

1. Use a colon before a list of items following an independent clause.
2. Use a colon in numbers giving the time, in salutations in business letters, and in labels used to signal important ideas.

Quotation Marks

1. A direct quotation represents a person's exact speech or thoughts and is enclosed in quotation marks.
2. An **indirect quotation** reports only the general meaning of what a person said or thought and does not require quotation marks.
3. Always place a comma or a period inside the final quotation mark of a direct quotation.
4. Place a question mark or an exclamation mark inside the final quotation mark if the end mark is part of the quotation; if it is not part of the quotation, place it outside the final quotation mark.

Titles

1. Underline or italicize the titles of long written works, movies, television and radio shows, lengthy works of music, paintings, and sculptures.
2. Use quotation marks around the titles of short written works, episodes in a series, songs, and titles of works mentioned as parts of collections.

Hyphens

1. Use a **hyphen** with certain numbers, after certain prefixes, with two or more words used as one word, and with a compound modifier that comes before a noun.

Apostrophes

1. Add an **apostrophe** and *s* to show the possessive case of most singular nouns.
2. Add an apostrophe to show the possessive case of plural nouns ending in *s* and *es*.
3. Add an apostrophe and *s* to show the possessive case of plural nouns that do not end in *s* or *es*.
4. Use an apostrophe in a contraction to indicate the position of the missing letter or letters.

GRAMMAR, USAGE, AND MECHANICS EXERCISES

Parts of Speech

Exercise A Classifying Nouns Identify the underlined nouns in the following sentences as *collective, compound, common* or *proper*, and *singular* or *plural*.

1. The <u>Milky Way</u> is one of several hundred million <u>galaxies</u>.
2. The <u>sun</u>, the closest star to the Earth, is a typical star.
3. <u>Supergiants</u> are the largest known <u>stars</u>.
4. A <u>committee</u> of astronomers gave numbers to some stars.
5. In the second century A.D., <u>Ptolemy</u> compiled the first catalog of stars.

Exercise B Classifying Pronouns Label the underlined pronouns in the following sentences as *personal, demonstrative, interrogative*, or *indefinite* and as *singular* or *plural*.

1. <u>Who</u> designated stars by Greek letters?
2. Johann Bayer listed <u>them</u> in a star atlas in 1603; <u>it</u> included <u>many</u> that Ptolemy had not cataloged.
3. John Flamsteed listed <u>these</u> stars according to <u>their</u> constellations.
4. Most of our modern catalogs are not like <u>those</u> used earlier; instead, <u>they</u> use copies of photographs.
5. <u>Which</u> of the charts includes the southern sky?

Exercise C Recognizing and Classifying Verbs Write the verbs in the following sentences. Label each one *action* or *linking*. Include and identify all helping verbs. Classify action verbs as *transitive* or *intransitive*.

1. Many stars vary their brightness when they expand and contract.
2. They can become very brilliant and then fade within days.
3. Some stars' cycles will last for years.
4. Most variations in brightness may be invisible to the human eye.

5. Scientists say that even the sun has a cycle of brightness.

Exercise D Recognizing Adjectives and Adverbs Label the underlined words in the following sentences as *adjectives* or *adverbs*. Then, write the word each one modifies.

1. The star called Rigel in the constellation Orion has a <u>bluish-white</u> tint.
2. Orion is located <u>almost squarely</u> on the celestial equator.
3. The stars form a picture of Orion, a hunter from <u>Greek</u> mythology.
4. He is standing with an <u>uplifted</u> club.
5. Three bright stars <u>accurately</u> represent his belt.
6. To the south, <u>three fainter</u> stars form his sword.
7. Another constellation, Pleiades, is a <u>loose</u> group of almost 3,000 stars.
8. The cluster was <u>initially</u> named by the Greeks after the mythological "Seven Sisters."
9. Observers can <u>sometimes</u> see up to twelve of the stars without a telescope.
10. Pleiades lies <u>375</u> light-years from our solar system.

Exercise E Recognizing Prepositions Write the prepositions in the following sentences, and then write the object of the preposition.

1. Tycho Brahe, a Danish astronomer, made measurements of the solar system.
2. This data was the most reliable until the invention of the telescope in the seventeenth century.
3. Brahe studied law and philosophy at universities in Copenhagen and Leipzig.
4. At night, he was busy with his observations of the stars.
5. Johannes Kepler, his assistant until 1601, used Brahe's data to formulate his three laws of planetary motion.

Exercise F Identifying Conjunctions

Write the conjunctions in the following sentences, and label them *coordinating* or *correlative*.

1. Both North Star and Pole Star are names for the star that roughly marks the direction of the North Pole.
2. Pole Star has been used by sailors, for they needed to find their direction when sailing at night.
3. It is used today for determining latitudes and other measurements.
4. Not only is Polaris the current North Star, but it also is part of the Little Dipper constellation.
5. Polaris is very accurate, but in the future, other stars will point more accurately to the North Pole.

Exercise G Recognizing Interjections

Write an interjection that replaces the feeling shown in parentheses in the following sentences.

1. __(surprise)__! Did you see that meteor shower last night?
2. __(hesitation)__, I was not sure what that was.
3. __(disappointment)__, did that happen while I was sleeping?
4. __(amazement)__! I could not believe my eyes.
5. __(agreement)__, it is a natural event.

Exercise H Identifying All the Parts of Speech

Write the part of speech of the underlined words in the following paragraph. Be as specific as possible.

These large comets <u>were</u> first <u>explained</u> by Tycho Brahe. Sir Isaac Newton and <u>Edmond Halley</u> made important observations <u>about</u> comets. The <u>American</u> astronomer Fred Whipple first described a comet as a "dirty <u>snowball</u>," a combination of ice and dust. <u>Gee,</u> that may not sound very scientific, <u>but</u> it is true. <u>Many</u> of the different comets pass by the Earth. Some are <u>easily</u> visible to the human eye.

Exercise I Revising Sentences

Revise each sentence according to the directions in parentheses.

1. Halley's Comet is a famous comet. (Add an adverb that modifies *famous*.)
2. Halley's Comet was discovered by Edmond Halley. (Replace *Halley's Comet* with a pronoun.)
3. Before he made his discovery, people believed that comets traveled at random, with no set path. (Replace *he* with a proper noun.)
4. Halley believed, however, that comets traveled regular patterns. (Add a preposition before *regular*.)
5. Halley's Comet takes a time—approximately seventy-seven years—to travel its orbit. (Add an adjective to modify *time* and another adjective to modify *orbit*.)

Exercise J Writing Application

Write a short narrative about a trip into outer space. Underline at least one noun, pronoun, verb, adjective, adverb, preposition, conjunction, and interjection. Then, label the part of speech of each as specifically as possible.

Phrases, Clauses, and Sentences

> **Exercise A** Recognizing Subjects, Predicates, and Sentence Types Copy these sentences, underlining each simple subject once and each simple predicate twice. Then, identify each sentence as *declarative, interrogative, imperative,* or *exclamatory.*

1. Look at this globe. Here is Australia down in the Southern Hemisphere.
2. Wow! What a surprise that is!
3. Aborigines first migrated there and remained undisturbed until the seventeenth century.
4. Did not the first European settlers arrive at Botany Bay in 1788?
5. Were they British convicts? Please answer the question.

> **Exercise B** Identifying Complements
Write the complements in the following sentences, and label each *direct object, indirect object, predicate noun,* or *predicate adjective.*

1. Australia's mountains are not high.
2. In fact, Australia is almost the world's flattest landmass.
3. Australians gave the interior the name *Outback.*
4. The Central-Eastern Lowlands is an area extending from the Great Dividing Range to the Great Western Plain.
5. The Nullarbor Plain seems strange with its caverns and tunnels.

> **Exercise C** Recognizing Phrases Identify the underlined phrases as *prepositional, appositive,* or *participial.*

1. The climate of Australia varies <u>from region</u> to region.
2. The southern states—<u>warm, temperate regions</u>—have four seasons.
3. <u>Located in the Southern Hemisphere,</u> Australia has seasons opposite those in the Northern Hemisphere.

4. Queensland, <u>on the north coast,</u> experiences a great deal of rain.
5. However, <u>in the drier grasslands,</u> unpredictable rainfall must be supplemented <u>by irrigation.</u>
6. The deserts, <u>making up most of central and western Australia,</u> receive even less rainfall.
7. <u>Applying many modern irrigation</u> techniques, Australia has increased its agricultural production.
8. The Australian Alps, <u>a mountain range</u> in <u>New South Wales,</u> receives heavy snowfall.
9. <u>Lying in the temperate zone,</u> Tasmania has heavy rainfall and frequent winter storms.
10. Hot and dry winds are common <u>in the southern states.</u>

> **Exercise D** Recognizing Clauses Identify the underlined clauses as *independent* or *subordinate.* Identify the subordinate clauses as *adjective* or *adverb.*

1. The platypus is an aquatic mammal of the Monotreme order <u>that has a bill like a duck.</u>
2. The spiny anteater is also categorized as a Monotreme <u>because it is an egg-laying mammal.</u>
3. While the kangaroo is a marsupial, <u>it is still a type of mammal.</u>
4. Possums and koalas are marsupials <u>that live in trees.</u>
5. Marsupials are animals that give birth to live young <u>even though the young are then nourished in an external pouch.</u>

Exercise E Recognizing Sentence Structure

Label each sentence *simple, compound,* or *complex.*

1. Kangaroos' powerful hind legs are used for hopping, and their thick, long tails are used for balancing.
2. The large red or gray kangaroo may stand as tall as seven feet.
3. Wallabies and kangaroo rats are smaller animals that are also members of the kangaroo family.
4. Although it does not bark, the dingo is a doglike animal.
5. Rabbits, foxes, and cats were introduced into Australia by Europeans.

Exercise F Varying Sentences

Rewrite the following sentences according to the instructions in parentheses.

1. Australia has two species of crocodiles. (Start with "Actually.")
2. The larger crocodile lives in the northern coastal swamps and can grow to be twenty feet long. (Revise the sentence so that it begins with "Living in the northern coastal swamp.")
3. Smaller species of crocodiles can be found living contentedly in inland fresh water. (Revise sentence to begin with "In inland fresh waters.")
4. More than 370 species of lizards are living in Australia. (Invert the subject-verb order.)
5. About 100 species of venomous snakes live in Australia. (Start with "Australia" as the subject, and change the verb as necessary.)

Exercise G Combining Sentences

Rewrite the following sentences according to the instructions in parentheses.

1. Australian waters contain hundreds of sharks. Some are a danger to humans. (Combine into a compound sentence.)
2. Edible shellfish are abundant. Oysters, abalone, and crayfish have been exploited. (Combine by turning one sentence into a subordinate clause.)
3. Seals live around the southern coast. They also inhabit the surrounding islands. (Combine by making a compound verb.)
4. The waters around Australia support many fish. There are also many aquatic mammals. (Combine sentences by creating a compound direct object.)
5. The Queensland lungfish breathes with a single lung. It does this instead of using gills. (Combine by changing one sentence into a phrase.)

Exercise H Identifying and Revising Sentence Problems

Label the error in each item as a *fragment, run-on, double negative, misplaced modifier,* or *common usage problem.* Then, correct the errors.

1. Believe the Aborigines were always in Australia.
2. By taking advantage of low sea levels that allowed land travel, researchers think the Aborigines migrated to Australia.
3. Tasmania was once part of Australia, a rise in sea level made Tasmania an island.
4. The Aborigines did not have no domesticated animals other than the dingo.
5. There most recent history features the use of tools.

Exercise I Writing Application

Write a short description of a place you have visited. Vary the length and structure of your sentences. Circle at least three phrases and three clauses. Try to avoid fragments, run-ons, double negatives, misplaced modifiers, and the common usage problems you have studied.

Usage

Exercise A Recognizing the Principal Parts of Verbs Identify the principal part used to form the underlined verbs in the following sentences as *present*, *present participle*, *past*, or *past participle*.

1. Steve is buying my birthday presents at the local shopping center.
2. He has found some of the lowest prices at one of the stores.
3. Last year, I think I paid too much for his gift.
4. First, I put it in layaway, and I went back to get it a week later.
5. This year, I hope to enter the stores only once because I am going to make a list.

Exercise B Recognizing Verb Tense
Identify the tense of each underlined verb or verb phrase in the following sentences. Then, write the principal part used to form the tense.

1. For our vacation, I have been making a list of things that I think I will need.
2. It seems as though summer has taken a long time to arrive.
3. I am looking forward to a shopping trip with my mom and my best friend.
4. I had been hoping we would go this weekend, and we are!
5. We will go to the outlet center that has opened several miles away.
6. Before the outlets opened, the location had been mainly farmland.
7. We were sorry to see the farms go, but we are happy now to buy some of our favorite brands at discounted prices.
8. By the time we finish, we will have shopped for hours.
9. Nowadays, you will find outlet centers just off interstate highways all across the country.
10. Discount stores have found success in Canada and Western Europe, as well.

Exercise C Identifying Pronoun Case
Identify the case of each personal pronoun in the following sentences as *nominative*, *objective*, or *possessive*.

1. Most of us shop at our local supermarkets.
2. I remember my great-grandmother telling me that she grew up in a town without a supermarket.
3. Her times were very different from ours.
4. Before the Great Depression of the 1930s, most people bought their food and household items in many different shops.
5. For example, a person would buy his or her meat at a butcher shop, bread at a bakery, and milk and cheese at a dairy.
6. When supermarkets arrived on the scene, combining self-service with lower prices, they experienced immediate growth.
7. In addition, the spread of the automobile meant that shoppers could drive to a store and fill their cars with packaged groceries.
8. Now, in one place, we can buy all our food, cleaning products, greeting cards, batteries, and much, much more.
9. You can see how the supermarket got its name!
10. The theory of supermarkets has spread to other types of stores; it is called "low-cost mass distribution."

Exercise D Revising to Eliminate Errors in Agreement Revise the following sentences, eliminating errors in agreement. If a sentence has no errors, write *correct*.

1. A common sight in stores is the "sale" sign.
2. There is chains in many types of businesses.
3. Each town and city has their own branches of certain fast-food restaurants, banks, movie theaters, gas stations, and supermarkets.
4. The products or services of each branch of a particular chain is almost always the same.
5. The chicken burrito that a person buys for their lunch at one fast-food restaurant will

be just like the chicken burrito sold at another branch of the same chain.

6. Each of us probably has our own favorites.
7. Developers of the first chain stores were not sure that they would be successful.
8. However, the lower prices and convenience has made chains very popular.
9. Usually in charge of a chain store is managers rather than an individual owner.
10. Managers make the day-to-day decisions concerning their particular stores.

▶ **Exercise E** Writing Sentences With Modifiers Write sentences according to the instructions. Be careful to use the correct forms of modifiers, and make sure your comparisons are complete and logical.

1. Using the comparative form of *expensive*, write a sentence about a shoe store.
2. Using the superlative form of *comfortable*, write a sentence about a new pair of shoes.
3. Using the superlative form of *friendly*, write a sentence about the salesperson.
4. Using the comparative form of *few*, write a sentence about job opportunities at this shoe store.
5. Using the comparative form of *far*, write a sentence about the distance of the store from your home.
6. Using the positive form of *good*, write a sentence about transportation into town.
7. Using the comparative form of *bad*, write about the service in another shoe store.
8. Using the superlative form of *much* as an adverb, describe the variety of styles in the shoe store.
9. Using the comparative form of *quickly*, write about a decision concerning a pair of shoes.
10. Using the superlative form of *good*, describe a purchase.

▶ **Exercise F** Revising to Eliminate Various Usage Errors Rewrite the following paragraph, correcting errors in agreement and in the usage of verbs, pronouns, and modifiers.

As usual, my parents, brothers, sister, and me had different ideas about where we should go this summer. Each of my two brothers has their own favorite place for fishing, while my sister was insisting on the beach. My parents and me have different ideas. My father thinks that us should see someplace new; he wanted to camp and fish at the shore. His idea is not the most popularest since the rest of us want to be closer to stores, movies, and other conveniences. My mother wants to visit a city because you can do so much there. I think we should of drawn straws instead of arguing for so long.

▶ **Exercise G** Writing Application Describe a store in which you like to shop. Use a consistent verb tense, and check carefully for problems in agreement or in the usage of verbs, pronouns, and modifiers.

Mechanics

Exercise A Proofreading Sentences to Correct Errors in End Marks, Commas, Semicolons, and Colons Proofread the following sentences, inserting end marks, commas, semicolons, and colons where necessary. Eliminate unnecessary punctuation. Some items are questions.

1. There is an old palace located in the heart of Venice Italy
2. Called the Doges' Palace it was the residence of the elected rulers
3. The waterfront portion was built in 1340 the great balcony was added in 1404
4. Whose paintings cover the inner waiting room the Hall of the Cabinet, and the Hall of the Senate
5. Many rooms and ceilings were decorated by these Italian painters Tintoretto Bellini and Tiepolo
6. The palace contained offices meeting rooms and law courts
7. It also served as a prison: and it even held the famous Casanova
8. Wow You mean the notorious Italian adventurer
9. The Doges' Palace is connected to the New Prisons by a small stone bridge the Bridge of Sighs
10. Do you know the origin of the bridge's name

Exercise B Proofreading Sentences for All the Rules of Punctuation Proofread the following sentences. Correct all punctuation errors. In the first sentence, the guide's words are directly quoted. Some items are questions.

1. Did you hear the guide say Windsor Castle is the primary residence of British kings and queens
2. Begun in 1474 Saint Georges Chapel was completed by King Henry VIII in 1528
3. Tradition says that the Round Tower is built on the site where King Arthurs

Knights of the Round Table met
4. Valuable paintings statues and decorations are found in these state apartments Saint George's Hall the Waterloo Chamber and the Throne Room
5. Old Windsor was home to the Anglo Saxon kings in fact William the Conqueror built a castle nearby
6. Is that where Edward III met with the Knights of the Garter
7. Leading from Home Park to Great Park the tree lined road is more than three miles long
8. Did you know there was a very destructive fire there in 1992
9. What I cannot believe it
10. An article in the International Herald Tribune said it destroyed Saint George's Hall and the Waterloo Chamber.

Exercise C Proofreading a Page to Correct Punctuation Errors Proofread these paragraphs, supplying missing punctuation and correcting errors in usage of end marks, commas, semicolons, quotation marks, hyphens, and apostrophes.

Neuschwanstein Castle in Germany is one of the worlds best known castles? With it's turrets and tall archways; it looks like a medieval castle As a friend of mine who visited it exclaimed This castle is a real fairy-tale fantasy come true

It sits high on a hilltop overlooking the Alps, and a deep gorge. The castle was built between—1869 and 1886—for King Ludwig II. The room's feature murals and detailed carvings. The woodcarving in Ludwigs bedroom took four-teen carpenters 4 1/2 years to complete Do you think you can pronounce *Neuschwanstein.*

Revise the following sentences, adding the missing capital letters.

1. castles in europe developed from the ancient roman idea of walled cities.
2. from spain to transylvania, castles were almost always built for defensive purposes.
3. the word *castle* also refers to large residences like william randolph hearst's castle in san simeon, california.
4. the area of nairnshire in northern scotland is well known for cawdor castle.
5. segovia, spain, located on the eresma river, is known for the alcazar, a famous castle.
6. in torun, poland, there are the ruins of a castle of ancient knights.
7. the wittelsbach family, a german dynasty, took their name from their castle in bavaria.
8. one wittelsbach was count otto vi, who served the emperor frederick I; he was made a duke in 1180.
9. in 1020 bishop werner built habsburg castle on the aare river.
10. later divided into the austrian and spanish branches, the habsburg family ruled in europe for hundreds of years.
11. a result of world war I was the banishment of emperor charles I.
12. in england, king george III bought buckingham palace but sometimes lived at saint james's palace.
13. another castle, balmoral castle, is the british royal residence in scotland.
14. in central japan, the city of osaka features a park built on the site of a sixteenth-century castle.
15. on an island near tokyo, iwatsuki is a castle town that was founded in 1458.

▶ **Exercise E** Revision Practice: Dialogue Write the following sentences as a dialogue, inserting the proper capitalization and punctuation and beginning a new paragraph with each new speaker.

stan i just read a book about castles but i am confused about the difference between a castle and a palace said rebecca
from what i remember from history class replied stan castles used to be the same as fortresses
kate added oh like the tower of london where they kept prisoners
right you must have read shakespeares *richard III* exclaimed stan
richard put prisoners in the tower added kate
thats true said stan however british royalty lived in the tower of london until the time of queen elizabeth I
wait a second kate said i saw the movie *elizabeth* but i do not remember the name of her castle
stan replied as time went on, *castle* came to mean the same thing as a large mansion
i think i see said kate some palaces were originally fortresses and were rebuilt as luxurious resorts
buckingham palace was built only as a residence but never to be a safe place during battle said stan

▶ **Exercise F** Writing Application Write a brief dialogue in which you and a friend discuss your dream castle or palace. Be sure to follow all the rules of capitalization and punctuation.

Index of Authors and Titles

Page numbers in *italics* refer to biographical information.

Index of Skills

Index of Features

Farrar, Straus and Giroux, Inc., and Faber and Faber Limited "Valediction" by Seamus Heaney. Published by Farrar, Straus & Giroux in the U.S. in *Poems 1965–1975* by Seamus Heaney, copyright © 1966, 1980 by Seamus Heaney. Published by Faber and Faber Ltd. in the U.K. in *Death of a Naturalist* by Seamus Heaney.

Golden Books Family Entertainment "The Bride of Pluto" (retitled "Demeter and Persephone") from *Golden Treasury of Myths and Legends* by Anne Terry White. Copyright © 1959 Western Publishing Company, Inc. All rights reserved.

Reid Goldsborough "Let the reader beware" from *Reading Today*, August/September 1997. Reprinted by permission of the author.

Harcourt, Inc. "The Enemy" from *Once*, copyright © 1966 and renewed 1968 by Alice Walker. Reprinted by permission of Harcourt Brace & Company. "Fog" from *Chicago Poems* by Carl Sandburg, copyright 1916 by Holt, Rinehart and Winston and renewed 1944 by Carl Sandburg. Excerpt from *In Search of Our Mother's Gardens: Womanist Prose*, copyright © 1983 by Alice Walker, and "Women" from *Revolutionary Petunias & Other Poems*, copyright © 1970 by Alice Walker. "Seventh Grade" from *Baseball in April and Other Stories*, copyright © 1990 by Gary Soto. Reprinted by permission of Harcourt, Inc. Excerpt from "The Tale of the Unknown Island" by José Saramago. Copyright © 1998, José Saramago, English translation copyright © 1999 by Margaret Jull Costa.

HarperCollins Publishers, Inc. "Winter" from *Cotton Candy on a Rainy Day* by Nikki Giovanni. Copyright © 1978 by Nikki Giovanni. Reprinted by permission of HarperCollins Publishers, Inc. "How the Snake Got Poison" from *Mules and Men* by Zora Neale Hurston. Copyright © 1935 by Zora Neale Hurston. Copyright renewed 1963 by John C. Hurston and Joel Hurston. "A Boy and a Man" from *Banner in the Sky* by James Ramsey Ullman. Copyright © 1954 by James Ramsey Ullman. From *An American Childhood* by Annie Dillard. Copyright © 1987 by Annie Dillard.

HarperCollins Publishers and The Estate of Shel Silverstein "Sarah Cynthia Sylvia Stout Would Not Take the Garbage Out" from *Where the Sidewalk Ends* by Shel Silverstein. Copyright © 1974 by Evil Eye Music, Inc.

Harvard University Press "I'm Nobody" (poem #288) from *The Poems of Emily Dickinson*, Thomas H. Johnson, Editor, Cambridge, Mass.: The Belknap Press of Harvard University Press, Copyright © 1951, 1955, 1979 by the President and Fellows of Harvard College. Reprinted by permission of the publishers and the Trustees of Amherst College.

John Hawkins & Associates Inc. "My Furthest-Back Person—The African" by Alex Haley, published July 16, 1972, by *The New York Times Magazine*. Copyright © 1972 by Alex Haley. Reprinted by permission of John Hawkins & Associates.

Heinemann Educational "Tenochtitlan: Inside the Aztec Capital" from *The Aztecs* by Jacqueline Dineen. Copyright © 1992 by Heinemann Educational Publishers. Reprinted by permission of Heinemann Educational Publishers.

Helmut Hirnschall "I Am a Native of North America" by Chief Dan George, from *My Heart Soars*. Copyright © 1974 by Clarke Irwin.

Edward D. Hoch "Zoo" by Edward D. Hoch, copyright © 1958 by King Size Publications, Inc.; © renewed by Edward D. Hoch. Reprinted by permission of the author.

Hodder and Stoughton Limited From *Pandas* by Gillian Standring. Copyright © 1991 by Wayland Inc. Reproduced by permission of Hodder and Stoughton Limited.

Henry Holt and Company, Inc. "Stopping by Woods on a Snowy Evening" from *The Poetry of Robert Frost*, edited by Edward Connery Lathem. Copyright 1923, © 1969 by Henry Holt and Co. Reprinted by permission of Henry Holt and Company, LLC.

Houghton Mifflin Company "St. Crispian's Day Speech" from *Henry V* by William Shakespeare, G. Blakemore Evans (Editor), *The Riverside Shakespeare*. Copyright © 1974 by Houghton Mifflin Company. "Phaethon, Son of Apollo," from *Greek Myths*. Copyright 1949, © renewed 1977 by Olivia E. Coolidge. "Victor Edmundo Villaseñor" by Jim & Terry Willard, with Jane Wilson, from *Ancestors: A Beginner's Guide to Family History & Genealogy*. Copyright © 1997 by KBYU TV. Reprinted by permission of Houghton Mifflin Company. All rights reserved.

International Paper Company "How to Enjoy Poetry" by James Dickey from *The Power of the Printed Word*.

Japan Publications, Inc. "On sweet plum blossoms," "Has spring come indeed?" and "Temple bells die out" by Bashō, from *One Hundred Famous Haiku* by Daniel Buchanan. Copyright © 1973.

Adam Kate for Sammy Sosa "Mi Amigo Mark" by Sammy Sosa from *Time*, December 22, 1998, Vol. 152. Copyright © 1998 by Time, Inc.

Alfred A. Knopf, a division of Random House, Inc. "Mother to Son" from *The Collected Poems of Langston Hughes* by Langston Hughes, copyright © 1994 by The Estate of Langston Hughes. Used by permission of Alfred A. Knopf, a division of Random House, Inc.

Alfred A. Knopf Children's Books, a division of Random House, Inc. "The People Could Fly" from *The People Could Fly: American Black Folktales* by Virginia Hamilton, copyright © 1985 by Virginia Hamilton. Used by permission of Alfred A. Knopf Children's Books, a division of Random House, Inc.

Maxine Kumin c/o Giles Anderson "The Microscope" by Maxine Kumin. Copyright © 1963 by The Atlantic Monthly Company, Boston, Mass. Reprinted by permission of the author.

Little, Brown and Company Publishers "The Real Story of a Cowboy's Life" from *The West* by Geoffrey Ward. Copyright © 1996 by The West Book Project, Inc. "Justin Lebo" from *It's Our World, Too!* by Phillip Hoose. Copyright © 1993 by Phillip Hoose. Reprinted by permission of Little, Brown and Company Inc. "The Hippopotamus" from *Verses From 1929 On* by Ogden Nash. First appeared in *Saturday Evening Post*. Copyright 1935 by the Curtis Publishing Company. Copyright 1949 by Ogden Nash; renewed 1976 by Frances Nash, Isabel Nash Eberstadt, and Linell Nash Smith.

Liveright Publishing Company "In Just" by E. E. Cummings, copyright 1923, 1951, © 1991 by the Trustees for the E. E. Cummings Trust. Copyright © 1976 by George James Firmage, from *Complete Poems: 1904–1962* by E. E. Cummings, edited by George J. Firmage. Used by permission of Liveright Publishing Corporation.

Naomi Long Madgett "Life" from *Remembrances of Spring: Collected Early Poems*, Copyright © 1993. Reprinted by permission of the author.

The National Oregon/California Trail Center Excerpt from The National Oregon/California Trail Center Web site (www.noctc.org), by The National OR/CA Trail Center.

Charles Neider Excerpt from "The Californian's Tale" by Mark Twain, from *The Complete Short Stories of Mark Twain*. Copyright © 1957 by Charles Neider.

Huge Noyes, on behalf of the Trustees of Alfred Noyes "The Highwayman" from *Collected Poems* by Alfred Noyes (J. B. Lippincott).

NTC Contemporary Books "No Gumption" from *Growing Up* by Russell Baker. Copyright © 1982 by Russell Baker.

The Oakland Press "Toned-down 'Christmas Carol' has more spirit" by John Sousanis, from *The Oakland Press*, November 29, 2000, Vol. 156, No. 280. Copyright © 2000 The Oakland Press.

Harold Ober Associates Inc. "Stolen Day" by Sherwood Anderson, originally published in *This Week Magazine*. Copyright 1941 by United Newspapers Magazine Corp. Copyright renewed 1968 by Elanor Copenhave Anderson.

Oregon-California Trails Association Excerpt from "The Alford-Cameron Gravesite, Bruff's Camp" by Randy Brown and Reg Duffin. Copyright © 1991, 1998 by Oregon-California Trails Association, Independence, Missouri.

Raymond R. Patterson "Martin Luther King" by Raymond R. Patterson. Copyright © 1971 by Raymond R. Patterson. Reprinted by permission of the author.

People Weekly "Picks & Pans: A Christmas Carol (TNT)," by Terry Kelleher, from *People Weekly*, December 6, 1999, Vol. 52. Used by permission. All rights reserved.

G. P. Putnam's Sons, a division of Penguin Putnam Inc. "Two Kinds" by Amy Tan from *The Joy Luck Club*. Copyright © 1989 by Amy Tan. Used by permission. "Our Finest Hour" from *The Osgood Files* by Charles Osgood. Copyright © 1986, 1987, 1988, 1989, 1990, 1991 by Charles Osgood.

Random House, Inc. "Melting Pot" from *Living Loud* by Anna Quindlen, Copyright © 1987 by Anna Quindlen. Used by permission of Random House, Inc.

Reader's Digest "How Do Rainmakers Make Rain?" from *How in the World?* Copyright © 1994 The Reader's Digest Association Limited. Used by Permission of The Reader's Digest Association, Inc., Pleasantville, NY, www.rd.com.

Marian Reiner for Eve Merriam "Onomatopoeia" from *It Doesn't Always Have To Rhyme* by Eve Merriam. Copyright © 1964, 1992 Eve Merriam. "Thumbprint" from *A Sky Full of Poems* by Eve Merriam. Copyright © 1964, 1970, 1973 by Eve Merriam. Copyright renewed ©1992 by Eve Merriam. Used by permission.

Rock and Roll Hall of Fame and Museum From "New Exhibit: Let the Good Times Roll: A Tribute to Rhythm and Blues" and from *Joe Whitburn's Top R&B Singles 1942–1988*, Menomonee Falls, WI, Record Research, Inc. 1988. Reprinted by kind permission of the Rock and Roll Hall of Fame and Museum, Cleveland, Ohio.

St. Martin's Press, Inc., and Harold Ober Associates, Inc. "Cat on the Go" from *All Things Wise and Wonderful* by James Herriot. Copyright © 1976, 1977 by James Herriot.

William Saroyan Foundation "The Hummingbird That Lived Through Winter" from *Dear Baby* by William Saroyan. Copyright © 1935, 1936, 1939, 1941, 1942, 1943, 1944 by William Saroyan. By permission of the Trustees of the Leland Stanford Junior University.

Scholastic, Inc. "Bat Attacks?" by Laura Allen for *Science World Magazine*, May 11, 1998. Copyright © 1998 by Scholastic, Inc. Reprinted by permission.

Scribner, a division of Simon & Schuster Inc. "False Dawn" from *Old New York: Four Novellas* by Edith Wharton. Copyright © 1924 by D. Appleton & Co., copyright renewed © 1951 by William R. Tyler. "A Day's Wait" from *Winner Take Nothing* by Ernest Hemingway. Copyright © 1933 Charles Scribner's Sons. Copyright renewed © 1961 by Mary Hemingway. Excerpts from "The Ancient Enmity" (retitled "Rattlesnake Hunt") from *Cross Creek* by Marjorie Kinnan Rawlings. Copyright © 1942 by Marjorie Kinnan Rawlings; copyright renewed © 1970 by Norman Baskin and Charles Scribner's Sons. Reprinted with the permission of Scribner, a division of Simon & Schuster, Inc.

Seiko Corporation Excerpt from "How to Use Your New Alarm Chronograph Timer" from *The Operation Instructions Manual*, Seiko Corporation.

Simon & Schuster Books for Young Readers, an imprint of Simon & Schuster Children's Publishing Division "The Lion and the Statue," "The Fox and the Crow," and "The Town Mouse and the Country Mouse" from *The Fables of Aesop, Selected, Told Anew and Their History Traced* by Joseph Jacobs. Copyright © 1964 Macmillan Publishing Company. "Papa's Parrot" by Cynthia Rylant from *Every Living Thing* by Cynthia Rylant. Copyright © 1985 Cynthia Rylant. Reprinted with the permission of Simon & Schuster Books for Young Readers, an imprint of Simon & Schuster Children's Publishing Division.

The Society of Authors as the Literary Representative of the Estate of James Stephens "Washed in Silver" from *Collected Poems*. Copyright © 1943 by James Stephens. Reprinted by permission of the Society of Authors as the Literary Representative of the Estate of James Stephens.

Gary Soto "Oranges" by Gary Soto. First appeared in *Poetry*, copyright © 1983 by The Modern Poetry Association.

Sports Illustrated From "Golden Girls" by Johnette Howard, *Sports Illustrated*, March 2, 1998. Copyright © 1998 by Time Inc. Reprinted courtesy of *Sports Illustrated*. All rights reserved.

Rosemary A. Thurber and The Barbara Hogensen Agency "The Night the Bed Fell" by James Thurber. Copyright © 1933, 1961 by James Thurber, from *My Life and Hard Times*, published by Harper & Row. Reprinted by arrangement with Rosemary Thurber and The Barbara Hogenson Agency. All rights reserved.

Time Inc. "Burning Out at Nine?" by Nadya Labi, from *Time*, November 23, 1998. Copyright © 1998 by Time Inc. Reprinted by permission.

U.S. Naval Institute Press "Master Chief Carl M. Brashear, Navy Diver" by Paul Stillwell, from the *Naval Institute History Reference & Preservation* website (www.usni.org/hrp/oralhistory/brashear.htm). Copyright 2001 U.S. Naval Institute, Annapolis, MD. Used by permission.

Universal Studios International, Holland Excerpt from "Billy Elliot" by Lee Hall. Copyright © 2000 Universal Studios Publishing Rights, a division of Universal Studios Licensing.

University of Notre Dame Press From *Barrio Boy* by Ernesto Galarza. Copyright © 1971 by University of Notre Dame Press.

Viking Penguin, a division of Penguin Putnam "Was Tarzan a Three-Bandage Man?" from *Childhood* by Bill Cosby. Copyright © 1991 by William H. Cosby. Reprinted by permission of Viking Penguin, a division of Penguin Putnam Inc.

Villard Books, a division of Random House From *"Into Thin Air"* by Jon Krakauer. Copyright © 1997 by Jon Krakauer. Excerpt from "The Boxer's Heart" by Kate Sekules. Copyright © 2000 by Kate Sekules.

Ralph Vincienza Ltd. "A Colony in the Sky" by Kim Stanley Robinson, from *Newsweek*, September 23, 1996. Copyright © 1996 by Newsweek Magazine.

John E. Wiley & Sons, Inc. "Moving Mountains" from *Earth Science for Every Kid* by Janice Van Cleave. Used by permission.

Writers & Artists Agency "The Monsters Are Due on Maple Street" by Rod Serling. Copyright © 1960 Rod Serling. Copyright ©1988 by Carolyn Serling, Jodi Serling and Anne Serling.

Writer's House "The Iceman" by Don Lessem from *The Iceman*. Copyright © 1994 by Don Lessem.

Note: Every effort has been made to locate the copyright owner of material reprinted in this book. Omissions brought to our attention will be corrected in subsequent editions.

Cover and Title Page: *The Picnic Grove,* Martha Walter, David David Gallery, Philadelphia/SuperStock **vi:** Robert Frerck/Odyssey Productions/Chicago **vii:** © George E. Jones III/Photo Researchers, Inc. **viii:** AP/Wide World Photos **ix:** Corel Professional Photos CD-ROM™ **x–xi:** Jeff Greenberg/Southern Stock/PictureQuest **xi:** Photo Researchers, Inc. **xii–xiii:** Paolo Koch/Photo Researchers, Inc. **xiv–xv:** Chad Ehlers/Tony Stone Images **xvi (t.):** United States Naval Institute **xvi (m.):** © The Stock Market/Jim Foster **xvi–xvii (b.):** Brian Parker/Tom Stack & Associates **xix:** UPI/CORBIS-BETTMANN **xxi:** Corel Professional Photos CD-ROM™ **1:** © Steve Dininno/Stock Illustration Source, Inc. **2 (b.):** © 1998 ABC, Inc. All rights reserved. **2 (t.):** Frank Orel/Tony Stone Images **4:** The Bettmann Archive **6:** "Then Came a Dog and Bit the Cat" from *Had Gadya (Tale of a Goat),* 1919, E. Lissitzky, The Jewish Museum/Art Resource, NY. © 2000 Artists Rights Society (ARS), New York/VG Bild-Kunst, Bonn. **8:** *La Cour d'une Ferme,* Marc Chagall, Christie's Images, London, UK/Bridgeman Art Library, London/New York, © 2000 Artists Rights Society (ARS), New York/ADAGP, Paris **10:** Thomas Victor **14:** Courtesy of Amy Tan **16:** UPI/CORBIS-Bettmann **19:** Mandarin Square: Badge with peacock-insignia-3rd civil rank. China, 17th–20th century, Unknown artist, Yale University Art Gallery **21:** *Chinese Girl Under Lanterns,* Winson Trang, Courtesy of the artist **24:** Courtesy of Amy Tan **27:** *Portrait,* Pamela Chin Lee, Courtesy of the artist **28:** Robert Foothorap **33:** Hal Mayforth **34:** Myrleen Ferguson/PhotoEdit **36:** Corel Professional Photos CD-ROM™ **38–39 (t.):** Frank Orel/Tony Stone Images **38 (b.):** Courtesy of the Library of Congress **39 (b.):** The Granger Collection, New York **40 (t.):** Michael P. Gadomski/Photo Researchers, Inc. **40 (b.):** © Faber & Faber Ltd. **44:** © 1998 ABC, Inc. All rights reserved. **46:** Betty Press/Panos Pictures **51:** © 1998 ABC, Inc. All rights reserved. **52–53:** © Faith Ringgold, 1986, *The Purple Quilt* (detail), 91" x 72", acrylic on canvas with pieced fabric borders **54:** AP/Wide World Photos **59, 60:** Courtesy of Victor Villaseñor Representations **61 (b.):** KBYU-TV **61 (t.):** Courtesy of Victor Villaseñor **62:** Culver Pictures, Inc. **64:** Corel Professional Photos CD-ROM™ **66:** CORBIS-BETTMANN **72:** Oscar Burriel/Photo Researchers, Inc. **74:** Herve Pelletier/SuperStock **76:** Larry Burrows/Life Magazine © Time Warner Inc.; **80:** The Granger Collection, New York **82:** Culver Pictures, Inc. **84:** Globe Photos **85:** *Three Fruit,* Ashton Hinrichs/SuperStock **86:** Dianne Trejo **94:** © Ian Shaw/Stone **100–101:** © David Ridley/Stock Illustration Source, Inc. **102, 104, 106, 109:** Corel Professional Photos CD-ROM™ **110:** Thomas Victor **114:** Vicky Kasala/The Image Bank **116:** David Young-Wolff/PhotoEdit **118:** Bob Daemmrich/The Image Works **120:** Macduff Everton/CORBIS **121:** Courtesy of the Author. Photo by Carolyn Soto **122:** *Sunday Afternoon,* Ralph Fasanella **124:** John Barrett/Globe Photos **128:** Chris Thomaidis/Tony Stone Images **130:** Photo Researchers, Inc. **131:** Courtesy of the Library of Congress **132–133:** Chris Thomaidis/Tony Stone Images **133 (b.):** *Rudyard Kipling,* oil on canvas, P. Burne-Jones, Courtesy of the National Portrait Gallery, London **134:** Photo by Bachrach **142:** *Organdy Collar,* 1936, Edmund Archer, Collection of Whitney Museum of American Art **144:** New York Public Library **145:** Nationwide News Service **146:** Corel Professional Photos CD-ROM™ **148:** CORBIS-Bettmann **153:** CORBIS **156:** ©1998 VCG/FPG International Corp. **162–163:** © Art Valero/Stock Illustration Source, Inc. **164 (l.):** Pal Hermansen/Tony Stone Images **164 (r.), 66:** Corel Professional Photos CD-ROM™ **168:** Alan Briere/SuperStock **170–171:** Hideki Fujii/The Image Bank **170: (inset top and bottom)** Corel Professional Photos CD-ROM™ **170: (in set middle)** Digital Imagery © Copyright 2001 PhotoDisc, Inc. **173:** Pal Hermansen/Tony Stone Images **178:** © Jean-Marc Boivin/Photo Researchers, Inc. **180–181:** Tony Stone Images **182:** © D.C. Lowe/Stone **185:** © Jean-Marc Boivin/Photo Researchers, Inc. **186:** AP/Wide World Photos **188:** Jose Azel/Aurora/PictureQuest **189:** AP/Wide World Photos **190:** Corel Professional Photos CD-ROM™ **191:** The Image Works **192:** ©1997 Linda M. Morre/Villard Books **196:** Courtesy of the Director, National Army Museum, London **198:** *Charge of the Light Brigade at the Battle of Balaklava,* 1854, Artist Unknown/SuperStock **200 (t.):** *Alfred Lord Tennyson,* c.1840, S. Laurence, Courtesy of the National Portrait Gallery, London **200 (b.):** Andre

Jenny/Focus Group/PictureQuest **201:** Thomas Victor **202:** © United Artists/Archive Photos **204:** *William Shakespeare,* (detail), Artist unknown, by courtesy of the National Portrait Gallery, London **209:** AP/Wide World Photos **210, 215:** © The Stock Market/Jeffrey W. Myers **218:** © IFA Bilderteam/eStock Photography/PictureQuest **219:** The Mark Twain House, Hartford, CT **220 (b.):** Thomas Victor **220 (t.):** Dennis Junor/Photo Network/PictureQuest **224, 226–227:** © R.G.K. Photography/Stone **227:** Dimitri Kessel/Life Magazine **228:** *La Bonne Aventure (Good Fortune),*1939, René Magritte, Gouache on paper, 33.5 x 40.7 cm., Museum Boymans-van Beuningen, Rotterdam, © 2000 C. Herscovici, Brussels/Artists Rights Society (ARS), New York **229:** Courtesy of the Library of Congress **230:** AP/Wide World Photos **235:** ©Visuals Unlimited **236:** Innerspace Visions **239:** Liaison Agency **242:** David Young-Wolff/PhotoEdit/PictureQuest **248–249:** *Signs,* Robert Vickrey, In the Collection of the Corcoran Gallery of Art **250 (r.):** Bill Bachmann/New England Stock Photo **250 (l.), 252:** "Briggs Suffocating" by James Thurber, Barbara Hogenson Agency, Photo by Eric H. Antoniou **256:** *My Life and Hard Times* Copyright © 1933 by James Thurber. Copyright © renewed 1961 by James Thurber. Reprinted by arrangement with Rosemary A. Thurber and The Barbara Hogenson Agency **258 (l.):** "Briggs and Rex" by James Thurber, Barbara Hogenson Agency, Photo by Eric H. Antoniou **258 (r.):** CORBIS-Bettmann **262, 264:** Dr. E.R. Degginger **267:** *Untitled,* Rob Wood, Illustration by Wood Ronsaville Harlin, Inc. **268:** *A New Planet,* K.F. Yuon, Tretiakov Gallery, Moscow, Russia/SuperStock **270:** Thomas Victor **274:** Digital Imagery © Copyright 2001 PhotoDisc, Inc. **276:** © Herman Eisenbeiss/Photo Researchers, Inc. **280:** UPI/CORBIS-BETTMANN **281:** Digital Imagery © Copyright 2001 PhotoDisc, Inc. **282:** Kansas State Historical Society, Topeka, Kansas **284:** Villard Books, photo © John Isaac **288:** Bryce Flynn/Stock, Boston/PNI **290–291:** © David Madison 1997 **293:** Jeff Greenberg/Stock, Boston **296, 297:** © David Madison 1997 **298:** Arte Público Press **299 (b.):** *Thomas Hardy* (detail), R.G. Eres, by courtesy of the National Portrait Gallery, London **299 (t.):** © Zandria Muench /Stone **300–301:** Bryce Flynn/Stock, Boston/PNI **303:** Bill Bachmann/New England Stock Photo **304:** SuperStock **305:** Richard Connelly **306 (b.):** Photo by Michael Nye **306 (t.):** Jeff Greenberg/Omni-Photo Communications, Inc. **310 (t.):** Jacket design: Daniel Rembert; Jacket photograph: Michael McLaughlin **310 (b.):** Cover art © 2000 Universal Studios Publishing Rights, Courtesy of Universal Studios Publishing Rights, a division of Universal Studios Licensing, Inc. All Rights Reserved. **311 (b.):** © Marion Ettlinger **311 (t.):** © Stewart Cohen/Stone **312:** Photofest **315 (all):** © Beverly Hesse Photo **319:** NASA **322:** Nancy Sheehan/PhotoEdit **328–329:** *Snap the Whip,* Winslow Homer, Butler Institute of American Art, Youngstown, Ohio, Bridgeman Art Library, London/SuperStock **330 (b.):** Christian Grzimek/OKAPIA/Photo Researchers, Inc. **330 (t.):** John Lei/Stock, Boston **332:** CBS Photo Archive **334–335:** Jeff Greenberg/Southern Stock/PictureQuest **336:** CBS Photo Archive **340:** *Happy Cat,* Private Collection/Christian Pierre/SuperStock **342:** Gunnar Kullenberg/SuperStock **346:** Christian Grzimek/OKAPIA/Photo Researchers, Inc. **350:** Hans Reinhard/OKAPIA/OKAPIA/ Photo Researchers, Inc. **354:** John Wyand **358:** Charles Gupton/Tony Stone Images **360:** © Tom & Dee Ann McCarthy/PhotoEdit **362:** Rollie McKenna **363:** John Lei/Stock, Boston **364:** *E. E. Cummings* (detail), 1958, Self Portrait, The National Portrait Gallery, Smithsonian Institution, Washington, D.C./Art Resource, New York; **365 (t.l.):** Photo Researchers, Inc. **365 (b.):** Photo by Victor Kumin **365 (t.r.):** Corel Professional Photos CD-ROM™ **366, 367 (t.):** Illustration from *Where the Sidewalk Ends* © 1974 by Evil Eye Music, Inc. Used by permission of HarperCollins Publishers **367 (b.):** AP/Wide World Photos **368:** *You Are Old, Father William,* 1865, Sir John Tenniel, The Granger Collection, New York **370 (b.):** New York Public Library Picture Collection **370 (t.):** *You Are Old, Father William,* 1865, Sir John Tenniel, The Granger Collection, New York **375:** © David Young-Wolff/Stone **378:** Steve Bly/Stone **382:** Photo by Patricia M. Hoch **383 (t.):** Corel Professional Photos CD-ROM™ **383 (b.):** UPI/ CORBIS-BETTMANN **384–385:** © The Stock Market/Paul Loven **386:** Courtesy of the Estate of Carl Van Vechten, Joseph Solomon, EXECUTOR, The National Portrait Gallery, Smithsonian

Institution, Washington, D.C./Art Resource, New York **390:** Cover illustration from *The Tale of the Unknown Island* by José Saramago, illustration copyright © 2000 by Peter Sis, reprinted by permission of Harcourt, Inc. **391:** Reuters NewMedia Inc./CORBIS **393:** Reuters/Gary Caskey/Archive Photos **396:** Andy Sacks/Stone **402–403:** *Negro Boys on the Quayside,* c.1880s, oil/panel 40x49 cm, David Norslup, © Corcoran Gallery of Art **404 (t.):** Clem Haagner/Photo Researchers, Inc. **404 (b.):** Hulton Getty Images/Tony Stone Images **406:** Paolo Koch/Photo Researchers, Inc. **409:** Clem Haagner/Photo Researchers, Inc. **410–411:** E. Hanumantha Rao/Photo Researchers, Inc. **413:** © Joel Simon/Stone **418–419:** Paolo Koch/Photo Researchers, Inc. **421:** R. Dev/Photo Researchers, Inc. **422:** *Rudyard Kipling,* oil on canvas, P. Burne-Jones, by Courtesy of the National Portrait Gallery, London **426:** © Hirz/Archive Photos **428–429:** *Nighthawks,* 1942, Edward Hopper, oil on canvas, 84.1 x 152.4 cm., Friends of American Art Collection 1942.51. photograph © 1998, The Art Institute of Chicago. All Rights Reserved. **432:** CORBIS-Bettmann **436:** Brian Parker/Tom Stack & Associates **438:** Digital Imagery © Copyright 2001 PhotoDisc, Inc. **441:** Corel Professional Photos CD-ROM™ **446:** United States Holocaust Memorial Museum **449:** George Kadish, courtesy of United States Holocaust Memorial Museum Photo Archives **450:** Main Commission for the Investigation of Nazi War Crimes, courtesy of United States Holocaust Memorial Museum Photo Archives **452:** Shraga Wainer, courtesy of United States Holocaust Memorial Museum Photo Archives **453:** Hikaru Iwasaki/United States Holocaust Memorial Museum **455:** Hulton Getty Images/Tony Stone Images **456:** Prentice Hall **460:** *Garden in the interior of a palace: a young lady and her servant,* from *Recueil de miniatures,* Giraudon/Art Resource, NY **462:** *Farmyard with woman milking cow,* from the *Da Costa Book of Hours,* Bruges, c. 1515, The Pierpont Morgan Library/Art Resource, NY **464:** *Four Piece Orchestra,* 1944, Ben Shahn, © Estate of Ben Shahn/Licensed by VAGA, New York, NY **466:** © 1990 Terry Heffernan **469:** *Three Studies of a Dancer in Fourth Position,* Charcoal and pastel with stumping, with touches of brush and black wash on greyish-tan laid paper with blue fibers (discolored from pinkish-blue). c. 1879/80, 48 x 61.5 cm. Bequest of Adele R. Levy, 1962.703. Photograph © 1994, The Art Institute of Chicago. All rights reserved. **470:** *Madame X,* 1993, Hung Liu, Courtesy Steinbaum Krauss Gallery, New York, New York **472:** © 1990 Terry Heffernan **474:** Permission granted by Troll Communications, LLC **475:** *Morning at the Jackson Ave. Ferry,* Gilbert Fletcher, Courtesy of the artist **478:** *Four Piece Orchestra,* 1944, Ben Shahn, © Estate of Ben Shahn/Licensed by VAGA, New York, NY **481:** *Disequilibrium,* 1987, Catherine Redmond, Courtesy of the artist **482:** Digital Imagery © Copyright 2001 PhotoDisc, Inc. **484:** John Craig Photo **489, 490:** Rock and Roll Hall of Fame and Museum, Michael Ochs Archives/Venice, CA **492:** Robert Dawson/Index Stock Imagery/PictureQuest **494:** *The Pond,* 1985, Adele Alsop, Courtesy of Schmidt Bingham Gallery, NYC. **496–497:** John Cancalosi/Stock, Boston/PictureQuest **498:** UPI/CORBIS-BETTMANN **506:** Comstock, Inc. **512–513:** *The Mellow Pad,* 1945–51, Stuart Davis, The Brooklyn Museum **514 (m.):** The Granger Collection, New York **514 (t.):** *Saturday Evening Post* Cover, August 10, 1935, Illustrated by G. Brehm, © The Curtis Publishing Company **514:** S. Dimmitt/Photo Researchers, Inc. **516:** *Buffalo,* 1992, Jaune Smith, Collection Eleanor and Len Flomenhaft, Courtesy Steinbaum Krauss Gallery, NYC **518:** S. Dimmitt/Photo Researchers, Inc. **521:** © Tom Bean/Stone **522:** AP/Wide World Photos **523:** John Lei/Omni-Photo Communications, Inc. **525:** © Richard Hutchings/PhotoEdit **527:** Mae Galarza **528–529:** Corel Professional Photos CD-ROM™ **530:** *Buffalo,* 1992, Jaune Smith, Collection Eleanor and Len Flomenhaft, Courtesy Steinbaum Krauss Gallery, NYC **531:** Alan Markfield/Globe Photos **532, 534:** UPI/CORBIS-BETTMANN **539:** The Granger Collection, New York **542:** *The Starry Night,* 1889, Vincent van Gogh, Oil on canvas, 29 x 36 1/4", Collection, The Museum of Modern Art, New York, Acquired through the Lillie P. Bliss Bequest **545:** *Simultaneous Contrasts: Sun and Moon,* 1913, Robert Delaunay, Oil on canvas, 53" diameter, Collection, The Museum of Modern Art, New York, Mrs. Simon Guggenheim Fund **547:** *The Starry Night,* 1889, Vincent van Gogh, Oil on canvas, 29 x 36 1/4", Collection, The Museum of Modern Art, New York, Acquired through the Lillie P. Bliss Bequest **548:** Thomas Victor **552:** © The

Stock Market/H. Armstrong Roberts **554:** *Saturday Evening Post* Cover, 1937, Illustrated by Frances Tipton Hunter, © The Curtis Publishing Company **556, 557:** Reprinted by permission of Don Congdon Associates, Inc. Copyright © 1982 by Russell Baker **559:** *Saturday Evening Post* Cover, March 28, 1931, © The Curtis Publishing Company, Illustrator: Norman Rockwell, Printed by permission of the Norman Rockwell Family Trust Copyright © 1931 the Norman Rockwell Family Trust **560 (b.):** *Saturday Evening Post* Cover, September 2, 1939, © The Curtis Publishing Company, Illustrator: Norman Rockwell. Printed by permission of the Norman Rockwell Family Trust Copyright © 1939 the Norman Rockwell Family Trust **560 (t.):** *Saturday Evening Post* Cover, August 10, 1935, Illustrated by G. Brehm, © The Curtis Publishing Company **561:** CORBIS-BETTMANN **562:** Annie Griffiths/DRK Photo **564:** Yuri Dojc/The Image Bank **566:** Thomas Victor **570, 572:** AP/Wide World Photos **574:** © Allsport/D. Stohmeyer **576:** Courtesy, William Lace **580, 581:** AFP/CORBIS **583:** Animals Animals © Zig Leszczynski **586:** © CORBIS/The Stock Market/Jose L. Palaez **594–595:** *Performers,* Freshman Brown, SuperStock **596:** Jim Baker as Ghost of Christmas Present in the Guthrie Theatre's 1975 production of *A Christmas Carol,* adapted by Barbara Field. Photo credit: Michal Daniel. **598:** Richard Ooms as Ebenezer Scrooge in the Guthrie Theatre's 1994 production of *A Christmas Carol,* adapted by Barbara Field. Photo credit: Michal Daniel. **605:** Charles Janasz as Bob Cratchit in the Guthrie Theatre's 1992 production of *A Christmas Carol,* adapted by Barbara Field. Photo credit: Michal Daniel. **608–609:** Bob Davis as Bob Cratchit and Nathaniel Fuller as Ebenezer Scrooge in the Guthrie Theatre's 1994 production of *A Christmas Carol,* adapted by Barbara Field. Photo credit: Michal Daniel. **612:** John Carroll Lynch as Marley and Richard Ooms as Ebenezer Scrooge in the Guthrie Theatre's 1994 production of *A Christmas Carol,* adapted by Barbara Field. Photo credit: Michal Daniel. **618:** Bob Davis as Bob Cratchit, Kevin James Kelly as Charles Dickens, and Richard Ooms as Ebenezer Scrooge in the Guthrie Theatre's 1994 production of *A Christmas Carol,* adapted by Barbara Field. Photo credit: Michal Daniel. **623:** CORBIS-BETTMANN **627:** Robert Houser/Index Stock Photography, Inc. **628:** Jim Baker as Ghost of Christmas Present in the Guthrie Theatre's 1975 production of *A Christmas Carol,* adapted by Barbara Field. Photo credit: Michal Daniel. **633:** The Guthrie Theatre **634:** Digital Imagery © Copyright 2001 PhotoDisc, Inc. **643:** The Cratchit family and Ebenezer Scrooge in the Guthrie Theatre's 1994 production of *A Christmas Carol,* adapted by Barbara Field. Photo credit: Michal Daniel. **646–647:** Richard Ooms as Ebenezer Scrooge in the Guthrie Theatre's 1994 production of *A Christmas Carol,* adapted by Barbara Field. Photo credit: Michal Daniel. **648:** Ebenezer Scrooge celebrating in the Guthrie Theatre's 1994 production of *A Christmas Carol,* adapted by Barbara Field. Photo credit: Michal Daniel. **654:** The Guthrie Theatre **664:** Mark C. Burnett/Stock, Boston **666–667:** Jean-Pierre Pieuchot/The Image Bank **670:** *Woman on telephone as seen through window,* William Low, Courtesy of the artist. **674:** *Overview of family walking dog on the street,* William Low, Courtesy of the artist **679:** *Streetlight,* 1930, Constance Coleman Richardson, © Indianapolis Museum of Art, Gift of Mrs. James W. Fesler **682–683:** Donald Carroll/The Image Bank **684:** UPI/CORBIS-BETTMANN **688:** CORBIS **691:** © Kenneth S. Lewis, Courtesy of Madeleine L'Engle **693:** © Graham Ford/Stone **694:** CORBIS **696:** Jonathan Nourak/PhotoEdit **702–703:** *Master of Midnight, Band Members Playing,* 24" x 36", collage, Phoebe Beasley/Omni-Photo Communications, Inc. **704 (m.):** Courtesy of the Library of Congress **704 (b.):** Philip Gould/CORBIS **706:** Ragnar Sigurdsson/Tony Stone Images **708:** Corel Professional Photos CD-ROM™ **708 (inset):** © Jeff Schultz/Alaska Stock Images **710:** Corel Professional Photos CD-ROM™ **712:** AP/Wide World Photos **713 (b.):** *James Stephens* (detail), Sir William Rothenstein, The Tate Gallery, London/Art Resource, NY **713 (t.):** Chad Ehlers/Tony Stone Images **714:** Courtesy of the author **718:** Garry McMichael/Photo Researchers, Inc. **720 (b.):** Sonja H. Smith **720 (t.):** Kennan Ward/CORBIS **721:** Dimitri Kessel/*Life* magazine **722 (b.):** The Granger Collection, New York **722 (t.l., t.r.):** Gary Conner/PhotoEdit **726:** Pearson Education/Modern Curriculum Press **729:** CORBIS-BETTMANN **730 (t.):** Courtesy of the Library of Congress **730 (b.):** William E. Stafford **734:** Robert Fried/Stock, Boston/PictureQuest **736:** Larry

Lipsky/Tom Stack & Associates **736 (inset):** *William Shakespeare* (detail), Artist unknown, by courtesy of the National Portrait Gallery, London **737:** Photo by Bachrach **738:** Arte Público Press **743:** CORBIS **745:** United States Naval Institute **746:** © The Stock Market/Jim Foster **748:** Colonial Williamsburg Foundation **749:** Courtesy of the Library of Congress **750 (t.):** *Carl Sandburg,* Miriam Svet, The National Portrait Gallery, Smithsonian Institution, Washington, D.C./Art Resource, New York **750 (b.):** © The Stock Market/Jim Foster **751:** Courtesy of Naomi Long Madgett **752–753:** Roger Werth/Woodfin Camp & Associates **754:** Patricia Allen-Wolk **763:** © The Stock Market/Lew Long **764:** Philip Gould/CORBIS **766:** Elena Rooraid/PhotoEdit/PictureQuest **772–773:** *Sleeping Beauty,* John Dixon Batten, Christie's Images, London/SuperStock **774 (t.):** The Granger Collection, New York **774 (inset):** Educational and Professional Publishing. **774 (b.), 776, 778:** Robert Frerck/Odyssey Productions/Chicago **780:** © Charles & Josette Lenara/CORBIS **782:** *The Volcanos,* 1905, Jose Maria Velasco, Galeria Arvil, Mexico. Courtesy of CDS Gallery, New York, Private Collection **784:** Courtesy of the author **789:** Educational and Professional Publishing **790:** Werner Forman Archive/Art Resource, NY **791:** Werner Forman Archive, Liverpool Museum, Liverpool/Art Resource NY **792:** The Bodleian Library, Oxford, MS. Arch. Selden, A.1, fol. 69r **793:** Erich Lessing/ART RESOURCE, N Y **798–799:** From *The People Could Fly* by Virginia Hamilton, illustrated by Leo and Diane Dillon. Illustrations copyright © 1985 by Leo and Diane Dillon. Reprinted by permission of Alfred A. Knopf, Inc. **801:** Prentice Hall **803:** The Granger Collection, New York **804–805:** © Papilio/CORBIS **806–807:** Corel Professional Photos CD-ROM™ **808:** Digital Imagery © Copyright 2001 PhotoDisc, Inc. **812, 815:** *Le Char d'Apollon (Apollo's Chariot),* Odilon Redon, Musée D'Orsay, Paris/Giraudon, Paris/SuperStock **817:** Courtesy, Houghton Mifflin Company **818:** *Demeter Mourning for Persephone,* 1906, Evelyn de Morgan, The De Morgan Foundation, London, UK/Bridgeman Art Library, London/New York **818–819:** © George Lepp/CORBIS **822–823:** Brian Parker/Tom Stack & Associates **823:** *Daedalus and Icarus:* French colored engraving, 1660, The Granger Collection, New York **824:** From Christina Hopkinson Baker, *Diary and Letters of Josephine Preston Peabody,* Riverside Press, MA **828:** Dr. Parvinder S. Sethi **829:** Corel Professional Photos CD-ROM™ **830:** Digital Imagery © Copyright 2001 PhotoDisc, Inc. **831 (t.):** Washington Square Press **831 (b.):** Bettmann/CORBIS **836:** Siteman/Monkmeyer **837 (t.):** Innerspace Visions **837 (b.):** © Visuals Unlimited

Staff Credits

The people who made up the *Prentice Hall Literature: Timeless Voices, Timeless Themes* team—representing design services, editorial, editorial services, market research, marketing services, media resources, online services and multimedia development, production services, project office, and publishing processes—are listed below. Bold type denotes the core team members.

Susan Andariese, Rosalyn Arcilla, Laura Jane Bird, Betsy Bostwick, **Anne M. Bray,** Evonne Burgess, **Louise B. Capuano, Pam Cardiff,** Megan Chill, Ed Cordero, Laura Dershewitz, Philip Fried, **Elaine Goldman,** Barbara Goodchild, Barbara Grant, **Rebecca Z. Graziano, Doreen Graizzaro,** Dennis Higbee, **Leanne Korszoloski,** Ellen Lees, David Liston, **Mary Luthi, George Lychock,** Gregory Lynch, Sue Lyons, **William McAllister,** Frances Medico, Gail Meyer, Jessica S. Paladini, Wendy Perri, Carolyn Carty Sapontzis, **Melissa Shustyk, Annette Simmons, Alicia Solis,** Robin Sullivan, Cynthia Sosland Summers, Lois Teesdale, **Elizabeth Torjussen, Doug Utigard,** Bernadette Walsh, Helen Young

The following persons provided invaluable assistance and support during the production of this program.

Gregory Abrom, Robert Aleman, Diane Alimena, Michele Angelucci, Gabriella Apolito, Penny Baker, Sharyn Banks, Anthony Barone, Barbara Blecher, Helen Byers, Rui Camarinha, Lorelee J. Campbell, John Carle, Cynthia Clampitt, Jaime L. Cohen, Martha Conway, Dina Curro, Nancy Dredge, Johanna Ehrmann, Josie K. Fixler, Steve Frankel, Kathy Gavilanes, Allen Gold, Michael E. Goodman, Diana Hahn, Kerry L. Harrigan, Jacki Hasko, Evan Holstrom, Beth Hyslip, Helen Issackedes, Cathy Johnson, Susan Karpin, Raegan Keida, Stephanie Kota, Mary Sue Langan, Elizabeth Letizia, Christine Mann, Vickie Menanteaux, Kathleen Mercandetti, Art Mkrtchyan, Karyl Murray, Kenneth Myett, Stefano Nese, Kim Ortell, Lissette Quiñones, Erin Rehill-Seker, Patricia Rodriguez, Mildred Schulte, Adam Sherman, Mary Siener, Jan K. Singh, Diane Smith, Barbara Stufflebeem, Louis Suffredini, Lois Tatarian, Tom Thompkins, Lisa Valente, Ryan Vaarsi, Linda Westerhoff, Jeff Zoda

Prentice Hall gratefully acknowledges the following teachers who provided student models for consideration in the program.

Barbara Abel, Dawn Akuna, Kathy Allen, Joan Anderson, Amy Bales, Lisa Cobb, Ann Collier-Buchanan, Janice Crews, Denise Donahue, Becky Dressler, Nicci Durban, Nancy Fahner, Margo Graf, Jan Graham, Carleen Hemric, Karen Hurley, Max Hutto, Lenore Hynes, Kim Johnson, Gail Kidd, Ashley MacDonald, Maureen MacDonald, Akiko Morimoto, Judy Plouff, Charlene Revels, Lynn Richter, Kathleen Riley, Sandy Shannon, Marilyn Shaw, Cheryl Spivak, Lynn Striepe, John Tierney, Vanna Turner, Pam Walden, Holly Ward, Jennifer Watson, Joan West, Virginia Wong